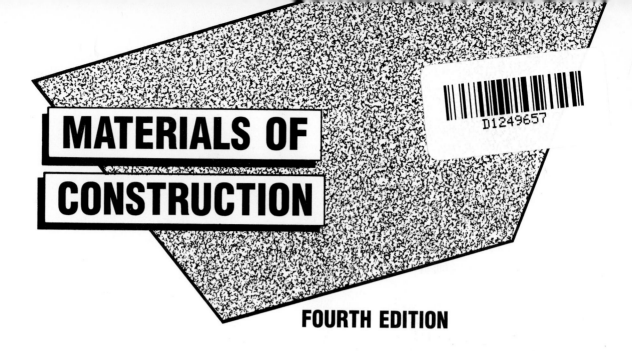

MATERIALS OF CONSTRUCTION

FOURTH EDITION

R. C. SMITH

C. K. ANDRES
Professional Engineer
Southern Alberta Institute
of Technology
Calgary, Alberta, Canada

GLENCOE

Macmillan/McGraw-Hill

New York, New York
Columbus, Ohio
Mission Hills, California
Peoria, Illinois

Library of Congress Cataloging-in-Publication Data

Smith, Ronald C.
    Materials of construction.

    Includes index.
    1. Building materials.   1. Andres, Cameron K.
II. Title.
TA403.S595   1987   691   87-22569
ISBN 0-07-058504-0

Materials of Construction, Fourth Edition

Imprint 1994

4 5 6 7 8 9 10 11 12 13 14 15   RAND 00 99 98 97 96 95 94

ISBN 0-07-058504-0

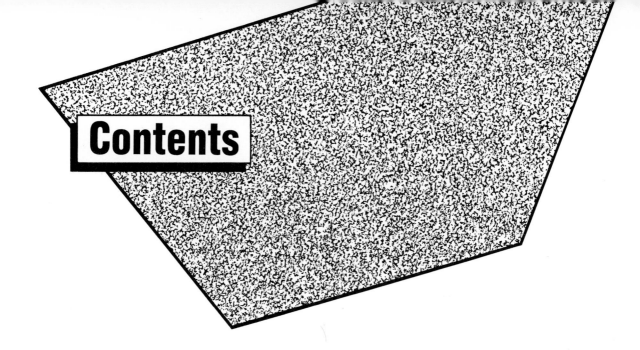

Contents

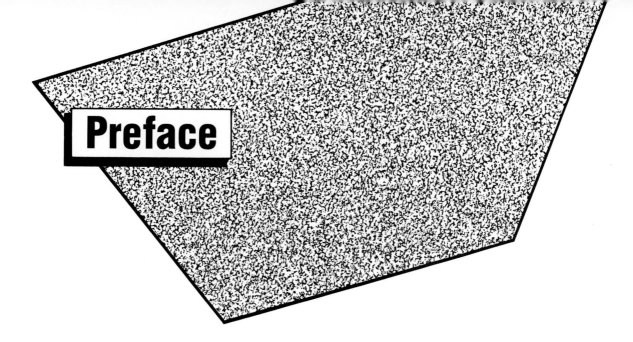

Preface

New advancements in technology have provided designers and planners with new materials and products, allowing for a wide variety of alternatives with which to meet the challenges and requirements of the construction industry.

To present this vast amount of knowledge in a more logical format and to provide added continuity in the discussion of materials and their applications, some reorganization of the text was necessary. As a result, the fourth edition of *Materials of Construction* provides the reader with a more focused presentation of the primary construction materials, their properties, and construction applications. For example, the application of wood products such as siding and shingles is discussed in the chapter entitled "Wood" rather than being included in a separate chapter dealing with exterior coverings.

Some of the soft conversions from traditional weights and measures to the SI metric system have now become standardized by government and industry and have been included where they are applicable as evidenced by the wood industry.

Since the purpose of this book is to introduce and describe material properties, products, and applications, this information will be of particular interest to those involved in vocational and technical education, as well as to those who have little or no formal training in building construction.

Although this text does not supersede those whose intent it is to examine one particular material exclusively, it is the hope of the authors that the material presented here will promote a search for more detailed information about specific materials and their properties. References included at the end of the chapters on wood, cement, ferrous metals, and plastics are intended to aid the reader in such a search. Also, manufacturers publish descriptions and detailed drawings on the recommended methods of using specific products, and interested persons should avail themselves of this technical information whenever necessary.

The authors wish to express their appreciation to many societies, associations, institutes, government agencies, and manufacturers for their generous contributions in the form of illustrations, new data, and material specifications. Without their assistance an undertaking of these proportions would have been impossible.

R. C. Smith
C. K. Andres

Acknowledgments

Acme Steel Co.

Acoustical Materials Association

Acrylic Plastics Ltd.

Alliance Wall Corp.

Alcan Canada Products Ltd.

Aluminum Association

American Concrete Institute

American Institute of Timber Construction

American Plywood Association

American Wood Preservers' Association

Anaconda Company

The Arborite Company, Division of Domtar Construction Materials, Ltd.

Besser Technical Center

Bethlehem Steel Co.

Better Finishes & Coatings Co.

Brick and Tile Manufacturing Association of Canada

Brick Institute of America

Bristol Products of Canada Limited

Building Stone Institute

Canadian Carpet Institute

Canadian Copper & Brass Development Association

Canadian Gypsum Co.

Canadian Industries Limited

Canadian Institute of Steel Construction

Canadian Lumbermen's Association

Canadian Lumber Standards Administration Board

Canadian Paint Manufacturers' Association

Canadian Pittsburgh Industries Ltd.

Canadian Prestressed Concrete Institute

Canadian Pulp and Paper Association

Canadian Sheet Steel Building Institute

Canadian Standards Association

Canadian Wood Development Council

Celotex Corp.

Chambers Brothers Company

Chisholm, Boyd & White Co.

CIBA-GEIGY Canada Ltd.

Ciment Fondu Lafarge Corp.

CIP Panel Boards Ltd.

Columbia Acoustics & Fireproofing Co.

Columbia Machine Inc.

Con-Force Products Ltd.

Consolidated Concrete Limited

Consolidated Red Cedar Shingle Association of B.C.

Coucil of Forest Industries of British Columbia

Cowin Steel Co.

Crown Zellerbach Corporation

Dominion Foundries and Steel, Limited
Domtar Construction Materials Ltd.
Donn Products Ltd.
Dow Chemical Co.
Edcon Block Company
Epco Inc.
Evertex Co. Ltd.
Expanded Shale, Clay and Slate Institute
Fiberglass Canada, Limited
Fiberglass R.P. Report (Canada)
Flintkote Company of Canada Limited
Garson Limestone Company
Gold Bond Building Products
Gypsum Association
Harris Manufacturing Co.
Hewitt-Robins, Inc.
Indiana Limestone Co.
Industrial Development Corp., Saskatchewan
Ingersoll-Rand Company
International Masonry Institute
International Panel Boards Limited
IXL Industries Ltd.
The Jeffrey Manufacturing Co.
Laminated Timber Institute of Canada
Libby-Owens-Ford Glass Co.
MacMillan Bloedel Ltd.
Masonite Canada Ltd.
Master Builders Co., Limited
McCready Products Ltd.
Minnesota Mining & Manufacturing Co.
Mississippi Glass Co.
Modern Plastics
Montreal Terra-Cotta Ltd.
Morrison Molded Fiber Glass Company
National Concrete Masonry Association
National Hardwood Lumber Association
National Lumber Grades Authority
National Research Council

Pilkington Bros., Ltd.
Pittsburgh Corning Corporation
Pittsburgh Plate Glass Co.
Plywood Manufacturers' Association of British Columbia
Portland Cement Association
Posey Iron Works, Inc.
PPG Industries Inc.
Pratt and Lambert
Robertson Irwin Ltd.
Rohm & Haas Plastics
Soiltest, Inc.
Sonoco Products Co.
Southern Forest Products Association
Southern Pine Association
Southern Pine Inspection Bureau
Steel Company of Canada, Ltd.
Stramit Corporation Ltd.
Structural Clay Products Institute
Stone Facings Ltd.
Sumner Rider and Associates Inc.
Sydney Steel Corp.
Terrazzo, Tile & Marble Association of Canada
Thiokol Chemical Corp.
3M Company
Tinius Olsen Co.
Tremco Manufacturing Co.
United States Ceramic Tile Co.
United States Department of Agriculture
United States Steel Corporation
Vermiculite Association, Inc.
Vermiculite Institute
Western Archrib Structures Ltd.
Western Forest Products Laboratory
Western Perlite Co., Ltd.
Westroc Industries Ltd.
W.R. Grace & Co. of Canada, Ltd.

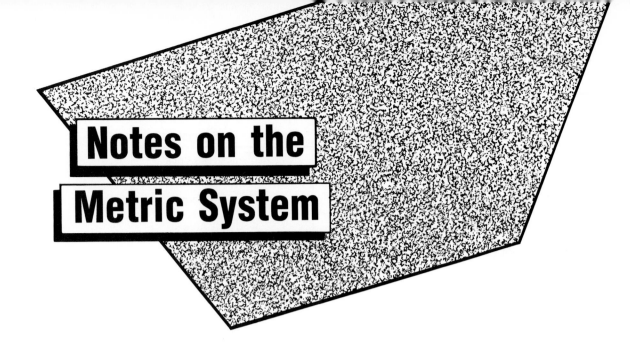

Notes on the Metric System

One of the most important recent innovations in the construction industry in North America has been the introduction, with the goal of total adoption, of the metric system of weights and measures. The overriding value of the metric system lies in its simplicity and universality. It is simple, because all relationships between the various units in the system work in powers of 10. It is nearly universal; most of the countries of the world, well over 95 percent of the world's population, use metric units and/or are converting to the International System of measurements (SI).

In 1960, the International Conference on Weights and Measures (CGPM) adopted the International System of Units, with the international abbreviation SI (Système International). The system is on its way to universal adoption.

There are seven basic types of measurement in SI: *length, mass, time, electric current, thermodynamic temperature,* the *amount of substance,* and *luminous intensity.* Other units have evolved to complete the metric system.

SI UNITS

Quantity	Name of Unit	Symbol
Length	meter	m
Mass	kilogram	kg
Time	second	s
Electric current	ampere	A
Thermodynamic temperature	kelvin	K
Amount of substance	mole	mol
Luminous intensity	candela	cd

There are also two supplementary units in SI: the unit of plane angle, the *radian,* and the unit of solid angle, the *steradian,* which have the symbols "rad" and "sr," respectively. All the other units in SI are called *derived units* and are expressed algebraically in terms of base units and/or supplementary units.

SOME DERIVED SI UNITS

Quantity	Name of Derived Unit	Symbol	Equivalent to
Force	newton	N	$kg \cdot m/s^2$
Pressure	pascal	Pa	N/m^2
Work, energy, quantity of heat	joule	J	$N \cdot m$
Power, heat flow rate	watt	W	J/s
Quantity of electricity	coulomb	C	$A \cdot s$
Electric potential	volt	V	W
Electric resistance	ohm	Ω	V/A
Electric capacitance	farad	F	C/V
Magnetic flux	weber	Wb	V/s
Inductance	henry	H	Wb/A
Magnetic flux density	tesla	T	Wb/m^2
Frequency	hertz	Hz	s^{-1}

There are other units outside SI which are also recognized because of their practical importance.

NON-SI UNITS FOR USE WITH SI

Quantity	Name of Unit	Symbol	Value in SI Units
Time	minute	min	1 min = 60 s
	hour	h	1 h = 3600 s
	day	d	1 d = 86,400 s
Plane angle	degree	°	$1° = (\pi/180)$ rad
	minute	'	$1' = (\pi/10800)$ rad
	second	"	$1'' = (\pi/64800)$ rad
Volume	liter	L or *l*	$1 \, l = dm^3$
Temperature	degree Celsius	°C	An interval of 1°C = 1 K By definition, 0°C = 273.15 K
Mass	tonne	t	$1 \, t = 10^3$ kg

Multiples and divisions of base units, derived units, and supplementary units may be expressed by adding a prefix. The prefix and the unit are always written as one word.

SOME COMMON PREFIXES

Prefix	Symbol	Means to Multiply by:	or by:
Mega	M	1 000 000	10^6
Kilo	k	1 000	10^3
Hecto	h	100	10^2
Deca	da	10	10
Deci	d	0.1	10^{-1}
Centi	c	0.01	10^{-2}
Milli	m	0.001	10^{-3}
Micro	μ	0.00001	10^{-6}

As the implementation of metric continues to grow throughout the construction industry in North America, more and more manufacturers are converting their products to SI units. The fourth edition of *Materials of Construction* incorporates the latest values where possible. However, not all industries are at the same level of transition and, therefore, not all have established metric standards for their products. Consequently, in some cases, the metric values used are soft conversions—simply a mathematical translation of the Imperial Units to their metric equivalents.

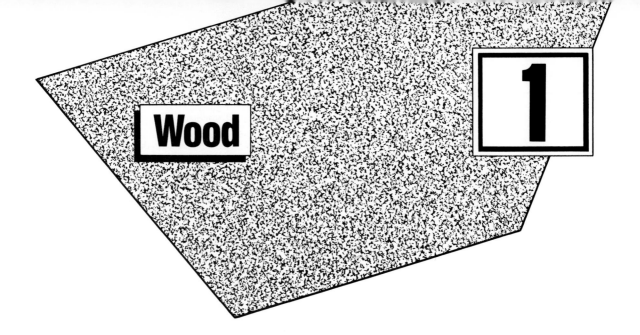

Wood

1

Throughout the ages wood has been used in countless ways—as a fuel, in musical instruments, in weapons, as a building material, and in transportation. In recent times, advanced technology has developed new materials which have replaced wood in many of its traditional applications. However, this same technology has created countless new uses for wood and its by-products that, until recently, were never considered. (See Fig. 1-1.)

To use any material efficiently and effectively, knowledge dealing with its physical and mechanical properties is vital. Wood is no exception. It is a very complex material, and when viewed under a microscope, its structure is more complicated than any skyscraper. (See Fig. 1-2.) From an engineering point of view, these complexities must be understood in order to predict the behavior of the wood when it is to be used as a structural material.

Some of the properties of wood that are of particular interest are as follows:

1. Wood is a *fibrous material* in which the fibers run longitudinally through the wood section. This produces a material that has good strength characteristics when loaded in flexure.

2. Wood is *viscoelastic*. Under relatively low stresses, it behaves elastically; that is, stresses are proportional to strains, but as the stresses increase, the strains become disproportionate and there is no evidence of a definite elastic limit. Under higher stresses, wood will creep over time, and water content and high temperatures will affect its strength characteristics.

3. Wood is *anisotropic*. Its properties are considerably different along the direction of the grain from those perpendicular to the grain.

4. Wood is *hygroscopic*. It will absorb moisture and will maintain a moisture content equal to that of the surrounding air. As a result, it will shrink and swell depending on the amount of moisture available.

Although the properties of wood may appear rather inconsistent for it to be used as a structural material, wood certainly has its place in the construction industry. It is easily worked, has great durability and beauty, and has great ability to absorb shocks from impact-type loads. In addition, wood does not corrode, is comparatively light in weight, and is adaptable to a countless variety of uses.

PHYSICAL PROPERTIES OF WOOD

As trees grow, they absorb carbon dioxide from the air, water and minerals from the soil, and by the process of photosynthesis, convert them into basic carbohydrate compounds to produce new wood

1

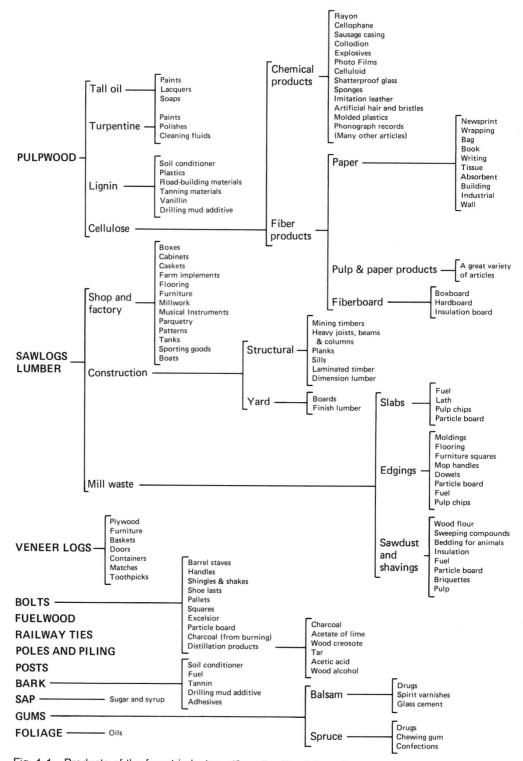

Fig. 1-1 Products of the forest industry. *(Canadian Wood Council)*

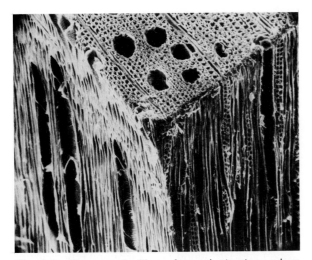

Fig. 1-2 The complexities of wood structure when viewed through an electron microscope. *(Forest Service, U.S. Department of Agriculture, Forest Products Laboratory, Madison, Wisconsin)*

cells. As the new cells are formed, the old cells cease to function and are preserved, forming that part of the tree known as wood. This phenomenon of self-preservation enables the tree to reach a size that allows it to be cut into sections and lengths of commerical value.

The tree stem is composed of two major components—the central core, or *stele*, and the outer protective shell, or *bark*. The central core provides the rigidity and the vascular system for food distribution, while the outer bark provides a protective cover for the active layer just below the inner surface of the bark. The central core, which makes up the major portion of the stem cross-section (see Fig. 1-3), consists of three major zones: (1) the pith, or inner core; (2) wood, or *xylem*; and (3) a very thin zone around the outside of the xylem known as the inner bark, or *phloem*. Between the inner bark and the xylem exists a very thin layer called

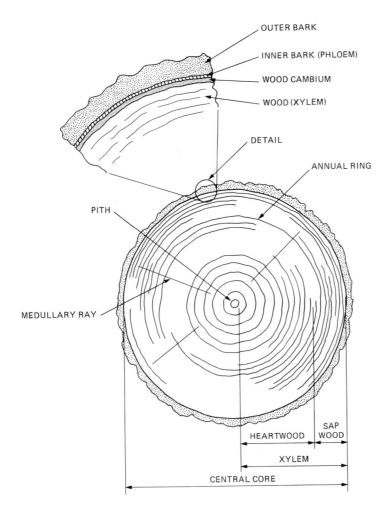

OUTER BARK
INNER BARK (PHLOEM)
WOOD CAMBIUM
WOOD (XYLEM)
DETAIL
ANNUAL RING
PITH
MEDULLARY RAY
HEARTWOOD
SAP WOOD
XYLEM
CENTRAL CORE

Fig. 1-3 Tree cross-section.

3

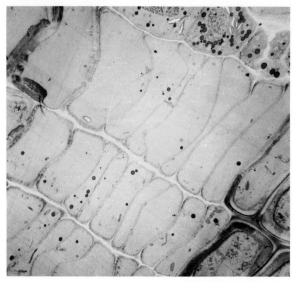

Fig. 1-4 Cambial zone of eastern white pine at approximately 1000X. The xylem is at the right, the phloem at the left. *(Forest Service, U.S. Department of Agriculture, Forest Products Laboratory, Madison, Wisconsin)*

the *vascular cambium* or wood cambium. (See Fig. 1-4.) This is the active layer where the new wood cells are produced. The cambium is composed of two types of cell structures: elongated longitudinal cells and short-ray cells. (See Fig. 1-5.) The cells subdivide in such a manner as to produce an increase in both the stem diameter and the stem circumference. The cells are composed mainly of cellulose and are bound together by a substance knows as *lignin*.

In each growing season, the cambium produces another layer of new wood. In climates where only one growing season exists, the new growth is known as an *annual ring*. (See Fig. 1-6.) Each growth ring is composed of early wood (springwood) and late wood (summerwood). Because of rapid growth, the springwood is lighter in color and is less dense than the summerwood.

The xylem of a tree is subdivided into two zones: *heartwood* and *sapwood*. When xylem is newly

Fig. 1-5 Macerated longitudinal cells of red oak. *(Forest Service, U.S. Department of Agriculture, Forest Products Laboratory, Madison, Wisconsin)*

Fig. 1-6 Annual rings of ponderosa pine magnified about 20X. *(Forest Service, U.S. Department of Agriculture, Forest Products Laboratory, Madison, Wisconsin)*

formed, the living cells provide the system through which food is distributed to all parts of the tree. Thus, the living portion of the xylem is the sapwood. As the tree adds new layers of growth, the older cells die, producing heartwood. Heartwood is usually darker in color than sapwood, is less permeable, and has a higher density. The darker color of the heartwood is due to biochemical changes, and the coloring, in many cases, is toxic to bacteria, providing a natural defense against decay.

The width of the sapwood may vary from $1\frac{1}{2}$ in (38 mm) in western red cedar, Douglas fir, and spruce to 3 in (35 mm) in ponderosa pine and many broad-leafed trees.

The xylem is composed of 50 percent cellulose, 15 to 30 percent hemicellulose, 15 to 35 percent lignin, and 5 to 30 percent ash and extractives such as tannin, turpentine, gums, and resins. If the lignin in the wood is chemically dissolved, the result is wood pulp.

Trees, generally, are divided into two groups: *hardwoods* and *softwoods*. Botanists refer to the former as deciduous. These trees are broad-leaved and normally shed their leaves in the fall. Softwoods are called conifers, trees that have needles rather than leaves and bear their seeds in cones. Except for the larches, the needles stay green through the winter and remain on the tree for 2 or more years.

The term "hardwood" or "softwood" applied to a particular species does not necessarily indicate the relative hardness of that particular species of wood. Some trees in the hardwood class, such as basswood or poplar, are softer than the average softwood species. Longleaf southern pine and Douglas fir, on the other hand, both in the softwood group, are harder than several of the hardwoods. The cells in softwoods are about 0.14 in (3.15 mm) long and about 0.0015 in (0.03 mm) in diameter, while those in hardwoods are usually much shorter.

Wood Grain

The term grain as applied to wood refers to the alignment of the wood cells with respect to the longitudinal axis of the tree stem. Straight-grained wood has wood fibers that predominantly run parallel to the longitudinal axis of the stem. A spiral grain is one that spirals around the longitudinal axis of the stem. The grain direction becomes evident by the appearance of the exposed plane when a piece of wood is split longitudinally.

Wood may be considered *close-grained* or *coarse-grained*. Close-grained wood has very narrow and inconspicuous annual rings, and wood of this nature has very closely spaced pores. Coarse-grained wood has wide annual rings with a noticeable difference between summerwood and springwood, and wood of this type is considered to have large pores. The variations in the grain determine the texture of the wood. An even texture is a result of uniformly distributed cells, while coarse texture results from large open elements such as exist in most hardwoods.

Moisture in Wood

Trees are living organisms, so they require water to sustain life. Wood in its natural state contains a substantial quantity of water in two forms: as bound water and as free water. Bound water is moisture that is held within the cell walls, and free water is that moisture which fills the cell cavities or *lumina*. The moisture content (MC) of wood is the weight of water contained in the wood expressed as a percentage of the oven-dry weight. In equation form it can be expressed as follows:

$$MC\% = \frac{\text{weight of water in the wood}}{\text{oven-dry weight}} \times 100$$

The weight of the water in the wood is obtained by subtracting the oven-dry weight of the wood from the wet weight. The standard procedure and conditions under which this test must be conducted are described in ASTM Standard D2016-74. Table 1-1 gives the average values for MCs in heartwood and sapwood of common trees in the green state.

When the cell walls become saturated but no moisture is present in the cell cavities, the wood is said to have reached its fiber-saturation point. Because all trees are different in structure, the fiber-saturation point varies between 25 and 30 percent MC in most cases. Maximum MC occurs when all the spaces in the cells are completely filled. In dense wood this occurs at about 60 percent moisture content, while some of the lighter and more porous woods can have a maximum MC of 200 percent.

Wood that is cut and left to dry will lose moisture

Table 1-1
MOISTURE CONTENT OF SOME COMMON TREES

Species	Moisture Content, %*	
	Heartwood	Sapwood
Hardwoods:		
Ash, white	46	44
Birch, yellow	74	72
Elm, American	95	92
Hickory, red	69	52
Maple, silver	58	97
Oak, white	64	78
Walnut, black	90	73
Poplar, yellow	83	106
Softwoods:		
Cedar, western	58	249
Fir, Douglas	37	115
Fir, white	98	160
Pine, ponderosa	40	148
Redwood, mature	86	210
Spruce, sitka	41	142

* Based on weight when oven dry.
SOURCE: Wood Handbook, United States Department of Agriculture Forest Service, 1974. Used with permission.

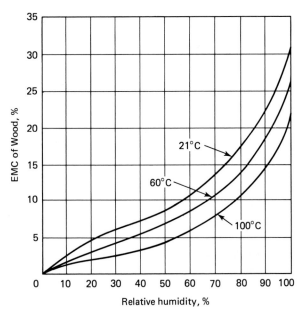

Fig. 1-7 Equilibrium moisture content of wood. *(Canadian Wood Council)*

until its MC is equal to that of the surrounding air. This is known as the equilibrium moisture content (EMC). The EMC of a piece of wood ranges between 5 and 12 percent, depending on the temperature and the relative humidity in the surrounding air. (See Fig. 1-7.)

Wood Shrinkage

When the MC falls below the fiber-saturation point, changes in the wood cells occur, producing distortions in the wood. This phenomenon is known as shrinkage. Different woods experience different amounts of shrinkage, with hardwoods being the most susceptible. Wood being *anisotropic*, the amount of shrinkage differs with respect to the three principal axes. (See Fig. 1-8.) Typical values for shrinkage from green to oven-dry conditions in each of the three directions are given in Table 1-2. Percent shrinkage in a particular direction can be calculated by the following expression:

$$\text{Percent shrinkage} = \frac{\text{change in length}}{\text{original length}} \times 100$$

Shrinkage in wood is not a permanent condition.

When dry wood is placed in water, it will absorb water and expand. Many a good piano has been ruined by being moved from a dry climate to a wet one and vice versa.

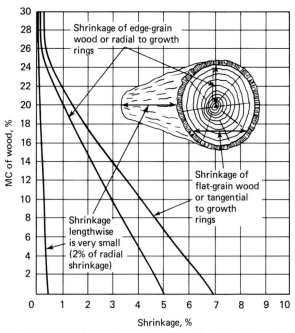

Fig. 1-8 Shrinkage of wood. *(Canadian Wood Council)*

6

Table 1-2
SHRINKAGE IN WOOD (Green to Oven Dry)

Direction	Shrinkage, %
Radial	3–6
Tangential	5–12
Longitudinal	0.1–0.2
Volumetric	7–18

Seasoning of Wood

To minimize the amount of dimensional change in finished wood products, drying of the wood (seasoning) is necessary. (See Fig. 1-9.) Seasoning is the procedure whereby the unfinished or rough material is dried to bring the MC of the wood into the same range as that of the anticipated service conditions.

A water content of 19 percent or less is considered as dry for material grading purposes. For finished products such as interior woodwork and

Fig. 1-9 Distortion of wood due to drying.

Fig. 1-10 Core temperature tester and moisture meter.
(Canadian Institute of Timber Construction)

flooring, MCs vary from 6 percent in dry climates to 11 percent in damp coastal climates. For exterior applications such as wood siding, framing, sheathing, and laminated timbers, MCs should be about 9 percent for dry areas and 12 percent for damp areas.

Moisture can be removed from wood by air drying, forced or natural, and by kiln drying. Thoroughly air-dried lumber has an average of 12.5 percent MC, while kiln-dried material contains less than 12 percent moisture and can have as little as 5 percent. The main advantage of kiln drying is the rate at which the desired MC can be achieved. For industrial applications, the measurement of MCs in wood products is accomplished by the use of an electric-moisture meter. (See Fig. 1-10.) An electric current is passed between two points on a piece of material, and the resulting resistance to the current passing through the wood is converted into an MC reading.

As seasoning of wood involves the removal of moisture, care must be taken to prevent damage to the wood structure during the drying process. If drying is not regulated properly, defects such as case hardening, checking, and collapse of the wood structure can occur.

Case hardening occurs when the outside of the wood section dries and sets around a wet inner core (see Fig. 1-11), producing tension stresses in the outer layer. As the moisture is removed from the inner core, the resulting shrinkage produces compression in the outer set layer. When sawing through such a piece, as shown in Fig. 1-10, the

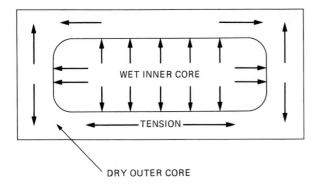

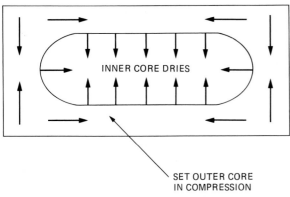

Fig. 1-11   Case hardening of wood section.

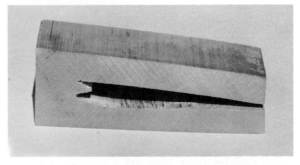

Fig. 1-12   Deformation due to case hardening.

Fig. 1-13   Collapse of wood structure due to drying.

piece will bind the saw blade. When the wedge is removed, the two prongs will bend inward as a result of the built-up stresses. (See Fig. 1-12.)

Checking is the occurrence of cracking across the grain and can be prevented by controlling the rate of moisture removal.

Collapse of the wood structure is produced when rows of cells collapse as a result of severe moisture removal. (See Fig. 1-13.) In extreme cases the material cross-section will appear caved in. Again, this damage can be prevented by careful regulation of the seasoning process.

When the MC of the wood falls below the fiber-saturation point, the cell walls stiffen, resulting in an increase in strength and density. Compression perpendicular to the grain is affected the most, while resistance to impact is the least affected.

Density of Wood

The amount of wood substance per unit volume varies from one species to another, as well as within a particular species because of the difference in the size of the cell cavities and the thickness of the cell walls. Nevertheless, an average specific gravity at air-dry condition has been determined for all species. Tables 1-3 and 1-4 provide values of the specific gravity for some of the more common species grown in North America.

MECHANICAL PROPERTIES OF WOOD

Wood has mechanical properties that are very susceptible to change from one part of the tree to another as well as from one type of tree to another. With the wood fibers running primarily in the longitudinal direction, wood can be considered an isotropic material. Using the fibers as a reference plane, wood exhibits different properties parallel to the fibers, perpendicular to the fibers, and tangentially to the fibers. (See Fig. 1-14.)

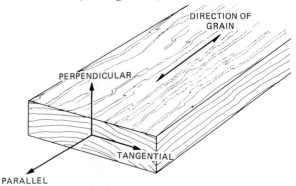

Fig. 1-14   The three principal directions of wood.

Tension

Wood exhibits its highest strength values in tension parallel to the grain. Because of the difficulty in doing actual tests in tension parallel to the grain, variations in results can be as high as 25 percent. Typical tension values of some common trees are listed in Table 1-5. These values are based on clear straight-grained samples at 12 percent MC. Variation in the grain, knots, and a different MC certainly would produce different values.

Tension capacity perpendicular to the grain is considerably lower than that parallel to the grain.

Table 1-3
MECHANICAL PROPERTIES OF COMMON HARDWOODS GROWN IN THE UNITED STATES*

Common Species Name	Specific Gravity	Modulus of Elasticity		Compression Parallel to Grain— Maximum Strength		Compression Perpendicular to Grain at Proportional Limit		Shear Parallel to Grain— Maximum Strength		Tension Perpendicular to Grain— Maximum Strength	
		psi × 10	GPa	psi	MPa	psi	MPa	psi	MPa	psi	MPa
Ash, white	0.60	1.74	12.000	7410	51.1	1160	8.0	1950	13.4	940	6.5
Aspen, quaking	0.38	1.18	8.100	4250	29.3	370	2.6	850	5.9	260	1.8
Birch, yellow	0.62	2.01	13.900	8170	56.3	970	6.7	1880	13.0	920	6.3
Cherry, black	0.50	1.49	10.300	7110	49.0	690	4.8	1700	11.7	560	3.9
Elm, American	0.50	1.34	9.200	5520	38.1	690	4.8	1510	10.4	660	4.6
Maple, silver	0.47	1.14	7.900	5220	36.0	740	5.1	1480	10.2	500	3.4
Oak, red	0.63	1.82	12.500	6760	44.6	1010	7.0	1780	12.3	800	5.5
Oak, white	0.68	1.78	12.300	7440	51.3	1070	7.4	2000	13.8	720	5.5
Sycamore	0.49	1.42	9.800	5380	37.1	700	4.8	1470	10.1	720	5.0

* Results obtained from small clear specimens with 12 percent moisture content.
SOURCE: Wood Handbook, United States Department of Agriculture Forest Service, 1974. Used with permission.

Table 1-4
MECHANICAL PROPERTIES OF COMMON SOFTWOODS GROWN IN THE UNITED STATES*

Common Species Name	Specific Gravity	Modulus of Elasticity		Compression Parallel to Grain— Maximum Strength		Compression Perpendicular to Grain at Proportional Limit		Shear Parallel to Grain— Maximum Strength		Tension Perpendicular to Grain— Maximum Strength	
		psi × 10	GPa	psi	MPa	psi	MPa	psi	MPa	psi	MPa
Cedar, western	0.32	1.11	7.70	4560	31.4	460	3.2	990	6.8	220	1.5
Fir, Douglas	0.48	1.95	13.40	7240	49.9	800	5.5	1130	7.8	340	2.3
Fir, white	0.39	1.49	10.30	5810	40.1	530	3.7	1100	7.6	300	2.1
Hemlock	0.45	1.64	11.30	7110	49.0	550	3.8	1250	8.6	340	2.3
Larch, western	0.52	1.87	12.90	7640	52.7	930	6.4	1360	9.4	430	3.0
Pine, lodgepole	0.41	1.34	9.20	5370	37.0	610	4.2	880	6.1	290	2.0
Pine, ponderosa	0.40	1.29	8.90	5320	36.7	580	4.0	1130	7.8	420	2.9
Pine, Virginia	0.48	1.52	10.50	6710	46.3	910	6.3	1350	9.3	380	2.6
Redwood, mature	0.40	1.34	9.20	6150	42.4	700	4.8	940	6.5	240	1.7
Spruce, Sitka	0.40	1.57	10.80	5610	38.7	580	4.0	1150	7.9	370	2.6
Spruce, white	0.40	1.34	9.20	5470	37.7	460	3.2	1080	7.4	360	2.5

* Results obtained from small clear specimens with 12 percent moisture content.
SOURCE: Wood Handbook, United States Department of Agriculture Forest Service, 1974. Used with permission.

Table 1-5
AVERAGE PARALLEL TO THE GRAIN TENSILE STRENGTHS OF COMMON SPECIES OF WOOD*

Name	Specific Gravity	Tensile Strength	
		Psi	MPa
Hardwoods:			
Elm, cedar	0.64	20,200	139.3
Oak, overcup	0.63	14,700	101.4
Sweetgum	0.52	17,300	119.3
Poplar, yellow	0.46	22,400	154.4
Softwoods:			
Fir, California red	0.39	13,100	90.3
Larch, western	0.55	19,400	133.8
Pine, eastern white	0.35	11,300	77.9
Spruce, Engleman	0.34	13,000	89.6

* Based on 12 percent moisture content and small, clear, straight-grained samples.
SOURCE: Wood Handbook, United States Department of Agriculture Forest Service, 1974. Used with permission.

This difference in strength is caused primarily by the lack of primary lateral connections between the individual longitudinal wood fibers. Failure in this mode produces a great deal of distortion as illustrated in Fig. 1-15.

Compression

The capacity of wood in compression parallel to the grain is conditional to the ability of the wood cells to resist buckling. As loading increases, the microscopic buckling that occurs in the cell walls is magnified to the point where failure will occur across the wood section. As Fig. 1-16 indicates, compression parallel to the grain is about one-half that of tension parallel to the grain. Compression perpendicular to the grain causes flattening of the wood cells, and a large amount of deformation can occur without any clear maximum load. (See Fig. 1-17.)

Shear

Three basic types of shear can occur in wood: shear parallel to the grain, shear perpendicular to the grain, and rolling shear. Shear parallel to the grain occurs in a plane parallel to the wood grain, with the resulting sliding occurring in the same direction. Shear perpendicular to the grain occurs when failure occurs in a plane normal to the grain. (See Fig. 1-18.) Rolling shear also occurs in a plane par-

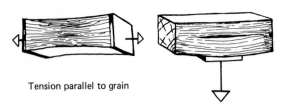

Tension parallel to grain

Tension perpendicular to grain

Fig. 1-15   Wood in tension. *(Canadian Wood Council)*

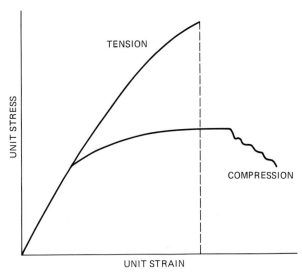

Fig. 1-16   Comparison of tension strength to compression strength of wood sample parallel to the grain.

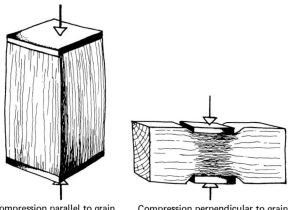

Compression parallel to grain   Compression perpendicular to grain

Fig. 1-17 Compression of wood. *(Canadian Wood Council)*

allel to the grain but the direction of sliding is at right angles to the grain in a plane parallel to the grain direction. (See Fig. 1-19.) Wood has a high resistance to shear perpendicular to the grain, and usually some other form of failure occurs before this type of shear failure occurs. Shear parallel to the grain must be considered when designing sections in flexure, and rolling shear must be dealt with when designing sections using plywood.

Bending Stresses

Bending stresses in sections are influenced by the fact that wood has different strength characteristics

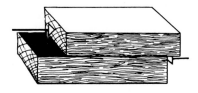

Longitudinal shear

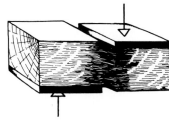

Vertical shear

Fig. 1-18 Shear parallel and perpendicular to the grain. *(Canadian Wood Council)*

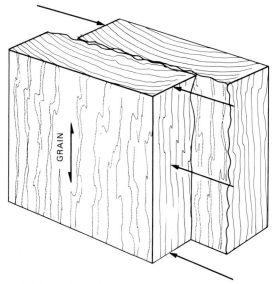

Fig. 1-19 Rolling shear.

in tension and compression. In homogeneous isotropic beams, stresses due to bending are assumed to vary linearly over the section. In wood this is true only for relatively small stresses. As the load is increased, the compressive strains cease to be proportional to the compressive stresses much sooner than those associated with tension (Fig. 1-20). The resulting maximum bending stresses that are developed are expressed as a *modulus of rupture*. In equation form:

$$\text{MOR} = \frac{M \times c}{I}$$

where

MOR is the modulus of rupture.
M is the applied moment.
c is the distance from the centroidal axis to the outermost fiber.
I is the moment of inertia.

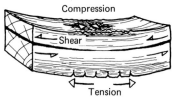

Fig. 1-20 Stresses in wood due to bending. *(Canadian Wood Council)*

11

Values for maximum bending stresses are higher than compression stresses parallel to the grain but are lower than tension stresses parallel to the grain.

Tables 1-3 and 1-4 list typical values of compression and tension and shear stresses for some of the more common species of trees grown in the United States.

Torsion

Torsion (longitudinal twisting, see Fig. 1-21) is not normally considered in wood design. The modulus of rigidity is the property that is used in determining torsion stresses due to twisting.

WOOD DISEASES

Various types of fungi are considered to be the chief causes of diseases in wood. These are low forms of plant growth, producing thin branching tubes which spread through the wood and use the cellulose, lignin, and other chemical compounds of the cell walls as food. This intrusion disintegrates the cell walls and reduces the strength of the wood. These fungi require food, air, moisture, and suitable conditions of temperature for development.

Three common wood diseases produced by various types of fungi are *sap stain, mold,* and *wood rot*. Certain fungi appear on green lumber, penetrate the wood with their threadlike roots (*hyphae*), and discolor the wood. They cease to be active after the lumber has been seasoned, and the wood is not appreciably weakened by this discoloration.

Other fungi cause molds which damage the wood mostly at the surface. Their roots pass through spaces between the bundles of fibers and take up the tree's nourishment instead of breaking down the cell walls. Such growths are usually found only near the surface of the sapwood.

Another kind of fungus causes rot, the destruction of the walls of the wood cells, by feeding on the cellulose or the lignin. When the cellulose is destroyed, a brittle, brownish, punky residue is left. When the lignin is dissolved, a soft, white mass of cellulose is left.

There are two stages in the progress of most types of decay; they differ somewhat in their characteristics and effects upon the wood. The first, *incipient decay,* is the result of early growth of the fungus; it usually shows up in the form of discoloration. The cell walls in this first stage are not injured enough to seriously affect the hardness or strength of the wood.

The second stage is *advanced decay;* in this case serious destructive action can easily be seen. *Brown rot* is one common type resulting in the destruction of the cellulose; *white rot* is the result when the lignin and other colored parts of the cell have been destroyed. Such rot appears in scattered spots, often with black margins.

The solution of the problems of stains and rot in wood is one of prevention rather than cure. The removal of moisture by kiln drying or subjecting the lumber to heat and dipping it in certain toxic materials or wood preservatives all help to prevent the growth of fungi.

INSECTS AND BORERS

Termites and the larvae of certain beetles can cause wood destruction, where they exist. Termites are normally found in warmer climates and wood beetles in regions or conditions of high humidity. Where these insects are a problem, preservatives which are effective against decay are usually equally effective against insects.

Other types of wood-boring organisms, known as *marine borers,* can cause severe damage to untreated timber in brackish or salt water. There are two types: a kind of *mollusk,* such as *teredo* and *bankia,* and *crustraceans*, such as *limnoria*. Timber to be used in such situations must be treated with a deep penetration of *creosote,* and care must be taken to prevent cutting or exposing areas where such borers might attack.

For a complete description of wood diseases and their cause and control, one should consult texts on this subject. Very good ones are published by the various forestry departments and forest-products laboratories across the country.

Fig. 1-21   Wood in torsion.   *(Canadian Wood Council)*

SAWN WOOD PRODUCTS

Merchantable timber is harvested (see Fig. 1-22), limbed, cut into logs, and transported to the sawmill. The logs are brought to the mill by truck, rail, barge, or tug and placed in a millpond for sorting (see Fig. 1-23) and held ready for sawing. Before the logs enter the sawmill they pass through a barker which removes the bark and rough protrusions, leaving the logs clean for the saw.

Sawn Lumber

In the sawmill, logs may be quartersawed or slash-sawed, to produce either *edge-grain* or *flat-grain* lumber. Large logs may be partially cut both ways to take full advantage of the material and still retain the best grain. (See Fig. 1-24.) Large logs may also be cut into *flitches* (see Fig. 1-25) at the headsaw, to be remanufactured at a later time into finished products. Some of the lumber will be sawn for kiln drying and some will be air dried.

Fig. 1-23 Logs sorted in millpond. *(Council of Forest Industries of B.C.)*

Lumber that is quartersawed (edge-grain or vertical-grain) has annual rings cutting the surface at angles from 45 to 90°. According to the National Lumber Grades Authority (NLGA) grading rules,

Fig. 1-22 Harvesting timber. *(Council of Forest Industries of B.C.)*

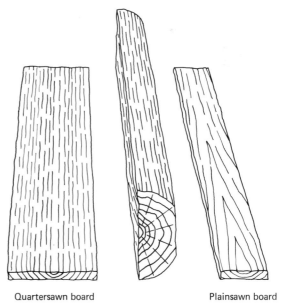

Quartersawn board   Plainsawn board

Fig. 1-24 Lumber from a log. *(Canadian Wood Council)*

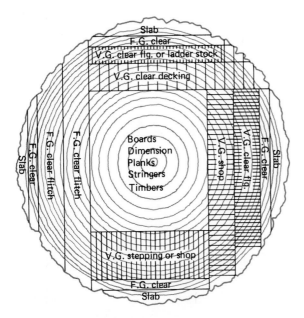

Fig. 1-25 Conversion of large log into lumber. *(Canadian Wood Council)*

Labels within figure:
Slab
F.G. clear
V.G. clear flg. or ladder stock
V.G. clear decking
V.G. shop
V.G. clear flg
F.G. clear
Slab
F.G. clear
Slab
F.G. clear flitch
F.G. clear flitch
Boards
Dimension
Planks
Stringers
Timbers
V.G. stepping or shop
F.G. clear
Slab

this is referred to as V.G. lumber. In slashsawed (flat-grain) lumber, the angle of the rings ranges from 0 to 45° with the surface. This is known in the grading rules as F.G. lumber. A piece of lumber containing both vertical and flat grain is classified as F.G. Any mixture of both vertical- and flat-grain material in a shipment is known as M.G.

Cross grain refers to lumber whose fibers do not run parallel to the edges of the board. Somewhere on the surface, the ends of the fiber bundles which have been cut appear as a rough spot, difficult to plane or finish. Diagonal grain refers to surface grain that runs at an angle to the edges of the board. Spiral grain is an arrangement of the fibers in a board which results from their growth in a spiral direction around the trunk of the tree. (See Fig. 1-26.)

To manufacture kiln-dried lumber, logs are sawed into rough lumber, which is first kiln dried and then surfaced (planed or dressed) to final finished size. Lumber to be air dried is sawed and dressed oversize while green, so that, after drying, it will be equivalent in size to lumber which has been surfaced dry. Lumber which has been dressed dry is stamped "S-DRY," while lumber dressed while still green is stamped "S-GRN." Figure 1-27 illustrates

two typical grade stamp facsimiles: one for the Pacific Lumber Inspection Bureau, Seattle, Washington, and the other for the Interior Lumber Manufacturing Association, Penticton, B.C. Lumber may also be remanufactured to produce special patterns, such as *shiplap, bevel siding,* or *tongue-and-groove decking.*

All this material is transported to domestic and foreign markets by truck, rail, and ship. Figure 1-28 illustrates a typical overseas shipment of lumber being loaded aboard a freighter from lumber barges.

SOFTWOOD LUMBER CLASSIFICATIONS

Standard softwood lumber is classified according to *species, use, extent of manufacturing,* and *size.*

The *species* commonly used for softwood lumber include Douglas fir, balsam fir, alpine fir, amabilis fir, grand fir, Pacific Coast hemlock, eastern hemlock, Sitka spruce, white spruce, Engelmann spruce, black spruce, red spruce, southern pine, white pine, western white pine, ponderosa pine, lodgepole pine, jack pine, red pine, western larch, tamarack, Pacific Coast yellow cedar, western red cedar, eastern white cedar, and California redwood.

Softwood lumber is classified by *use* into three groups:

1. **Yard lumber.** Lumber of those grades, sizes, and patterns which are generally intended for use in ordinary construction or general building purposes. (See Fig. 1-29.)

2. **Structural lumber.** Lumber which is at least 2 in (50 mm) in nominal width and thickness, to be used where working stresses are required.

3. **Factory and shop lumber.** Lumber that is produced or selected primarily for remanufacturing purposes.

Softwood lumber is also classified according to the *extent of manufacture* as follows:

1. **Rough lumber.** Lumber which has not been dressed but has been sawed, edged, and trimmed.

2. **Dressed (surfaced) lumber.** Lumber which has been dressed by a planer in order to

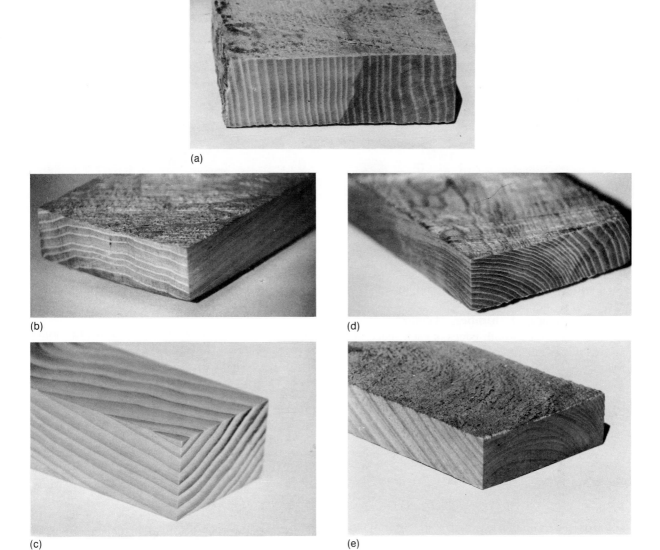

Fig. 1-26 Grain patterns in wood. *(a)* Edge grain, *(b)* flat grain, *(c)* cross grain, *(d)* spiral grain, *(e)* diagonal grain.

obtain a smooth surface and uniformity of size. It may be dressed on one side (S1S), on two sides (S2S), on one edge (S1E), on two edges (S2E), or on a combination of sides and edges (S1S1E, S1S2E, S2S1E, or S4S).

3. Worked lumber. Lumber which, in addition to being dressed, has been further shaped as follows:

a. Matched lumber. Lumber which has a tongue on one edge and a matching groove on the

ILMA® S-DRY **1**
0 0   S—P—F

Interior Lumber
Manufacturers
Association

NLGA RULE
No 1
0 0   S-GRN
HEM-FIR-N

Pacific Lumber
Inspection Bureau

Fig. 1-27 Typical grade-stamp facsimiles. *(Canadian Lumber Standards Administration Board)*

Fig. 1-28 Loading lumber aboard ship from barges. *(Council of Forest Industries of B.C.)*

opposite edge, to provide a close-fitting joint between two pieces. Material may be end-matched as well.

   b. Shiplapped lumber. Lumber which has been rabbeted on both edges of each piece, so that two pieces will fit together with a close-lapped joint.

   c. Patterned lumber. Lumber that has been shaped to a pattern or molded form, in addition to being dressed, matched, or shiplapped or any combination of these.

Softwood lumber is classified according to *size* by nominal sizes and by dressed sizes. Nominal sizes include the following:

1. Boards. Lumber less than 2 in (50 mm) in nominal thickness and 2 in (50 mm) or more in nominal width.

2. Dimension. Lumber from 2 in (50 mm) to, but not including, 5 in (127 mm) in nominal thickness and 2 in (50 mm) or more in nominal width. Dimension lumber may be further classified as *framing, studs, rafters, planks,* and *joists.*

3. Timbers. Lumber which is 5 in (127 mm) or more nominally in least dimension. Timbers may be further classified as *girders, stringers, beams, posts, sills, caps,* and *purlins.*

Dressed sizes of softwood lumber equal or exceed the minimum sizes shown in Tables 1-6 through 1-11. Notice that Table 1-11 deals exclusively with western red cedar and eastern white cedar.

The *minimum-dressed* dry sizes referred to in Tables 1-6 through 1-11 are manufactured from corresponding *rough dry* sizes. "Rough" means "before dressing" and "dry" means "at a moisture content of not more than 19 percent at the time of dressing."

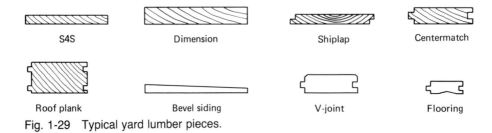

| S4S | Dimension | Shiplap | Centermatch |
| Roof plank | Bevel siding | V-joint | Flooring |

Fig. 1-29 Typical yard lumber pieces.

Table 1-6
NOMINAL AND MINIMUM-DRESSED DRY SIZES OF FINISH, FLOORING, CEILING, PARTITION, AND STEPPING AT 19 PERCENT MAXIMUM MOISTURE CONTENT
(The thicknesses apply to all widths and all widths to all thicknesses except as modified.)

Item	Thicknesses			Face Widths		
	Nominal[a]	Minimum Dressed		Nominal	Minimum Dressed	
		Inches	Millimeters[c]		Inches	Millimeters[c]
Finish	$\frac{3}{8}$	$\frac{5}{16}$	8	2	$1\frac{1}{2}$	38
	$\frac{1}{2}$	$\frac{7}{16}$	11	3	$2\frac{1}{2}$	64
	$\frac{5}{8}$	$\frac{9}{16}$	14	4	$3\frac{1}{2}$	89
	$\frac{3}{4}$	$\frac{5}{8}$	16	5	$4\frac{1}{2}$	114
	1	$\frac{3}{4}$	19	6	$5\frac{1}{2}$	140
	$1\frac{1}{4}$	1	25	7	$6\frac{1}{2}$	165
	$1\frac{1}{2}$	$1\frac{1}{4}$	32	8	$7\frac{1}{4}$	184
	$1\frac{3}{4}$	$1\frac{3}{8}$	35	9	$8\frac{1}{4}$	210
	2	$1\frac{1}{2}$	38	10	$9\frac{1}{4}$	235
	$2\frac{1}{2}$	2	51	11	$10\frac{1}{4}$	260
	3	$2\frac{1}{2}$	64	12	$11\frac{1}{4}$	286
	$3\frac{1}{2}$	3	76	14	$13\frac{1}{4}$	336
	4	$3\frac{1}{2}$	89	16	$15\frac{1}{4}$	387
Flooring[b]	$\frac{3}{8}$	$\frac{5}{16}$	8	2	$1\frac{1}{8}$	29
	$\frac{1}{2}$	$\frac{7}{16}$	11	3	$2\frac{1}{8}$	54
	$\frac{5}{8}$	$\frac{9}{16}$	14	4	$3\frac{1}{8}$	79
	1	$\frac{3}{4}$	19	5	$4\frac{1}{8}$	105
	$1\frac{1}{4}$	1	25	6	$5\frac{1}{8}$	130
	$1\frac{1}{2}$	$1\frac{1}{4}$	32			
Ceiling[b]	$\frac{3}{8}$	$\frac{5}{16}$	8	3	$2\frac{1}{8}$	54
	$\frac{1}{2}$	$\frac{7}{16}$	11	4	$3\frac{1}{8}$	79
	$\frac{5}{8}$	$\frac{9}{16}$	14	5	$4\frac{1}{8}$	105
	$\frac{3}{4}$	$\frac{11}{16}$	18	6	$5\frac{1}{8}$	130
Partition[b]	1	$\frac{23}{32}$	18	3	$2\frac{1}{8}$	54
				4	$3\frac{1}{8}$	79
				5	$4\frac{1}{8}$	105
				6	$5\frac{1}{8}$	130
Step-ping[b]	1	$\frac{3}{4}$	19	8	$7\frac{1}{4}$	184
	$1\frac{1}{4}$	1	25	10	$9\frac{1}{4}$	235
	$1\frac{1}{2}$	$1\frac{1}{4}$	32	12	$11\frac{1}{4}$	286
	2	$1\frac{1}{2}$	38			

[a] For nominal thicknesses under 1 in (25 mm), the board measure count is based on the nominal surface dimensions (width by length). With the exception of nominal thicknesses under 1 in, the nominal thicknesses and widths in this table are the same as the board measure or count sizes.

[b] In tongue-and-grooved flooring and in tongue-and-grooved shiplapped ceiling of $\frac{5}{16}$-in, $\frac{7}{16}$-in, and $\frac{9}{16}$-in (8, 11, 14 mm) dressed thicknesses, the tongue or lap shall be $\frac{3}{16}$-in (5 mm) wide, with the overall widths $\frac{3}{16}$-in (5 mm) wider than the face widths shown in Table 1-6. In all other worked lumber of dressed thicknesses of $\frac{5}{8}$-in to $1\frac{1}{4}$-in (16 to 32 mm) the tongue shall be $\frac{1}{4}$-in (6 mm) wide or wider in tongue-and-grooved lumber, and the lap $\frac{3}{8}$-in (16 mm) wide or wider in shiplapped lumber, and the overall widths shall be not less than the dressed face widths shown in Table 1-6 plus the width of the tongue or lap.

[c] Metric equivalents are approximate and included for information only.

SOURCE: Canadian Standards Association.

Table 1-7

NOMINAL AND MINIMUM-DRESSED DRY SIZES OF SIDING AT 19 PERCENT MAXIMUM MOISTURE CONTENT
(The thicknesses apply to all widths and all widths to all thicknesses.)

Item	Thicknesses			Face Widths		
	Nominal[a]	Minimum Dressed		Nominal	Minimum Dressed	
		Inches	Millimeters[b]		Inches	Millimeters[b]
Bevel siding	$\frac{1}{2}$	$\frac{7}{16}$ butt, $\frac{3}{16}$ tip	11, 5	4	$3\frac{1}{2}$	89
	$\frac{9}{16}$	$\frac{15}{32}$ butt, $\frac{3}{16}$ tip	12, 5	5	$4\frac{1}{2}$	114
	$\frac{5}{8}$	$\frac{9}{16}$ butt, $\frac{3}{16}$ tip	14, 5	6	$5\frac{1}{2}$	140
	$\frac{3}{4}$	$\frac{11}{16}$ butt, $\frac{3}{16}$ tip	18, 5	8	$7\frac{1}{4}$	184
	1	$\frac{3}{4}$ butt, $\frac{3}{16}$ tip	19, 5	10	$9\frac{1}{4}$	235
				12	$11\frac{1}{4}$	286
Bungalow siding	$\frac{3}{4}$	$\frac{11}{16}$ butt, $\frac{3}{16}$ tip	18, 5	8	$7\frac{1}{4}$	184
				10	$9\frac{1}{4}$	235
				12	$11\frac{1}{4}$	286
Rustic drop siding— shiplapped, $\frac{3}{8}$-in lap (10 mm)	$\frac{5}{8}$	$\frac{9}{16}$	14	4	3	76
	1	$\frac{23}{32}$	18	5	4	102
				6	5	127
Rustic drop siding— shiplapped, $\frac{1}{2}$-in lap (13 mm)	$\frac{5}{8}$	$\frac{9}{16}$	14	4	$2\frac{7}{8}$	73
	1	$\frac{23}{32}$	18	5	$3\frac{7}{8}$	98
				6	$4\frac{7}{8}$	124
				8	$6\frac{5}{8}$	168
				10	$8\frac{5}{8}$	219
				12	$10\frac{5}{8}$	270
Rustic and drop siding— dressed and matched	$\frac{5}{8}$	$\frac{9}{16}$	14	4	$3\frac{1}{8}$	79
	1	$\frac{23}{32}$	18	5	$4\frac{1}{8}$	105
				6	$5\frac{1}{8}$	130
				8	$6\frac{7}{8}$	175
				10	$8\frac{7}{8}$	225

[a] For nominal thicknesses under 1 in, the board measure count is based on the nominal surface dimension (width by length). With the exception of nominal thicknesses under 1 in, the nominal thicknesses and widths in this table are the same as the board measure or count sizes.
[b] Metric equivalents are approximate and included for information only.
SOURCE: Canadian Standards Association.

SOFTWOOD LUMBER GRADES

Grading is a system of classifying lumber in order to provide the proper material for a specific end use. To make the system as simple as possible, a limited number of grades have been established but with enough differentiation to satisfy the needs of users.

Softwood lumber is graded according to its *use*, and the first division separates it into the three use classifications: *yard lumber, factory lumber,* and *structural lumber.*

Yard Lumber

Yard lumber is lumber of those grades, sizes, and patterns which are generally intended for ordinary construction and general building purposes. It is first classified on the basis of *quality,* with the two basic quality classifications being Selects and Commons.

Select is specified as being lumber of good appearance and finishing qualities which is (1) suitable for natural finishes or (2) suitable for paint finishes.

Common is specified as being lumber which is suitable for general construction and utility purposes. It may be used for (1) standard construction or (2) less-exacting construction.

Yard lumber is then divided into a number of categories, which include V.G. (vertical grain), F.G. (flat grain), and/or M.G. (mixed grain) finishing materials, boards, light framing, and studs.

Table 1-8
NOMINAL AND MINIMUM-DRESSED SIZES OF BOARDS, DIMENSION, AND TIMBERS
(The thicknesses apply to all widths and all widths to all thicknesses.)

Item	Nominal (Thickness)	Dry Inches	Dry Millimeters[a]	Green Inches	Green Millimeters[a]	Nominal (Face Width)	Dry Inches	Dry Millimeters[a]	Green Inches	Green Millimeters[a]
Boards	1	11/16	18	3/4	19	2	1 1/2	78	1 9/16	40
	1 1/4	1	25	1 1/32	26	3	2 1/2	63	2 9/16	65
	1 1/2	1 1/4	32	1 9/32	32	4	3 1/2	89	3 9/16	90
						5	4 1/2	114	4 5/8	118
						6	5 1/2	140	5 5/8	143
						7	6 1/2	165	6 5/8	168
						8	7 1/4	184	7 1/2	190
						9	8 1/4	210	8 1/2	216
						10	9 1/4	235	9 1/2	241
						11	10 1/4	260	10 1/2	267
						12	11 1/4	286	11 1/2	292
						14	13 1/4	336	13 1/2	343
						16	15 1/4	387	15 1/2	394
Dimension	2	1 1/2	38	1 9/16	40	2	1 1/2	38	1 9/16	40
	2 1/2	2	51	2 1/16	52	3	2 1/2	64	2 9/16	65
	3	2 1/2	64	2 9/16	65	4	3 1/2	89	3 9/16	90
	3 1/2	3	76	3 1/16	78	5	4 1/2	114	4 5/8	118
						6	5 1/2	140	5 5/8	143
						8	7 1/4	184	7 1/2	190
						10	9 1/4	235	9 1/2	241
						12	11 1/4	286	11 1/2	292
						14	13 1/4	336	13 1/2	343
						16	15 1/4	387	15 1/2	394
Dimension	4	3 1/2	89	3 9/16	90	2	1 1/2	38	1 9/16	40
	4 1/2	4	102	4 1/16	103	3	2 1/2	64	2 9/16	65
						4	3 1/2	99	3 9/16	90
						5	4 1/2	114	4 5/8	118
						6	5 1/2	140	5 5/8	143
						8	7 1/4	184	7 1/2	190
						10	9 1/4	235	9 1/2	241
						12	11 1/4	286	11 1/2	292
						14			13 1/2	343
						16			15 1/2	394
Timbers	5 & thicker			1/2 off	13 off	5 & wider			1/2 off	13 off

[a] Metric equivalents are approximate and included for information only.
SOURCE: Canadian Standards Association.

FINISHING MATERIALS Finishing materials are subdivided into several classes, based on use: *finish, ceiling and siding, casing and base, flooring, stepping, clear paneling,* and window and door *jambs and sills.* All are normally produced kiln dried (K.D.), in V.G., F.G., and/or M.G.

Finish, 2 in (38 mm) and thinner in thickness and 2 in (38 mm) and wider, is produced in all species except western red cedar. Figure 1-30 illustrates the shape. It is divided into two grades—C and Better and D—based on quality and appearance.

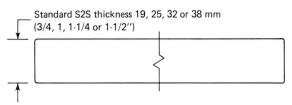

Fig. 1-30 Finish profile.

Standard S2S thickness 19, 25, 32 or 38 mm (3/4, 1, 1-1/4 or 1-1/2")

Table 1-9
NOMINAL AND MINIMUM-DRESSED SIZES OF (2-IN AND UNDER) SHIPLAP, CENTER MATCH, AND D & M (The thicknesses apply to all widths and all widths to all thicknesses.)

Item	Thicknesses					Face Widths				
	Nominal	Minimum Dressed				Nominal	Minimum Dressed			
		Dry		Green			Dry		Green	
		Inches	Milli-meters[a]	Inches	Milli-meters[a]		Inches	Milli-meters[a]	Inches	Milli-meters[a]
Shiplap, $\frac{5}{8}$-in lap (16 mm)	1	$\frac{3}{4}$	19	$\frac{25}{32}$	20	4	$3\frac{1}{8}$	79	$3\frac{3}{16}$	81
						6	$5\frac{1}{8}$	130	$5\frac{1}{4}$	133
						8	$6\frac{7}{8}$	175	$7\frac{1}{8}$	181
						10	$8\frac{7}{8}$	225	$9\frac{1}{8}$	232
						12	$10\frac{7}{8}$	276	$11\frac{1}{8}$	283
						14	$12\frac{7}{8}$	327	$13\frac{1}{8}$	334
						16	$14\frac{7}{8}$	378	$15\frac{1}{8}$	384
Shiplap, $\frac{1}{2}$-in lap (13 mm)	5	$\frac{3}{4}$	19	$\frac{25}{32}$	20	4	3	76	$3\frac{1}{16}$	78
						6	5	127	$5\frac{1}{8}$	130
						8	$6\frac{3}{4}$	171	7	178
						10	$8\frac{3}{4}$	222	9	229
						12	$10\frac{3}{4}$	273	11	279
						14	$12\frac{3}{4}$	324	13	330
						16	$14\frac{3}{4}$	375	15	381
Center-match, $\frac{1}{4}$-in tongue (6 mm)	1	$\frac{3}{4}$	19	$\frac{25}{32}$	20	4	$3\frac{1}{8}$	79	$3\frac{3}{16}$	81
	$1\frac{1}{4}$	1	25	$1\frac{1}{32}$	26	5	$4\frac{1}{8}$	105	$4\frac{1}{4}$	108
	$1\frac{1}{2}$	$1\frac{1}{4}$	32	$1\frac{9}{32}$	32	6	$5\frac{1}{8}$	130	$5\frac{1}{4}$	133
						8	$6\frac{7}{8}$	175	$7\frac{1}{8}$	181
						10	$8\frac{7}{8}$	225	$9\frac{1}{8}$	332
						12	$10\frac{7}{8}$	276	$11\frac{1}{8}$	383
2-inch D & M, $\frac{5}{8}$-in tongue (16 mm)	2	$1\frac{1}{2}$	38	$1\frac{9}{16}$	40	4	3	76	$3\frac{1}{16}$	78
						6	5	127	$5\frac{1}{8}$	130
						8	$6\frac{3}{4}$	171	7	178
						10	$8\frac{3}{4}$	222	9	229
						12	$10\frac{3}{4}$	273	11	279
2-inch shiplap, $\frac{1}{2}$-in lap (13 mm)	2	$1\frac{1}{2}$	38	$1\frac{9}{16}$	40	4	3	76	$3\frac{1}{16}$	78
						6	5	127	$5\frac{1}{8}$	130
						8	$6\frac{3}{4}$	171	7	178
						10	$8\frac{3}{4}$	222	9	229
						12	$10\frac{3}{4}$	273	11	279

[a] Metric equivalents are approximate and included for information only.
SOURCE: Canadian Standards Association.

Ceiling and siding, 2 in (38 mm) and thinner and 3, 4, 6, and 8 in (64, 89, 140, and 184 mm) and wider, is produced S2S, with edges tongue-and-grooved, shiplapped, or otherwise patterned, in all species except western red cedar. It is divided into three grades—C and Better, D, and E—based on quality and appearance. Ceiling and siding patterns are illustrated in Fig. 1-31.

Casing and base, 1 in (19 mm) thick and 2 in (38 mm) or wider, is usually run to a pattern, with the reverse side hollow or *scratched* (roughened). It is divided into three grades—C and Better, D, and E—based on the quality and appearance of the face and edges. Figure 1-32 indicates some typical casing and base patterns.

Flooring, 2 in (38 mm) and thinner and 3, 4, and 6 in (64, 89, and 140 mm) wide, is produced S2S, with tongue-and-groove edges. The reverse side

Table 1-10
WORKED LUMBER[a] SUCH AS FACTORY FLOORING, HEAVY ROOFING, DECKING, AND SHEET PILING (The thicknesses apply to all widths and all widths to all thicknesses.)

Item	Thicknesses[b]					Face Widths				
		Minimum Dressed					Minimum Dressed			
	Nominal	Dry		Green		Nominal	Dry		Green	
		Inches	Milli-meters[c]	Inches	Milli-meters[c]		Inches	Milli-meters[c]	Inches	Milli-meters[c]
Tongue-and-grooved	$2\frac{1}{2}$	2	51	$2\frac{1}{16}$	52	4	3	76	$3\frac{1}{16}$	78
	3	$2\frac{1}{2}$	64	$2\frac{9}{16}$	65	6	5	127	$5\frac{1}{8}$	130
	$3\frac{1}{2}$	3	76	$3\frac{1}{16}$	78	8	$6\frac{3}{4}$	171	7	178
	4	$3\frac{1}{2}$	89	$3\frac{9}{16}$	90	10	$8\frac{3}{4}$	222	9	229
	$4\frac{1}{2}$	4	102	$4\frac{1}{16}$	103	12	$10\frac{3}{4}$	273	11	279
Shiplap	$2\frac{1}{2}$	2	51	$2\frac{1}{16}$	52	4	3	76	$3\frac{1}{16}$	78
	3	$2\frac{1}{2}$	63	$2\frac{9}{16}$	65	6	5	127	$5\frac{1}{8}$	130
	$3\frac{1}{2}$	3	76	$3\frac{1}{16}$	78	8	$6\frac{3}{4}$	171	7	178
	4	$3\frac{1}{2}$	89	$3\frac{9}{16}$	90	10	$8\frac{3}{4}$	222	9	229
	$4\frac{1}{2}$	4	102	$4\frac{1}{16}$	103	12	$10\frac{3}{4}$	273	11	279
Grooved-for-splines	$2\frac{1}{2}$	2	51	$2\frac{1}{16}$	52	4	$3\frac{1}{2}$	89	$3\frac{9}{16}$	90
	3	$2\frac{1}{2}$	64	$2\frac{9}{16}$	65	6	$5\frac{1}{2}$	140	$5\frac{5}{8}$	143
	$3\frac{1}{2}$	3	76	$3\frac{1}{16}$	78	8	$7\frac{1}{4}$	184	$7\frac{1}{2}$	190
	4	$3\frac{1}{2}$	89	$3\frac{9}{16}$	90	10	$9\frac{1}{4}$	235	$9\frac{1}{2}$	241
	$4\frac{1}{2}$	4	102	$4\frac{1}{16}$	103	12	$11\frac{1}{4}$	286	$11\frac{1}{2}$	292

[a] In worked lumber of nominal thicknesses of 2 in and over, the tongue shall be $\frac{5}{8}$ in (16 mm) wide in tongue-and-grooved lumber and the lap $\frac{1}{2}$ in (13 mm) wide in shiplapped lumber, with the overall widths $\frac{5}{8}$ in (16 mm) and $\frac{1}{2}$ in (13 mm) wider, respectively, than the face widths shown in the above table. Double tongue-and-grooved decking may be manufactured with a $\frac{5}{16}$-in (8 mm) tongue.

[b] See Table 1-9 for information on 2-in dimension.

[c] Metric equivalents are approximate and included for information only.

SOURCE: Canadian Standards Association.

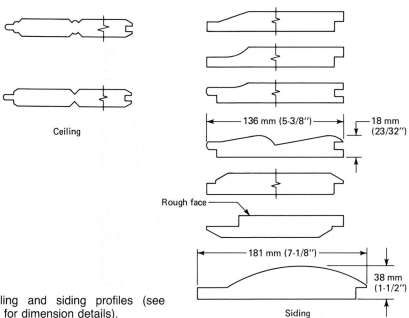

Fig. 1-31 Ceiling and siding profiles (see Grading Rules for dimension details).

Table 1-11
GREEN SIZE REQUIREMENTS FOR WESTERN RED CEDAR AND EASTERN WHITE CEDAR

Thicknesses			Widths		
Nominal	Minimum Dressed		Nominal	Minimum Dressed	
	Inches	Millimeters[a]		Inches	Millimeters[a]
$\frac{5}{8}$ dry	$\frac{21}{32}$	17	3	$2\frac{9}{16}$	65
1	$\frac{25}{32}$	20	4	$3\frac{9}{16}$	90
2	$1\frac{9}{16}$	40	5	$4\frac{9}{16}$	116
$2\frac{1}{2}$	$2\frac{1}{16}$	52	6	$5\frac{9}{16}$	141
3	$2\frac{9}{16}$	65	7	$6\frac{9}{16}$	167
$3\frac{1}{2}$	$3\frac{1}{16}$	78	8	$7\frac{3}{8}$	187
4	$3\frac{9}{16}$	90	10	$9\frac{3}{8}$	238
$4\frac{1}{2}$	$4\frac{1}{16}$	103	12	$11\frac{3}{8}$	289
			14	$13\frac{7}{16}$	341
			16	$15\frac{7}{16}$	392

[a] Metric equivalents are approximate and are included for information only.
SOURCE: Canadian Standards Association.

may be partially surfaced, hollow, or scratched. Flooring is divided into three grades—C and Better, D, and E—based on quality and appearance. Figure 1-33 illustrates softwood flooring profiles.

Stepping, 2 in (38 mm) or less in thickness and $7\frac{1}{4}$ in (184 mm) and wider, is made S2S1E and *bullnosed* on the opposite edge. (See Fig. 1-34.) It is divided into two grades—C and Better and D—based on finish, strength, and wearing ability.

Clear paneling, $\frac{23}{32}$ in (18 mm) in thickness and $5\frac{3}{8}$, $7\frac{1}{8}$, $9\frac{1}{8}$, or $11\frac{1}{8}$ in (140, 184, 235, and 286 mm) in width, is produced in all species except western red cedar. It is graded under finish rules, in one face grade. (See Fig. 1-35 for paneling patterns.)

Door and window jamb and sills, 2 in (38 mm) in thickness and various widths, are graded under the finish rules, in one face grade. Figure 1-36 illustrates the shapes.

For details on the allowable defects and specifications for each grade in each class of finishing material, consult "Standard Grading Rules," published by the National Lumber Grades Authority.

BOARDS   Boards are included in a category called *boards, sheathing, and form lumber,* which may be rough or surfaced, plain-edged, shiplapped, or tongue-and-grooved, under 2 in (38 mm) in thickness and 2 in (38 mm) and wider. They are produced in five grades: Select Merchantable, Construction, Standard, Utility, and Economy. The exact characteristics and limiting provisions of each are given in grading and dressing rules. The top grade

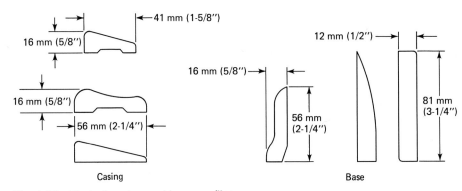

Fig. 1-32   Typical casing and base profiles.

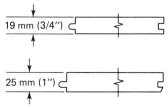

Fig. 1-33 Softwood flooring profiles (see Grading Rules for dimension details).

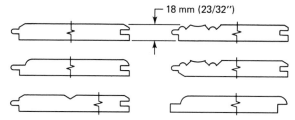

Fig. 1-35 Clear paneling profiles (see Grading Rules for dimension details).

in this category is recommended for high-class work and exposed use, both inside and out, and will usually be of the finest appearance. Construction grade is widely used for subfloors, walls, roof sheathing, and form work. The remaining grades are quite serviceable but have less importance placed on appearance and presence of defects. Manufacturers recommend the best use for each grade.

LIGHT FRAMING   Lumber in this category is produced 2 to 4 in (38 to 89 mm) thick and 2 to 4 in (38 to 89 mm) wide, in random lengths. It is divided into four grades—Construction, Standard, Utility, and Economy—all of which are *stress rated* except Economy. The characteristics permitted and the limiting provisions for each grade are detailed in "Standard Grading Rules."

Pieces in Construction grade are of good appearance but are graded primarily for strength and serviceability and are widely used for general framing purposes. Standard light framing is used for essentially the same purposes as, or in conjunction with, Construction grade, although the limiting provisions are somewhat less stringent.

Utility light framing is used where a combination of good strength and economical construction is desired and may be used for such purposes as *studding, rafters, braces, blocking,* and *plates. Economy* grade is suitable for temporary or low-cost construction and for such things as *bracing, blocking, cribbing,* etc.

STUDS   This category of yard lumber is produced in thicknesses of 2 to 4 in (38 to 89 mm), in widths up to 4 in (89 mm), and in lengths of 10 ft (3 m) and shorter. It is divided into two grades: Stud and Economy Stud.

The Stud grade is limited in characteristics which affect strength and stiffness so that the grade is suitable for use in load-bearing walls. The value of the *fiber stress* in bending for this grade is 26 percent of that allowed for clear, straight-grained wood, and the value of the recommended *modulus of elasticity* is 80 percent of that allowed for clear wood. The Economy grade is not stress rated and its uses are limited to those recommended for Economy light framing.

Factory Lumber

Factory or shop lumber is lumber which has been produced or selected primarily for remanufacturing purposes and normally includes Door Stock. Factory lumber includes material 2 in (38 mm) and less in thickness, 5 in (114 mm) and greater in

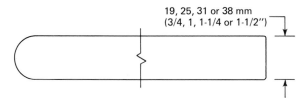

Fig. 1-34 Stepping profile (see Grading Rules for dimension details).

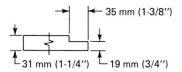
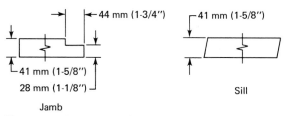

Fig. 1-36 Jamb and sill profiles (see Grading Rules for dimension details).

width, and in random lengths of 4 ft (1.2 m) or more. The grading rules apply to all species except western red cedar and divide the material into four grades: Select Shop, No. 1 Shop, No. 2 Shop, and No. 3 Shop.

The various grades, valued for their *cutting* qualities, are based on the quality and percentage of cuttings obtainable from each piece. Cuttings are of two sizes: (1) $9\frac{1}{2}$ in (241 mm) or wider and 18 in (457 mm) or longer and (2) 5 in (125 mm) or wider and 3 ft (1 m) or longer. They are divided into three grades: A cuttings must be clear both sides, with bright sapwood admitted; B cuttings must have a face equal to B and Better Industrial; C cuttings are *sash cuttings* $2\frac{1}{2}$ in (64 mm), $3\frac{1}{2}$ in (89 mm), and $4\frac{1}{2}$ in (114 mm) wide and 28 in (711 mm) and over in length. Select Shop consists of at least 70 percent A and/or B cuttings. No. 1 Shop consists of 50 to 70 percent of A and/or B cuttings. No. 2 Shop consists of $33\frac{1}{3}$ to 50 percent A and/or B cuttings. No. 3 Shop admits all factory-lumber-type pieces below the grade of No. 2 Shop, if they contain at least 10 percent of mixed A and/or B cuttings and 30 percent or more of mixed C cuttings or 50 percent of C cuttings.

Structural Timber

Structural timber is lumber which is 2 in (38 mm) or more in nominal thickness and width, intended for use in situations in which working stresses are required. As a result, such lumber is *stress graded*, and to accomplish this, minimum strength is assured through the allocation to each grade of what are known as safe allowable working stresses. These are obtained from *basic stresses,* compiled as the result of individual tests on thousands of small, clear specimens.

By limiting the size and position of defects and characteristics such as *knots, checks, splits,* and *slope of grain,* strength ratios can be established for any grade and safe, allowable working stresses allocated to that grade. The properties for which allowable stresses are allocated include *bending, compression, tension, shear,* and *relative stiffness* (modulus of elasticity). These allowable working stresses vary with the different species and within the grades in each category.

Since a number of softwood lumber species have characteristics similar to one another and can be used together or interchangeably, certain commercial species are combined into a single species designation and marketed under a group name. (See Fig. 1-27.) For example, Douglas fir and western larch are grouped together in a designation known as D Fir-L. Table 1-12 lists common commercial species groups and the characteristics of each group.

Structural lumber is divided into a number of categories: *structural light framing, structural joists and planks, decking, beams and stringers,* and *posts and columns.* Each category is divided into one or more grades, each of which is described in detail in "Standard Grading Rules." Tables 1-13 and 1-14 (p. 27 and p. 31) list working stresses for common species and species combinations, in each category and grade for which working stresses are given, for both light framing and structural lumber. (See the notes under the tables.)

HARDWOOD LUMBER

Hardwood lumber is produced from *deciduous* trees, those that drop their leaves each year, including *alder, ash, basswood, beech, birch, butternut, cherry, cottonwood, elm, gum, hickory, locust, magnolia, mahogany, maple, oak, pecan, poplar, sycamore, tupelo,* and *walnut.*

Hardwood lumber is produced in a variety of categories, including *boards*—Construction and Utility—*dimension lumber, finishing lumber,* and *structural timbers,* which are used for many purposes, such as *flooring, wall paneling, interior trim and moldings, stair rails, risers* and *treads, furniture* (including pianos), *plywood veneers, wagon stock, railway car stock, mine stock,* and *sheet piling.*

Standard Hardwood Rules and Grades

Because of the differing inherent qualities, growth characteristics, and end uses of hardwoods, the grading methods are substantially different from those used for grading softwoods. Whereas a softwood board is generally graded as a whole piece, a hardwood board is graded on its usable content, aside from any undesirable parts containing any of the standard defects. Thus the term *cutting* is introduced into hardwood grading. A cutting is a portion of a board or plank obtained by cross-cutting

Table 1-12
SOFTWOOD SPECIES AND GROUPS

Commercial Species Group Designation	Grade Stamp Identification	Species in Combination	Wood Characteristics
Most common			
Spruce-Pine-Fir	S-P-F	Spruce (all species except Coast Sitka spruce) Lodgepole pine Jack pine Alpine fir Balsam fir	Woods of similar characteristics. They work easily, take paint easily, and hold nails well. Generally white to pale yellow in color.
Douglas fir-Larch (North)[1]	D Fir-L (N)	Douglas fir Western larch	High degree of hardness and good resistance to decay. Good nail holding, gluing, and painting qualities. Color ranges from reddish-brown to yellowish-white.
Hem-Fir (North)[1]	Hem-Fir (N)	Western hemlock Amabilis fir	They work easily, take paint well, and hold nails well. Good gluing characteristics. Color ranges pale yellow-brown to white.
Less common			
Eastern hemlock-Tamarack (North)[1]	Hem-Tam (N)	Eastern hemlock Tamarack	Mostly used for general construction. Fairly hard and durable. Color ranges yellowish-brown to whitish.
Coast species	Coast Species, or often marked individually as: D Fir (N) Larch (N) W Hem (N) Am Fir (N) G Fir (N)	Douglas fir Western larch Western hemlock Amabilis fir Grand fir	See characteristics within previous groups that they are listed in.
	C Sitka	Coast Sitka spruce	A light, resilient wood that works and takes paint easily, and holds nails well. Creamy white to light pink in color with large proportion of clear wood.
Western cedars (North)[1]	W Cedar (N)	Western red cedar Pacific coast yellow cedar	Woods with exceptional resistance to decay. Relatively weak in strength. High in appearance qualities, they work easily and take fine finishes. Each species has distinct and easily recognizable colorations; red cedar varies from reddish-brown heartwood to light sapwood, and yellow cedar has a uniform warm yellow color.
Northern species	North Species, or often marked individually as: R Pine (N) P Pine	All species above plus: Red pine Ponderosa pine	See characteristics of previous groups. Fairly strong and easy to work, it takes a good finish. Holds nails and screws well. Moderately durable; it seasons with little checking or cupping. Sapwood is pale yellow; heartwood pale brown to reddish tinge.

Table 1-12 (continued)
SOFTWOOD SPECIES AND GROUPS

Commercial Species Group Designation	Grade Stamp Identification	Species in Combination	Wood Characteristics
Northern species	W W Pine	Western white pine	Softest of the Canadian pines, it works and finishes exceptionally well. Not as strong as most pines but does not tend to split or splinter. Good nail-holding properties. Low shrinkage, better than all other Canadian species except the cedars. Takes stains, paints, and varnishes well. Color of sapwood almost white; heartwood creamy white to light straw brown.
	East White Pine (E W Pine) (N)	Eastern white pine	
Northern aspen[2]	N Aspen	Trembling aspen Largetooth aspen Balsam poplar	Light woods of moderate strength, they work easily, finish well, and hold nails well. Generally light in color, varying from almost white to grayish-white.
Black cottonwood[2][3]	B Cot	Black cottonwood	Characteristics similar to those of northern aspen group, but it is lower in strength and stiffness. No specified strength provided for black cottonwood.

NOTES: **1.** Designation "North" or "N" in the grade mark provides regional identification for lumber exported to U.S.
        2. Northern aspen species group and black cottonwood are technically hardwoods, but are graded and marketed under softwood standards.
        3. Normally not marketed in Canada.
SOURCE: CWC Datafile WS-1, Canadian Wood Council. Used with permission.

or ripping or both (diagonal cuttings are not permitted) and may be designated as *clear-face* or *sound.* A clear-face cutting is a cutting which has one clear face and a sound reverse side. A sound cutting is free from rot, pith, shake, and wane.

Because of its relative scarcity, hardwood lumber is produced in a much greater range of lengths, widths, and thicknesses than softwoods, including very thin slabs, called *flitches,* which are often used to cover less expensive woods (see Table 1-15 on page 35).

The standard grades of hardwood lumber are Firsts, Seconds, Selects, No. 1 Common, No. 2 Common, Sound Wormy, No. 3A Common, and No. 3B Common. Firsts and Seconds are usually combined as one grade, with various percentages of Firsts being required in the combined grade, depending on the species. For example, in Philippine mahogany, 40 percent of the combined grade must be Firsts; in plain oak, $33\frac{1}{3}$ percent of the combined grade must be Firsts.

Selects and No. 1 Common may be combined as one grade with some species, and No. 3A Common and No. 3B Common may be combined as No. 3 Common.

The grading rules covering Firsts and Seconds are generally as follows:

1. Widths may be 6 in (140 mm) and wider.

2. Lengths may be 8 to 16 ft (2.4 and 4.8 m), admitting 30 percent of 8 to 11 ft (2.4 to 3.3 m), of which one-half may be 8 and 9 ft (2.4 and 2.7 m).

3. No piece shall be admitted which contains pith exceeding in length the number of inches equal to the length of the board in feet (82 mm per meter of length).

4. Wane exceeding in length one-twelfth of the length of the piece will not be admitted; splits must not exceed in length the number of inches equal to twice the length of the board in feet (164 mm per meter of length).

(Text continued on p. 34.)

Table 1-13
ALLOWABLE STRESSES FOR LIGHT FRAMING AND STRUCTURAL LUMBER (Metric—MPa) (Dry)

Grade Category	Commercial Species or Species Group Designation	Grade	Bending		Compression		Tension Parallel to Grain	Mod-ulus of Elasticity
			Stress at Extreme Fiber	Longitu-dinal Shear	Parallel to Grain	Per-pendic-ular to Grain		
Light framing 38 × 89 mm only	D Fir-L	Construction Standard Utility	7.6 4.1 2.1	0.62	7.9 6.55 4.1	3.2	4.5 2.4 1.0	9,928
	Hem-Tam	Construction Standard Utility	6.9 3.8 1.7	0.62	7.2 5.9 3.8	2.8	4.1 2.4 1.0	7,653
	S. pine	Construction Standard Utility	6.9 4.0 1.9	0.7 0.62 0.62	7.6 6.2 4.0	2.8	4.1 2.4 1.0	9,653
	S. pine mixed species	Construction Standard Utility	6.55 3.9 1.7	0.59	8.0 6.5 4.5	1.9	3.9 2.1 0.9	7,894
	Hem-Fir	Construction Standard Utility	5.5 3.1 1.4	0.48	6.55 5.2 3.4	1.6	3.4 1.7 0.7	8,894
	Coast species	Construction Standard Utility	5.5 3.1 1.4	0.41	5.9 4.8 3.1	1.6	3.1 1.7 0.7	8,894
	S-P-F	Construction Standard Utility	5.2 3.1 1.4	0.45	5.5 4.5 3.1	1.7	3.1 1.7 0.7	7,446
	W. cedar	Construction Standard Utility	5.5 3.1 1.4	0.48	6.2 4.5 3.4	1.9	3.1 1.7 0.7	6,688
Structural light fram-ing Stud 38 × 89 mm only	D Fir-L	Select Struct. No. 1 No. 2 No. 3 Stud	15.2 12.75 10.7 5.9 5.9	0.62	11.0 8.6 6.9 4.1 4.1	3.2	8.6 7.6 6.2 3.4 3.4	12,410 12,410 11,169 9,928 9,928
	Hem-Tam	Select Struct. No. 1 No. 2 No. 3 Stud	13.8 11.7 9.65 5.5 5.5	0.62	10.0 7.9 6.2 3.8 3.8	2.79	8.3 6.9 5.9 3.1 3.1	9,584 9,584 8,618 7,653 7,653
	S. pine	D. Select Struct. Select Struct. No. 1 Dense No. 1 No. 2 Dense No. 2 No. 3 Dense No. 3 Stud	16.2 13.8 13.8 11.7 11.4 9.6 6.4 5.3 5.3	0.69 0.69 0.69 0.69 0.62 0.62 0.62 0.62 0.62	12.4 10.7 10.0 8.6 7.9 6.7 4.6 4.0 4.0	3.27 2.79 3.27 2.79 3.27 2.79 3.27 2.79 2.79	9.3 7.9 7.9 6.9 6.7 5.7 3.6 3.1 3.1	12,410 11,721 12,410 11,721 11,032 11,032 10,342 9,653 9,653
	S. pine mixed species	Select Struct. No. 1 No. 2 No. 3 Stud	12.8 11.1 9.0 5.1 5.1	0.59	11.5 9.0 7.0 4.5 4.5	1.91	7.7 6.4 5.1 3.0 3.0	9,866 9,866 8,915 7,894 7,894

Table 1-13 (continued)

Grade Category	Commercial Species or Species Group Designation	Grade	Bending		Compression		Tension Parallel to Grain	Modulus of Elasticity
			Stress at Extreme Fiber	Longitudinal Shear	Parallel to Grain	Perpendicular to Grain		
Structural light framing Stud 38 × 89 mm only	Hem-Fir	Select Struct. No. 1 No. 2 No. 3 Stud	11.0 9.3 7.9 4.1 4.1	0.48	8.9 7.2 5.5 4.4 4.4	1.62	6.5 5.5 4.5 2.4 2.4	11,169 11.169 9,997 9,584 9,584
	Coast species	Select Struct. No. 1 No. 2 No. 3 Stud	11.0 9.3 7.6 4.1 4.1	0.41	8.3 6.55 5.2 3.1 3.1	1.62	6.2 5.5 4.5 2.4 2.4	11,169 11,169 9,997 8,894 8,894
	S-P-F	Select Struct. No. 1 No. 2 No. 3 Stud	10.3 9.0 7.2 4.1 4.1	0.45	7.9 6.2 4.8 3.1 3.1	1.67	6.2 5.2 4.1 2.4 2.4	9,308 9,308 8,412 7,446 7,446
	W. cedar	Select Struct. No. 1 No. 2 No. 3 Stud	10.7 9.0 7.6 4.1 4.1	0.48	9.0 6.9 5.5 3.4 3.4	1.93	6.2 5.2 4.5 2.4 2.4	8,343 8,343 7,515 6,688 6,688
Structural joists and planks 38 to 89 mm thick, 114 mm and wider	D Fir-L	Select Struct. No. 1 No. 2 No. 3	12.75 11.0 9.0 5.2	0.62	9.65 8.6 7.2 4.5	3.2	8.6 7.2 5.9 3.4	12,410 12,410 11,169 9,928
	Hem-Tam	Select Struct. No. 1 No. 2 No. 3	11.7 10.3 8.3 4.8	0.62	8.6 7.9 6.55 3.4	2.8	7.9 6.9 5.5 3.1	9,584 9,584 8,618 7,653
	S. pine	D. Select-Struct. Select Struct. No. 1 Dense No. 1 No. 2 Dense No. 2 No. 3 Dense No. 3	15.2 12.75 12.75 11.0 10.7 9.0 6.0 5.2	0.65	12.75 11.0 11.7 10.0 9.65 8.3 5.9 5.0	3.27 2.8 3.27 2.8 3.27 2.8 3.27 2.8	10.0 8.3 8.6 7.2 5.5 4.65 3.1 2.75	13,100 12,410 13,100 12,410 11,721 11,032 10,342 10,342
	S. pine mixed species	Select Struct. No. 1 No. 2 No. 3	11.0 9.4 7.9 4.3	0.58	10.0 9.0 7.5 4.5	1.9	6.2 5.5 5.1 3.0	9,859 9,859 8,915 7,894
	Hem-Fir	Select Struct. No. 1 No. 2 No. 3	9.65 8.3 6.55 3.8	0.48	7.9 7.2 5.9 3.8	1.62	6.55 5.5 4.5 2.3	11,169 11,169 9,997 8,894
	Coast species	Select Struct. No. 1 No. 2 No. 3	9.3 7.9 6.55 3.8	0.41	7.2 6.55 5.5 3.1	1.62	6.2 5.2 4.1 2.4	11,169 11,169 9,997 8,894

Table 1-13   (continued)

Grade Category	Commercial Species or Species Group Designation	Grade	Bending		Compression		Tension Parallel to Grain	Modulus of Elasticity
			Stress at Extreme Fiber	Longitudinal Shear	Parallel to Grain	Perpendicular to Grain		
Structural joists and planks 38 to 89 mm thick, 114 mm and wider	S-P-F	Select Struct. No. 1 No. 2 No. 3	9.0 7.6 6.2 3.4	0.45	6.9 6.2 5.2 3.1	1.69	5.8 5.2 4.1 2.4	9,308 9,308 8,412 7,446
	W. cedar	Select Struct. No. 1 No. 2 No. 3	9.0 7.9 6.2 3.8	0.48	7.9 6.9 5.9 3.4	1.9	6.2 5.2 4.1 2.4	8,343 8,343 7,515 6,688
Decking, 38 to 89 mm thick, 140 mm and wider	D Fir-L	Select Commercial	12.4 10.7			3.2		12,410 11,169
	Hem-Tam	Select Commercial	11.7 9.65			2.8		9,584 8,618
	S. pine	D. Stand. Decking Select Decking D. Select Decking Comm. Decking D. Comm. Decking	13.8 9.65 11.4 9.65 11.4	0.69 0.62 0.62 0.62 0.62	10.0 6.7 7.9 6.7 7.9	3.3 2.8 3.3 2.8 3.3	7.9 5.7 6.7 5.7 6.7	12,410 11,032 11,032 11,032 11,032
	S. pine mixed spec.	Select Commercial	10.7 9.0			1.9		9,866 8,915
	Hem-Fir	Select Commercial	9.3 7.9			1.6		11,169 9,997
	Coast species	Select Commercial	9.0 7.6			1.6		11,169 9,997
	S-P-F	Select Commercial	8.6 7.2			1.7		9,308 8,412
	W. cedar	Select Commercial	9.0 7.6			1.9		8,343 7,515
Beams and stringers, 114 mm and thicker, depth more than 51 mm greater than thickness	D Fir-L	Select Struct. No. 1	11.7 9.3	0.59	7.6 6.2	3.2	6.9 4.8	11,859
	Hem-Tam	Select Struct. No. 1	10.69 8.6	0.59	6.9 5.9	2.8	6.2 4.5	8,963
	S. pine	No. 1 Dense SR No. 1 SR No. 2 Dense SR No. 2 SR	10.7 9.3 8.6 7.6	0.76 0.65	6.4 5.3 5.0 4.3	2.2 1.9 2.2 1.9	7.2 6.0 5.9 5.9	11,032 10,342 9,653
	S. pine mixed spec.	Select Struct. No. 1	9.8 8.1	0.55	8.0 6.5	1.89	6.0 4.3	8,839

Table 1-13 (continued)

Grade Category	Commercial Species or Species Group Designation	Grade	Bending		Compression		Tension Parallel to Grain	Modulus of Elasticity
			Stress at Extreme Fiber	Longitudinal Shear	Parallel to Grain	Perpendicular to Grain		
Beams and stringers, 114 mm and thicker, depth more than 51 mm greater than thickness	Hem-Fir	Select Struct. No. 1	8.6 6.9	0.45	6.2 5.2	1.62	5.2 3.4	9,997
	Coast species	Select Struct. No. 1	8.3 6.9	0.38	5.9 4.8	1.62	4.8 3.4	9,997
	S-P-F	Select Struct. No. 1	7.9 6.55	0.41	5.5 4.5	1.7	4.8 3.4	8,343
	W. cedar	Select Struct. No. 1	8.3 6.55	0.45	6.2 5.2	1.9	4.8 3.4	7,722
Posts and timbers, 114 × 114 mm and larger, depth not more than 51 mm greater than thickness	D Fir-L	Select Struct. No. 1	10.7 8.3	0.79 0.59	8.3 7.2	3.2	7.2 5.5	11,859 10,687
	Hem-Tam	Select Struct. No. 1	10.0 7.6	0.79 0.59	7.2 6.55	2.8	6.55 4.8	9,170 8,274
	S. pine	No. 1 Dense Sr	10.7	0.76	6.4	2.2	7.2	11,032
		No. 1 SR	9.3		5.3	1.9	6.0	10,342
		No. 2 Dense SR	8.6	0.65	5.0	2.2	5.9	9,653
		No. 2 SR	7.6		4.3	1.89	5.0	
	S. pine mixed spec.	Select Struct. No. 1	9.4 6.8	0.76 0.55	8.5 7.5	1.9	6.4 4.7	8,846 7,963
	Hem-Fir	Select Struct. No. 1	7.9 6.2	0.62 0.45	6.55 5.9	1.62	5.5 4.1	9,997 8,963
	Coast species	Select Struct. No. 1	7.9 5.9	0.52 0.38	6.2 5.5	1.62	5.2 3.8	9,997 8,963
	S-P-F	Select Struct. No. 1	7.6 5.5	0.59 0.41	5.9 5.2	1.69	5.2 3.8	7,722 7,515
	W. cedar	Select Struct. No. 1	7.6 5.9	0.62 0.45	6.55 5.5	1.93 6	5.2 3.8	7,722 6,964

NOTES:
1. Allowable fiber stress in bending for decking applies only when the plank is loaded on the wide face.
2. Allowable fiber stress in bending for beams and stringers applies only when the member is loaded on the narrow face.
3. When beams and stringers are loaded on the wide face, the allowable unit stresses for bending at the extreme fiber for Select Structural grade must be modified by the factor 0.88 and for No. 1 grade by 0.77. The modulus of elasticity for No. 1 grade must be modified by the factor 0.90.
4. If post and timber sizes are graded to beam and stringer requirements, design values for beams and stringers apply.
5. An approximate value for modulus of rigidity may be estimated as 0.065 times the modulus of elasticity.

SOURCE: Canadian Wood Council and S.P.I.B.

Table 1-14
ALLOWABLE STRESSES FOR LIGHT FRAMING AND STRUCTURAL LUMBER
(Imperial—psi) (Dry)

Grade Category	Commercial Species or Species Group Designation	Grade	Bending — Stress at Extreme Fiber	Bending — Longitudinal Shear	Compression — Parallel to Grain	Compression — Perpendicular to Grain	Tension Parallel to Grain	Modulus of Elasticity
Light framing 2 × 4 in only	D Fir-L	Construction Standard Utility	1100 600 300	90	1150 950 600	460	650 350 150	1,440,000
	Hem-Tam	Construction Standard Utility	1000 550 250	90	1050 850 550	405	600 350 150	1,110,000
	S. pine	Construction Standard Utility	1000 575 275	100 90 90	1100 900 575	405	600 350 150	1,400,000
	S. pine mixed species	Construction Standard Utility	950 560 250	85	1160 940 650	275	560 310 125	1,145,000
	Hem-Fir	Construction Standard Utility	800 450 200	70	950 750 500	235	500 250 100	1,290,000
	Coast species	Construction Standard Utility	800 450 200	60	850 700 450	235	450 250 100	1,290,000
	S-P-F	Construction Standard Utility	750 450 200	65	800 650 450	245	450 250 100	1,080,000
	W. cedar	Construction Standard Utility	800 450 200	70	900 750 500	280	450 250 100	970,000
Structural light framing, Stud and Appearance grade 2 × 4 in only	D Fir-L	Select Struct. No. 1 No. 2 No. 3 Stud	2200 1850 1550 850 850	90	1600 1250 1000 600 600	460	1250 1100 900 500 500	1,800,000 1,800,000 1,620,000 1,440,000 1,440,000
	Hem-Tam	Select Struct. No. 1 No. 2 No. 3 Stud	2000 1700 1400 800 800	90	1450 1150 900 550 550	405	1200 1000 850 450 450	1,390,000 1,390,000 1,250,000 1,110,000 1,110,000
	S. pine	D. Select Struct. Select Struct. No. 1 Dense No. 1 No. 2 Dense No. 2 No. 3 Dense No. 3 Stud	2350 2000 2000 1700 1650 1400 925 775 775	100 100 100 100 90 90 90 90 90	1800 1550 1450 1250 1150 975 675 575 575	475 405 475 405 475 405 475 405 405	1350 1150 1150 1000 975 825 525 450 450	1,800,000 1,700,000 1,800,000 1,700,000 1,600,000 1,600,000 1,500,000 1,400,000 1,400,000

Table 1-14   (continued)

Grade Category	Commercial Species or Species Group Designation	Grade	Bending		Compression		Tension Parallel to Grain	Modulus of Elasticity
			Stress at Extreme Fiber	Longitudinal Shear	Parallel to Grain	Perpendicular to Grain		
Structural light framing, Stud and Appearance grade 2 × 4 in only	S. pine mixed species	Select Struct.	1860		1670		1120	1,431,000
		No. 1	1610		1305		930	1,431,000
		No. 2	1300	85	1015	285	745	1,293,000
		No. 3	745		650		435	1,145,000
		Stud	745		650		435	1,145,000
	Hem-Fir	Select Struct.	1600		1300		950	1,620,000
		No. 1	1350		1050		800	1,620,000
		No. 2	1150	70	800	235	650	1,450,000
		No. 3	600		500		350	1,390,000
		Stud	600		500		350	1,390,000
	Coast species	Select Struct.	1600		1200		900	1,620,000
		No. 1	1350		950		800	1,620,000
		No. 2	1100	60	750	235	650	1,450,000
		No. 3	600		450		350	1,290,000
		Stud	600		450		350	1,290,000
	S-P-F	Select Struct.	1500		1150		900	1,350,000
		No. 1	1300		900		750	1,350,000
		No. 2	1050	65	700	245	600	1,220,000
		No. 3	600		450		350	1,080,000
		Stud	600		450		350	1,080,000
	W. cedar	Select Struct.	1550		1300		900	1,210,000
		No. 1	1300		1000		750	1,210,000
		No. 2	1100	70	800	280	650	1,090,000
		No. 3	600		500		350	970,000
		Stud	600		500		350	970,000
Structural joists and planks and Appearance grade, 2 to 4 in thick, 5 in and wider	D Fir-L	Select Struct.	1850		1400		1250	1,800,000
		No. 1	1600		1250		1050	1,800,000
		No. 2	1300	90	1050	460	850	1,620,000
		No. 3	750		650		500	1,440,000
	Hem-Tam	Select Struct.	1700		1250		1150	1,390,000
		No. 1	1500		1150		1000	1,390,000
		No. 2	1200	90	950	405	800	1,250,000
		No. 3	700		500		450	1,110,000
	S. pine	D. Select Struct.	2200		1850	475	1450	1,900,000
		Select Struct.	1850		1600	405	1200	1,800,000
		No. 1 Dense	1850		1700	475	1250	1,900,000
		No. 1	1600	95	1450	405	1050	1,800,000
		No. 2 Dense	1550		1400	475	800	1,700,000
		No. 2	1300		1200	405	675	1,600,000
		No. 3 Dense	875		850	475	450	1,500,000
		No. 3	750		725	405	400	1,500,000
	S. pine mixed species	Select Struct.	1600	85	1450	275	900	1,430,000
		No. 1	1365		1300		795	1,430,000
		No. 2	1115		1085		745	1,293,000
		No. 3	620		650		430	1,145,000
	Hem-Fir	Select Struct.	1400	70	1150	235	950	1,620,000
		No. 1	1200		1050		800	1,620,000
		No. 2	950		850		650	1,450,000
		No. 3	550		550		350	1,290,000

Table 1-14   (continued)

Grade Category	Commercial Species or Species Group Designation	Grade	Bending		Compression		Tension Parallel to Grain	Modulus of Elasticity
			Stress at Extreme Fiber	Longitudinal Shear	Parallel to Grain	Perpendicular to Grain		
Structural joists and planks and Appearance grade, 2 to 4 in thick, 5 in and wider	Coast species	Select Struct.	1350	60	1050	235	900	1,620,000
		No. 1	1150		950		750	1,620,000
		No. 2	950		800		600	1,450,000
		No. 3	550		450		350	1,290,000
	S-P-F	Select Struct.	1300	65	1000	245	850	1,350,000
		No. 1	1100		900		750	1,350,000
		No. 2	900		750		600	1,220,000
		No. 3	500		450		350	1,080,000
	W. cedar	Select Struct.	1300	70	1150	280	900	1,210,000
		No. 1	1150		1000		750	1,210,000
		No. 2	900		850		600	1,090,000
		No. 3	550		500		350	970,000
Decking, 2 to 4 in thick, 6 in and wider	D Fir-L	Select	1800			460		1,800,000
		Commercial	1550					1,620,000
	Hem-Tam	Select	1700			405		1,390,000
		Commercial	1400					1,250,000
	S. pine	D. Stand. Deck.	2000	100	1450	475	1150	1,800,000
		Select Deck.	1400	90	975	405	825	1,600,000
		D. Select Deck.	1650	90	1150	475	975	1,600,000
		Comm. Decking	1400	90	975	405	825	1,600,000
		D. Comm. Deck.	1650	90	1150	475	975	1,600,000
	S. pine mixed species	Select	1550			275		1,431,000
		Commercial	1300					1,293,000
	Hem-Fir	Select	1350			235		1,620,000
		Commercial	1150					1,450,000
	Coast species	Select	1300			235		1,620,000
		Commercial	1100					1,450,000
	S-P-F	Select	1250			245		1,350,000
		Commercial	1050					1,220,000
	W. cedar	Select	1300			280		1,210,000
		Commercial	1100					1,090,000
Beams and stringers 5 in and thicker, depth more than 2 in greater than thickness	D Fir-L	Select Struct.	1700	85	1100	460	1000	1,720,000
		No. 1	1350		900		700	
	Hem-Tam	Select Struct.	1550	85	1000	405	900	1,300,000
		No. 1	1250		850		650	
	S. pine	No. 1 Dense SR	1550	110	925	315	1050	1,600,000
		No. 1 SR	1350		775	270	875	1,500,000
		No. 2 Dense SR	1250	95	725	315	850	1,400,000
		No. 2 SR	1100		625	270	725	

Table 1-14 (continued)

Grade Category	Commercial Species or Species Group Designation	Grade	Bending		Compression		Tension Parallel to Grain	Modulus of Elasticity
			Stress at Extreme Fiber	Longitudinal Shear	Parallel to Grain	Perpendicular to Grain		
Beams and stringers 5 in and thicker, depth more than 2 in greater than thickness	S. pine mixed species	Select Struct. No. 1	1425 1175	80	1160 940	275	870 620	1,282,000
	Hem-Fir	Select Struct. No. 1	1250 1000	65	900 750	235	750 500	1,450,000
	Coast species	Select Struct. No. 1	1200 1000	55	850 700	235	700 500	1,450,000
	S-P-F	Select Struct. No. 1	1150 950	60	800 650	245	700 500	1,210,000
	W. cedar	Select Struct. No. 1	1200 950	65	900 750	280	700 500	1,120,000
Posts and timbers 5 × 5 in and larger, depth not more than 2 in greater than thickness	D Fir-L	Select Struct. No. 1	1550 1200	115 85	1200 1050	460	1050 800	1,720,000 1,550,000
	Hem-Tam	Select Struct. No. 1	1450 1100	115 85	1050 950	405	950 700	1,330,000 1,200,000
	S. pine	No. 1 Dense SR No. 1 SR No. 2 Dense SR No. 2 SR	1550 1350 1250 1100	110 95	925 775 725 625	315 270 315 270	1050 875 850 725	1,600,000 1,500,000 1,400,000
	S. pine mixed species	Select Struct. No. 1	1360 990	110 80	1230 1085	275	930 680	1,283,000 1,155,000
	Hem-Fir	Select Struct. No. 1	1150 900	90 65	950 850	235	800 600	1,450,000 1,300,000
	Coast species	Select Struct. No. 1	1150 850	75 55	900 800	235	750 550	1,450,000 1,300,000
	S-P-F	Select Struct. No. 1	1100 800	85 60	850 750	245	750 550	1,210,000 1,090,000
	W. cedar	Select Struct. No. 1	1100 850	90 65	950 800	280	750 550	1,120,000 1,010,000

NOTES:
1. Allowable fiber stress in bending for decking applies only when the plank is loaded on the wide face.
2. Allowable fiber stress in bending for beams and stringers applies only when the member is loaded on the narrow face.
3. When beams and stringers are loaded on the wide face, the allowable unit stresses for *bending at the extreme fiber* for Select Structural grade must be modified by the factor 0.88 and for No. 1 grade by 0.77. The *modulus of elasticity* for No. 1 grade must be modified by the factor 0.90.
4. If post and timber sizes are graded to beam and stringer requirements, design values for beams and stringers apply.
5. An approximate value for modulus of rigidity may be estimated as 0.065 times the *modulus of elasticity*.

SOURCE: Canadian Wood Council and S.P.I.B.

5. The average diameter of a knot or hole must not exceed the number of inches equal to one-third of the length of the piece in feet (27 mm per meter of length).

6. Warp and cup will not be admitted if sufficient to prevent the board from dressing two sides to standard thickness.

7. The minimum size cutting allowed from a piece will be 4 in (89 mm) wide by 5 ft (1.5 m) long or 4 in (75 mm) wide by 7 ft (2.1 m) long.

Firsts admits pieces that will yield $91\frac{2}{3}$ percent clear-face cuttings as follows: 4 to 9 ft (1.2 to 2.7 m) surface measure in one cutting; 10 to 14 ft (3 to 4.2 m) in two cuttings; 15 ft (4.5 m) and over in three cuttings.

Seconds admits pieces that will yield $83\frac{1}{3}$ percent or $91\frac{2}{3}$ percent clear-face cuttings as follows: 4 to 7 ft (1.2 to 2.1 m) surface measure, $83\frac{1}{3}$ percent in one cutting; 8 to 11 ft (2.4 to 3.3 m) in two cuttings; 12 to 15 ft (3.6 to 4.5 m) in three cuttings; 16 ft (4.8 m) and over in four cuttings, except that pieces 6 to 15 ft (1.8 to 4.5 m) surface measure will admit one additional cutting to yield $91\frac{2}{3}$ percent.

Seconds also admits pieces 6 to 9 in (140 to 216 mm) wide, of 6 to 12 ft (1.8 to 3.6 m) surface measure, that will yield 97 percent in two clear-face cuttings of any length, full width of the board.

For particulars on all species and grades of hardwood, consult *Hardwood Grading Rules,* available from the National Hardwood Lumber Association.

Table 1-15
STANDARD THICKNESSES FOR HARDWOOD LUMBER

Rough		Surfaced	
Millimeters	Inches	Millimeters	Inches
9.5	$\frac{3}{8}$	4.5	$\frac{1}{16}$
12.5	$\frac{1}{2}$	8.0	$\frac{5}{16}$
16.0	$\frac{5}{8}$	11.0	$\frac{7}{16}$
19.0	$\frac{3}{4}$	14.0	$\frac{9}{16}$
25.0	1	21.0	$\frac{13}{16}$
32.0	$1\frac{1}{4}$	27.0	$1\frac{1}{16}$
38.0	$1\frac{1}{2}$	33.0	$1\frac{5}{16}$
44.0	$1\frac{3}{4}$	38.0	$1\frac{1}{2}$
50.0	2	44.0	$1\frac{3}{4}$
62.5	$2\frac{1}{2}$	57.0	$2\frac{1}{4}$
75.0	3	70.0	$2\frac{3}{4}$
87.5	$3\frac{1}{2}$	83.0	$3\frac{1}{4}$
100.0	4	95.0	$3\frac{3}{4}$

SOURCE: National Hardwood Lumber Association.

LUMBER DEFECTS

Lumber defects, flaws in the wood which affect either the strength or the appearance or both, can have many causes. One has already been discussed—wood diseases. Another is the action of animal parasites. Defects also can be caused by too-rapid seasoning, faulty manufacturing, or some nat-

ural growth of the wood. The most common defects are as follows:

Checks. These are lengthwise separations in the wood, occurring across the annual ring. (See Fig. 1-37.)
Shakes. Lengthwise separations in the wood, occurring between annual rings. (See Fig. 1-37.)

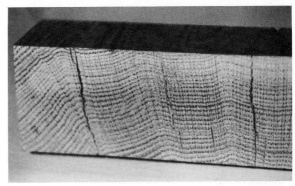

(a)

(b)

(c)

Fig. 1-37 Some lumber defects; *(a)* checks, *(b)* shakes, *(c)* wane.

Wane. Bark or other soft material left on the edge of a board. (See Fig. 1-37.)

Knots. Cross-sections or longitudinal sections of tree branches that have been cut with the board. There are several kinds of knots, including round, spike, sound, pin, loose, and cluster.

Pitch Pocket. An accumulation of tree sap in a well-defined opening between annual rings.

Bark Pocket. Bark partially or wholly encased in the wood.

Sap Streak. A heavy accumulation of sap in the fibers of the wood, producing a distinctive streak of color.

Splits. A lengthwise separation of the wood, caused by handling.

Torn Grain. A condition in which part of the surface has been chipped or torn out below the line of cut.

Skips. An area that failed to surface when the piece went through the planer.

Machine Burn. An area that has been darkened by overheating due to machine rollers.

Warp. A condition in which the flat, plane surface has been distorted in some manner. An edge-wise deviation is called a *crook;* a flat deviation is a *bow;* a deviation across the width is a *cup.* (See Fig. 1-38.)

Wormholes. Small holes caused by wood borers.

Sap Stain. Described in wood diseases.

Incipient or **Advanced Decay.** Described in wood diseases.

MACHINE STRESS-RATED LUMBER

Visual grading of lumber is still the most common method in determining the grade of a piece of sawn lumber, but in many instances, to ensure that ma-

Fig. 1-38   Types of warp.   *(Council of Forest Industries of B.C.)*

Crook   Bow   Cup   Twist

terial will perform as required, a more accurate method of determining allowable stresses is required. A new method, using a machine fitted with a small computer to record deflections, has been developed to determine the actual stresses that a piece of material can develop. Material can be processed at the rate of 1200 ft (365 m) per minute with deflection readings being taken every 6 in (150 mm).

The machine has not eliminated visual inspection completely, as the material is fed into the machine on the flat and is evaluated on that basis only. The edges of the material must be inspected for knots to ensure that a proper correlation exists between the machine rating on the flat and performance of the material in flexure on edge. Other flaws in the wood such as wanes, warp, and checks must also be dealt with visually.

At present there are 14 stress levels or f-E classifications recognized by the National Lumber Grades Authority with five of these being currently produced. The f-E designation relates directly to the allowable stresses in the material. For example, a 1450f-1.3E stress grade designates an allowable bending stress of 1450 psi (10.0 MPa) and a modulus of elasticity of 1.3 million psi (9000 MPa).

The use of *machine stress-rated* (MSR) lumber, for now, is limited to trusses and component systems which require materials that have consistent strength characteristics. As the supply of MSR material increases, certainly its use will increase. With the supply of good quality timber on the decline, the use of machine stress grading will allow for better use of existing material and provide the required consistency.

SHAKES AND SHINGLES

Two traditional wood products that are still used extensively because of their versatility and durability are shakes and shingles. (See Figs. 1-39 and 1-40.)

Shingles

Several species of wood are used to make wood shingles, including some pines, redwood, and red cedar, but by far the largest proportion of wood shingles on the market are made from western red

Fig. 1-39   Cedar shake siding.   *(Council of Forest Industries of B.C.)*

Fig. 1-40   Typical shingled roof.   *(Council of Forest Industries of B.C.)*

MANUFACTURE   Cedar logs are first cut into 16-18-, or 24-in (400-, 450-, or 600-mm) lengths (see Fig. 1-41) and cut into blocks of the proper size for the shingle machine. Every effort is made to produce blocks which have an edge-grain face, as illustrated in Fig. 1-42.

Fig. 1-41   Cutting shingle blocks.   *(Consolidated Red Cedar Shingle Association of B.C.)*

cedar. There are a number of reasons for this choice. In proportion to its weight, which is quite light when dry, cedar has unusually high crushing strength. The trees grow slowly, and as a result the wood has narrow annual rings. This, in turn, results in a fine, evenly grained wood with uniform texture. Cedar trees grow very large, with relatively few knots, so that shingles free from blemishes and distorted grain can be produced in large quantities. Most important is the fact that cedar has a low coefficient of expansion and contraction owing to changes in moisture conditions. This means that cedar shingles, in changing from a wet to an air-dry condition, are less likely to split or check than most woods.

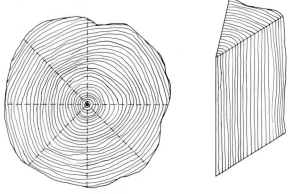

Fig. 1-42   Shingle block with edge-grain face.

Upright machines then saw these blocks into shingles, alternating the feed so that a tapered shingle with the butt either up or down is cut at each stroke. The operator clips the edges of each shingle at right angles to the butt and cuts out defects, if any, during this clipping operation. At the same time, the operator tries to ensure that no shingle is more than 14 in (355 mm) or less than 3 in (75 mm) wide.

GRADING   Shingles then go directly to graders who grade them according to clearly defined grading rules, which are outlined briefly in Table 1-16. (See Fig. 1-43.)

PACKING AND DRYING   After grading, shingles are packed in bundles (see Fig. 1-44) according to

Fig. 1-44   Packing shingles.   *(Council of Forest Industries of B.C.)*

length and grade. The number of courses of shingles in each end of the bundles is indicated in Table 1-16. The shingle packs are sent to the dry kiln (see Fig. 1-45), where moisture content is reduced to a minimum.

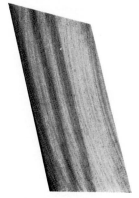

Fig. 1-43   No. 1 blue label shingle.

Fig. 1-45   Packed shingles going to dry kiln.

38

Table 1-16
RED CEDAR SHINGLE GRADES

Grade	Length		Thickness (at butt)		No. of Courses per Bundle	Bdls./ Cartons per Square	Description
	Milli- meters	Inches	Milli- meters	Inches			
No. 1 Blue Label	400 (Fivex) 450 (Perfections) 600 (Royals)	16 18 24	10 11 13	0.40 0.45 0.50	20/20 18/18 13/14	4 bdls. 4 bdls. 4 bdls.	The premium grade of shingles for roofs and sidewalls. These top-grade shingles are 100% heartwood, 100% clear, and 100% edge-grain.
No. 2 Red Label	400 (Fivex) 450 (Perfections) 600 (Royals)	16 18 24	10 11 13	0.40 0.45 0.50	20/20 18/18 13/14	4 bdls. 4 bdls. 4 bdls.	A good grade for many applications. Not less than 10" clear on 16" shingles (250 mm clear on 400-mm shingles), 11" clear on 18" shingles (280 mm clear on 450-mm shingles), and 16" clear on 24" shingles (400 mm clear on 600-mm shingles). Flat grain and limited sapwood are permitted in this grade. Reduced weather exposures recommended.
No. 3 Black Label	400 (Fivex) 450 (Perfections) 600 (Royals)	16 18 24	10 11 13	0.40 0.45 0.50	20/20 18/18 13/14	4 bdls. 4 bdls. 4 bdls.	A utility grade for economy applications and secondary buildings. Not less than 6" clear on 16" and 18" shingles (150 mm clear on 400- and 450-mm shingles), 10" clear on 24" shingles (250 mm clear on 600-mm shingles). Reduced weather exposure recommended.
No. 4 Under- coursing	400 (Fivex) 450 (Perfections)	16 18	10 11	0.40 0.45	14/14 or 20/20 14/14 or 18/18	2 bdls. 2 bdls. 2 bdls. 2 bdls.	A utility grade for undercoursing or double-coursed sidewall applications or for interior accent walls.
No. 1 or No. 2 Rebutted- Rejointed	400 (Fivex) 450 (Perfections) 600 (Royals)	16 18 24	10 11 13	0.40 0.45 0.50	33/33 28/28 13/14	1 carton 1 carton 4 bdls.	Same specifications as above but machine trimmed for exactly parallel edges with butts sawn at precise angles. Used for sidewall application where tightly fitting joints between shingles are desired. Also available with smooth sanded face.

SOURCE: Council of Forest Industries of B.C.

COVERING CAPACITY OF SHINGLES The area of roof which can be covered by one bundle of shingles depends on the *exposure* (the portion of shingle exposed to the weather), and the amount of roof shingle that should be exposed to the weather depends on the *pitch of the roof* and the

Table 1-17
SHINGLE EXPOSURE

Pitch	Maximum Exposure Recommended for Roofs: (Imperial)								
	No. 1 Blue Label, in			No. 2 Red Label, in			No. 3 Black Label, in		
	16	18	24	16	18	24	16	18	24
3 in 12 to 4 in 12	$3\frac{3}{4}$	$4\frac{1}{4}$	$5\frac{3}{4}$	$3\frac{1}{2}$	4	$5\frac{1}{2}$	3	$3\frac{1}{2}$	5
4 in 12 and steeper	5	$5\frac{1}{2}$	$7\frac{1}{2}$	4	$4\frac{1}{2}$	$6\frac{1}{2}$	$3\frac{1}{2}$	4	$5\frac{1}{2}$

Pitch	Maximum Exposure Recommended for Roofs: (Metric)								
	No. 1 Blue Label, mm			No. 2 Red Label, mm			No. 3 Black Label, mm		
	400	450	600	400	450	600	400	450	600
14° to 18°	95	105	145	90	100	140	75	90	125
18° and steeper	125	140	190	100	115	165	90	100	140

SOURCE: Council of Forest Industries of B.C.

length of the shingle. Table 1-17 outlines the maximum exposure recommended for roofs in all three roofing shingle grades.

Table 1-18 gives the approximate coverage of one bundle of shingles for a given exposure and length of shingle.

Wood Shakes

Shakes are used for the same purpose as shingles but are split rather than sawed from the cedar blocks. This produces a much rougher face than is the case with shingles.

Three types of shakes are made: *hand-split-and-resawn* (see Fig. 1-46), *taper split,* and *straight split.*

HAND-SPLIT-AND-RESAWN SHAKES Hand-split-and-resawn shakes are made by cutting blanks of the proper thickness from the block (see Fig. 1-47) and ripping them diagonally on a bandsaw. (See Fig. 1-48.) Table 1-19 gives lengths and grades.

The coverage which may be obtained with hand-split shakes of various lengths and types is indicated in Tables 1-20 and 1-21.

TAPER-SPLIT SHAKES Taper-split shakes are produced by hand splitting. A shingle-like taper is achieved by reversing the block, end-for-end, with each split. Shakes must be graded to produce 100 percent edge grain.

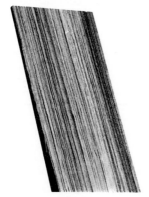

Fig. 1-46   No. 1 hand-split-and-resawn shake.

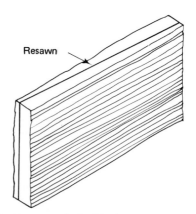

Fig. 1-47   Resawn shake blank.

40

Table 1-18
SHINGLE COVERAGE

Approximate Coverage of One Bundle of Shingles Based on These Weather Exposures (Imperial)

Length and Thickness	3½″	4″	4½″	5″	5½″	6″	6½″	7″	7½″	8″	8½″	9″	9½″	10″	10½″	11″	11½″	12″	12½″	13″	13½″	14″	14½″	15″	15½″	16″
16″ × 5/2″	17.5	20	22.5	25[a]	27.5	30	32.5	35	37.5[c]	40	42.5	45	47.5	50	52.5	55	57.5	60[b]	—	—	—	—	—	—	—	—
18″ × 5/2¼″	15.9	18	20.4	22.6	25[a]	27.2	29.5	31.7	34	36.4	38.6[c]	40.8	43.1	45.4	47.8	50	52.3	54.5	56.7	59	61.4	63.6[b]	—	—	—	—
24″ × 4/2″	11.6	13.3	15	16.6	18.3	20	21.6	23.2	25[a]	26.6	28.3	30	31.6	33.3	35	36.6	38.3[c]	40	41.6	43.3	45	46.6	48.3	50	51.6	53.3

Approximate Coverage in m^2 of One Bundle Based on the Following Weather Exposures (Metric)

Length and Thickness	90 mm	100 mm	115 mm	125 mm	140 mm	150 mm	165 mm	180 mm	190 mm	200 mm	215 mm	225 mm	240 mm	250 mm	265 mm	280 mm	290 mm	305 mm	315 mm	330 mm	340 mm	355 mm	365 mm	380 mm	390 mm	405 mm
400 mm × 10 mm	1.69	1.88	2.16	2.35[a]	2.63	2.82	3.10	3.38	3.57[c]	3.76	4.04	4.23	4.51	4.70	4.98	5.26	5.45	5.73[b]	—	—	—	—	—	—	—	—
450 mm × 11 mm	1.52	1.69	1.95	2.11	2.37[a]	2.54	2.79	3.04	3.21	3.38	2.64[c]	3.81	4.06	4.23	4.48	4.74	4.90	5.16	5.33	5.58	5.75	6.00[b]	—	—	—	—
600 mm × 13 mm	1.14	1.27	1.46	1.59	1.78	1.90	2.09	2.28	2.41[a]	2.54	2.73	2.85	3.04	3.17	3.36	3.55	3.68[c]	3.87	4.00	4.19	4.31	4.50	4.63	4.82	4.95	5.14[c]

[a] Maximum exposure recommended for roofs.
[b] Maximum exposure for double-coursing No. 1 grade on sidewalls.
[c] Maximum exposure recommended for single-coursing No. 1 and No. 2 grades on sidewalls.
SOURCE: Council of Forest Industries of B.C.

Table 1-19
RED CEDAR HAND-SPLIT SHAKES

Grade	Length and Thickness: Millimeters	Length and Thickness: Inches	No. of Courses per Bundle (465 mm Pack)	No. of Bundles per Square	Description
No. 1 Hand-split-and-resawn	380, starter-finish course	15, starter-finish	9/9	5	These shakes have split faces and sawn backs. Cedar logs are first cut into desired lengths. Blanks or boards of proper thickness are split and then run diagonally through a bandsaw to produce two tapered shakes from each blank.
	450 × 13, medium resawn	18 × ½ to ¾	9/9	5	
	450 × 19, heavy resawn	18 × ¾ to 1¼	9/9	5	
	600 × 9, hand split	24 × ⅜	9/9	5	
	600 × 13, medium resawn	24 × ½ to ¾	9/9	5	
	600 × 19, heavy resawn	24 × ¾ to 1¼	9/9	5	
No. 1 Taper split	600 × 13, taper split	24 × ½ to ⅝	9/9	5	Produced largely by hand using a sharp-bladed steel froe and a wooden mallet. The natural shinglelike taper is achieved by reversing the block, end-for-end, with each split.
No. 1 Straight split	450 × 9, true-edge[a] straight split	18 × ⅜ true-edge[a]	14 straight[b]	4	Produced in the same manner as taper-split shakes except that by splitting from the same end of the block the shakes acquire the same thickness throughout.
	450 × 9, straight split	18 × ¾	19 straight[b]	5	
	600 × 9, straight split	24 × ⅜	16 straight[b]	5	

[a] Exclusively sidewall product, with parallel edges.
[b] Packed in 20″ wide (505 mm) frames.
SOURCE: Council of Forest Industries of B.C.

Fig. 1-48   Taper-splitting shake blanks.

Table 1-20
HAND-SPLIT SHAKES COVERAGE
(Imperial Measures) [in feet squared]

Length and Thickness	Approximate Coverage of One Bundle of Hand-Split Shakes Based on These Weather Exposures											
	$5\frac{1}{2}''$	$6\frac{1}{2}''$	$7''$	$7\frac{1}{2}''$	$8''$	$8\frac{1}{2}''$	$10''$	$11\frac{1}{2}''$	$13''$	$14''$	$15''$	$16''$
$18'' \times \frac{1}{2}''$ to $\frac{3}{4}''$ hand-split-and-resawn	11[a]	13	14	15[b]	16	17[f]	20	23	26	28[d]	—	—
$18'' \times \frac{3}{4}''$ to $1\frac{1}{4}''$ hand-split-and-resawn	11[a]	13	14	15[b]	16	17[f]	20	23	26	28[d]	—	—
$24'' \times \frac{3}{8}''$ hand split	—	13	14	15[c]	16	17	20[e]	23[f]	—	—	—	—
$24'' \times \frac{1}{2}''$ to $\frac{3}{4}''$ hand-split-and-resawn	—	13	14	15[a]	16	17	20[b]	23[f]	26	28	30	32
$24'' \times \frac{3}{4}''$ to $1\frac{1}{4}''$ hand-split-and-resawn	—	13	14	15[a]	16	17	20[b]	23[f]	26	28	30	32
$24'' \times \frac{1}{2}''$ to $\frac{5}{8}''$ taper split	—	13	14	15[a]	16	17	20[b]	23[f]	26	28	30	32
$18'' \times \frac{3}{8}''$ true-edge straight split	—	—	—	—	—	—	—	—	—	20	26.5	28[d]
$18'' \times \frac{3}{8}''$ straight split	13[a]	15	16	18[a]	19	20[f]	23.7	27	30.5	33	35.5	38[d]
$24'' \times \frac{3}{8}''$ straight split	—	13	14	15[a]	16	17	20	23	—	—	—	—
15″ starter-finish course	Use supplementary with shakes applied not over 10″ weather exposure											

[a] Maximum exposure recommended for 3-ply roof construction.
[b] Maximum exposure recommended for 2-ply roof construction.
[c] Maximum exposure recommended for roof pitches of 4/12 to 8/12.
[d] Maximum exposure recommended for double-coursing on sidewalls.
[e] Maximum exposure recommended for roof pitches of 8/12 or steeper.
[f] Maximum exposure recommended for single-coursing on sidewalls.
SOURCE: Council of Forest Industries of B.C.

Table 1-21
HAND-SPLIT SHAKES COVERAGE
(Metric Measures) [in meters squared]

Length and Thickness	Approximate Coverage in Square Meters of One Bundle of Hand-Split Shakes Based on the Following Weather Exposures											
	140 mm	165 mm	180 mm	190 mm	200 mm	215 mm	250 mm	290 mm	330 mm	355 mm	380 mm	405 mm
450 × 13 mm medium resawn	1.02[a]	1.21	1.32	1.39[b]	1.46	1.57[f]	1.83	2.12	2.41	2.60[d]	—	—
450 × 19 mm heavy resawn	1.02[a]	1.21	1.32	1.39[b]	1.46	1.57[f]	1.83	2.12	2.41	2.60[d]	—	—
600 × 9 mm hand split	—	1.21	1.32	1.39[c]	1.46	1.57	1.83[e]	2.12[f]	—	—	—	—
600 × 13 mm medium resawn	—	1.21	1.32	1.39[a]	1.46	1.57	1.83[b]	2.12[f]	2.41	2.60	2.78	2.96
600 × 19 mm heavy resawn	—	1.21	1.32	1.39[a]	1.46	1.57	1.83[b]	2.12[f]	2.41	2.60	2.78	2.96
600 × 13 mm taper split	—	1.21	1.32	1.39[a]	1.46	1.57	1.83[b]	2.12[f]	2.41	2.60	2.78	2.96
450 × 9 mm true-edge straight split	—	—	—	—	—	—	—	—	—	2.27	2.43	2.59[d]
450 × 9 mm straight split	1.22[a]	1.43	1.56	1.65[a]	1.74	1.87[f]	2.17	2.52	2.87	3.08	3.30	3.53[d]
600 × 9 mm straight split	—	1.21	1.32	1.39[a]	1.46	1.57	1.83	2.12	2.41	2.60	2.78	2.96
380 mm starter-finish course	Use supplementary with shakes applied not over 250 mm weather exposure											

[a] Maximum exposure recommended for 3-ply roof construction.
[b] Maximum exposure recommended for 2-ply roof construction.
[c] Maximum exposure recommended for roof pitches of 18° to 33.5°.
[d] Maximum exposure recommended for double-coursing on sidewalls.
[e] Maximum exposure recommended for roof pitches of 33.5° or steeper.
[f] Maximum exposure recommended for single-coursing on sidewalls.
SOURCE: Council of Forest Industries of B.C.

STRAIGHT-SPLIT SHAKES   Straight-split shakes are also hand split, but the splitting is done from one end of the block only, resulting in shakes which are approximately the same thickness throughout. They are also 100 percent edge grain.

GROOVED-SIDEWALL SHAKES   Grooved shakes are manufactured from shingles and are machine-grooved. (See Fig. 1-49.) Edges are dressed parallel, producing shakes which can be fitted quite precisely for interior finish. They are also used for exteriors. Grading of grooved shakes is outlined in Table 1-22 and the coverage provided by them in Table 1-23.

MANUFACTURED WOOD PRODUCTS

In order to make timber more competitive with other materials such as steel and reinforced concrete, new products using wood as the main component have been developed. With large trees being at a premium, it has become advantageous to use smaller sections glued together to produce large timber girders that are much more uniform in strength and appearance than regular sawn timber

Fig. 1-49   No. 1 grooved-sidewall shake.

Table 1-22
RED CEDAR GROOVED-SIDEWALL SHAKES
(Grade No. 1, Blue Label)

Length	Courses Per Carton	Cartons Per Square[a]	Description
16″ (400 mm)	66 (16/17)	2	Machine-grooved shakes are manufactured from shingles and have striated faces and parallel edges. Used on interior and exterior walls.
18″ (450 mm)	56 (14/14)	2	
24″ (600 mm)	48 (12/12)	2	

[a] Also marketed in one-carton squares.
SOURCE: Council of Forest Industries of B.C.

sections. By-products such as wood chips and sawdust, which at one time were burned or left to decay, are now being combined with resins to produce various types of sheathing. Trees that are too small to be cut into useful framing sizes are converted into paper and paper products such as insulation. These manufactured products provide new alternatives to the construction industry, which is continually seeking materials that are cost-efficient yet durable and maintenance-free.

Glued Laminated Timber

Glued laminated timber is a structural timber product obtained by gluing together a number of laminations of lumber so that the grain direction of all the laminations is parallel to the longitudinal direction of the member. The use of stress-rated material produces a product that has better strength qualities than sawn timber, has a greater range of spans and cross-sectional sizes, and can be shaped and curved to enhance its appearance as well as its application. Glulam sections, as they are commonly known, can be classified in two general categories: *archribs* and *glulam timbers.*

Archribs are relatively small, laminated members used as a framework in light construction projects. (See Fig. 1-50.) Ribs are generally made in two designs: (1) the arch rafter, with gothic arch shape, and (2) the shed rafter, whose shape is a curve and straight-line combination. (See Fig. 1-51.) Rafter

Table 1-23
GROOVED-SIDEWALL SHAKE EXPOSURE

Length	Approximate Coverage in Square Meters of One Carton of Machine-Grooved Shakes Based on the Following Weather Exposures							
	255 mm	280 mm	305 mm	330 mm	355 mm	380 mm	405 mm	415 mm
400 mm	7.77	8.53	9.30[a]	—	—	—	—	—
450 mm	6.67	7.33	7.98	8.63	9.29[a]	—	—	—
600 mm	5.66	6.22	6.77	7.33	7.88	8.44	8.99	9.21

Length	Approximate Coverage of One Square of Machine-Grooved Shakes Based on the Following Weather Exposures							
	10″	11″	12″	13″	14″	15″	16″	16½″
16″	83	92	100[a]	—	—	—	—	—
18″	—	78	86	93	100[a]	—	—	—
24″	—	—	—	—	85	91	97	100[a]

[a] Maximum exposure recommended for double-coursing on sidewalls.
SOURCE: Council of Forest Industries of B.C.

Fig. 1-50 Typical structure built using archribs. *(Western Archrib Structures)*

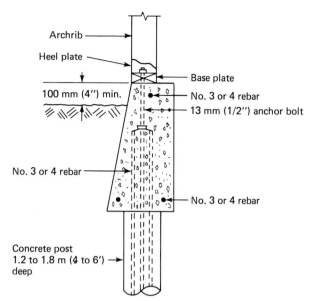

Fig. 1-52 Typical archrib foundation anchor.

widths will generally be from $1\frac{1}{2}$ to 5 in (38 to 127 mm), in varying depths based on the number of laminations and depending on the span and load. Maximum spans for this type of section are in the range of 70 ft (21 m). Rafter spacings will vary from 24 to 96 in (600 to 2400 mm), depending on the spans and loads. The rafters may rest directly on a foundation, anchored as illustrated in Fig. 1-52, or they may rest on top of conventional framing as in Fig. 1-50.

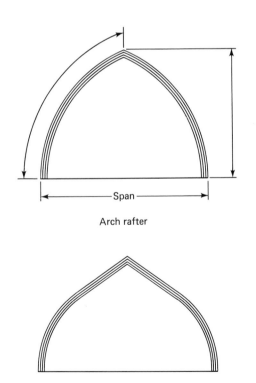

Fig. 1-51 Typical archrib shapes.

Generally, glulam timbers are much larger in size, but they are manufactured in sizes that range from $4\frac{1}{2}$ in (114 mm) to over $78\frac{3}{4}$ in (2000 mm) in depth and widths vary in standard increments from 3 to $14\frac{1}{4}$ in (80 to 365 mm). The basic glulam section is produced as a straight rectangular shape but can be manufactured in various arch types. Glulam sections are classified according to grade: service grade, which is based on the service conditions under which the section must perform; stress grade, which determines the type of stresses that the section will predominantly resist; and appearance, which dictates the quality of finish that will result. Table 1-24 outlines the three classifications and the typical grades included in each.

MANUFACTURE OF GLUED LAMINATED TIMBER Douglas fir and southern pine are the most used species for the manufacture of glulam sections, primarily because of their superior strength, but western larch, lodgepole pine, and spruce are also used. In the United States, the manufacture of glulams is done in accordance with American Institute of Timber Construction specification AITC 117-84—Manufacturing, and American National Standard ANSI/AITC A190.1-1983, Structural Glued Laminated Timber. In Canada, manufacture is controlled by Canadian Standards Association standard, CSA Standard 0122-M, Structural Glued-Laminated Timber.

Table 1-24
GLULAM CLASSIFICATIONS AND GRADES

Classification	Grades		Description	
Service grade	Interior grade		Employs moisture resistant (usually casein) glue or waterproof glue (usually resorcinol); used for interior applications where the equilibrium moisture content will not exceed 15%.	
	Exterior grade		Employs waterproof (usually a resorcinol) glue; used for exposed exterior applications and interior applications subject to highly humid conditions. This grade should also be used when the member may be exposed for a period of time between manufacture and end use.	
Stress grade	Bending grade	24f-E 24f-EX	Contains D Fir-L, or Hem-Fir and D Fir-L	Used for members subjected to bending as the principal stress, such as beams and arches. Specify EX when members subject to positive and negative moments or when members subject to combined bending and axial load.
		20f-E 20f-EX	Contains D Fir-L, or Lodgepole Pine-Spruce	
	Compression grade	16c-E	Contains D Fir-L	Used for members stressed principally in axial compression, such as columns.
	Tension grade	18t-E	Contains D Fir-L	Used for members stressed principally in axial tension, such as bottom truss chords.
Appearance grade	Industrial grade		Intended for use where appearance is not of primary concern such as in industrial buildings; laminating stock may contain natural characteristics allowed for specified stress grade; sides planed to specified dimensions but occasional "misses" and rough spots allowed; may have broken knots, knot holes, torn grain, checks, wane, and other irregularities on surface.	
	Commercial grade		Intended for painted or flat-gloss varnished surfaces; laminating stock may contain natural characteristics allowed for specified stress grade; sides planed to specified dimensions and all squeezed-out glue removed from surface; knot holes, loose knots, voids, wane, or pitch pockets are not replaced by wood inserts or filler on exposed surface.	
	Quality grade		Intended for high-gloss transparent or polished surfaces, displays natural beauty of wood for best aesthetic appeal; laminating stock may contain natural characteristics allowed for specified stress grade; sides planed to specified dimensions and all squeezed-out glue removed from surface; may have tight knots, firm heart stain, and medium sap stain on sides; slightly broken or split knots, slivers, torn grain, or checks on surface filled; loose knots, knot holes, wane, and pitch pockets removed and replaced with non-shrinking filler or with wood inserts matching wood grain and color; face laminations free of natural characteristics requiring replacement; faces and sides sanded smooth.	

NOTES: 1. A member cannot be fabricated from a mixture of service grades.
2. Appearance grades are not related to quality of materials in a member or its overall strength, only to appearance.
3. To obtain a desired result, the specifier need only describe requirements by listing the required grade for each of the three classifications.

SOURCE: CWC Datafile WS-2, Canadian Wood Council. Used with permission.

After arrival at a laminating plant, the lumber is regraded as laminating stock, and as such, is assigned one of four grades, depending on such characteristics as *knots, checks, splits, slope of grain, wane, warp,* and *pitch pockets.*

The moisture content of the laminating stock, prior to gluing, must range between 7 and 16 percent, with the range in the laminations for any one member not exceeding 5 percent.

Two thicknesses of laminating stock, 1 in (25 mm) and 2 in (50 mm), are surfaced to exact dimensions of $1\frac{1}{2}$ in (38 mm) and $\frac{3}{4}$ in (19 mm), with a thickness tolerance of 0.016 in (0.39 mm). Standard finished widths of laminating stock are 3, 5, $6\frac{3}{4}$, $8\frac{3}{4}$, $8\frac{3}{4}$, and $10\frac{3}{4}$ in (75, 125, 169, 219, and 269 mm). For members wider than that, two pieces are edge glued to produce the required width.

For long members, laminations must be end-jointed to form a single unit, and this is done by *scarfing* or *finger jointing.* Scarfing involves cutting the ends of two meeting pieces diagonally across their edge and joining the two by means of a *plain* scarf, *doweled* scarf, or *hooked* scarf. (See Fig. 1-53.) Finger jointing involves cutting two meeting ends, as illustrated in Fig. 1-54, either parallel or perpendicular to the wide face, and fitting them together with glue.

After grading and end jointing, the laminations are given a coating of *glue* and assembled into structural members. The method of assembling the grades of laminations within a member depends on

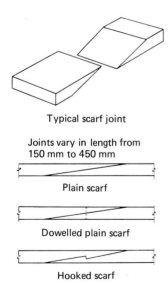

Typical scarf joint

Joints vary in length from
150 mm to 450 mm

Plain scarf

Dowelled plain scarf

Hooked scarf

Fig. 1-53   Scarf joints.

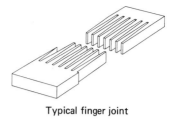

Typical finger joint

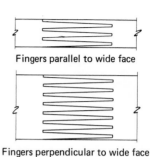

Fingers parallel to wide face

Fingers perpendicular to wide face

Fig. 1-54   Finger joints.

the end use of the member. Set procedures for placing the various grades for all conditions are laid down in the "Standard Grade Rules." Flat-grain and edge-grain lumber may be mixed in any proportion or combination in a member without affecting its strength or stiffness characteristics.

Laminations are bonded together with one of two types of adhesive, depending on the conditions of service. A *moisture-resistant adhesive*—usually *casein*—may be used for interior uses where the EMC in service will average 15 percent or less over a period of a year. For members which are to have exterior exposure or interior exposure to continuously humid conditions, a *waterproof adhesive*—usually a *resorcinol*—is used. Moisture-resistant adhesives cure by the dissipation of the moisture in the adhesive into the atmosphere, while waterproof adhesives cure by polymerization.

Laminations are clamped together in a jig, under pressure of 100 to 150 psi (690 to 1030 kPa), and cured at room temperatures or higher, depending on the type of adhesive used and the length of time allocated for curing.

After the adhesive has set, the members are removed from the jig and surfaced both sides. The ends are trimmed to provide a precise length, and, depending on the appearance grade required, the surfaces of the member are further finished by *filling, patching, surfacing,* and *sanding.* The member is *drilled, dapped,* and *grooved* to accommodate

Fig. 1-55 Low-V arches
wrapped for protection.
*(Plywood Manufacturing
Association of B.C.)*

connecting hardware and marked for the job. Unless specifications are to the contrary, a moisture-retardant coating is applied; for paint and quality appearance grades, the member is wrapped to pro-

vide greater protection during transit and erection. (See Fig. 1-55.)

GLULAM UTILIZATION Glued laminated timber is used in a wide range of applications, from bridges (see Fig. 1-56) to buildings to wharves and transmission towers. Many of the applications are outlined in Table 1-25.

GLULAM TYPES A large percentage of the glulam members manufactured are in the form of straight members, such as *beams* and *columns* (see Fig. 1-57). But glulam can be manufactured to suit many curved shapes as well, such as *curved beams, arches,* and *trusses,* as well as a variety of special products. Arches are made in several shapes, including *circular* (see Fig. 1-58), *parabolic, gothic, tudor* (see Fig. 1-59), and *bowstring.* Figure 1-60 illustrates the versatility of glulam, showing it in use for both roof members and furniture.

ADVANTAGES OF GLUED LAMINATED TIMBER

1. Design freedom. The designer has a wide latitude in creating structural shapes which express the structure's function and intended use.

2. Economy. Timber construction has historically been recognized as an economical method of

Fig. 1-56 Glued laminated timber bridge. *(American Institute of Timber Construction)*

Fig. 1-57 Post-and-beam construction using glued laminated timber. *(Southern Forest Products Association)*

building. Glulam members can be used to provide long, clear spans which require no interior walls or supports.

3. Ease of installation. Glulam members are made in a plant to job specifications and arrive on

Fig. 1-58 Laminated circular arches. *(T.P.L. Industries, Ltd.)*

Table 1-25
TYPICAL USES OF GLULAM SECTIONS

Application	Type of Building or Structure
Industrial	Buildings using chemical processes Warehouses, factory buildings Bulk storage buildings Bridges—highway, railway Ramps—gangways, loading Conveyor structures Transmission towers, crossarms Falsework and formwork Ship keels, frames, and stems Wharf structures Track ties
Agricultural	Storage facilities—grain, equipment Barns and sheds
Commercial	Shopping centers Stores Motels Restaurants Showrooms
Recreational	Arenas Curling rinks Swimming pools Lodges Club rooms Stadiums Bowling alleys
Institutional	Schools Hospitals
Religious	Churches Seminaries
Residential	Houses Apartment buildings

SOURCE: Canadian Wood Council.

the site ready for installation. Mobile construction equipment is normally used for installation.

4. Durability. Members made of wood, properly designed and constructed and, where necessary, pressure-treated with chemical preservatives, will perform satisfactorily for long periods of time.

5. Chemical resistance. Wood is a relatively inert material and, under normal conditions, not subject to chemical change or deterioration. Thus timber can often be used where the danger of

Fig. 1-59 Tudor (high-V) arches.

chemical deterioration may eliminate the use of other structural materials.

6. Safety. Heavy, smooth-faced timbers are difficult to ignite, they burn slowly, and the unburned

Fig. 1-60 Typical uses of glued laminated timber. *(Southern Forest Products Association)*

50

portions retain their strength. Also, timber, with its great ability to absorb impact loads and temporary overloads, provides safety under high wind and shock conditions.

7. Efficient utilization. Because of the laminating process, better utilization of the available supplies is possible. Higher grades of lumber are placed in the sections of highest stress, and lower grades where stresses are lower.

8. Energy conservation. Comparisons reveal that wood requires much less fuel for conversion from the raw state to finished product than does any comparable industrial building material.

9. Resources conservation. Since wood is a renewable resource, products made from it may be used continuously, without fear of final disappearance of the base material.

PLYWOOD

Plywood is made by bonding together thin layers of wood—*veneers*—in pairs about a central core in such a way that the grain of each layer is at right angles to the grain of each adjacent layer. In most plywoods, an odd number of layers is used to give a balanced construction and reduce the tendency to cupping. The outside veneers are called the *faces* or *backs;* the center layer, the *core;* and, where more than three plies are used, those in between, the *crossbands.* Generally, in the manufacture of softwood plywood, the same species or species group is used throughout, whereas, in hardwood plywood, a less expensive core and crossbands may be used with the hardwood face and back. The veneers are united under high pressure and temperature with a high-strength glue to produce panels of various sizes and thicknesses.

Softwood Plywood

MANUFACTURE Selected logs are cut into $8\frac{1}{2}$-ft (2.6-m) or $10\frac{1}{2}$-ft (3.2-m) lengths, called *peeler blocks,* and are debarked. Blocks are placed in a lathe and rotated at a constant surface speed against a long steel blade, which peels the veneer from the block in a continuous, thin sheet. (See Fig. 1-61.)

As veneer is produced, it goes to semiautomatic *clippers,* which cut the strip into various widths.

Fig. 1-61 Veneer strip coming from mounted peeler block. *(Georgia Pacific)*

Fig. 1-63 Veneer dryer. *(Plywood Manufacturing Association of B.C.)*

The clipper can also be operated manually to cut out defective pieces of veneer. From the clipper, pieces are graded and sorted into stacks of *heartwood* and *sapwood*. (See Fig. 1-62.) This is necessary because the heartwood and sapwood have widely differing moisture contents and require different drying cycles.

The material is then *dried* to approximately 5 percent moisture content (see Fig. 1-63) and graded again into three grades—A, B, and C—based

on the presence of *defects, patching compound,* used to patch or fill small defects, and *patches,* which are used to replace knots and other defects. (See Fig. 1-64.) The strips are then edge-glued together, by means of a high-frequency gluing machine, into a continuous sheet, which is clipped into standard widths.

Sound veneer then moves to the *glue spreader,* where the crossband veneers are coated with a waterproof phenol-formaldehyde resin glue and laid

Fig. 1-62 Sorting heartwood and sapwood strips from clipper. *(Georgia Pacific)*

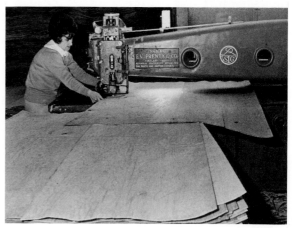

Fig. 1-64 Veneer patching machine in action. *(Georgia Pacific)*

51

Fig. 1-65 Crossbands coming from glue spreader. *(Plywood Manufacturing Association of B.C.)*

Fig. 1-67 Plywood panels trimmed to size. *(Plywood Manufacturing Association of B.C.)*

at right angles to the adjacent sheets on either side. (See Fig. 1-65.)

The veneer *sandwiches* then go to a *hot press,* where they are subjected to a pressure of 200 psi (1379 kPa) at a temperature of 266°F (149°C) to set and cure the glue and produce a plywood suitable for use under conditions of extreme exposure to moisture. (See Fig. 1-66.) From the hot press, the panels go to trimmers (see Fig. 1-67), which cut them to the required dimensions, usually 4 × 8 ft (1200 × 2400 mm).

If they are to be marketed as sheathing grades, the panels then go directly to the grader. If they are to be produced as sanded grades, panels go through a *sander,* which sands both faces smooth simultaneously (see Fig. 1-68), after which they are graded.

PLYWOOD GRADES (CANADA)   In Canada, softwood plywood is manufactured in seven grades, based in general on the quality of the veneers used for the face and back of the panels. (See Table 1-26.) Included in them are two grades of *overlaid*

Fig. 1-66 Veneer sandwiches entering hot press. *(Plywood Manufacturing Association of B.C.)*

Fig. 1-68 Plywood panels going to sander. *(Plywood Manufacturing Association of B.C.)*

Table 1-26
STANDARD PLYWOOD GRADES AND USES

Grade[a]	Veneer Grades			Characteristics	Typical Applications
	Face	Inner Plies	Back		
Good two sides (G2S)	A	C	A	Sanded. Best appearance both faces. May contain neat wood patches, inlays, or synthetic patching material.	Furniture, cabinet doors, partitions, concrete forms, opaque paint finishes.
Good one side (G1S)	A	C	C	Sanded. Best appearance one side only. May contain neat wood patches, inlays, or synthetic patching material.	Where appearance of one exposed surface is important. Floor underlayment where sanded surface desired. Concrete forms.
Select sheathing tight face (SEL TF)	B	C	C	Unsanded. Uniform surface.	Underlayment and combined subfloor and underlayment. Hoarding. Construction use where sanded material is not required. Concrete forms where smooth surface is not necessary.
Select Sheathing (SELECT)	B	C	C	Unsanded. Uniform surface with minor open splits.	
Sheathing (SHG)	C	C	C	Unsanded. Face may contain limited size knots, knotholes, and other minor defects.	Roof, wall, and floor sheathing. Hoarding. Construction use where sanded material or uniform surface not required.
High-density overlaid 60/60 (HDO 60/60)	B[b]	C	B[b]	Smooth, resin-fiber overlaid surface. Further finishing not required.	Bins, tanks, boats, furniture, signs, displays, forms for architectural concrete.
Medium-density overlaid (one or both sides) (MDO1S) (MDO2S)	C[b]	C	C[b]	Smooth, resin-fiber overlaid surface. Best paint base.	Siding, soffits, paneling, built-in fittings, signs, any use requiring superior paint surface.

[a] All grades, including overlays, bonded with waterproof, phenolic resin glue.
[b] Permissible openings filled.

plywood: *medium-density* and *high-density* overlaid plywood.

Medium-density overlaid plywood consists of a finished panel covered on one or both sides with a cellulose-fiber coating containing 17 to 22 percent thermosetting phenol or melamine resin solids, resulting in a bonded surface not less than 0.011 in (0.28 mm) in thickness. Such a surface is smooth and uniform and intended for high-quality paint finishes.

High density overlaid plywood consists of a finished panel coated on both sides with the same type of coating, containing not less than 45 percent resin solids, having a thickness of not less than 0.012 in (0.30 mm), and weighing not less than 60 lb per 1000 ft^2 (290 g/m^2). The surface is hard and smooth and such that further finish by paint or varnish is not necessary.

PLYWOOD GRADES (U.S.) In the United States, plywood is manufactured in two types, *exterior* and *interior*, based on the kind of glue used. Each type is produced in a number of grades, based in general on the quality of the veneers used in each.

Exterior plywood has a *fully waterproof glueline* and has back and inner plies of a higher quality veneer than those used for interior plywood. Interior plywood basically is made with a *moisture-*

Table 1-27
EXTERIOR PLYWOOD GRADES

Panel Grade Designations	Minimum Veneer Quality			Surface
	Face	Back	Inner Plies	
Marine, A-A, A-B, B-B, HDO, MDO				See regular grades
Special exterior, A-A, A-B, B-B, HDO, MDO				See regular grades
A-A	A	A	C	Sanded 2 sides
A-B	A	B	C	Sanded 2 sides
A-C	A	C	C	Sanded 2 sides
B-B (concrete form)				
B-B	B	B	C	Sanded 2 sides
B-C	B	C	C	Sanded 2 sides
C-C Plugged	C Plugged	C	C	Touch-sanded
C-C	C	C	C	Unsanded
A-A high-density overlay	A	A	C Plugged	——
B-B high-density overlay	B	B	C Plugged	——
B-B high-density concrete form overlay	B	B	C Plugged	——
B-B medium-density overlay	B	B	C	——
Special overlays	C	C	C	——

SOURCE: American Plywood Association.

resistant glueline but is also made with *intermediate* glue and with *exterior* glue.

The veneers used in both types are graded according to quality, as follows:

Grade N intended for natural finishes
Grade A suitable for painting
Grade B solid and free from open defects
Grade C has sanding defects which will not impair the strength or serviceability of the panel
Grade C Plugged has small holes and other defects, plugs and patches
Grade D has any number of defects and patches, provided that they do not seriously impair the strength or serviceability of the panel

Exterior plywood should be used in conditions in which the material will be permanently exposed to the weather or to moisture. In situations where moderate delays may occur in providing protection for the plywood or where contact with water or high humidity may occur temporarily, interior panels with intermediate glue may be used. Where durability is required for delays in providing protection, interior panels with exterior glue may be used.

Exterior type plywood grades are outlined in Table 1-27 and interior type grades in Table 1-28.

For a more complete description of types and grades of plywoods and veneers, see U.S. Product Standard PS 1-74, available from the American Plywood Association.

PLYWOOD SPECIALTIES In addition to the standard sanded or unsanded and overlaid, square-edged panels, softwood plywood is also manufactured in a number of specialty types, including *decorative* panels, *tongue-and-grooved* plywood, and *concrete form* panels.

Decorative panels include *embossed, brushed, grooved, striated, factory-stained,* and *coated* panels. Designs cover a wide range from a *beach-weathered timber* effect, achieved by removing some of the soft springwood from the surface by machine brushing, to medium-density overlaid plywood grooved to create a vertical plank effect.

Table 1-28
INTERIOR PLYWOOD GRADES

Panel Grade Designations	Minimum Veneer Quality			Surface
	Face	Back	Inner Plies	
N-N	N	N	C	Sanded 2 sides
N-A	N	A	C	Sanded 2 sides
N-B	N	B	C	Sanded 2 sides
N-D	N	D	D	Sanded 2 sides
A-A	A	A	D	Sanded 2 sides
A-B	A	B	D	Sanded 2 sides
A-D	A	D	D	Sanded 2 sides
B-B	B	B	D	Sanded 2 sides
B-D	B	D	D	Sanded 2 sides
Underlayment	C Plugged	D	C & D	Touch-sanded
C-D Plugged	C Plugged	D	D	Touch-sanded
Structural I C-D				Unsanded
Structural I C-D plugged, underlayment				Touch-sanded
Structural II C-D				Unsanded
Structural II C-D plugged, underlayment				Touch-sanded
C-D	C	D	D	Unsanded
C-D with exterior glue	C	D	D	Unsanded

SOURCE: American Plywood Association.

Tongue-and-grooved plywood (T&G) is usually a Sheathing or Select Sheathing grade, with a tongue cut along one long edge and a corresponding groove along the other. T&G profiles are designed so that panels butt at the tip of the tongue, leaving a $\frac{1}{32}$ in (0.75 mm) gap on the face and underside between panels. These panels are made to ensure the transmission of loads without the use of blocking at unsupported joints. T&G panels are usually made in thicknesses of $\frac{1}{2}$, $\frac{5}{8}$, and $\frac{3}{4}$ in (12, 15, and 18 mm).

PLYWOOD SIZES AND THICKNESSES Plywood of all standard grades is normally manufactured in panels 48×96 in (1200×2400 mm), though some mills will make panels 60×120 in (1500×3000 mm) to special order. T&G panels are made from 48-in (1200-mm) panels, resulting in a $47\frac{1}{2}$-in (1187-mm) net width.

Panels longer than 120 in (3000 mm) are available with *stress joints*. Two or more panels have the meeting ends cut to a slope of not more than 1 to 8, and the tapered cuts are glued together with waterproof, thermosetting phenol-formaldehyde or melamine glue to form a continuous sheet. Standard panel thicknesses are outlined in Table 1-29.

PLYWOOD PROPERTIES The ability of plywood to bend depends on the thickness of the material, its moisture content, and, to some extent, on the number of defects in the panel. Table 1-30 gives the average *cold bend radii* of various thicknesses of Douglas fir plywood, without soaking.

For load durations which are other than normal, the *allowable unit stresses* for Douglas fir plywood must be modified by the factors given in Table 1-31. Allowable unit stresses given in Table 1-32 are based on the normal duration of the full design load.

Hardwood Plywood

Plywood is made from many species of hardwood, including poplar, birch, beech, ash, mahogany, walnut, rosewood, elm, and many others. Except with poplar, the usual procedure is first to grade the veneers and then to use various combinations of veneers to make different grades of plywood.

Table 1-29
NOMINAL PLYWOOD PANEL THICKNESSES

Sanded Grades			Unsanded Grades		
Thickness		Minimum Number of Plies	Thickness		Minimum Number of Plies
Milli-meters	Inches		Milli-meters	Inches	
6	$\frac{1}{4}$	3	8	$\frac{5}{16}$	3
9.5	$\frac{3}{8}$	3	9.5	$\frac{3}{8}$	3
13	$\frac{1}{2}$	5	13	$\frac{1}{2}$	3
16	$\frac{5}{8}$	5	16	$\frac{5}{8}$	5
17.5	$\frac{11}{16}$	5	17.5	$\frac{11}{16}$	5
19	$\frac{3}{4}$	5	19.	$\frac{3}{4}$	5
Over 19	Over $\frac{3}{4}$	7	Over 19	Over $\frac{3}{4}$	7

NOTE: Metric equivalents approximate and for information only.

The veneers are classified into three grades: Red (Good), Blue (Sound), and Black (Backing). The specifications for each grade are as follows:

Red. The veneer shall be tightly and smoothly cut, containing the natural character markings inherent to the species, unselected for uniformity of color if one piece. If not one piece, the joints shall be matched to avoid sharp contrasts in color and grain. Blurs, occasional pin knots, slight mineral streaks, slight natural discolorations, sapwood, and inconspicuous small patches shall be permitted. Knots other than pin knots, wormholes, splits, open joints, sand-throughs, cross breaks, rough and lifting grain, shake, doze, and other forms of decay shall not be permitted. Voids and gaps or other openings under the face plies of Good grade (G) shall not show through the face in such a way as to result in an undesirable appearance. Voids in other inner plies shall not exceed in width the thickness of the ply in which they occur.

Blue. The veneer shall be tightly cut but need not be matched in color or for grain at the joints. Mineral streaks, stain discoloration, sapwood, patches, small areas of doze in early stages if sound, wormholes, open joints not exceeding the thickness of the face veneer cross breaks, gum spots, small bark pockets, sound tight knots not exceeding $\frac{3}{4}$ in (18 mm) average diameter, open knotholes not exceeding $\frac{1}{8}$ in (3 mm) diameter, and small areas of rough and lifting grain are permitted. The fore-

Table 1-30
COLD BEND RADII OF DOUGLAS FIR PLYWOOD

Plywood Thickness		Parallel to Face Grain		Perpendicular to Face Grain	
Milli-meters	Inches	Meters	Inches	Meters	Inches
6	$\frac{1}{4}$	1.22	48	0.41	16
8	$\frac{5}{16}$	1.52	60	0.61	24
9.5	$\frac{3}{8}$	2.13	84	0.91	36
13	$\frac{1}{2}$	2.74	108	1.83	72
16	$\frac{5}{8}$	3.76	148	2.44	96
19	$\frac{3}{4}$	4.87	192	3.65	144

NOTE: Metric equivalents approximate and for information only.
SOURCE: Council of Forest Industries of B.C.

Table 1-31
MODIFICATION OF ALLOWABLE UNIT STRESSES WITH DURATION OF LOADING

Duration of Loading	Modification Factor	Typical Applications
Continuous	0.90	Tanks, bins, retaining walls, floors continuously subjected to full design load; support of dead loads.
Normal	1.00	Most floors, bridges, miscellaneous structures; some retaining walls.
2-month	1.15	Structures subjected to snow loads; some temporary structures.
7-day	1.25	Some concrete formwork and falsework.
1-day	1.33	Wind and earthquake loads; some concrete formwork.
Instantaneous	2.00	Impact loads.

NOTES: 1. Factors listed are not cumulative.
2. Factors are not applicable to modulus of elasticity
3. Continuous application of full design load means that condition of loading under which a structure is subjected to more or less continuous full design load, as obtains in most storage occupancies.
4. Normal application of full design load means that condition of loading under which a structure is subject to the full design load only occasionally (as is generally the case in assembly, residential, business, and commercial occupancies and undermoving loads such as in bridges), such that the cumulative period of full-design-load application does not exceed 10 years.
5. Typical applications shown are included only for the guidance of the designer.
SOURCE: Council of Forest Industries of B.C.

going defects generally occur singly, and a combination of more than three types of defects is not permitted. *The defects in this grade of panel should be such that minor filling and/or patching will provide a suitable high-quality painting surface.* Veneer containing brashness, shake, sand-throughs, face overlaps, excessive doze, and any other form of decay is not permitted.

Black. The veneer may contain brash wood, shake, sand-throughs, compression failures, doze, loose and rough cuttings, open knotholes up to $1\frac{1}{2}$ in (38 mm) diameter, splits not exceeding $\frac{1}{4}$ in (6 mm) wide, which may extend the full length of the panel. The veneer of this grade is used chiefly as the back ply with Good and Sound grade veneers.

The grades of plywood commonly made by using various combinations of the above three grades of veneer are: Good Both Sides (G2S), Good One Side

Sound One Side (G/So), Good One Side Backing One Side (G1S), Sound Both Sides (So2S), Sound One Side Backing One Side (So1S). The grade is marked on each plywood panel by means of a color code consisting of two parallel colored lines appearing on the *left* side of each panel end. G2S is represented by two red lines, G/So by one red line and one blue line, G1S by one red and one black line, So2S by two blue lines, and So1S by one blue and one black line. In addition, the type of glue bond is indicated by black lines on the *right* side of each panel end. One black line represents exterior waterproof glue; two black lines indicate interior highly water-resistant glue.

WAFERBOARD

Waferboard is made by binding wood chips together with phenolic resin or urea formaldehyde glue in the form of a board 4 ft (1200 mm) wide.

The chips are produced by feeding pieces of log—often poplar—into a *disc waferizer* (see

57

Table 1-32
ALLOWABLE UNIT STRESSES FOR DOUGLAS FIR PLYWOOD UNDER NORMAL DURATION OF LOAD

Type of Stress		Allowable Unit Stress, MPa		Allowable Unit Stress, p	
		Service Condition		Service Condition	
		Dry	Wet	Dry	Wet
Extreme fiber in bending					
Face grain parallel to span	3 or 4 plies	14.82	11.72	2,150	1,700
Face grain parallel to span	5 or more plies	14.13	11.38	2,050	1,650
Face grain perpendicular to span	3 or more plies	11.03	8.96	1,600	1,300
Tension					
Parallel to face grain	3 or 4 plies	12.06	9.65	1,750	1,400
Parallel to face grain	5 or more plies	10.34	8.27	1,500	1,200
Perpendicular to face grain	3 or more plies	8.27	6.89	1,200	1,000
Compression					
Parallel to face grain	3 or 4 plies	15.51	12.41	2,250	1,800
Parallel to face grain	5 or more plies	13.44	10.69	1,950	1,550
Perpendicular to face grain	3 or more plies	11.38	8.96	1,650	1,300
Bearing on face					
Normal to plane of plies		1.62	1.31	235	190
Shear in plane of plies					
Parallel or perpendicular to face grain		0.344[a]	0.344[a]	50[b]	50[b]
Shear through thickness					
Parallel or perpendicular to face grain		1.48	1.27	215	185
Modulus of elasticity					
Face grain parallel to span		15,030	13,376	2.18×10^6	1.94×1
Face grain perpendicular to span		11,790	10,135	1.71×10^6	1.47×1
Shear through thickness modulus					
Parallel to face grain		563.3	563.3	81,700	81,700
Perpendicular to face grain		499.0	499.0	72,400	72,400

[a] May be increased to 0.5 MPa for plywood having individual ply thickness of 4.2 mm or less.
[b] May be increased to 65 psi for plywood having an individual ply thickness of 0.165″ or less.
SOURCE: Council of Forest Industries of B.C.

Fig. 1-69), which cuts the pieces into thin *wafers* about 1½ in (38 mm) square and from 0.01 to 0.05 in (0.25 to 1.27 mm) thick. They are dried, separated according to thickness into *core* and *face* wafers (thick wafers form the core), and fed to the production line. There they are given a coating of glue and then blown onto a steel forming table—first a layer of face wafers, then two layers of core wafers, followed by a final layer of face wafers. The board passes through a hot press which heats and polymerizes the glue, laminating the wafers into a solid board. The result is a versatile, general-purpose building material, made in panels 4 ft (1200 mm) wide and 8 to 16 ft (2.4 to 4.8 m) long, in thicknesses of $\frac{1}{4}$, $\frac{5}{16}$, $\frac{3}{8}$, $\frac{1}{2}$, $\frac{5}{8}$, and $\frac{3}{4}$ in (6, 8, 9.5, 12, 16, and 19 mm).

Panels are made in two types: *plain* and *patterned*. Plain panels may be unsanded, sanded one side, or sanded two sides, square- or lapped-edge. (See Fig. 1-70.) Patterned panels have one grooved face, with either evenly spaced or random grooving. (See Fig. 1-71.)

Waferboard has a variety of applications, both exterior and interior. Uses include sheathing for walls (see Fig. 1-72) and roof, subflooring, fence paneling, and commerical exteriors and interiors. The board lends itself to a range of stain and paint finishes, an advantage for interior use, while at the

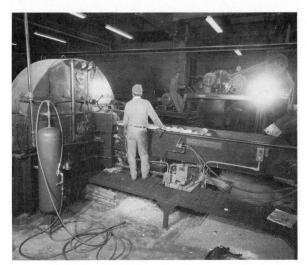

Fig. 1-69 Disc waferizer. *(Department of Industry and Information, Regina, Saskatchewan)*

same time its weather resistance makes it valuable as an outdoor material.

PARTICLE BOARD

Particle board is so called because it is made from relatively small particles, as compared to the chips used in chipboard. Red cedar particles are combined with thermosetting urea formaldehyde resin under heat and pressure to form a high-grade, medium-density board suitable for many uses in the construction field.

The particles are graduated from coarse at the center of the board to fine at the surface to help produce a product with a smooth, dense surface. Both surfaces are sanded, and one surface and the edges may be filled to provide a still smoother, denser surface for particular uses.

Particle board is made in a range of thicknesses including $\frac{1}{4}$, $\frac{5}{16}$, $\frac{3}{8}$, $\frac{1}{2}$, $\frac{5}{8}$, $\frac{11}{16}$, $\frac{3}{4}$, 1 and $1\frac{1}{8}$ in (6, 8, 9.5, 12, 16, 17.5, 19, 25, and 28.5 mm) in various panel sizes including the standard 48 × 96 in (1200 × 2400 mm). Other panel sizes available are 24 × 48 in (600 × 1200 mm) and 48 × 48 in (1200 × 1200 mm). In addition, panels may be made to special order in sizes up to 50 × 144 in (1250 × 3600 mm).

One of the common uses of standard particle board is for floor underlay, using annular-grooved underlay flooring nails, divergent-point staples, or

Fig. 1-70 Waferboard with lapped edge. *(MacMillan Bloedel)*

Fig. 1-71 Waferboard in plank pattern. *(MacMillan Bloedel)*

Fig. 1-72 Waferboard wall sheathing. *(MacMillan Bloedel)*

polyvinyl acetate adhesive for fastening. (See Fig. 1-73.) The board is also used for cabinets (see Fig. 1-74), for shelving, as core stock in millwork and furniture manufacturing, and as a base to which may be applied wood veneers, plastic laminates, printed wood-grain patterns, chalkboard coating, or a sealer-primer compound which produces a surface suitable for painting or lacquer.

HARDBOARD

Hardboard is made from processed wood chips. Chips of controlled size are subjected to high-pressure steam in pressure vessels. When the pressure is released, the chips "explode" and the cellulose and lignin are separated from the unwanted elements. The cellulose fibers and lignin are then mixed into a homogeneous mass and formed into a continuous board which is cut up into convenient lengths. These are pressed into uniform, hard, grainless sheets in heated presses.

Three grades of board are produced: *standard, tempered,* and *low-density.* In each case the stan-

Fig. 1-73 Particle board for underlayment. *(Allcraft Foundation; photo by Bruce Tilden)*

Fig. 1-74 Particle board for cabinets. *Allcraft Foundation; photo by Bruce Tilden*

60

dard product is smooth on one side with a burlap-like impression on the back (screen) side. It is also available smooth on both sides.

Standard Hardboard

Standard hardboard has a density of about 60 lb/ft^3 (961 kg/m^3), but it is flexible enough to be easily bent. Light brown in color, it is produced in thicknesses of $\frac{1}{8}$, $\frac{3}{16}$, $\frac{1}{4}$, and $\frac{5}{16}$ in (3, 4.75, 6, and 8 mm). Panels are 48 in (1200 mm) wide and are available in lengths of 4, 6, 8, 10, 12, and 16 ft (1.2, 1.8, 2.4, 3, 3.65, and 4.875 m).

This grade of hardboard is not suitable for exterior work but has many interior applications. In addition to the plain, smooth surface, the board is produced in a variety of surface patterns, including wood grain, and a variety of textures, including plank pattern and the texture illustrated in Figure 1-75.

Tempered Hardboard

Tempered hardboard is made by impregnating standard board with a tempering compound of oils and resin and baking it to polymerize the tempering material. The result is a board with a density of about 70 lb/ft^3 (1121 kg/m^3), which has considerably greater durability and strength than standard hardboard. It is also stiffer and more brittle but has improved machining qualities and much greater resistance to water penetration, making it suitable for exterior use. Thicknesses include those of standard hardboard plus $\frac{3}{8}$ in (9.5 mm).

In addition to the smooth finish, tempered hardboard is also made in a number of embossed patterns, including leather, and grooved patterns, including tile and vertical plank. A black hardboard is made by treating the board with black dye during manufacture.

Low-Density Hardboard

Low-density hardboard weighs from 50 to 55 lb/ft^3 (800 to 880 kg/m^3) and is not as strong or durable as standard hardboard. It is produced in thicknesses of $\frac{3}{16}$ and $\frac{1}{4}$ in (4.75 and 6 mm), in widths of 48 in (1200 mm), and in lengths of 4, 6, 8, and 10 ft (1.2, 1.8, 2.4, and 3 m).

MEDIUM-DENSITY FIBERBOARD

This product, sometimes called medium-density hardboard, is a material similar to tempered hardboard but made in $\frac{3}{8}$-in (9.5-mm) thickness, for use as a cladding material. It is produced in a wide

Fig. 1-75 Hardboard decorative wall panel. *(Masonite Corp.)*

Fig. 1-76 Medium-density fiberboard embossed in stucco pattern. *(Masonite Corp.)*

variety of textured patterns imitating traditional house finishes, for example, *stucco* (see Fig. 1-76), *rough-sawn wood, vertical plank, shakes* (see Fig. 1-77), and smooth *horizontal lap siding*.

PHENOLIC PARTICLE BOARD

This is a product with similarities to both waferboard and particle board, but made with phenolic resin glue, resulting in a very smooth, hard surface, suitable for the direct application of thin vinyl flooring. It has higher linear expansion than plywood or waferboard, and it is used mainly in factory-built housing.

VENEER-FACED PARTICLE BOARD

This is a product which is made by facing a core of particle board with thin veneers of selected softwoods or hardwoods. The hardwood-faced panels are used for such things as *cabinets, interior wall paneling,* and *partition panels* (see Fig. 1-78).

INSULATING FIBERBOARD

Insulating fiberboard is made from three types of fiber: wood, sugar cane, and asbestos.

Wood fibers are produced by two methods. One method consists of pressing logs against a grindstone which breaks down the wood into fibers by the shearing and rubbing action of the stone against the wood. About 45 percent of the wood fiber used is manufactured by this process.

In the second process, logs are first made into

Fig. 1-77 Medium-density fiberboard. This is displayed here in shake pattern. *(Masonite Corp.)*

Fig. 1-78 Hardwood-faced particle-board panels.

chips about $\frac{5}{8}$ in (16 mm) long. The chips are charged into pressure vessels called digesters where they are softened with live steam. The softened chips are then fed between two discs, one stationary and one rotating, and the shearing action of the rotating disc breaks the chips down into fibers.

Fibers from both processes are mixed and diluted with water so that oversized fibers can be screened out and returned for further processing. The mixture is stored in tanks and fed to a forming machine, which consists of a vat and a rotating drum covered with stainless steel wire mesh. The drum picks up the fibers to form a sheet of uniform thickness.

The surface of the drum, under the mesh, is lined with suction compartments under 15 in (380 mm) of vacuum, which draw the fibers firmly against the mesh and remove excess water. As the sheet is discharged from the drum, it passes through several sets of press rolls, is cut into panels of the desired length, and is fed into drying kilns. From these panels two basic grades of board are made: *sheathing* grade and *insulating* grade (see below).

Cane fiberboard is made by shredding cane and processing the fibers in much the same way as in the digesting process used with wood fibers. The same types of board are made as are made from wood fibers.

Sheathing Grade

Sheathing grade insulating board weighs about 18.25 lb/ft^3 (292 kg/m^3) and is made in two types, one having both faces and all edges coated with asphalt and the other with the fibers impregnated with asphalt during manufacture.

The sheathing board is made 48 in (1200 mm) wide, $\frac{7}{16}$, $\frac{1}{2}$, and $\frac{5}{8}$ in (11, 12, and 16 mm) thick, and 8 and 9 ft (2.4 and 2.7 m) long. This type of board is intended for interior use over frame or masonry construction and for insulation and sound control where moisture is a factor.

Insulating Grade

Insulating grade board has a density of about 17.5 lb/ft^3 (280 kg/m^3) and is made up as insulating panels, decorative panels, decorative ceiling tile, V-notch plaster base, and roof insulation. Standard thicknesses of this type of board are $\frac{1}{2}$, $\frac{5}{8}$, $\frac{3}{4}$, and 1 in (12, 16, 19, and 25 mm), but thicker panels for roof insulation are made by laminating two or more thin sheets with asphalt cement.

As insulating panels, the board is made 48 in (1200 mm) wide and from 4 to 16 ft (1.2 to 4.875 m) long.

One common type of decorative panel is $\frac{1}{2}$ in (12 mm) thick, 23, 24, or 26 in (300, 400 or 600 mm) wide, and 8, 9, or 10 ft (2.4, 2.7, or 3m) long. The edges are tongue-and-grooved, and the surface may be natural, white-coated, or white-finished.

Ceiling tiles are made various sizes, with tongue-and-grooved edges and the same choices of finish as decorative panels. They are intended to be applied over strapping which is nailed at right angles to the ceiling joists, over solid backing, and in suspended ceiling systems.

A special insulating board is also manufactured which has a sheet of hardboard glued to one or both faces. It is intended for use where a hard, paintable surface is required.

BUILDING PAPERS

Paper has been used by the Chinese as early as 2000 B.C. Since that time, much development and mechanization has taken place in the production of paper such that it has become a common commodity. The construction industry has been quick to adapt the unique properties of paper in the development of paper products that enhance the construction process and help to produce a better quality end result.

In building construction, paper is used for sheathing, roofing, and insulation; in making asphalt shingles, laminated and corrugated building products, and concrete-form materials; as a moisture and vapor barrier; as a cushioning material; as wallpaper; as an envelope or sheath for other materials; and as a fireproofing material.

Most paper is made from *cellulose fibers,* although a certain amount is also produced from asbestos fiber. The largest source of cellulose fibers is wood pulp, obtained from a group of trees which includes white and black spruce, balsam fir, lodgepole pine, jackpine, eastern and western hemlock, and Douglas fir. Wastepaper, jute waste, manila hemp, rags, straw (particularly wheat straw), and bagasse (cane and corn stalks) are also utilized. Many building papers are made from coarse materials such as wastepaper and jute waste, but, depending on specific requirements, certain amounts of the better pulps are blended with these. Although the finest grades of paper are still made from rags, the large majority of paper is produced from coniferous softwoods.

The process includes harvesting of the trees, transportation and delivery to a pulp mill, usually in either 4- or 8-ft (1.2- or 2.4-m) lengths, and transformation of the wood into pulp. Wood pulp is manufactured by three principal methods: the *mechanical,* or *groundwood,* method, the *chemical* method, and the *semichemical* method.

Mechanical Pulp

Mechanical pulp, sometimes referred to as *groundwood,* accounts for about 40 percent of the industry's total production. It is produced by forcing logs against huge, revolving abrasive stones or by grinding steamed wood chips in a grinding mill.

Pulp produced by the mechanical method has almost identical composition to the original wood. It is the cheapest form of pulp produced, because 90 percent or better of original raw material is used, compared to 50 percent or more in the chemical process. It takes 80 ft^3 (2.26 m^3) of wood to produce 1 ton (0.9 t) of pulp by the mechanical method, as compared to 150 ft^3 (4.24 m^3) by the chemical method.

No chemicals are required, and equipment for making this type of pulp is less expensive. However, because of the process involved, fibers produced by this method are shorter and weaker than those produced by other methods. As a result, paper made from mechanical pulp tends to be weaker and, with time, to become brittle. Most of the production is used in the manufacture of newsprint, although mechanical pulp is used in the making of paperboard and some felt papers.

Chemical Pulp

Three basic types of chemical pulp are produced: *sulfite, sulfate,* and *soda* pulp, each with its own peculiar characteristics.

SULFITE   Sulfite pulp accounts for about 12 percent of the total production. It is produced by cooking chips from low-resin-content coniferous trees under heat and pressure, in a solution of calcium, magnesium, or ammonium bisulfite, containing sulfur dioxide.

It is produced in both bleached and unbleached grades, and used in a wide variety of papers. Papers from bleached grades are used for many book, bond, writing, and tissue papers, as well as some varieties of paperboard. Unbleached sulfite is made into two grades of paper: *news* grade and *paperboard* grade.

SULFATE   Sulfate—sometimes called *kraft*—pulp accounts for about 45 percent of pulp production. It is produced by cooking chips of almost any kind of wood in a solution of about equal parts of caustic soda and sodium sulfide. Sulfate pulp is known best for its strength, and the unbleached grades are used chiefly in the manufacture of *kraft* papers, used in wrapping paper, building paper, bags, and paperboard. Semibleached and bleached sulfate pulp are used to produce a multitude of paper products.

SODA   Soda pulp is produced by cooking chips, mainly from deciduous trees, in a caustic soda solution under pressure. The pulp is relatively pure cellulose, bleaches well, but produces paper of only medium strength. It is often used in combination with other types of chemical pulp.

Semimechanical Pulp

Semimechanical pulp accounts for about 2.5 percent of production, but is on the increase because there is a relatively high yield (up to 75 percent) and because a variety of woods, including hardwoods, can be used. The pulp is usually unbleached and used, to a large extent, for the manufacture of corrugating medium, for use in corrugated board.

Miscellaneous Pulp

The production of pulp from material other than wood is carried out by various methods, depending on the material, and used in the production of a variety of products. *Rag pulp* is used to make the highest grades of paper. Pulp made from *wastepaper* is mainly used in the manufacture of some grades of building and roofing paper and building board. Production from this source will continue to grow as the necessity for recycling becomes more evident in our society.

Pulp Treatment

Before the pulps made by the processes just described can be made into paper having desirable characteristics, they must be treated to improve their papermaking qualities. This process is known as *beating* and *refining* and varies somewhat, depending on the particular pulp being treated and the type of paper to be made.

BEATING   Beating consists of passing pulp, suspended in water, under a heavy revolving drum studded with metal bars which rub the fibers against bars set in a bed plate. This rubbing and cutting action separates the fibers, reduces them to the proper length, and frays the ends and side walls. This fraying enables the fibers to mat together to form a uniform sheet.

During the beating stage, various nonfibrous additives are introduced into the pulp. Depending on the additive used, these increase the resistance of paper to water penetration, increase the tensile strength and wet strength, help to increase absorbency and opacity, and help to decrease the tendency of fibers to collect in bundles. Rosin and wax emulsions are added to increase resistance of paper to water penetration. Mineral fillers such as clay and calcium carbonate are added to increase opacity and softness of the paper. The addition of starch increases bursting and tensile strength. Sodium silicate increases the firmness or stiffness of paper as well as its strength.

REFINING   Most pulps which have been through the beater are passed through a final refining machine, called a Jordan, before they are ready to be made into paper. Pulp passes from the beaters to a vat, where more water is added and the mixture kept stirred to prevent fibers from settling out. From this vat the pulp is pumped to the Jordan, which consists of a cone-shaped shell fitted on the inside with a series of bars or ribs (Fig. 1-79) inside which a ribbed cone is rotated at high speed. The fibers are rubbed between the sets of bars. This cuts them to length, further frays the fiber walls, and curls or crimps them. The object is to create fibers with greater matting power.

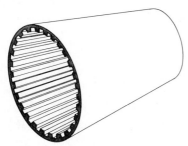

Fig. 1-79   Inside of Jordan outer shell.

After passing through the Jordan, the pulp is further diluted with water and run through fine screens to separate dirt, sand, and fiber bundles. It is now ready for the paper machine, where the paper is formed.

Papermaking

There are two types of paper machine: the *Fourdrinier* and the *cylinder.* Most paper products, with the notable exception of paperboards, are made on a Fourdrinier machine.

FOURDRINIER PROCESS   The papermaking process is begun on this machine by running very highly diluted pulp (97.5 to 99.5 percent water), known as *paperstock,* onto an endless belt made of wire mesh containing 3000 to 6000 openings per square inch (465 to 930 openings per square centimeter). Water drains away through the holes, assisted by suction under the wire at certain points.

As a result, a film of interlaced fibers is deposited on the wire belt. Even distribution of fibers across the sheet is improved by a lateral shaking motion of the frame carrying the belt. The thickness of the sheet of paper being formed, and hence its weight, is determined by the rate at which paper stock is allowed to flow onto the belt and the speed of belt travel. This may vary from 50 to 2000 ft/min (15.25 to 610 m/min). Various widths of sheet are made, from 50 to over 300 in (127 to over 7620 mm), while the weight of paper may vary from about 2 to 12 lb per 100 ft^2 (0.098 to 0.58 kg/m^2).

After it leaves the wire belt, the wet sheet of paper is picked up on an endless belt of woolen felt and carried to heavy rolls which press more water from it. It then passes through a long series of rotating heated rollers, supported by a layer of canvas which travels with the paper. Here practically all the remaining water is driven out and the paper is ready for the finishing that is required. (See Fig. 1-80.)

When paper is required to be smooth and dense, it is passed through a series of polished steel rollers called *calender rolls.* The smoothness and density of the paper are controlled by the pressure on the rollers and the number of times the sheet is passed between them. For most building papers, smoothness is not a prime consideration and softness and absorbency, rather than density, are desirable qualities.

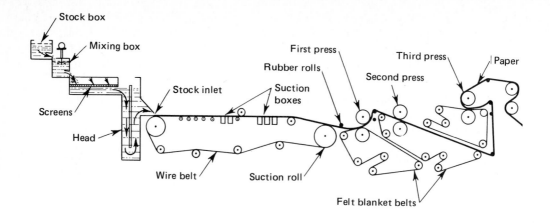

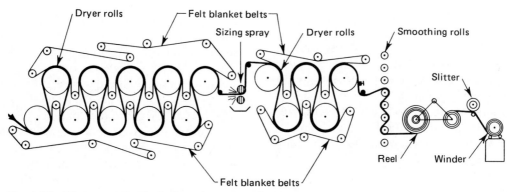

Fig. 1-80 Diagrammatic illustration of papermaking process.

CYLINDER PROCESS The cylinder machine has a cylinder mold, which is covered with fine wire cloth, revolving in a vat of paper stock. The pulp suspension is flowed onto the surface of the cylinder, where fiber matting takes place and water is drained off. Altering the length of time that the mat remains on the cylinder controls the thickness of the paper sheet. From the point at which the sheet leaves the cylinder, the process is similar to the Fourdrinier process.

Paper from the paper machines or the calender rolls is wound into large rolls. These may be later rewound into smaller rolls or cut into narrower widths as required for further processing. (See Fig. 1-81.)

Paper Treatment

Many building papers go through further processing to produce products designed for specific jobs. These processes include saturating the paper with asphalt or asphalt emulsion (see Fig. 1-82), coating

the surface with a layer of asphalt (see Fig. 1-83), embedding crushed slate in an asphalt surface coating, coating the surface with wax, laminating two sheets of paper together with a layer of asphalt, and laminating a sheet of paper and a sheet of copper

Fig. 1-81 Rewound rolls of building paper. *(Domtar Pulp & Paper Products, Ltd.)*

Fig. 1-82 Paper starting on the asphalting process. *(Domtar Pulp & Paper Products, Ltd.)*

foil together with asphalt. Another process involves the forming of a corrugated sheet of paper and laminating it between two flat sheets.

Types of Paper

SHEATHING PAPER   Two types of sheathing paper are produced. One is a plain paper and the other an asphalt-impregnated or coated felt or kraft

Fig. 1-83 Paper with first asphalt coat. *(Domtar Pulp & Paper Products, Ltd.)*

paper. Two kinds of plain sheathing are made, one a low-cost paper made from a mixture of semichemical pulp and wastepaper and the other a tough paper made from kraft pulp. The first is normally produced in rolls 36 in (900 mm) wide, containing 400 ft^2 (37.2 m^2), and weighing about 3.75 lb per 100 ft^2 (0.18 kg/m^2). Kraft sheathing is produced in two widths and several weights. A strong, tough sheathing is made in widths of 36 and 72 in (900 and 1800 mm), in rolls of 400 and 800 ft^2 (37.2 and 74.4 m^2), weighing 10.75 lb per 100 ft^2 (0.52 kg/m^2). A lighter kraft, in 36-in (900-mm) rolls of 400 ft^2 (37.2 m^2), weighing 4 lb per 100 ft^2 (0.19 kg/m^2), is also common.

Asphalt-impregnated and coated papers are made from felt and kraft papers. Various amounts of asphalt are used per hundred square feet of paper so that papers of various weights are made, from 4 to 10 lb per 100 ft^2 (0.19 to 0.49 kg/m^2). These are what are known as *breather* papers, impervious to water but not to water vapor. Rolls are generally 36 in (900 mm) wide and contain 400 ft^2 (37.2 m^2) of paper.

ROOFING PAPERS   Two types of roofing papers are made: those which are used in making a built-up roof, generally called *roofing felts,* and what is known as *rolled* roofing, a heavy, mineral-surfaced paper used as a final roof covering. Both are made largely from mechanical pulp produced by grinding steamed wood chips in a grinding mill. The method yields long fibers which produce paper with good saturating properties. Generally, rag pulp is added to give extra strength and absorbency.

Roofing felts are usually produced in rolls 36 in (900 mm) wide, in various weights from 3 to 20 lb per 100 ft^2 (0.14 to 0.97 kg/m^2). Rolled roofing is made 18 and 36 in (450 and 900 mm) wide, in various weights from 45 to 120 lb per 100 ft^2 (2.2 to 5.85 kg/m^2).

INSULATING PAPER   The primary objective in the production of this type of paper is to secure bulk and entrapped air with as much strength as possible. Insulating papers are made both from wood pulp and from asbestos fiber.

Wood-fiber insulating paper is made from ground-wood or bagasse with some wastepaper pulp added. The paper is usually gray, produced in rolls 36 in (900 mm) wide weighing about 9 lb per 100 ft^2

(0.44 kg/m²). It is used for insulating walls, ceilings, and floors.

Insulating paper made from asbestos fibers is a soft, pliable paper used for insulating pipes carrying steam, boilers, and other vessels with high temperatures. It is produced in various weights from 5 to 10 lb per 100 ft² (0.24 to 0.48 kg/m²).

A heavier asbestos-felt paper is produced for use as a built-up roofing material. It is saturated with asphalt and produced in rolls 36 in (900 mm) wide weighing approximately 15 lb per 100 ft² (0.73 kg/m²).

CUSHIONING PAPER   This is much the same as wood-fiber insulating paper, but less attention is paid to strength. Its chief use is for cushioning under linoleum, carpets, or slate roofing. Two grades are commonly made: 12- and 16-oz (340- and 454-g) paper; the first weighs about 8 lb per 100 ft² (0.39 kg/m²), and the second about 11 lb per 100 ft² (0.54 kg/m²). Both are put up in rolls 36 in (900 mm) wide.

VAPOR-BARRIER PAPER   These papers, which are intended to prevent the passage of moisture vapor through walls, ceilings, and floors, are made in three different types. One, a waxed paper, is made from strong, light kraft in three grades commonly known as X, XX, and XXX. The first weighs about 2 lb per 100 ft² (0.10 kg/m²), the second about 3 lb per 100 ft² (0.15 kg/m²), and the third about 4 lb per 100 ft² (0.19 kg/m²). All are made up in rolls 36 in (900 mm) wide.

The second type consists of two thicknesses of paper laminated together with a film of asphalt. Two kinds of paper are used: one a kraft paper, the other a mixture of groundwood pulps treated by the sulfite and the kraft methods. Rolls are 36 in (900 mm) wide, contain 400 ft² (37.2 m²), and weigh from 2 to 6.5 lb per 100 ft² (0.1 to 0.32 kg/m²).

The third type consists of a sheet of kraft paper laminated to copper foil by an asphalt film. This is a heavy-duty material used both for vapor barrier and for flashing. It is available in rolls from 6 to 60 in (150 to 1500 mm) wide, in weights of 1, 2, and 3 oz/ft² (0.03, 0.06, and 0.09 g/cm²).

LAMINATING PAPER   This is a special, high-strength kraft paper made for use in the production of plastic laminates. The thin, strong paper is im-

pregnated with liquid plastic resin, and several sheets are laminated together under heat and pressure to form the base for the plastic sheet.

CONCRETE-FORM PAPER   Two different types of concrete forms are made from paper. One is made from strong kraft paper in the form of a spiral tube. It is used for column forms and for ducts and core forms in concrete floors. (See Fig. 1-84.)

The other type is a boxlike form made from corrugated container paper. (See Fig. 1-85.) This is unbleached kraft paper sized with rosin and coated with wax sizing and starch to make it abrasion-

Fig. 1-84   Paper tube void forms.

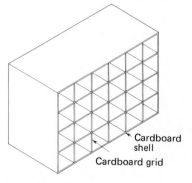
Fig. 1-85   Paper box forms.

68

resistant. The boxes are approximately 16 × 32 in (400 × 800 mm), of various depths, reinforced with a gridwork of the same paper. These forms are used in forming ribbed concrete slabs.

WALLPAPER Paper from which decorative wallpaper is made is produced in two grades: No. 1 Hanging and No. 2 Hanging. No. 1 Hanging is made from bleached sulfite or bleached soda pulp, mixed with not more than 20 percent high-quality groundwood. Talc is used as a filler, rosin and sodium silicate as sizing. The paper is coated with a clay film bound to the paper with casein, and the design is printed over the clay coating.

No. 2 Hanging is from 72 to 90 percent groundwood and the rest unbleached sulfite. Little filler is used, but the paper must be sufficiently sized to stand the application of water paste without wetting or breaking through.

ENVELOPE PAPER Paper is used as an outer covering or envelope for a number of building materials. One of these is gypsum board, composed of a layer of calcined gypsum covered on both sides by a sheet of kraft paper. A number of insulating materials are enveloped in a kraft paper cover, sometimes plain, sometimes asphalted.

FIREPROOFING PAPER Paper to be used for fireproofing is made from asbestos fibers, since this is an incombustible material. The material may be in the form of a matted paper, similar to asbestos insulating or roofing paper, or it may be in the form of a cloth woven from thread spun from asbestos fibers.

PAPERBOARD Paperboard, commonly known as *cardboard*, is a paper product in increasing demand, used for every kind of packaging, from heavy cases to containers for small items on department-store shelves. It is divided into two broad categories: *boxboard* and *container board.*

Boxboard is produced as a sheet, sometimes identical in substance and quality throughout and sometimes composed of layers made from different types of pulp. There are three classifications of boxboard: *folding, set-up,* and *miscellaneous.* Folding boxboard is made into a variety of folding cartons, whereas set-up boxboard is used where more rigid containers are required. Miscellaneous boxboard includes paperboard of many kinds, used for hundreds of products, from pie plates to bottle caps to wallboard.

Container board is also divided into three classifications: *liner, corrugating,* and *container chipboard,* all of which are used almost entirely in the manufacture of shipping cases.

Linerboard is hard, firm, and strong, manufactured in two forms: *kraft liner,* produced from kraft pulp, and *jute liner,* sometimes called *testboard,* made from kraft pulp and repulped paper.

Corrugating board is the fluted product used in corrugated shipping cases. It emerges flat from the paperboard machine and is later backed on both sides with linerboard and used to make light, strong packing cases.

Container chipboard is produced from wastepaper as a single sheet, several of which are later laminated together to form solid fiber shipping cases, as opposed to corrugated cases.

WOOD PRODUCTS APPLICATIONS

The use of wood in construction is not limited to structural-type applications with which most people are familiar. Because of the many wood products that are available, the application of wood in buildings can be seen in every phase of the construction process. From formwork for the pouring of concrete to finely finished floors and cabinets, the use of wood products is almost unlimited.

The use of preservatives, finishes, and retardants has greatly increased the versatility of wood products, both for interior as well as exterior applications. The next few pages will deal with some of the nonstructural uses of wood products in construction to illustrate the wide range of these applications.

Wood Siding

Several wood species are used in making siding, but the two most common ones are redwood and cedar.

Redwood siding is manufactured in three styles: *tongue-and-groove, shiplap,* and *bevel,* with each style having several patterns. (See Fig. 1-86.) Those styles are classified in four grades: Clear All Heart V.G., Clear All Heart, A-Grade V.G. (which contains some clear sapwood), and A Grade (which contains clear sapwood and flat grain).

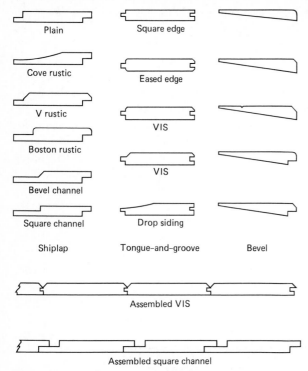

Plain
Square edge
Cove rustic
Eased edge
V rustic
VIS
Boston rustic
VIS
Bevel channel
Square channel
Drop siding
Shiplap
Tongue–and–groove
Bevel

Assembled VIS

Assembled square channel

Fig. 1-86   Redwood siding patterns.

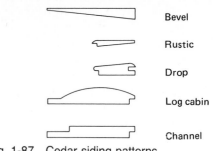

Bevel

Rustic

Drop

Log cabin

Channel

Fig. 1-87   Cedar siding patterns.

Much of the cedar siding is made from western red cedar. This particular wood exhibits the smallest shrinkage of any of the softwoods. This factor, in addition to its very low fiber saturation point, results in very small changes in size and shape with humidity changes. Because it is such a stable wood, it has practically no tendency to cup and pull loose from fastenings. Its heat-transmission coefficient gives it one of the highest insulating values of all the commonly used softwoods. Cedar takes stain, paint, or varnish finishes exceptionally well, but in some areas red cedar products are used with no finishing at all.

Cedar siding is manufactured with either a *dressed* or *saw-textured* finish, in five styles: *bevel, rustic, drop, log-cabin,* and *channel*. (See Fig. 1-87.) Beveled cedar siding is graded Clear V.G. Heart, A, B, Rustic, and C. The remainder of the cedar sidings are graded Clear Heart, A, and B. In all the cedar sidings there is also a Glued-up grade, in which the pieces are end glued or edge glued or both but otherwise interchangeable with one-piece stock of the same grade.

Boards and Battens

A board-and-batten exterior finish is one in which boards of various kinds—redwood, cedar, cypress, fir—rough-sawn or planed, are applied to a wall vertically, with narrow strips of the same material nailed over the vertical joints. A variation of this system is the use of vertical plank siding. This is $\frac{3}{4}$- and $1\frac{1}{2}$-in (19- and 38-mm) material, usually redwood or cedar, with tongue-and-grooved edges and various arrangements of molding cuts on the face. (See Fig. 1-34.) Plank for this purpose are manufactured in both clear and knotty grades.

Plywood Exterior Finish

Any exterior grade of plywood can be used for exterior finishing purposes. It may be applied in panels with the long edges vertical and the joints covered by battens, or it can be cut in strips and applied horizontally.

However, plywood is produced with several textured surfaces, particularly for exterior finishing. Usually such plywood is made in a $\frac{3}{8}$-in (9.5-mm) thickness and may be applied either vertically, in the full panel, or horizontally in overlapping strips 16 in (450 mm) wide, depending on the type of texture.

Another type is made with a resin-impregnated cellulose fiber overlay on one or both sides, as required. A hard, smooth surface suitable for painting is produced. It is available in thicknesses from $\frac{5}{16}$ to $\frac{3}{4}$ in (8 to 19 mm), with the thinner panels being used for exterior cladding over sheathing, while the thicker ones are normally applied in 12 or 16 in (300 or 400 mm) wide, horizontal, overlapping strips. (See Fig. 1-88.)

Still another type is made in vertical-plank pattern and may be produced in its natural surface, pre-

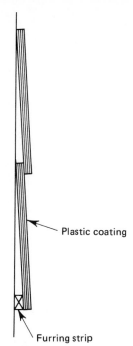

Fig. 1-88   Resin-coated plywood applied horizontally.

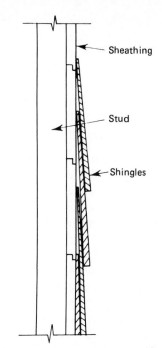

Fig. 1-89   Single-coursed sidewall shingles.

stained in several colors or overlaid with the resin-impregnated coating mentioned above.

Shingles and Shakes

Red cedar shingles and shakes, very well known roofing materials, are also used for exterior wall finish. (See Fig. 1-39.)

Either the single- or the double-course method can be used in applying shingles or shakes to sidewalls. Single coursing is similar to roof shingling except that recommended exposures are greater. The maximum recommended exposure for 16-in (400-mm) shingles on sidewalls is $7\frac{1}{2}$ in (190 mm); for 18-in (450-mm) shingles it is $8\frac{1}{2}$ in (212 mm); and for 24-in (600-mm) shingles it is $11\frac{1}{2}$ in (290 mm). (See Fig. 1-89.)

Maximum recommended weather exposure for single-coursed shakes, for wall application, is as follows: for 18-in (450-mm) shakes, $8\frac{1}{2}$ in (212 mm); for 24-in (600-mm) shakes, $11\frac{1}{2}$ in (290 mm); and for 32-in (800-mm) shakes, 15 in (375 mm).

Double coursing involves applying two courses of shingles or a course of shingles and a course of shakes, one over the other. This provides a heavy

shadow line at the butts (see Fig. 1-90) and allows for still wider exposure.

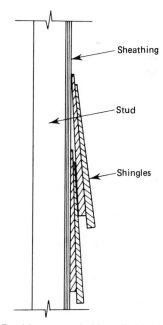

Fig. 1-90   Double-coursed sidewall shingles.

The recommended exposure for 16-in (400-mm), double-coursed shingles is 10 in (250 mm); for 18-in (450-mm) shingles it is 11 in (275 mm); and for 24-in (600-mm) shingles it is 14 in (350 mm). When double-coursed, 18-in (450-mm) shakes may be exposed 14 in (350 mm), and 24-in (600-mm) shakes up to 20 in (500 mm).

Hardboard Siding

Tempered hardboard strips of 12 and 16 in (300 and 400 mm) are often used as siding. They are made in lengths of 4, 8, and 12 ft (1.2, 2.4, and 3.65 m). Three methods of application are used. One consists of applying the strips in the same way that beveled siding is applied. Another involves the use of a rabbeted wood strip at the bottom of each course to accentuate the shadow line. (See Fig. 1-91.) In the third method, preformed metal strips hold the siding in place and produce a deep shadow line. Holes in the metal strips serve to provide ventilation behind the board. (See Fig. 1-92.)

Wood Finishes

Interior finishing materials can be divided into two basic groups: those used to cover walls, floors, and ceilings, and those used as trim materials. Examples of the latter include door and window casings, door jambs, beam and column caps, baseboards, window and door sills, stair treads, nosing, and posts, as well as various beads and moldings.

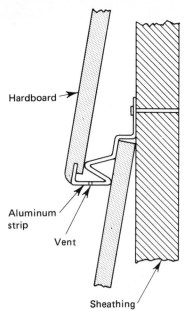

Fig. 1-92   Vented hardboard siding.

Wall and ceiling coverings may be in the form of boards or sheets. Boards are produced from various species including pine, fir, redwood, cedar, ash, beech, and mahogany in 1- and 2-in nominal (19- and 38-mm) thicknesses. Boards of 1-in nominal (19 mm) range in width from 2- to 12-in nominal (38 to 286 mm) and in lengths from 4 to 10 ft (1.2 to 3 m). The faces may be plain or rough-sawn or molded in a variety of patterns, some of which are illustrated in Fig. 1-93. For actual widths, thicknesses, depth of groove, width of bead, width and depth of chamfer, etc., a grading rules manual should be consulted. Material of this type is normally plain sawn with clear or knotty face. It is kiln dried and may be factory sealed or sealed and prefinished with synthetic lacquer.

Such items as door jamb or beam and column covers may be shaped from 2-in (50-mm) boards, as indicated in Fig. 1-94.

Plywood wall paneling is made from a number of softwoods including fir, pine, and spruce, as well as from various hardwoods such as walnut, birch, beech, ash, oak, mahogany, and teak. Softwood plywoods may be plain, textured, patterned, or have a wood grain printed on the surface. Hardwood panel surfaces may be plain, V-grooved, or laid out in a vertical, random-plank pattern. Plywood panel

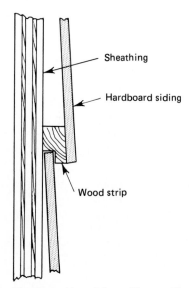

Fig. 1-91   Hardboard lap siding with wood furring strip.

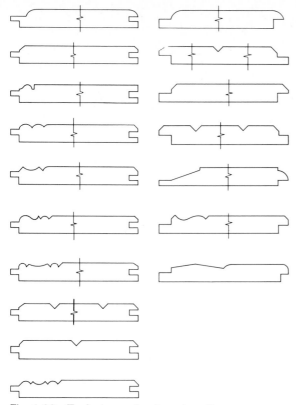

Fig. 1-93   Typical paneling board profiles.

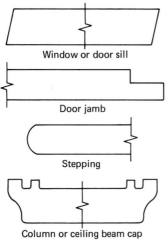

Window or door sill

Door jamb

Stepping

Column or ceiling beam cap

Fig. 1-94   Typical trim materials from 2-in (50-mm) boards.

thicknesses include $\frac{1}{4}$, $\frac{3}{8}$, $\frac{7}{16}$, $\frac{1}{2}$, $\frac{5}{8}$, and $\frac{3}{4}$ in (6, 9.5, 11, 12, 16, and 19 mm), and panels are normally made 4 ft (1200 mm) wide by 7, 8, 9, or 10 ft (2.1, 2.4, 2.7, or 3 m) in length. The edges may be left square,

or they may be tongue-and-grooved, shiplapped, or beveled. Square-edged panels may meet with a fitted butt joint, have the joint covered with a batten, or have edges separated and covered by a small molding.

Wood trim materials are usually made from either fir or mahogany but may be run from any species of wood desired. A large number of stock trim materials and moldings are manufactured, some of the more common ones being illustrated in Fig. 1-95. A complete list of stock items may be obtained on request from lumber manufacturers or retailers.

Softwood Flooring

Softwood flooring is available in $\frac{3}{4}$- and 1-in (19- and 25-mm) actual thicknesses and in 3-, 4-, and 6-in nominal (54-, 79-, and 130-mm) widths. Softwood strip flooring is designated K.D. Flooring, V.G., F.G., and/or M.G. and is available in three grades: C and better, D, and E. All three are normally supplied kiln dried, surfaced on two sides, tongue-and-grooved, with partially surfaced or hollow back.

Grade C and better flooring is recommended where a combination of good appearance and good wearing qualities are required. Grade D flooring is used where serviceability and good wearing qualities are required but appearance is not of primary importance. Grade E flooring, which is normally mixed grain, is used where economy is important and is often used for subflooring, sheathing, and lining.

Decking

Lumber that spans between supporting beams to support loads is commonly known as *decking*. It can be tongue-and-grooved boards or planks placed on the flat or lumber placed on edge. (See Fig. 1-96.) Material that is placed on the flat is known as *plank* decking, while material placed on edge is designated as *laminated* decking. Wood species used for decking include western red cedar, Douglas fir, hemlock, and members of the spruce-pine-fir group. Cedar is usually used where appearance is a concern (see Fig. 1-97), and the harder species are usually used for flooring where resistance to wear is important.

Plank decking is available in three thicknesses: 2, 3-, and 4-in nominal (38-, 64-, and 89-mm) and in widths of 6- and 8-in nominal (127 and 171 mm) for the 2-in (38-mm) thickness and 6-in nominal

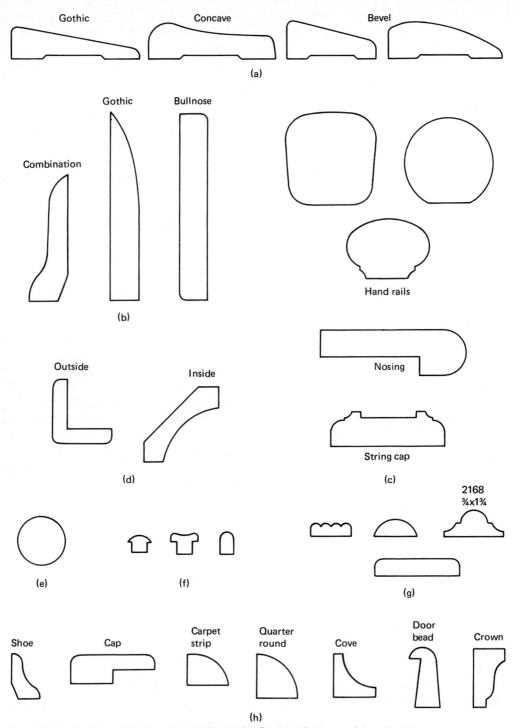

Gothic Concave Bevel

(a)

Combination Gothic Bullnose

Hand rails

(b)

Outside Inside

Nosing

String cap

(d) (c)

2168
¾x1¾

(e) (f) (g)

Shoe Cap Carpet strip Quarter round Cove Door bead Crown

(h)

Fig. 1-95   Typical wood trim and moldings. *(a)* Casing, *(b)* base, *(c)* stair parts, *(d)* corners, *(e)* round, *(f)* dividers, *(g)* battens, *(h)* moldings.

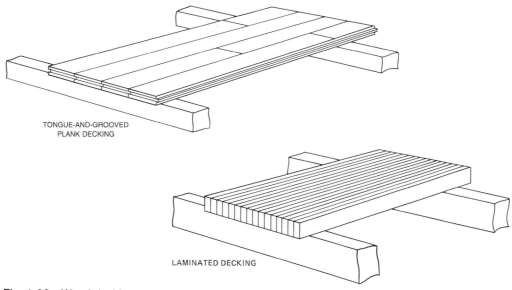

TONGUE-AND-GROOVED
PLANK DECKING

LAMINATED DECKING

Fig. 1-96   Wood decking types.

(133 mm) for the 3- and 4-in (64- and 89-mm) thicknesses. (See Fig. 1-98.) Plank decking comes in two grades: select and commercial. Select grade is used where aesthetics and high strength are a concern, whereas the commercial grade is used where appearance and strength are not as critical. Select grade is used where its natural beauty is used to best advantage as illustrated in Fig. 1-99.

Laminated decking is dimensioned lumber placed on edge to produce a surface that has high resistance to wear and vibration. Laminated decking can be of any softwood species that may be readily available and has been used successfully in bridge decks and loading ramps and as roof decking.

Hardwood Strip Flooring

Many hardwood species are used to manufacture strip flooring, but the more common ones are maple, birch, beech, red and white oak, and walnut. The material is kiln dried and made with tongue-

Fig. 1-97   Exposed plank decking.

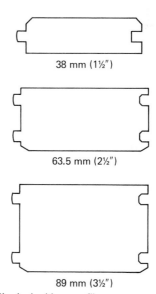

38 mm (1½″)

63.5 mm (2½″)

89 mm (3½″)

Fig. 1-98   Plank decking profiles.

Fig. 1-99 Natural beauty of wood decking. *(Canadian Institute of Timber Construction)*

and-grooved edges and ends (end matched) and usually has a channeled or grooved bottom surface. (See Fig. 1-100.)

A variety of flooring thicknesses and face widths are made. The standard thicknesses and common uses are given in Table 1-33. In addition to these, extra-thick narrow flooring is made for bowling alleys.

Birch, maple, and beech flooring have similar grading standards and are available in First, Second, Third, and Fourth grades; quality shorts; and combination grades. Shorts consist of First- and Second-grade material in 9- and 18-in (225- and 450-mm) lengths. There are two combination grades: prime and mill run. Prime combination grade consists of 60 percent First and 40 percent Second grade. Mill run is a combination of First, Second, and Third grades. Specifications for all grades are described in grading rules for hardwood flooring.

Oak flooring is first divided into two types, quartersawn and plain sawn, and each type has its own grades. Quartersawn flooring is available in three grades: First grade, Sap Clear First grade, and

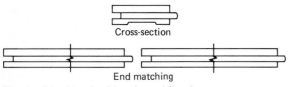

Fig. 1-100 Matched hardwood flooring.

Second grade. In Sap Clear First grade, the face must be practically free of defects, but unlimited bright sapwood is allowed. The details of specifications for each grade are listed in grading rules for hardwood flooring.

Plain-sawn oak flooring grades are First grade, Second grade, No. 1 Common, No. 2 Common, Prime-Quality Shorts, Mill-Run grade, and No. 1 Common and Better Shorts. Detailed specifications are given for each.

Strip flooring is also available in what is known as Colonial Plank, strips of various widths with round inserts of some contrasting wood. (See Fig. 1-101.) Usual thickness is $\frac{25}{32}$ in (20 mm); widths range from 3 to 8 in (75 to 200 mm). Edges are tongue-and-grooved, and the ends are grooved with splines supplied.

Parquet Flooring

Parquet flooring consists of blocks of hardwood of various sizes which can be laid in a number of patterns such as herringbone, basket weave, and squares. (See Fig. 1-102.) Common thickness is $\frac{25}{32}$ in (20 mm), and dimensions of blocks are normally $2\frac{1}{4} \times 6\frac{3}{4}$, 9, $11\frac{1}{4}$, $13\frac{1}{2}$, $15\frac{3}{4}$, and 18 in (56 × 170, 225, 275, 338, 394, and 450 mm) or 18 × 18 in

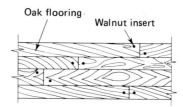

Fig. 1-101 Colonial plank flooring.

Fig. 1-102 Parquet flooring in square pattern.

Table 1-33
HARDWOOD STRIP FLOORING THICKNESSES

Thickness				Uses
Nominal		Actual		
Inches	Milli-meters	Inches	Milli-meters	
$\frac{3}{8}$	9.5	$\frac{11}{32}$	8.7	Residential office floors
$\frac{1}{2}$	13	$\frac{15}{32}$	11.9	
$\frac{13}{16}$	20.5	$\frac{25}{32}$	19.8	
$1\frac{1}{16}$	27	$\frac{33}{32}$	26	Dance floors, gymnasia, skating rinks, schools, churches
$1\frac{5}{16}$	33.3	$\frac{41}{32}$	32.5	
$1\frac{11}{16}$	42.8	$\frac{53}{32}$	42	

(450 × 450 mm). Blocks may be blind nailed or fastened to the subfloor with mastic.

Grading rules formulated for parquet flooring made from various hardwoods are available from national lumbermen's associations.

Hardboard Finishing Panels

Tempered hardboard is treated in many ways to produce interior facing panels, usually 4 × 7 ft (1200 × 2100 mm) or 4 × 8 ft (1200 × 2400 mm), and $\frac{1}{4}$ in (6 mm) thick. One treatment consists of printing a wood-grain pattern on the face and grooving at irregular intervals along the board to represent random planking. Boards are also produced with an embossed-leather-grain pattern pressed on the face. Both of these are fastened to the wall with nails.

Another type of treatment consists of covering the hardboard with a plastic film printed in a wide variety of wood, stone, and fabric patterns and then applying a coating of baked-on melamine plastic. Such panels are made with tongue-and-grooved edges and can be applied over solid backing with contact adhesives or fastened to studs with special clips, as shown in Fig. 1-103. Boards are also covered with a baked-on enamel coating, applied in 4-in squares to represent ceramic wall tile.

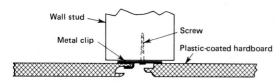

Fig. 1-103   Clip fasteners for hardboard panels.

Fiberboard Panels

Fiberboard panels may be used as interior finish on ceilings or on walls, particularly above dado level. Wall panels are 4 × 7 ft (1200 × 2100 mm) or 4 × 8 ft (1200 × 2400 mm), $\frac{1}{2}$ in (12 mm) thick, with a factory-sealed or prepainted surface and square or beveled edges. Boards are held in place with finishing nails driven at an angle to the surface.

For ceilings, the boards may be in the form of tile, in strips 16 × 32 in (400 × 800 mm), 16 × 48 in (400 × 1200 mm), or 16 × 96 in (400 × 2400 mm); or in 4 × 8 ft (1200 × 2400 mm) panels, which are held in place by adhesives to a solid surface or by a suspended ceiling frame. (See Fig. 1-104.)

PRESSURE-TREATED TIMBER

Wood is generally recognized as a relatively abundant structural material—a renewable resource—with several advantages such as lightness, ease of fabrication, resilience, and wear resistance. However, its useful life may be limited under adverse service conditions, such as dampness, exposure to fire or weather, or the presence of wood-destroying insects, such as termites, carpenter ants, or marine borers of various kinds.

To counteract these adverse conditions, wood may be pressure-treated with preservatives or fire retardants. The preservatives include *creosote* and *creosote solutions, oil-borne chemicals,* and *water-borne inorganic compounds,* while the fire retardants usually consist of *water-soluble salts.* Each

77

Fig. 1-104   Suspended fiberboard ceiling panels.

preservative has its own properties and so its own best uses. Some knowledge of each one is required in order to specify correctly for the job at hand.

Preservatives

Creosote is a dark brown distillate of coal tar, containing more than 160 compounds, each of which has been proved to be toxic to wood-destroying fungi, insects, and marine borers. Creosote's greatest value, therefore, is in its multiplicity of toxic compounds, which increase its inhibiting effect. In addition to being dependable and generally available, creosote is nonleachable, has low volatility, and protects against some chemicals. These qualities provide permanence under a variety of service conditions, ease of impregnation, and readily determined depth of penetration. It is the only preservative recognized for marine work.

Creosote–coal-tar mixtures are often used for economy, in proportions of up to 50 percent coal tar. This provides adequate protection in many cases. Creosote–coal-tar solutions are detailed in CSA 080.P2.

Creosote-petroleum mixtures also do an adequate job under a variety of circumstances. Not less than 50 percent creosote in the mixture is required by CSA 080.P3. These mixtures are used in construction where such a high degree of protection given by similar quantities of straight creosote are not required. Costs of mixtures are less than costs of straight creosote, the difference depending on the relative costs and amounts of creosote and petroleum.

Oil-borne preservatives of known toxicity, such as *pentachlorophenol,* are often used instead of creosote with some materials, because the treated wood is lighter in color and cleaner to handle. Usually 5 percent pentachlorophenol by weight is mixed with the prescribed petroleum product. Wood so treated is initially brown in color but eventually turns silver.

Water-borne preservatives have the greatest value where cleanliness in handling, paintability, or absence of odor is required. Widely used water-borne preservatives include *chromated copper arsenate, fluor chrome arsenate phenol,* and *chromated zinc chloride.* These have varying resistance to leaching, and this may be a consideration when specifying.

In order to produce the most economical and efficient retention of preservative, the wood should first be uniformly seasoned before treatment. Then the material to be treated—lumber, plywood, piling, poles, ties, or posts—is loaded on rail trams which are run into large steel cylinders (see Fig. 1-105), and the door is clamped shut to produce a vacuum/pressure-tight seal.

Several processes are used to provide impregnation of the wood. In one, vacuum is first applied to the cylinder and the preservative admitted under vacuum. As a result, a large quantity of preservative is drawn into the cells of the sapwood and outer heartwood, where it is most needed for effective protection. (See Fig. 1-106.) In another process, preservative is admitted at atmospheric pressure. In a third, the cylinder is first pressurized to force some air into the wood cells and the preservative is introduced at above atmospheric pressure. In the two latter processes, the cylinder is finally put under vacuum to remove excess preservative from the surface.

Fig. 1-105 Charge of treated piles withdrawn from pressure cylinder. *(Canadian Institute of Timber Construction)*

Fig. 1-106 Pile cutoff, showing deep penetration of preservative. *(Canadian Institute of Timber Construction)*

Fig. 1-107 Pile head protected by moisture barrier. *(Canadian Institute of Timber Construction)*

Uses of Pressure-Treated Timber

Pressure-treated timber is used in a wide variety of situations. Pressure-treated piles (large poles) are used in the building of *wharves* and *breakwaters* and as *channel markers, bridge timbers,* and *utility poles.* It should be noted that when pile ends must be cut off during construction, the pile head should be protected by a moisture barrier placed over the cut end. (See Fig. 1-107.) Smaller poles are used for *fencing, guard rail posts, farm structures* (see Figs. 1-108 and 1-109), and *light standards.*

Fig. 1-108 Pole building frame. *(Canadian Institute of Timber Construction)*

Fig. 1-109 Pole building complete. *(Canadian Institute of Timber Construction)*

Fig. 1-111 Pressure-treated timber used in wood foundation. *(Canadian Institute of Timber Construction)*

Pressure-treated sawn timber is used for *boat planking, tanks, viaducts* (see Fig. 1-110), *roof decks, retaining walls, highway guard rails, glulam timbers,* and *house foundations.* (See Fig. 1-111.)

Pressure-treated plywood is used for *decking, farm structures, water tanks,* and *house foundations.* (See Fig. 1-112.)

Other uses for pressure-treated timber include *railroad ties, floor blocks* (see Fig. 1-113), *bleachers, crossarms, sign posts,* and *mine timbers.*

Fire Retardants

Fire retardants are odorless chemical formulations which, when dissolved in water and impregnated into wood under pressure, reduce *flame spread, fuel contributed,* and *smoke developed* to a point where the treated woods perform favorably in comparison to other building materials normally considered noncombustible. Colorless treatments are available for natural finishes, while others give a slightly brownish color to the wood.

Fig. 1-110 Viaduct made with pressure-treated timber. *(Canadian Institute of Timber Construction)*

Fig. 1-112 Pressure-treated plywood used in wood foundations. *(Koppers Co., Inc.)*

Fig. 1-113 Pressure-treated wood blocks as flooring. *(Canadian Institute of Timber Construction)*

The effects obtained by treating wood with a fire retardant are brought about by one or more reactions which result when the salts are exposed to the heat of a fire. As the salts decompose, they produce a nonflammable gas which mixes with combustible gases to inhibit flaming and form a vapor blanket along the surface. As the salts decompose, heat is absorbed from the attacking fire. And, as the salts melt, they form an inert glazed skin which shuts off the air needed for combustion.

As a result of these reactions, wood pressure-treated with fire retardant is difficult to ignite, is resistant to flaming and smoldering, seldom supports combustion itself, and contributes a sharply reduced amount of heat to the growth of the fire. When wood which has been treated with fire retardant is used on building interiors, it may be a significant factor in saving lives and property.

GLOSSARY

asbestos A mineral occurring in long, delicate fibers or in fibrous masses; it is incombustible, nonconducting, and chemically resistant.

bagasse Residue of cane or corn stalks after the juice has been extracted.

calender rolls Highly polished steel rollers used to smooth the surface of paper or plastics.

cambium layer Layer of growing cells, just under the bark of a growing tree.

cellulose An inert substance, the chief ingredient of cell walls in plants.

chipboard Rigid board made from wood chips mixed with thermosetting adhesive.

deciduous tree A tree with broad leaves.

dry kiln An oven used for removing moisture from lumber.

edgings	Trimmings containing bark, cut from the edges of boards.
emulsion	A milky fluid made by suspending particles of material in a watery liquid.
factory lumber	Lumber that is intended for remanufacture.
flitch	In sawmill jargon, a large timber to be recut into smaller units.
Fourdrinier	An endless-belt-type papermaking machine.
groundwood	Wood pulp made by grinding wood blocks against abrasive stones.
homogeneous	Consisting of similar material throughout.
impregnating	Saturating.
Jordan	A final refining machine used in the processing of wood pulp.
jute	Glossy fiber of the jute plant.
kraft	A strong, usually brown paper made from sulfate pulp.
modulus of elasticity	The property of a material that indicates its resistance to bending.
modulus of rigidity	The property of a material that indicates its resistance to torsion.
polymerize	To change into another compound having the same elements but with more complex molecules and different physical properties.
rosin	The hard, amber-colored residue left after distilling off the volatile oil of turpentine.
sheathing paper	Paper used to provide an airtight barrier over walls, floors, etc.
structural lumber	Lumber carefully graded for strength and used in structurally designed construction.
tempered hardboard	Hardboard that has its density and its resistance to water penetration increased.
yard lumber	Lumber commonly used for building purposes.

REVIEW QUESTIONS

1. List five properties of wood that have created a demand for it as a building material. Which one of these do you consider to be the most important?

2. a. How can one tell the age of a tree by examination?

b. List two other facts one could tell about the tree from examination.

3. a. List common hardwoods whose wood is not hard and common softwoods whose wood is not soft.

b. Explain the reason for these apparent contradictions.

4. a. In general terms, what does wood grain mean?

b. Draw a vertical cross-section of a piece of edge-grain flooring.

5. List seven factors to be considered when grading lumber.

6. What is the practical lower limit of moisture content achieved by air drying? By kiln drying?

7. a. What are the three general use classifications of structural lumber?

b. How is each of the three intended to be loaded?

c. How does the grading of structural lumber differ from grading of yard or factory lumber?

8. a. Explain what is meant by glued laminated timber.

b. List six advantages of glued laminated timber when compared to sawn timber.

9. a. What is the basic material used in the manufacture of most commonly used papers?

b. What is the main source of this material?

c. How does paper made from asbestos fiber differ from most others?

10. a. Explain what is meant by chemical pulp.

b. How does it differ from semichemical pulp?

11. a. What type of tree is used in making sulfite pulp?

b. Give two reasons for the increase in production of semichemical pulp.

12. List five wood-pulp additives and state the purpose of each.

13. What is the basic purpose of a Jordan in the pulp-refining process?

14. Outline the major use of each of the following types of building paper:

a. Asphalt-impregnated paper.

b. Waxed paper.

15. Outline the basic features of roofing felt and rolled roofing.

16. Explain the difference between insulating paper made from wood fiber and that made from asbestos fiber.

17. Explain what is meant by envelope paper and give two examples of its use in construction materials.

18. How does the density of standard hardboard compare with tempered hardboard?

19. Explain why tempered hardboard can be used for exteriors while standard hardboard is not satisfactory for this use.

20. Outline two differences between insulation-grade fiberboard and sheathing-grade fiberboard.

21. Compare wall coverings of solid wood to those of plywood from the standpoint of the following:

a. Size of units.

b. Surface characteristics.

c. Method of application.

22. a. List 10 commonly used stock moldings.

b. Draw a cross-section of each.

c. Indicate the primary use of each.

23. Distinguish between the terms "roof decking" and "roofing."

24. Give five reasons why cedar is so widely used in the manufacture of shingles.

25. Explain the difference between shingles and shakes.

26. a. Outline two basic reasons for using pressure-treated timber.

b. Explain the basic differences between creosote-type preservatives and oil-borne preservatives.

27. a. What are the four most important properties of plywood that give it an advantage over sawn lumber?

b. Explain the term "stress joint" in long plywood panels.

SELECTED SOURCES OF INFORMATION

Abitibi Paper Co. Ltd., Toronto, Ont.
American Institute of Timber Construction, Englewood, Calif.
American Plywood Association, Tacoma, Wash.
American Wood Preservers' Association, Washington, D.C.
Bennett, Ltd., Chambly, Que.
Bowaters Newfoundland, Ltd., Corner Brook, N.F.
British Columbia Forest Products, Ltd., Vancouver, Brit. Col.
Building Products of Canada, Ltd., Halifax, N.S.

California Redwood Association, San Francisco, Calif.
Canadian Institute of Timber Construction, Ottawa, Ont.
Canadian International Paper Co., Montreal, Que.
Canadian Lumbermen's Association, Ottawa, Ont.
Canadian Pulp & Paper Association, Montreal, Que.
Canadian Wood Council, Ottawa, Ont.
Council of Forest Industries of British Columbia, Vancouver, Brit. Col.
Crown Zellerbach Canada, Ltd., Vancouver, Brit. Col.
Domtar Pulp & Paper Products, Ltd., Montreal, Que.
International Panel Boards, Ltd., Montreal, Que.
MacMillan, Bloedel, Powell & River, Ltd., Vancouver, Brit. Col.
Masonite Canada, Ltd., Gatineau, Que.
National Lumber Manufacturers' Association, Washington, D.C.
Southern Pine Association, New Orleans, La.
United States Plywood Corporation, New York, N.Y.
U.S. Department of Agriculture, Forest Service, Washington, D.C.
Welsh Plywood Corporation, Memphis, Tenn.
West Coast Lumbermen's Association, Portland, Oreg.
Western Forest Products Laboratory, Vancouver, Brit. Col.

REFERENCES

1. Dietz, A. G. H., E. L. Schaffer, D. S. Gromala, *Wood As a Structural Material,* The Pennsylvania State University, 1982.
2. Panshin, A. J., Carl de Zeeuw, *Textbook of Wood Technology,* McGraw-Hill Book Company, New York, N.Y., 1980.
3. *Structure and Properties, CWC Datafile SP-1,* Canadian Wood Council, Ottawa, Ont., 1981.
4. Wangaard, F. F., *Wood: Its Structure and Properties,* The Pennsylvania State University, 1981.
5. U.S. Forest Products Laboratory, *Wood Handbook, (Agriculture Handbook; No. 72),* United States Department of Agriculture, Washington, D.C., 1974.

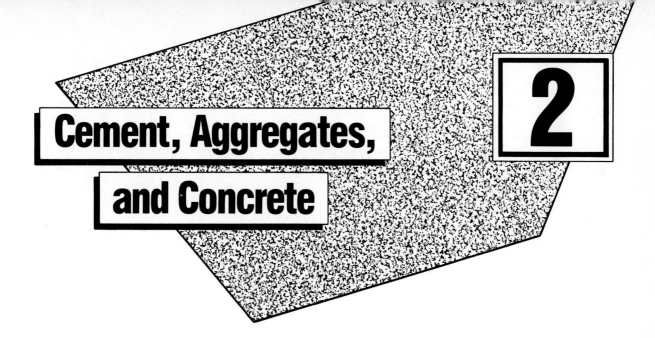

Cement, Aggregates, and Concrete

2

Cements have been known and used for at least two thousand years. The Romans used a great deal of this material in their construction projects, many of which still stand. The cements they used were natural and pozzolan cements, made from naturally occurring mixtures of limestone and clay and from a mixture of slaked lime and volcanic ash containing silica.

CEMENTS
Portland Cement

It was not until 1824 that the first step was made in producing the type of cement with which we are familiar today. The inventor, Joseph Aspdin, produced a powder made from the calcined mixture of limestone and clay. He called it portland cement because when it hardened it produced a material resembling stone from the quarries near Portland, England.

This method of making cement has been improved upon since that time, but the basic process has remained. Modern portland cement is made from materials which must contain the proper proportions of *lime, silica, alumina,* and *iron* with minor amounts of magnesia and sulfur trioxide. Table 2-1 indicates the range of oxide composition usually found in normal portland cements.

The ingredients come from a variety of raw materials, the typical ones being indicated in Table 2-2. The magnesia and sulfur trioxide may be pres-

ent in one or more of the ores or other raw materials listed.

Depending on the location of the cement-manufacturing plant, available raw materials are pulverized and mixed in proportions such that the resulting mixture will have the desired chemical composition.

When limestone and clay are the two basic ingredients, the proportions will be approximately 4 parts limestone to 1 part of clay. Limestone is quarried and transported to a large gyratory, or "jaw crusher," for primary reduction in size. It then passes through a hammer mill, where further reduction takes place, and from there it goes to rock storage. From storage, the crushed rock is fed to a tube mill, along with the clay or crushed shale. In the wet process, water is also added at this point, so that the product of the tube mill is *slurry,* a

Table 2-1
OXIDE COMPOSITION OF TYPE 10 (ASTM TYPE I) OR NORMAL PORTLAND CEMENT

Oxide Ingredient	Range, %
Lime, CaO	60–66
Silica, SiO_2	19–25
Alumina, Al_2O_3	3–8
Iron, Fe_2O_3	1–5
Magnesia, MgO	0–5
Sulfur trioxide, SO_3	1–3

SOURCE: Portland Cement Association.

Table 2-2

TYPICAL SOURCES OF RAW MATERIAL USED IN THE MANUFACTURE OF PORTLAND CEMENT

Components			
Lime	**Silica**	**Alumina**	**Iron**
Cement rock	Sand	Clay	Iron ore
Limestone	Traprock	Shale	Iron calcine
Marl	Calcium silicate	Slag	Iron dust
Alkali waste	Quartzite	Fly ash	Iron pyrite
Oyster shell	Fuller's earth	Copper slag	Iron sinters
Coquina shell		Aluminum ore	Iron oxide
Chalk		refuse	Blast furnace flue
Marble		Staurolite	dust
		Diaspore clay	
		Granodiorite	
		Kaolin	

SOURCE: Portland Cement Association.

blended mixture of very finely ground raw materials and water. The slurry is stored in tanks, under constant agitation and fed into huge rotary kilns, 11 to 12 ft (3.35 to 3.65 m) in diameter, from 200 to 455 ft (61 to 139 m) long, with a slope of about $\frac{1}{2}$ in/ft (40 mm/m). The kilns are fired with crushed coal or gas from the discharge end, so that the material which is being fed in advances against the heat blast as the kiln rotates.

At about 425°C, the excess water is driven off and then, further along the kiln, at about 870°C, the limestone breaks down into calcium oxide and carbon dioxide. Finally, at about 1480°C and about 30 ft (9 m) from the discharge end, the initial melting stage of the materials is reached, known as the point of *incipient fusion*. Here *sintering* takes place and a *clinker* is formed. The clinker is cooled, is crushed, has about 3 percent crushed gypsum added, and is fed into a *tube mill*. Here it is ground so fine that nearly all of it passes through a 200-mesh (75-μm) sieve. The cement is finally bagged or loaded in bulk into railway cement cars or cement trucks. Figure 2-1 illustrates the complete process.

Portland cement is a *hydraulic cement*. That is, it reacts with water (*hydrates*) to produce a substance that is durable, resists the effects of water, and continues to gain strength as long as moisture is present. It will continue to gain strength even when completely submerged in water. Compared to hydraulic limes, the strength gain is quite rapid and much greater in value.

When lime and silica are heated to the sintering temperature in the presence of alumina and ferric oxide, four basic components of cement are formed:

Tricalcium silicate, $3CaO \cdot SiO_2$ (C_3S)
Dicalcium silicate, $2CaO \cdot SiO_2$ (C_2S)
Tricalcium aluminate, $3CaO \cdot Al_2O_3$ (C_3A)
Tetracalcium aluminoferrite, $4CaO \cdot Al_2O_3 \cdot Fe_2O_3$ (C_4AF)

The clinker compounds that are formed by sintering are responsible for the hydration process. In their pure form the tricalcium and dicalcium silicates tend to set quite slowly. In direct contrast, the tricalcium aluminate develops a *flash set*. Because of the speed at which this reaction takes place and the amount of heat that is liberated, this compound in its pure form is of little value. Even in small quantities, this compound can set off a *flash set* in the entire cement mass. This phenomenon was not a serious problem when cement was not ground as finely as today's cement. In fact, the setting time for cement was usually quite prolonged. However, as cements became finer, the setting rate accelerated, making the problem of flash set much more prevalent. Through experimentation it was found that a small quantity of gypsum would counteract this detrimental reaction. This discovery was of great importance in that now the rate of hydration could be stabilized and controlled.

In addition to the four main compounds, some free lime along with some other minor components are produced in the sintering process. The amount of free lime produced is that portion of the lime that is not used by the acidic oxides during the sintering process. The free lime, however, does not behave in the same manner as hydraulic lime. Because of its glazed surface structure, it resists reacting with water, thus retarding the slaking action that normally occurs relatively quickly in hydraulic limes. Even after grinding the lime into a very fine powder, the slaking process is delayed until after setting of the cement has occurred. Since the slaking process produces an increase in volume, the resulting stresses may be such as to produce fracture. This is known as "unsoundness due to free lime." To ensure that this does not occur in industrial applications, the content of free lime must be controlled within an accuracy of $\pm$ 0.1 percent during the cement manufacturing process.

Although small in quantity, the addition of gypsum must also be done with some care. As its prime purpose is to react with the tricalcium aluminate, the quantity added must correspond to the amount of tricalcium aluminate available. If free gypsum remains in the cement after sintering, it will react with moisture in the setting process and produce gypsum expansion similar to that of the free lime.

Other constituents, though minor in quantity, also have a bearing on the final properties of cement. Magnesium oxide (MgO), when slaked, will produce the same effects as lime but with more serious consequences. Its reaction with water is much slower, and the effects can take years to become evident. To minimize its effects its quantity is limited to 5 percent of the total. The greenish-gray color of cement is due to the presence of this compound.

Alkalis in the form of K_2O and Na_2O are usually present in the raw materials in some quantity. In large concentrations they may react with some aggregate types and produce aggregate degradation. However, this is not a common occurrence.

Moisture is another minor constituent that does have an effect on the properties of cement. During the manufacturing process some moisture is absorbed by the clinker to produce *ignition loss*. This condition is the hydration of some of the clinker during sintering. When kept below 5 percent of the total, its effects on the hardening properties of the final product are negligible. Improper storage, where the cement will come in contact with moisture, produces a much greater loss of ignition than that developed during the manufacturing process.

TYPES OF PORTLAND CEMENT   The amounts of the four basic ingredients can be varied to produce different types of portland cement, each with some unique characteristics. The three most common types are (1) Type 10 (ASTM Type I), normal portland cement; (2) Type 30 (ASTM type III), high-early-strength portland cement; and (3) Type 50 (ASTM Type V), sulfate-resistant portland cement. In addition, two other types are made: (1) Type 20 (ASTM Type II), moderate portland cement, and (2) Type 40 (ASTM Type IV), low-heat-of-hydration portland cement. (See Table 2-3.)

Normal portland (Type 10) is used for general construction work when the special properties of the other types are not required. It is normally used for reinforced-concrete buildings, bridges, pavements, and sidewalks where the soil conditions are normal, for most concrete masonry units, and for all uses where the concrete is not subject to special sulfate hazard or where the heat generated by the hydration of the cement is not objectionable.

Table 2-3
TYPICAL COMPOUND COMPOSITION AND FINENESS OF PORTLAND CEMENTS

Type	Compound Composition, %				Fineness,[a] cm^2/g
	C_3S	C_2S	C_3A	C_4Af	
10 Normal	50	24	11	8	1800
20 Moderate	42	33	5	13	1800
30 High-early-strength	60	13	9	8	2600
40 Low-heat	26	50	5	12	1900
50 Sulfate-resistant	40	40	4	9	1900

[a] Fineness as determined by Wagner turbidimeter test.

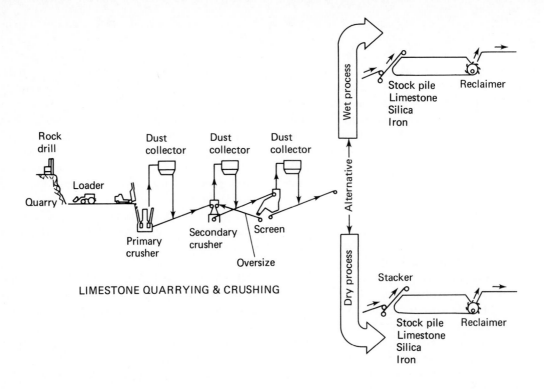

LIMESTONE QUARRYING & CRUSHING

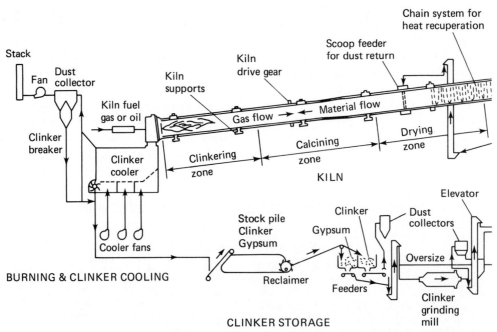

BURNING & CLINKER COOLING

CLINKER STORAGE

Fig. 2-1 Flowchart of portland cement manufacturing process. *(Canada Cement Lafarge)*

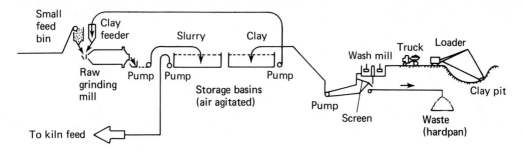

KILN FEED PREPARATION (Wet process)

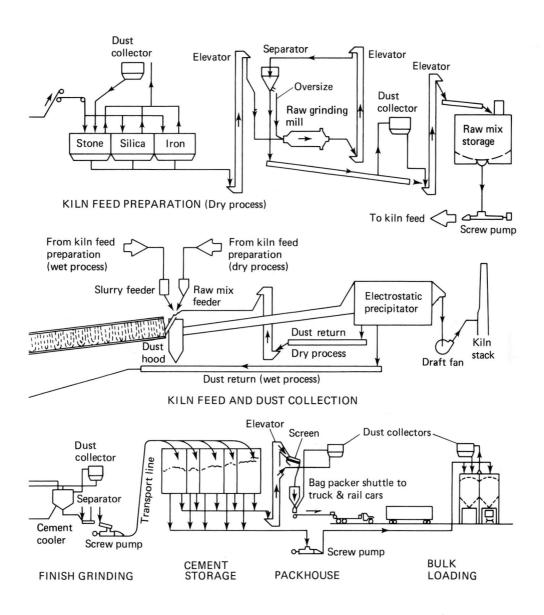

KILN FEED PREPARATION (Dry process)

KILN FEED AND DUST COLLECTION

FINISH GRINDING   CEMENT STORAGE   PACKHOUSE   BULK LOADING

Moderate portland (Type 20) has better resistance to the action of sulfates than normal portland and is used where sulfate concentrations in groundwaters are higher than normal but not unusually severe. It also generates heat at a slower rate than normal portland and is used in mass concrete work. Its use will minimize temperature rise, a property which is particularly important when concrete is being placed in hot weather.

High-early-strength cement (Type 30) is used where higher strengths are required at early periods, usually of a week or less. It is particularly useful where it is required to remove forms as soon as possible or when the structure must be brought into service quickly. High early strength makes it possible to reduce the period of protection for concrete during cold weather.

Low-heat portland (Type 40) is a special cement for use where the amount and rate of heat generated must be minimized. Strength is also developed at a slower rate. It is intended for use in massive concrete structures, such as large dams, where the temperature rise resulting from heat generated during hydration is a critical factor.

Sulfate-resistant cement (Type 50) is intended for use in structures subject to attack by sulfate concentrations in some waters, such as may be found in certain manufacturing plants or in the groundwater in some areas. It is also resistant to the action of seawater.

The rate at which the strength of concrete increases varies according to the type of cement used. Table 2-4 gives the approximate strength values of concrete for each of the five types at four time periods. Concrete made with normal portland cement is the basis for comparison.

PROPERTIES OF PORTLAND CEMENT   Normally, during the manufacture of cement, quite close limits are placed on the chemical composition and some of the physical properties of the material. Frequent tests are carried out on the cement itself, either on hardened cement paste or on concrete made from the cement, to maintain the quality within specification limits. Figure 2-2 illustrates a typical control laboratory checking on the properties of the product.

One of the important physical properties of cement is its *fineness*. Fineness affects the rate of hydration: the finer the cement, the faster strength development takes place. The effects of greater fineness on strength are particularly noticeable during the first 7 days. Also, as fineness increases, the amount of water required for a constant slump concrete decreases, to the limits reached by the higher ranges of fineness in high-early-strength cement.

Soundness is a physical property tested by determining the ability of a hardened cement paste to retain its volume after setting. Lack of soundness or a delayed destructive expansion is caused by too much hard-burned free lime or magnesia in the cement.

Setting time is an important characteristic of cement which must be regulated. It is necessary for concrete to remain plastic long enough for finishing operations to be carried out. In practical circumstances, the length of time that a concrete mixture will remain plastic is usually more dependent on the amount of mixing water used and the atmospheric temperature than on the setting time of the cement.

False set is a characteristic which results in loss of plasticity, without much heat being developed, a

Table 2-4
APPROXIMATE RELATIVE STRENGTH OF CONCRETE AS AFFECTED BY TYPE OF CEMENT

Types of Portland Cement	Compressive Strength—Percent of Strength of Normal (Type I) Portland-Cement Concrete			
	1 Day	7 Days	28 Days	3 Months
10 Normal	100	100	100	100
20 Moderate	75	85	90	100
30 High-early-strength	190	120	110	100
40 Low-heat	55	55	75	100
50 Sulfate-resistant	65	75	85	100

Fig. 2-2 Typical cement laboratory. *(Portland Cement Association)*

short time after the concrete is mixed. Further mixing without the additional use of water usually restores plasticity. The use of chemical admixtures may delay the occurrence of false set.

The ability of cement to develop *compressive strength* in a concrete mixture is one of its most important characteristics. Compressive strength is determined by making tests on 2-in (50-mm) mortar cubes, in which a standard sand is used. Strength tests at various ages indicate the strength-producing characteristics of the cement but should not be used to try to predict concrete strengths accurately because of the great number of variables that may occur in a number of concrete mixtures. To accurately determine compressive strength, tests should be made on concrete samples made from the particular ingredients to be used.

Heat of hydration is the heat produced by the chemical reaction between cement and water. In the main, the amount of heat generated depends on the chemical composition of the cement. The rate of heat generation is affected by the fineness of the cement, the chemical composition, and the temperature during hydration. In some structures with considerable mass, the rate and amount of heat generated are significant. If the heat is not rapidly dissipated, an undesirable rise in temperature may occur, which may be accompanied by thermal expansion. A subsequent drop in temperature may then create undesirable stresses in the structure. On the other hand, a rise in temperature may be

beneficial in cold weather, helping to maintain favorable curing conditions. The approximate amount of heat generated during the first seven days by each of the five types of cement, based on 100 percent for Type 10 or normal portland cement, are shown in Table 2-5.

Loss on ignition is a test carried out on portland cement to determine how much weight a sample will lose when heated to 900 to 1000°C. Normally the loss will be in the neighborhood of 2 percent. The maximum allowable is 4 percent.

The *specific gravity* of portland cement is generally about 3.15. Cements made from materials other than limestone and clay may vary somewhat from that figure. Specific gravity is not an indication of the quality of the cement. It is used in calculating mix designs.

Insoluble residue in cement must be determined

Table 2-5
COMPARATIVE AMOUNTS OF HEAT GENERATED DURING FIRST 7 DAYS BY FIVE TYPES OF CEMENT

Cement Type	Heat Generated, %
Type 10 or normal	100
Type 20 or moderate	80–85
Type 30 or high-early-strength	Up to 150
Type 40 or low-heat	40–60
Type 50 or sulfate-resistant	60–75

through tests. The maximum allowable is 0.85 percent.

Cement is also tested to ensure that the contents of sulfuric anhydride and magnesia are kept within limits. The maximum allowable for sulfuric anhydride is 2 percent and for magnesia 4 percent.

Consistency tests on cement paste are carried out using the Vicat-needle technique, and *tensile* tests are carried out on standard shapes of hardened mortar, using the standard sand.

All these tests are outlined in ASTM.

Aluminous Cement

For many years research has been conducted in an attempt to produce a structural hydraulic cement which would not liberate free lime during and after hydration. Elimination of free lime was desired primarily in order to provide a cement for making concrete which would not be attacked by seawater and injurious groundwaters. It was discovered that a cement with a high content of alumina (Al_2O_3), with approximately equal parts of Al_2O_3 and CaO, would meet this requirement.

This cement is now produced commercially by completely melting a mixture of bauxite (aluminum ore) and a calcareous material (chalk or limestone). The molten material is tapped from the furnace continuously and cast into pigs similar in shape to the iron pigs from a blast furnace. The pigs are crushed and ground to a fine powder (not as fine as portland cement) in a ball mill. The resulting product, without addition of any other materials, is called *Ciment Fondu* (melted cement).

The chemical composition of Ciment Fondu is considerably different from that of portland cement. The Al_2O_3 content is about 40 percent, the content of CaO slightly lower. The SiO_2 content is less than 6 percent. Quite wide variations in these amounts are possible without changing the characteristics of the cement, but the ratio of Al_2O_3 to CaO is not less than 0.85 or greater than 1.3.

The initial set of Ciment Fondu is slower than that of portland cement. The average initial setting times are from 2 to 4 h, and the final set takes place about 30 min later. After the final set, the extremely fast hardening process begins, and within 24 h the concrete has developed the 28-day strength of similar concrete made with portland cement.

Although Ciment Fondu could be used in nearly every situation in which portland cement is used, it is particularly valuable where concrete must be put into service in a short time. Repairs to sewers and concrete water mains, for example, can be made overnight. Machine foundations and floors can be put to use the day after placing. Airport runways can be repaired with little or no disruption of traffic.

The fact that Ciment Fondu generates considerable heat gives it great practical value in cold-weather work. Freezing must be prevented during the first few hours until the concrete begins to generate its own heat. After that, with a normal mix and reasonable bulk, the concrete will generate enough heat to keep the mass from freezing, even at temperatures several degrees below freezing.

Because Ciment Fondu liberates no free lime during hydration, the concrete is highly resistant to attacks by sulfates. It also resists many of the chemicals produced in processing plants better than concrete made with portland cement.

The other important characteristic of Ciment Fondu is its ability to retain binding power when subjected to heat. Thus concrete made with Ciment Fondu and refractory aggregates is useful for flue linings, combustion chambers for domestic furnaces, door linings for annealing furnaces, furnace foundations, etc. Generally it is limited to service below 1370°C.

SPECIAL CEMENTS
White Portland Cement

White portland cement is manufactured according to the specifications of ASTM C150 or CSA A5 and is very similar to normal portland except in color. It is made from specially selected raw materials containing negligible amounts of iron and manganese oxide, and the manufacturing process is controlled to produce a pure white, nonstaining cement. It is used primarily for architectural purposes such as curtain-wall and facing panels, decorative concrete, stucco, tile grout, or wherever white or colored concrete or mortar is specified.

Masonry Cement

Masonry cement has been specially designed to produce better mortar than that made with normal portland cement or with a lime-cement combination.

It is made by grinding together a carefully proportioned mixture of normal portland cement clinker and high-calcium limestone. To the finely ground product an air-entraining agent, a plasticizing agent, and a set retarder are added.

The mortar made with this cement has particularly good plasticity and workability, good adhesion and bond, and has adequate strength to meet the requirements of ASTM C91 or CSA A8. It also offers great resistance to efflorescence and has good appearance.

Air-Entraining Portland Cement

Sometimes small amounts of certain air-entraining agents are added to the clinker and ground with it to produce air-entraining cements. Three types of air-entraining portland cement are specified in ASTM C150: Types 10A, 20A, and 30A. They correspond to cement Types 10, 20, and 30, except for the addition of the air-entraining agents.

Concrete made with these cements contains millions of minute well-distributed and completely separated air bubbles. The entrained air resulting from the use of these cements should range from about 4 percent for concrete with large-size aggregate to 6 or 7 percent for concrete with $\frac{3}{8}$-in (9-mm) maximum size coarse aggregate.

Concrete containing entrained air has proved to be more resistant to severe frost and to the effects of salt applied to sidewalks and pavements for ice and snow removal.

Oil-Well Cement

This is a special portland cement used for sealing oil wells. It must be slow-setting and resistant to high temperatures and pressures. There are specifications for oil-well cements (AP 1 Standard 10A) which cover requirements for eight classes, each of which is applicable for use at a certain range of well depths.

Waterproofed Portland Cement

Waterproofed portland cement is normally produced by adding a small amount of a stearate, usually calcium or aluminum, to the cement clinker during the final grinding. It is made in both white and gray color.

Plastic Cement

Plastic cements are made by adding plasticizers to Type 10 or Type 20 cement during the manufacturing process, up to 12 percent of total volume. Such cements are commonly used for making mortar, plaster, and stucco.

Expansive Cement

Expansive cement is a hydraulic cement which expands during the initial hardening period. At present there are three types of expansive cement, designated as Types K, M, and S, all of which may have their expansive properties varied over a considerable range.

Expansive cements can be used to compensate for the volume decrease in concrete due to shrinkage and also to induce tensile stress in reinforcement used for prestressing purposes.

Regulated-Set Cement

Regulated-set cement is a modified portland cement—a hydraulic cement with a setting time which can be controlled from approximately 1 to 2 min to about 60 min, with corresponding rapid early-strength development. Concrete made with such a cement is in most ways similar to comparable mixes made with standard portland cement.

Blended Hydraulic Cements

There are two kinds of blended hydraulic cements: those made with blast furnace slag and those containing a pozzolan. ASTM C595 specifies two types of blast furnace slag cement: IS and IS-A, the latter containing an air-entraining agent. A selected quality of granulated blast furnace slag is either ground with portland cement clinker or blended with portland cement to produce these products.

There are four types of portland pozzolan cements: IP, IP-A, P, and P-A, the two bearing the "A" suffix containing an air-entraining agent. They are made by intergrinding portland cement clinker with a suitable pozzolan, by blending portland cement or portland blast furnace slag cement and a pozzolan, or by a combination of intergrinding and blending.

Types IS, IS-A, IP, and IP-A can be used in general-purpose concrete construction, when the specific properties of the other types are not required. Types P and P-A are used in massive structures, such as dams, piers, or large footings, where early high strengths are not required.

AGGREGATES USED IN CONCRETE

Concrete can be considered to be an artificial stone made by binding together particles of some inert material with a paste made of cement and water. These inert materials are the *aggregate*. Among the materials used for this purpose are sand, gravel, crushed stone, air-cooled blast furnace slag, expanded clay, shale, slate and slag, vermiculite, perlite, pumice, scoria and diatomite, barite, limonite, magnetite, hematite, and iron and steel punchings. All of these vary in weight and strength. The strength, durability, and weight of the concrete depend on the type of aggregate used.

Sand, gravel, crushed stone, and air-cooled blast furnace slag produce what are called *normal-weight* concretes, weighing from 135 to 160 lb/ft³ (2160 to 2560 kg/m³). Specifications for these aggregates are contained in ASTM C33 and CSA A23.1.

Expanded clay, shale, slate, and slag are used to make *structural lightweight* concrete, an ever-more popular commodity, weighing from about 85 to 115 lb/ft³ (1360 to 1840 kg/m³), and a large proportion of the concrete blocks being produced. Specifications for such aggregates are contained in ASTM C330 and in CSA A23.1.

Lightweight aggregates such as pumice, scoria, perlite, vermiculite, and diatomite are used to produce *insulating* concrete, used for its insulative properties rather than its structural strength. Such concrete will weigh from about 15 to 90 lb/ft³ (240 to 1440 kg/m³). Specifications for these are contained in ASTM C332.

Hematite, barite, limonite, magnetite, and iron and steel punchings are used to make *heavyweight* concrete, which may weigh from 175 to 400 lb/ft³ (2800 to 6400 kg/m³). It is used where weight is as important a factor as structural strength or where the concrete is to be used as a radiation shield. Specifications for such aggregates are to be found in ASTM C637.

Properties of Stone Aggregates

Sand, gravel, and crushed stone fall into this category and make up a large percentage of the aggregates used in concrete. Since they generally constitute from 60 to 80 percent of the volume of concrete, their characteristics influence the properties of concrete. They should therefore meet certain requirements if the concrete is to be strong, durable, and economical.

They must be of the proper shape, either rounded or approximately cubical in shape, clean, hard, strong, and well graded. They must possess chem-

ical stability and in many cases exhibit abrasion resistance and resistance to freezing and thawing.

SHAPE AND SURFACE TEXTURE   The particle shape and the surface texture of aggregates influence the properties of fresh concrete more than those of hardened concrete. Sharp, angular, and rough aggregate particles require more paste to make good concrete than do rounded ones. Flat, slivery pieces make concrete more difficult to finish and should be limited to not more than 15 percent of the total. This requirement is particularly important for crushed fine aggregate, since material made in this way contains more flat and elongated particles.

CLEANLINESS OF AGGREGATES   Particles should be free from coatings of clay or other fine material and from organic impurities which may affect the setting of the cement paste. In the case of coarse aggregate, visual inspection will often disclose the presence of such deleterious materials, but where doubt exists, the aggregate should be tested. However, it is not so easy to inspect fine aggregate in the same way, and standard tests may be carried out to determine the amount of silt and organic material present in the aggregate. The test to measure the amount of fine material present, called a *silt test,* is carried out as follows:

Place 2 in (5 cm) of the sand to be tested in a 1-qt (1-L) jar and then fill the jar three-quarters full with clean water. Place the top on the jar and shake the contents well. Allow the jar to sit for several hours. As the solid material settles out of the water, the very fine particles will be deposited last in a layer on top of the sand. When the water is clear again, measure the depth of the silt deposit. If it exceeds $\frac{1}{8}$ in (3 mm), the aggregate contains too much *fines* and should not be used for concrete without washing. Figure 2-3 shows a sample of fine aggregate with an excessively thick layer of silt on top.

A *colorimetric test* determines whether fine aggregate contains injurious amounts of organic matter. Fill a 12-oz (340-g) prescription bottle to the $4\frac{1}{2}$-oz (130-g) level with the fine aggregate to be tested. Fill to the 7-oz (200-g) level with a 3 percent solution of sodium hydroxide. Shake the contents well and allow to stand for 24 h. If the liquid, which was originally clear, is colored, it indicates the pres-

Fig. 2-3 Silt test. *(Portland Cement Association)*

Fig. 2-5 Set of sand screens and shaker. *(Soiltest, Inc.)*

ence of some organic matter. A color that ranges from light to dark straw indicates that the amount of organic matter is not serious. If the color ranges from dark straw to chocolate brown, the aggregate is not suitable for concrete unless the organic matter is removed by washing. Figure 2-4 illustrates three samples: in one the solution is clear, in one there is slight discoloration, while in the third the solution has turned very dark.

AGGREGATE GRADING   Grading, or particle-size distribution, is an important feature of aggregates and is determined by a *sieve analysis,* as specified by ASTM C136 and CSA A23.2.2. The sieves used include the following sizes: Nos. 4, 8, 16, 30, 50, and 100 (5 mm, 2.5 mm, 1.25 mm, 630 μm, 315 μm, and 160 μm) for fine aggregate and 6 in, 3 in, $1\frac{1}{2}$ in, $\frac{3}{4}$ in, $\frac{3}{8}$ in, and No. 4 (150 mm, 75 mm, 37.5 mm, 19 mm, 9.5 mm, and 4.75 mm) for coarse aggregate. Figures 2-5 and 2-6 illustrate typical ag-

Fig. 2-4 Colorimetric test. *(Portland Cement Association)*

Fig. 2-6 Set of coarse aggregate screens and shaker.

95

gregate screen sets and the equipment used to operate them.

Limits are usually specified for the percentage of material passing each sieve, the limits being indicated in Fig. 2-7, which shows them for fine aggregates and one designated size of coarse aggregate. Notice that most of the fine aggregates pass through a No. 4 (4.75-mm) sieve, but a very large percentage of the coarse aggregates are retained on a No. 4 (4.75-mm) sieve.

Grading limits and maximum size of aggregates are important because they affect relative aggregate proportions, cement and water requirements, workability, economy, porosity, shrinkage, and durability of concrete. In general, aggregates which conform to the grading limits produce the most satisfactory results, a fact which may be explained by the *minimum voids theory*.

This theory is illustrated in Fig. 2-8, in which one beaker is filled with 1-in (25-mm) aggregate, one with ⅜-in (9.5-mm) aggregate, and one with a mixture of the two. Each beaker is accompanied by a graduate which contains the exact amount of water required to fill the voids in each case. It can be seen that when a beaker has aggregate of one size only, the amount of water needed to fill the voids remains fairly constant. But when the aggregate sizes are mixed, the amount of water required is reduced. If more sizes were added to the combined sizes, the reduction in water required would be still greater. Since the void content of the aggregates determines the amount of cement paste required,

it is desirable to keep void content as low as possible.

To check the gradation of a specific sample of fine aggregate, weigh out a 1000-g dry sample and pass it through the fine-aggregate sieves, arranged in order as illustrated in Fig. 2-9. Weigh the amount of material retained on each sieve and calculate the percentage of each. The results should correspond to the gradations shown in Table 2-6.

To find the cumulative percentage retained on each sieve, add the percentage retained on each one to the total retained on the sieves above. For example, suppose that a 1000-g sample yielded the following amounts on each sieve after screening:

Sieve No.	Amount Retained, g
4 (5 mm)	40
8 (2.5 mm)	121
16 (1.25 mm)	214
30 (630 μm)	251
50 (315 μm)	209
100 (160 μm)	136

The percentage of the sample retained in each sieve would be as follows:

Sieve No.	Percent Retained
4 (5 mm)	4.0
8 (2.5 mm)	12.1
16 (1.25 mm)	21.4
30 (630 μm)	25.1
50 (315 μm)	20.9
100 (160 μm)	13.6

Percent passing, by weight

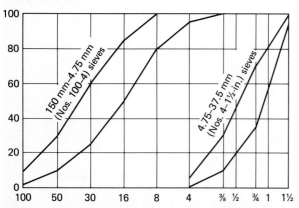

Fig. 2-7 Specified grading limits for fine aggregate and one size of coarse aggregate. *(Portland Cement Association)*

25 mm (1") 9.5 mm (³/₈") Combination

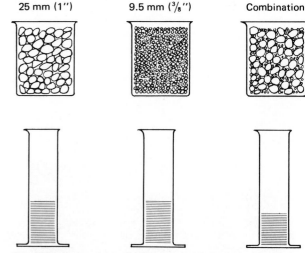

Fig. 2-8 Illustration of minimum voids theory. *(Portland Cement Association)*

Fig. 2-9 Passing sand through sieves. *(Soiltest, Inc.)*

Then the cumulative percentages would be as shown below:

Sieve No.	Percent Retained (Cumulative)
4 (5 mm)	4.0
8 (2.5 mm)	16.1
16 (1.25 mm)	37.5
30 (630 μm)	62.6
50 (315 μm)	83.5
100 (160 μm)	97.1

Another test made on fine aggregate determines the relative fineness or coarseness of the material: a *fineness modulus test.* A 500-g sample is taken and screened. The percentage retained on each

Table 2-6
GRADATION RANGE IN FINE AGGREGATE

Sieve Size No.	Percent Retained (Cumulative)
4 (5 mm)	0–5
8 (2.5 mm)	10–20
16 (1.25 mm)	20–40
30 (630 μm)	40–70
50 (315 μm)	70–88
100 (160 μm)	92–98

screen and the cumulative percentages are calculated as above. The cumulative percentages are totaled and divided by 100. The resulting number is the fineness modulus number. Allowable fineness modulus numbers range from 2.30 to 3.10. Numbers from 2.30 to 2.60 indicate a fine sand; those from 2.61 to 2.90, medium sand; and those from 2.91 to 3.10, coarse sand.

MOISTURE CONTENT OF AGGREGATES   Two types of moisture are recognized in aggregates: absorbed moisture and surface moisture. Absorbed moisture is that which is taken in by the voids in aggregate particles and may not be apparent on the surface, while surface moisture is that which clings to the surface of the particle.

The absorption and surface moisture of aggregates need to be determined in order to control the net water content of a concrete mix and to make adjustments in batch weights of the materials. The moisture conditions of aggregates are designated as follows:

Oven-Dry. In this condition they are fully absorbent.

Air-Dry. Particles are dry at the surface but contain some interior moisture. They are therefore somewhat absorbent.

Saturated Surface-Dry. In this condition there is no water on the surface, but the particle contains all the interior moisture it will hold. It will neither absorb moisture from nor contribute moisture to the mix.

Damp or Wet. The particles contain an excess of moisture on the surface and will contribute moisture to a mix.

The amount of moisture in fine aggregate is determined by a *moisture test.* Again, a 500-g sample is taken, placed in a shallow pan, and dried by gas jets in an oven or by pouring methyl hydrate over the sample and burning it off. Drying continues until the sample no longer continues to lose weight. Now, loss in weight/dry weight × 100 = percentage of total moisture. From this total subtract 1 for adsorbed moisture (moisture contained in the surface crevasses of the aggregate particles), and the result is the percentage of free moisture in the sample.

Surface moisture in fine aggregate is the cause of

a phenomenon known as *bulking* of sand. Surface moisture holds the particles apart, causing an increase in volume over the same amount of sand in a surface-dry condition. The amount of bulking will depend on the fineness of the sand, and the percentage of bulking over the dry volume is illustrated in Fig. 2-10.

SPECIFIC GRAVITY

The specific gravity of an aggregate is another characteristic of the material which needs to be determined. It is not a measure of aggregate quality but is used in making calculations related to mix design. The specific gravity of most normal-weight aggregates will range from 2.4 to 2.9. Test methods for determining specific gravity of both coarse and fine aggregates are described in ASTM C127 and C128. CSA A23.2.6 describes a test for specific gravity of fine aggregate.

HARDNESS OF AGGREGATES

The hardness of aggregates is expressed in terms of their resistance to abrasion. This characteristic is important if the aggregate is used in concrete intended for such purposes as heavy-duty floors. A common method of making this test is described in ASTM C131 or C535 and consists of placing a specified quantity of the aggregate to be tested in a revolving steel drum. The percentage of material worn away during the test is then determined.

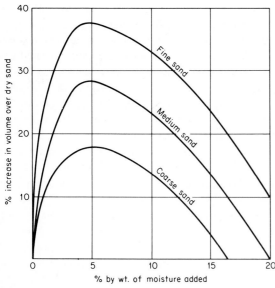

Fig. 2-10 Bulking in sand.

STRENGTH OF AGGREGATES

One measure of the strength of an aggregate is its resistance to freeze-thaw. This resistance is an important characteristic in concrete which is exposed to severe weather. The freeze-thaw resistance of an aggregate is related to its porosity, absorption, and pore structure. If a particle of the aggregate absorbs so much water that there is not enough pore space available, it will not accommodate the expansion which takes place when the water freezes and the particle will fail. Freeze-thaw tests on aggregates are commonly carried out on specimens of concrete made with the aggregate and will be described under the section dealing with tests on concrete.

Another test of the strength of aggregates is their ability to withstand compressive stresses. This test is made by subjecting hardened concrete specimens made with the aggregate in question to compression testing. This is also described under tests on concrete.

CHEMICAL STABILITY OF AGGREGATES

Aggregates need to be chemically stable so that they will neither react chemically with cement nor be affected chemically by outside influences. In some cases aggregates with certain chemical constituents react with alkalis in cement. This reaction may cause abnormal expansion and resultant cracking of concrete. There are three tests used for testing aggregates for reactivity to alkali: ASTM C227, ASTM C289, and ASTM C586.

BULK UNIT WEIGHT OF AGGREGATES

The bulk unit weight of an aggregate is the weight of the amount of material which can be placed in a 1-ft^3 (28.3-L) container. The amount may vary, depending on the method used to fill the container, and specifications for determining bulk unit weight are given in ASTM C29 and CSA A23.2.10. The normal range of bulk unit weight for aggregates for normal-weight concrete is from 75 to 110 lb/ft^3 (1200 to 1760 kg/m^3).

AGGREGATE SAMPLES FOR TESTING

Samples of aggregates to be tested should be as representative as possible. To ensure this, a quantity of the material should be taken from a number of locations in the stockpile. The total sample should be thoroughly mixed and then passed through a splitter. This piece of equipment (see Figs. 2-11 and 2-12) divides the whole sample into two equal parts. One half of the sample is then discarded and the other half passed through the splitter again. This procedure is repeated until a final sample of the required size is obtained.

Table 2-7 on page 101 provides a summary of the characteristics of aggregates on which tests should be made, the importance of taking the tests, the sources of test information, and the requirement of the specification.

Fig. 2-11 Aggregate splitting equipment. *(Soiltest, Inc.)*

Fig. 2-12 Splitting a fine aggregate sample. *(Soiltest, Inc.)*

Structural Lightweight Aggregates

EXPANDED AGGREGATES   Most structural lightweight aggregates are produced by one of three methods: in a *rotary kiln*, on a *sintering grate*, or by *water treatment*.

By the first method, crushed shale or slate and pelletized or extruded clay are passed through a rotary kiln at about 1090°C. Gases within the material expand, forming thousands of tiny air cells within the mass. When the materials cool and solidify, these cells remain, each surrounded by a hard, vitreous, waterproof membrane. Each piece of material is likewise surrounded by a vitreous shell.

In the sintering process, raw material is crushed, screened, and mixed with a small amount of combustible material such as finely ground coal or coke. The mixture is spread evenly over a traveling grate and the fuel ignited. As the grate travels over blowers and the temperature increases, the same reactions take place as in the kiln. Usually the resulting sintered material is made up of larger pieces and has to be crushed for use.

Expanded slag aggregate is produced by using controlled amounts of moisture on molten blast furnace slag. The moisture may be in the form of water or steam, but in the process, the slag expands to form relatively large particles of aggregate, which are crushed to proper size.

CINDER AGGREGATE   Cinders to be used for concrete aggregate should come from anthracite coal and should be free from such harmful impurities as sulfides, unburned coal, and fine ashes. Concrete made from cinders is not used for structural purposes, but floor and roof slabs, fire walls, fireproofing concrete, and masonry blocks are made from it.

Properties of Lightweight Aggregates

UNIT WEIGHT   The unit weight of lightweight aggregates will range from 35 to 70 lb/ft^3 (560 to 1120 kg/m^3), depending on the type of aggregate, gradation, particle shape, and specific gravity. A maximum loose dry weight for structural lightweight aggregates is specified in ASTM C330, the limits being 70 lb/ft^3 (1120 kg/m^3) for fine aggregate, 55 lb/ft^3 (880 kg/m^3) for coarse aggregate, and 65 lb/ft^3 (1040 kg/m^3) for combined fine and coarse.

ABSORPTION   Over a 24-h period lightweight aggregates may absorb water in the amount of 5 to 20 percent of their own dry weight, depending on the type of aggregate and its pore structure. A tendency of this sort must be taken into account when concrete is made with lightweight aggregate. To make lightweight mixtures as uniform as possible, however, aggregates should be *prewetted,* but not *saturated,* 24 h before they are to be used.

PARTICLE SIZE, SHAPE, AND SURFACE TEXTURE   In the case of expanded shale, variously known as *berculite* or *baydite,* particles form in various sizes from very fine to $\frac{3}{4}$ in (19 mm) and other aggregates are crushed to similar sizes. The product is screened into two commercial sizes: *Fine*—0 to $\frac{3}{8}$ in (0 to 9.5 mm) and *Coarse*—$\frac{3}{8}$ to $\frac{3}{4}$ in (9.5 to 19 mm). A *Combined* grade is produced by mixing the two.

   Products of the kiln tend to have rounded or cubical shape and relatively smooth surface, while crushed aggregates will have angular shape and rough-textured surfaces. The latter types will require a larger percentage of fines to provide for proper workability of the concrete.

GRADATION   ASTM C330 outlines the specifications for gradation of lightweight aggregates. As with normal-weight aggregates, well-graded lightweight aggregates will have minimum void content and so require a minimum of cement paste to make a proper mix.

BULK SPECIFIC GRAVITY   The bulk specific gravity of lightweight aggregates is generally in the range of 1.0 to 2.4. But because that range is so wide and because it is often difficult to obtain an accurate rating for a specific aggregate, design methods for structural lightweight concrete use the concept of *specific gravity factors.* This concept takes into account the moisture conditions of the aggregate at the time of mixing.

Insulating Lightweight Aggregates

PERLITE   Perlite is a nonmetallic mineral, a siliceous volcanic rock, containing combined water. The rock is crushed and heated quickly to just over 815°C, which causes the crude perlite particles to expand and turn white. The combined water vaporizes to form microscopic cells in the heat-softened particles. The result, on cooling, is a honeycomb structure containing a great many sealed cells which give it strength, lightness, and resistance to water penetration. The material, which weighs from $7\frac{1}{2}$ to 15 lb/ft^3 (120 to 240 kg/m^3), is screened into various sizes for use as loose fill, plaster aggregate, and concrete aggregate.

VERMICULITE   Vermiculite is a micalike mineral chemically known as hydrated magnesium-aluminum-iron silicate. It is composed of many very thin layers, with a minute amount of water between each pair. The crude ore is crushed to controlled sizes and heated in a furnace to about 1090°C. The water is turned to steam, forcing the layers apart and expanding the individual granules to at least twelve times their original size. (See Fig. 2-13.) As each granule expands, its traps within itself thousands of dead air cells, and it is these which provide a large part of the insulation value of the material.

   The granules are graded in four sizes. Size 1 ranges from $\frac{3}{8}$ in to No. 16 sieve (9-5 to 1.18 mm), Size 2 from No. 4 to No. 30 sieve (4.75 to 600 μm), Size 3 from No. 8 to No. 100 sieve (2.36 mm to

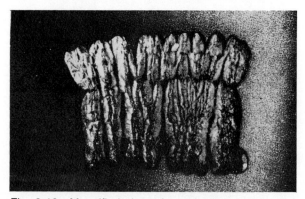

Fig. 2-13   Magnified view of vermiculite granule after expansion.

Table 2-7
CHARACTERISTICS OF AGGREGATES

Characteristic	Significance of Importance	Test or Practice, ASTM and CSA Designation	Specification Requirement
Resistance to abrasion	Index of aggregate quality; warehouse floors, loading platforms, pavements	C131 C535	Max. percent loss[a]
Resistance to freezing and thawing	Structures subjected to weathering	C666, C671	Max. number of cycles or period of frost immunity
Chemical stability	Strength and durability of all types of structures	C227 (mortar bar) C342 (mortar bar) C289 (chemical) C586 (aggregate prism) C295 (petrographic)	Max. expansion of mortar bar[a] Aggregates must not be reactive with cement alkalis[a]
Particle shape and surface texture	Workability of fresh concrete		Max. percent flat and elongated pieces
Grading	Workability of fresh concrete; economy	C136 A23.2.2	Max. and min. percent passing standard sieves
Bulk unit weight	Mix design calculations; classification	C29 A23.2.10	Max. or min. unit weight (special concretes)
Specific gravity	Mix design calculations	C127 (coarse aggregate) C128 (fine aggregate) A23.2.6	
Absorption and surface moisture	Control of concrete quality	C70, C127, C128, C566 A23.2.11	

[a] Aggregates not conforming to specification requirements may be used if service records or performance tests indicate they produce concrete having the desired properties.
SOURCE: Portland Cement Association.

150 μm), and Size 4 from No. 16 to No. 100 sieve (1.18 mm to 150 μm). Sizes 1 and 2 are normally used as insulating concrete aggregate.

DIATOMITE Diatomite, otherwise known as diatomaceous earth, is a material composed largely of the silicified skeletons of microscopic one-celled animals.

PUMICE Pumice is a variety of volcanic slag, filled with minute cavities and very light in weight. It is crushed and used to make a very light concrete aggregate.

SCORIA Scoria is another variety of light volcanic slag, but "scoria" is also the name given to the slag resulting from the reduction of certain ores. Both materials are crushed to make an insulating concrete aggregate.

Heavyweight Aggregates

BARITE Barite is an ore containing barium sulfate, with a specific gravity of 4.3 to 4.6, often called *heavy spar*.

HEMATITE Hematite is an iron ore, containing Fe_2O_3, also a very heavy material.

LIMONITE   Limonite is another iron ore, containing hydrous ferric oxide, $2Fe_2O_3 \cdot 3H_2O$, also with high specific gravity.

MAGNETITE   Magnetite is still another iron ore, containing Fe_3O_4, and another heavyweight.

DESIGN AND CONTROL OF CONCRETE
Design of Normal-Weight Concrete

In order to produce concrete that will do its job properly, a great deal of attention must be paid to concrete design—determining the correct amounts of each of the ingredients which should be used in any given case. Mixtures must be designed to give the most practical and economical combination of materials that will produce the necessary plasticity and workability and at the same time produce concrete of the required strength and durability.

The designing of concrete mixtures is based primarily on the *water-cement ratio theory* and the *absolute-volume system* of calculating material amounts. Attention, of course, also must be paid to exposure and placing conditions.

The water-cement ratio theory states that the strength of concrete is inversely proportional to the amount of water used per unit of cement. This means that if, for example, 0.68 lb of water per pound of cement (680 g of water per kilogram of cement) will produce concrete capable of developing 2500 psi (17.2 MPa) in 28 days, then less water per unit will produce stronger concrete and more water will produce concrete of lesser strength. Table 2-8 shows the probable compressive strength that can be expected in 28 days for various amounts of water per unit of cement and for both plain and air-entrained concrete.

The durability of concrete—its ability to withstand frequent freezing and thawing cycles, wide ranges of temperature, alternate wetting and drying, the action of seawater and ground salts, the abrasion of traffic—and its permeability (its watertightness) are also affected by the water-cement ratio. Table 2-9 gives the recommended water-cement ratios to be used for a variety of exposure conditions and thicknesses of section, for both plain and reinforced concrete. When both compressive-strength and exposure conditions are involved, the designer must choose the smaller of the two recommended water-cement ratios for his design.

The maximum size of coarse aggregate, the preferred fineness modulus of fine aggregate, and the proportions of fine to coarse depend on the placing conditions, the thickness of the section, and the requirements of finishing. But the amounts of aggregates to be used with a given cement paste are calculated by the absolute-volume method. The absolute volume of a loose material is the actual total volume of solid matter in all the particles, without taking into account the space occupied by voids

Table 2-8
COMPRESSIVE STRENGTH OF CONCRETE FOR VARIOUS WATER-CEMENT RATIOS

Water-Cement Ratio, Pounds/Pound of Cement	Probable Compressive Strength at 28 Days, psi		Water-Cement Ratio, Grams/Kilogram Cement	Probable Compressive Strength at 28 Days, MPa	
	Plain Concrete	Air-Entrained Concrete		Plain Concrete	Air-Entrained Concrete
0.75	2000	1600	750	15.4	12.3
0.68	2500	2000	680	19.3	15.4
0.62	3000	2400	620	23.2	18.5
0.56	3500	2800	560	27	21.6
0.50	4000	3200	500	31	24.7
0.45	4500	3600	450	34.7	27.8
0.41	5000	4000	410	38.6	31
0.38	5500	4400	380	42.5	34
0.34	6000	4800	340	46.3	37

Table 2-9
MAXIMUM PERMISSIBLE WATER-CEMENT RATIOS FOR DIFFERENT TYPES OF STRUCTURES AND DEGREES OF EXPOSURE

| Type of Structure | Severe Wide Range in Temperature, or Frequent Alterations of Freezing and Thawing (Air-Entrained Concrete Only) | | | Mild Temperature Rarely Below Freezing; Rainy; Arid | | |
| | | At Waterline or Within Range of Fluctuating Water Level or Spray | | | At Waterline or Within Range of Fluctuating Water Level or Spray | |
	Air	Fresh Water	Seawater or Sulfates[a]	Air	Fresh Water	Seawater or Sulfates[a]
Thin sections, such as railings, curbs, sills, ledges, ornamental or architectural concrete-reinforced piles, pipe, and all sections with less than 1-in concrete cover over reinforcing	0.49 lb/lb (490 g/kg)	0.44 lb/lb (440 g/kg)	0.4 lb/lb (400 g/kg)	0.53 lb/lb (530 g/kg)	0.49 lb/lb (490 g/kg)	0.4 lb/lb (400 g/kg)
Moderate sections, such as retaining walls, abutments, piers, girders, beams	0.53 lb/lb (530 g/kg)	0.49 lb/lb (490 g/kg)	0.44 lb/lb[b] (440 g/kg)	c	0.53 lb/lb (530 g/kg)	b
Exterior portions of heavy (mass) sections	0.58 lb/lb (580 g/kg)	0.49 lb/lb (490 g/kg)	0.44 lb/lb[b] (440 g/kg)	c	0.53 lb/lb (530 g/kg)	0.44 lb/lb[b] (440 g/kg)
Concrete deposited by tremie under water	—	0.44 lb/lb (440 g/kg)	0.44 lb/lb (440 g/kg)	—	0.44 lb/lb (440 g/kg)	0.44 lb/lb (440 g/kg)
Concrete slabs laid on the ground	0.53 lb/lb (530 g/kg)	—	—	c	—	—
Concrete protected from the weather, interiors of buildings, concrete below ground	c	—	—	c	—	—
Concrete which will later be protected by enclosure or backfill but which may be exposed to freezing and thawing for several years before such protection is offered	0.53 lb/lb (530 g/kg)	—	—	c	—	—

[a] Soil or groundwater containing sulfate concentrations of more than 0.2 percent.
[b] When sulfate-resistant cement is used, maximum water-cement ratio may be increased by 0.05 lb/lb (50 g/kg) of cement.
[c] Water-cement ratio should be selected on basis of strength and workability requirements.
NOTE: Air-entrained concrete should be used under all conditions involving severe exposure and may be used under mild exposure conditions to improve workability of the mixture.

between the particles. Absolute volume is computed from the weight of the material and its specific gravity. The formula is as follows:

$$\text{Absolute volume} = \frac{\text{weight of loose dry material}}{\text{specific gravity} \times \text{unit weight of water}}$$

For example, the absolute volume of 100 lb of cement, whose specific gravity is 3.15, would be

$$\text{Absolute volume} = \frac{100}{3.15 \times 62.4} = 0.508 \text{ ft}^3$$

Again for example, the absolute volume of 45.4 kg of cement, whose specific gravity is 3.15, would be

$$\text{Absolute volume} = \frac{45.4}{3.15 \times 1000} = 0.014 \text{ m}^3$$

If the volume of the water and the absolute volume of the cement required for a unit of concrete (1 yd^3 or 1 m^3) plus air content, if any, are added together, the result is the absolute volume of the cement paste and air in a unit of concrete. If that figure is subtracted from the volume of a unit of concrete, the remainder will represent the absolute volume of the aggregates required for a unit of concrete.

Publications by the Portland Cement Association and the American Concrete Institute give full details on working out a concrete-mix design by absolute volume.

Design of Structural Lightweight Concrete

Structural lightweight aggregate is being widely used to replace normal-weight aggregates in the production of structural concrete because it reduces weight by about one-third with no loss of structural strength for comparable cement contents. Because of the light weight and its insulating value, due to its cellular structure, it is also used for plaster stucco and gunite aggregate. It has high resistance to heat and for this reason is used for refractory linings, fireproofing of structural steel, and for the construction of other concrete surfaces exposed to high temperatures. The concrete made from such aggregate also has better sound absorption and acoustical properties than that made with normal-weight aggregate.

Because of their comparative lightness, lightweight aggregates have a greater tendency to segregate than normal-weight aggregates. Overvibration of the concrete should be avoided, because this causes the coarser particles to rise to the surface and results in a surface which is difficult to finish. A Vinsol resin air-entraining agent is recommended to improve the workability of the concrete and to reduce segregation. Air entrainment should normally range from 4 to 6 percent.

Designing a concrete mix using structural lightweight aggregate requires a different method from that used with normal-weight aggregate. Because of the difficulties involved in determining a satisfactory value for specific gravity and absorption of the aggregate, a method of proportioning is suggested which does not require the use of these values. The determination of the proportions of cement, water, and aggregates to attain the required strengths and workability is carried out by mixing trial batches based on volume proportions. Table 2-10 gives the recommended proportions to be used in trial batches.

It is advisable to use an air-entraining agent of good quality to improve workability and reduce segregation. The recommended air content is from 4 to 6 percent.

Design of Insulating Lightweight Concrete

Vermiculite concrete can be made with or without sand. The mix design will depend on the use to

Table 2-10
TRIAL BATCHES USING STRUCTURAL LIGHTWEIGHT AGGREGATE

Maximum Size Aggregate		Required 28-Day Strength		Cement		Loose Dry Aggregate			
						Cubic Yards		Cubic Meters	
Inches	Millimeters	psi	MPa	lb/yd^3	kg/m^3	Fine (0 to $\frac{3}{8}$ in)	Coarse ($\frac{3}{8}$ to $\frac{3}{4}$ in)	Fine (0 to 9.5 mm)	Coarse (9.5 to 19 mm)
$\frac{3}{4}$	19	2000	15.4	460	273	20	12	0.74	0.44
$\frac{3}{4}$	19	2500	19.3	499	296	19.8	11.8	0.73	0.43
$\frac{3}{4}$	19	3000	23	547	324	19.6	11.7	0.72	0.43
$\frac{3}{4}$	19	3500	27	586	347	19.5	11.7	0.72	0.43
$\frac{3}{4}$	19	4000	30.8	634	376	19.3	11.7	0.71	0.43
$\frac{3}{4}$	19	5000	38.6	744	441	19	11.5	0.70	0.42
$\frac{3}{8}$	9.5	2000	15.4	503	298	32.6		1.2	
$\frac{3}{8}$	9.5	2500	19.3	543	322	32.3		1.19	
$\frac{3}{8}$	9.5	3000	23	591	350	32		1.18	

(a)

(b)

Fig. 2-14 *(a)* Filling slump cone, *(b)* tamping slump cone. *(Soiltest, Inc.)*

Control of Concrete Mixes

Freshly mixed concrete and hardened and cured concrete are regularly subjected to a number of tests to ensure that the specifications for that concrete have been achieved.

SLUMP TEST Freshly mixed concrete must be checked to ensure that the specified slump is being attained consistently. This is done by taking slump tests. A standard slump cone 12 in (30.5 cm) high and 8 in (20 cm) in diameter at the bottom, is used (see Fig. 2-14). The cone is filled in three equal layers, each being tamped 25 times with a $\frac{5}{8}$-in (16-mm) bullet-nosed tamping rod. Figure 2-14*a* and *b* illustrates the process of filling and tamping a slump cone.

When the cone has been filled and leveled off, it is lifted carefully (see Fig. 2-15*a*). The amount of slump is then measured (see Fig. 2-15*b*).

(a)

(b)

Fig. 2-15 *(a)* Lifting cone, *(b)* measuring slump. *(Soiltest, Inc.)*

which the concrete is to be put; manufacturers and the Vermiculite Institute publish design specifications for most uses of vermiculite concrete. For example, for vermiculite-sand concrete for floors on ground, specifications call for 88 lb (40 kg) portland cement, 3 ft³ (0.084 m³) stabilized vermiculite-concrete aggregate, and 2 ft³ (0.056 m³) concrete sand. Enough water must be added to produce a slump of not less than 3 or more than 5 in (7.5 to 12.5 cm).

For a vermiculite concrete floor on ground, 88 lb (40 kg) portland cement to not more than 6 ft³ (0.168 m³) of vermiculite is recommended. Enough water should be used to produce a slump of 6 in (15 cm). This usually amounts to about 17 to 19 U.S. gal (63.5 to 68 L or 14 to 15 English gal).

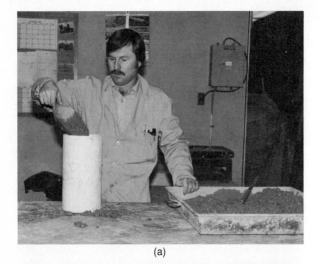

(a)

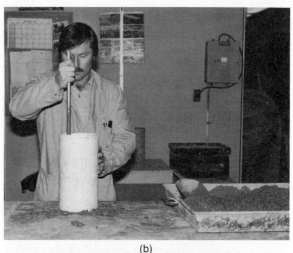

(b)

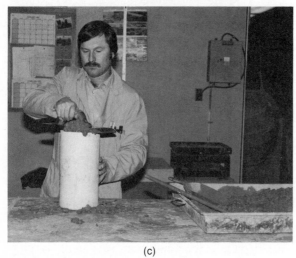

(c)

Fig. 2-16 *(a)* Filling test cylinder, *(b)* tamping cylinder, *(c)* leveling off.

COMPRESSIVE-STRENGTH TEST The compressive-strength test of cylindrical concrete specimens is the most common quality-control test of concrete. The tests may be conducted for any time interval but generally are based on 7- and 28-day curing periods.

Concrete specimens are usually cylindrical with a length equal to twice the diameter. The standard size is 12 in (30.5 cm) high and 6 in (15.25 cm) in diameter, if the coarse aggregate does not exceed 2 in (50 mm) in size. (See Fig. 2.16*a*.) The mold is filled in three equal layers, each one being rodded 25 times with a standard tamping rod (Fig. 2-16*b*). When the mold is full, it is struck off level (Fig. 2-16*c*) and covered with a glass or metal plate to prevent evaporation. The specimens are removed from the mold after 24 h and placed in the curing location for the designated period. Some will be placed in a curing cabinet under moist, warm conditions, and some may be placed in field conditions.

At the end of the curing period the specimens are subjected to a compression test. First the ends are capped with a thin layer of sulfur to provide completely even bearing surfaces at both ends. Figure 2-17*a*, *b*, *c*, and *d* illustrates the procedure for capping the test specimens.

Each specimen is then placed on a compression-testing machine and loaded to rupture. Figure 2-18 shows a typical compression tester in operation.

FLEXURAL-STRENGTH TEST Tests are also made on concrete to determine its flexural (bending) strength. The test specimen is in the form of a beam with a length at least 2 in (50 mm) greater than three times the depth. The minimum cross-sectional dimension must be at least three times the maximum size of the coarse aggregate used and in no case less than 6 × 6 in (150 × 150 mm).

The mold should be filled in two equal layers, with each layer rodded one stroke for each 2 in^2 (13 cm^2) of area. The edges are spaded as shown in Fig. 2-19*c*. The top must be finished off with a wood or metal float. Figure 2-19*a*, *b*, *c*, and *d* illustrates quite clearly the procedure in forming a flexure specimen.

After the specified curing period, during which the specimen should be kept in a moist condition at a temperature between 15 and 27°C, it is tested. The machine subjects the specimen to third-point

Fig. 2-17 *(a)* Test cylinder, *(b)* capping compound, *(c)* one end being capped, *(d)* capping complete. *(Soiltest, Inc.)*

Fig. 2-18 Compression-testing machine.

loading and the piece is broken under the load. The load required to rupture the specimen is read as ultimate flexural strength in pounds per square inch (kilopascals). Figure 2-20*a, b, c,* and *d* describes the procedure for making the flexural test.

CONSISTENCY TEST   A consistency test, also known as a ball penetration test, is also carried out on fresh concrete. The apparatus consists of a cylinder with a half-round bottom and an attached handle. The complete unit weighs about 31 lb (14 kg). A frame guides the handle and serves as a reference for measuring the depth of penetration. The instrument is set on a freshly placed, smooth concrete surface, and the ball is set on the level concrete surface with the handle vertical. The ball is allowed to settle under its own weight; after the weight has come to rest, the ball penetration is read to the nearest $\frac{1}{4}$ in (6 mm). A minimum of three

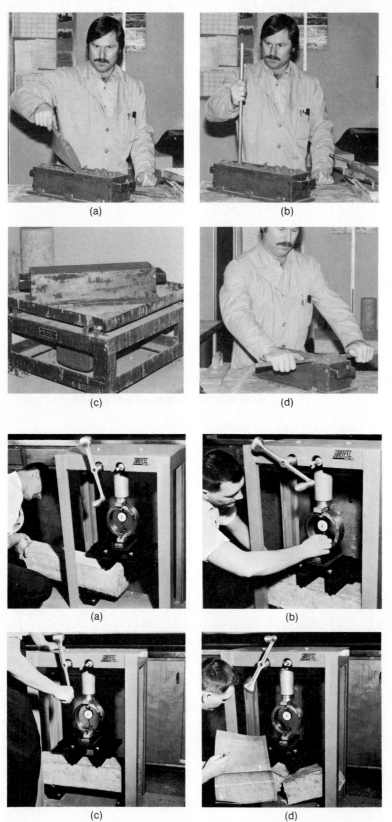

Fig. 2-19 *(a)* Preparing test beam, *(b)* tamping concrete, *(c)* consolidating concrete, *(d)* leveling off concrete.

(a)

(b)

(c)

(d)

(a)

(b)

(c)

(d)

Fig. 2-20 *(a)* Placing test specimen, *(b)* machine being adjusted, *(c)* applying test load, *(d)* beam broken. *(Soiltest, Inc.)*

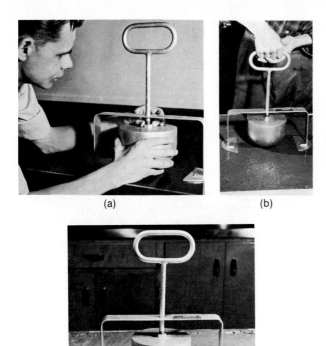

(a)   (b)

(a)

(b)

(c)

Fig. 2-21 *(a)* Ball penetration tester, *(b)* setting tester in place, *(c)* ball penetrates concrete. *(Soiltest, Inc.)*

readings should be taken from each batch or location. Figure 2-21*a, b,* and *c* depicts the instrument and its use.

AIR-CONTENT TEST The air content of concrete is determined by the use of an air meter, such as the one illustrated in Fig. 2-22. The container is filled in three equal layers, with each one tamped 25 times. (See Fig. 2-22*a.*) When the container is full, the top is struck off level and the lid put on and locked in place. Accompanying instructions describe the steps to take to obtain a reading.

ABRASION TEST In addition to making abrasion tests on aggregates, tests are also made on hardened concrete specimens to determine their resistance to *wear,* or abrasion. The tests are carried out by rolling steel balls, under pressure, over the surface of the specimen for a given number of revolutions and then determining the loss in weight due to this

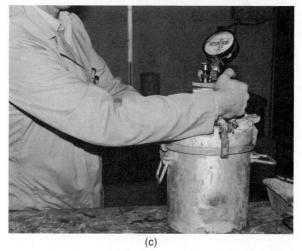

(c)

Fig. 2-22 *(a)* Consolidating concrete for air-content test, *(b)* leveling off concrete, *(c)* obtaining an air-content reading.

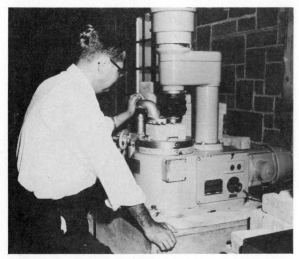

Fig. 2-23 Making an abrasion test. *(Portland Cement Association)*

action. Figure 2-23 illustrates how such a test is carried out.

WATERTIGHTNESS TEST   In many situations, it is important that concrete be watertight, and watertightness depends primarily on the amount of

Fig. 2-24 Testing for watertightness of concrete paste. *(Portland Cement Association)*

cement and mixing water used in the paste and on the length of the moist-curing period. Tests are made by subjecting discs of mortar to water pressure under controlled conditions. The amount of water which leaks through the disc is collected and measured. Figure 2-24 shows a watertightness test in operation.

FREEZE-THAW TEST   One of the prime requirements of exposed concrete is resistance to weathering and particularly to the destructive effects of alternate freezing and thawing while the concrete is moist or wet.

It has been shown that air-entrained concrete withstands freeze-thaw cycles better than concrete with no air entrainment. Tests are carried out in the laboratory, in which the specimens are put through a long series of freeze-thaw cycles, to determine the mix design and the percentage of air entrainment in the mix that will produce the best results. The amount of weight loss in the specimens is recorded to provide comparison. Figures 2-25 and 2-26 illustrate two types of freeze-thaw test equipment, one a *chest* type and the other a *cabinet* type. Figure 2-27 indicates, by the amount of surface material eroded, the difference between air-entrained and non-air-entrained concrete in their resistance to freeze-thaw cycles.

Concrete Mixing, Transportation, Placing, Finishing, and Curing

After all the tests have been made and the mix design has been formulated, the concrete must be mixed, transported to its final location, placed, finished, and cured. All of these steps must be properly carried out if the finished product is to reach its design potential.

MIXING   Concrete should be thoroughly mixed so that aggregate particles are well distributed throughout the mix and each one is surrounded by a film of paste. Figure 2-28 provides a cross-sectional view of well-distributed aggregate in a mix. Thorough mixing also ensures that maximum flowability consistent with the design is achieved.

Fig. 2-25   Chest-type freeze-thaw tester.   *(Soiltest, Inc.)*

Fig. 2-26   Cabinet-type freeze-thaw tester.   *(Soiltest, Inc.)*

Fig. 2-27   Samples of freeze-thaw cycle specimens. *(Portland Cement Association)*

TRANSPORTATION AND PLACING   Good transportation, handling, and placing techniques are essential for good results. Improper handling and rough usage will result in segregation—the separation of paste and aggregates—and ultimately a poor product.

The type of transportation used and the method of placing the concrete will depend on the particular situation. Included in the possible choices are

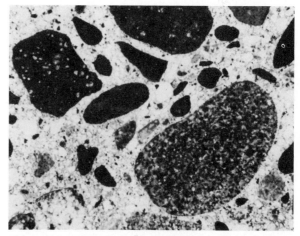

Fig. 2-28   Well-distributed aggregate in hardened concrete.   *(Portland Cement Association)*

Fig. 2-29 Concrete buggy.
(Gar-Bro Manufacturing)

concrete buggies (see Fig. 2-29) for short hauls, *transit mix trucks* (Fig. 2-30) for long-distance transportation, *concrete pumps* (Fig. 2-31) for otherwise difficult locations, and *concrete tremies* (Fig. 2-32) for placing concrete under water.

Whether one of these or some other choice is selected, the prime objective is to get the concrete to its destination and in place as smoothly and quickly as possible.

With the concrete in place, it must be consoli-

Fig. 2-30 Transit mix truck.

Fig. 2-31 Concrete pump.
(Portland Cement Association)

dated and brought to the proper level. Figure 2-33 illustrates the use of a vibrator to consolidate concrete and pipe screeds to assist in leveling.

FINISHING   Concrete finishing is as much an art as it is a science. Every surface has its own require-

Fig. 2-32 Concrete tremie. *(Portland Cement Association)*

Fig. 2-33 Concrete vibrator and screeds in use.

113

Fig. 2-34   Gas-powered concrete trowel.

ments depending on its final use. Horizontal surfaces such as floors have much different requirements than do wall surfaces, for example. Floors may have a troweled finish (see Fig. 2-34) or even a ground finish in some instances where tolerances are critical (Fig. 2-35). One type of ground concrete floor finish that produces a surface with a mottled appearance such as illustrated in Fig. 2-36 is known as terrazzo. A base slab, reinforced with wire mesh, is cast first, on which a layer of cement and sand, mixed very dry, is spread, worked flat, and compacted. This forms a cushion on which the terrazzo topping is placed.

A gridwork, consisting of thin strips of brass, bronze, aluminum, or plastic, is laid on the sand-cement cushion, bedded in, and leveled. The grid stands up approximately 1 in (25 mm) above the surface and is so arranged that the floor area is divided into a number of squares or rectangles of equal size. Grids should be so arranged that a strip will run above and parallel to each floor beam and completely circle each column rising from the floor.

The topping mix is then made up, consisting of cement, sand, and marble chips or an abrasive material such as coarse aggregate. It is mixed as dry as is practical for placing. This topping is spread over the floor and compacted until it is level with the top of the grid strips. After the topping has cured sufficiently, the surface is ground and polished by machine.

Fig. 2-35   Concrete surface grinder.

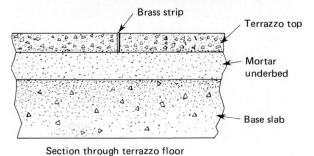

Section through terrazzo floor

Fig. 2-36   Terrazzo floor.

114

Fig. 2-37   Broom finish on concrete.

Terrazzo has a tendency to be slippery, so on ramps, elevator entrances, and other locations where nonslip surface is required, abrasive aggregates such as aluminum oxide should be used. By the use of white cement, colored pigments, and carefully chosen marble chips of one or more colors, a great variety of effects can be produced.

Exterior horizontal surfaces such as sidewalks usually have a textured finish such as illustrated in Fig. 2-37, where a stiff broom is used to provide a slip-resistant surface. In some instances patterns may be imprinted onto the surface to provide additional relief.

Finishes for vertical surfaces, on the other hand, can be quite varied. Exposed concrete interior walls are usually given a plain finish. (See Fig. 2-38.) After the formwork is removed and tie holes and other irregularities are filled with grout, the surface is

Fig. 2-38   Exposed concrete finish for interior walls.

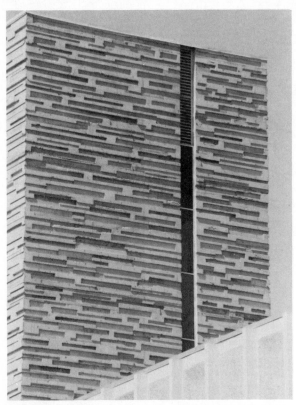

Fig. 2-39   Patterned concrete surface on exterior wall.

rubbed down with an abrasive stone to produce a smooth and attractive surface. No additional finishing is required.

Patterned surfaces on exterior walls are normally produced by special treatment of the form face. Formliners of wood, steel, plastic, or expanded polystyrene are used in various shapes to produce the required patterns or images to be imprinted on the face of the exposed concrete. (See Fig. 2-39.) A textured finish can be achieved by bush hammering (Fig. 2-40) or by sandblasting. An exposed aggregate concrete finish (Fig. 2-41) is obtained by coating the forms with a retarder (preventing the cement near the surface from setting) and then washing the concrete surface with a high-pressure water jet immediately after stripping. This removes the fine aggregates near the surface leaving the large aggregate exposed.

A very common finish that can be applied to almost any surface is stucco. Stucco is a type of plaster made of portland cement that produces a very durable surface that may be patterned and painted if so desired. It can be applied directly to concrete or masonry, but over wood sheathing some type of wire must be used to tie the sheathing and stucco together. Either a woven wire mesh or

Fig. 2-40   Bush-hammered concrete surface. *(Portland Cement Association)*

Fig. 2-41   Exposed aggregate surface. *(Portland Cement Association)*

116

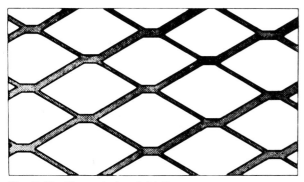
Fig. 2-42 Expanded metal lath.

expanded metal lath (see Fig. 2-42) may be used, but in either case the mesh should not be less than $\frac{1}{4}$ in (6 mm) away from the sheathing and completely embedded in the first stucco coat.

Stucco is applied in three coats, all of which are composed of 1 volume of portland cement to 3 to 5 volumes of clean, sharp sand. To this may be added $\frac{1}{4}$ volume of *hydrated lime, hydrated lime putty, slaked lime putty,* or 2 to 3 lb (0.9 to 1.36 kg) of *diatomaceous earth* to increase plasticity.

Mineral color may be added to the finish coat, or prepared dry stucco already colored and available for finish coats may be used.

A variety of treatments can be given to the finish coat to produce certain textures. Among those commonly used are French trowel, Italian finish, Modern American, spatter dash, English cottage, and travertine. (See Fig. 2-43.) Consult a stucco manual for an illustration of these and other stucco textures. Coarse, colored pebbles may be sprayed against the newly applied finish coat to produce a pebble dash finish.

CURING   Finally, concrete must be properly cured—allowed to gain its design strength—and to do this, the right conditions must be provided and maintained. These include a warm temperature, preferably from 10 to 25°C, and moist conditions. When these things have all been done, a last check may be made on the concrete to confirm whether or not it has reached, or is reaching, its design strength. This check may be made with a concrete test hammer, illustrated in Fig. 2-44, which is designed to give a compressive strength reading on hardened concrete in place.

Fig. 2-43 Stucco finish.

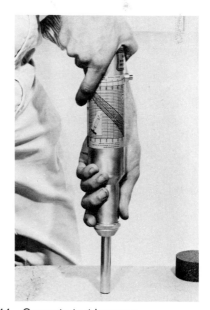
Fig. 2-44 Concrete test hammer.

117

GLOSSARY

abrasive aggregates	Concrete aggregates in which the particles have abrasive qualities.
absolute volume	The volume of the solid particles of a loose granular material.
air-entraining agent	A material which introduces tiny air bubbles into a concrete mixture.
ASTM	American Society for Testing Materials.
calcine	To become powdery by the action of heat.
clinker	A stage in the manufacture of cement in which the ingredients are fused into small pieces.
CSA	Canadian Standards Association.
cumulative percentage	The sum of all preceding percentages in a series.
diatomaceous earth	Material containing silica formed from the skeletons of single-celled animals.
fineness modulus	Relative fineness or coarseness.
flexural strength	Strength in bending.
haydite	A lightweight aggregate made from vitrified shale.
incipient fusion	Initial stage of the melting process.
nailing concrete	Cellular concrete or concrete made with vermiculite aggregate, into which nails can be driven.
perlite	A light mineral consisting of volcanic glass.
pozzolan cement	A cement made from volcanic rock containing a large proportion of silica.
sintering	Reduction to a cinderlike state by semiliquefaction.
tremie	A long, funnel-topped pipe used to deposit concrete on the bottom of a body of water.
vitreous shell	Glass- or ceramic-like covering.

REVIEW QUESTIONS

1. Define each of the following terms:
   a. Pozzolan cement
   b. Incipient fusion
   c. Hydration

2. a. Name the four basic ingredients of portland cement.
   b. List five types of portland cement produced.
   c. Basically, how are these five types produced?
   d. What are the main ingredients of aluminous cement?
   e. List four advantages to be gained in using concrete made with aluminous cement over concrete made with portland cement.
   f. How does masonry cement differ from normal portland cement?

3. What do the results of each of the following tests, made on fine aggregate, indicate?
   a. Colorimetric test
   b. Fineness modulus test
   c. Silt test

4. Name five types of aggregate, other than stone, which are used in making concrete.

5. Briefly outline the *design* of a concrete mixture.

6. What two major difficulties are encountered in designing concrete containing lightweight aggregates by the absolute-volume method?

7. Describe briefly the test specimens made to determine compressive strength and those used to determine flexural strength.

8. **a.** What is the purpose of making and testing both *lab-cured* and *field-cured* concrete specimens?

   b. What is the purpose of a sulfur cap placed on specimens to be tested for compressive strength?

   c. What is the purpose of a ball penetration test on fresh concrete?

   d. What unit compressive strength is indicated if a 6 × 12-in (15 × 30-cm) cylindrical specimen of concrete ruptures at a 26,000-lb (57,379.5-kg) load?

9. Give two reasons for using wire with a stucco exterior finish.

10. Draw a section through a floor with a terrazzo topping showing all the components of the floor.

SELECTED SOURCES OF INFORMATION

American Concrete Institute, Detroit, Mich.
Canada Cement Lafarge Co., Montreal, Que.
Expanded Shale, Clay and Slate Institute, Washington, D.C.
Portland Cement Association, Skokie, Ill.
Vermiculite Institute, Chicago, Ill.
Perlite Institute, New York, N.Y.

REFERENCES

1. Bye, G. C., *Portland Cement Composition, Production and Properties,* Pergamon Press, Oxford, England, 1983.
2. Czernin, Wolfgang, *Cement Chemistry and Physics for Civil Engineers,* Crosby Lockwood & Son Ltd., London, 1962.
3. *Hydraulic Cement Pastes: Their Structure and Properties. Proceedings of a Conference Held at University of Sheffield 8–9 April 1976,* Cement and Concrete Association, Wexham Springs, Slough, 1976. Distributed by Scholium International Inc., Flushing, N.Y.
4. Witt, J. C., *Portland Cement Technology,* Chemical Publishing Company, Inc., New York, N.Y., 1966.

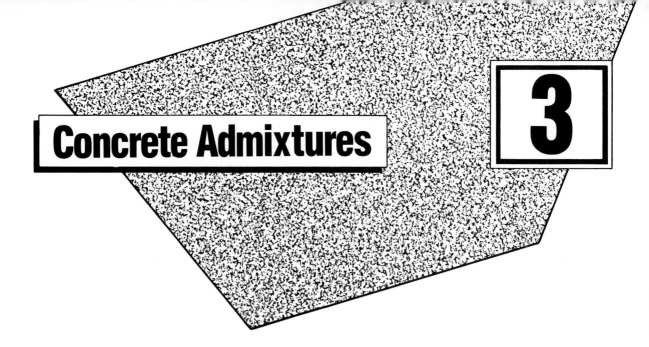

Concrete Admixtures

3

In addition to the basic ingredients of concrete—cement, water, and aggregates—other materials are often added to the mix or applied to the surface of freshly placed concrete to produce some special result. These materials, known as *concrete admixtures,* may be used for any one of the following reasons:

1. To speed up the initial set of concrete

2. To retard the initial set

3. To make the concrete more resistant to deterioration due to repeated freezing and thawing cycles

4. To prevent the bleeding of water to the surface of concrete

5. To improve the workability of the mix

6. To improve the hardness or denseness of the concrete surface

7. To render the concrete more watertight

8. To improve the bond between two concrete surfaces

9. To inhibit the set of cement paste

10. To produce a colored surface

11. To produce a nonskid surface

12. To prevent the evaporation of water from the newly placed concrete

13. To help develop all the potential strength of a given water-cement paste

14. To decrease the weight of concrete per cubic foot

ACCELERATORS

An admixture which is used to speed up the initial set of concrete is called an *accelerator.* Such a material may be added to the mix to increase the rate of early-strength development for several reasons. For example, this will allow earlier removal of forms and in some cases reduce the whole curing period. With proper protection it will partly compensate for the retardation of strength development due to low temperatures. This does not mean, however, that an accelerator makes it possible to place concrete in cold weather without proper protection.

The most common accelerator is calcium chloride ($CaCl_2$), but other materials are also used for this purpose. Among them are some of the soluble carbonates, silicates, fluosilicates, and triethanolamine.

Calcium chloride should be added to the mix in solution form by dissolving it in part of the mixing water and should be restricted to not more than 2 percent by weight of cement. If it is added to the concrete in dry form, all the dry particles may not be completely dissolved during mixing, with the result that undissolved lumps can cause "pop-outs" or dark spots in hardened concrete.

The addition of not more than 2 percent calcium chloride to a mix has no significant corrosive effect on ordinary steel reinforcement, provided the concrete is of high quality. It does, however, increase the resistance of concrete to erosive and abrasive action. On the other hand, shrinkage of concrete due to drying is likely to be increased when calcium chloride is used.

The use of calcium chloride or admixtures containing soluble chlorides is not recommended in prestressed concrete because of the possible corrosion hazards. It may also cause serious corrosion of aluminum embedded in steel, especially if the aluminum is in contact with embedded steel and the concrete is in a moist condition. Similarly, soluble chlorides should not be used where galvanized steel will be in permanent contact with the concrete. Also, calcium chloride should not be used in concrete which will be subjected to alkali-aggregate reaction or exposed to soils or water containing sulfates, in order to avoid lowering the resistance of concrete to sulfate attack.

Set accelerators made from the other chemicals named above are produced under a variety of trade names, in conformity with standards set by the ASTM. Some are in nonhygroscopic powder form, while others are in concentrated solutions. Because they contain no chlorides, they are useful where potential corrosion of embedded or stressed steel must be avoided. Such accelerators should also be used—when necessary—in concrete which will be in contact with steel-clad or zinc-coated steel decks, where it is important to avoid corrosion. Manufacturers of the various products supply details of amounts to be used.

Some of the accelerators containing fluosilicates and triethanolamine can produce a very pronounced accelerating effect. Some are capable of reducing the period during which concrete remains plastic to less than 10 min. Sternson's Quicksets, for example, added to neat portland cement, produce setting in a matter of seconds. This makes this type of accelerator valuable for making cement plugs to stop pressure leaks.

Aluminous cement is accelerated by the use of small amounts of portland cement. The portland cement is actually used as an accelerator in this case. The combination usually recommended for field use is about 70 percent aluminous cement and 30 percent portland cement. Some experimenting has been done, using small amounts of aluminous cement (5 to 20 percent) to accelerate the setting time of portland cement.

RETARDERS

The function of a *retarder* is to delay or extend the setting time of the cement paste in concrete. In hot weather hydration is accelerated by the heat, thus cutting down the time available to place, consolidate, and finish the concrete. This speedup of hydration means that some of the water usually available to provide plasticity is used by the cement. Therefore more water is required for equal slump, which in turn means lower concrete strength. High temperatures, low humidity, and wind cause rapid evaporation of water from the mix during summer. This drying of the concrete leads to cracking and crazing of the surface.

An initial set retarder will hold back the hydration process, leaving more water for workability and allowing concrete to be finished and protected before drying out. A retarder usually has water-reducing characteristics as well, making further reductions possible in the water-cement ratio.

There are also other reasons for using a retarder. For example, in bridge construction, girders or beams are designed with a camber and will be deflected as the load of the bridge deck is applied. Paving bridge decks is a relatively slow operation, and deflection takes place progressively as the load is increased. Concrete placed initially may be partially set before paving is complete if a retarder is not used. As further deflection takes place, this concrete, being no longer plastic, will be subjected to stress and may crack.

In casting prestressed members, a retarder is often important. Since prestress beds are usually quite long—300 ft (90 m) or more—it takes a considerable time to place and consolidate the entire member. It is desirable to keep the concrete plastic until vibrating is completed to ensure a good bond between concrete and prestressed steel along the entire length of the bed. It is also believed that steam, used to cure prestressed members, is more effective if the concrete has not passed a certain point in the hydration process. An initial set retarder will help to ensure this.

Fig. 3-1 Air-entraining agent increases slump. *(Soil-test, Inc.)*

Retarders are also helpful for concrete that has to be hauled long distances in transit mix trucks, to ensure that it reaches its destination in a plastic and placeable condition.

A wide variety of chemicals have a retarding effect on the normal setting time of portland cement. Some act as retarders when used in certain quantities and as accelerators when used in others. The more commonly known retarders are carbohydrate derivatives and calcium ligninsulfonate, used in fractions of a percent by weight of the cement. One of these is a highly purified metallic salt of a modified ligninsulfonic acid in the form of a brown liquid. It is used at the rate of 8 fluid oz (227 mL) per sack of cement at 21°C. This amount will extend

the vibration time and retard the set by 2 to 4 h. As a general rule, the addition rate should be increased or decreased by 1 oz (28 mL) per sack for each 5°C increase or decrease in temperature from 21°C. The use of retarding agents is not generally recommended if the temperature is below 15°C.

In general, some reduction in the early-strength development of concrete that contains retarders occurs during the first 1 to 3 days. The effects on the other properties of concrete, such as shrinkage, cannot be predicted, and therefore tests of retarders should be made with the materials to be used under job conditions as they are likely to exist.

AIR-ENTRAINING AGENTS

The introduction of controlled amounts of air into a mix has proved to be an important advance in concrete engineering. It is generally recognized that proper amounts of entrained air result in *improved workability* (see Fig. 3-1), *easier placing, increased durability, better resistance to frost action, improved flow* in concrete pump lines, and *reduction in bleeding and water gain.*

The increased resistance to frost action is particularly marked where freezing conditions are severe or where salts are used for ice removal. (See Fig. 3-2.) The reduced tendency for bleeding and water gain indirectly aids in promoting durability, because uniformity is increased and weak sections at the top of vertical lifts can be eliminated.

Air-entrained concrete contains microscopic bubbles of air formed with the aid of a group of chemicals called *surface active agents,* materials which have the property of reducing the surface tension of water. This property enables water to

Fig. 3-2 Comparison of *(left)* plain vs. *(right)* air-entrained concrete subjected to frost action.

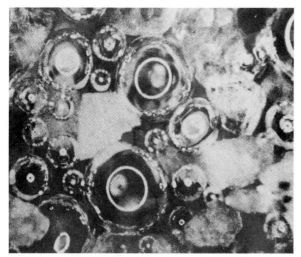

Fig. 3-3 Air bubbles in concrete mix magnified 250X.

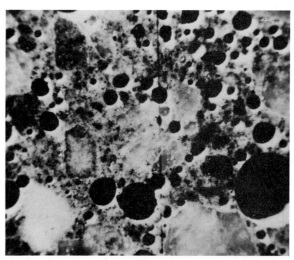

Fig. 3-4 Magnified view of hardened, air-entrained concrete. *(Portland Cement Association)*

hold air when agitated, resulting in a foam. (See Fig. 3-3.) A large number of these compounds are available, but only a relatively few may be used satisfactorily in concrete. Among them are a number of natural wood resins, various sulfonated compounds, neutralized Vinsol resin, some fats and oils, and some polyethylene oxide polymers.

A satisfactory air-entraining agent must not react chemically with cement. It must be able to produce air bubbles of a certain size, from approximately 0.01 to 0.001 in (0.25 to 0.025 mm) in diameter (see Fig. 3-4), which will not break too rapidly. These entrained air bubbles constitute a definite part of the fine aggregate and, like water and fine sand, lubricate the concrete. They also act like ball bearings to help concrete to move more easily.

Air entrainment, while improving durability and plasticity, may have an adverse effect on the strength of the concrete. Within the normal range of air contents (see Table 3-1), the decrease in strength usually is about proportional to the amount of entrained air. The maximum reduction in compressive strength rarely exceeds 15 percent, and in the case of flexural strength the maximum reduction is about 10 percent. These figures are for equal cement content and with the sand and water

Table 3-1
AIR-ENTRAINED CONCRETE

Mixture	Coarse Aggregate, Maximum Size	Optimum Air Content, % By Volume
Sand mortar (masonry)	No coarse aggregate; max No. 4 sieve (5 mm)	14 ± 2
Sand mortar (concrete)	No coarse aggregate; max No. 4 sieve (5 mm)	9 ± .5
Concrete	$\frac{1}{2}$ in (12.5 mm)	7.5 ± 1.5
Concrete	1 in (25 mm)	6 ± 1.5
Concrete	$1\frac{1}{2}$ in (37.5 mm)	4.5 ± 1.5
Concrete	3 in (75 mm)	3.5 ± 1

content reduced by the amount permitted by the increased workability of an air-entrained mix.

The amount of entrained air which will normally be most beneficial will vary, depending on the maximum size of coarse aggregate used in the mix. Table 3-1 gives the generally recognized optimum volume of entrained air in a number of mixes. The air content of a concrete mixture can be measured by an air meter, available in a number of styles.

Air-entraining agents made from the modified salts of a sulfonated hydrocarbon tend to plasticize a concrete mix. As a result, they are particularly useful where aggregates which tend to produce harsh concrete or natural sand deficient in fines are used in producing concrete.

Another type, made from neutralized Vinsol resin, is used in mass concrete and concrete used in highway pavements. Highway-paving concrete characteristically has high cement content and low slump, and an air-entraining agent which will improve placing and finishing conditions is important. On the other hand, mass concrete will normally be a lean, stiff mix with a low sand factor and will be difficult to place. Again, an air-entraining agent which will be effective for such mixtures and will improve placing conditions is necessary.

Air-entrained concrete can also be made by using an air-entraining portland cement. This type of portland cement contains an air-entraining agent which has been mixed and ground with the raw material during the manufacture of the cement. A specification covering this type of cement has been issued by the American Society for Testing Materials.

SUPERPLASTICIZERS

When cement and water are mixed, the cement particles tend to gather in clumps known as cement *agglomerates.* This clumping action prevents thorough mixing of the cement and the water, producing a loss in the workability of the concrete mix as well as preventing complete hydration of the cement. This means that less than the full potential strength of the cement paste will be developed. In some instances, in 28 days of curing, only 50 percent of the cement content has hydrated.

The relatively large clumps of cement have rough, abrasive surfaces requiring larger quantities of water to produce a workable concrete mix. This, in turn, increases the water cement ratio, resulting in a weaker mix. Water trapped between the clumps

bleeds to the surface as the concrete begins to set, leaving voids that later become passages for infiltration by free moisture.

A *superplasticizer* is a substance that disperses the clumps by coating each cement particle, thus separating and dispersing the cement in the water phase. This coating also induces a negative charge on the cement particles, causing them to repel one another. The final effect is that the workability of the concrete mix is improved without increasing the water/cement ratio or producing excessive bleeding and segregation.

Three types of superplasticizers are currently available: (1) sulfonated naphthalene formaldehydes (SNF), (2) sulfonated melamine formaldehydes (SMF), and (3) modified ligninsulfonates. They are added to the concrete mix in liquid form much like other admixtures.

The advantages that result from the use of this type of admixture can be summarized as follows:

1. Keeping the water and cement content constant, a highly workable mix is produced.

2. Reducing the water content and keeping the cement content and workability the same produces a lower water/cement ratio concrete of higher strength.

3. Reducing the water and cement content at a constant water/cement ratio but maintaining workability produces a concrete that develops the same strength but uses less cement.

Normally, the addition of a superplasticizer has no adverse effect on the concrete mix except in lean mixes with high slumps. In these types of mixes it is advisable to check the *combined fines* content. For example, a concrete mix using $\frac{3}{4}$ in (20 mm) maximum aggregate should have a combined fines content of at least 380 lb/yd^3 (450 kg/m^3). Mixes that are deficient in fines can be upgraded by adding fly ash or sand.

Superplasticized mixes lose slump rather quickly. The superplasticizer is normally added at the site to ensure that placing is completed before any loss of slump occurs. The addition of a water-reducing retarder, ASTM Type D, has proved successful in slowing down the loss of slump in mixes. The two chemicals work together as far as the plasticizing action is concerned, resulting in smaller quantities of the more expensive superplasticizer to produce the same effect. Figure 3-5 illustrates the delaying action of a retarder on slump loss in a superplasticized concrete.

CONCRETE HARDENERS

Plain concrete is used as a wearing surface in a wide variety of applications ranging from residential floor slabs to buildings housing heavy industry. As a result the concrete surface is subject to every kind of wear and abuse, such as impact, abrasion, and attack by salts and aggressive liquids. Over a period of time, the surface of the slab will begin to dust and crumble under the applied loads and eventually reach such a state of disrepair that it will no longer be serviceable.

To prolong the life expectancy of the concrete surface, in addition to proper curing and finishing, concrete hardeners are added to the concrete mix. Hardeners come in two forms: as *chemical additives* and as *metallic aggregates.*

Chemical hardeners are liquids containing silicofluorides or fluosilicates and a wetting agent. The latter reduces the surface tension of the liquid and allows it to penetrate the pores of the concrete more easily. The silicofluorides or fluosilicates combine chemically with the free lime and calcium carbonate which are present in the concrete and bind the fine particles into a flintlike topping, which is highly resistant to wear and dusting.

Metallic hardeners are specially processed and graded iron particles which are dry-mixed with portland cement, spread evenly over the surface of freshly floated concrete, and worked into the surface by floating. The result is a hard, tough topping which is highly resistant to wear and less brittle than normal concrete. Figure 3-6 illustrates the difference in wearing ability between floors made with and without metallic aggregates. The regular concrete floor surface on the right has deteriorated badly after 5 years of usage, while the adjoining floor section on the left, subject to the same traffic but made with metallic aggregate, is still in good condition.

Metallic aggregates are normally applied to the freshly cast surface as a shake and worked into the top by float and trowel. Various amounts can be used, depending on the type of use. Recommendations on the amount of metallic aggregate to be applied under various conditions of usage are given in Table 3-2.

Metallic aggregate topping may be finished to produce a nonskid surface by using a wooden or cork float, which leaves a slightly roughened surface. Nonskid surfaces can also be produced by using abrasive-type aggregates, such as aluminum oxide and silicon carbide, in the topping.

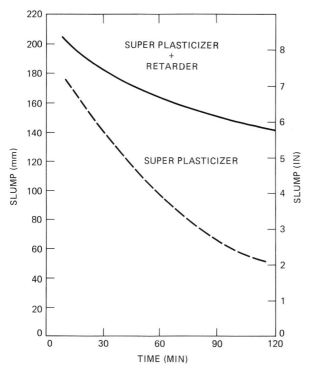

Fig. 3-5 Slump loss in concrete containing superplasticizer versus retarder plus superplasticizer.

Fig. 3-6 Comparison of concrete floors with and without metallic aggregates. *(Master Builders Co.)*

125

Table 3-2
AMOUNT OF METALLIC AGGREGATE FOR VARIOUS USES OF FLOOR

Type of Traffic	Amount Of Metallic Aggregate	
	lb/ft^2	kg/m^2
Heavy foot traffic	0.5	2.4
Light wheel traffic	0.75	3.65
Medium wheel traffic	1.00	4.88
Heavy wheel traffic	1.25	6.1
Extra-heavy wheel loads	10.0	48.8
Extra-heavy impact	20.0	97.6

SOURCE: Master Builders Co.

The use of metallic aggregates also results in the production of floors that are nonsparking. Frictional sparks resulting from the striking of metal on stone are eliminated, and by having the right degree of conductivity metallic aggregate floors overcome the hazard of static sparks.

WATER-REDUCING ADMIXTURES

A water-reducing admixture is a material used to reduce the amount of water necessary to produce a concrete of a given consistency or to increase the slump for a given water content. A typical one is made from the metallic salts of ligninsulfonic acids.

More water than is actually required for the hydration of the cement must be used in any given concrete mix in order to give it placeability. Unless the water content is carefully controlled, excess water may bleed to the surface of the concrete, causing segregation or surface laitance, or may evaporate, leaving voids which decrease strength and increase permeability. Excess water will also dilute and weaken the cement paste. Therefore, an agent which will decrease the amount of water required while maintaining consistency and workability is a useful addition to the mix.

Some water-reducing admixtures may also retard the setting time of concrete, while others have little or no effect. Tests may be required to determine the effects of any given water-reducing agent on the setting time. Some of them also introduce entrained air into the concrete.

An increase in the strength of concrete can usually be obtained, using a water-reducing agent, if the water content is reduced for a given mix to maintain a given slump and if the cement content is maintained as specified.

Concrete made with some water-reducing admixtures shows significant increases in drying shrinkage, in spite of the reduction in water content. Again, testing may be necessary to determine the effect of any given product in this regard.

CONCRETE WATERPROOFERS

Water under pressure and in contact with one surface of the concrete can be forced through channels between the inner and outer surfaces. A measure of the amount of water passing in this way is a measure of permeability; any admixture used to reduce this flow is really a *permeability reducer*.

Water also can pass through concrete by the action of capillary forces. If one side is exposed to moisture and the other to air, the water reaching the dry side evaporates, resulting in a flow of moisture through the concrete. Materials used to reduce or stop this type of flow are more properly called *dampproofers*.

Before water can pass by either of these means there must be channels through which it can travel. It is possible, through careful design, placing, and curing of concrete, to make it impermeable without using an admixture. But for some types of concrete, lean mixes in particular, it is often advantageous to use an admixture to reduce permeability.

The production of concrete of low permeability depends largely on uniform placing of the material and some means of preventing or limiting bleeding. Air-entraining agents increase the plasticity of concrete and therefore help to make placing easier and more uniform. They also reduce bleeding by holding the water in films about the air bubbles. For these reasons air-entraining agents may also be considered as permeability-reducing agents. It is also believed that the small disconnected voids produced by air entrainment break up the capillaries in the concrete and therefore offer a barrier to the passage of water by capillary action. This means that an air-entraining agent may also be classed as a *dampproofing agent*.

A cement dispersal agent may also be considered as a permeability reducer, since it also tends to reduce voids formed when water is trapped in groups of cement particles.

Water repellents are also used as dampproofing agents. Materials commonly used for this purpose are compounds containing calcium or ammonium stearate, calcium or ammonium oleate, or butyl stearate. These substances are generally combined with lime or calcium chloride. Because these materials are water repellents, their effectiveness depends on the uniformity of distribution throughout the concrete.

Another type of concrete waterproofer consists of a film applied to the surface, preferably the one adjacent to the water source. Several materials are used for this purpose, the three most common ones being those containing asphalt or sodium silicate and one which contains a metallic aggregate.

The asphaltic products, thick viscous liquids, form an impervious coating over the surface. The sodium silicate compounds enter the surface pores and form a gel which prevents water from entering the concrete. The metallic-aggregate type of waterproofer consists of fine cast-iron particles, to which is added a chemical that causes them to oxidize rapidly when mixed with portland cement and wetted. It is applied over a concrete surface in the form of a slurry; rapid oxidation results in an expansion of the iron particles, causing them to knit the coating to the surface by means of the many tiny fingers thrust out in the process of oxidation. Successive coats build up a thin but dense watertight film over the surface.

BONDING AGENTS

When fresh concrete is placed against another concrete surface already set and at least partially cured, it is often difficult to obtain a bond between the two surfaces unless special precautions are taken. Fresh concrete shrinks when setting, and unless there is a very good bond this shrinkage makes the new concrete pull away from the old surface. If the old surface is treated so that the aggregates are exposed and clean, the cement paste in newly placed concrete will bond to them in the same way that it bonds to the aggregates in the new mix. A cement-paste slurry is often applied to such an old surface immediately before placing new concrete

to increase the amount of paste available at the surface for bonding purposes.

Where such a treatment cannot be applied, bonding agents can be used to join the two surfaces. Two types of bonding agent are in common use, one in which the bonding is accomplished by a metallic aggregate and the other consisting of a synthetic latex emulsion.

The metallic-aggregate bonding agent is similar to a permeability reducer made with the same materials, except that in the bonding agent, the iron particles are larger. Bonding takes place through the oxidation and subsequent expansion of the iron particles. The tiny fingers that thrust out into both the old and the new concrete bind them together.

There are a number of types of synthetic latex bonding agents, but basically they consist of a highly polymerized synthetic liquid resin dispersed in water. Since it is an emulsion, a bonding agent must lose water for its adhesive ingredients to set. When it is sprayed or painted on a concrete surface, the pores in the concrete absorb the water and allow the resin particles to coalesce and bond. When a bonding agent is mixed with cement paste or a mortar, the water is used in the hydration of the cement and the resin is left to bind to both surfaces involved.

Another type of bonding agent, which is not an admixture, is applied to the surface of hardened concrete just before fresh concrete is placed over it. One of these is a two-component polysulfide-epoxy material which produces a bond that may be stronger than the concrete itself.

CONCRETE COLORING AGENTS

There is a considerable demand for colored concrete surfaces in modern construction, and a number of methods of producing these have been developed. One, of course, is to use concrete paint, applied after the concrete surface has been neutralized, either through exposure or by using a neutralizing agent such as zinc sulfate.

Another method is to add pigments to the concrete while it is still fresh as in the case of exposed concrete floors. Pigments are produced from natural and synthetic mineral oxides and are used in

Table 3-3
MINERAL OXIDE COLORING AGENTS

Color Required	Coloring Agent
Blues	Cobalt oxide
Browns	Brown oxide of iron
Buffs	Synthetic yellow oxide of iron
Greens	Chromium oxide
Reds	Red oxide of iron
Grays, blacks	Black iron oxide

conjunction with a topping mix of sand and a water-reducing agent. This mix is then applied to the concrete surface as a dry shake and troweled into the concrete to produce a uniform color and a smooth finish. Table 3-3 gives examples of some of the more common coloring agents and the colors that they produce.

The natural metallic oxides of materials such as cobalt, chromium, and iron produce very distinctive colors, as do the ochers and the umbers. In powder form they are readily mixed with other materials in the topping mix and once troweled into the concrete produce a very uniform finish.

The coloring agents made with synthetic oxides are usually a mixture of the oxide with one or more additional drying ingredients. The color is sometimes mixed with fine pure silica sand and applied by shaking the mixture over the freshly poured and floated surface. The coloring mixture is floated in, troweled, and cured like any other concrete surface. The colors are also available mixed with metallic aggregate. In this case the material is mixed dry with cement and applied as a dry shake over the surface. The mix is floated, troweled, and cured as before.

A semipaste type of admixture is available which may be added to plain or air-entrained concrete mixes to darken them. Depending on the amount of admixture used, a range of shades from light gray to black may be obtained.

SET-INHIBITING AGENTS

Specifications sometimes require that concrete surfaces be produced in which the aggregates are exposed for architectural effect. Exposed aggregates also provide a good bonding surface for concrete toppings. Normally these aggregates will be covered by a coating of cement-sand mortar which

bonds to them as curing progresses and results in a smooth, uniformly colored surface.

Certain inhibiting agents will prevent the cement paste from bonding to the surface aggregates but will not interfere with the set throughout the remainder of the concrete. Two materials are used for this purpose: a liquid which is applied to forms for vertical surfaces immediately before placing concrete and a powder which is applied directly to freshly placed horizontal surfaces. In the latter case, the depth of penetration of the inhibitor depends on the amount used per 100 square feet (9 square meters). Usual rates of application will vary from $1\frac{1}{2}$ to 3 lb per 100 ft^2 (85 to 175 g/m^2) of surface.

After 3 or 4 days of curing, the retarded surface concrete should be hosed or brushed off, exposing clean aggregate and leaving a roughcast effect.

NONSKID SURFACES

Well-troweled concrete surfaces can be made very smooth, and under certain conditions these surfaces tend to be slippery. A nonskid surface can be produced in several ways. One is to leave out the steel troweling operation during the floor-finishing process. Instead the floor can be finished with wood or cork floats which will leave a rough surface. This can be done either with a plain concrete floor or with a floor topped with a metallic-aggregate coating.

Another method is to use an abrasive material in the topping, applied as a dry shake in much the same way as metallic-aggregate topping is applied. The abrasive material is floated into the top, and the steel trowel operation is omitted. Materials commonly used for this purpose are fine particles of flint, aluminum oxide, silicon carbide, and emery.

SURFACE-SEALING AGENTS

Surface-sealing agents are used for two purposes. One is to form a watertight coating which will prevent water from evaporating from a concrete surface and allow it to be retained for hydration. The other is to seal the pores of a concrete surface after it has hardened in order to prevent the passage of water and the absorption of spilled materials such as oil, grease, or paint.

Sealing agents used to prevent water evaporation are usually liquid waxes which can be sprayed over the surface but which are easily removed after curing is complete. The type of sealer applied after the concrete is cured is used primarily to reduce maintenance. This kind of sealer may be a heavy-bodied wax which is rubbed into the surface or a synthetic resin emulsion. Both must be reapplied periodically because of normal wear on the floor.

A number of other products, such as quick-drying liquid polymers, perform both functions; that is, they may be used to seal and cure new concrete floors or to seal old floors for easier maintenance.

GAS-FORMING AGENTS

Under normal conditions concrete undergoes settlement and drying shrinkage, which, in some situations, can result in undesirable characteristics in the hardened concrete. For example, voids on the underneath side of forms, blockouts, reinforcing steel, or other embedded parts such as machinery bases may interfere with the bond and allow passage of water and reduce uniformity and strength.

One method of reducing such voids is to add an expanding agent to the concrete. Aluminum powder, when added to mortar or concrete, reacts with the hydroxides in hydrating cement to produce very small bubbles of hydrogen gas. This action, when properly controlled, causes a slight expansion in plastic concrete or mortar and thus reduces or eliminates voids caused by settlement. The effect on the strength of the concrete depends to a large extent on the restraint offered to expansion. With complete restraint imposed, the strength is not affected appreciably. Very small amounts of aluminum powder are used for this purpose, usually about 1 teaspoon (5 ml) per sack of cement.

When larger amounts of powder are used, the expansion is greatly increased, resulting in a lightweight, low-strength concrete. Such concrete is useful for floor and roof slabs, fire walls, nonbearing partitions, etc. Aluminum powder for this purpose is used at a rate of approximately $\frac{1}{4}$ lb (113 g) per sack of cement.

POZZOLANIC ADMIXTURES

A pozzolan (see Chap. 2), finely ground and in the presence of moisture, will react with calcium hydroxide at ordinary temperatures to form compounds which have cementitious properties. A number of natural materials such as diatomaceous earth, opaline cherts and shales, tuffs and pumicites, and some artificial materials such as fly ash are used as pozzolans. Fly ash is a fine residue which results from the combustion of powdered coal and may contain various amounts of carbon, silica, sulfur, alkalis, and other ingredients. These materials are sometimes used in structures where it is desirable to avoid high temperature or in structures exposed to seawater or water containing sulfates. These pozzolanic materials are generally substituted for 10 to 35 percent of the cement. This substitute produces concrete that is more permeable but much more resistant to the action of salt, sulfate, or acid water. Strength gain is usually slower than for normal concrete.

Pozzolans may be added to concrete mixes—rather than substituting for part of the cement—to improve workability, impermeability, and resistance to chemical attack. The results depend on the aggregates used in the concrete. Where the aggregates are deficient in fine material, the results are best.

Some pozzolans have been found to reduce the expansion caused by alkali-aggregate reaction in concrete and mortar. The expansion is caused by the interaction of alkali in portland cement and certain siliceous types of aggregates. The result of this action is excessive expansion and pattern cracking of the concrete.

The amount of suitable pozzolan required to control this type of expansion varies with the type of aggregate used and the alkali content of the cement. Normally protection can be obtained by using quantities ranging from 2 to 35 percent by weight of the cement. In the case of a few specific pozzolans of high opal content, less than 15 percent by weight is sufficient to prevent expansion.

Pozzolans vary considerably in their effect on concrete mixes and should be tested in conjunction with the aggregates and cement to be used in a given situation to determine their suitability. They will have varying effects on the water required, on strength development, and on heat development, as well as on durability, shrinkage, and other properties of concrete. Excessive amounts of some of the components of fly ash may adversely affect the strength, durability, and air content of concrete.

For more information on admixtures, see the CSA special publication A266.4, called *Guidelines for the Use of Admixtures in Concrete.*

GLOSSARY

aluminous cement	Cement made from aluminum ore.
bleeding	The migration of mixing water to the surface of freshly poured concrete.
camber	A convexity built into a beam or girder.
concrete bond	The knitting together of two concrete surfaces.
hydration	The chemical action between cement and water which results in the hardening of concrete.
initial set	The original stiffening of the cement paste which results in the concrete losing its plasticity.
lean mix	A concrete mix with a low proportion of cement to aggregates.
permeability	A measure of the rate of the passage of water through concrete.
plasticity	Ability of freshly mixed concrete to flow.
plasticizer	A material added to increase the plasticity of a concrete mix.
polymer	A compound formed by the union of two or more molecules having the same elements.
shake	Material applied to a floor by sprinkling over the surface.
water gain	Absorption of water by hardened concrete.

REVIEW QUESTIONS

1. **a.** Give a concise definition of a concrete admixture.

    b. List reasons for the use of admixtures in concrete.

2. **a.** What is the basic purpose of an accelerator?

    b. How does an accelerator do its job?

    c. What is the material most commonly used as an accelerator?

3. Give two important reasons for using a retarder in concrete.

4. **a.** What is air-entrained concrete?

    b. List three important purposes for which an air-entraining agent is used.

    c. Explain how air entrainment of concrete reduces water bleeding and how air entrainment increases workability of concrete.

5. **a.** What is meant by cement dispersal?

    b. Name one commonly used dispersal agent.

6. Explain how chemical concrete hardeners differ in their action from metallic hardeners.

7. **a.** Explain what is meant by concrete permeability.

    b. Name two methods by which permeability may be reduced.

8. List three reasons for using metallic aggregates in a concrete floor topping.

9. **a.** Explain what is meant by a concrete bonding agent.

    b. Under what conditions is a bonding agent advisable?

    c. Name two types of concrete bonding agent.

10. What is the purpose of using a neutralizing agent such as zinc sulfate on a concrete surface?

11. Explain the reason for using a set inhibitor.

12. Describe how a nonskid surface can be produced by the use of abrasive material.

13. **a.** What is pozzolan?

    b. Why are pozzolans used in concrete mixtures?

SELECTED SOURCES OF INFORMATION

Calcium Chloride Association, Detroit, Mich.
G. F. Sterne & Sons, Brantford, Ont.
Master Builders Co., Cleveland, Ohio
Portland Cement Association, Chicago, Ill.
Sika Chemical Corporation, Passaic, N.J.
W. R. Grace & Co., LaSalle, Que.

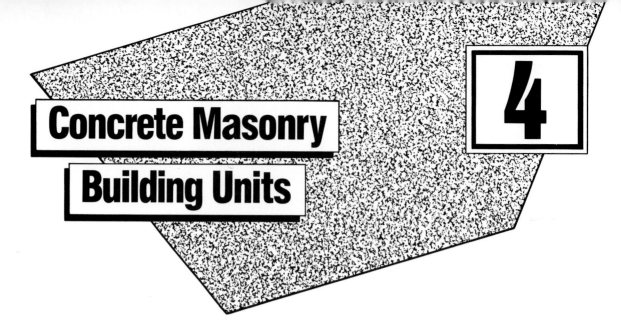

Concrete Masonry Building Units

4

Concrete masonry building units—solid and hollow modular concrete block—widely accepted as a building material, are designed and manufactured for use in all types of masonry construction. They are made from both lightweight and heavyweight materials, in a great variety of sizes and shapes. Some of the uses are exterior and interior load-bearing walls, fire walls, party walls, curtain walls, panel walls, partitions, backing for other masonry facing materials, fireproofing over structural steel members, piers, pilasters, columns, retaining walls, chimneys and fireplaces, concrete floor units, fillers for ribbed concrete floors, and patio paving units.

As the industry continues to grow, new shapes and uses are being developed, and in recent years, more block is being designed for use in the architectural, as well as in the structural field. (See Fig. 4-1.)

BLOCK TYPES

Concrete blocks may first be classified according to their *weight,* which will depend on the materials from which they are made. Those materials include *sand, gravel, crushed stone, air-cooled slag, expanded slag, expanded clay, expanded shale, pumice, scoria,* and *cinders.* The weight class of a block is based on the density of the concrete that the block contains. A block is considered *normal-weight* if it weighs more than 125 lb/ft^3 (2000 kg/m^3), *medium-weight* if it weighs beween 105 to 125 lb/ft^3 (1680 and 2000 kg/m^3), and *lightweight* if it weighs 105 lb/ft^3 (1680 kg/m^3) or less. The use of lightweight aggregates can reduce the weight of blocks about 20 to 45 percent, compared to the weight of similar units made with normal-weight aggregates, with no loss of structural strength.

Blocks may also be classified according to *type:* (1) hollow load-bearing block, (2) solid load-bearing block, (3) hollow non-load-bearing block, (4) concrete brick, and (5) specialty block.

A hollow block is one in which the net concrete cross-sectional area parallel to the bearing face is less than 75 percent of the gross cross-sectional area, while solid units have a net concrete cross-sectional area of 75 percent or more.

Generally, specifications require load-bearing blocks to have minimum face-shell thicknesses of $\frac{3}{4}$ to $1\frac{1}{2}$ in (19 to 38 mm) and minimum web thicknesses of $\frac{3}{4}$ to $1\frac{1}{4}$ in (19 to 32 mm), depending on the width of the block. Normally, non-load-bearing units are not subject to these requirements, except that the face shell cannot be less than $\frac{1}{2}$ in (13 mm).

Concrete brick and some split-block units are made 100 percent solid, though some concrete

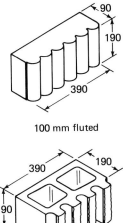

100 mm fluted

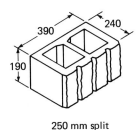

200 mm ribbed

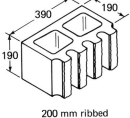

250 mm split

Fig. 4-1 Concrete block shapes. *(Edcon Block Co.)*

brick may have a depression—a *frog*—in one bearing face.

Specialty blocks are those made with odd shapes, such as manhole blocks, drainage tile, grass pavers, etc.

Blocks may also be categorized by their normal uses, for example, *wall and partition* block, *pilaster* block, *chimney* block, *lintel* block, *bond-beam* block, *jamb or sash* block, *decorative* block, *floor* block, *utility* block, and *systems* block.

BLOCK SIZES

Most blocks are made in modular sizes. That simply means that the actual dimensions of a block plus the thickness of the mortar in which it is laid conform to a well-recognized unit of measurement—a module. In the imperial system, the basic module is 4 in, while in the International System of Units (the SI metric system) it is 100 mm.

In the metric system, the mortar joint is 10 mm thick. Therefore a standard modular block is made 390 mm long, so that, center-to-center of mortar joints, the measurement will be 400 mm—four modules. (See Fig. 4-2.)

Concrete blocks are made in a wide variety of sizes and shapes to fit many different construction needs. Many are made in half- as well as full-length units, and half-height blocks are also available in many areas. Consult the local manufacturer's bro-

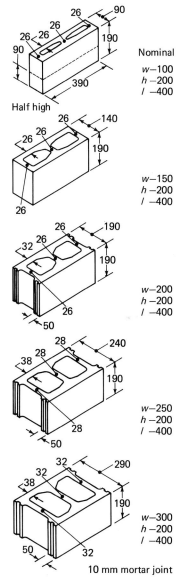

Fig. 4-2 Recommended basic SI metric modular units based on a 100-mm module. *(Besser Co.)*

133

chure for the sizes and shapes of blocks available. Figure 4-3 shows a number of typical blocks in metric modular sizes.

BLOCK TERMINOLOGY

The terminology used with regard to concrete block has been standardized to a considerable degree. For example, blocks are usually referred to by their *modular* dimensions. Thus, the first block shown in Fig. 4-2 is called a 4 × 8 × 16 (100 × 200 × 400 mm) block. Figure 4-4 illustrates standard block terminology.

BLOCK MANUFACTURE

Normally, the ingredients for concrete blocks are mixed in a paddle-type mixer, and the very dry mix is fed into a block-forming machine (see Fig. 4-5), where the blocks are molded under heavy pressure and vibration. They are then transported to a curing room, or *autoclave*, where they are cured by steam, and from there to a storage yard.

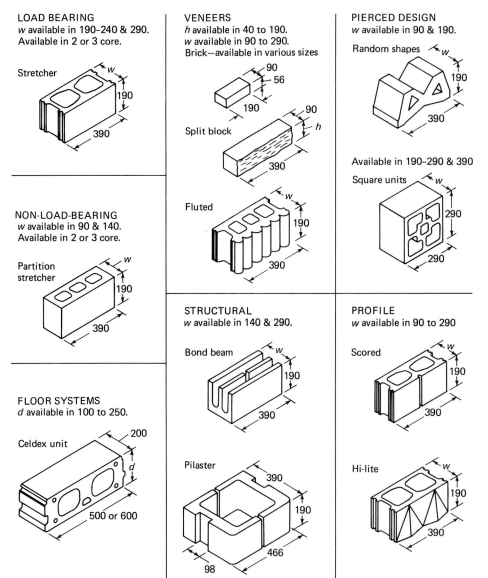

LOAD BEARING
w available in 190–240 & 290.
Available in 2 or 3 core.

Stretcher

NON-LOAD-BEARING
w available in 90 & 140.
Available in 2 or 3 core.

Partition stretcher

FLOOR SYSTEMS
d available in 100 to 250.

Celdex unit

VENEERS
h available in 40 to 190.
w available in 90 to 290.
Brick—available in various sizes

Split block

Fluted

STRUCTURAL
w available in 140 & 290.

Bond beam

Pilaster

PIERCED DESIGN
w available in 90 & 190.

Random shapes

Available in 190–290 & 390

Square units

PROFILE
w available in 90 to 290

Scored

Hi-lite

Fig. 4-3   Typical sizes and shapes of metric modular concrete block.   *(Besser Co.)*

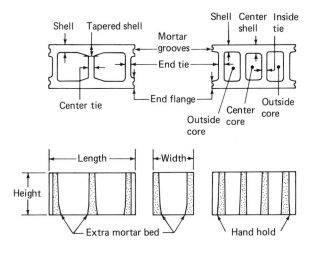

Note: The following nomenclature is the same for 2-core and 3-core block. The 2-core has been used here for illustration.

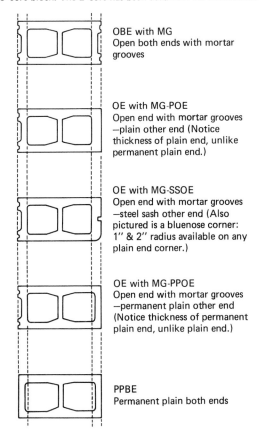

OBE with MG
Open both ends with mortar grooves

OE with MG-POE
Open end with mortar grooves —plain other end (Notice thickness of plain end, unlike permanent plain end.)

OE with MG-SSOE
Open end with mortar grooves —steel sash other end (Also pictured is a bluenose corner: 1″ & 2″ radius available on any plain end corner.)

OE with MG-PPOE
Open end with mortar grooves —permanent plain other end (Notice thickness of permanent plain end, unlike plain end.)

PPBE
Permanent plain both ends

Fig. 4-4 Standard block nomenclature. In practice, the first dimension of a concrete masonry unit represents the thickness; the second, the height; the third, length. (Besser Co.)

Fig. 4-5 Block-making machine. (Columbia Machine, Inc.)

BLOCK PROPERTIES

Concrete blocks are made to comply with certain requirements, notably with regard to *compressive strength, rate of absorption, moisture content, weight,* and *thermal expansion.* These are laid down by local or national building codes and by the applicable specifications of ASTM, CSA, or other specifying agencies. (See Table 4-1.)

Compressive-strength requirements provide a measure of the block's ability to carry loads and withstand structural stresses. Absorption requirements provide a measure of the density of the concrete, while the moisture-content requirements are intended to indicate whether the unit is sufficiently dry for use in wall construction. Concrete shrinks slightly with loss of moisture, down to an air-dry condition. If moist units are placed in a wall and this natural shrinkage is restrained, as is often the case, tensile and shearing stresses are developed which may result in cracking. Units should be dried to at least the moisture-content limitations of the applicable specifications.

The weight is an indication of the type of block and an important consideration in calculating the dead loads in the structure. A hollow load-bearing

Table 4-1
PROPERTIES OF CONCRETE BLOCK MADE WITH VARIOUS AGGREGATES

Imperial Modular Units

Aggregate (Graded $\frac{3}{8}$ in to 0 in)		Weight of Concrete, lb/ft³	Weight 8 × 8 × 16 in Unit Pounds	Compressive Strength (Gross Area), lb/in²	Water Absorption of Concrete, lb/ft³	Thermal Expansion Coefficient in/in/°F × 10⁻⁶
Type	Density (Air-Dry), lb/ft³					
Sand and Gravel	130–145	135	40	1200–1800	7–10	5.0
Limestone	120–140	135	40	1100–1800	8–12	5.0
Air-cooled blast furnace slag	100–125	120	35	1100–1500	9–13	4.6
Expanded clay, shale, and slag	75– 90	85	25	1000–1500	12–15	4.5
Expanded blast furnace slag	80–105	95	28	700–1200	12–16	4.0
Cinders (coal ash)	80–105	95	28	700–1000	12–18	2.5
Pumice (volcanic ash)	60– 85	75	22	700– 900	13–19	4.0
Scoria (volcanic ash)	75–100	95	28	700–1200	12–16	4.0

Metric Equivalent of Imperial Modular Units

Aggregate (Graded: 9.53 mm to 0)		Weight of Concrete, kg/m³	Weight 200 × 200 × 400 mm Unit Kilograms	Compressive Strength[a] (Gross Area), kg/cm² (N/mm²)[b]	Water Absorption of Concrete, kg/m³	Thermal Expansion Coefficient mm/mm/°C
Type	Density (Air-Dry), kg/m³					
Sand and gravel	2083–2323	2163	18.1	8.4–126.6 (8.27–12.41)	112–160	9.0×10^{-6}
Limestone	1922–2243	2163	18.1	77.3–126.6 (7.58–12.41)	128–192	9.0×10^{-6}
Air-cooled blast furnace slag	1602–2003	1922	15.9	77.3–105.5 (7.58–10.34)	144–208	8.3×10^{-6}
Expanded clay, shale, and slate	1202–1442	1362	11.3	70.3–105.5 (6.90–10.34)	192–240	8.1×10^{-6}
Expanded blast furnace slag	1282–1682	1522	12.7	49.2–84.4 (4.83–8.27)	192–256	7.2×10^{-6}
Cinders (coal ash)	1282–1682	1522	12.7	49.2–70.3 (4.83–6.90)	192–288	4.5×10^{-6}
Pumice (volcanic ash)	961–1362	1202	10.0	49.2–63.3 (4.83–6.21)	208–304	7.2×10^{-6}
Scoria (volcanic ash)	1202–1602	1522	12.7	49.2–84.4 (4.83–8.27)	192–256	7.2×10^{-6}

[a] Multiply these values by 1.8 to obtain approximate corresponding values of strength of the concrete (strength of unit on net area).
[b] The standard unit for stress as set by the International System of Units (SI) is newton per square meter. It is more significant to express the strength performance for masonry in newton per square millimeter. (1 newton/millimeter² = 10⁶ newton/meters.²)
SOURCE: Besser Technical Center, from Figure 30, American Savings and Loan Institute. *Construction Lending Guide*. Section 205, 1966.

concrete block 8 × 8 × 16 in (200 × 200 × 400 mm) will weigh approximately 40 lb (18 kg) when made with regular aggregate and 22 to 35 lb (10 to 16 kg) with lightweight aggregate.

The coefficient of thermal expansion provides a means of calculating the amount of expansion which will take place in a unit or a structure owing to specified increases in temperature.

The insulation value of concrete block has been determined by a variety of tests. Table 4-2 shows the insulation values for various types of block walls, with several types of interior finish.

The overall coefficient of heat transmission, *U*, represents the amount of heat transmitted in British thermal units per hour per square foot per degree Fahrenheit (watts per square meter per degree centigrade) for each degree difference in temperature between the air on the warm and cool sides of the

Table 4-2
COEFFICIENTS OF HEAT TRANSMISSION (*U*) FOR VARIOUS WALLS

British Thermal Units Per Hour Per Square Foot Per Degree Fahrenheit

Basic Wall Construction[a]		Plain Wall No Plaster	Interior Finish		
			Wall Direct	½ in Plaster on:	
				¾ in Furring With:	
				⅜ in Plasterboard	½ in Rigid Insulation
Concrete masonry (cores not filled)	8-in sand and gravel or limestone	0.53	0.49	0.31	0.22
	8-in cinder	0.37	0.35	0.25	0.19
	8-in expanded slag, clay, or shale	0.33	0.32	0.23	0.18
	12-in sand and gravel or limestone	0.49	0.45	0.30	0.22
	12-in cinder	0.35	0.33	0.24	0.18
	12-in expanded slag, clay, or shale	0.32	0.31	0.23	0.18
Concrete masonry (cores filled with insulation[b])	8-in sand and gravel or limestone	0.39	0.37	0.26	0.19
	8-in cinder	0.20	0.19	0.16	0.13
	8-in expanded slag, clay, or shale	0.17	0.17	0.14	0.12
	12-in sand and gravel or limestone	0.34	0.32	0.24	0.18
	12-in cinder	0.20	0.19	0.15	0.13
	12-in expanded slag, clay, or shale	0.15	0.14	0.12	0.11

Watts Per Square Meter Per Degree Celsius

Basic Wall Construction[a]		Plain Wall No Plaster	Interior Finish		
			Wall Direct	12 mm Plaster on:	
				19 mm Furring With:	
				9 mm Plasterboard	12 mm Rigid Insulation
Concrete masonry (cores not filled)	200 mm sand & gravel or limestone	3.01	2.78	1.76	1.25
	200 mm cinder	2.10	1.99	1.42	1.08
	200 mm expanded slag, clay, or shale	1.87	1.82	1.31	1.02
	300 mm sand & gravel or limestone	2.78	2.56	1.70	1.25
	300 mm cinder	1.99	1.87	1.36	1.02
	300 mm expanded slag, clay, or shale	1.82	1.76	1.31	1.02
Concrete masonry (cores filled with insulation[b])	200 mm sand & gravel or limestone	2.21	2.10	1.48	1.08
	200 mm cinder	1.14	1.08	0.91	0.74
	200 mm expanded slag, clay, or shale	0.97	0.97	0.79	0.68
	300 mm sand & gravel or limestone	1.93	1.82	1.36	1.02
	300 mm cinder	1.14	1.08	0.85	0.74
	300 mm expanded slag, clay, or shale	0.85	0.79	0.68	0.62

[a] All concrete masonry shown in this table are hollow units. All concrete masonry wall surfaces exposed to the weather have two coats of portland cement base paint. Surfaces of all walls exposed to the weather subject to a wind velocity of 24.14 kilometers/hour.

[b] Values based on dry insulation. The use of vapor barriers or other precautions must be considered to keep insulation dry.

SOURCE: Besser Technical Center, from Table 2, Portland Cement Association. "Concrete Masonry Handbook for Architects, Engineers, and Builders," 1951.

Table 4-3
REDUCTION FACTORS IN SOUND TRANSMISSION THROUGH

Imperial Modular Units		
Walls of Hollow Concrete Masonry	**Weight Per Square Foot of Wall Area, lb**	**Average Reduction Factor, dB**
3 in cinder, $\frac{5}{8}$ in plaster on both sides[a]	32.2	45.1
4 in cinder, $\frac{5}{8}$ in plaster on both sides[a]	35.8	45.6
4 in cinder, 1 in plaster[b]	32.3	47.0
8 in expanded slag, 1 in plaster[b]	56.0	52.6
4 in Celocrete,[e] $\frac{1}{2}$ in plaster on both sides[c]	30.0	42.6
8 in Celocrete,[e] unplastered[c]	28.6	43.7
8 in Celocrete,[e] $\frac{1}{2}$ in plaster on both sides[c]	40.0	52.9
Cavity wall, two 4 in Celocrete,[e] $\frac{1}{2}$ in plaster on one inner face[c]	45.0	57.1
3 in Haydite,[e] unplastered[c]	—	36.0
3 in Haydite,[e] 1 in plaster[c]	—	42.0
4 in Haydite,[e] unplastered[c]	—	37.0
4 in Haydite,[e] 1 in plaster[c]	—	43.0
6 in Haydite,[e] unplastered[c]	—	44.8
6 in Haydite,[e] 1 in plaster[c]	—	48.5
8 in Haydite,[e] unplastered[c]	—	47.8
8 in Haydite,[e] 1 in plaster[c]	—	50.5
12 in Haydite,[e] unplastered[c]	—	52.0
12 in Haydite,[e] 1 in plaster[c]	—	54.0
4 in pumice, $\frac{1}{2}$ in plaster on both sides[d]	25.3	37.4
4 in pumice, $\frac{1}{2}$ in plaster on one side only	20.4	34.6
4 in Waylite,[e] $\frac{1}{2}$ in plaster on both sides[c]	31.0	50.0
8 in Waylite,[e] $\frac{1}{2}$ in plaster on both sides[c]	47.0	53.0
3 in Waylite,[e] 2 coats cement paint each side[c]	16.75	44.1
4 in Waylite,[e] unpainted[c]	16.5	33.2
4 in Waylite,[e] 2 coats cement paint each side[c]	16.5	46.7
6 in Waylite,[e] unpainted[c]	21.0	39.7
6 in Waylite,[e] 2 coats cement paint each side[c]	21.0	52.2
Cavity wall, two 3 in Waylite,[e] $\frac{3}{8}$ in plaster on one exposed face[c]	17.0	56.1

[a] National Bureau of Standards Report BMS 17.
[b] Data reported in *Acoustics and Architecture* by Paul E. Sabine.
[c] Tests conducted at Riverbank Laboratories.
[d] National Bureau of Standards Supplement to Report BMS 17.
[e] Celocrete and Waylite are expanded blast furnace slags, Haydite is expanded shale.
SOURCE: Besser Technical Centre, from Table 5, Portland Cement Association, "Concrete Masonry Handbook for Architects, Engineers, and Builders," 1951.

wall. It may be seen from Table 4-2 how the insulating value of concrete block walls can be affected by the type of construction, kind of wall finish, type of aggregate used, use of insulating fill in core blocks, and the use of air spaces. (See also Chap. 13.)

A great deal of attention is being paid in recent years to the reduction of noise in buildings, and studies have been and are being conducted to determine the sound-absorbing qualities of various building materials. Results have shown that concrete blocks with open surface texture tend to absorb sound more readily than smooth-faced ones and that paint applied to block walls tends to reduce the sound-control values, with spray painting having less effect than brush painting.

WALLS OF HOLLOW CONCRETE MASONRY

Metric Equivalents of Imperial Modular Units

Walls of Hollow Concrete Masonry	Weight Per Square-Meter of Wall Area, kg	Average Reduction Factor, dB
75 mm cinder, 16 mm plaster on both sides[a]	157.2	45.1
100 mm cinder, 16 mm plaster on both sides[a]	174.8	45.6
100 mm cinder, 25 mm plaster[b]	157.7	47.0
200 mm expanded slag, 25 mm plaster[b]	273.4	52.6
100 mm Celocrete,[e] 12 mm plaster on both sides[c]	146.5	42.6
200 mm Celocrete,[e] unplastered[c]	139.6	43.7
200 mm Celocrete,[e] 12 mm plaster on both sides[c]	195.3	52.9
Cavity wall, two 100 mm Celocrete,[e] 12 mm plaster on one inner face[c]	219.7	57.1
75 mm Haydite,[e] unplastered[c]	—	36.0
75 mm Haydite,[e] 25 mm plaster[c]	—	42.0
100 mm Haydite,[e] unplastered[c]	—	37.0
100 mm Haydite,[e] 25 mm plaster[c]	—	43.0
150 mm Haydite,[e] unplastered[c]	—	44.8
150 mm Haydite,[e] 25 mm plaster[c]	—	48.5
200 mm Haydite,[e] unplastered[c]	—	47.8
200 mm Haydite,[e] 25 mm plaster[c]	—	50.5
300 mm Haydite,[e] unplastered[c]	—	52.0
300 mm Haydite,[e] 25 mm plaster[c]	—	54.0
100 mm pumice, 12 mm plaster on both sides[d]	123.5	37.4
100 mm pumice, 12 mm plaster on one side only	99.6	34.6
100 mm Waylite,[e] 12 mm plaster on both sides[c]	151.3	50.0
200 mm Waylite,[e] 12 mm plaster on both sides[c]	229.5	53.0
75 mm Waylite,[e] 2 coats cement paint each side[c]	81.8	44.1
100 mm Waylite,[e] unpainted[c]	80.6	33.2
100 mm Waylite,[e] 2 coats cement paint each side[c]	80.6	46.7
150 mm Waylite,[e] unpainted[c]	102.5	39.7
150 mm Waylite,[e] 2 coats cement paint each side[c]	102.5	52.2
Cavity wall, two 75 mm Waylite,[e] 9 mm plaster on one unexposed face[c]	83.0	56.1

The ability of walls to resist the transmission of sound is important. Hollow blocks made with light-weight aggregate have very good sound-reduction factors, in most cases. Table 4-3 gives the reduction factors in sound transmission through various types of lightweight, hollow concrete blocks. Table 4-4 shows the relation between sound transmission loss through a wall and the hearing conditions on the quiet side. Chapter 14 provides further information on acoustical materials.

In order to qualify as a useful construction material, the product in question must have a reasonable ability to resist the passage of fire. Materials are tested and given a *fire-resistance rating*. Table 4-5 indicates the fire-resistance rating of concrete block made with various types of aggregate.

Table 4-4

RELATION BETWEEN SOUND TRANSMISSION LOSS THROUGH A WALL AND HEARING CONDITIONS ON QUIET SIDE[a]

Transmission Loss, dB	Hearing Condition	Rating
30 or less	Normal speech can be understood quite easily and distinctly through the wall.	Poor
30 to 35	Loud speech can be understood fairly well. Normal speech can be heard but not easily understood.	Fair
35 to 40	Loud speech can be heard but it is not easily intelligible. Normal speech can be heard only faintly, if at all.	Good
40 to 45	Loud speech can be faintly heard but not understood. Normal speech is inaudible.	Very good, recommended for dividing walls between apartments.
45 or more	Very loud sounds such as loud singing, brass musical instruments, or a radio at full volume can be heard only faintly or not at all.	Excellent, recommended for band rooms, music practice rooms, radio and sound studios.

[a] This table is based on the assumption that a noise corresponding to 30 dB is continuously present on the listening side and that noises passing through the wall are audible despite this noise level. A decibel is roughly equivalent to the smallest change in sound energy that the average ear can detect, and 30 dB corresponds approximately to the average background noise in a quiet apartment.
SOURCE: Portland Cement Association.

BLOCK USES

Wall and Partition Blocks

These are the units used to build the bearing and nonbearing walls and partitions in concrete block construction. They may be laid up with either *face-shell* or *full mortar bedding*. (See Fig. 4-6.) For most concrete masonry work with hollow units, it is common practice to use only face-shell bedding. Full mortar bedding is used to lay the first course of blocks on a footing or foundation wall and to lay solid units and concrete brick. It is used for columns, piers, or pilasters built of blocks which are to carry heavy loads and for blocks whose cores are to be grouted.

Wall blocks include a number of shapes with special uses in wall construction. One of them is an *L-corner* block, used in one method of laying block at a corner. (See Fig. 4-7.) Another is a *bullnose* block, which is used to produce rounded corners to help eliminate chipping. *Sill* blocks may be used to form a *sill* or bottom ledge for a window opening

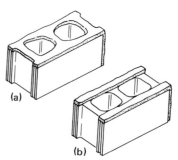

Fig. 4-6 *(a)* Full mortar bedding, *(b)* face-shell mortar bedding.

140

Table 4-5

CONCRETE MASONRY ESTIMATED FIRE-RESISTANCE RATING

Imperial Modular Units

Aggregate Type	Minimum Equivalent Thickness, Inches For Rating Of			
	1 h	2 h	3 h	4 h
Pumice	1.8	3.0	4.0	4.7
Expanded slag	2.2	3.3	4.2	5.0
Expanded shale or clay	2.5	3.7	4.7	5.5
Limestone, scoria, cinders, or unexpanded slag	2.7	4.0	5.0	5.9
Calcareous gravel	2.8	4.2	5.3	6.2
Siliceous gravel	3.0	4.5	5.7	6.7

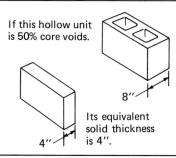

If this hollow unit is 50% core voids.

8"

Its equivalent solid thickness is 4".

4"

Equivalent thickness is the solid thickness that would be obtained if the same amount of concrete contained in a hollow unit were re-cast without core holes.

Calculating Estimated Fire Resistance. Example:
An 8" hollow masonry wall is constructed of expanded slag units reported to be 55%* solid. What is the estimated fire resistance of the wall? (modular units)

Eq Th = 0.55 x 7.625 in = 4.19 inches. From table: 3 h fire resistance requires 4.20 inches. Use minus 3 h est. resistance.

Metric Equivalents of Imperial Modular Units

Aggregate Type	Minimum Equivalent Thickness, Millimeters For Rating Of			
	1 h	2 h	3 h	4 h
Pumice	45.72	76.20	101.60	119.38
Expanded slag	55.88	83.82	106.68	127.00
Expanded shale or clay	63.50	93.98	119.38	139.70
Limestone, scoria, cinders, or unexpanded slag	68.58	101.60	127.00	149.86
Calcareous gravel	71.12	106.68	134.62	157.48
Siliceous gravel	76.20	114.30	114.78	170.18

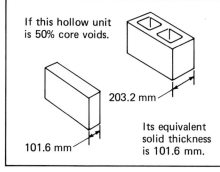

If this hollow unit is 50% core voids.

203.2 mm

Its equivalent solid thickness is 101.6 mm.

101.6 mm

Equivalent thickness is the solid thickness that would be obtained if the same amount of concrete contained in a hollow unit were re-cast without core holes.

Calculating Estimated Fire Resistance. Example:
A 203.2 mm hollow masonry wall is constructed of expanded slag units reported to be 55%* solid. What is the estimated fire resistance of the wall? (modular units)

Eq Th = 0.55 x 193.68 mm = 106.43 mm. From table: 3 h fire resistance requires 106.68 mm. Use minus 3 h est. resistance.

From National Concrete Masonry Association, TEK Report No. 6, "Estimating the Fire Resistance of Concrete Masonry," 1966.

*Percentage solid can be calculated from net area or net volume values as determined by ASTM C 140 "Methods of Testing Concrete Masonry Units."

Source: Besser Technical Centre

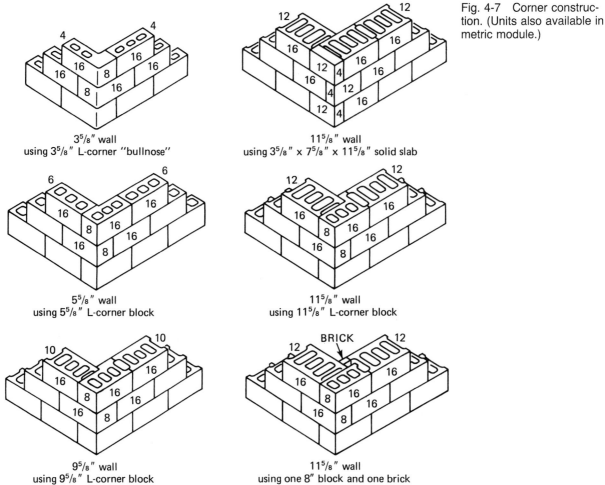

3⁵/₈" wall
using 3⁵/₈" L-corner "bullnose"

11⁵/₈" wall
using 3⁵/₈" x 7⁵/₈" x 11⁵/₈" solid slab

5⁵/₈" wall
using 5⁵/₈" L-corner block

11⁵/₈" wall
using 11⁵/₈" L-corner block

9⁵/₈" wall
using 9⁵/₈" L-corner block

11⁵/₈" wall
using one 8" block and one brick

in a block wall, while *coping* blocks *cap* a wall and shed water from it to the roof, as illustrated in Fig. 4-8.

In order to eliminate cracking of block walls, which may result from stresses in them, *control joints* are introduced into the walls at specified intervals to absorb movement, relieve stresses, and so prevent cracking. Figure 4-9 illustrates two typ-

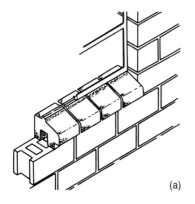

(a)

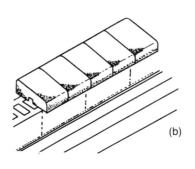

(b)

Fig. 4-8 (a) Sill blocks, (b) coping blocks.

142

ical control joints in block walls, one in a plain wall and one at a window opening.

Bond-Beam Blocks

One method of strengthening block walls is by the use of *bond beams*, continuous concrete beams around the perimeter of a wall at designated levels. They are formed by laying a course of bond-beam blocks on the wall, introducing reinforcing bar into the cavity, and filling it with concrete or grout. (See Fig. 4-10.) There are two types of bond-beam block in use: the *low-web* block and the *channel* block.

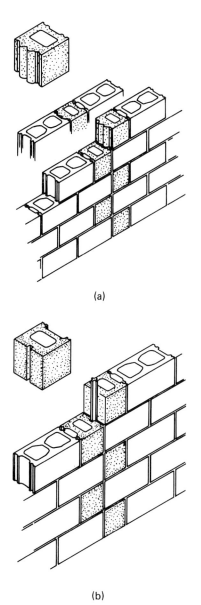

(a)

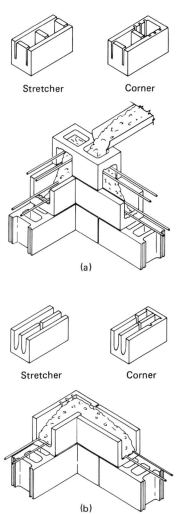

(b)

Fig. 4-9 Control joints. *(a)* Controls volume change of wall. Placed at specific intervals, this block relieves stresses in wall. *(b)* A steel sash masonry unit is used in conjunction with a cross-shaped rubber extrusion, to produce an easily installed control joint. *(Besser Co.)*

Stretcher   Corner

(a)

Stretcher   Corner

(b)

Fig. 4-10 Forming bond beams. *(a)* Closed bottom and grooves for rebar permit construction of a continuous reinforced concrete beam, 8 or 16 in (200 or 400 mm) deep around entire building. Can be tied in with vertical column for exceptionally strong walls. *(b)* Closed bottom with longitudinal center rib. Courses of this style keep wall from cracking due to volume changes. Bond beams can be used above or below window openings, can serve as lintels, and can support loads in flexure. Therefore, the name, bond-beam block.

Pilaster Blocks

Good construction practices require that long, load-bearing block walls be stabilized, and this may be done by the introduction of pilaster blocks into the walls at specified intervals. These blocks may be used with or without a reinforced-concrete core. In addition to providing greater lateral strength to a wall, pilaster blocks also provide a greater bearing area for beams and girders carried on the wall. Some pilaster blocks are made in identical halves for easier handling, for ease in placing around preinstalled *rebar*, or for use as control-joint blocks. Figure 4-11 shows two types of pilaster block being used: the flush wall pilaster and the full pilaster.

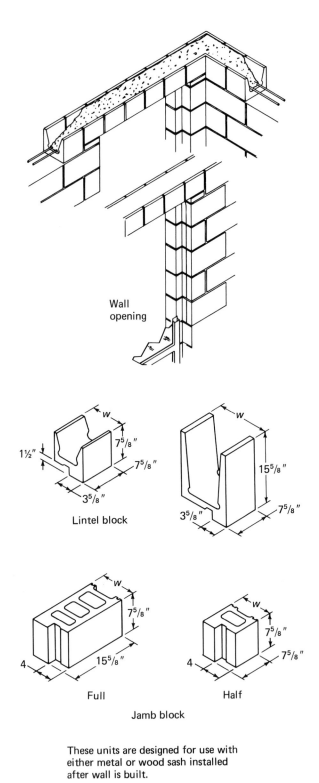

Wall opening

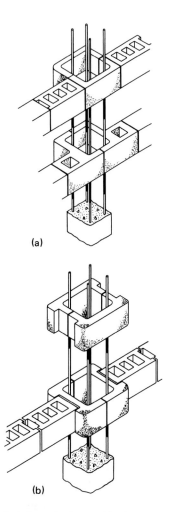

(a)

(b)

Fig. 4-11   Reinforced pilaster block.

Lintel block

Full   Half

Jamb block

These units are designed for use with either metal or wood sash installed after wall is built.

Fig. 4-12   Lintel and jamb blocks.   *(Besser Co.)*

144

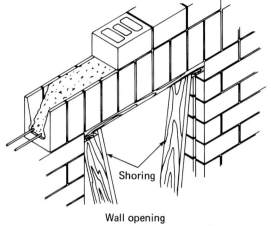

Shoring

Wall opening

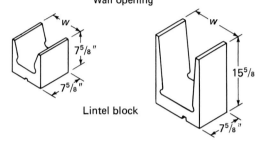

Lintel block

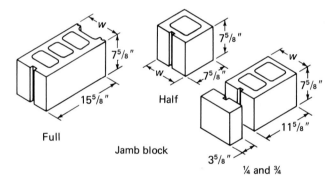

Full

Half

Jamb block

¼ and ¾

These units are intended for openings with metal sash only. Windows must be installed as the wall is erected.

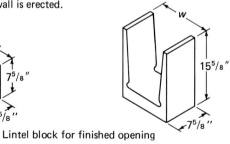
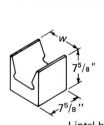

Lintel block for finished opening

Where no windows or doors are used, these units produce finished masonry opening.

Fig. 4-12 (continued)

Lintel Blocks

Lintel blocks may be used for two purposes. The main purpose is to form a reinforced support (lintel) over openings in block walls. (See Fig. 4-12.) Various styles and sizes are made, the choice depending on the span and the load above the opening. Lintel blocks may also be used to form bond beams. *Precast* lintels and sills are available for use over and under openings in concrete block construction.

Jamb or Sash Blocks

This type of block (see Fig. 4-12) is intended to be used to form the sides of openings in block walls. It is made in two *styles,* the choice depending on whether wood or metal sash is to be used in the opening, and in four standard *lengths.*

Acoustical Blocks

Additional noise control and acoustical correction may be obtained by the use of concrete blocks designed specifically for that purpose. (See Fig. 4-13). They derive their good sound-absorption qualities from a patented *cavity-slot* construction. The cavities are closed at the top, and the slots allow the closed cavities to act as damped resonators. They are made in standard modular dimensions, in three types, as indicated in Fig. 4-13. Types B and BB have incombustible fibrous fill in the cavities. *Sound blocks,* as they are called, have their maximum sound absorption at low frequencies, with peak absorption at under 100 Hz. They are useful in many situations, such as industrial plants,

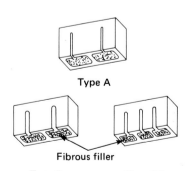

Type A

Fibrous filler

Type B   Type BB

Fig. 4-13 Acoustical block. *(Edcon Block Co.)*

Table 4-6
SOUND-ABSORPTION COEFFICIENTS OF SOUND BLOCKS

Size, mm	Type	Surface	Cavities/ Slots	Frequency, Hz						NRC Range
				125	250	500	1000	2000	4000	
100	A-1	Unpainted	2/2	0.19	0.83	0.41	0.38	0.42	0.40	0.45–0.55
150	A-1	Painted	2/2	0.62	0.84	0.36	0.43	0.27	0.50	0.45–0.55
200	A-1	Painted	2/2	0.97	0.44	0.38	0.39	0.50	0.60	0.40–0.50
100	B	Painted	2/2	0.20	0.95	0.85	0.49	0.53	0.50	0.65–0.75
150	B	Painted	2/2	0.31	0.97	0.56	0.47	0.51	0.53	0.60–0.70
200	B	Painted	2/2	0.74	0.57	0.45	0.35	0.36	0.34	0.40–0.50
200	BB	Painted	3/3	0.60	0.72	0.56	0.48	0.46	0.47	0.50–0.60

NOTE: The sound-absorption values shown in the table above were determined in accordance with ASTM methods by the acoustical laboratories of Geiger & Hamme, Inc., Ann Arbor, Mich.
SOURCE: Edcon Block.

gymnasiums, natatoriums, mechanical equipment rooms, fan rooms, etc. Table 4-6 indicates the sound-transmission-loss characteristics of this type of block.

A very effective sound-absorptive treatment for walls has been developed by using the type of construction illustrated in Fig. 4-14. The sound-absorption values resulting from this method of construction are indicated in Table 4-7.

For further information on acoustical materials, see Chap. 14.

Decorative Blocks

Standard blocks may be laid in such a way as to produce a decorative surface, as illustrated in Fig. 4-15. To further enhance the aesthetics of exposed concrete block, patterns are designed into the exposed face. Figure 4-16 illustrates a number of these decorative blocks that are available. Standard blocks may also be covered with a metal or plastic cap (Fig. 4-17) to produce a surface that is easily cleaned. Another variation, to produce a rough

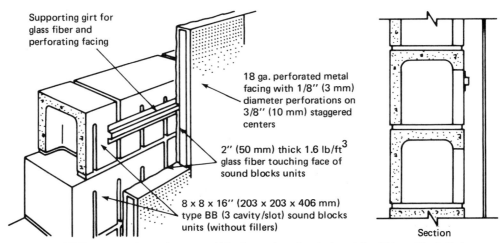

Fig. 4-14   Wall construction using sound blocks and perforated metal.   *(Edcon Block Co.)*

Supporting girt for glass fiber and perforating facing

18 ga. perforated metal facing with 1/8″ (3 mm) diameter perforations on 3/8″ (10 mm) staggered centers

2″ (50 mm) thick 1.6 lb/ft^3 glass fiber touching face of sound blocks units

8 x 8 x 16″ (203 x 203 x 406 mm) type BB (3 cavity/slot) sound blocks units (without fillers)

Section

Table 4-7
SOUND-ABSORPTION COEFFICIENTS OF WALL INDICATED IN FIG. 4-14

125 Hz	250 Hz	500 Hz	1000 Hz	2000 Hz	4000 Hz	NRC Range
0.80	0.97	1.02	0.90	0.77	0.71	85–95

NOTE: The sound-absorption values shown in the table above were determined in accordance with ASTM Designation C423-66 by Geiger and Hamme Acoustical Laboratories for the system shown in Fig. 4-14.

rocklike finish, is the split block. (See Fig. 4-18.) These blocks are made to be split in two, using the rough face exposed to produce an effective finish. The added benefit of many of these units is that not only are they attractive but they can be incorporated into the structure as load-carrying structural members.

Pierced blocks may be used for a special purpose: to make a *pierced* wall, which acts as a sunscreen. They may also be used for garden walls and fences. (See Fig. 4-19.)

Glazed face block is another type of decorative block which has one or both faces glazed with a compound containing at least 75 percent graded silica sand, with added color pigment, which is cast onto the base block by an external heat-polymerization process. The glazing material is returned around the ends of the block, as shown in Fig. 4-20, resulting in the use of a 6-mm mortar joint in modular coursing. The finish is available on a wide variety of block shapes, a few of which are illustrated in Fig. 4-20, and in numerous standard colors.

These blocks are useful not only from a decorative standpoint. Since the glazed face has high impact resistance, good ductility, good abrasion resistance, and high resistance to most chemicals and

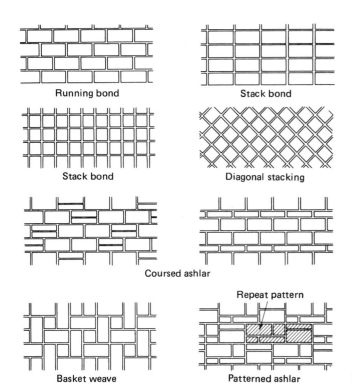

Running bond

Stack bond

Stack bond

Diagonal stacking

Coursed ashlar

Repeat pattern

Basket weave

Patterned ashlar

Fig. 4-15 Wall patterns with standard block.

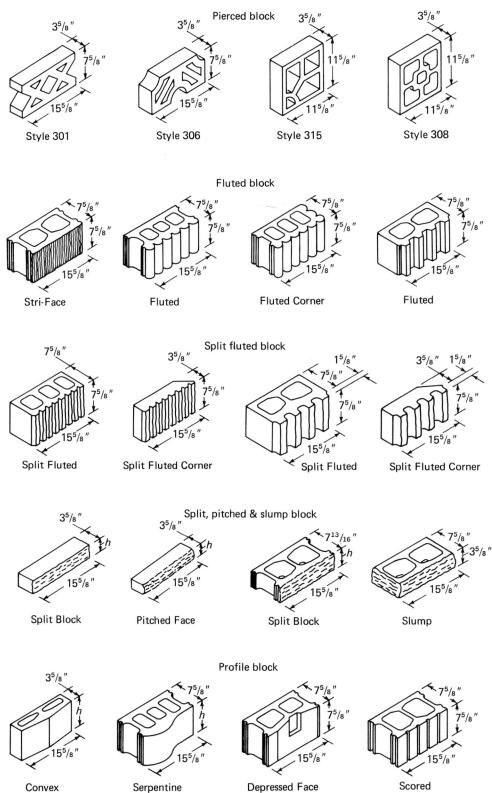

Fig. 4-16 Typical decorative block. (Available in metric dimensions.) *(Besser Co.)*

Fig. 4-17 Steel covers for concrete blocks.

Fig. 4-19 Garden wall using split block and pierced block. *(National Concrete Masonry Assoc.)*

Fig. 4-18 Split block surface.

to steam, they are useful in situations where a high degree of sanitation is a prime consideration. For this reason they are often used in dairies, meat-packing plants, washrooms, etc.

Floor Blocks

Floor blocks are made in various thicknesses for use in constructing light-, medium-, and heavy-duty concrete floors. Two kinds are made: *filler* type, for

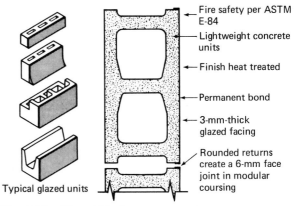

Typical glazed units

Fire safety per ASTM E-84

Lightweight concrete units

Finish heat treated

Permanent bond

3-mm-thick glazed facing

Rounded returns create a 6-mm face joint in modular coursing

Fig. 4-20 Glazed block. *(Edcon Block Co.)*

use in a *ribbed* floor, and *plank* type, used when a *flat* block deck is required. Figure 4-21 illustrates both types.

Standard lightweight blocks may be used to form a ribbed concrete floor, the method used to form the ribs illustrated in Fig. 4-22.

Chimney Blocks

Chimney blocks are intended as an alternative to brick or various types of steel chimneys. In addition to *regular* chimney blocks (see Fig. 4-23), *flue* blocks, to accommodate the furnace exhaust flue; *clean-out* blocks, to allow for the removal of soot from the bottom of the chimney; and *cap* blocks, to cover the cavities in the regular blocks and to provide a finished appearance to the chimney, are also available.

Utility Blocks

Utility blocks are made for such purposes as laying *sidewalks, paving* (both flat and slopes), providing *grass pavers* and *stepping stones,* and building

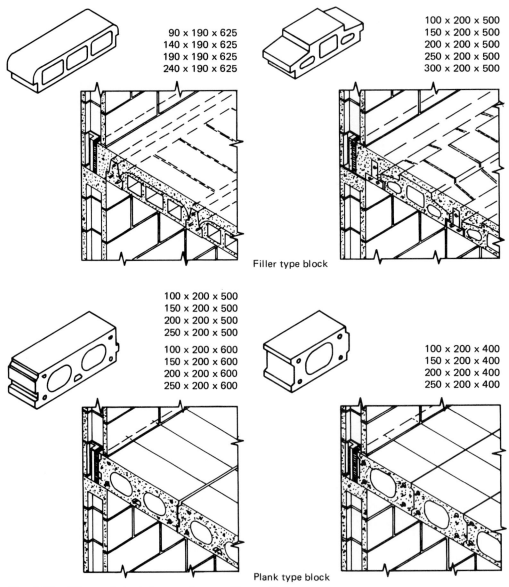

Fig. 4-21   Filler and plank floor systems.   *(Besser Co.)*

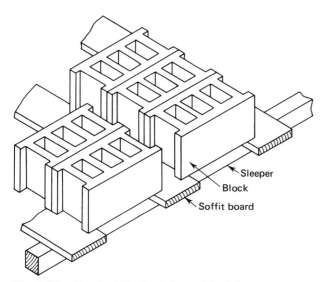

Fig. 4-22   Standard blocks to form ribbed floor.

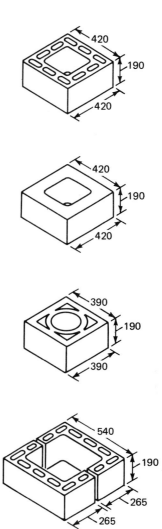

Fig. 4-23   Chimney block styles.

manholes and *septic tanks.* Figure 4-24 illustrates some typical utility blocks in common use.

Also illustrated in Fig. 4-24 is concrete drain tile, used in place of ceramic or plastic tile to drain the perimeter of foundations or in field drainage systems.

SYSTEMS BLOCK

One of the results of research by the construction industry into ways of increasing productivity has been the development of the *systems* block (see Fig. 4-25), with double tongue and groove, which allows all vertical joints to be laid dry, if desired. The horizontal joint mortar, either conventional cement mortar or epoxy mortar placed with a caulking gun, can be applied much more quickly. By using a staggered stack pattern of erection, the block can be laid with no mortar in either the vertical or horizontal joints. In such a system, the mortar is applied in a thin coat to the inside and outside surfaces of the wall.

BLOCK MORTARS

Conventional mortars for concrete block masonry are composed primarily of sand, water, portland cement, and lime. Each component contributes in producing the final properties of the mortar. The portland cement provides strength and durability; the lime content determines the workability and

elasticity, and provides additional water retention. Both cement and lime contribute to the bond strength of the mortar. The sand acts as a filler and contributes to the compressive strength of the mortar as well as reducing the shrinkage due to setting and drying. Sand adds body to the mortar, allowing it to retain its shape before curing is complete. Water is the mixing fluid and is necessary for the hydration of the cement.

As for all materials used in structural components, standards are available for masonry mortars to ensure consistency and strength. The American Society for Testing and Materials provides specifications for the proportioning of the materials that

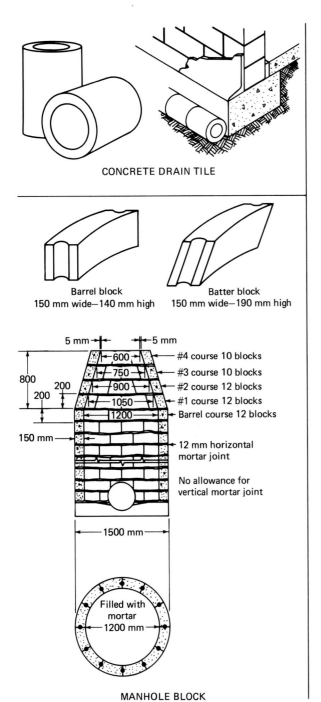

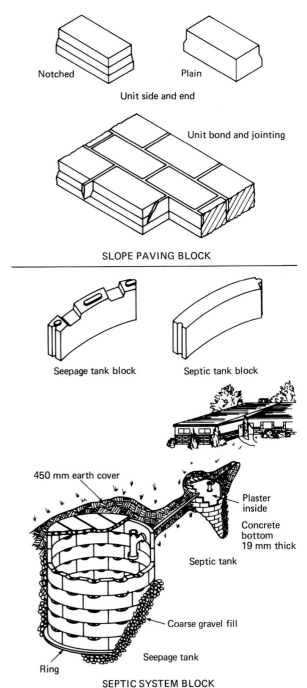

Fig. 4-24 Utility block. *(Besser Co.)*

are used in mortars. (See Table 4-8.) Each mortar type is used for specific construction applications based on its strength.

Type M mortar is a high-strength mortar and is used for structures below grade or in buildings where extreme forces due to lateral earth pressure, earthquakes, or high winds are expected. The average 28-day compressive strength of this mortar is 2500 psi (17 MPa). Type S mortar is used in structures requiring high bond strength in flexure. The

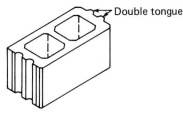

Fig. 4-25   Systems block.   *(Besser Co.)*

compressive strength of this mortar averages 1800 psi (12.5 MPa). Type N mortar can be used for general construction above grade. Average compressive strength is 750 psi (5.0 MPa). Type O mortar is used in non-load-bearing walls and in partitions. Average compressive strength is 350 psi (2.5 MPa). Type K mortar is a low-strength mortar used only where building codes allow its use in interior non-load-bearing partitions. It has an average compressive strength of only 75 psi (0.5 MPa).

A combination of portland cement and lime can be used to formulate all five types. Masonry cement can be used to formulate Types N and O, but portland cement must be added to the masonry cement in the case of Types M and S to achieve the high strengths. Which combination of materials is used depends on preference and availability.

Properties of mortars, especially in the plastic state, are based on field performance rather than on quantitative limits. Workability is the property of mortar that determines the rate at which the mason can work. Workable mortar must spread easily, adhere to the masonry, and squeeze out of the mortar joints. It must have sufficient strength to support the weight of the masonry and yet make alignment easy. Workability is dependent on the amount of water in the mix, because the water content affects the consistency.

Aggregates also affect the workability of the mortar. Well-graded aggregates—100 percent passing a No. 4 (5.0-mm) sieve, 95 to 100 percent passing a No. 8 (2.5-mm) sieve, 25 percent maximum passing a No. 100 (150-m) sieve, and 10 percent maximum passing a No. 200 (80-m) sieve—will provide a mortar that has good workability characteristics. Sand that is deficient in fines produces a harsh mix, while excess fines produce a weak mortar. Well-graded sand helps to prevent segregation, which in turn reduces bleeding. An air-entraining admixture can be added to help increase the workability, as will additional lime.

Water retentivity is the measure of the ability of the mortar to remain plastic while in contact with an absorbent unit. This allows the mason time to align the unit before the mortar stiffens. Water retentivity is improved by the addition of lime, air

Table 4-8
RECOMMENDED MORTAR MIXES

Specification	Mortar Type	Parts by Volume		
		Portland Cement	Masonry Cement	Hydrated Lime or Lime Putty
For plain masonry, ASTM C270 CSA A179-M	M	1 1	1 ——	—— $\frac{1}{4}$
	S	$\frac{1}{2}$ 1	1 ——	—— $\frac{1}{4}$–$\frac{1}{2}$
	N	—— 1	1 ——	—— $\frac{1}{2}$–$1\frac{1}{4}$
	O	—— 1	1 ——	—— $1\frac{1}{4}$–$2\frac{1}{2}$
	K	1	——	$2\frac{1}{2}$–4
For reinforced masonry, ASTM C476	PM PL	1 1	1 ——	—— $\frac{1}{4}$–$\frac{1}{2}$

entrainment, or the addition of fines within allowable limits.

Hardening of plastic mortar is the property which defines the resistance to deformation as the mortar sets. Consistency is the prime concern so as to allow the mason time to tool the joints to a uniform finish and color. Because of the specifications placed on portland cement during manufacture, the use of portland cement or masonry cement under normal temperatures provides ample time for the mason to complete the finishing of the mortar joints.

Properties of hardened mortar determine the performance of the finished product. Two properties of major concern are *compressive strength* and *bond strength.*

Compressive strength of mortar is rarely a problem. Bond strength, on the other hand, is the single most critical property and is quite dependent on the quality of the workmanship. "Bond" is defined as the ability of the hardened mortar to adhere to the masonry units without cracking and is low in value compared to the compressive strength as it depends on the tensile characteristics of the mortar. A mortar having a compressive strength of 2500 psi (17.5 MPa) will develop only 100 psi (0.7 MPa) in bond. Good workability will ensure that proper contact is established between the mortar and the units producing the best possible bond.

Mortar may lose water due to evaporation if not used immediately after mixing. Water may be re-added to improve the workability, provided that hardening of the mortar has not begun. For best results mortar should be placed within $2\frac{1}{2}$ h of mixing.

Durability is the ability of mortar to resist cycles of freezing and thawing. Types M, S, and air-entrained mortars are best suited for this type of application.

In some cases, conventional mortar is being replaced by a powerful adhesive known as *organic mortar.* This is usually an epoxy product, applied to masonry joints with a caulking gun in a thin layer approximately $\frac{1}{16}$ in (1.5 mm) thick. This means that block laid up with such a mortar system must be manufactured practically full nominal size in order to maintain modularity.

Surface Bonding

The technique of applying a thin coat of mortar to a block wall laid up without mortar in the joints is called *surface bonding.* The mortar may be a cement mortar which is reinforced with glass fibers and applied in a coat from $\frac{1}{16}$ to $\frac{1}{8}$ in (1.5 to 3 mm) thick. The surface coat on each side of the blocks bonds them together into a strong, composite structure and also serves as a protective, waterproof shield. Color pigment may be added to the surface-bonding mortar, eliminating the necessity for painting.

Surface-bonded walls are as strong in bending flexure as walls built with conventional mortar joints. They are less resistant to vertical compressive loads, however, unless the blocks have had their meeting surfaces ground.

Also available are bonding mortars which are factory-prepared products requiring only the addition of water to prepare them for use. Such mortars may be applied either by trowel or by spraying.

BLOCK PANELS

Another technique developed in the concrete block industry is that of assembling blocks into prefabricated panels which can then be installed as a single unit. (See Fig. 4-26.) The blocks may be laid in conventional mortar, laid in organic mortar, or surface-bonded, as described above.

There are two methods in use for the assembly of prefabricated block panels. One is a manual method, in which blocks may be assembled into a panel without any mortar, after which reinforcing steel is introduced into the cores and grouted. A variation of the manual method, involving the laying of the blocks in a panel with organic mortar, may be employed when the panel is to be used for a facing application.

The other method involves the use of a block-laying machine, which is located in a factory. The machine lays the blocks, inserts the joint reinforcement, makes the bed and head joints, and tools them. Walls up to 12 to 20 ft (3.6 to 6 m) may be assembled by this method much faster than could be done manually. Panels made by either method may be faced with brick or other facing material before erection.

Quality concrete masonry construction depends not only on high-quality masonry units but also on good design, good mortar, and good workmanship. Suggested specifications for handling and laying concrete blocks of all kinds are available from man-

Fig. 4-26 Prefabricated concrete block wall panel. *(International Masonry Institute)*

ufacturers' associations. Information on suitable mortars, good mortar bedding, and methods of making mortar joints is also available. In addition, literature covering patterns and bonds, control joints, block ties, waterproofing, and block cleaning may be obtained from the same sources.

GLOSSARY

bond beam	A beam that ties an upper and lower section of wall together giving them added stiffness.
cement-lime mortar	Mortar made with a proportion of slaked lime added to the cement.
control joint	A continuous horizontal or vertical joint between sections of a structure, built in to relieve stresses in the sections.
Imperial system	System of weights and measures based on inches, pounds, gallons, etc.
flue	An enclosed passage—pipe—to carry a current of air or gas.
heat polymerization	A change in molecular structure, taking place as a result of chemical action in the presence of heat.
Hz	Abbreviation for Hertz, the unit of measurement of the frequency of sound, represented by one cycle per second.
lintel	A beam over an opening in a wall.
masonry cement	A cement made specifically for mortar and containing a high percentage of finely ground, high-calcium limestone.
module	A small measurement, taken as a unit of measure for regulating proportions.

155

organic mortar	A powerful synthetic adhesive, made largely from epoxy resins, used in place of conventional cement mortar.
party wall	A wall which is common to two buildings.
pierced wall	A wall made from screen blocks, containing regular openings.
pilaster	A built-in column in a masonry wall, intended to stiffen the wall.
pumice	A variety of volcanic glass, full of minute cavities and very light.
scoria	Light slag or slaglike lava.
septic tank	A tank used for the collection and disintegration of domestic sewage, where a municipal sewage disposal system is not available.
SI	*Système International,* or International System of Units: the form of the metric system used by most industrial nations.
water retentivity	Ability of a mortar to retain the mixing water for hydration purposes.

REVIEW QUESTIONS

1. Outline ASTM specifications with regard to the following:

    a. Compressive strength of load-bearing concrete blocks.

    b. Allowable absorption rate of load-bearing blocks.

    c. Moisture content of blocks.

2. Describe the difference between face-shell and full-mortar bedding of blocks.

3. **a.** Explain why blocks with open surface texture have better sound-absorbing qualities than smooth-faced blocks.

    b. Why does paint applied to blocks tend to reduce their sound-control value?

4. **a.** Explain why good water retentivity of mortar used in laying blocks is important.

    b. Name two ways of improving the water retentivity of mortar.

5. **a.** What is the purpose of a bond beam in a block wall?

    b. Describe the method used to form a lintel over an opening in a block wall by the use of lintel blocks.

    c. What is the alternative to the use of lintel blocks?

6. **a.** What is the difference between a flush wall pilaster block and a full pilaster block?

    b. Give two reasons for using pilasters in a block wall.

7. Explain the significance of the development of the *systems* block.

8. Outline three advantages of using prefabricated concrete block panels in construction.

9. List four factors basic to the construction of a good-quality block wall.

SELECTED SOURCES OF INFORMATION

Besser Company, Alpena, Mich.
Canada Cement Co., Montreal, Que.
Consolidated Concrete, Limited, Calgary, Alta.
Edcon Block Co., Edmonton, Alta.
Expanded Shale, Clay and Slate Institute, Washington, D.C.
International Masonry Institute, Washington, D.C.
National Concrete Masonry Association, Washington, D.C.
Portland Cement Association, Chicago, Ill.

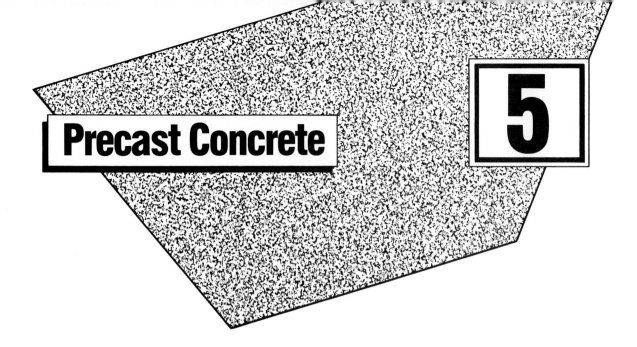

Precast Concrete

5

The concept of building with concrete structural members which have been cast and cured in a factory, rather than in place on the site, has found general acceptance and grown into a widespread industry. These prefabricated, reinforced units go under the general heading of *precast concrete,* and the rapid growth in the use of this system is one of the important developments in the construction industry. While originally the system was involved with the *structural* members of a building, a further step has been the development of *architectural precast concrete,* in which the members are not only designed for structural purposes and precast, but are designed and made for architectural purposes as well. In many cases, the same member which is carrying a building load is also providing the exterior finish for the building.

ADVANTAGES OF PRECAST

The system has gained popularity for a number of reasons:

1.   Casting and curing conditions, as well as concrete design, can be rigidly controlled, resulting in consistently high-quality concrete.

2.   Close supervision and control of materials and a specialized work force in a centralized plant also help to produce a high-quality product.

3.   Finishing work on concrete surfaces can be done more easily and efficiently in a plant than in position on the site.

4.   The cost of form work is reduced, since it can be set up on the ground rather than being suspended or supported in position.

5.   Where mass production of a unit is possible, forms can be made very precisely of wood, steel, or plastic, to ensure long life and, where necessary, very smooth surfaces.

6.   Structural members can be mass produced in a plant while excavations and foundation work are taking place at the site. Precast concrete members are then delivered as called for in work schedules and, in most cases, erected directly from truck bed to the structure without rehandling at the site.

7.   Because of superior reinforcing techniques, the load-carrying ability of a member may be increased while at the same time reducing its dead load by reducing the amount of concrete required.

8.   Plant production is not normally subject to delays due to adverse weather conditions, as are job site operations.

STRUCTURAL PRECAST

Precast structural members fall into two general classifications: *normally reinforced* and *prestressed.*

157

Fig. 5-1 Normally rein-
forced precast wall section.
(Portland Cement Association)

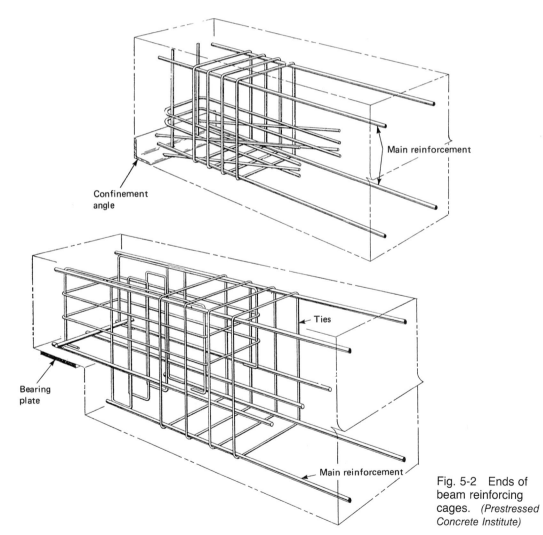

Confinement
angle

Main reinforcement

Bearing
plate

Ties

Main reinforcement

Fig. 5-2 Ends of
beam reinforcing
cages. *(Prestressed
Concrete Institute)*

158

Prestressed units are again divided into two groups: those which are *pretensioned* and those which are *posttensioned.*

Structural units which are normally precast include *floor* and *roof slabs, columns, girders, beams, joists, wall panels, bearing piles,* and *stairs.*

Normally Reinforced Precast

Normally reinforced precast units are those in which at least a major part of the reinforcement is placed in much the same form as it might be in a cast-in-place concrete member. Such units may be divided into two classes. One group includes the type of wall panel which is cast on a flat surface on the job site and raised into position in what is known as *tilt-up* construction. (See Fig. 5-1.)

The other group includes units which, because of their size or the fact that they may be few in number, cannot be economically prestressed, or, because of the way in which they will be loaded, do not require prestressing. Very large or unique girders and beams and many columns fall into this category.

Normally reinforced precast units are designed according to accepted reinforced concrete practice, the main difference being that the reinforcing may be made up as a unit, often called a *cage,* and placed in position in the completed form. (See Fig. 5-2.) In addition, the member will have the benefit of carefully designed and placed high-strength concrete, and a number of units may subsequently be tied together by posttensioning. (See Fig. 5-3.)

In the case of columns, the reinforcing may include provision for a bracket or *corbel,* which will support the end of a beam, or it may include provision for the insertion of the end of a structural steel member. (See Fig. 5-4.)

Prestressed Precast Concrete

A prestressed concrete unit is one into which engineered stresses have been introduced *before* it has been subjected to a load. This is done by introducing cables—*strands*—made of high-tensile steel wire into the unit, either *before* or *after* the concrete has been placed, and stressing them with powerful hydraulic jacks.

PRETENSIONED PRECAST The pretensioning technique is usually employed where mass production of a particular shape is feasible, frequently because standard shapes and sizes for such items have

Fig. 5-3   Posttensioned spandral beams.   *(Prestressed Concrete Institute)*

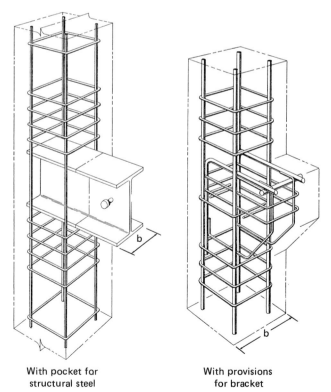

With pocket for
structural steel

With provisions
for bracket

Fig. 5-4   Reinforcing cages for precast concrete columns.   *(Prestressed Concrete Institute)*

been established. This means that the same *bed* and *form* and the same *stressing facilities* may be reused many times.

The form is built between two end *abutments,* made of a heavy steel framework or reinforced concrete, which are built into each end of the casting bed. The high-tensile steel-reinforcing strands are stretched through the form, anchored at one end to the *dead-end* abutment, and passed through the live-end abutment to the stressing equipment installed behind it. A predetermined stress is applied to each strand and a clamp is applied which bears on the outside face of the live-end abutment, so that the stress is maintained on the strand after the jack has been removed.

Concrete is then placed in the form, encasing the stressed strands, as illustrated in Fig. 5-5. As the concrete sets, it bonds to the stressed steel, and when it has reached a specified strength, the ends of the stressed strands are released and the stress is transferred to the concrete through the bond between concrete and steel. The action of the highly stressed strands produces a high compressive stress in the lower portion of the member and a tensile stress in the upper portion. It also pro-

Fig. 5-5   Placing concrete for a pretensioned member. *(Portland Cement Association)*

Fig. 5-6   Camber in pretensioned roof slabs.   *(Portland Cement Association)*

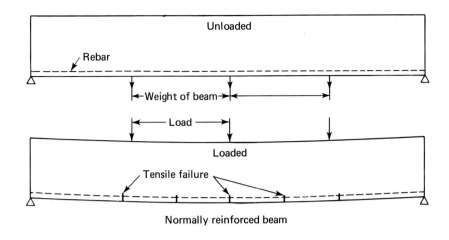

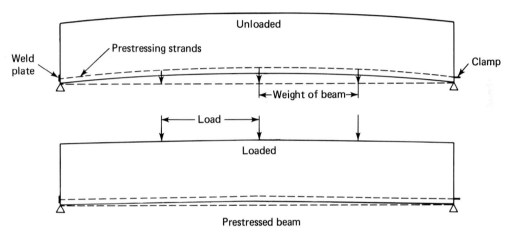

Fig. 5-7 Normally reinforced versus prestressed beam.

duces a slight arch or *camber* in the member, as may be seen in the units shown in Fig. 5-6. The difference between a normally reinforced concrete beam and a pretensioned one, *unloaded* and *under load,* is illustrated in Fig. 5-7.

Members which are relatively small in cross-section or which can readily be mass produced are normally pretensioned. They include *double T, single T, hollow-core,* and *flat* slabs; *rectangular, L-shaped,* and *inverted T* beams; *AASHO girders;* and *prestressed columns* and *bearing piles.* (See Fig. 5-8.)

Double T slabs are made in widths of 8 and 10 ft (2.44 and 3.04 m) in depths of 14 to 32 in (350 to 800 mm) and in lengths (*spans*) up to 100 ft (30.5 m). The flange thickness is normally 2 in (50

mm), but the widths of webs vary, depending on the width of the member. Double T's are intended primarily as floor and roof slabs and may rest on top of a wall or beam, as shown in Fig. 5-9, or the ends may be carried by an inverted T, or *ledger* beam, as shown in Fig. 5-10. In the first case, the slabs are anchored by welding, between a plate cast into the bottom of the web and one in the top of the wall or beam. In the second case, they are anchored by weld plates between slabs and beam.

Single T slabs are made in widths of 8, 10, and 12 ft (2.44, 3.04, and 3.66 m), in depths of 24 to 48 in (600 to 1200 mm), and in spans which reach up to 125 ft (38 m). The tapered flange has an edge depth of $1\frac{1}{2}$ (38 mm) and the web a standard width of 8 in (200 mm).

161

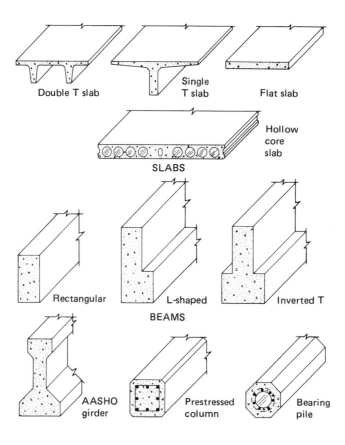

Fig. 5-8 Standard pre-stressed structural shapes.

Double T slab

Single T slab

Flat slab

Hollow core slab

SLABS

Rectangular

L-shaped

Inverted T

BEAMS

AASHO girder

Prestressed column

Bearing pile

Fig. 5-9 Double T roof slabs resting on wall. *(Prestressed Concrete Institute)*

162

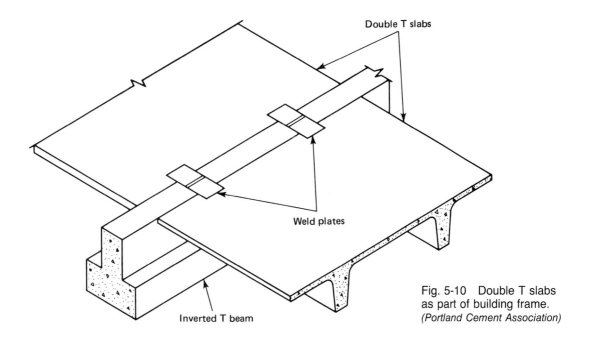

Fig. 5-10 Double T slabs as part of building frame. *(Portland Cement Association)*

Double T slabs

Weld plates

Inverted T beam

Single T's are used as floor and roof slabs, but also as framing members, as indicated in Fig. 5-11. There the spaces between the slabs are filled with cast-in-place concrete to form the decks. Slabs are normally supported on column corbels (See Fig. 5-11), on pilasters fixed to the inside of bearing walls, by resting on top of the wall, or by having the end of the web project into a pocket on a bearing wall, as illustrated in Fig. 5-12.

Hollow-core slabs vary in core design, depending on the manufacturer, and are available in a range of widths from 16 in to 8 ft (406 mm to 2.44 m). Depths range from 4 to 12 in (100 to 300 mm). The span is based on a span-to-depth ratio, and the recommended maximum ratio for roof slabs is *50,* while for floors *40* is the recommended maximum ratio. Such slabs will usually be supported by a wall

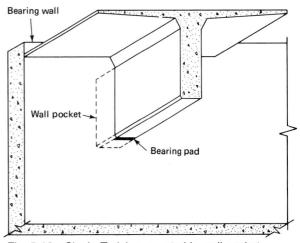

Fig. 5-11 Single T slabs as part of building frame. *(Portland Cement Association)*

Fig. 5-12 Single T slab supported in wall pocket.

Bearing wall

Wall pocket

Bearing pad

163

or by a ledger beam, with anchorage being provided by weld plates.

Flat slabs are normally 4 ft (1200 mm) wide, are 4 in (100 mm) thick, and are produced in spans of 12 to 19 ft (3.65 to 5.79 m). They are used mainly for roof slabs where short spans are required.

Rectangular, L-shaped, and *inverted T beams* are all available in lengths of 16 to 50 ft (4.875 to 12.25 m). Rectangular beams are made in depths of 16 to 40 in (400 to 1000 mm) and in widths of 12 to 16 in (300 to 400 mm). Depths of L-shaped beams range from 20 to 60 in (500 to 1500 mm), with a bottom width of 18 in (450 mm) and a top width of 12 in (300 mm). Similarly, depths of inverted T beams range from 20 to 60 in (500 to 1500 mm), with a bottom width of 24 in (600 mm) and a top width of 12 in (300 mm).

AASHO girders are made in three depths: 36 in (900 mm), 45 in (1125 mm), and 54 in (1350 mm), with corresponding thickness dimensions. Spans range from 30 to 64 ft (9.14 to 19.5 m).

Prestressed columns are made with two strengths of concrete: 5000 and 6000 psi (34.5 and 41.4 MPa). Also, by using three different prestressing strand arrangements, namely, four strands of $\frac{7}{16}$-in (11-mm), four strands of $\frac{1}{2}$-in (13-mm), or eight strands of $\frac{1}{2}$-in (13-mm), columns of varying strengths are produced. All these arrangements are found in all the standard column sizes, which range from 10 × 10 in (250 × 250 mm) to 24 × 24 in (600 × 600 mm), in increments of 2 in (50 mm), resulting in a wide range of design-load capabilities.

Prestressed concrete bearing piles are made in four concrete strengths—5000, 6000, 7000, and 8000 psi (34.5, 41.4, 48.25, and 55.2 MPa)—and in three shapes—square, octagonal, and round. The square and octagonal piles may be solid or hollow and are available in sizes of 10 × 10 in (250 × 250 mm) to 24 × 24 in (600 × 600 mm). Round piles are hollow, with outside diameters of 36, 48, and 54 in (900, 1200, and 1350 mm) and core diameters of 26, 38, and 44 in (650, 950, and 1100 mm), respectively. Piles can be ordered in lengths desired.

CONNECTIONS   The design of the connections for precast concrete units plays an important part in the overall effectiveness of the system. Over the years, field experience, laboratory tests, and structural analysis have resulted in the establishment of a number of basic connection systems: *welding, bolting, pinning* or *doweling, grouting,* and *post-tensioning.* (See Fig. 5-13.) Nearly all connections are adaptations of one of these systems, and every precast concrete structural member is produced with a predetermined, built-in method of connecting it to other members. Members are also provided with bearing plates, where necessary, to provide for the even distribution of load from one to the other.

Figure 5-14 illustrates one typical connection for each of the basic connection situations, namely, *column-to-foundation, beam-to-column, column-to-column, slab-to-beam,* and *slab-to-wall.*

For complete information on *dimensions, allowable loads, section properties, cambers, deflections,* and *connections* for all the prestressed structural members mentioned above, consult the *PCI Design Handbook,* published by the Prestressed Concrete Institute.

POSTTENSIONED PRECAST   Posttensioning is a method used to apply prestressing to concrete after it has hardened. Its greatest use is with cast-in-place construction, such as concrete floors or bearing walls, but it is also used in precast members, either as a means of prestressing an individual member or as a means of providing continuity connections for two or more members.

Posttensioning of precast concrete members involves placing and curing a precast member which contains normal reinforcement (see Fig. 5-2) and, in addition, a number of channels through which poststressing *strands* or *bars* may be passed. (See Fig. 5-15.) The channels are generally formed by suspending inflated tubes through the form and casting around them. When the concrete has set, they are deflated and removed.

After the concrete has reached a specified strength, the posttensioning *tendons* are inserted into the channels and anchored at one end. They are then stressed from the opposite end by a portable hydraulic jack (see Fig. 5-16) and anchored by one of several automatic gripping devices.

If members are posttensioned individually, this is normally done at the plant. If two or more members are to be positioned together, the operation must be carried out after they have been erected.

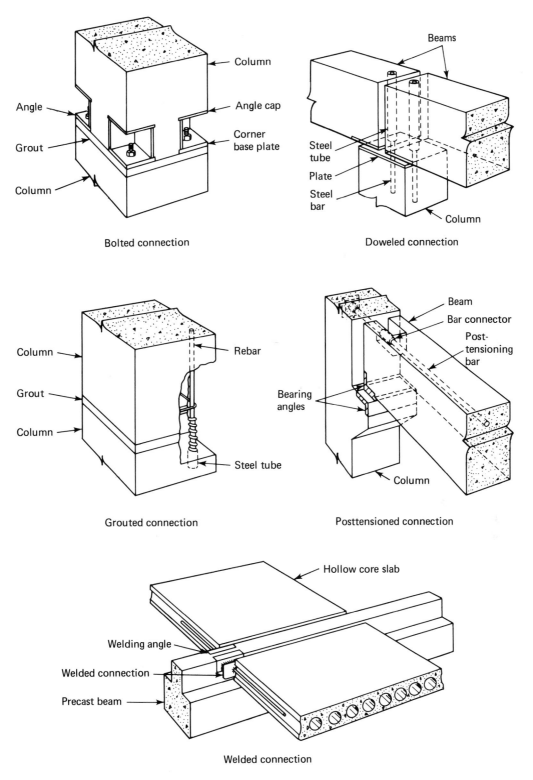

Bolted connection

Doweled connection

Grouted connection

Posttensioned connection

Welded connection

Fig. 5-13   Basic connection systems for precast.

165

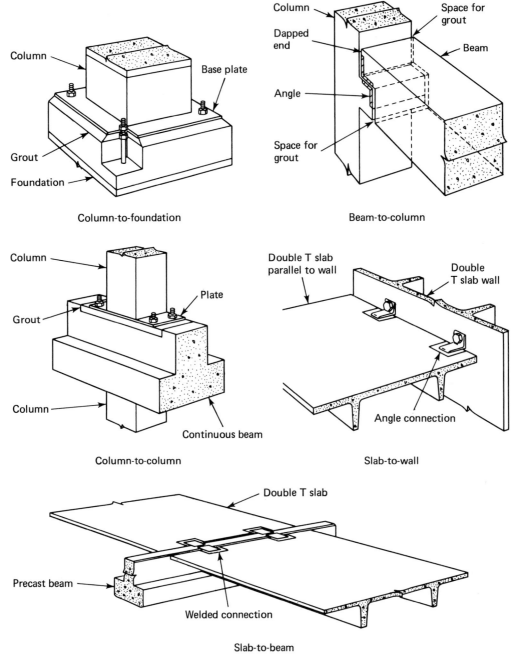

Column-to-foundation

Beam-to-column

Column-to-column

Slab-to-wall

Slab-to-beam

Fig. 5-14 Typical structural precast connections.

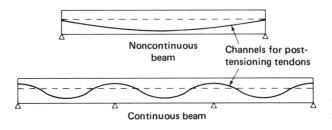

Fig. 5-15 Channels for posttensioning tendons.

166

Fig. 5-16 Posttensioning large single girder. *(Portland Cement Association)*

ARCHITECTURAL PRECAST

Precast concrete units were originally intended to act as a building frame, performing the same functions as wood or steel framing members. But advances in *design* and in *prestressing* and *manufacturing techniques* have made it possible and economical to produce precast units which are not only the load-bearing components of a building but which, at the same time, provide the exterior finish for that building.

There are two principal methods by which this type of unit can be produced. One is the *tilt-up* method, already described, in which the finish desired on the face may be introduced into the slab when it is being cast. The other is the same *central-plant* type of operation used to produce structural precast, except that shapes are not necessarily so standardized and, in many cases, special attention is paid to the color, texture, or profile (see Fig. 5-17) of the exterior face.

There are some distinct advantages to producing

Fig. 5-17 Precast panels with high-profile face. *(Precast Concrete Institute)*

167

Fig. 5-18 Architectural precast units made from one master mold. *(Prestressed Concrete Institute)*

Fig. 5-19 Telecommunications tower. *(Prestressed Concrete Institute)*

architectural precast building units in a central plant. They include the following:

1. Design freedom. The styles and designs of buildings may be widely diversified, ranging from the use of one master mold to produce units for an entire building (see Fig. 5-18) to unique structures, such as the one shown in Fig. 5-19.

2. The high degree of quality control, of both the ingredients and the finishing techniques.

3. The shapes, sizes, and configurations of units for one building may be as diversified or similar as the designer wishes.

4. The possibility of including in the precast units some or all of the services which are normally installed after erection, such as *glazing, mechanical services,* and *interior finish.* (See Fig. 5-20.)

5. The speed with which a building can be closed in, reducing costs and allowing earlier access by the service trades.

Architectural Wall Panels

A great deal of architectural precast production is in the form of wall panels. While a wide variety of shapes is possible, most wall panels may be classified as *double T, flat panel, window* or *mullion-type panel,* or *ribbed panel.* (See Fig. 5-21.)

Fig. 5-20 Architectural precast wall with glazing included. *(Prestressed Concrete Institute)*

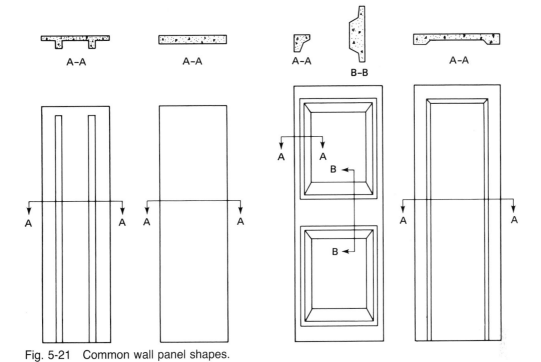

Fig. 5-21   Common wall panel shapes.

The *double T panel* is an adaptation of the double T structural member used in floor and roof sections. Although they may be made to suit a particular situation, double T's are made in standard dimensions of 48 and 96 in (1200 and 2400 mm) wide, in depths of 12, 14, 17, and 25 in (300, 350, 425, and 625 mm), with flange thicknesses of 2 or 3 in (50 or 75 mm). They are often made with a corbel cast on the flange face to facilitate the support of intermediate floor members. (See Fig. 5-22.)

Flat panels have many uses, ranging from small *fascia pieces* to *shear walls* to large *curtain walls* and *load-bearing walls* supporting one or more floors. Multistory load-bearing flat panels have corbels or other types of supports built in to carry the floor and roof loads. Design tables are available for flat panels, based on 12 in (300 mm) widths and 6 or 8 in (150 or 200 mm) thicknesses, using 5000 or 6000 psi (34.5 or 41.4 MPa) concrete, for both prestressed and normally reinforced panels.

Window or *mullion panels* are usually custom-made for a particular project and are the most complex type of architectural panel to design. Prestressing may not be possible in some cases because of the nature of the forms and the difficulty of obtaining concentric prestress forces. As a result, these panels are normally reinforced with mild steel. (See Fig. 5-23.) Such panels may be one story in height

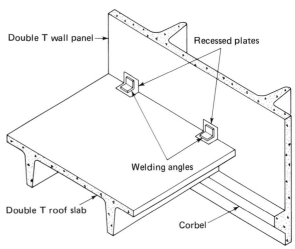

Fig. 5-22   Roof slab supported by corbel.   *(Prestressed Concrete Institute)*

169

Fig. 5-23 Reinforcing cage. *(R-T-P, Inc.; Photo by Irene Fertik)*

or they may be multistoried (see Fig. 5-24), though usually the length will not exceed 45 ft (13.7 m), owing to difficulties in handling. The problems of handling large panels in the plant may be alleviated by the use of tilt-up forms, such as that shown in Fig. 5-25.

Ribbed panels have no openings but, like double T's, are stiffened by monolithically cast *mullions* or *ribs.* However, unlike double T's, the flat portion of the panel is usually from 4 to 6 in (102 to 152 mm) in thickness. Ribbed panels may be prestressed or normally reinforced, depending on the design, and may be used as curtain wall or in a load-bearing capacity. They are commonly used in commercial and industrial applications where no win-

dows are required but an attractive exterior is desired.

Corners

The design of corners in buildings which use architectural precast wall panels requires some special attention. Mitered meeting edges on the panels themselves are difficult to make and fit satisfactorily, owing to the difficulty of casting the thin lip on a mitered edge, and frequently some other design is chosen. Figure 5-26 illustrates a number of alternative corner designs. In Fig. 5-27, the two halves of a corner unit have been preassembled at the plant before erection.

Fig. 5-24 Two-story architectural precast wall panel. *(Precast Concrete Institute)*

Fig. 5-25 Tilt-up form for architectural precast wall panel. *(Prestressed Concrete Institute)*

Other Uses for Architectural Precast

In addition to its use in curtain wall and load-bearing panels, architectural precast concrete has a number of other uses, including *decorative columns* (see Fig. 5-28), *fences, sunscreens, column*

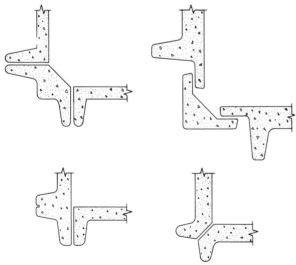

Fig. 5-26 Corner designs for architectural precast wall panels.

Fig. 5-27 Preassembled corner unit for architectural precast wall panels. *(Prestressed Concrete Institute)*

covers, street furniture (see Fig. 5-29), *light standards, planters, railings,* and *sculptures* (see Fig. 5-30).

Surface Finishes

One of the major advantages of using architectural precast concrete is the opportunity to provide a great variety of surface finishes, both in color and texture. Colors are varied by using *white cement, color pigments, colored aggregates,* and *synthetic coatings,* either alone or in combination.

Fig. 5-28 Architectural precast decorative column. *(Prestressed Concrete Institute)*

171

Fig. 5-31 Architectural precast wall panels with ribbed face. *(Prestressed Concrete Institute)*

A desired surface texture is produced by *casting on a smooth surface,* using a *ribbed or textured form face* (see Fig. 5-31), *casting on a sand-molded surface* (see Fig. 5-17), *sand blasting, exposing the aggregate to various degrees* (see Fig. 5-32), or *grinding* (see Fig. 5-33). Color or surface texture variations on an individual panel may be highlighted by the use of ribs and recesses.

Fig. 5-29 Architectural precast furniture. *(Prestressed Concrete Institute)*

Fig. 5-30 Architectural precast street sculptures. *(Prestressed Concrete Institute)*

Fig. 5-32 Architectural precast panel with exposed aggregate. *(Prestressed Concrete Institute)*

172

Fig. 5-33 Ground and polished architectural precast wall panel. *(Prestressed Concrete Institute)*

Connections

Connections for architectural precast concrete units may be as varied as the units themselves. A typical floor system-to-wall panel connection is shown in Fig. 5-22.

If the panels are for curtain wall, the connections must be between the panel and the structural frame. If the panels are load-bearing, placed one above the other, connections between them will probably be by *weld plates* or *dowels*. In either case, panels must be equipped with *lifting hardware*, which is often attached to the panel by means of *concrete inserts*, cast into the panel.

GLOSSARY

AASHO	American Association of State Highway Officials.
abutment	A buttress which provides support at the extreme end of a structure.
bearing pile	A polelike member, driven into the ground and used to support part of the load of a building.
reinforcing cage	An arrangement of reinforcing bars, wired or welded together to fit the reinforcing requirements of a particular member.
camber	A slight convex curve in a structural member.
concrete insert	A threaded device cast into concrete to receive a threaded bolt.
continuity connection	A connection designed to allow two or more members, joined together, end-to-end, to act as one.
mullion	A bar designed to divide windows or other openings.
prefabricated	Manufactured or built prior to assembly.
structural members	Those components of a building which carry the loads of the building.
tendon	A steel rod or strand used in prestressing concrete members.

REVIEW QUESTIONS

1. List three major advantages of *precasting* concrete structural members.

2. Outline the main difference between *pretensioned* and *posttensioned* concrete units.

3. Under what conditions is posttensioning normally carried out?

4. Explain what is meant by *normally reinforced* structural members.

5. Explain what happens when the design load is applied to a previously unloaded, pretensioned, horizontal member.

SELECTED SOURCES OF INFORMATION

Con-Force Ltd., Calgary, Alta.
Portland Cement Association, Skokie, Ill.
Prestressed Concrete Institute, Chicago, Ill.

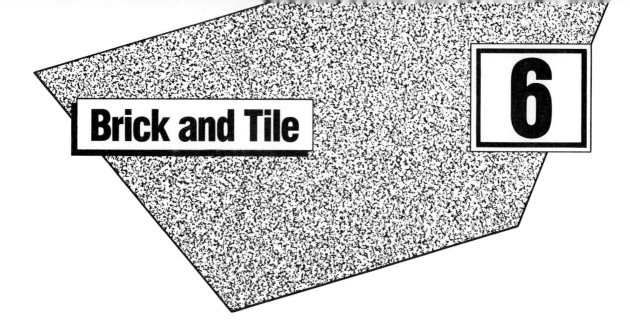

Brick and Tile

6

BRICK
Manufacture of Brick

Brick is one of the oldest building materials known, and the manufacture of these basic building units still follows the same basic procedures of the past. Modern plants have been made much more efficient, however, as a result of technological advances during the past hundred years. A more complete knowledge of raw materials and their properties, better kilns and control of burning, and more and better machinery have all aided the development of a highly efficient industry.

The basic ingredient of brick is clay—clay which has some specific properties. It must have plasticity when mixed with water, so that it can be molded or shaped; it must have sufficient tensile strength to keep its shape after forming; and clay particles must fuse together when subjected to sufficiently high temperatures.

Clay occurs in three principal forms, all of which have similar chemical compositions but different physical characteristics: (1) surface clays, (2) shales, and (3) fireclays.

Surface clays, as the name implies, are found near the surface of the earth. They may be upthrusts of older deposits or of more recent, sedimentary formation. Shales are clays which have been subjected to high pressure until they have become relatively hard. Fireclays are found at deeper levels than the other types and usually have more uniform physical and chemical qualities. Their most important characteristic is their ability to withstand high temperatures.

Clays are complex materials, but basically they are compounds of silica and alumina with varying amounts of metallic oxides and other ingredients. They may be divided into two classes, depending on basic composition: (1) calcareous clays and (2) noncalcareous clays. The calcareous clays contain about 15 percent calcium carbonate and burn to a yellowish color. Noncalcareous clays are composed of silicate of alumina, with feldspar and iron oxide, the oxide content varying from 2 to 10 percent. These clays burn buff, red, or salmon, the color depending largely on the iron oxide content.

The manufacturing process has seven phases: (1) mining or *winning* and storage of raw material, (2) preparing raw material, (3) forming units, (4) drying, (5) glazing, (6) burning and cooling, and (7) drawing and storing the finished product.

MINING AND STORAGE   Most clays are mined from open pits, although some fireclays are obtained by underground mining. The material is transported by rail or truck to the plant site where, if the clay is in large lumps, it first undergoes preliminary crushing. (See Fig. 6-1.) It is then elevated

Fig. 6-1 Clay being transported from car dump to crusher. *(Hewitt-Robins)*

to storage (see Fig. 6-2), and it is at this stage that blending of clays takes place to minimize variations in chemical composition and physical properties.

PREPARING RAW MATERIALS

From the storage bins, clay passes to crushers, where stones are removed and the material is reduced to relatively small pieces, no larger than 2 in (50 mm) in diameter.

Conveyors, controlled by a central console operator (see Fig. 6-3), then carry the crushed clay to grinders, where it is reduced to a very fine flour and thoroughly mixed. The ground clay passes over a vibrating screen which passes only the material which has been ground finely enough. The coarse particles are returned to the grinder for further processing, while the fine material is elevated to storage.

FORMING

The first step in the forming process is *tempering,* the mixing of the clay with water in a pug mill. The amount of water used depends on the method being used to form the units. There are three principal methods in use: (1) the stiff-mud process, (2) the soft-mud process, and (3) the dry-press method.

In the *stiff-mud process,* only enough water is used to produce plasticity, usually from 12 to 15 percent by weight. The plastic clay goes through a deairing machine to remove air pockets and bubbles. This also increases workability and strength.

The clay is then forced by an auger through a *die,* which produces a continuous column of clay of the proper size and shape and, at the same time, imparts the desired texture to the surface. These three operations are combined in a *pug mill* and *extruder,* like that illustrated in Fig. 6-4.

The clay column passes through an automatic cutter (see Fig. 6-5), which cuts off units of the

Fig. 6-2 Crushed clay going to storage. *(Hewitt-Robins)*

Fig. 6-3 Console operator controlling clay conveyors to grinder. *(Hewitt-Robins)*

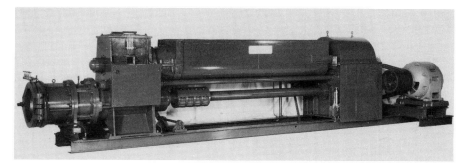

Fig. 6-4 Pug mill and extruder. *(Chambers Bros.)*

Fig. 6-5 Automatic brick cutter. *(Chambers Bros.)*

proper length. These are carried by belt to an inspection area, where good units are unloaded onto *drier cars* and the imperfect ones are returned to the pug mill for reprocessing.

A great deal of industry's brick and all structural clay tile are manufactured by the stiff-mud process.

The *soft-mud process* is used for making brick only and is employed with clays which contain too much natural water for the stiff-mud process. Twenty to thirty percent water is used in tempering, and the bricks are formed in molds. This is the oldest method of production. Molds are lubricated with sand or water. Brick made with sanded molds is *sand struck;* brick made with water-lubricated molds is *water struck.*

The *dry-press process* uses the least water in tempering, the maximum being about 10 percent. The relatively dry mix is fed to machines which form the bricks in steel molds under high pressure, much the same way in which concrete blocks are produced. (See Fig. 6-6.)

DRYING When the units come from the forming machines, they contain from 7 to 30 percent moisture, most of which is removed in drier kilns.

Drying causes shrinkage, which must be allowed for when the bricks are being formed so that the finished product will be the proper size.

Fig. 6-6 Dry-press brick machine. *(Chisholm, Boyd & White Co.)*

177

Drier-kiln temperatures range from 38 to 204°C, and the drying time varies from 24 to 48 h, depending on the type of clay. Heat is usually provided by the exhaust heat from the burning kilns. In all cases the heat and humidity are carefully regulated to avoid too-rapid shrinkage, which causes excessive cracking.

GLAZING   When bricks are to be glazed, it is usually done at the end of the drying period, although low-fire glazes can be applied after the brick has been burned. Ceramic glazing consists of spraying a coating of a mixture of mineral ingredients on one or more surfaces of the brick. The glaze melts and fuses to the brick at a given temperature, producing a glasslike coating which is available in almost any color.

BURNING AND COOLING   Burning is a very important step in the manufacture of brick. The time required varies from 40 to 150 h, depending on the type of kiln, the type of clay, the type of glaze if any, and other variables. A number of kiln types are in use now, the main ones being tunnel kilns and periodic kilns. In the tunnel kiln, dried bricks pass through various temperature zones on special cars. In periodic kilns the temperature is varied periodically—raised and then lowered by steps—until the burning is complete.

Bricks must be set on the kiln cars or in the kilns in a prescribed pattern which allows free circulation of hot kiln gases. Fuel may be natural gas, oil, or coal.

Burning may be divided into six general steps: *water-smoking, dehydration, oxidation, vitrification, flashing,* and *cooling.* Although temperatures vary, depending on the type of material, each step occurs in a definite temperature zone.

Water-smoking (evaporating free water) takes place at temperatures up to about 204°C; dehydration at temperatures from about 149 to 982°C; oxidation from 538 to 982°C; and vitrification from 871 to 1315°C.

Near the end of the burning process the bricks may be flashed to produce color variations. This is done by injecting natural gas at the appropriate time or place. When this extra fuel burns, patches and variations in color are formed throughout the stack of bricks.

Cooling takes from 48 to 72 h, depending on the type of kiln; it must be carefully controlled because the rate of cooling has a direct effect on color and because too-rapid cooling will cause cracking and checking in the brick.

DRAWING AND STORING   Drawing is the process of unloading a kiln after the bricks are cool. At this time they are normally sorted, graded, packaged, and taken to storage yards or loaded on trucks or railcars for shipment.

Brick Types, Sizes, and Designs

The unit universally known as a common brick has, in the past, been made in a variety of sizes, depending on the material and the locality. But as the need for standardization became apparent and particularly the need to conform to the generally recognized *4-in building module,* most structural clay products have been so standardized by nationally recognized product specifications.

Like concrete block, structural clay products are designated by their nominal dimensions, but their modular or *specified* dimensions are such that, measured center-to-center of mortar joints, the measurement will be equal to one or more standard 4-in (100-mm) modules.

A standard Imperial-measure nominal size for common brick was adopted—$4 \times 2\frac{1}{4} \times 8$ in—from which modular dimensions could be developed which would be adaptable to a 4-in module; for example, $3\frac{5}{8} \times 2\frac{1}{6} \times 7\frac{1}{2}$ in. Thus *three thicknesses, two widths,* or *one length,* plus the thickness of $\frac{1}{2}$-in mortar joints, would equal 2 modules: 8 in. (See Fig. 6-7.) Similar dimensions could be devel-

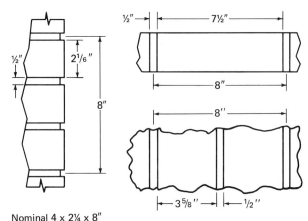

Nominal 4 x 2¼ x 8″

Fig. 6-7   Modular dimensions with $\frac{1}{2}$-in mortar joint.

oped which could be used with $\frac{3}{8}$-in mortar joints.

With the introduction of the metric system, the recommended standard metric nominal size for common brick would be 100 × 67 × 200 mm. The modular dimensions, which would be adaptable to a 100-mm module, would be 90 × 57 × 190 mm. Thus three thicknesses, two widths, or one length of brick, plus the thickness of 10-mm mortar joints, would equal 2 modules: 200 mm. (See Fig. 6-8.)

COMMON BRICK

Common brick is used primarily as structural material where strength and durability, rather than appearance, are the important factors. Three grades of common brick are made, as follows:

Grade SW brick is intended for use where high resistance to frost action is desired: for wet locations, below ground, and where the brick may be frozen when permeated with water. The compressive strength rating is 3000 psi (20.7 MPa).

Grade MW brick is intended for use in relatively dry locations, exposed to temperatures below freezing. The compressive strength rating is 2500 psi (17.2 MPa). In general, brick used in the exterior face of a wall above ground should conform to this grade.

Grade NW brick is intended for use as a back-up or interior masonry where no freezing occurs. The compressive rating is 1500 psi (10.3 MPa).

Two common designs are found in standard brick, depending on whether it is *wire-cut* (extruded) or *pressed* (dry-press) brick. (See Fig. 6-9.)

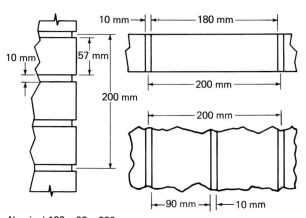

Nominal 100 x 60 x 200 mm

Fig. 6-8   Modular dimensions with 10-mm mortar joint.

Wirecut   Pressed

Fig. 6-9   4-in nominal (90-mm) modular standard brick.

BRICK TYPES AND SIZES

In addition to standard brick, there are a number of other types in common use. Some are old designs which have been standardized for modern use, while others have been developed mainly for architectural purposes. Several are produced in more than one size. Types include *Titan, Norman, Roman, Saxon, Monarch, Giant,* and *3-in.* (See Fig. 6-10.) Table 6-1 lists types and available sizes.

Brick Textures

Common brick is normally made with smooth surfaces, but bricks to be used for facing are very often given some type of surface treatment—a texture applied as the column of clay leaves the die in the stiff-mud process, a glaze, or a color variation produced by flashing.

Table 6-1
BRICK TYPES AND SIZES

Brick Type	Modular Dimensions	
	Inches	Millimeters
Standard	$3\frac{5}{8} \times 2\frac{1}{4} \times 7\frac{5}{8}$	90 × 57 × 190
3 in (75 mm)	$3 \times 2\frac{1}{4} \times 7\frac{5}{8}$	75 × 57 × 190
Norman	$3\frac{5}{8} \times 2\frac{1}{4} \times 11\frac{5}{8}$	90 × 57 × 290
	$5\frac{5}{8} \times 2\frac{1}{4} \times 11\frac{5}{8}$	140 × 57 × 290
	$7\frac{5}{8} \times 2\frac{1}{4} \times 11\frac{5}{8}$	190 × 57 × 290
Titan	$3\frac{5}{8} \times 2\frac{1}{2} \times 7\frac{5}{8}$	90 × 63 × 190
	$3\frac{5}{8} \times 2\frac{1}{2} \times 11\frac{5}{8}$	90 × 63 × 290
	$5\frac{5}{8} \times 2\frac{1}{2} \times 11\frac{5}{8}$	140 × 63 × 290
Roman	$3\frac{5}{8} \times 1\frac{5}{8} \times 7\frac{5}{8}$	90 × 40 × 190
	$3\frac{5}{8} \times 1\frac{5}{8} \times 11\frac{5}{8}$	90 × 40 × 290
Saxon	$3\frac{5}{8} \times 3\frac{5}{8} \times 11\frac{5}{8}$	90 × 90 × 290
Monarch	$3 \times 3\frac{5}{8} \times 15\frac{5}{8}$	75 × 90 × 390
	$3\frac{5}{8} \times 3\frac{5}{8} \times 15\frac{5}{8}$	90 × 90 × 390
Giant	$3\frac{5}{8} \times 3\frac{5}{8} \times 15\frac{5}{8}$	90 × 90 × 390
	$5\frac{5}{8} \times 3\frac{5}{8} \times 15\frac{5}{8}$	140 × 90 × 390
	$7\frac{5}{8} \times 3\frac{5}{8} \times 15\frac{5}{8}$	190 × 90 × 390

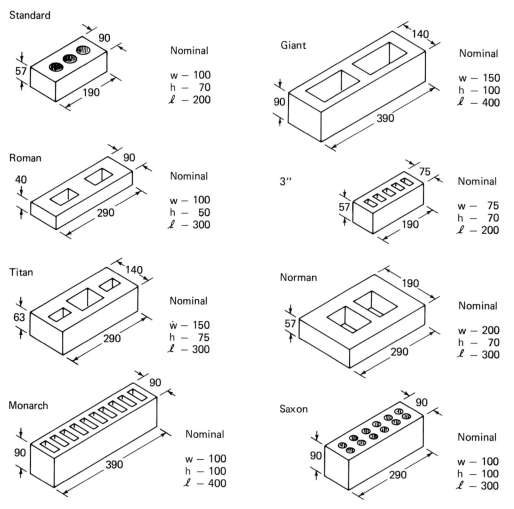

Fig. 6-10 Brick types and recommended metric modular sizes.

Standard

90
57
190

Nominal

w — 100
h — 70
ℓ — 200

Giant

140
90
390

Nominal

w — 150
h — 100
ℓ — 400

Roman

40
90
290

Nominal

w — 100
h — 50
ℓ — 300

3″

75
57
190

Nominal

w — 75
h — 70
ℓ — 200

Titan

140
63
290

Nominal

$\dot{w}$ — 150
h — 75
ℓ — 300

Norman

190
57
290

Nominal

w — 200
h — 70
ℓ — 300

Monarch

90
90
390

Nominal

w — 100
h — 100
ℓ — 400

Saxon

90
90
290

Nominal

w — 100
h — 100
ℓ — 300

Textures are applied by attachments which cut, scratch, brush, roll, or otherwise roughen the surface. (See Fig. 6-9.)

Glazes are sprayed on the brick before or after burning. Typical ones are *ceramic glaze,* described previously, and *salt glaze,* consisting of a solution of sodium iron silicate. Salt glaze is transparent, and so the color of the brick is presented under a lustrous gloss.

Flashing of brick has been described in a previous section.

Brick Bonds

The term *bond,* used in connection with brick masonry, can be used in three different ways. The method of laying up bricks in a wall in order to form some distinctive pattern or design is referred to as the *pattern bond.* The method by which the individual units in a brick structure are tied together, either by overlapping or by metal ties, is known as the *structural bond.* The adhesion of mortar to bricks or to steel reinforcements used in conjunction with them is called the *mortar bond.*

STRUCTURAL BOND   Bricks are used in walls (1) to form a *solid* brick wall at least two widths of brick in thickness; (2) to build a *cavity* wall, which consists of *wythes* of brick separated by a 1- or 2-in (25- or 50-mm) cavity or a wythe of brick and another backup material separated by a cavity; and (3) to face a wall of some other material with a *veneer* of brick, usually 4 in (100 mm) thick. In all cases there must be some method of tying the units to one another or to the backup material to form a solid structure. This is done by providing a *structural bond.*

In solid walls, the structural bond is provided by *header* bricks, which reach through the wall and tie it together. (See Fig. 6-11.) In cavity walls, the two wythes of brick are tied by metal ties. (See Fig. 6-12.)

Structural bond for brick veneer over wood backup can be accomplished in different ways depending on the veneer being used. For the 4-in (100-mm) standard brick veneer, two methods can be used. One is to lay up the brick over the paper-covered sheathing, using metal ties nailed to the sheathing to hold the brick in place. The other is to nail paper-backed wire mesh over the wall studs, apply a 1-in (25-mm) coating of mortar, and set the bricks with their back ends embedded in the mortar. (See Fig. 6-13.)

When a thin brick veneer is used, it is set into a mortar base that has been applied over a stucco wire backing as illustrated in Fig. 6-14.

Composite walls of brick and concrete block can be reinforced by either using header bricks, as shown in Fig. 6-15, or by using metal ties, as illustrated in Fig. 6-16. Cavity walls of brick and block are reinforced in the same manner.

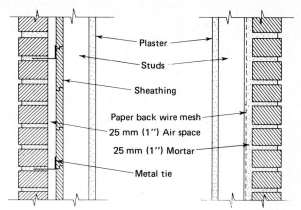
Fig. 6-13 Structural tie for brick veneer over wood sheathing.

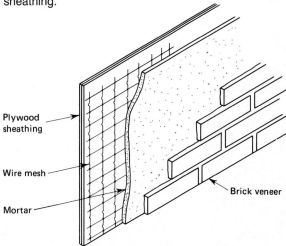
Fig. 6-14 Thin brick veneer set in mortar backing.

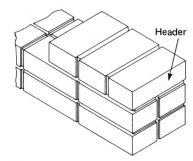
Fig. 6-11 Structural header.

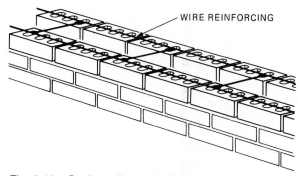
Fig. 6-12 Cavity-wall structural tie.

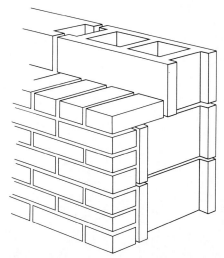
Fig. 6-15 Header brick as structural tie with concrete block as backup.

181

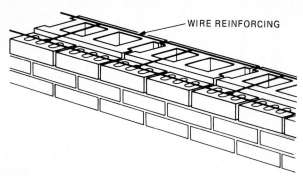

Fig. 6-16 Structural tie for brick and block composite wall.

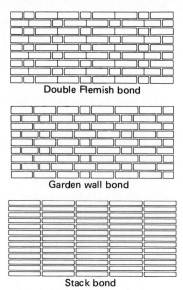

Fig. 6-18 Pattern bond variations.

PATTERN BOND   Five basic pattern bonds are most commonly used in brickwork today: *running bond, common bond, Flemish bond, English bond,* and *English cross bond.* (See Fig. 6-17.) Variations of these basic pattern bonds include *double Flemish, garden wall, stack* (see Fig. 6-18), and many others, some of which are particularly adapted to Roman and Norman brick (see Fig. 6-19).

MORTAR BOND   The building of structures from brick is possible only because a *mortar bond* develops between the mortar and the brick. The strength of brick walls and their ability to resist water penetration depend to a large extent on the strength and completeness of the mortar bond.

The mortar should be mixed with the minimum amount of water that is possible to use and still maintain the proper plasticity. If mixed mortar loses water by evaporation and stiffens, additional water may be added and the mortar remixed. However, water should not be added to mortar which has begun to stiffen because the *set* has begun; all mortar should be used within 2 h after mixing, under normal temperature conditions.

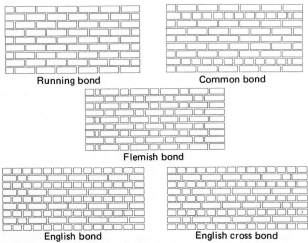

Fig. 6-17 Basic pattern bonds.

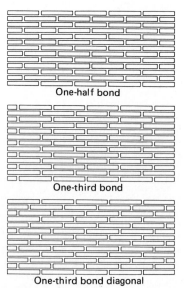

Fig. 6-19 Patterns suited to Roman or Norman brick.

Most building codes recognize four types of mortar for use with brick, each with a specific purpose. These are as follows:

Type M Mortar. This mortar is suitable for general use and is recommended specifically for masonry below grade and in contact with earth. It consists of 1 part portland cement, $\frac{1}{4}$ part hydrated lime or lime putty, 3 parts sand by volume *or* 1 part portland cement, 1 part masonry cement, and 6 parts sand by volume.

Type S Mortar. This is also a general-purpose mortar bond and is recommended where high resistance to lateral force is required. It consists of 1 part portland cement, $\frac{1}{2}$ part hydrated lime or lime putty, $4\frac{1}{2}$ parts sand by volume *or* $\frac{1}{2}$ part portland cement, 1 part masonry cement, and $4\frac{1}{2}$ parts sand by volume.

Type N Mortar. This mortar is suitable in exposed masonry above grade and is recommended specifically for exterior walls subjected to severe exposure. It consists of 1 part portland cement, 1 part hydrated lime or lime putty, 6 parts sand by volume *or* 1 part masonry cement, and 3 parts sand by volume.

Type O Mortar. This mortar is recommended for load-bearing walls of solid units where the compressive stresses do not exceed 100 psi (0.69 MPa) and the masonry will not be subjected to freezing and thawing in the presence of excess moisture. It consists of 1 part portland cement, 2 parts hydrated lime or lime putty, 9 parts sand by volume *or* 1 part masonry cement, and 3 parts sand by volume.

MORTAR JOINTS   Mortar joints may be treated in any one of several ways to provide some extra effect in a brick wall. Figure 6-20 shows six types of tooled mortar joints in common use, particularly for exterior work. Tooled joints compress the mortar tightly against the brick, increasing the resistance to rain penetration, while the concave joint, V-joint, and weathered joints also shed water from the joint.

A type of mortar joint frequently used with interior brickwork—an *extruded joint*—is illustrated in Figure 6-24.

Special Brick Shapes

In order to provide greater flexibility in design, a number of special brick shapes are made by several manufacturers of brick. They include *corner units, angled brick, inside radial brick, outside radial brick, fluted brick, solid brick, bullnose brick,* with either single or double bullnose, and *corner brick,* three courses high.

These units are normally made to order, and the local brick plant should be consulted for items available. (See Fig. 6-21.)

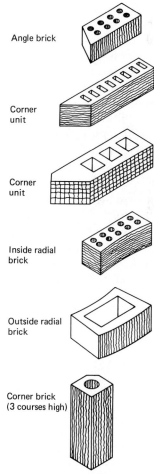

Angle brick

Corner unit

Corner unit

Inside radial brick

Outside radial brick

Corner brick (3 courses high)

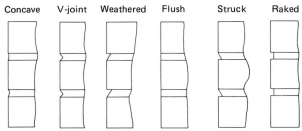

Concave   V-joint   Weathered   Flush   Struck   Raked

Fig. 6-20   Tooled mortar joints.

Fig. 6-21   Some special brick shapes.

Properties of Brick Units and Brick Masonry

All properties of brick are affected by the composition of the raw material used and the manufacturing processes involved. Those properties include *color, texture, size, strength,* and *absorption rate.* Strength tests include tests in *compression, tension, shear,* and *transverse strength.*

COLOR   The color of a burned brick depends on its *chemical composition,* the *heat* of the kiln, and the method used to *control the burning.* All clays containing iron will burn red if exposed to an oxidizing fire. If it is burned in a reducing atmosphere, the same clay will take on a purple tint, owing to the ferrous silicate content. If the same clay is underburned, salmon colors are produced. Overburning produces dark red brick. Buff clays produce the buff and brown bricks, depending on the temperature of burning.

TEXTURE   Texture is produced by the *surface treatment* the clay is given as it leaves the extruding die. A smooth texture is produced by the pressure of clay against the sides of the steel die. But in the stiff-mud process, rough textures may be applied to the clay as it leaves the die. These include *scored finishes,* in which the clay surface is grooved; *combed finishes,* produced by placing parallel scratches on the surface; and *rough-texture* finishes, produced by wire cutting or wire brushing the clay surface as it emerges from the die.

SIZE   Most clays shrink during drying and burning from 4.5 to 15 percent, and allowances are made for this when the units are molded. Shrinkage will vary, depending on the *composition of the clay,* its *fineness,* the *amount of water* added, and the *kiln temperature.* As a result, absolute size uniformity is impossible, and consequently specifications normally include permissible variations in size.

STRENGTH OF BRICK   The strength characteristics of brick also vary with the raw materials and the manufacturing processes involved. For example, the compressive strength of brick varies from 1500 to 20,000 psi (10.3 to 137.9 MPa).

Similarly, transverse strength—the strength of a brick when it acts as a beam, supported at both ends—varies from 114 to an average maximum of 2890 psi (0.79 to an average maximum of 19.9 MPa). The value for transverse strength is usually expressed as the *modulus of rupture.*

Tests indicate that the tensile strength of brick is between 30 and 40 percent of the transverse strength, while punching shear tests of brick indicate strengths in shear from 30 to 40 percent of the net compressive strength. Table 6-2 gives some average physical properties of brick.

WATER ABSORPTION OF BRICK   The water absorption of a brick is defined as the weight of water, expressed as a percentage of the dry weight, which is taken up under a given test method. The water is taken in through pores which act as capillaries to suck water into the unit. This initial rate of absorption, or *suction,* of a brick has an important effect on the bond between brick and mortar. Tests indicate that maximum bond strength is obtained when suction rate at the time of laying is about 0.7 oz/min (20 g/min). When brick has a greater suction rate than that, it should be wetted before laying, to reduce the suction.

The method of determining the suction rate of brick consists of partially immersing the unit to a depth of $\frac{1}{8}$ in (3 mm) in water for 1 min. It is then removed and weighed, and the final weight is compared to the dry weight.

Table 6-2
AVERAGE PHYSICAL PROPERTIES OF BRICK

Absorption		Modulus of Rupture				Compressive Strength				Tensile Strength		Shear Strength	
		Flatwise		Edgewise		Flatwise		Edgewise					
5 h Boil, %	48 h Cold, %	psi	MPa	psi	MPa	psi	Mpa	psi	Mpa	psi	MPa	psi	MPa
17.4	14	1064	7.3	1105	7.6	4700	32.4	5430	37.4	389	2.7	1850	12.7

Table 6-3
ALLOWABLE COMPRESSIVE STRESSES IN BRICK MASONRY

Solid Brick Masonry	Allowable Compressive Stresses, With Mortar Type							
	M		S		N		O	
	psi	MPa	psi	MPa	psi	MPa	psi	MPa
Over 10,000 psi (69 MPa)	500	3.4	450	3.1	350	2.4	250	1.7
8000–10,000 psi (55–69 MPa)	400	2.75	350	2.4	300	2.0	200	1.4
4500–8000 psi (31–55 MPa)	250	1.7	250	1.7	200	1.4	150	1.0
2500–4500 psi (17–31 MPa)	175	1.2	180	1.24	150	1.0	110	0.75
1500–2500 psi (10–17 MPa)	125	0.86	140	0.96	100	0.69	75	0.5

PROPERTIES OF BRICK MASONRY   The physical properties of the brick units determine the properties of walls made from them, and these are further affected by the properties of the mortar, the workmanship, and the design of the walls themselves. For example, much of the brick manufactured has compressive strengths of over 4500 psi (13 MPa), but when it is combined with mortar in a wall, the allowable compressive stresses in the wall will vary from 75 to 500 psi (0.5 to 3.4 MPa), owing to the limiting mortar factor. Table 6-3 indicates some typical allowable compressive stresses in brick masonry walls.

HEAT TRANSMISSION IN A BRICK WALL   The ability of a wall assembly to resist the passage of heat is one of the important considerations in choosing both materials for a wall and the method to be used in assembling those materials. While in many of the modern buildings heat loss and heat gain are largely controlled by glass area, the structure of exterior walls to control the inside surface temperature of the wall and to prevent condensation is an important factor to consider. Table 6-4 outlines the coefficients of heat transmission and the resistances of several brick-wall assemblies. (See also Chap. 13.)

FIRE RESISTANCE OF A BRICK WALL   The ability of a material to resist fire is related to its ability to resist the passage of heat. In addition, for load-bearing construction, there is also the necessity for the material to be able to continue carrying a load after it has been subjected to the heat of a fire.

Wall, floor, and partition assemblies are given fire ratings, in terms of hours, based on standard fire tests. The maximum rating included in most codes is 4 h. Table 6-5 gives fire ratings for various thicknesses of two types of brick wall.

SOUND TRANSMISSION OF A BRICK WALL   The ability of a wall or floor assembly to resist the passage of sound from one side to the other is an important consideration in choosing wall materials. Walls inhibit noise transmission by absorbing sound, by reflecting it, but far more important, by preventing the passage of sound from one side of a wall to the other by diaphragm action.

Sound absorption is the conversion of sound energy into heat enegy and is accomplished mainly by the use of acoustical materials. Most clay products absorb little sound, owing to their high density and stiffness.

Sound reflectance is the "bouncing back" of sound waves when they have encountered a solid

Table 6-4
COEFFICIENTS OF HEAT TRANSMISSION (*U*) AND RESISTANCES (*R*) OF VARIOUS BRICK WALLS

Wall Type	$U - 1/R$	$R - 1/U$
6-in (150-mm) solid brick	0.72	1.38
8-in (200-mm) solid brick	0.55	1.82
12-in (300-mm) solid brick	0.43	2.34
10-in (250-mm) brick cavity wall	0.36	2.77

Table 6-5
MINIMUM THICKNESS OF BRICK WALLS FOR FIRE RATINGS

Wall Type	Minimum Thickness for Fire-Resistance Rating of:						
	$\frac{1}{2}$ h	$\frac{3}{4}$ h	1 h	$1\frac{1}{2}$ h	2 h	3 h	4 h
Solid brick units, 80% solid and over: actual overall thickness	2.5″ (63.5 mm)	3″ (76 mm)	3.5″ (89 mm)	4.3″ (109 mm)	5″ (127 mm)	6″ (152 mm)	7″ (178 mm)
Cored brick units, less than 80% solid: equivalent thickness	2″ (51 mm)	2.4″ (61 mm)	2.8″ (71 mm)	3.4″ (86 mm)	4″ (102 mm)	4.8″ (122 mm)	5.6″ (142 mm)

surface. It is a major concern in the design of such buildings as auditoriums.

The passage of sound by diaphragm action is caused by the sound waves on one side of a wall causing the wall to vibrate like a diaphragm. The vibrating wall causes the air on the other side to vibrate, producing new sound waves. Therefore, the greater the ability of a wall to resist vibration, the greater its ability to resist the passage of sound. This resistance is related to the weight of the wall: the transmission loss for homogeneous walls is proportional to the logarithm of the weight of the wall. The initial doubling of the weight produces the greatest increase in transmission loss. Further increases in weight produce proportionately smaller losses.

The sound transmission loss of a wall or floor assembly is expressed in decibels, 1 dB being the minimum noise level audible to the normal human ear. In comparison, 10 dB is equivalent to the rustle of leaves.

Table 6-6 lists the weights and average reduction factors of a number of brick-wall assemblies. (See also Chap. 14.)

Prefabricated Brick Panels

Prefabrication of building units of various kinds has become a widely used technique in the construction industry, and the brick industry has contributed to the total with prefabricated brick panels, for use in curtain wall construction.

A number of recent developments have made prefabrication of brick masonry much more feasible. Among them are (1) the development and acceptance of a rational design method for brick masonry; (2) improved quality control in the

Table 6-6
SOUND TRANSMISSION LOSS OF VARIOUS BRICK WALLS

Type of Wall	Weight of Wall		Average Reduction Factor, dB
	1b/ft²	kg/m²	
$2\frac{1}{4}$-in (57-mm) brick, plastered both sides	31.6	154	48.8
$2\frac{1}{4}$-in (57-mm) brick, furring strips, gypsum board and plastered both sides	38.2	186.5	55.2
$2\frac{1}{4}$-in (57-mm) brick, furring strips, $\frac{1}{2}$-in (50-mm) insulating board and plastered both sides	33.3	162.5	54.6
4-in (100-mm) brick, gypsum plaster, smooth lime finish both sides	49.0	239	53.7
8-in (200-mm) brick, plastered both sides, brown coat and white finish	87.0	425	57.2

manufacture of brick masonry units; (3) the development of new brick units; (4) increased control in the performance of portland cement–lime mortar; and (5) the development of several high-bond mortar additives, which have greatly improved the bonding ability of mortar.

Several manufacturing methods are used in brick panel prefabrication but, in general, they involve either *hand laying* or *casting.*

HAND LAYING   The hand-laying method of prefabrication is carried out in the same way as conventional brick laying, except that the work is usually carried out in a plant set up for the purpose. (See Fig. 6-22.) The laying may be done by hand or with power equipment and with conventional or high-bond mortar.

CASTING   The casting method of prefabrication requires a form, into which bricks are placed in proper position, either by hand or by machine. The form is then filled with grout in such a way that, when the grout has set, the unit constitutes a precast panel with a grout back and brick face.

PANEL FITTINGS   Prefabricated panels usually require some type of *reinforcement,* which may be horizontal or vertical or both. Hollow brick units

are required for the panel when vertical reinforcement is used. In addition, *anchors, inserts, connection devices,* and *lifting devices* must be included in the panel as it is being laid.

HIGH-BOND MORTAR   High-bond mortar is a mortar containing a synthetic resin additive—a liquid saran polymer—which greatly increases the bonding and the compressive and tensile strength characteristics of the mortar.

The recommended proportions for mortar using the additive are as follows:

Mortar additive	4 gal (15 L)
Mortar sand	$3\frac{1}{4}$ ft^3 (92 L)
Portland cement	1 bag (40 kg)
Workability additive	50 lb (22.65 kg)
Water	As required, up to a max. of 4 gal (15 L)

Brick Masonry Curtain Walls

Density, high compressive strength, and wide variation in color allow brick units to be used in a variety of ways. On exterior walls they provide a long-lasting, maintenance-free surface that is pleasing in appearance. On interior walls, brick is used for much the same reasons. Used as a finish on a

Fig. 6-22   Prefabricating brick panels. *(International Masonry Institute)*

187

feature wall, it adds warmth to any room. Figure 6-23 illustrates the effect that can be produced using different colored bricks and conventional mortar joints, while Fig. 6-24 illustrates a roughcast effect using extruded mortar joints.

Traditionally, because of the high compressive strength of brick masonry, brick walls were normally incorporated into the structural frame of the building as load-carrying members as well as to provide a durable finished exterior. In recent times, with materials such as steel and reinforced concrete being used for the structural frame, masonry has been used as curtain wall material. In this application, the brick needs only to support its own dead weight and horizontal forces due to wind if used on exterior walls.

Anchorage must be provided for the brick to ensure that any lateral loads that may be applied to the brick are transferred to the structural frame. Various ingenious methods have been developed to accomplish this requirement. If the frame is of reinforced concrete, metal ties are usually employed to anchor the ends of the curtain-wall sections to the concrete columns. These consist of flat metal straps, one end of which can be anchored to the column, while the other end is laid into a mortar joint between courses of brick. A metal keyway is cast into the sides of the column to accommodate the end of the tie. (See Fig. 6-25.) The brick and spandrel beam may be bonded simply by a mortar joint between them, or a keying system such as illustrated in Fig. 6-26 may be used.

In a building with a steel frame, the curtain wall may be placed so as to enclose the steel (Fig. 6-27), or the frame may be exposed as shown in Fig. 6-28. Again, metal anchors welded to the steel frame are used to tie the curtain wall to the structure.

A recent development in curtain wall design has been to prefabricate brick curtain walls complete

Fig. 6-23 Brick color variations produce an interesting effect.

Fig. 6-24 Extruded mortar joints.

188

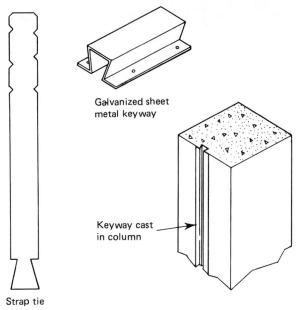

Strap tie

Fig. 6-25 Brick strap tie and keyway.

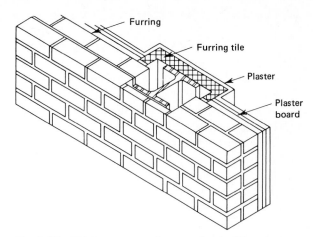

Fig. 6-27 Brick veneer wall conceals steel frame.

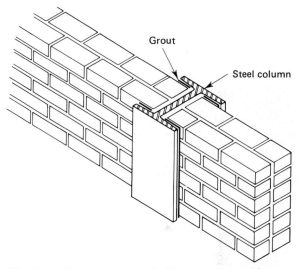

Fig. 6-28 Brick veneer wall with exposed steel frame.

with insulation and interior framing. This approach allows for better control of working conditions during the laying up of the bricks and reduces the amount of time spent in the field. Figure 6-29 illustrates an example of the shapes that can be prefabricated.

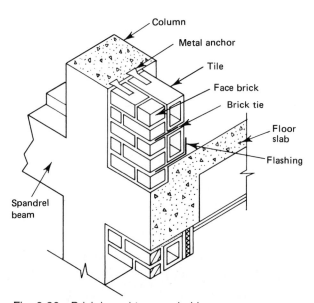

Fig. 6-26 Brick keyed to spandrel beam.

Fig. 6-29 Prefabricated brick panels.

TILE

Clay tile is manufactured from the same materials as brick and formed by extrusion using the stiff-mud process. The difference between clay tile and brick is the amount of core area that is removed. Bricks are considered as solid units (core area removed not to exceed 25 percent of the total cross-sectional area), while the clay tiles are considered hollow units. (See Fig. 6-30.)

Although many types have been developed for various uses including load-bearing wall tile, partition tile, back-up tile, furring tile, fireproofing tile, floor tile, structural clay facing tile, and structural glazed facing tile, their use has declined over the years with the increased availability of lightweight concrete masonry blocks. In many areas clay tile use is limited to renovation work and many manufacturers produce tile only by request.

TERRA-COTTA

Terra-cotta, meaning "fired earth," is a clay product which has been used for architectural decorative purposes since the days of ancient Greece and Rome. Modern terra-cotta is machine-extruded and molded or pressed. The machine-made product, usually referred to as *ceramic veneer,* is a unit with flat face and flat or ribbed back. (See Fig. 6-31.) The

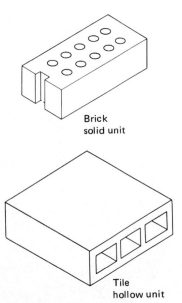

Fig. 6-30   Solid versus hollow units.

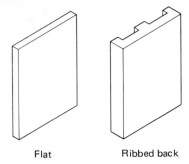

Fig. 6-31   Ceramic veneer.

molded or pressed units, called *architectural terra-cotta,* are available in sculptured, as well as plain, faces.

Ceramic Veneer

Ceramic veneer is made in two types, *adhesion* type and *anchor* type. Adhesion-type units are held to the wall by the bond of the mortar to the ceramic veneer back and to the backing wall. Anchor type are held by mortar and by wire ties between the terra-cotta and the wall behind.

Adhesion-type ceramic veneer is available in face sizes up to 600 in² (0.385 m²) with maximum widths of 24 in (600 mm) and lengths up to 36 in (900 mm). The thickness is limited to $1\frac{5}{8}$ in (40 mm). The actual face dimensions will vary with the manufacturer and, of course, with the overall dimensions of the structure for which the facing is intended. It can be applied over brick or tile, concrete, metal, or wood surfaces by setting it in a mortar coat applied over the surface of the wall. (See Fig. 6-32.)

Anchor-type ceramic veneer is used where the architect desires a larger slab than those available in adhesion-type veneer. The slab thickness will range from 2 to $2\frac{1}{2}$ in (50 to 62 mm), and the face dimensions, within reason, are a matter of choice.

The back of the units is scored or ribbed, and anchor holes are provided in the *bed* edges. One method of anchoring this type of terra-cotta involves the use of heavy copper wire loops. The wire is passed around a pencil rod fastened to the backing wall, and the ends of the loop are bent down to fit into the anchor holes in the edge of the unit. (See Fig. 6-33.) The spaces between the back of the terra-cotta units and the backing wall are

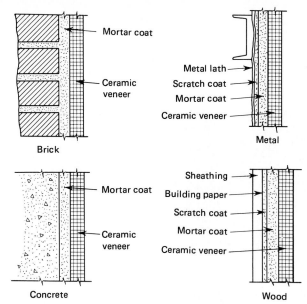

Fig. 6-32 Typical ceramic-veneer applications.

poured full of grout to provide mortar bond and to hold the anchors in place.

Architectural Terra-Cotta

Architectural terra-cotta units are made to order. Before they are made, detailed drawings must be prepared showing *size, shape, profile, joint sizes,* and location and *type of anchors* and *hangers, expansion joints,* etc. Relatively light architectural terra-cotta units may be anchored to the wall in the same manner as anchor-type ceramic veneer (see Fig. 6-33), while heavier ones are anchored in the same manner as stone veneer.

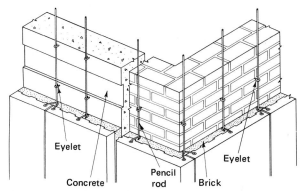

Fig. 6-33 Anchoring system for ceramic veneer or architectural terra-cotta.

CLAY TILE APPLICATIONS

Much like brick, clay tile is durable and inert and has a wide range of applications. Glazed, it produces a surface that is aesthetically pleasing and easily cleaned. Unglazed, it has a warm appearance that blends in with the surroundings. In applications such as roofing, it will last almost indefinitely. (See Fig. 6-34.) Various shapes and sizes are available, depending on the intended use.

Terra-Cotta Facing

The type of terra-cotta commonly used with light frame buildings is known as *vitrolite*. It is made from china clay in thin sections $\frac{11}{32}$, $\frac{7}{16}$, and $\frac{3}{4}$ in (8, 11, and 19 mm) thick, in squares of 4 to 24 in (100 to 600 mm), and in various rectangular sizes as well. Common colors include *white, black, red, tan, blue, green,* and *gray.* The face side is mechanically ground and polished to produce a bright, mirrorlike finish.

Asphaltic mastic is used to attach the vitrolite units to exterior surfaces, leaving joints of approximately $\frac{1}{16}$ in (1.5 mm). These are later filled with joint cement and painted. Direct contact with metal, concrete, or other hard substances should be avoided.

Clay Tile Flooring

Tiles for flooring are manufactured as glazed or unglazed units. Different types are available for varying floor conditions, including quarry tile, pavers, packinghouse tile, galley tile, faience, ceramic mosaic, and glazed interior tile. (See Fig. 6-35.)

Several methods are used to bond floor tiles to the subfloor. When the subfloor is concrete, one common method is to set the tiles in Type A cement mortar. Once the tiles are in place and the mortar has hardened, grout is poured on the surface and rubbed into the joints. Organic adhesives or inorganic bonding coats are used when the tiles are placed on wood or asphaltic subfloors.

QUARRY TILE   Quarry tile is hard, dense, unglazed tile made either by the dry-press or extrusion method. Usually clays are used which, when burned, produce red, brown, and buff colors. The tiles are made in square and oblong shapes, from $\frac{1}{2}$ to $\frac{3}{4}$ in (12 to 20 mm) thick. Square sizes are $2\frac{3}{4}$, 4, 6, 8, and 9 in (70, 100, 150, 200, and 225 mm),

Fig. 6-34   Unglazed roofing tiles.

Fig. 6-35   Clay tile flooring.

while oblong tiles are $2\frac{3}{4} \times 6$ in (70×150 mm), $3\frac{3}{4} \times 8$ in (95×200 mm), 4×8 in (100×200 mm), and 6×9 in (150×225 mm). In conjunction with these, a number of shapes of trim tile are made, including *straight base, cove base, internal-* and *external-angle base,* and *double bullnose.*

PAVER TILE   Paver tile is similar to quarry tile but with a thickness of $\frac{3}{8}$ to $\frac{5}{8}$ in (9.5 to 16 mm). Square pavers are 3, 4, $4\frac{1}{4}$, and 6 in (75, 100, 106, and 150 mm) square, while oblong ones are 3×6 in (75×150 mm). These tiles are intended for a little lighter duty than quarry tiles.

PACKINGHOUSE TILE   Packinghouse tile is intended for heavy, industrial uses, with a thickness of $1\frac{1}{4}$ to $1\frac{5}{8}$ in (32 to 41 mm) and 4×8 in (100×200 mm) dimensions.

GALLEY TILE   Galley tile is a special quarry tile with an indented pattern on the face. Its thickness is from $\frac{5}{8}$ to $\frac{3}{4}$ in (16 to 19 mm); usual face dimensions are 6×6 in (150×150 mm).

FAIENCE   Faience is a hard, durable glazed tile made with a comparatively uneven surface. Thicknesses vary from $\frac{1}{2}$ to $\frac{5}{8}$ in (12 to 16 mm), and face dimensions are $4\frac{1}{4} \times 4\frac{1}{4}$ in (106 × 106 mm) and 6×6 in (150 × 150 mm). These tiles are intended for both interior and exterior use, provided they pass the Standard Weather Test.

CERAMIC MOSAIC   Ceramic mosaic consists of small pieces of glazed or unglazed tile, arranged in patterns like those illustrated in Fig. 6-36, in a standard *sheet unit*. In some cases a paper backing is used to hold the pieces together, while in others they are bonded to a preformed rubber grid. The latter sheet units are 9×9 in (225 × 225 mm), while the ones on a paper back are approximately 12×24 in (300 × 600 mm). All have a nominal thickness of $\frac{1}{4}$ in (6 mm).

These small tiles are made in a variety of shapes, including *square, rectangular, hexagon,* and *octagon.*

GLAZED INTERIOR TILE   Glazed interior tile has a glasslike finish, a hard matte glaze that is produced in a wide variety of colors. The nominal thickness is $\frac{3}{8}$ in (9.5 mm), and tiles are made 3, $4\frac{1}{4}$, and 6 in (75, 106, and 150 mm) square; $2\frac{1}{16} \times 4\frac{1}{4}$ in (52 × 106 mm) oblong; 3 in (75 mm) hexagonal; and $4\frac{1}{4}$ in (106 mm) octagonal.

Roofing Tile

Roofing tiles are basically a terra-cotta product, designed to be applied to a roof in a similar manner to shingles. But because of their weight—900 to 1325 lb per 100 ft^2 (44 to 65 kg/m^2)—wood sheathing and strong, well-braced roof frames are necessary.

The tiles are made in a variety of styles, including *French* tile, *Spanish* tile, *Roman* tile, *English* tile, *Mission* tile, and *shingle* tile. Dimensions vary from one style to another and range from 12 to 16 in (300 to 400 mm) long and 9 to 12 in (225 to 300 mm) wide. (See Fig. 6-37.)

Glazed and unglazed tiles are available in the colors normally associated with burned-clay products.

All clay tile should be laid over an asphalt felt base and fastened with copper nails. Elastic cement is used to caulk joints that are otherwise not watertight.

Ceramic Wall Tile

Ceramic wall tiles are available in many sizes and shapes (Fig. 6-38), are usually $\frac{3}{8}$ in (9.5 mm) thick, and are used in kitchens, bathrooms, washrooms, laboratories, and feature walls, or as a dado or wainscot with other materials covering the upper part of the wall. Ceramic mosaic—small pieces of plain

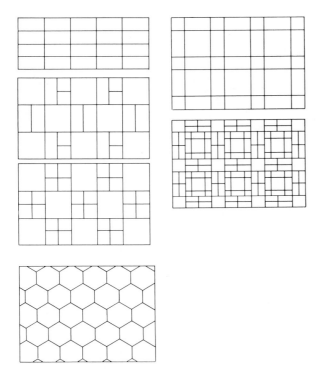

Fig. 6-36   Ceramic mosaic patterns.

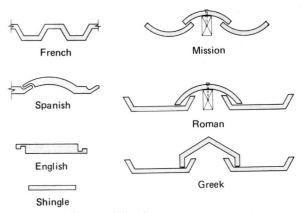

Fig. 6-37   Clay roof tile shapes.

193

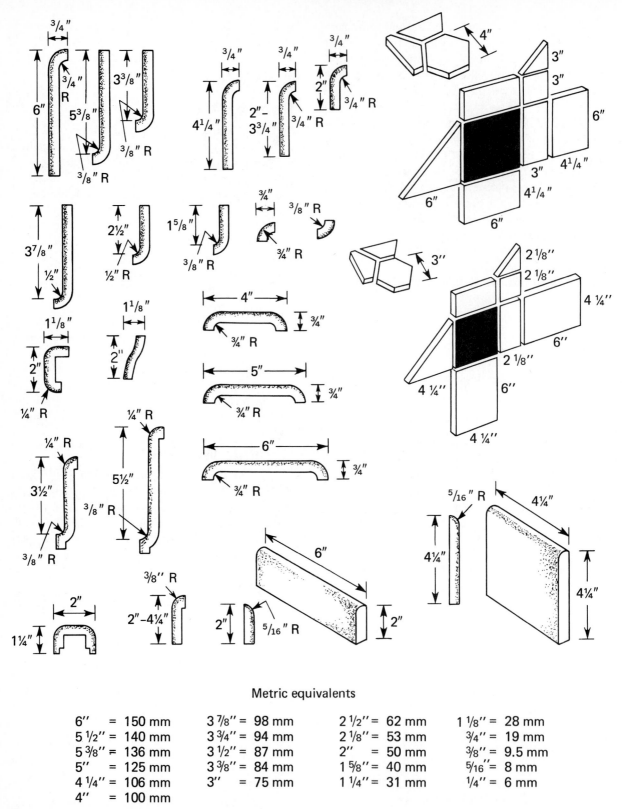

Metric equivalents

6″ = 150 mm	3 7/8″ = 98 mm	2 1/2″ = 62 mm	1 1/8″ = 28 mm
5 1/2″ = 140 mm	3 3/4″ = 94 mm	2 1/8″ = 53 mm	3/4″ = 19 mm
5 3/8″ = 136 mm	3 1/2″ = 87 mm	2″ = 50 mm	3/8″ = 9.5 mm
5″ = 125 mm	3 3/8″ = 84 mm	1 5/8″ = 40 mm	5/16″ = 8 mm
4 1/4″ = 106 mm	3″ = 75 mm	1 1/4″ = 31 mm	1/4″ = 6 mm
4″ = 100 mm			

Fig. 6-38   Ceramic wall tile sizes and shapes.

or colored tile mounted on a net backing—is used in the same manner.

CLAY MASONRY SOLAR SCREENS

Solar screens may be made from brick or tile units originally intended for some other purpose or from *screen tiles* made especially for this purpose. The latter are made in a wide variety of patterns, sizes, and colors, glazed and unglazed. Figure 6-39 illustrates some of the patterns available.

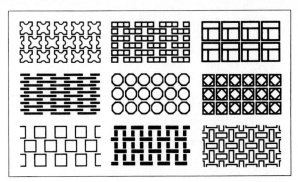

Fig. 6-39   Typical clay-masonry solar-screen patterns.

GLOSSARY

backup wall	A wall to support a facing material.
cladding	External covering of a building.
curtain wall	A wall panel that does not contribute to the structural integrity of a building.
feldspar	A crystalline mineral, aluminum silicate, with potassium, sodium, calcium, or barium.
furring	The building out or leveling of a surface.
pencil rod	A thin rod used as an anchor for stone or terra-cotta facing.
pug mill	A machine for mixing clay with water.
salt glaze	Transparent glazing.
solar screen	A pierced wall, made from masonry or tile units, intended to act as a sunshade.
spandrel beam	A load-carrying beam on the exterior wall of a building spanning over a series of openings.
veneer	A surface coating.
vitrification	The process of changing to a glassy substance through heat.
winning	Mining or removal of clay.
wythe	A 4-in thickness of brick wall.

REVIEW QUESTIONS

1. What are the basic properties which clay must have to be suitable for making brick?

2. What is the reason for blending two or more clays in the process of manufacturing brick?

3. **a.** What is meant by tempering clay?
   b. Where is this done?

4. **a.** Which process is most commonly used in molding brick?
   b. What is the purpose of the die at the end of a pug mill?

5. Explain why heat and humidity must be carefully controlled in brick-drying kilns.

6. What is meant by each of the following terms:
   a. Flashing brick
   b. Textured brick
   c. Ceramic glaze

7. Explain the meaning of these terms:
   a. Pattern bond
   b. Structural bond
   c. Mortar bond

8. Illustrate by means of a sketch the difference between English bond and Dutch bond.

9. Why should brick be soaked before being laid up in a wall?

10. What is the basic difference between brick and tile?

11. What is a curtain wall?

12. By means of careful diagrams, illustrate how a brick curtain wall can be secured to spandrel beams and columns of a reinforced concrete structural frame.

13. Outline two basic differences between ceramic veneer and architectural terra-cotta.

14. Explain the reasons for the following:
   a. There is a maximum allowable area and thickness for adhesion-type ceramic veneer.
   b. Architectural terra-cotta is a relatively costly type of facing material.

SELECTED SOURCES OF INFORMATION

Brick and Tile Manufacturers' Association of Canada, Toronto, Ont.
Division of Building Research, N.R.C., Ottawa, Ont.
Federal Seaboard Terra Cotta Corporation, New York, N.Y.
Medicine Hat Brick & Tile Co. Ltd., Medicine Hat, Alta.
Structural Clay Products Institute, Washington, D.C.
United States Ceramic Tile Co., Canton, Ohio

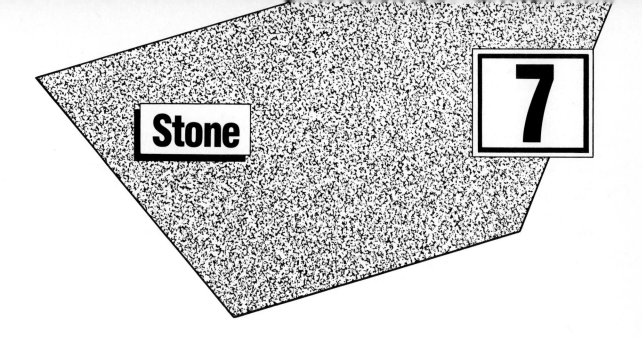

Stone

7

Stone, like brick, is one of the oldest building materials known. Since the dawn of recorded history, stone has been regarded as the preferred material in the construction of permanent buildings. It was, in fact, the predominant material used in the construction of such buildings before the turn of the twentieth century. Since that time, however, stone has assumed a new role. Rather than being used as a basic structural material, it began to be developed as a facing material, used in comparatively thin slabs over a skeleton framework of steel or concrete. Thus the inherent qualities of stone which brought it into prominence—*beauty, permanence, adaptability, economy*—have been put to use, while at the same time the great weight of a solid stone structure has been substantially reduced.

CLASSIFICATION OF STONE
Geological Origin
Rock can be divided into three general categories, depending on its geological origin: (1) *igneous,* (2) *sedimentary,* and (3) *metamorphic.* Igneous rock was formed as the result of the cooling of molten matter. Sedimentary rock was formed by the action of water, either depositing minerals at the bottom of a water body or depositing them on the earth's surface. The latter took place when water flowed to the surface from the earth's interior,

bringing minerals which were deposited as the water evaporated. Metamorphic rocks have been changed from their original structure by the action of extreme pressure, heat, moisture, or various combinations of these forces.

Composition
Rock can be classified according to its composition. Although a great many minerals occur in rock formations throughout the world, stone used in construction comes from rock that usually falls into one of three classifications: (1) rock containing mainly *silica,* (2) rock containing chiefly *silicates,* and (3) rock containing *calcareous* minerals.

The main silica mineral is *quartz,* the most abundant mineral on the earth's surface. It is the chief constituent of sand and is found in most clays and in several of the building stones.

Silicate minerals include *feldspar, hornblende, serpentine,* and *mica.* Feldspar is a silicate of alumina in combination with lime or potash. Depending on the combination, colors may be red, pink, or clear. Hornblende is a silicate of alumina with lime or iron. It is a strong, tough mineral appearing in green, brown, and black crystals. Mica is mainly silicate of alumina but may be in combination with other minerals such as iron or potash. It appears in soft, usually clear crystals that split easily into flat flakes. Serpentine, a silicate of magnesia, appears often in combination with lime. It is light green or yellow in color and has well-defined planes along which it splits readily.

The calcareous minerals include *calcite,* which is basically carbonate of lime, and *dolomite,* a carbonate of lime in combination with varying amounts of magnesia.

Commercial Forms

Stone used for building purposes also can be classified according to the form in which it is available commercially: (1) rubble (fieldstone), (2) dimension (cut stone), (3) flagstone (flat slabs), and (4) crushed rock. Rubble includes rough fieldstone which may merely have been broken into suitable sizes, or it may include irregular pieces of stone that have been roughly cut to size. Dimension stone makes up the largest portion of the stone used in building; it consists of pieces that have been cut or finished according to a set of drawings. Flagstone consists of thin pieces $\frac{1}{2}$ in (12 mm) and up in thickness, which may or may not have had their face dimensions cut to some particular size. Crushed stone consists of pieces varying in size from $\frac{3}{8}$ to 6 in (9.5 to 152 mm) and is used to a large extent in the concrete industry.

Building-Stone Requirements

Despite the abundance of rock, relatively few stones satisfy the requirements as building stones. The important requirements are (1) strength, (2) hardness, (3) workability, (4) durability, (5) color and grain, (6) porosity and texture, (7) ease of quarrying, and (8) accessibility.

Many stones satisfy the requirements of strength. For most purposes in building, a compressive strength of 5000 psi is satisfactory. In a few instances good shear strength is important. Hardness is vitally important only where the stone is to be used in floors, steps, walks, etc.; but hardness does have a bearing on workability. It varies all the way from soft sandstone, which can be easily scratched, to some stones harder than steel. Workability is important since the ease of producing the required sizes and shapes has a direct bearing on the cost. Durability—the ability of the stone to withstand the effects of rain, spray, wind, dust, frost action, heat, and fire—determines the maintenance-free life of a stone structure. This will vary from about 10 to 200 years. Color is very important from the standpoint of aesthetics and location but is also partially a matter of taste and fashion. The grain or surface appearance of stone affects its desirability for decorative purposes.

Porosity has a direct bearing on the ability of the stone to withstand frost action and the marking and staining caused by the dissolving of some mineral constituents in water. Texture, the fineness of grain, affects workability and therefore cost. Fine-textured rock splits and dresses more readily than coarse rock. For many ornamental purposes, also, the texture is important.

The ease of quarrying is a prime consideration in judging the suitability of stone for building. The bedding and joint planes must be such that the stone can be produced in sizable, sound blocks. The rock exposure should be free from closely spaced joints, cracks, and other lines of weakness. Deep and irregular weathering is also undesirable. The nearness of the deposit to the surface is also important. Building stone is seldom obtained from underground. Accessibility also affects cost. Transportation over long distances is expensive but in some cases becomes a necessity.

BUILDING STONES

Stone which does, in general, satisfy the foregoing requirements and which is commonly used in building includes *argillite, granite, greenstone, quartzite, limestone, travertine, marble, serpentine, sandstone, slate, schist,* and some *natural lavas.*

Argillite

Argillite is a metamorphic rock, formed from clay. It differs from shale in that it has undergone metamorphosis, and it differs from slate in that it has no well-defined cleavage lines. Its main ingredients are silicon dioxide, iron oxide, and aluminum oxide, with small amounts of calcium, magnesium, and sodium oxides. Its weight is in the range of 165 to 175 lb/ft^3 (2640 to 2800 kg/m^3), and its compressive strength ranges from 33,000 to 45,500 psi (255 to 350 MPa). Colors range from deep red to purple to deep blue, with seam face colors of gray, buff, tan, and russet.

Argillite is produced mainly in the form of hand-cut ashlar and rubble, though some is used for flatwork, such as floor tile, wall base, and window trim. (See Fig. 7-1.) The ashlar is produced in 6- and

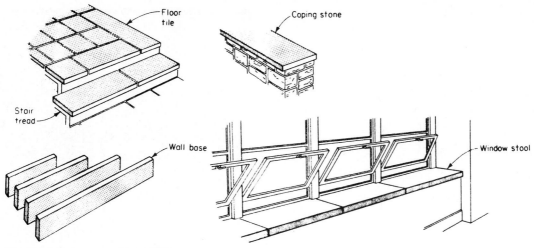

Fig. 7-1 Some uses for argillite.

8-in (150- and 200-mm) veneers, from 2 to 12 in (50 to 300 mm) high and up to 36 in (900 mm) long.

Granite

Granite is of igneous origin, composed of *quartz, feldspar, bornblende,* and *mica.* It is generally very hard, strong, durable, and capable of taking a high polish. Its main chemical ingredients are silicon dioxide and aluminum oxide, with varying amounts of iron, potassium, sodium, and calcium oxides. The weight varies from 165 to 200 lb/ft^3 (2643 to 3204 kg/m^3), average compressive strength from 18,000 to 40,000 psi (139 to 309 MPa), and water absorption from 0.002 to 0.2 percent by weight.

Finishes may vary from the rough-sawed or natural surface to a mirror-smooth, polished surface. Colors include red, pink, yellow, green, blue, white, black, and brown.

Granite has a wide variety of uses in building, including flooring, interior and exterior wall facing, column and mullion facings (see Fig. 7-2), stair treads and flagstone, as well as for ashlar and rubble veneers. For wall paneling, it is produced in several forms, including large, single slabs, extending from floor to floor, up to 6 ft (1800 mm) wide and $2\frac{1}{4}$ to 4 in (57 to 100 mm) thick, and smaller units, usually 3 to 4 in (75 to 100 mm) thick, custom cut to size. Pieces may also be cut to fit a specific member. (See Fig. 7-3.)

Ashlar is produced in thicknesses of 4 to 8 in (100 to 200 mm), in heights of 4 to 13 in (100 to 325 mm), with lengths averaging twice the height. Because of its extreme hardness, granite is difficult to cut to an exact thickness. Therefore, a tolerance of $\frac{3}{8}$ in (9.5 mm) is usually required from the nominal thickness.

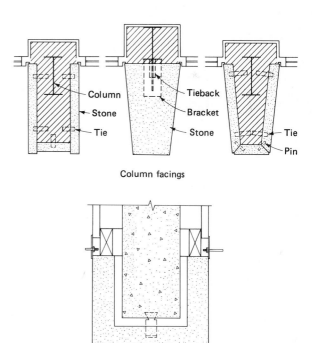

Fig. 7-2 Typical column and mullion facings.

199

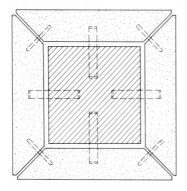

4-piece column facing
(a)

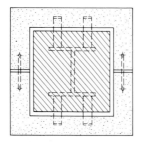

2-piece column facing
(b)

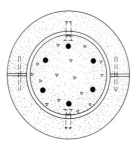

Round column facing
(c)

Fig. 7-3   Stone cut to fit columns. *(a)* four-piece column facing, *(b)* two-piece column facing, *(c)* round column facing.

Other uses for granite include facings for bridges, curb and paving stones, riprap, landscaping products, rubble facing (see Fig. 7-4), and a mosaic-type facing made by setting small cut or broken pieces of stone into the face of a precast concrete panel.

Greenstone

Greenstone is a heavy, close-grained stone, showing no visible seams, found largely in the Allegheny

Fig. 7-4   Granite random rubble facing.

mountain range. Its basic ingredients are silicon, with aluminum, iron, calcium, and manganese oxides, with small amounts of sodium, potassium, and titanium oxides. Greenstone weighs about 180 lb/ft^3 (2880 kg/m^3) and has a compressive strength of 30,000 to 50,000 psi (230 to 385 MPa). The color ranges from pea green to dark moss green, with some copper tones. Production is mainly in the form of rubble for veneer and landscaping boulders, in sizes ranging from 5 to 800 lb (2 to 365 kg).

Quartzite

Quartzite is a type of stone which is sometimes confused with granite but is quite different in composition; it is a stone which is harder than some granites. It is made up of grains of quartz sand cemented together with silica and is usually distinguishable by its coarse, crystalline appearance. The two main ingredients are alumina and silica, with lesser, varying amounts of iron and calcium oxides and magnesium. Its weight ranges from 160 to 170 lb/ft^3 (2563 to 2723 kg/m^3), and its compressive strength from 20,000 to 47,500 psi (154 to 440 MPa). The absorption rate varies quite widely, from almost zero to a high of about 1.5 percent by weight.

Because of its coarse appearance, quartzite is often used where a rustic effect is required. Colors include ivory, tan, red, gray, brown, and buff. Characteristically, each stone contains several colors with striated markings.

Quartzite is most often used in ashlar veneer, in thicknesses of 2 to 4$\frac{1}{2}$ in (50 to 115 mm), with heights of 1 to 8 in (25 to 200 mm), in random lengths up to about 48 in (1200 mm). It is also available for treads, mantels, hearths, and copings in standard thickness of 2$\frac{1}{4}$ in (57 mm), custom cut in widths up to 24 in (600 mm), and lengths up to 10 ft (3000 mm).

Limestone

Limestone is a sedimentary rock, with three distinct types being found:

Oolitic limestone is a calcite-cemented calcareous stone formed of shells and shell fragments, particularly noncrystalline in nature. It has no cleavage lines and is usually very uniform in composition and structure.

Dolomitic limestone is rich in magnesium carbonate and frequently somewhat crystalline in character. It usually has greater compressive and tensile strength than oolitic limestones, with greater variety of texture.

Crystalline limestone is predominantly composed of calcium carbonate crystals. It has high compressive and tensile strength, is very low in absorption, and has a smooth texture. The color is a fairly uniform light gray.

Some of the better known limestones are *Carthage* and *Miami Valley* limestone, which are crystalline limestones; *Kasota stone, Mankota stone, Winona stone,* and *Niagara limestone,* which are dolomitic limestones; and *Indiana limestone, Tyndallstone, Corodova limestone, Shadow Vein, Cottonwood,* and *Golden Shell* limestones, which are oolitic limestones. Some of the latter are quite interesting, owing to the fact that the fossil shapes are clearly visible in the face of the cut stone.

Limestones are composed mainly of two basic ingredients—*calcium carbonate* and *magnesium carbonate*—with silica, aluminum oxide, and iron oxide, together with other elements in lesser amounts, present in most limestones. The calcium carbonate may range from as high as 97 percent in some limestones to a low of about 48 percent in others. The amount of magnesium carbonate varies from about 1.2 percent as a low to about 43 percent in some stones.

The weight of limestone varies quite widely, according to the type, from 125 to 180 lb/ft^3 (2000 to 2880 kg/m^3), with compressive strength ranging all the way from a low of 2500 psi (19 MPa) to a high of about 25,000 psi (193 MPa). The rate of water absorption also varies greatly, from a low of about 0.25 to a high of about 7.5 percent.

Limestone is one of the most commonly used building stones and is produced in all three types: *dimension* (cut) stone, *ashlar,* and *rubble.* It is put to a great many uses, including paneling, ashlar veneer, window stools and sills, copings, facings of all kinds, rubble facing, flagstone, hearths, mantels, and sculpture.

Panels are produced up to 16 ft (4800 mm) long by 6 ft (1800 mm) wide, in thicknesses of 2$\frac{1}{4}$ in (57 mm) to 8 in (200 mm). Insulated spandrel panels are produced by cementing glass-fiber insulation to the back of a 2-in (50-mm) limestone panel. A sandwich panel can be produced by covering that insulation with a thin metal or rigid plastic sheet.

Ashlar is usually produced in thicknesses of 2$\frac{1}{4}$ in (57 mm) to 8 in (200 mm), in widths of 2 to 10 in (50 to 250 mm), and in lengths of 6 in (150 mm) to 3 ft (900 mm).

Travertine

Travertine is also a sedimentary rock, composed mainly of calcium carbonate. It has been formed at the earth's surface through the evaporation of water from hot springs. It is used as an interior decorative stone because of its pleasing texture and its tendency to show small, natural pockets on a cut surface. Colors include off-white, gray to creamy buff, and light to dark tan.

Travertine is produced primarily as ashlar veneer, rubble, and rustic cut stone, in thicknesses of 3 to 5 in (75 to 125 mm) in ashlar, 6 to 8 in (150 to 200 mm) in rubble, and 4 in (100 mm) in rustic cut stone. Face dimensions vary, up to a maximum of about 24 in (600 mm) in length.

Marble

Marble is an example of a metamorphic rock, one that has been changed from its original structure. In this case limestone and dolomite have been recrystallized to form marble. A number of types of marble have come to be recognized, among them *carrara, parian, numidian, onyx, Vermont,* and *brecciated* marbles.

The colors of marble range from pure white through all shades of gray to black, including violet, red, yellow, pink, and green. The great range of colors is due to the presence of various oxides of iron, silica, graphite, mica, and carbonaceous matter, which are scattered through the rock in streaks, blotches, or grains. Brecciated marbles are made up of small fragments embedded in a colored paste or cementing material. Certain varieties of marble deteriorate quite readily when exposed to the weather and are suitable only for interior work.

Marble is used mainly for wall or column facing and for flooring. Wall facing is done by paneling or by ashlar veneer. Initial costs of paneling have been cut by producing precast lightweight concrete panels faced with a $\frac{7}{8}$-in (22-mm) veneer of marble.

Average compressive strength of marble varies from 12,000 to 21,000 psi (93 to 162 MPa), while the weight is in the range of 185 to 190 lb/ft^3 (2963 to 3043 kg/m^3). The absorption rate is in the range of 0.001 to 0.06 percent.

Serpentine

Serpentine is an igneous rock which takes its name from the mineral serpentine, its chief constituent. The mineral, a magnesium silicate, is olive green to greenish black, but impurities may give the rock other colors.

Serpentine has a fine grain, is dense and homogeneous in structure, and is free from cleavage planes. Some types are subject to deterioration due to weathering and are therefore confined to use in interiors or in sheltered locations.

The black serpentine is highly resistant to chemical attack, and therefore polished surfaces hold their polish without deterioration. For the same reason it is useful for wainscot work because it is not discolored by moisture.

It is possible to cut this stone into relatively thin sections of $\frac{7}{8}$ to $1\frac{1}{4}$ in (22 to 32 mm), and it is therefore relatively inexpensive as a stone paneling. In those thicknesses, it is also used for windowsills, stools, and stair treads and landings.

Sandstone

Sandstone is a sedimentary class of stone, made up of silica grains cemented together. The cement may be silica, iron oxide, or clay; the hardness and durability of the particular sandstone depends on the type of cement. Other materials such as mica, lime, and feldspar appear in some sandstones, resulting in considerable variation in color and texture. Some common sandstones are *berea* sandstone, *linroc* stone, *ledgestone, Kaibab* sandstone, *Pearl* sandstone, *Delaware Valley* sandstone, *Briar Hill* sandstone, and *Walpole* stone. Colors include gray, buff, light brown, brown, russet, copper, red, and purple.

The basic elements in sandstone are 70 to 95 percent *silicon dioxide* and 2 to 10 percent *aluminum oxide.* Accompanying them in smaller amounts, of varying percentages, are calcium, iron, and magnesium oxides.

Some sandstones are quite porous, with as much as 30 percent of their volume composed of pores, with the result that there is quite a wide variation in weight, which ranges from 140 to 165 lb/ft^3 (2242 to 2643 kg/m^3). The compressive strength also varies widely, from 4000 to 14,000 psi (31 to 108 MPa). Because of the relatively porous nature of sandstone, absorption rates range from 1.5 to 6 percent by weight.

A large percentage of the production of sandstone is in ashlar veneer and rubble. Ashlar is normally produced in 4-, 6-, and 8-in (100-, 150-, and 200-mm) thicknesses, though there is some production of $\frac{1}{2}$-in (13-mm) thin veneer. Units will vary from 1 to 10 in (25 to 250 mm) in height and up to 36 in (900 mm) in length.

Panels are produced in some types of sandstone, in thicknesses ranging from $2\frac{1}{4}$ to 4 in (57 to 100 mm) and in face sizes up to 8 ft (2400 mm) long and 4 ft (1200 mm) wide. Larger sizes may be custom cut on request.

Because of their structure, sandstones lend themselves to textured finishes, such as split face or chipped face. Rubbed finishes and hammered finishes are also available.

Slate

Slate is a metamorphic rock, formed by the metamorphosis of clays and shales which have been deposited in layers. A unique characteristic of the material is the relative ease with which it may be separated into thin, tough sheets, called *slates*, $\frac{1}{2}$ in (6 mm) or more in thickness. Colors include black, green, red, gray, and purple; in some cases the color changes after long exposure.

The basic ingredients include *silicon dioxide*, 45 to 56 percent; *aluminum oxide*, 16 to 25 percent; *iron oxide*, 5 to 8 percent; *potassium oxide*, 3 to 6.5 percent; magnesium oxide, 2 to 4 percent, with smaller amounts of titanium, calcium, and sulfur. The weight ranges from 175 to 180 lb/ft^3 (2800 to 2880 kg/m^3), and the compressive strength from 16,000 to 24,000 psi (124 to 185 MPa). The water absorption rate is small: from 0.15 to 0.25 percent.

Slate is normally produced in three textures—*natural cleft, sand rubbed,* and *honed*—and three main types—*dimension slate, random flagging,* and *roofing tile*. Common uses include flooring, flagstones, interior and exterior wall facing, windowsills and stools, counter tops, coping and caps, and roofing tile.

Dimension slate is produced in thicknesses of $\frac{3}{4}$ to 2 in (19 to 50 mm), in widths of 4 to 48 in (100 to 1200 mm), and in lengths up to 90 in (2250 mm). Random flagging contains approximately $1\frac{1}{2}$ ft^2 (0.1 m^2) per piece. Roofing tile is normally 12 in (300 mm) wide, 14 to 24 in (350 to 600 mm) long, and comes in thicknesses of $\frac{1}{4}$, $\frac{3}{8}$, and $\frac{1}{2}$ in (6, 9.5, and 13 mm).

When used as roofing tile, the slabs are cut into various lengths and widths (for random style) and predrilled for nailing. The surface may be left in a textured state or it may be ground smooth.

Slate may be laid over a surface of nailing concrete, over gypsum decking, or over wood decking. Heavy felt paper, 15 to 65 lb (6.75 to 29.5 kg), depending on the thickness of the slate, is used as an underlay. Slates are placed with a 3-in (75-mm) lap and held in place with copper nails.

Schist

Schist is also a metamorphic rock of foliated structure, which splits easily into slabs or sheets. Its composition varies, depending on the basic material on which the process of metamorphosis took place. Colors include green, red, gold, brown, white, gray, and blue.

In most cases, the basic components will be about 85 percent silica, with the remainder made up of iron and magnesium oxides. Weights range from 150 to 170 lb/ft^3 (2400 to 2725 kg/m^3), and the compressive strength is about 17,000 psi (131 MPa).

Most of the production is in the form of rubble veneer and flagstone, the veneer in thicknesses of 2 to $4\frac{1}{2}$ in (50 to 115 mm) and the flagstone of $\frac{3}{4}$ to $1\frac{1}{2}$ in (19 to 36 mm). Face sizes range from very small to about 5 ft^2 (0.5 m^2). Uses include interior and exterior wall facing, fireplaces, sidewalks and patios, and landscaping.

Natural Lavas

In various areas, the lava flow from ancient volcanoes has left rock deposits which have proven useful as building stone. A unique feature of most of them is their relative lightness; some weigh only one-fifth as much as granite.

Some of the lightweight stone used in construction includes *featherock, corkstone,* and some *scorias*. Their composition is largely silica. The weights of these stones vary from about 40 lb/ft^3 (640 kg/m^3) for featherock and scorias to about 100/ft^3 (1600 kg/m^3) for corkstone. Production is mainly in the form of rubble veneer, in thicknesses of 1 to 4 in (25 to 100 mm), in random face sizes.

PRODUCTION OF STONE

The process of removing stone from its natural bed is known as quarrying, and the method of quarrying will depend to some extent on the nature of the stone. Some stone is stratified horizontally, and the horizontal demarcations between the strata are known as *bedding planes*. In other stone, the vertical separations are more visible, and they are called *joint planes*. In some stone both are apparent, as in Fig. 7-6, where both bedding planes and joint planes are clearly visible.

In one method of stone removal, holes are drilled close together at right angles to the bedding planes or joint planes or both. Wedges are then driven into the holes to split the rock along the drilled line.

Another method involves a system illustrated in Fig. 7-5. After the overburden has been removed, *channel machines* are brought in to outline the boundaries of the quarry. The machines have a chisel mounted on one or both sides and, traveling on temporary tracks, they cut channels, or *canals,* 10 ft (3 m) deep into the stone, one down each side and one down the center. (See Fig. 7-5.)

Next, the first three lateral cuts are made. This may be done with a channel machine, but more often a wire saw is used. (See Fig. 7-6.) A wire saw consists of a $\frac{1}{4}$-in (6-mm) wire strung between pulleys mounted top and bottom on frames which are anchored in the center canal and one or the other of the side canals. The saws use quartz sand as a cutting agent; they are simply the transport vehicle, serving to carry the sand through the cut.

The long blocks thus formed are cut into shorter lengths. The outside corner one—the *key block*—is removed first by placing wedges every few feet along the top of the cut and driving them down to tilt the block and break it loose at the bottom of the cut. Large tongs grasp the block, and a crane removes it from the quarry. The remainder of the blocks from the first three cuts are removed in a similar manner. Finally the entire quarry is cut into

Fig. 7-6 Wire saws in action. *(Indiana Limestone Co.)*

blocks of approximately 4 ft (1.2 m) wide by means of the wire saws.

The stone blocks thus produced (see Fig. 7-7) are transported from the quarry by truck and taken to a plant where the stone panels, etc., required are cut from them. Power saws (*chat* saws, *shot* saws, and *diamond* saws) are used to cut the blocks to the required dimensions. Each type of saw produces a surface texture which is different from the others.

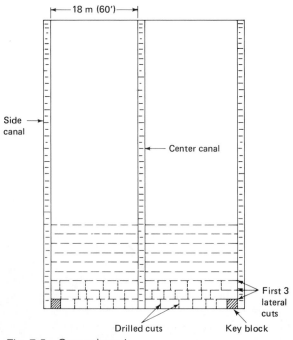

Fig. 7-5 Quarry layout.

Fig. 7-7 Large stone block loaded for removal from quarry. *(Indiana Limestone Co.)*

Stone Surface Finishes

In addition to the sawn finishes, a number of other surface treatments can be applied to a stone face. Machine finishes include a planer finish, carbo-finish, rubbed finish, and various machine-tool finishes. A carbo-finish is a very smooth finish produced by the use of a Carborundum machine instead of a planer. A rubbed finish requires the rubbing of the stone with an abrasive after it has been planed.

A variety of hand finishes are also applicable to cut stone. They include the bush-hammer, peen-hammer, patent-hammer, pick-point, crandalled, and hand-rubbed finishes. (See Fig. 7-8.)

STONE CONSTRUCTION

The building industry today uses stone largely as a facing material for large buildings with steel or concrete frames. When used as facing, stonework may be divided into four general categories: *paneling, veneer, trim,* and *stone flatwork.* Veneer may be applied in one of two ways: in *ashlar* patterns or as *rubble.*

Paneling

Paneling, sometimes known as dimension stone, is used as curtain wall material to provide a finished exterior on structural frames. Panels can be solid slabs supported directly by the structural frame as illustrated in Figs. 7-9 and 7-10, or they can be

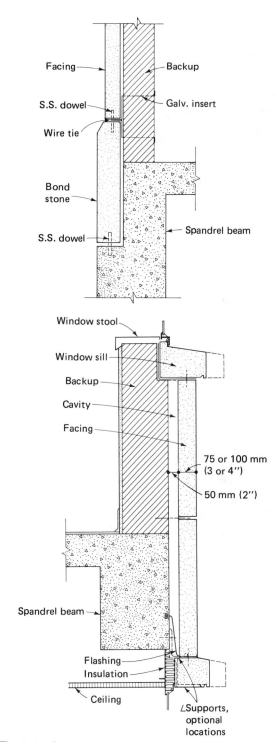

Fig. 7-9   Stone panels supported over backup wall.

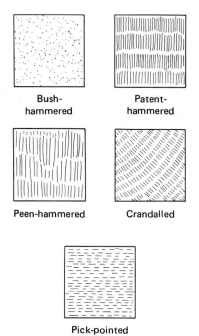

Fig. 7-8   Hand finishes on stone.

205

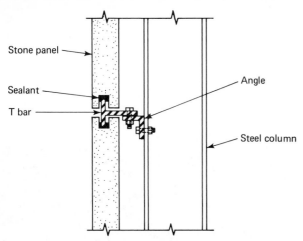

Fig. 7-10   Stone panels supported on steel frame.

incorporated into insulated sandwich panels.

Solid stone slabs vary in thickness from 1 to 5 in (25 to 125 mm), with bond stones up to 8 in (200 mm) thick. The face area also varies, depending on the type of stone, the quarry from which it is produced, and the slab thickness. In general, maximum size is about $108 \times 156 \times 5$ in ($2700 \times 3900 \times 125$ mm), but the actual size will depend on the specifications for the particular project.

Because of their weight, stone panels must have adequate support to ensure that no movement will occur once they are set in place. Panels are usually supported by bond stones or by structural steel angles (see Figs. 7-9 and 7-10), and stone panels used for facing soffits are supported as shown in Fig. 7-11.

Panels supported as shown in Fig. 7-9 are secured to the backup wall by ties which have one end anchored in the backup wall material and the other set in holes drilled in the edge of the stone panels.

(See Fig. 7-12.) Stones under 30 in (750 mm) in height require two anchors per stone in the top bed for widths of 24 in (600 mm) or more, one anchor per stone for widths less than 24 in. Two anchors should be provided top and bottom for stones that are over 30 in (750 mm) in height, no matter what the width.

Stone sandwich panels may have a facing of limestone, granite, or marble and are made in two ways. One method is to bond 2 in (50 mm) of rigid insulation to 2 in (50 mm) of stone. The back may or may not be covered with some type of rigid board, such as hardboard or asbestos-cement board. Such panels are made to order, but the practical maximum width would be 48 in (1200 mm), with a maximum area of about 25 ft³ (2.3 m²).

The other type of stone sandwich panel consists of 2 in (50 mm) of glass fiber insulation between a 2-in (50-mm) slab of stone and a thin metal pan backing.

Stone sandwich panels are usually supported by some type of subframe (see Fig. 7-13), which, in turn, is attached to the building frame by one of the methods illustrated in Fig. 7-14.

Veneer

Stone veneering involves the use of relatively small pieces of stone of various thicknesses, fastened to the surface of a backup wall, such as block, brick, tile, or concrete with some type of stone anchor. It may be one of a type shown in Fig. 7-15, a galvanized-wire tie such as that illustrated in Fig. 7-16, or a system like that shown in Fig. 7-17. In the latter the horizontal joint reinforcement used in the block backup has a projecting third rod, with hooks attached, which tie the stone to the wall.

(Text continued on page 210.)

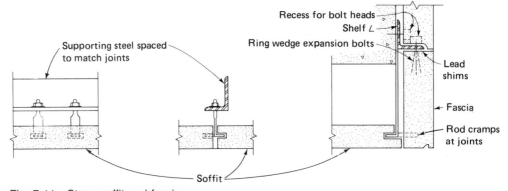

Fig. 7-11   Stone soffit and fascia.

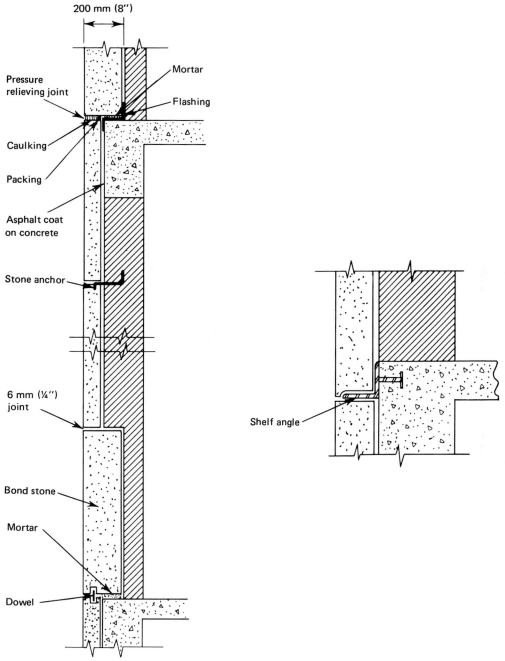

200 mm (8")

Pressure
relieving joint

Mortar

Flashing

Caulking

Packing

Asphalt coat
on concrete

Stone anchor

6 mm (¼")
joint

Bond stone

Mortar

Dowel

Shelf angle

Fig. 7-12   Stone facing on masonry backup.

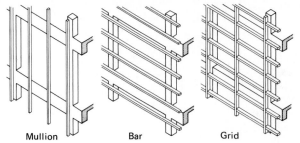

Mullion   Bar   Grid

Fig. 7-13   Curtain wall subframes.

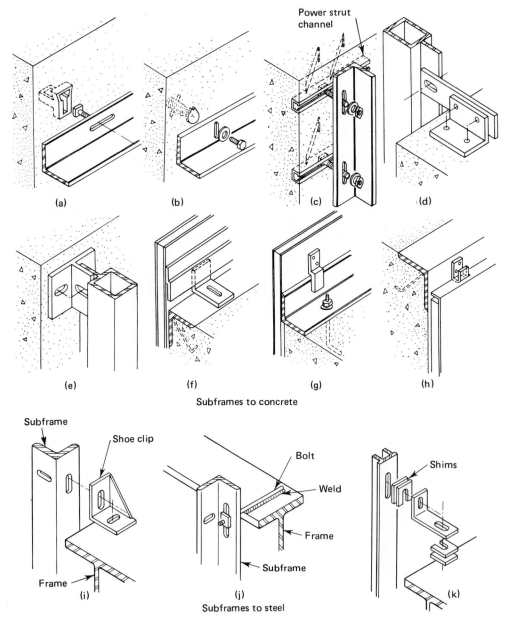

Fig. 7-14   Subframe anchoring systems.

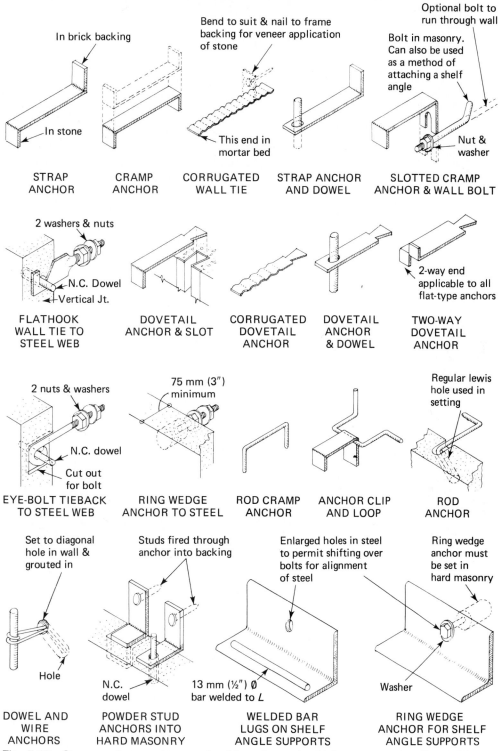

In brick backing

In stone

STRAP ANCHOR

CRAMP ANCHOR

Bend to suit & nail to frame backing for veneer application of stone

This end in mortar bed

CORRUGATED WALL TIE

STRAP ANCHOR AND DOWEL

Optional bolt to run through wall

Bolt in masonry. Can also be used as a method of attaching a shelf angle

Nut & washer

SLOTTED CRAMP ANCHOR & WALL BOLT

2 washers & nuts

N.C. Dowel

Vertical Jt.

FLATHOOK WALL TIE TO STEEL WEB

DOVETAIL ANCHOR & SLOT

CORRUGATED DOVETAIL ANCHOR

DOVETAIL ANCHOR & DOWEL

2-way end applicable to all flat-type anchors

TWO-WAY DOVETAIL ANCHOR

2 nuts & washers

N.C. dowel

Cut out for bolt

EYE-BOLT TIEBACK TO STEEL WEB

75 mm (3") minimum

RING WEDGE ANCHOR TO STEEL

ROD CRAMP ANCHOR

ANCHOR CLIP AND LOOP

Regular lewis hole used in setting

ROD ANCHOR

Set to diagonal hole in wall & grouted in

Hole

DOWEL AND WIRE ANCHORS

Studs fired through anchor into backing

N.C. dowel

POWDER STUD ANCHORS INTO HARD MASONRY

Enlarged holes in steel to permit shifting over bolts for alignment of steel

13 mm (½") Ø bar welded to L

WELDED BAR LUGS ON SHELF ANGLE SUPPORTS

Ring wedge anchor must be set in hard masonry

Washer

RING WEDGE ANCHOR FOR SHELF ANGLE SUPPORTS

Fig. 7-15 Stone anchors and supports. All anchors should be noncorrosive if possible, especially in coastal regions with salty air, where supporting angles should also be of non-corrosive metal. Rusting anchors increase in size and diameter, developing tremendous stresses which can split the stone at the anchor slots.

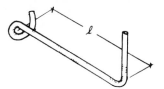

For use in vertical joints

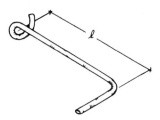

For use in horizontal joints

Fig. 7-16   Galvanized wire ties.

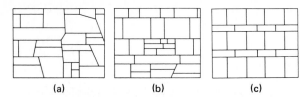

Fig. 7-18   Ashlar veneer. *(a)* Broken ashlar, *(b)* irregular coursed ashlar, *(c)* regular coursed ashlar.

Ashlar requires the use of cut stone and includes broken ashlar, irregular coursed ashlar, and regular coursed ashlar (see Fig. 7-18). Support is provided in much the same way as for stone panels, and galvanized-wire ties provide anchors to the back-up wall.

Two styles of rubblework are used: random and coursed. In the first case no attempt is made to produce either horizontal or vertical course lines. Spaces too small for a regular stone are filled with *spalls*, and bond stones must be provided for structural bonding, unless ties are being used for this purpose. In coursed rubblework, horizontal course lines are maintained, but no vertical course lines used. (See Fig. 7-19.)

As an interior finish, stone veneer is used in feature walls such as entranceways and as a finish on fireplaces. (See Figs. 7-20 and 7-21.) Granite, marble, limestone, sandstone, slate, and quartzite are all available in a wide range of colors and textures for use in these applications. Stones that can be used to enhance the aesthetics of any interior include bluestone, a fine-grained sandstone with a deep color; greenstone, a stone with a hard, abrasive structure; and travertine, a particular type of limestone.

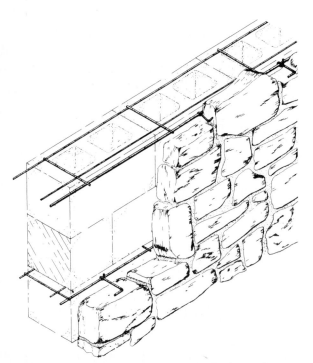

Fig. 7-17   Wall reinforcement and anchoring system.

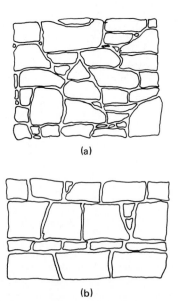

(a)

(b)

Fig. 7-19 Rubble veneer. *(a)* Random rubble, *(b)* coursed rubble.

Fig. 7-20 Stone veneer on fireplace.

Stone veneers such as these are normally 1 to 2 in (25 to 50 mm) in thickness and have custom-cut face areas. They can be placed in an ashlar or rubble pattern and are anchored to the backup wall with standard stone anchors. Lightweight rock such as featherock, a natural lava rock weighing only 30 to 40 lb/ft^3 (480 to 640 kg/m^3), can be applied to a wall using common portland cement mortar.

Fig. 7-21 Marble veneer in office building foyer.

Fig. 7-22 Lightweight stone panels used as an interior finish.

Lightweight panels using natural aggregates embedded in a substrate of fiberglass-reinforced sand, resin, and filler are also used to provide a pleasing and durable finish. (See Fig. 7-22.) Similar panels are available as exterior finishes because of their durability and resistance to weathering.

Stone Trim

Stone trim refers to those pieces of cut stone which are used for such specific purposes as *base, window stool, stair treads* (see Fig. 7-1), *copings,* and similar items that are normally regarded as *finishing.* Figure 7-23 illustrates a number of typical stone trim items.

Stone Flatwork

Stone floors, walks, and patios are made by covering a base of stone, concrete, brick, or tile with flagstones. They may be random flagstone, trimmed flagstone, trimmed rectangular, or square and rec-

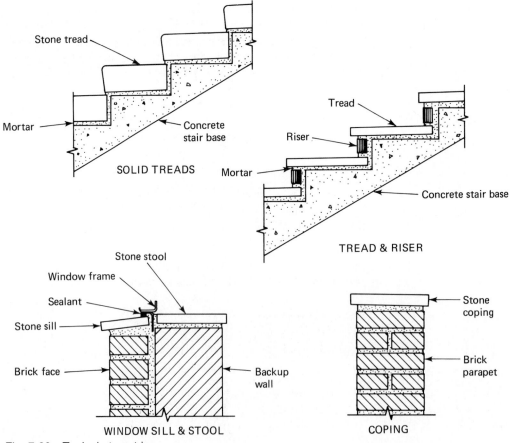
Fig. 7-23 Typical stone trim.

Fig. 7-24   Random flag-
stone floor.

tangular. Random flagstone consists of natural irreg-
ularly shaped pieces laid without any attempt at
pattern. (See Fig. 7-24.) Trimmed flagstones consist
of natural random pieces, a percentage of which
have one or two edges saw trimmed. Trimmed rectangular flagstones have four straight sawn edges
with right-angle corners but are of no specific dimensions. Square and rectangular flagstones have
straight edges, right-angle corners, and are cut to
specific sizes, often 4×4 in (100×100 mm) or
6×6 in (150×150 mm), but they may be cut
to any specified size.

GLOSSARY

bedding plane   The position and direction of the joints between strata or layers of rock.

chat saw   A stone saw using small pieces of hard steel as the cutting agent.

cleavage lines   Natural lines of weakness along which stone can be broken most easily.

diamond saw   A large circular saw, having commercial diamonds fixed to its edge to act as cutting teeth.

joint plane   The position and direction of the breaks or joints in an individual rock layer, roughly perpendicular to the bedding plane.

shelf angle   A metal angle projecting from a back up wall which acts as a support for facing material.

shot saw   A stone using chilled steel shot as the cutters.

spall   A small stone used to fill a space between two stones in rubble veneer.

subframe   A light frame attached to the structural frame for the purpose of carrying a curtain wall.

REVIEW QUESTIONS

1. **a.** Explain what is meant by a "metamorphic rock."

b. Show why marble is an example of metamorphic rock.

2. Why are relatively few stones used as building stones?

3. What is meant by the following:
   a. The porosity of a stone
   b. The texture of a stone

4. Explain why stone is today largely limited to a facing material.

5. How does oolitic limestone basically differ from other types of limestone?

6. What is the chief use of travertine as a building stone?

7. What kinds of stone are most commonly used for exterior work?

8. Illustrate by diagram one method of anchoring a stone facing to a concrete backup wall.

9. **a.** What is a bond stone?
   b. What is a stone anchor?

SELECTED SOURCES OF INFORMATION

Adirondak Stone Quarries Inc., Malone, N.Y.
Building Stone Institute, Indianapolis, Ind.
Chicago Cut Stone Contractors' Association, Chicago, Ill.
Cold Springs Granite Co., St. Cloud, Minn.
Garson Limestone Co., Ltd., Winnipeg, Man.
Indiana Limestone Co., Bedford, Ind.
Sinclair Cut Stone Co., Hamilton, Ont.
Tennessee Marble Co., Knoxville, Tenn.

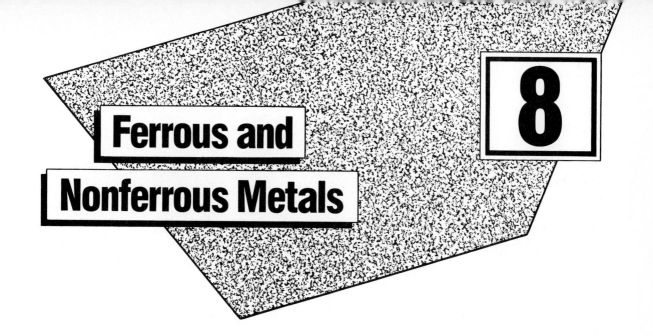

Ferrous and Nonferrous Metals

8

FERROUS METALS
Iron Production

Three basic raw materials are needed in large quantities for the production of iron—iron ore, coal, and limestone. The operations of the mines and quarries are, in themselves, major industries. Figures 8-1 and 8-2 illustrate the type of facilities that are required to provide raw materials for the production of iron.

Iron in its natural state is not found as a pure metal but as an oxide of iron. *Hematite* (Fe_2O_3), *magnetite* (Fe_3O_4), *siderite* (Fe_2CO_3), *limonite* ($Fe_2O_3 + nH_2O$), and *taconite* are primary ores that are used in the commercial production of iron. Taconite, the most abundant source of iron in North America, is a hard quartz containing from 20 to 40 percent iron.

The iron ore, usually obtained by open pit mining, goes through primary crushing and concentrating at the mine. In the case of the taconite, the ore is ground to a fine powder and mixed with water to form a slurry. The iron oxide is then removed magnetically, formed into mud pellets about $\frac{1}{2}$ in (12 mm) in diameter, and sintered, producing a concentrate containing about 65 percent iron.

Limestone and dolomite are quarried, crushed, screened, and shipped to the steel plant in various sizes for use in the sinter plant, as flux material in the blast furnaces, and in the making of refractory brick. Coal is converted into coke in coke ovens for use as fuel in the blast furnace.

The process of converting the iron oxides to iron is accomplished in the *blast furnace*. (See Fig. 8-3.) The furnace is charged with alternate layers

Fig. 8-1 Unloading coal at steel plant. *(Steel Co. of Canada, Ltd.)*

215

Fig. 8-2 Iron ore on storage dock. *(Steel Co. of Canada, Ltd.)*

of iron ore, coke, and limestone (see Fig. 8-4) in a ratio of approximately 60 percent iron ore, 25 percent coke, and 15 percent limestone and dolomite.

Air, preheated to 760 to 1150°C, is forced

Fig. 8-3 Blast furnace from outside. *(Dominion Foundries & Steel, Ltd.)*

through the furnace to drive off the surface moisture contained by the raw materials and to facilitate in the combustion of the coke. The resulting gases, mainly carbon monoxide (CO), pass through the charge in the first step of the reduction process. In the case of the coke, carbon and oxygen combine to produce carbon monoxide, as indicated by the following equation:

$$2C + O_2 \rightarrow 2CO$$

If hematite ore is used, its partial reduction due to the carbon monoxide can be expressed as

$$3Fe_2O_3 + CO \rightarrow 2Fe_3O_4 + CO_2$$

While this partial reduction is occurring, the flux materials are also being transformed. Due to the increasing temperature, the limestone is being calcined in preparation for combination with the nonmetallic substances in the iron ore to produce slag. For the limestone, the reaction is expressed as

$$CaCO_3 \rightarrow CaO + CO_2$$

and for the dolomite, the expression becomes

$$MgCO_3 \rightarrow MgO + CO_2$$

As the charge descends into the furnace and the temperature increases, a small amount of carbon is used up by the iron oxide (a result of incandescent

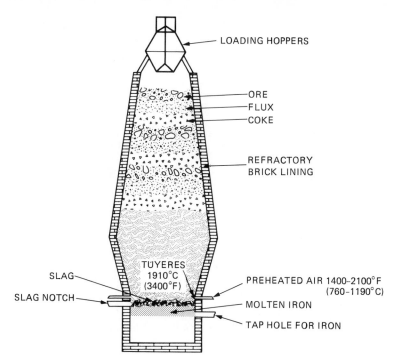

Fig. 8-4 Schematic of a blast furnace.

LOADING HOPPERS

ORE
FLUX
COKE

REFRACTORY
BRICK LINING

SLAG

SLAG NOTCH

TUYERES
1910°C
(3400°F)

PREHEATED AIR 1400–2100°F
(760–1190°C)

MOLTEN IRON

TAP HOLE FOR IRON

carbon coming in contact with the iron ore), resulting in the complete reduction of the iron oxide to metallic iron:

$$Fe_2O_3 + 3C \rightarrow 2Fe + 3CO$$

Once the charge reaches the hearth, further reduction of the nonmetallic materials occurs and the oxides of manganese, silicon, and phosphorus are reduced by combining with carbon:

$$MnO + C \rightarrow Mn + CO$$
$$SiO_2 + 2C \rightarrow Si + 2CO$$
$$P_2O_5 + 5C \rightarrow 2P + 5CO$$

Due to the intense heat at this point in the furnace, the iron becomes molten and the nonmetallic materials combine to form slag. The amounts of manganese (Mn), silica (Si), and phosphorus (P) that are released by the reduction process are responsible for the various amounts of impurities in the iron.

A final, important function of the slag is to remove sulfur from the molten iron. The amount of sulfur that the slag can extract from the iron depends on the temperature in the hearth and the basicity of the slag. The resulting equation is

$$FeS + CaO + C \rightarrow CaS + Fe + CO$$

The molten iron and slag are drawn off at regular intervals from the bottom of the furnace. (See Fig. 8-5.) The whole cycle of the charge, from the time

Fig. 8-5 Molten iron drawn from blast furnace. *(Steel Co. of Canada, Ltd.)*

217

it is loaded into the top of the furnace to the time it is drawn off, ranges between 5 and 8 h. Once a blast furnace is put into operation, the process is continuous and the furnace is not shut down until refractory relining is necessary.

The product of the blast furnace is known as *pig iron*—the basis for all ferrous metals and alloys. It is basically metallic iron containing about $3\frac{1}{2}$ to 4 percent carbon and small amounts of manganese, silica, and phosphorus. To produce 2200 lb (1 metric ton) of pig iron, it takes approximately 2800 lb (1270 kg) of iron ore, 1300 lb (600 kg) of coke, 825 lb (375 kg) of limestone, 16,000 lb (7260 kg) of air, 480,000 lb (21,800 kg) of water, and 27 million Btu (28,500,000 kJ) of heat. Natural gas is sometimes used as a fuel to lower the quantity of coke.

CAST IRON Cast iron is produced by reheating pig iron and removing some of the impurities. It is an alloy of iron, silica, and carbon. The carbon content is between 1.7 and 4.5 percent, and the properties of cast iron are modified through heat treatment.

There are several types of cast iron, but the most common are the *gray* and *white* cast irons. When cast iron is cooled, some of the carbon combines with the iron to form iron carbide and the remainder of the carbon remains as free carbon. The slower the rate of cooling, the less iron carbide is formed and the greater the amount of free carbon. When a sample of this type of cast iron is fractured, the fracture appears gray in color. If the rate of cooling is increased, much more of the carbon will combine with the iron, leaving less in the form of free carbon. When fractured, this type of cast iron has an almost white appearance and is known as white cast iron.

In general, cast iron is usually quite brittle. (See Fig. 8-6.) It is relatively weak in tension and strong in compression, thereby having limited use as a construction material. Its primary uses are in castings, machine bases, and pipe.

Iron-Carbon Alloys

Pure iron is known as *allotropic*, that is, as it cools from the molten state the arrangement of its atoms changes. Pure iron solidifies at about 1540°C. At this temperature the atoms are in a *body-centered cubic* arrangement. (See Fig. 8-7.) In this state, the

Fig. 8-6 Brittle failure of cast iron (on *right*) in tension compared to ductile failure of steel (on *left*).

iron is known as delta (δ) iron or δ-*ferrite*. As the iron continues to cool a change in the arrangement of the atoms occurs at about 1400°C. The atoms are rearranged in a *face-centered cubic* (see Fig. 8-7) and the iron is known as gamma (γ) iron or *austenite*. In this stage the iron is nonmagnetic. As cooling continues, another change occurs at about 910°C. The iron reverts back to a body-centered cubic, but it does not regain its magnetic qualities until the temperature drops to 770°C.

When carbon is added to iron, it combines with the iron in various ways (depending on the temperature), disrupting the original properties of the iron. The amount of carbon plays an important role in establishing the final properties of the alloy. This combination of iron and carbon is known as an iron-carbon alloy.

Figure 8-8 is a simplified phase diagram for iron and carbon to help illustrate the effect of temper-

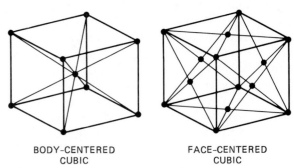

BODY-CENTERED CUBIC   FACE-CENTERED CUBIC

Fig. 8-7 Atomic arrangements of iron.

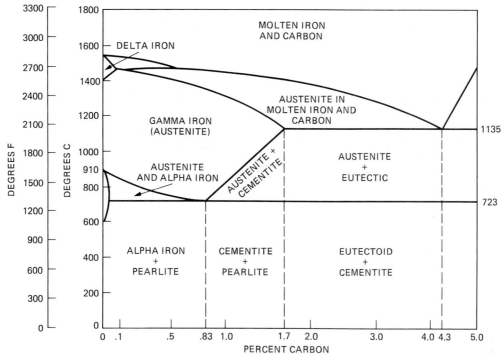

Fig. 8-8   Iron-carbon phase diagram.

ature on an iron-carbon alloy. For example, gamma iron with 0 percent carbon transforms to alpha iron at about 910°C, but as the carbon content increases to 0.83 percent, the transformation temperature drops to 723°C. Below 723°C, and a carbon content of less than 0.83 percent, a composition of alpha iron and pearlite exists. The *pearlite* is a *eutectoid* mixture composed of alpha iron and *cementite.* Increasing the carbon content above 0.83 percent, the mixture transforms to a combination of cementite and pearlite.

By understanding the effects of temperature on the alloy, it is possible to vary the interaction between the carbon and the iron to produce an alloy with properties that are most appropriate for a particular application. Between 0.008 and 1.7 percent carbon content, the alloy is considered a steel (known as low carbon steel) and above 1.7 percent carbon content, the alloy is considered a cast iron. Figure 8-9 illustrates the effects that can be produced on the tensile properties of an AISI 1030 low carbon steel by heat treating. Table 8-1 lists variations in tensile properties and machinability of AISI

1030 and 1035 carbon steels that result from different methods of working and heat treatment. Because the interaction of iron and carbon is affected by temperature and the rate at which temperature changes occur, carbon-steel alloys are one of the most versatile alloys produced.

STEEL FURNACES   Several types of furnaces are used in the production of steel, including the *open-hearth furnace,* the *Bessemer converter,* the *electric furnace,* and the *basic oxygen furnace.* The open-hearth furnace has been the traditional large producer of steel, but in recent years the basic oxygen furnace, because of its speed of production, has been gaining in popularity.

The *open-hearth furnace* is called "open" because the charge is exposed to the sweep of flames over the surface. Molten pig iron, scrap iron and steel, limestone, and high-grade iron ore are all charged into an open-hearth furnace. Limestone is put in first to act as a flux; then the scrap (see Fig. 8-10) and the iron ore are introduced. When they

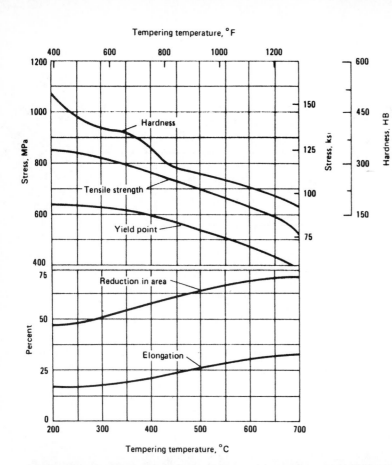

Fig. 8-9 AISI 1030: Effect of tempering temperature on tensile properties. Normalized at 925°C; reheated to 870°C; quenched in water. Specimens were treated in 1.0-in (25-mm) diameter and machined to 0.505 in (12.8 mm) for testing. Tests were conducted using test specimens machined to English units. As-quenched hardness was 514 HB. Elongation was measured in 2 in (50 mm). (From *Engineering Properties of Steel*, American Society for Metals, 1982, p. 23. Used with permission.)

Fig. 8-10 Charging scrap into open-hearth furnace. *(Steel Co. of Canada, Ltd.)*

Table 8-1
TENSILE PROPERTIES AND MACHINABILITY OF AISI 1030 AND 1035 STEELS

Condition or Treatment	Size Round		Tensile Strength		Yield Strength		Elongation,[a] %	Reduction in Area, %	Hardness, HB	Average Machinability Rating,[b]
	in	mm	ksi	MPa	ksi	MPa				
AISI 1030:										
Hot rolled	0.75–1.25	19–32	68	470	38	260	20	42	137	—
Cold drawn	0.75–1.25	19–32	76	525	64	440	12	35	149	70
As rolled	—	—	80	550	50	345	32	57	179	—
Normalized at 925°C (1700°F)	—	—	76	525	50	345	32	61	149	—
Annealed at 845°C (1550°F)	—	—	67	460	50	345	31	58	126	—
AISI 1035:										
Hot rolled	0.75–1.25	19–32	72	495	40	275	18	40	143	—
As rolled	0.75–1.25	19–32	85	585	54	370	30	53	183	65
Water quenched from 845°C (1550°F), tempered at 540°C (1000°F)	0.75–1.25	19–32	103	710	89	615	16	40	207	—
Cold drawn	0.75–1.25	19–32	80	550	67	460	12	35	163	65
As cold drawn	0.63–0.88	16–22	85	585	75	515	13	35	170	—
	0.88–1.25	22–32	80	550	70	485	12	35	163	—
	1.25–2	32–50	75	515	65	450	12	35	149	—
	2–3	50–75	70	485	60	415	10	30	143	—
Cold drawn, low temperature, stress relieved	0.63–0.88	16–22	90	620	80	550	13	35	179	—
	0.88–1.25	22–32	85	585	75	515	12	35	170	—
	1.25–2	32–50	80	550	70	485	12	35	163	—
	2–3	50–75	75	515	65	450	10	30	149	—
Cold drawn, high temperature, stress relieved	0.63–0.88	16–22	80	550	60	415	16	45	163	—
	0.88–1.25	22–32	75	515	60	415	15	45	149	—
	1.25–2	32–50	70	485	60	415	15	40	143	—
	2–3	50–75	65	450	55	380	12	35	131	—

[a] In 50 mm (2 in)
[b] Based on AISI 1212 steel as 100% average machinability.
SOURCE: From *Engineering Properties of Steel*, American Society for Metals, 1982, p. 23. Used with permission.

have begun to melt, molten pig iron is added. (See Fig. 8-11.)

For the melting process, fuel oil or natural gas serves as fuel; it is injected along with hot air. Refining takes from $3\frac{1}{2}$ to 7 h, at temperatures up to 1650°C. Continuous sampling is carried out by laboratory technicians to ensure that the steel adheres to specifications, for each *heat* of steel is made to a specific formula. In Fig. 8-12, technicians are using spectrographic equipment in the chemical control of steel production. During the process, it may be necessary to remove some elements and add others. Impurities are removed by the use of oxidizing agents such as limestone. Burnt lime may be added to hasten the absorption of sulfur and phosphorus.

In some open-hearth furnaces, oxygen is injected through the furnace roof. As a result of doing this, greater heat is produced and the furnace heat time is reduced.

The *Bessemer converter* is a huge pot, set on massive trunnions so that it can be tilted (Fig. 8-13). The scrap and molten pig iron are charged into the converter first, through the top, and then the limestone or other fluxes are added. Air and fuel are injected from the bottom. When the steel is ready, it is tapped off through a port in the side of the converter.

The *basic oxygen furnace* (see Fig. 8-14) resembles a Bessemer converter, but, instead of using air injected at the bottom, pure oxygen is blown in

Fig. 8-11 Charging molten pig iron into open-hearth furnace. *(Steel Co. of Canada, Ltd.)*

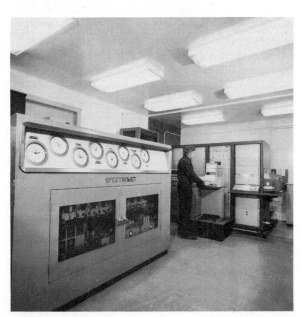

Fig. 8-12 Spectrographic equipment in steel control laboratory. *(Sydney Steel Corp.)*

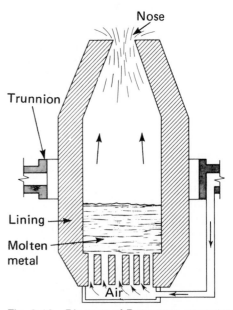

Fig. 8-13 Diagram of Bessemer converter.

Nose

Trunnion

Lining

Molten metal

Air

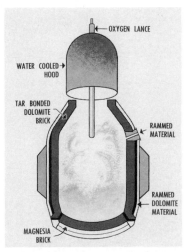

Fig. 8-14 Diagram of basic oxygen furnace. *(Bethlehem Steel)*

Fig. 8-16 Scrap metal being charged into basic oxygen furnace. *(Bethlehem Steel)*

from the top. The process was pioneered in North America in 1954, but it had been used previously in Europe for a number of years. The principal raw material used is molten pig iron from a blast furnace (see Fig. 8-15), though some scrap metal is used as well (see Fig. 8-16). *Lime,* rather than limestone, is used as the fluxing agent, with fluorspar also being added.

With the furnace returned to a vertical position, the oxygen lance is lowered and the oxygen is turned on to a flow of up to 6000 ft^3/min (2832 L/s) and at a pressure of 160 lb/in^2 (1100 kPa). This causes very rapid burning to remove the carbon and other impurities and allows the production of a batch of steel within a period of about one hour.

Electric furnaces have long been used for producing alloy, tool, and other specialty steels, but recently larger heats of carbon steel have also been made in these furnaces. The roof of an electric furnace is pierced so that three carbon or graphite electrodes can be lowered into the furnace. Heat is produced by the arcs between the huge electrodes and the charge in the furnace.

When specialty steels are being made, the charge is mostly selected scrap, along with some iron ore. To this are added the ingredients necessary to make the special alloy. When carbon steel is being made, very high-grade, prereduced ore, containing up to 98 percent iron, is the charge.

INGOTS When it is ready, the molten steel is drawn from the furnace in giant ladles (Fig. 8-17), from which it is poured into ingot molds. This pouring into molds is known as *teeming.*

The molds containing the ingots are transported to a stripper building, where they are allowed to

Fig. 8-15 Molten pig iron being charged into oxygen furnace. *(Bethlehem Steel)*

Fig. 8-17 Teeming a heat of steel from ladle into ingot molds. *(Sydney Steel Corp.)*

Fig. 8-18 Removing molds from ingots. *(Steel Co. of Canada, Ltd.)*

cool. The molds are then removed (Fig. 8-18), and the ingots placed in soaking pits (see Fig. 8-19), where they are reheated to a uniform temperature high enough for rolling. Ingots vary in size from about 9 to 23 tons (8 to 21 t).

A great variety of products used in the construction industry are made from these ingots. They include rolled structural shapes, rods, bars, plates, pipe, wire, bolts, rivets, nails, sheet steel, and many others. Subsequent treatment of the ingots depends to a considerable extent on which of these products is to be made from them.

SHAPING STEEL   Hot ingots go into a blooming mill (see Fig. 8-20), where they receive their first shaping between huge rolls. If the steel is to be made into sheets or other flat products, the ingot is formed into a rectangular slab (Fig. 8-21). If it is to become bars, rods, rolled structural shapes, etc., the ingot is formed into a bloom, roughly square in section.

A bloom which is to be made into a rolled shape is heated to 1200°C in a continuous reheating fur-

Fig. 8-19 Ingot being placed in soaking pit. *(Steel Co. of Canada, Ltd.)*

224

Fig. 8-20 Blooming mill and operator. *(Steel Co. of Canada, Ltd.)*

nace. It then passes through a series of rolls; as it does so, the grooves and raised areas on the rolls give it shape. A bloom may make as many as 26

passes through the rolls before it is turned into an S-shaped beam.

When *rods and bars* are being made, the bloom is further reduced to a billet (Fig. 8-22) by passing through a series of billet rolls, becoming smaller in cross-section and greater in length with each stand of rolls. Finally, the billets are cut into the required lengths and passed on to the rod or bar mills. Before being rolled into rods or bars, billets are heated in a three-zone furnace and passed into the roll stands of a bar mill. (See Fig. 8-23.)

Slabs formed in the blooming mill are rolled into plates of various widths, usually from 24 to 120 in (600 to 3000 mm) and in thicknesses of from $\frac{3}{16}$ to 6 in (5 to 150 mm). Steel to be rolled thinner than plate goes to a hot-strip mill, where it is further reduced in thickness. Steel strips from there may be still further reduced by being passed through a cold-reduction mill (see Fig. 8-24), where they may be made as thin as 0.007 in (0.18 mm) and rolled into *coils.* Sheets cut from these coils go into many diversified products, such as tin plate, galvanized sheets, steel decking, and automobile stampings.

Cold-reduced steel for tin products must be ductile. It is made so by controlled heating and cooling in a continuous annealing furnace, as indicated in

Fig. 8-21 Slab leaving the blooming mill. *(Steel Co. of Canada, Ltd.)*

Fig. 8-22 Billet mill roll stands. *(Steel Co. of Canada, Ltd.)*

225

Fig. 8-23   Bars being fed into bar-mill roll stands.   *(Steel Co. of Canada, Ltd.)*

Fig. 8-24   Five-stand cold rolling mill.   *(Dominion Foundaries & Steel, Ltd.)*

Fig. 8-25, which shows cold-rolled strip steel being fed into an annealing line. Cold-rolled sheets are galvanized by being passed through a *galvanizing pot* and cooling tower like that illustrated in Fig. 8-26.

New Techniques in Steelmaking

The need for better steel for advanced industrial equipment and highly sophisticated alloy and specialty steels for use in the world's new technologies in aerospace and nuclear energy has led to the development of a number of new processes in steelmaking. These new processes may be divided into two categories. In one, molten metal is taken from conventional furnaces and worked to remove many impurities quickly before the steel solidifies. Among these processes are *vacuum stream degassing, vacuum ladle degassing, argon-oxygen decarburization,* and *vacuum oxygen decarburization.* The second category of processes involves remelting steel and other raw materials and subjecting them to refining and purifying forces of a quite radical nature. Included in this group are *electron-beam processing, vacuum-induction melting, consumable-electrode melting,* and *electroslag melting.*

VACUUM STREAM DEGASSING   In vacuum stream degassing, ladles of molten steel from conventional furnaces are taken to vacuum chambers with a small ladle above and molds below. The steel is dropped through a hole in the bottom of the furnace ladle into the small one on top of the vacuum chamber. The small—*pony*—ladle controls the flow of molten metal into the receptacles contained in the vacuum chamber. There the stream of steel is broken up into *droplets* instantaneously when it is exposed to the vacuum within the chamber. During the droplet stage, substantial amounts of the undesirable gases escape from the steel and are drawn off by the vacuum pump before the metal solidifies in the mold below.

VACUUM LADLE DEGASSING   In this degassing system, the furnace ladle is set beneath a heated vacuum vessel containing a descending suction nozzle. The entire vessel is lowered into the ladle of molten steel (see Fig. 8-27), which is forced through the suction nozzle into the heated vacuum chamber. Gases are removed in the vacuum vessel, which is then raised so that the molten steel flows

Fig. 8-25 Cold-rolled steel fed into an annealing furnace. *(Steel Co. of Canada, Ltd.)*

back into the ladle. This is repeated several times until all the steel in the ladle has been processed.

ARGON-OXYGEN DECARBURIZATION In this process, a small refining vessel shaped like a Bessemer converter contains two tubes, called *tuyeres,*

Fig. 8-26 Galvanizing pot and cooling tower. *(Steel Co. of Canada, Ltd.)*

Fig. 8-27 Vacuum vessel being lowered into molten steel. *(Sydney Steel Corp.)*

227

which allow *oxygen* and *argon* to enter the bath of molten steel simultaneously. The introduction of the argon dilutes the carbon-oxygen in the melt, so that, in the case of stainless steel, for example, the affinity of carbon for oxygen is increased and the oxidation of the added chromium is thus minimized. The argon also stirs the molten steel, promoting rapid equilibrium between the slag and the metal, without affecting the steel in any way, since it is inert.

VACUUM OXYGEN DECARBURIZATION A vessel full of molten steel is placed in an *induction* stirrer, which induces a stirring action in the melt. A roof, pierced by an oxygen lance and equipped for vacuum degassing, is placed over the vessel, and the metal is degassed while being stirred. Then a second roof, equipped with heating electrodes, is placed over the vessel and alloys, and other additives are added through the heating roof and thoroughly mixed by the stirring.

ELECTRON-BEAM MELTING Steel is melted in an induction-heated crucible inside a vacuum chamber. Partially degassed metal from this crucible is transferred to an induction-heated ladle in an adjoining vacuum chamber. An electron beam strikes the steel to keep it molten while it flows over a series of water-cooled copper hearths. As it flows, the vacuum removes impurities and the refined steel is continuously cast into ingots.

VACUUM-INDUCTION MELTING The vacuum-induction process melts and refines steel in an induction furnace located inside a vacuum chamber. The charge, usually *scrap,* is charged into the furnace and melted, and the gaseous impurities are removed by the vacuum pump. The re-refined steel is poured into a trough which carries it to a holding ladle in an adjoining vacuum chamber. From there it can be cast into molds.

CONSUMABLE-ELECTRODE MELTING In this process, a solid steel cylinder is lowered on a control rod into a vertical vacuum chamber. The control rod acts as a cathode and carries an electric current to the steel cylinder. The bottom half of the chamber is a water-cooled mold, which acts as an anode. When current is applied, the steel cylinder acts like a great *electrode* and the end of it melts.

As the molten metal drops into the water-cooled mold below, the gaseous impurities are drawn off by the vacuum in the chamber.

ELECTROSLAG MELTING In this process the steel cylinder—electrode—is suspended in a chamber with its lower end surrounded by molten slag. When current is applied and the end of the electrode melts, the melted steel drops through the liquid slag, which removes the impurities, and collects in a pool below, where it solidifies in a water-cooled mold. Figure 8-28 illustrates the basic operation in each of the eight processes outlined above.

Kinds of Steel

There is an almost infinite number of kinds of steel available, since it is possible to make steel to perform under most known conditions. There are special grades of steel to perform at ultra-high temperatures and some for very low temperatures. There are steels for strength, for electrical conductivity, for electrical resistance. There are steels to resist impact, corrosion, or abrasion, steels to take and hold a sharp edge, and steels to cut other steels. Consequently, steels have been grouped into a number of classifications, based on the content of modifying elements. They are as follows:

Carbon Steel. A steel that owes its properties mainly to the presence of carbon, without substantial amounts of other alloying elements, except manganese.

Alloy Steel. So classified when the content of alloying elements exceeds certain limits or in which a definite range of alloying elements is specified.

High-Strength Low-Alloy Steel. One of a group with chemical composition specially developed to provide better mechanical properties and better resistance to atmospheric corrosion that can be obtained from normal carbon steels.

Stainless and Heat-Resisting Steels. Steels which provide outstanding resistance to heat and corrosion by the addition of chromium and nickel to the carbon steel.

Tool Steels. Either carbon or alloy steels which are capable of being hardened and tempered for use as cutting and stamping tools.

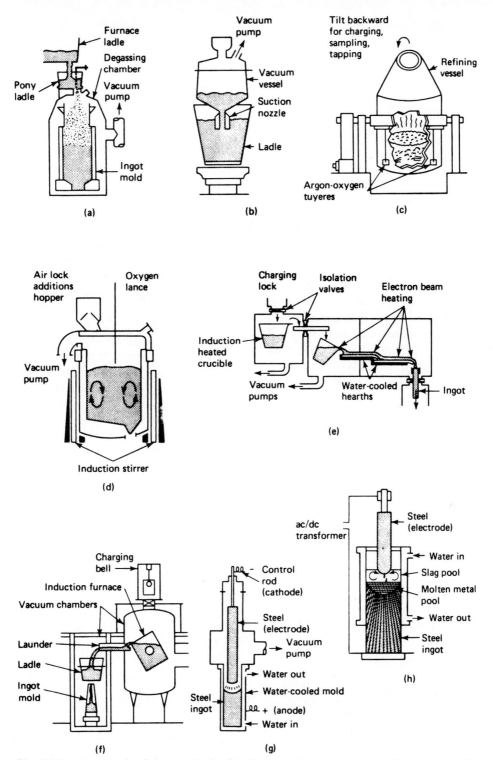

Fig. 8-28 New steel refining methods. *(a)* Vacuum stream degassing, *(b)* vacuum ladle degassing, *(c)* argon-oxygen decarburization, *(d)* vacuum oxygen decarburization, *(e)* electron-beam melting, *(f)* vacuum-induction melting, *(g)* consumable-electrode melting, *(h)* electroslag melting.   *(American Iron & Steel Institute)*

Steel Alloying Elements

Pure iron, without any additives, is too ductile to be of much use in most applications. Even plain carbon steels exhibit changes in physical properties when exposed to extreme cold, cyclical loadings, and corrosive environments. (See Fig. 8-29.) To enhance the basic properties of iron and plain carbon steels, small amounts of various materials, known as alloys, are added.

ALUMINUM   The major use of aluminum in steelmaking is as a *deoxidizer,* often in conjunction with other deoxidizing agents. It restricts grain growth and is widely used as a deoxidizer to control grain growth.

CARBON   Carbon is, by far, the most important element in steel, and as the content of carbon increases, up to about 0.90 percent, its response to heat treatment and its depth of hardening increases. In the *"as-rolled"* condition, increasing the carbon content *increases* the *hardness, strength,* and *abrasion resistance* of steel but *decreases* the *ductility, toughness, impact properties,* and *machinability.*

In general, carbon steel may be divided into three classes, depending on the amount of carbon present: *mild* or *low carbon steel,* with carbon content not exceeding 0.25 percent; *medium carbon steel,* with carbon content of 0.25 to 0.50 percent; and *high carbon steel,* with carbon content from 0.50 to about 0.90 percent.

CHROMIUM   Chromium contributes to the heat treatment of steel by increasing strength and hardness. It increases resistance to both corrosion and abrasion. Chromium steels maintain their strength at high temperatures.

COLUMBIUM   Columbium is used in carbon steels to develop higher tensile properties. It also combines with carbon to provide better corrosion resistance and is often used for this purpose in stainless steels.

MANGANESE   By its chemical action with sulfur and oxygen, manganese makes it possible to roll hot steel and is therefore next in importance to carbon as an alloying element. It has a strengthening effect on iron and increases the response of steel to heat treatment. It also increases the machinability of machining steels but tends to decrease the ductility of low carbon drawing steels.

MOLYBDENUM   Molybdenum raises the temperature at which steel coarsens and promotes its ability to harden. It increases the high temperature strength of steel, improves its resistance to creep, and improves the corrosion resistance of stainless steels.

NICKEL   Nickel improves the ability of steel to harden and increases its toughness after tempering. It is particularly useful in strengthening unhardened steels and improving impact strength at low temperatures. It is used in conjunction with chromium in stainless steels.

PHOSPHORUS   Phosphorus strengthens steel but reduces its ductility. It improves the machinability of steels high in sulfur content and, under some conditions, may help to increase corrosion resistance.

SILICON   Silicon is one of the main steel *oxidizers* and is commonly added to steel for this purpose. In amounts up to about 2.5 percent, it increases the ability of steel to harden. In lower carbon electrical steels, silicon is used to promote the crystal structure desired in annealed sheets.

SULFUR   Sulfur added to steel increases its machinability but may decrease the ductility of low carbon drawing steel. Its detrimental effect in hot rolling is offset by manganese.

TITANIUM   Titanium is used in stainless steels for stabilization by holding the carbon in combination. It is also used for special single-coat enameling steels. In low-alloy structural steels, its use, in conjunction with other alloys, promotes fine grain

Fig. 8-29   Charpy impact samples show effects of temperature on mild steel. The sample on the left, impacted at +20°C, exhibits ductile failure, while the sample on the right, impacted at −50°C, exhibits brittle failure.

structure and improves the strength of the steel in the "as-rolled" condition.

VANADIUM   Vanadium is a mild *deoxidizing* agent, and its addition to steel results in a fine grain structure, which is maintained at high temperatures. It effectively promotes strength at high temperature. Vanadium steels have improved fatigue values and a good response to heat treatment. In unhardened steel, it is used for strengthening.

CHEMICAL COMBINATIONS OF ALLOYS   Steels have various specified chemical combinations of alloys, depending on their use. Table 8-2 summarizes the specified chemical combinations of alloys for a number of structural steels used in building and in bridge, tower, and storage-tank construction. Since the amount of data which can be conveniently shown in Table 8-2 is limited, the specifications should be consulted when more detailed information is required.

Table 8-2
SPECIFIED CHEMICAL COMPOSITIONS[a]

| Steel Standard | Grade or Product | Chemical Requirements (Heat Analysis), % All Percentages Are Maximal Unless Otherwise Indicated | | | | | | | | | |
		C	Mn	P	S	Si	Cu	V	Ni	Cr	Other[b]
CSA G40.21	33G	0.26	1.20	0.05	0.05	0.35	e	0.10[j]	—	—	—
	42W[i]	0.26	0.30/1.20	0.04	0.05	0.35	e	0.10[j]	—	—	—
	44W	0.22	0.50/1.50	0.04	0.05	0.35	e	0.10[j]	—	—	—
	50W	0.23	0.50/1.50	0.04	0.05	0.35	e	0.10[j]	—	—	—
	55W[i]	0.23	0.50/1.50	0.04	0.05	0.35	e	0.10[j]	—	—	—
	60W	0.23	0.50/1.50	0.04	0.05	0.35	e	0.10[j]	—	—	—
	44T	0.22	0.80/1.50	0.03	0.04	0.15/0.40	e	0.10[j]	—	—	—
	50T	0.22	0.80/1.50	0.03	0.04	0.15/0.40	e	0.10[j]	—	—	N—0.02[h]
	50R	0.16	0.75	0.50/0.15	0.04	0.75	0.20/0.60	0.10[j]	0.90	0.30/1.25	—
	50A	0.20	0.75/1.35	0.03	0.04	0.15/0.40	0.20/0.60	0.10[j]	0.90	0.70	—
	100Q	0.20	1.50	0.03	0.04	0.15/0.35	e	—	—	—	Boron 0.0005/0.005
ASTM A36	Shapes	0.26	—	0.04	0.05	—	0.20 min[c]	—	—	—	—
	Plates	0.25 to 0.29 (varies)	0.80/1.20 (varies)	0.04	0.05	0.15/0.30[d]	0.20 min[c]	—	—	—	—
	Bars	0.26 to 0.29 (varies)	0.60/0.90	0.04	0.05	—	0.20 min[c]	—	—	—	—
ASTM A572	42	0.21									N—0.015[h]
	45	0.22									C_b—0.005/0.05
	50	0.23	1.35	0.04	0.05	0.30[g]	0.20 min[c]	0.01/0.15	—	—	V/N—4 min
	55	0.25									
	60	0.26									
	65	0.26									
ASTM A588	A[f]	0.10/0.19	0.90/1.25	0.04	0.05	0.15/0.30	0.25/0.40	0.02/0.10	—	0.40/0.65	—

[a] Actual specifications should be consulted for complete details.
[b] Additional alloying elements may be added with prior approval of the purchaser.
[c] When specified.
[d] Silicon range not required in all thicknesses.
[e] Copper content of 0.20% minimum may be specified.
[f] One of 7 chemical compositions permitted.
[g] Silicon range 0.15/0.30 for plates over $1\frac{1}{2}$ in thick.
[h] Permissible but not mandatory.
[i] Hollow sections only.
[j] C_b and V, singly or in combination.
SOURCE: Canadian Institute of Steel Construction.

All Percentages Are Maximal Unless Otherwise Indicated

Steel Products

Rolled and welded structural shapes are among the most important steel products used in building construction. They include the following: *S* (standard beam) shapes; *W* (wide-flange) shapes; *WWF* (welded wide-flange) shapes; *HP* (bearing pile) shapes; *M* (miscellaneous) shapes; *C* (channel) shapes; *T*'s (structural T), cut from W, M, or WWF shapes; *L* (angle), equal or unequal leg; *HSS* (hollow structural section), square, rectangular or round; *Pipe, Bar* (flat, square, or round); and *Plate.* (See Fig. 8-30.)

Metric dimensions have already been established for a number of these steel products, including *plate, sheet, bar, rod, wire,* and *WWF shapes* (which are made from plate), and these are available from major steel companies. For example, Table 8-3 lists metric thicknesses for *carbon* and *high-strength low-alloy* plate.

Table 8-4*a* and *b* illustrates one section of the wide-flange shapes tables, in which properties and dimensions are given in both Imperial and metric units.

Table 8-5 lists metric conversion factors which may be used for those steel products for which metric tables are not yet available.

Since it is desirable to have a standard method of identifying these various shapes, a designation system has been established, which is recognized by everyone involved in the steel industry. As indicated above, a letter or letters designates the shape of the majority. For most of them, further identification is provided in the Imperial system by quoting the *nominal depth in inches* and the *weight* of the member in *pounds per lineal foot.* In the metric system, the depth is in *millimeters* and the *weight* in *kilograms per meter.* The remainder—angles, pipe, plate, bars, and HHS—are further identified by their dimensions. Table 8-6 gives one example of a standard designation for each of the rolled and welded structural shapes.

S SHAPES S shapes are designated according to their depth and are made in a variety of sizes from 3 to 24 in (76 to 610 mm). Most of them are made in two different weights per unit of length, the

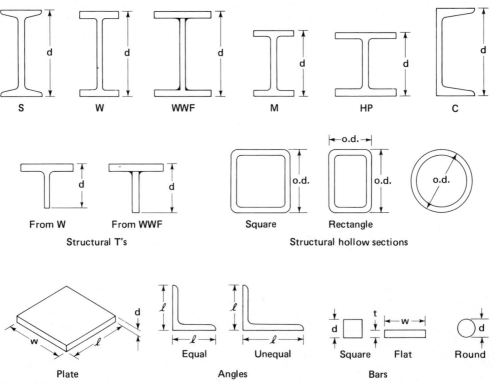

Fig. 8-30 Structural rolled and welded shapes.

Table 8-3
THICKNESSES FOR CARBON AND HIGH-STRENGTH LOW-ALLOY PLATE

English Decimal Equivalent in Inches	Millimeters	English Decimal Equivalent in Inches	Millimeters
0.1969	5	1.3780	35
0.2165	5.5	1.4961	38
0.2362	6	1.5748	40
0.2756	7	1.7717	45
0.3150	8	1.9685	50
0.3543	9	2.1654	55
0.3937	10	2.3622	60
0.4331	11	2.7559	70
0.4724	12	3.1496	80
0.5512	14	3.5433	90
0.6299	16	3.9370	100
0.7087	18	4.3307	110
0.7874	20	4.7244	120
0.8661	22	5.1181	130
0.9843	25	5.5118	140
1.1024	28	5.9055	150
1.1811	30	6.2992	160
1.2598	32		

difference being achieved by changing the width of the flange and the thickness of the web, as illustrated in Fig. 8-31. Thus the depth dimension of the member remains constant. Properties and dimensions tables similar to those shown in Table 8-4,

Increasing weight in S shape

Increasing weight in W shape

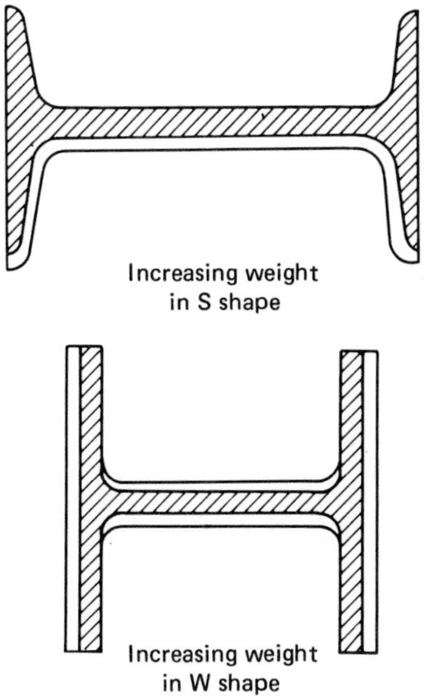

Fig. 8-31 Increasing weights per unit of length in rolled shapes.

produced by steel companies and institutes of steel construction, provide complete data for designing and detailing for these and other rolled shapes.

W SHAPES W shapes are made in a wider range of sizes and weights than S shapes. The regular series are made in depths of $4\frac{1}{8}$ to $36\frac{3}{4}$ in (105 to 933 mm), in a variety of weights. For example, 14-in (356-mm) W shapes alone are rolled in 47 different weights per unit of length. Weights are changed by altering the width and thickness of the flange and the thickness of the web, as illustrated in Fig. 8-31. Thus the depth dimension of that member does not stay constant, only one weight of the group being actually 14 in (356 mm) deep.

The flanges of most W shapes are rectangular in cross-section—some are made with a 5 percent slope—as opposed to S shapes, whose flanges have a $16\frac{2}{3}$ percent slope.

WWF SHAPES These shapes are produced by welding plates together. Hot-rolled plates are flame-cut automatically to the required widths. An assembly machine holds a web plate and two flange plates in the correct position, while heavy rolls press them together and propel them forward. Automatic weld-

(Text continued on page 238.)

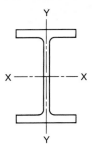

Table 8-4a
WIDE-FLANGE SHAPES, PROPERTIES, AND DIMENSIONS (W460–W410) (SI UNITS)

PROPERTIES

Designation[a]	Dead Load, kN/m	Total Area, mm²	Axis X - X				Axis Y - Y				Torsional Constant J, 10³ mm⁴	Warping Constant C_w, 10⁹ mm⁶
			I_x, 10⁶ mm³	S_x, 10³ mm³	r_x, mm	Z_x, 10³ mm³	I_y, 10⁶ mm⁴	S_y, 10³ mm³	r_y, mm	Z_y, 10³ mm³		
W460:												
X177[b]	1.73	22,600	910	3,780	201	4,280	105	735	68.2	1,130	4,410	5,440
X158[b]	1.54	20,100	796	3,350	199	3,780	91.4	643	67.4	989	3,120	4,670
X144[b]	1.41	18,400	726	3,080	199	3,450	83.6	591	67.4	906	2,440	4,230
X128[b]	1.26	16,400	637	2,730	197	3,050	73.3	520	66.9	796	1,720	3,670
X113[b]	1.10	14,400	556	2,400	196	2,670	63.3	452	66.3	691	1,180	3,150
W460:												
X106	1.03	13,500	488	2,080	190	2,390	25.1	259	43.1	405	1,460	1,260
X97	0.947	12,300	445	1,910	190	2,180	22.8	237	43.1	368	1,130	1,140
X89	0.876	11,400	410	1,770	190	2,010	20.9	218	42.8	339	907	1,040
X82	0.804	10,400	370	1,610	189	1,830	18.6	195	42.3	303	691	918
X74	0.728	9,450	333	1,460	188	1,650	16.6	175	41.9	271	517	813
X67[c]	0.668	8,680	300	1,320	186	1,500	14.6	153	41.0	239	412	709
X61[c]	0.598	7,760	259	1,150	183	1,310	12.2	129	39.7	202	289	588
W460:												
X68[b]	0.672	8,730	297	1,290	184	1,490	9.41	122	32.8	192	509	463
X60[b]	0.584	7,590	255	1,120	183	1,280	7.96	104	32.4	163	335	388
X52[b]	0.510	6,630	212	943	179	1,090	6.34	83.4	30.9	131	210	306
W410:												
X149[b]	1.46	19,000	619	2,870	180	3,250	77.7	586	63.9	900	3,220	3,200
X132[b]	1.29	16,800	538	2,530	179	2,850	67.4	512	63.3	785	2,260	2,730
X114[b]	1.12	14,600	462	2,200	178	2,460	57.2	439	62.6	671	1,490	2,300
X100[b]	0.977	12,700	398	1,920	177	2,130	49.5	381	62.4	581	994	1,960
W410:												
X85	0.833	10,800	315	1,510	171	1,730	18.0	199	40.8	310	926	717
X74	0.735	9,550	275	1,330	170	1,510	15.6	173	40.4	269	637	614
X67	0.662	8,600	246	1,200	169	1,360	13.8	154	40.1	239	469	540
X60	0.584	7,580	216	1,060	169	1,190	12.0	135	39.8	209	328	468
X54	0.524	6,810	186	924	165	1,050	10.1	114	38.5	177	226	388
W410:												
X46	0.453	5,890	156	773	163	885	5.14	73.4	29.5	115	192	197
X39	0.384	4,990	127	634	160	730	4.04	57.7	28.5	90.6	111	154

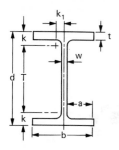

Nominal Mass, kg/m	Theoretical Mass, kg/m	Depth d, mm	Width b, mm	Flange				Distances, mm					Surface Area (m²) per Meter of Length	
				Mean Thickness t		Web Thickness w								Minus Top of
				mm	mm	mm	mm	a	T	k	k₁	d − 2t	Total	Top Flange
177	177.3	482	286	26.9	27	16.6	17	135	395	44	24	428	2.07	1.79
158	157.7	476	284	23.9	24	15.0	15	135	395	41	23	428	2.06	1.77
144	144.6	472	283	22.1	22	13.6	14	135	395	39	22	428	2.05	1.76
128	128.4	467	282	19.6	20	12.2	12	135	394	37	21	428	2.04	1.76
113	113.1	463	280	17.3	17	10.8	11	135	396	34	21	428	2.02	1.74
106	105.8	469	194	20.6	21	12.6	13	91	393	38	22	428	1.69	1.50
97	96.6	466	193	19.0	19	11.4	11	91	394	36	21	428	1.68	1.49
89	89.3	463	192	17.7	18	10.5	10	91	393	35	21	428	1.68	1.48
82	81.9	460	191	16.0	16	9.9	10	91	394	33	21	428	1.66	1.47
74	74.2	457	190	14.5	14	9.0	9	91	395	31	20	428	1.65	1.46
67	68.1	454	190	12.7	13	8.5	8	91	394	30	20	428	1.65	1.46
61	60.9	450	189	10.8	11	8.1	8	91	394	28	20	428	1.64	1.45
68	68.5	459	154	15.4	15	9.1	9	73	396	32	20	428	1.51	1.36
60	59.6	455	153	13.3	13	8.0	8	73	396	30	19	428	1.50	1.35
52	52.0	450	152	10.8	11	7.6	8	72	395	28	19	428	1.49	1.34
149	149.3	431	265	25.0	25	14.9	15	125	348	42	23	381	1.89	1.63
132	132.1	425	263	22.2	22	13.3	13	125	348	39	22	381	1.88	1.61
114	114.5	420	261	19.3	19	11.6	12	125	349	36	21	381	1.86	1.60
100	99.6	415	260	16.9	17	10.0	10	125	348	34	20	381	1.85	1.59
85	85.0	417	181	18.2	18	10.9	11	85	347	35	21	381	1.54	1.35
74	74.9	413	180	16.0	16	9.7	10	85	347	33	21	381	1.53	1.35
67	67.5	410	179	14.4	14	8.8	9	85	348	31	20	381	1.52	1.34
60	59.5	407	178	12.8	13	7.7	8	85	347	30	20	381	1.51	1.33
54	53.4	403	177	10.9	11	7.5	8	85	347	28	20	381	1.50	1.32
46	46.2	403	140	11.2	11	7.0	7	67	347	28	19	381	1.35	1.21
39	39.2	399	140	8.8	9	6.4	6	67	347	26	19	381	1.35	1.21

[a] Nominal depth in millimeters and mass in kilograms per meter.
[b] Not available from Canadian mills.
[c] Produced exclusively by Algoma Steel.
SOURCE: *Handbook of Steel Construction,* 1985, Canadian Institute of Steel Construction, Toronto. Used with permission.

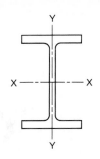

Table 8-4b
WIDE-FLANGE SHAPES, PROPERTIES, AND DIMENSIONS (IMPERIAL UNITS)

PROPERTIES

Designation[a]	Nominal Mass, lb/ft	Total Area, in²	Axis X - X				Axis Y - Y				Torsional Constant J, in⁴	Warping Constant C_w, in⁶
			I_x, in⁴	S_x, in³	r_x, in	Z_x, in³	I_y, in⁴	S_y, in³	r_y, in	Z_y, in³		
W460:												
X177[b]	119	35.1	2,190	231	7.90	261	253	44.9	2.68	69.1	10.6	20,300
X158[b]	106	31.1	1,910	204	7.84	230	220	39.3	2.66	60.5	7.48	17,400
X144[b]	97	28.5	1,750	188	7.84	211	201	36.1	2.66	55.3	5.86	15,800
X128[b]	86	25.3	1,530	166	7.78	186	175	31.6	2.63	48.4	4.10	13,600
X113[b]	76	22.3	1,330	146	7.72	163	152	27.6	2.61	42.2	2.83	11,700
W460:												
X106	71	20.8	1,170	127	7.50	145	60.3	15.8	1.70	24.7	3.48	4,700
X97	65	19.1	1,070	117	7.48	133	54.8	14.4	1.69	22.5	2.73	4,240
X89	60	17.6	984	108	7.48	123	50.1	13.3	1.69	20.6	2.17	3,860
X82	55	16.2	890	98.3	7.41	112	44.9	11.9	1.66	18.5	1.66	3,430
X74	50	14.7	800	88.9	7.38	101	40.1	10.7	1.65	16.6	1.24	3,040
X67[c]	45	13.4	719	80.5	7.33	91.3	34.8	9.31	1.61	14.5	.986	2,620
X61[c]	41	12.1	623	70.4	7.18	80.1	29.3	7.87	1.56	12.3	.696	2,190
W460:												
X68[b]	46	13.5	712	78.8	7.26	90.7	22.5	7.43	1.29	11.7	1.22	1,710
X60[b]	40	11.8	612	68.4	7.20	78.4	19.1	6.35	1.27	9.95	.809	1,440
X52[b]	35	10.3	510	57.6	7.04	66.5	15.3	5.10	1.22	8.06	.505	1,140
W410:												
X149[b]	100	29.4	1,490	176	7.12	198	186	35.7	2.52	54.9	7.73	11,900
X132[b]	89	26.2	1,300	155	7.04	175	163	31.5	2.49	48.1	5.45	10,300
X114[b]	77	22.6	1,110	134	7.01	150	138	26.8	2.47	41.1	3.57	8,570
X100[b]	67	19.7	954	117	6.96	130	119	23.3	2.46	35.5	2.39	7,300
W410:												
X85	57	16.8	758	92.3	6.72	105	43.1	12.1	1.60	18.9	2.22	2,660
X74	50	14.7	659	81.1	6.70	92.0	37.2	10.5	1.59	16.3	1.52	2,270
X67	45	13.3	586	72.7	6.64	82.3	32.8	9.33	1.57	14.5	1.11	1,990
X60	40	11.8	518	64.7	6.63	72.9	28.9	8.26	1.56	12.7	.793	1,740
X54	36	10.6	448	56.5	6.50	64.0	24.5	7.02	1.52	10.8	.544	1,460
W410:												
X46	31	9.12	375	47.2	6.41	54.0	12.4	4.49	1.17	7.03	.460	739
X39	26	7.68	301	38.4	6.26	44.2	9.59	3.49	1.12	5.48	.261	565

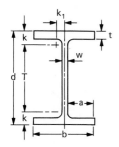

Nominal Mass, kg/m	Depth d (in)	(in)	Flange Width b (in)	(in)	Flange Thickness t (in)	(in)	Web Thickness w (in)	(in)	Distances, in — a	T	k	k_1	d − 2t	Surface Area (ft²) per Foot of Length — Total	Minus Top of Top Flange
177	18.97	19	11.27	11 1/4	1.06	1 1/16	.655	5/8	5 1/4	15 1/2	1 3/4	15/16	16 7/8	6.81	5.87
158	18.73	18 3/4	11.20	11 1/4	.940	15/16	.590	9/16	5 1/4	15 1/2	1 5/8	15/16	16 7/8	6.76	5.82
144	18.59	18 5/8	11.15	11 1/8	.870	7/8	.535	9/16	5 1/4	15 1/2	1 9/16	7/8	16 7/8	6.72	5.80
128	18.39	18 3/8	11.09	11 1/8	.770	3/4	.480	1/2	5 1/4	15 1/2	1 7/16	7/8	16 7/8	6.68	5.76
113	18.21	18 1/4	11.03	11	.680	11/16	.425	7/16	5 1/4	15 1/2	1 3/8	13/16	16 7/8	6.64	5.72
106	18.47	18 1/2	7.64	7 5/8	.810	13/16	.495	1/2	3 5/8	15 3/8	1 9/16	7/8	16 7/8	5.54	4.90
97	18.35	18 3/8	7.59	7 5/8	.750	3/4	.450	7/16	3 5/8	15 3/8	1 1/2	7/8	16 7/8	5.51	4.88
89	18.24	18 1/4	7.56	7 1/2	.695	11/16	.415	7/16	3 5/8	15 3/8	1 7/16	7/8	16 7/8	5.49	4.86
82	18.11	18 1/8	7.53	7 1/2	.630	5/8	.390	3/8	3 5/8	15 3/8	1 3/8	7/8	16 7/8	5.46	4.84
74	17.99	18	7.49	7 1/2	.570	9/16	.355	3/8	3 5/8	15 3/8	1 5/16	13/16	16 7/8	5.44	4.81
67	17.86	17 7/8	7.48	7 1/2	.499	1/2	.335	5/16	3 5/8	15 3/8	1 1/4	13/16	16 7/8	5.41	4.79
61	17.70	17 3/4	7.45	7 1/2	.425	7/16	.320	5/16	3 5/8	15 3/8	1 3/16	13/16	16 7/8	5.38	4.76
68	18.06	18	6.06	6	.605	5/8	.360	3/8	2 7/8	15 1/2	1 1/4	13/16	16 7/8	4.97	4.46
60	17.90	17 7/8	6.02	6	.525	1/2	.315	5/16	2 7/8	15 1/2	1 3/16	13/16	16 7/8	4.94	4.43
52	17.70	17 3/4	6.00	6	.425	7/16	.300	5/16	2 7/8	15 1/2	1 1/8	3/4	16 7/8	4.90	4.40
149	16.97	17	10.43	10 3/8	.985	1	.585	9/16	4 7/8	13 5/8	1 11/16	15/16	15	6.21	5.34
132	16.75	16 3/4	10.36	10 3/8	.875	7/8	.525	1/2	4 7/8	13 5/8	1 9/16	7/8	15	6.16	5.30
114	16.52	16 1/2	10.30	10 1/4	.760	3/4	.455	7/16	4 7/8	13 5/8	1 7/16	7/8	15	6.11	5.25
100	16.33	16 3/8	10.23	10 1/4	.665	11/16	.395	3/8	4 7/8	13 5/8	1 3/8	13/16	15	6.07	5.21
85	16.43	16 3/8	7.12	7 1/8	.715	11/16	.430	7/16	3 3/8	13 5/8	1 3/8	7/8	15	5.04	4.45
74	16.26	16 1/4	7.07	7 1/8	.630	5/8	.380	3/8	3 3/8	13 5/8	1 5/16	13/16	15	5.00	4.41
67	16.13	16 1/8	7.03	7	.565	9/16	.345	3/8	3 3/8	13 5/8	1 1/4	13/16	15	4.98	4.39
60	16.01	16	6.99	7	.505	1/2	.305	5/16	3 3/8	13 5/8	1 3/16	13/16	15	4.95	4.37
54	15.86	15 7/8	6.98	7	.430	7/16	.295	5/16	3 3/8	13 5/8	1 1/8	13/16	15	4.92	4.34
46	15.88	15 7/8	5.52	5 1/2	.440	7/16	.275	1/4	2 5/8	13 5/8	1 1/8	13/16	15	4.44	3.98
39	15.69	15 3/4	5.50	5 1/2	.345	3/8	.250	1/4	2 5/8	13 5/8	1 1/16	3/4	15	4.41	3.95

[a] Nominal depth in millimeters and mass in kilograms per meter.
[b] Not available from Canadian mills.
[c] Produced exclusively by Algoma Steel.

SOURCE: *Handbook of Steel Construction*, 1985, Canadian Institute of Steel Construction, Toronto. Used with permission.

Table 8-5
CONVERSION FACTORS FOR STEEL PRODUCTS

	Imperial	SI Metric	From Imperial to SI Metric Multiply by:	From SI Metric to Imperial Multiply by:
Linear measurement	Inch	Millimeter	<u>25.4</u>	0.039 37
	Mil	Micrometer	<u>25.4</u>	0.039 37
	Foot	Meter	<u>0.304 8</u>	3.280 84
	Yard	Meter	<u>0.914 4</u>	1.093 61
	Mile	Kilometer	1.609 34	0.621 37
Area	Square inch	Square millimeter	<u>645.16</u>	0.001 55
	Square inch	Cubic millimeter	<u>6.451 6</u>	0.155 00
	Square foot	Square meter	0.092 903	10.763 91
	Square yard	Square meter	0.836 13	1.195 99
Volume and liquid capacity	Cubic inch	Cubic centimeter	16.387 06	0.061 024
	Cubic foot	Cubic meter	0.028 37	35.314 67
	Cubic yard	Cubic meter	0.764 55	1.307 95
	Fluid ounce (Cdn.)	Milliliter	28.413 06	0.035 195
	Gallon (Cdn.)	Liter	4.546 09	0.219 97
	Gallon (U.S.)	Liter	3.785 41	0.264 17
Weight (mass)[a]	Ounce	Gram	28.349 52	0.035 274
	Pound	Kilogram	0.453 59	2.204 62
	Ton (short)	Tonne	0.907 18	1.102 31
Weight (mass)[a] per unit length	Pound/foot	Kilogram/meter	1.488 16	0.671 97
Coating weight	Ounce/square foot	Gram/square meter	305.152	0.003 277
Force	Pound-force	Newton	4.448 22	0.224 81
	Kip-force	Kilonewton	4.448 22	0.224 81
Pressure and stress	psi	Megapascal	0.006 8948	145.039
	ksi	Megapascal	6.894 76	0.145 04
Torque and bending movement	Inch pound	Newton meter	0.112 99	8.850 75
	Foot pound	Newton meter	1.355 82	0.737 56
Energy	Foot pound	Joule	1.355 82	0.737 56
Temperature	°F (Fahrenheit)	°C (Celsius)	$\frac{5}{9}$(°F − 32)	$\frac{9}{5}$°C + 32

[a] Mass is the correct term for grams, kilograms, and tones in the SI metric system and will probably be used by the technical community. It is anticipated that in general usage the term "weight" will be retained.

NOTE: Underlined values are exact.

SOURCE: Stelco, Ltd.

ing heads, which are adjacent to the pressure rolls, produce the four welds required while the member travels through the rolls.

These shapes are produced in two categories—those intended for beams and those intended for columns—in depths of $13\frac{3}{4}$ to $47\frac{1}{4}$ in (350 to 1200 mm) in a variety of weights. For example, in the $47\frac{1}{4}$-in (1200-mm) group, there are five weights, ranging from 176 to 326 lb/ft (263 to 487 kg/m).

C SHAPES   c shapes (channels) are manufactured in two categories: *standard* and *miscellaneous.* Standard channels are made in depths of 3 to 15 in (76 to 381 mm), while the miscellaneous channels range from 3 to 18 in (76 to 457 mm) in depth. Each depth is made in two or more weights per unit length, with the weight being altered by altering the width of the flange and the thickness of the web, thus maintaining a constant depth.

Table 8-6
STANDARD DESIGNATIONS FOR ROLLED AND WELDED SHAPES

Shape	Designation	
	Imperial	Metric
WWF shape	WWF47 × 326	WWF1200 × 487
S shape	S15 × 42.9	S381 × 64
W shape	W24 × 76	W610 × 113
M shape	M8 × 37.7	M203 × 56
C shape	C9 × 13.4	C229 × 20
HP shape	HP14 × 73	HP356 × 109
T shape		
cut from WWF shape	WWT10 × 124	WWT254 × 185
cut from W shape	WT5 × 10.5	WT127 × 15.6
cut from M shape	MT4 × 9.25	MT102 × 13.7
Equal leg angle		
(leg dimension × thickness)	L3 × 3 × $\frac{1}{4}$	L76 × 76 × 6
Unequal leg angle		
(leg dimension × thickness)	L6 × 4 × $\frac{1}{2}$	L152 × 152 × 13
Plate		
(width × thickness)	Pl 0.18 × 0.551	Pl 0.457 × 14
Square bar (side)	Bar 1 ⏛	Bar 25 ⏛
Flat bar		
(width × thickness)	Bar $2\frac{1}{2}$ × $\frac{1}{4}$	Bar 64 × 6
Round bar (diameter)	Bar $1\frac{1}{4}$ ⌀	Bar 32 ⌀
Pipe		
(outside dia. × thickness)	Pipe 12.75 OD × 3.75	Pipe 70 OD × 95
HSS (square)		
(outside dimension × thickness)	HSS 4 × 4 × 0.375	HSS 102 × 102 × 9.5
HSS (rectangular)		
(outside dimensions × thickness)	HSS 8 × 4 × 0.551	HSS 204 × 102 × 14

NOTE: Metric equivalents approximate and for information only.

T SHAPES Structural T's are produced by splitting the webs of various beams—W, WWF, or M shapes—either by shearing or flame cutting. Those cut from W shapes range in depth from 3.95 to 18.36 in (100 to 466 mm). WWT shapes range in depth from 6.89 to 10.8 in (175 to 274 mm). All are made in a number of weights per unit of length.

M SHAPES M shapes are made in *wide-flange* design but in depth-width-weight combinations which differ from all the regular series of structural members. Depths range from 4 to 14 in (102 to 356 mm), in one, two, or three weights per unit of length.

HP SHAPES HP shapes are specially made for use as bearing piles. Since, in this function, they are acting as columns, all are made with depth and width dimensions nearly equal. Also, they are generally made with a greater unit weight than com-

parable units in other shapes. For example, a 10-in (254-mm) HP shape weighs 57 lb/ft (85 kg/m), compared to 49 lb/ft (73 kg/m), 9 lb/ft (13 kg/m), or 35 lb/ft (52 kg/m) for a 10-in (254-mm) depth in a W shape, M shape, or S shape, respectively.

HP shapes are made in depths of 8 to $14\frac{1}{4}$ in (203 to 362 mm). Their weights range from 36 lb/ft (54 kg/m) to 117 lb/ft (174 kg/m).

HSS SHAPES Hollow structural sections are made in accordance with structural-steel-material specifications by two general methods: *seamless* process and *welding* process. In the seamless process, a hot billet is either *pierced* to form a hollow bloom, which is subsequently rolled over a mandrel, or *extruded* through a die. Welded sections are made from flat-rolled steel formed to shape and welded by *furnace* welding, *electric-resistance,* or *electric-fusion* welding processes.

Round HSS are produced in diameters of $1\frac{3}{64}$ to

16 in (27 to 406 mm), in two or more weights per unit of length. The weight differences are achieved by altering the wall thickness of the section and vary from 1.01 to 82.8 lb/ft (1.5 to 123 kg/m).

Square HSS are made in sizes of 1×1 in (25×25 mm) to 12×12 in (305×305 mm), in various weights per unit length. Weights vary from 1.12 lb/ft (1.66 kg/m) to 76 lb/ft (113 kg/m).

Rectangular HSS are produced in sizes of 2×1 in (51×25 mm) to 12×8 in (305 to 203 mm), in weights ranging from 1.81 lb/ft (2.7 kg/m) to 62.4 lb/ft (93 kg/m).

PIPE Pipe is usually produced to steel-piping-material specifications, rather than to structural-steel-material specifications. One class of pipe which is suitable for general structural purposes is that produced in accordance with ASTM Standard A53, known as *welded* and *seamless steel pipe*.

Steel pipe is made by two different methods. Small-diameter pipe can be either seamless or welded, while large-diameter pipe is electrically welded.

Seamless pipe is made by forcing a solid hot rod over a pointed mandrel to form a hollow tube. The tube is then rolled and stretched to produce pipe of the correct diameter and wall thickness.

Either hot-rolled or cold-rolled steel strip, called *skelp,* can be used to make resistance-welded pipe or tubing. Coils of skelp are welded together end to end, and rolls form the strip into a continuous cylinder. The meeting edges are resistance-welded. After cooling, the pipe is passed through cold straightening equipment and hydraulically tested to a pressure of at least 1000 psi (7.7 MPa). Pipe to be used for carrying water is galvanized to resist corrosion.

Small-diameter pipe is made in diameters of $\frac{1}{2}$ in (13 mm) to 12 in (305 mm), with each diameter in three standard weights: standard (STD), extra strong (XS), and double extra strong (XXS). Those weights range from 0.85 lb/ft (1.26 kg/m) for standard $\frac{1}{2}$-in (13-mm) pipe to 125.49 lb/ft (187 kg/m) for double extra strong 12-in (305-mm) pipe.

To make large-diameter pipe, plates of the proper width have their edges beveled and are then placed in a press which forms them into cylinders. The two edges are welded together, and the pipe is brought to its final diameter by hydraulically expanding the welded shell against a retaining jacket.

ANGLES Both equal- and unequal-legged angles are rolled in various sizes. Equal-leg angles range from 1×1 in (25×25 mm) to 8×8 in (203×203 mm), with each size made in two or more weights per unit length. Weights are changed by altering the thickness of the legs. Unequal-leg angles range in size from $1\frac{1}{4} \times 1\frac{3}{4}$ in (32×44 mm) to 9×4 in (229×102 mm), with each size in three or more weights.

BARS The term "bar" includes four categories of products:

1. Rounds, squares, and hexagons of all sizes, normally $\frac{1}{16}$ in (1.6 mm) to 12 in (305 mm)

2. Flat-rolled steel, up to and including 6 in (152 mm) in width and $\frac{13}{64}$ in (5 mm) or over in thickness

3. Flat-rolled steel, over 6 in (152 mm) and up to and including 8 in (203 mm) in width and 0.25 in (6 mm) and over in thickness

4. Bar-size shapes under 3 in (76 mm) in maximum dimension

Hot-rolled flat bars are available from many mills in most necessary thicknesses and lengths. They usually have width increments of $\frac{1}{2}$ in (13 mm) and thickness increments of $\frac{1}{16}$ in (1.6 mm).

PLATE Plate, normally produced from hot-rolled steel, is classified in two ways. One classification is determined by the method of ordering, as follows:

1. Plate ordered to thickness
  a. Over 8 in (203 mm) in width and 0.25 in (6 mm) in thickness
  b. Over 48 in (1219 mm) in width and 0.180 in (4.5 mm) in thickness

2. Plate ordered to weight
  a. Over 8 in (203 mm) in width and 9.62 lb/ft^2 (104 kg/m^2) or heavier
  b. Over 48 in (1219 mm) in width and 7.53 lb/ft^2 (81 kg/m^2) or heavier

The other type of classification is based on the method of production. *Universal mill plates* have their edges rolled straight and parallel within the specified tolerance limits. *Sheared plates* are rolled with horizontal rolls only and have their edges *sheared* to the proper dimension.

Table 8-7
PROPERTIES OF REINFORCING BARS

Standard Bars				Metric Bars			
Bar Designation	Weight, lb/ft	Diameter, in	Cross-Sectional Area, in	Bar Designation	Mass, kg/m	Diameter, mm	Cross-Sectional Area, mm
No. 3	0.376	0.375	0.11	No. 10	0.785	11.3	100
No. 4	0.668	0.500	0.20	No. 15	1.570	16.0	200
No. 5	1.043	0.625	0.31	No. 20	2.355	19.5	300
No. 6	1.502	0.750	0.44	No. 25	3.925	25.2	500
No. 7	2.044	0.875	0.60	No. 30	5.495	29.9	700
No. 8	2.670	1.000	0.79	No. 35	7.850	35.7	1000
No. 9	3.400	1.128	1.00	No. 45	11.755	43.7	1500
No. 10	4.303	1.270	1.27	No. 55	19.625	56.4	2500
No. 11	5.313	1.410	1.56				
No. 14	7.650	1.693	2.25				
No. 18	13.600	2.257	4.00				

SOURCE: Reinforcing Steel Institute of Ontario.

SHEET PILING   Sheet piling is another type of rolled section in common use. Sections are made to interlock and are available in several shapes, some of which are shown in Fig. 8-32.

REINFORCING STEEL   Reinforcing steel is produced as deformed bars in standard sizes (see Table 8-7). The bar sizes are normally available in three grades—40, 50, and 60—having minimum yield strengths of 40,000, 50,000, and 60,000 psi, respectively. In Canada, metric bars are available in similar grades—300, 350, and 400—having minimum yield strengths of 43,600 psi (300 MPa), 50,800 psi (350 MPa), and 58,000 psi (400 MPa), respectively. A weldable grade, Grade 400W, is also produced. Higher strengths are produced on request if sufficient quantities warrant the special production run.

Reinforcing bars are produced from three kinds of steel based on ASTM bar specifications A615, A616, and A617: billet steel, rail steel, and axle steel. Reinforcing bars may be galvanized or covered with epoxy to prevent corrosion when used in harsh environments such as in bridge decks and parking structures. (See Fig. 8-33.)

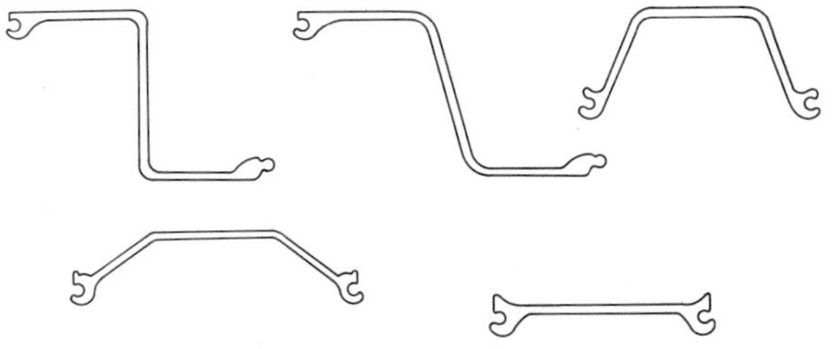

STEEL WIRE   Steel wire is one of the steel industry's most versatile products. Altogether there are over 150,000 uses for wire, some of the common ones in the construction industry being *nails, bolts, screws, cables, springs, wire fabric, block reinforcement* (see Fig. 8-34), and *fences.* Accordingly, steel wire must be made in every conceivable degree of strength, hardness, and ductility.

Fig. 8-32   Sheet piling shapes.

Fig. 8-33   Deformed reinforcing bars, epoxy-coated.

Fig. 8-34 Horizontal block reinforcement. *(United States Steel)*

Wire is normally made from hot-rolled rods which are first pickled in an acid bath to remove the scale. The rods are then cold-drawn through special tungsten carbide dies into wire of widely varying shapes, diameters, and qualities. Wire diameters range from about 0.006 to 1 in (0.15 to 25 mm). (See Fig. 8-35.) Table 8-8 gives standard wire sizes for four specific uses.

Where corrosion resistance is important, as, for example, in fence wire, the strands are zinc-coated for protection. Wire for mechanical springs is hardened and oil-tempered. Wire with very high tensile strength is twisted into cables to be used for reinforcing prestressed concrete products.

NAILS AND SCREWS Wire in coils is fed into nail-making machines, where it is cut to length, headed, and pointed to form nails of all sizes and styles.

In the manufacture of screws, high-speed cold-heading machines automatically cut wire of the required diameter to length and form a head on each cut length. Another machine makes the proper

6mm = .236 inches

Fig. 8-35 Steel wire. *(United States Steel)*

Table 8-8
STANDARD WIRE SIZES IN COLD-DRAWN, CARBON STEEL WIRE

Equivalent Inches	Milli- meters	Premier High Carbon Screen		Premier Mechanical Spring		Recessed, Special Recessed, and Special Head Screw		Rivet	
		Sizes Drawn	Tolerance Size ±, mm	Sizes Drawn	Tolerance Size ±, mm	Sizes Drawn	Tolerance Size ±, mm	Sizes Drawn	Tolerance Size ±, mm
0.984	25					X	0.05	X	0.05
0.945	24					X	0.05	X	0.05
0.906	23					X	0.05	X	0.05
0.866	22					X	0.05	X	0.05
0.827	21					X	0.05	X	0.05
0.787	20					X	0.05	X	0.05
0.748	19					X	0.05	X	0.05
0.709	18					X	0.05	X	0.05
0.669	17					X	0.05	X	0.05
0.630	16					X	0.05	X	0.05
0.591	15	X	0.075	X	0.075	X	0.05	X	0.05
0.551	14	X	0.075	X	0.075	X	0.05	X	0.05
0.512	13	X	0.075	X	0.075	X	0.05	X	0.05
0.472	12	X	0.05	X	0.05	X	0.038	X	0.038
0.433	11	X	0.05	X	0.05	X	0.038	X	0.038
0.394	10	X	0.05	X	0.05	X	0.038	X	0.038
0.354	9	X	0.05	X	0.05	X	0.038	X	0.038
0.315	8	X	0.05	X	0.05	X	0.038	X	0.038
0.295	7.5	X	0.05	X	0.05	X	0.038	X	0.038
0.276	7	X	0.05	X	0.05	X	0.038	X	0.038
0.256	6.5	X	0.05	X	0.05	X	0.038	X	0.038
0.236	6	X	0.05	X	0.05	X	0.038	X	0.038
0.217	5.5	X	0.05	X	0.05	X	0.038	X	0.038
0.197	5	X	0.05	X	0.05	X	0.038	X	0.038
0.177	4.5	X	0.05	X	0.05	X	0.038	X	0.038
0.157	4	X	0.05	X	0.05	X	0.038	X	0.038
0.138	3.5	X	0.05	X	0.05	X	0.038	X	0.038
0.118	3	X	0.05	X	0.05	X	0.038	X	0.038
0.110	2.8	X	0.05	X	0.05	X	0.038	X	0.038
0.098	2.5	X	0.05	X	0.05	X	0.038	X	0.038
0.087	2.2	X	0.05	X	0.05	X	0.038	X	0.038
0.079	2	X	0.05	X	0.05	X	0.038	X	0.038
0.071	1.8	X	0.025	X	0.025	X	0.025	X	0.025
0.063	1.6	X	0.025	X	0.025	X	0.025	X	0.025

SOURCE: United States Steel.

depression in the head (slot, cross, or square hole). The blanks are then rolled between opposing dies to form the thread and produce a finished screw.

BOLTS AND NUTS Bolts and nuts used for non-structural purposes may be either *hot-forged* or *cold-formed* from wire of the appropriate diameter. To make bolts, the wire is fed into an automatic bolt-making machine, which cuts to length, heads, trims, points, and, in many cases, rolls the thread. In some cases, however, the thread may be die cut.

High-strength structural bolts, used in steel construction, are made according to six different specifications, as follows:

1. ASTM A307 Grade A. A low carbon steel bolt in diameters of $\frac{1}{4}$ to 1 in (6 to 25 mm), having a proof load of 60 ksi (kips per square inch) (414 MPa).

2. ASTM A325 Type 1. Standard structural bolt of medium carbon steel, quenched and tempered, in diameters of $\frac{1}{2}$ to $1\frac{1}{2}$ in (13 to 38 mm). Diameters up to and including 1 in (25 mm) have a proof load of 85 ksi (586 MPa), while those over that diameter have a proof load of 74 ksi (510 MPa). (A kip equals 1000 lb.)

3. ASTM A325 Type 2. A low carbon, martensite, boron steel. Sizes and strength provided on request.

4. ASTM A325 Type 3. Weathering steel, quenched and tempered, sizes and proof load identical to those of Type 1.

5. ASTM A325 Galvanized. Hot-dipped galvanized standard structural bolt, medium carbon steel, quenched and tempered. Sizes and strength provided on request.

6. ASTM A490. Quenched and tempered alloy steel. Bolts and nuts are the same dimensions as those of A325. They provide greater clamping force and shear strength for use with new high-strength steels. Diameters are from $\frac{1}{2}$ to $1\frac{1}{2}$ in (13 to 38 mm), having a proof load of 120 ksi (827 MPa).

Table 8-9 illustrates identifying marks for ASTM A325 and A490 bolts, nuts, and washers.

Basic dimensions (see Fig. 8-36) for all types of structural bolts are given in tables provided by the major steel companies.

SPIRAL REINFORCEMENT   A special column-reinforcing material, in the form of a spiral, is made from intermediate or hard-grade hot-rolled coils, corresponding to CSA specification G30.1-1954 or ASTM specification A432, and from cold-drawn wire meeting ASTM specification A82. (See Fig. 8-37.)

Spirals are available in wire diameters of $\frac{1}{4}$, $\frac{3}{8}$, $\frac{1}{2}$, $\frac{5}{8}$, and $\frac{3}{4}$ in (6, 9, 13, 16, and 19 mm). The diameters of spirals range from 10 to 40 in (254 to 1016 mm). A spiral is held at its proper spacing or *pitch* in a column form by *spacer bars.*

WELDED WIRE FABRIC   Another type of reinforcing material is known as welded wire fabric. It consists of parallel longitudinal wires welded to transverse wires at regular intervals, produced on a type of *loom.* The cold-drawn wire sizes vary from W1.4 (fine) to W20 (heavy) and are listed in tables produced by manufacturers which give wire gauge numbers and diameters.

Fabric is commonly identified by the term style, which refers to the spacing of both longitudinal and transverse wires, as well as the gauge of each. The spacing varies from 2 to 12 in (100 to 300 mm) in both directions, and the spaces may be square or rectangular. For example, a fabric identification might read 6 × 12 in (150 × 300 mm) − W2.0 × W4.0. The first figure indicates that the longitudinal wires are 6 in (150 mm) on center (o.c.), the second that transverse wires are 12 in (300 mm) o.c. The third figure refers to the gauge of the longitudinal, and the fourth to the gauge of the transverse wires.

Wire fabric is put up in *rolls* or in *flat sheets,* depending on the gauge of the material. Rolls are normally 5 or 6 ft (1.5 or 1.8 m) wide and 200 ft (60 m) long. Sheets are made up to 32 ft (9.75 m) long but are not usually over 8 ft (2.4 m) wide.

The fabric made with the heavier gauges of wire,

Fig. 8-37   Spiral reinforcement.

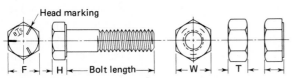

Fig. 8-36   Basic bolt dimensions.

244

Table 8-9
BOLT AND NUT IDENTIFYING MARKS

IDENTIFICATION		ASTM DESIG-NATION	MATERIAL	HEAT TREAT-MENT
BOLT	NUT			
		A325 Type 1 bolt	Medium carbon steel	Quenched and tempered
		A325 Type 1 nut		—
		A325 Type 3 bolt and nut	Low alloy steel	Quenched and tempered
		A490 Bolt	Alloy steel	Quenched and tempered
		A194 nut grade 2H	Medium carbon steel	
WASHERS		A325 Type 1 & A490 washer	Medium carbon steel	Quenched and tempered
A325 Type 1, A490	A325 Type 3	A325 Type 3 washer	Low alloy steel	Quenched and tempered

commonly known as structural fabric, is used as primary reinforcement in structural slabs and similar members. Structural fabric can be made to order in material heavier than the W20 wire used in welded wire fabric. Both can be made with either plain or deformed wire.

STEEL STRAPPING Steel strapping is made from high-tensile-stress flat wire in a number of sizes ranging from $\frac{1}{2}$ in (13 mm) to 2 in (50 mm), often in two different breaking strengths for a given width. This type of strapping is used for, among other things, banding column forms to keep them from bulging under the pressure of freshly placed concrete. (See Fig. 8-38.) Strapping is tightened in place by means of a tightener and held in position by a metal seal which is placed over the two lapped ends and clamped tightly by a sealing tool.

OPEN-WEB STEEL JOISTS Open-web steel joists are playing an increasingly important role in building construction. Many building owners are

Fig. 8-38 Steel banding. (*Acme Steel Co.*)

demanding the greatest possible flexibility of interior design. Large open areas, long column-free spans, movable partitions, etc., are all becoming a necessity in modern schools and office buildings. These requirements can be met to a large extent by the use of open-web steel joists.

Such joists are actually a lightweight type of *Warren truss,* made in several different styles, one of which is illustrated in Fig. 8-39. Two basic types are made: *shortspan* and *longspan.* Shortspan joists are made in lengths of 4 to 48 ft (1.2 to 14.6 m), with depths ranging from 8 to 24 in (200 to 600 mm). The joist weight varies from 4 lb/ft (5.9 kg/m) for an 8-in (200-mm) depth to 13 lb/ft (19.35 kg/m) for a 24-in (600-mm) depth. Tables are available which give the weight and safe load for all the various lengths and depths.

Longspan joists are made of heavier material, in lengths of 22 to 96 ft (6.7 to 29.25 m). Depths range from 18 to 48 in (450 to 1200 mm) and weights from 13 to 68 lb/ft (19.35 to 101 kg/m). Safe-load tables are also available for these.

A number of accessories are made which are a part of a complete joist installation. Bottom-chord extensions carry the bottom chords to the wall for ceiling application. Joist bridging holds joists in alignment. Steel rod is often used for this purpose. Bridging anchors secure the ends of bridging lines to masonry walls. Header angles are available to form floor or roof openings, and outriggers are used to extend the top chord beyond a wall for an overhanging roof.

Figure 8-40 illustrates a typical installation of longspan joists to support a roof structure.

SHEET STEEL   Hot- and cold-rolled steel sheets are versatile products of the steel industry. They are made in a range of thicknesses and used to manufacture a wide variety of products. The thickness of sheet steel is commonly referred to as its

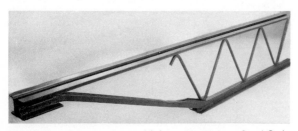

Fig. 8-39   Open-web steel joist.   *(Bethlehem Steel Co.)*

Fig. 8-40   Long-span open-web steel joists.   *(Bethlehem Steel Co.)*

gauge, which is an indication of both thickness and weight. Common gauge numbers run from 3 to 38, though some products are rolled in heavier gauge than 3 and some lighter than 38. Table 8-10 indicates weights and thicknesses of some common sheet-steel gauges.

Hot-rolled sheets are usually made in the heavier gauges and used for products in which strength and durability are the most important characteristics. Culverts and expanded metal decking are typical examples of products made from hot-rolled sheet.

Cold-rolled sheets are manufactured from hot-rolled steel strip of various compositions, which has been pickled to remove the scale and edge-trimmed to the proper width dimension. Cold-rolling then reduces the sheets to the required thickness, which varies with the type of steel and the end product for which the sheet is made. Table 8-11 gives standard thicknesses for some basic steel sheets. Since cold rolling tends to harden the metal, cold-rolled sheet is annealed (see Fig. 8-25) and stored in rolls, ready for the final manufacturing process (see Fig. 8-41). Among the products made from cold-rolled sheet steel for the construction industry are *roofing, siding, decking, curtain-wall panels, partition panels, wall* and *ceiling tile, framing members* (studs and joists), *ribbed floor pans, pipe, eaves-trough, soffit systems,* and *window frames.*

Table 8-10
COMMON SHEET STEEL GAUGES

Gauge Number	Weight		Approximate Thickness	
	oz/ft²	kg/m²	in	mm
3	160	48.76	0.2391	6
4	150	45.71	0.2242	5.7
6	130	39.62	0.1943	4.9
8	110	33.52	0.1644	4.2
10	90	27.43	0.1345	3.4
12	70	21.33	0.1046	2.6
14	50	15.23	0.0747	1.9
16	40	12.20	0.0598	1.5
18	32	9.75	0.0478	1.2
20	24	7.31	0.0359	0.91
22	20	6.09	0.0299	0.76
24	16	4.87	0.0239	0.61
26	12	3.65	0.0179	0.45
28	10	3.05	0.0149	0.38
30	8	2.44	0.0120	0.30
32	6.5	1.98	0.0097	0.25
34	5.5	1.68	0.0082	0.21
36	4.5	1.37	0.0067	0.17
38	4	1.22	0.0060	0.15

Fig. 8-41　Cold-rolled sheet steel in storage.　*(Dominion Foundaries & Steel, Ltd.)*

Construction Applications

The strength of steel and the ease with which it can be shaped and formed make it a natural material for use in construction applications. Steel, in its various types, is used in every phase of the construction process—from the basic structural frame in a high-rise building to the stainless-steel sink in the kitchen.

STEEL ROOFING　Roofing sheets are made from mild steel that may or may not be coated to prevent corrosion. The most common coatings used are zinc, tin, lead, or some combination of the three. Steel coated with zinc is known as *galvanized;* coated with tin, it is known as bright plate; and when coated with 75 percent lead and 25 percent tin, it is known as terneplate. Several styles are produced, in a number of gauges, usually from 20 to 30, two of which are illustrated in Fig. 8-42. Sheets are generally 26 or 27 in (660 or 685 mm) wide and provide 24 in (600 mm) of actual coverage when properly lapped. Usual lengths are from 5 to 16 ft (1.5 to 4.875 m).

247

Table 8-11
STANDARD THICKNESSES FOR SOME BASIC STEEL SHEETS

Minimum Thickness		Hot-Rolled Sheet	Cold-Rolled Sheet	Galvanized Steel Sheet	Long Terne Sheet	Aluminum Coated Sheet
Equivalent Inches	Milli-meters					
0.3937	10.0	*				
0.3543	9.0	*				
0.3150	8.0	*				
0.2756	7.0	*				
0.2362	6.0	X				
0.2165	5.5	X				
0.1969	5.0	X				
0.1890	4.8	X				
0.1772	4.5	X				
0.1654	4.2	X				
0.1575	4.0	X		*		
0.1496	3.8	X		*		
0.1378	3.5	X		*		
0.1260	3.2	X	*	*		
0.1181	3.0	X	*	*		
0.1102	2.8	X	*	*		
0.0984	2.5	X	*	*		
0.0866	2.2	X	*	X		
0.0787	2.0	X	*	X		
0.0709	1.8	X	X	X		*
0.0630	1.6	X	X	X	*	*
0.0551	1.4		X	X	*	*
0.0472	1.2		X	X	*	*
0.0433	1.1		X	X	*	*
0.0394	1.0		X	X	*	*
0.0354	0.90		X	X	*	*
0.0315	0.80		X	X	*	*
0.0276	0.70		X	*	*	*
0.0256	0.65		X	*	*	*
0.0236	0.60		X	*	*	*
0.0217	0.55		X	*	*	*
0.0197	0.50		X	*	*	*
0.0177	0.45		*	*	*	
0.0157	0.40		*	*	*	
0.0138	0.35				*	

* Not available in high-strength low-alloy steel.
SOURCE: United States Steel.

Galvanized sheet metal for roofing is produced in a variety of thicknesses, or *gauges*, and in a number of *coating classes*, depending on the amount of zinc used per square unit of sheet. The number of each coating class represents the amount of zinc coating used in producing sheets which meet the minimum test requirements.

Galvanized sheets for roofing are manufactured in lengths of 6 to 10 ft (1.8 to 3 m), with each length being available in widths of 24, 30, and 36 in (600, 750, and 900 mm).

Terneplate for roofing is produced in several thicknesses and in three coating weights, namely, 0.29, 0.73, and 1.47 oz/ft^2 (88, 223, and 449 g/m^2)

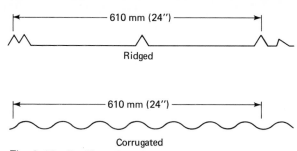

Fig. 8-42 Profiles of roofing sheets.

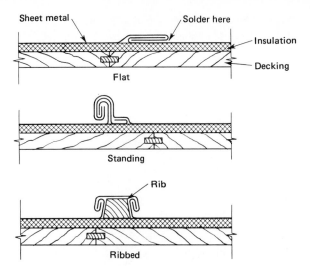

Fig. 8-43 Sheet metal roofing seams.

of tin-lead coating. Plates are normally made 14 × 20 or 20 × 28 in (350 × 500 or 500 × 700 mm), but seamless terneplate roofing is also made in 50-ft (15.2-m) lengths, 20 in (500 mm) wide. Machines are available for turning up both edges of such strips at once to form a pan for a standing rib seam.

To ensure a waterproof skin, different types of joints have been developed depending on the material thickness and the application. For light gauge material, the seams can be formed on the job site, or if the sheets are corrugated, lapping may be all that is required to ensure that no leaking occurs. In thicker material, the joint may be preformed in the plant during the manufacturing process.

Field-fabricated joints are varied but fall into three basic categories: flat, standing, and ribbed. Flat seams are used when the roof is flat or low-sloped, since they can be readily soldered for additional sealing. Roofs with a slope over 18° may have un-soldered standing seams. (See Fig. 8-43.) Ribbed seams are used with heavier metal for appearance or where expansion of the roofing material may be of concern.

STEEL SIDING Siding sheets are made in corrugated, as well as a number of ribbed, styles, one of which is shown in Fig. 8-44. Sheets may be galvanized or prepainted, generally 24 in (610 mm) in net width and from 5 to 12 ft (1.5 to 3.65 m) in length.

STEEL DECKING Formed-steel decking is a widely used sheet-steel product. It is produced in a great variety of shapes and styles, using various thicknesses of metal, ranging from 12 to 22 gauge. Depending on the depth, sections are made in spans of 4 to 36 ft (1.2 to 11 m).

Two basic styles are made: open-faced decking (see Fig. 8-45) and cellular decking, as illustrated

Fig. 8-44 Prepainted steel siding. *(Custom Steel Building Co.)*

249

Fig. 8-45   Open-faced steel decking.   *(Robertson-Irwin, Ltd.)*

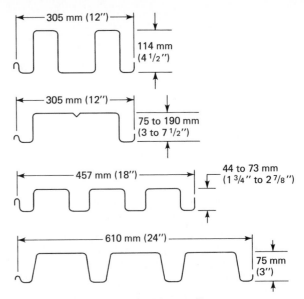

Fig. 8-47   Some steel decking profiles.

in Fig. 8-46. Cellular decking not only provides greater strength but also allows easy distribution of electric systems and outlets. Figure 8-47 illustrates a number of the shapes and depths in which steel decking is available.

Steel deck provides a base for several types of floor or roof. A concrete slab may be cast over a steel deck, or a built-up roof may be applied directly over decking. Wood flooring can be applied also, using wood sleepers anchored to the decking.

Corrugated roofing sheets are also utilized as decking for flat roofs with light loads. In such cases the corrugated deck is used as a base on which to cast a concrete slab (see Fig. 8-48) or as a base for a built-up roof.

Still another type of decking is made with light gauge steel. (See Fig. 8-49.) It is used to provide a walking surface in such locations as between-floor spaces in large buildings.

Fig. 8-46   Cellular steel decking.

LIGHT STEEL FRAMING   Another important use of sheet steel is in the manufacture of steel joists and studs. They are used, not only in commercial and industrial buildings, but in residential construction as well.

Steel joists have the advantage of not being subject to change in shape due to changes in moisture conditions; their use thus results in more stable floors. The joists shown in Fig. 8-50 are made from

Fig. 8-48   Placing concrete slab over corrugated steel decking.   *(Bethlehem Steel Co.)*

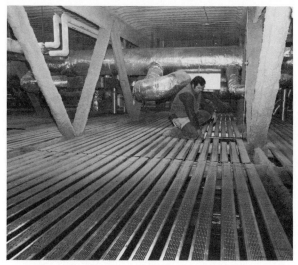

Fig. 8-49 Spaced steel decking. *(United States Steel)*

Fig. 8-51 Steel studs in place. *(United States Steel)*

16-gauge galvanized sheet steel, $9\frac{1}{4}$ in (235 mm) in depth.

Fabricated by several manufacturers, steel studs may differ in detail, but basically they are roll-formed sections made from 25-gauge galvanized sheet steel, with prepunched service holes. They are available in three standard sizes: $1\frac{5}{8}$, $2\frac{1}{2}$, and $3\frac{5}{8}$ in (41, 63, and 92 mm). The narrow stud is used where savings in floor area are of prime importance.

The larger sizes give proportionally stiffer walls and are used for greater floor-to-ceiling heights.

The use of steel studs for framing is illustrated in Fig. 8-51. Wall framing may be preassembled in the shop or on site in much the same manner as wood framing. Studs and plates are cut to the required lengths and held together with self-drilling screws. Because of the light weight of the individual members, entire wall sections are easily lifted into place

Fig. 8-50 Lightweight steel joists used in conjunction with lightweight steel deck. *(United States Steel)*

and assembled. The size of stud members depends on anticipated wall loads and double stud partition walls can be used to accommodate service piping. Rigidity of wall sections may be enhanced by the use of horizontal spacers between studs and the addition of tension straps. Electrical wiring is passed through prepunched holes and is secured by plastic clips. Sheathing is readily attached to the studs by self-drilling metal screws.

RIBBED FLOOR PANS   Among the materials used for forms for *ribbed-slab* concrete floors are sheet steel *pans* and *domes.* Two systems are used for *one-way ribs:* the *slip-out* system, illustrated in Fig. 8-52, in which the pans rest on ledgers nailed to the sides of floor joists, and the *adjustable* system, shown in Fig. 8-53, in which the pans are nailed to the sides of the joists. In both systems, *end caps,* such as those shown in Fig. 8-54, cover the ends of pan rows.

For *two-way* ribbed slabs, *dome* pans are used. They may rest on a solid plywood deck, as illustrated in Fig. 8-55, or on spaced supports.

CURTAIN-WALL AND PARTITION PANELS Once steel is rolled into sheets, it is easily shaped into various profiles as was illustrated in the sections dealing with siding and decking. Another application where steel is most useful is in the production of curtain-wall panels—components of a non-load-bearing wall system. Two panel types are produced: *single-skin* and *sandwich* panels.

Fig. 8-53   Pans set in adjustable system.   *(Cowin Steel Co.)*

Single-skin panels are very similar to roofing, siding, and decking panels in that they are formed into various profiles to add stability and strength to the panels. They are usually textured and/or prepainted and applied in the vertical direction (Fig. 8-56). Some of the shapes that are available are shown in Fig. 8-57.

Sandwich panels (see Fig. 8-58) consist of a face skin, formed into some profile (Fig. 8-59), backed by a layer of insulated material, which in turn is covered by a back-up material. Two types of sandwich panels are made: open-end and closed sandwich. In one case the core insulation is completely surrounded, while in the other, only the two faces are covered. Figure 8-60 illustrates the construction

Fig. 8-52   Setting pans for one-way concrete joist system.   *(Cowin Steel Co.)*

Fig. 8-54   End caps for floor pans.   *(Cowin Steel Co.)*

Fig. 8-55 Dome pans on solid deck for two-way concrete joist system. *(Cowin Steel Co.)*

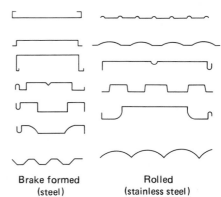

Brake formed   Rolled
(steel)   (stainless steel)

Fig. 8-57 Metal single-skin facing panel profiles.

of a typical sandwich panel of each type.

In addition to insulation, sandwich panel cores often contain a stabilizing core member in the form of a sheet of hardboard, asbestos-cement board, or other rigid material.

Many of the steel panels have an exterior finish of porcelain enamel, though for some uses, galvanized steel is provided, while aluminum facings may be plain, etched, or anodized.

Sizes vary widely from one manufacturer to another. Panel thicknesses range from $\frac{3}{4}$ to 4 in (19 to 100 mm), widths from 12 to 36 in (300 to 900 mm); lengths up to 60 ft (18.25 m) are available in some types. Figure 8-59 illustrates a few of the many shapes in open and closed panels.

Sheet steel is also used to produce partition panels. In many instances the sheet is prepainted and used to cover both sides of some type of rigid

Fig. 8-56 Steel single-skin facings.

Fig. 8-58 Steel sandwich panels. *(Hunter-Douglas, Ltd.)*

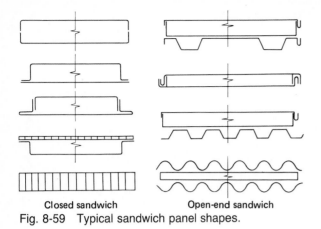

Closed sandwich   Open-end sandwich

Fig. 8-59 Typical sandwich panel shapes.

board which provides stiffness to the panel. (See Fig. 8-61.)

Weathering Steel

One of the newer grades of steel that merits special mention is one known as *weathering steel*. It forms its own protection against atmospheric corrosion and thus requires no painting. In addition, it undergoes a unique color transformation during the weathering process, from orange to brown and finally to blue-gray.

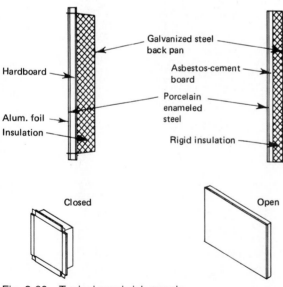

Closed   Open

Fig. 8-60 Typical sandwich panels.

Fig. 8-61 Steel partition panels. *(Steel Co. of Canada, Ltd.)*

As a result of these characteristics it is used on bridges, buildings, and other applications, both structurally and for decorative effect. It is not recommended for structures exposed to recurrent wetting by salt water; in most indoor locations there is not enough moisture in the air for appreciable oxidation of the steel to occur. Its performance in submerged or buried applications will not be significantly different from that of mild steel.

Weathering steel in plates, bars, and shapes meets the chemical and mechanical property requirements of ASTM Specification A588, Grade C, and ASTM Specification A242, Type 2, for high-strength low-alloy structural steels, with improved atmospheric corrosion resistance. In sheets, the steel meets the chemical and mechanical property requirements of ASTM Specification A374 (cold-rolled) and ASTM Specification A375 (hot-rolled).

In the initial stages, water runoff from exposed weathering-steel surfaces will contain soluble corrosion products which precipitate on contact with alkaline surfaces, such as concrete, unglazed brick, and galvanized surfaces, causing staining. It is therefore necessary to make provisions for protecting such exposed surfaces when weathering steel is being used.

NONFERROUS METALS
Aluminum

Aluminum is a relatively new material, compared with iron, but it is finding increased use in the building industry. The process now used for extracting aluminum from its ore, bauxite, requires tremendous amounts of electricity—about 10 kWh for each pound of metal. As a consequence, any large aluminum-extraction industry must be located near the source of abundant low-cost electric power, at present hydroelectric power.

The ore is strip-mined in various parts of the world, and shipped to smelters located near large hydroelectric power developments. In North America, two of the large smelters are at Kitimat, B.C., and Arvida and Isle Maligne, Que. Other essential ingredients in the manufacture of aluminum are petroleum coke, cryolite, and fluorspar.

Aluminum Ore Reduction

The reddish brown ore is washed and treated in a soda solution to yield a chalky white powder called alumina, containing a high concentration of aluminum. This material is fed into a reduction furnace (pot), where it is dissolved in a bath of molten cryolite, to which aluminum fluoride has been added.

The reduction furnace is lined with a paste of coke which is baked until hard. Carbon blocks are suspended in the molten cryolite, and as electricity flows from the carbon blocks through the molten cryolite to the carbon lining of the furnace, it provides the necessary action to separate the alumina into aluminum and oxygen.

COMMERCIALLY PURE ALUMINUM   Aluminum has a number of unique characteristics in the field of construction metals. It is light—about one-third the weight of steel or copper—but by itself, has relatively low strength. Excellent corrosion resistance is one of aluminum's most important characteristics. Its surface also lends itself to many types of finish.

It has high electrical conductivity and is an efficient heat conductor. It is also a good reflector of heat, light, and other forms of radiant energy. It is easy to weld but is not heat-treatable.

ALUMINUM ALLOYS   The mechanical strength and other properties of aluminum may be improved by the addition of one or more of a number of elements, under closely controlled conditions, to produce a number of aluminum alloys. Each alloying element, added alone or in combination with others, imparts specific characteristics to the alloy produced.

A small amount of manganese increases the strength of aluminum, while silicon or magnesium or both together produce alloys which have good corrosion resistance and much improved strength, approaching that of mild steel.

Copper and zinc are used to produce alloys with high strength-to-weight ratios. Nickel, chrominum, titanium, cadmium, and tin may also be used in small quantities to produce special characteristics.

The various aluminum products are usually designated by number codes. These indicate whether or not the material is alloyed and the minimum aluminum content of unalloyed material or the major alloying element and the amount of that element contained in alloyed material.

WROUGHT AND FOUNDRY ALLOYS   Aluminum alloys are divided into two major groupings, *wrought alloys* and *foundry alloys,* depending on which manufacturing process each one is suited for. Wrought alloys are those which are suited to such manufacturing processes as extrusion or forging, while foundry alloys lend themselves to die casting and various molding processes. Each group is further subdivided into heat-treatable and non-heat-treatable, depending on whether or not the alloys can be further strengthened by heat treatment.

CHARACTERISTICS OF ALUMINUM ALLOYS One of the outstanding characteristics of wrought alloys is their ability to withstand severe physical deformation while they are being worked, either hot or cold. The strength of all wrought alloys is increased by working cold, but with those alloys which are heat-treatable, better results are obtained by heat treatment or by a combination of heat treatment and cold working. The strongest alloys are found among those which are heat-treatable. Other characteristics of aluminum alloys depend on the type of alloying constituent.

ALUMINUM-COPPER ALLOYS   The alloys containing copper may also contain varying amounts of manganese and magnesium, producing a high-strength alloy, but one of the least easily formed, except in the annealed condition. They can be welded by the resistance welding process only, are heat-treatable, and in general, offer less resistance to corrosion than the other alloys.

ALUMINUM-MANGANESE AND/OR MAGNE-SIUM ALLOYS   Alloys with manganese as the only alloying constituent are slightly less ductile than pure aluminum, have better mechanical properties and good corrosion resistance, and are not heat-treatable. The alloys using magnesium only are also non-heat-treatable but contain the most favorable combination of strength, ductility, and corrosion resistance.

ALUMINUM-SILICON ALLOYS   Aluminum-silicon alloys have a low melting point and high fluidity and are therefore useful in the wire form as a filler for welding or brazing. They turn to a pleasing gray color when anodized and are therefore popular for making architectural shapes. These alloys are not heat-treatable. When silicon or silicides are used as the alloying elements in conjunction with magnesium, alloys are produced which are relatively easy to fabricate and have good strength, corrosion resistance, and finishing characteristics. These alloys may also have small amounts of manganese, chromium, or copper added to improve strength. All are heat-treatable.

ALUMINUM-ZINC ALLOYS   Alloys using zinc and magnesium or zinc, magnesium, and copper as the alloying elements are the strongest of all the aluminum alloys, with strength-to-weight ratios better than those of some of the high-tensile steels.

ALUMINUM-TIN ALLOYS   Aluminum-tin alloys have excellent compressive and fatigue strengths and have good heat conductivity. Because they also have good resistance to corrosion by internal-combustion-engine lubricants and good antifriction

characteristics, they are useful in the manufacture of engine parts. When copper and nickel are added to these, alloys are produced which are used to make bearings capable of withstanding high speeds, loads, and temperatures. All of this group of alloys are non-heat-treatable.

FABRICATION OF ALUMINUM PRODUCTS   The molten aluminum from the reduction-furnace pot is siphoned into rectangular molds, producing *ingots* of various sizes. These are shipped to various production plants which manufacture one or more aluminum products. The main fabricating operations for converting aluminum ingot are rolling, extruding, forging, and casting. In some cases, the products made by these operations may go directly into use in the construction or other industries. In other cases, they may undergo further fabricating to alter their cross-section, or they may undergo forming operations such as spinning or bending to alter their shape.

When plate, sheet, bars, or rods are to be produced, *rolling* is the fabricating process used. Ingots are rolled hot to give the metal plasticity and to reduce rolling pressure. (See Fig. 8-62.) In the case of sheet and plate, ingots from 2 to 25 in (50 to 635 mm) in thickness are hot rolled in a sheet mill to an intermediate thickness of $\frac{1}{4}$ to 1 in (6 to 25 mm). Later these may be further reduced in thickness by cold rolling. Products of a sheet mill are classified according to their thickness. *Plate* is 0.25 in (6 mm) thick and thicker, *sheet* is from 0.006 to 0.25 in (0.15 to 6 mm) thick, and *foil* is less than 0.006 in (0.15 mm) in thickness.

For the production of rods and bars, ingots are hot-rolled to shape the metal into rods, usually $\frac{3}{8}$ in (9 mm) in diameter. Further reduction is done by cold rolling.

Extrusion is the fabricating process used to produce such products as structural shapes, aircraft shapes, architectural shapes, and electrical bus conductors. A preheated cylindrical ingot is placed in a hydraulic extrusion press, usually in the range of 1250 to 2500 tons (1135 to 2265 t) capacity (see Fig. 8-63) and forced through a steel die to produce a member of the desired cross-section. It may be solid or hollow (see Fig. 8-64) and may vary from a simple symmetrical shape to an intricate asym-

Fig. 8-62 Hot-rolling aluminum ingot. *Alcan, Ltd.)*

Fig. 8-63 Hydraulic extrusion press. *(Alcan, Ltd.)*

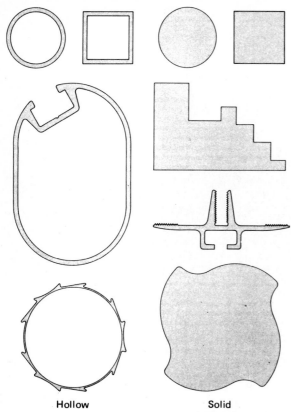

Hollow   Solid

Fig. 8-64 Solid and hollow aluminum shapes. *(Alcan, Ltd.)*

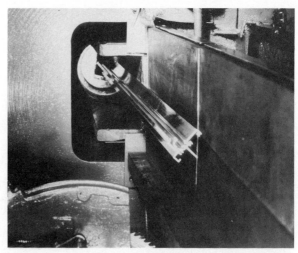

Fig. 8-65 Asymmetrical extruded aluminum shape. *(Alcan, Ltd.)*

metrical form. (See Fig. 8-65.) To produce high-strength extruded shapes, heat-treatable alloys must be used, because conventional extrusion does not impart much work hardening.

PROPERTIES OF ALUMINUM

Table 8-12 provides a comparison of the general physical properties of the aluminum alloys used in structures and those of steel, while Table 8-13 indicates the physical constants of practically pure aluminum.

A number of the characteristics which are common to many of the aluminum alloys give to them important structural values. For example, the fact that most of the alloys can be easily fabricated and parts easily joined is important from a structural standpoint. Most such alloys may be machined, pierced, sawed, or sheared with conventional equipment at high operating speeds. Bolting, riveting, and welding are all suitable methods of joining aluminum component parts. Aluminum welds are free from brittle failure at low temperatures, and

stress relieving after welding is not necessary. Adhesives may also be used to bond aluminum parts together or to bond aluminum to other materials, such as is required in the manufacture of sandwich panels.

The surface of aluminum is such that it lends itself to many types of finish, such as painting, porcelain enameling, or mechanical surface texturing. It may also be chemically treated to produce matte or bright surfaces or electrochemically treated to provide for permanent coloring.

The resistance of aluminum to corrosive attack is due to the fact that the bare aluminum surface is covered by a thin, inert layer of aluminum oxide, which gives excellent protection to the metal beneath. This characteristic reduces the need for maintenance and makes it possible to use the metal in many corrosive and abrasive conditions. Structures made from most of the aluminum alloys may be used in almost any industrial environment. Because of this corrosion resistance and because the corrosion products which are generated are non-poisonous and colorless, aluminum alloys are widely used in the food and chemical industries.

ALUMINUM IN CONSTRUCTION

Because it is light, noncorrosive, has a good strength-to-weight ratio, and is easily formed and extruded, aluminum has a wide range of uses in construction. It can be formed into structural shapes, extruded into architectural shapes, and cast into a variety of miscellaneous shapes.

Table 8-12
COMPARISON OF PHYSICAL PROPERTIES OF ALUMINUM AND STEEL

Physical Properties Used for Design Purposes	Aluminum		Steel	
	Imperial	Metric	Imperial	Metric
Modulus of elasticity	1×10^7 psi	68947 MPa	3×10^7 psi	206842 MPa
Shear modulus of elasticity	4×10^6 psi	27579 MPa	1.2×10^7 psi	82737 MPa
Poisson's ratio	0.33	0.33	0.28	0.28
Weight	0.1 lb/in^3	0.0027 kg/cm^3	0.29 lb/in^3	0.008 kg/cm^3
Weight of shape (6.45 cm^2) (1 in^2 in area)	1.2 lb/ft	1.77 kg/m	3.5 lb/ft	5.18 kg/m
Weight of plate 25.4 mm (1 in) thick	14.4 lb/ft^2	70.2 kg/m^2	41 lb/ft^2	200 kg/m^2
Coefficient of linear expansion	0.000023	0.000023	0.000013	0.000013

Structural shapes, some of which are illustrated in Fig. 8-66, are used as structural members in building construction in the same way that steel structural members are used. Both riveting and welding are used to make connections.

Architectural shapes, a few of which are indicated in Fig. 8-67, are those which are used for decorative effect or for finishing purposes. Typical uses would be for *door and window jambs, curtain-wall panel frames, thresholds, treads, handrails,* door and window *stiles, rails, muntins and bars, mullions, railings,* and *gravel stops.*

One of the most significant features of the extrusion process is the ease with which it is able to produce *mating fits*—shapes that *fit, snap, slide,* or *hook* together to facilitate assembly. Four types of fit are illustrated in Fig. 8-68. In addition, where mechanical joining of parts is necessary, *slots, holes,* and *threads* for mechanical fasteners can be extruded as an integral part of a structural or architectural shape. (See Fig. 8-69.) These features mean a reduction in the time required to erect such building components. Figure 8-70 illustrates the use of such interlocking units in the construction of the

Table 8-13
PHYSICAL CONSTANTS OF ALUMINUM 99.95% MINIMUM PURITY

Properties	Imperial	Metric
Density at 68°F (20°C)	0.0975 lb/in^3	2.70 g/c^3
Melting point	1220°F	660°C
Boiling point at 760 mm mercury	4221°F	2327°C
Thermal conductivity at 77°F (25°C)	1540 Btu/h/ft^2/ in thickness/°F	0.53 g cal/s/cm^2/ cm thickness/°C
Mean specific heat, 32–212°F (0–100°C)	0.225 Btu/lb/°F	0.225 cal/g/°C
Coefficient of linear thermal expansion, 68–212°F (20–100°C)	0.00001322/°F	0.0000239/°C
Latent heat of fusion	167 Btu/lb	93 cal/g
Modulus of elasticity (Young's)	10,000,000 psi	68947 MPa
Modulus of rigidity (shear)	3,790,000 psi	26131 MPa
Poisson's ratio	0.33	0.33
Electrical resistivity at 68°F (20°C)	15.8 Ωcmil/ft^a	0.00000263 Ω/cm^3
Temperature coefficient of electrical resistivity at 68°F (20°C)	0.00238 Ω/°F	0.00429 Ω/°C
Magnetic susceptibility at 64°F (18°C)		+0.00000065

^{a} 1 mil is the area of a circle 1 mil (0.001 in) in diameter. Hence the area of a solid wire in circular mils is equal to the diameter of the wire in mils, squared.

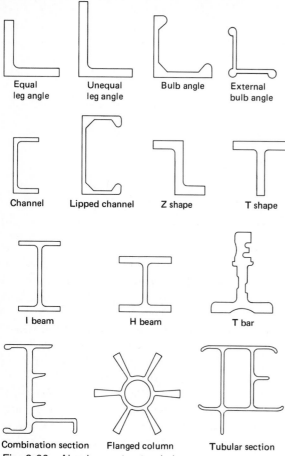

Fig. 8-66 Aluminum structural shapes. *(The Aluminum Association)*

Labels in figure 8-66:
Equal leg angle · Unequal leg angle · Bulb angle · External bulb angle
Channel · Lipped channel · Z shape · T shape
I beam · H beam · T bar
Combination section · Flanged column · Tubular section

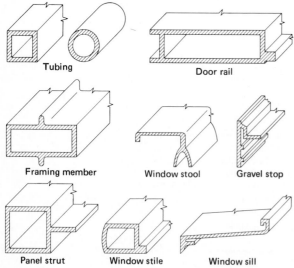

Fig. 8-67 Some aluminum architectural shapes.

Labels in figure 8-67:
Tubing · Door rail
Framing member · Window stool · Gravel stop
Panel strut · Window stile · Window sill

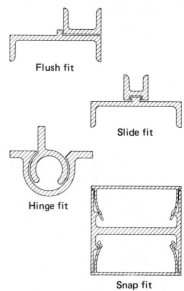

Fig. 8-68 Mating fits in aluminum extrusions. *(Alcan, Ltd.)*

Labels in figure 8-68:
Flush fit · Slide fit · Hinge fit · Snap fit

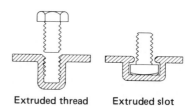

Fig. 8-69 Mechanical fasteners in aluminum extrusion. *(Alcan, Ltd.)*

Labels in figure 8-69:
Extruded thread · Extruded slot

curtain walls for a large office building.

Aluminum, in sheet form, is one of the most widely used auxiliary materials in construction. It is available in a variety of thicknesses (see Table 8-14) and can be used as flashing, roof drains, weather stripping, chimney caps, air ducts, louver blades, backing for built-up curtain wall panels, shingles, roofing, and siding.

When used as roofing, it is available as plain sheet material in natural finish, in polished and oxide finishes, painted on one side or both, and in a variety of surface patterns. Mechanical joints are the most practical method of joining aluminum sheeting, although welding can be used with heavier gauges to produce strong weatherproof joints. Care must be taken when aluminum is subjected to temperature changes because it has a high thermal coefficient of expansion and the connections must be

Fig. 8-70   Interlocking aluminum components.   *(Alcan, Ltd.)*

able to compensate for the movement that will occur. Figures 8-71 and 8-72 illustrate typical mechanical joints that are used in splicing aluminum sheeting.

Sheet aluminum is also treated in several ways to improve its appearance and to increase its resistance to weather and corrosion. One of these treatments is called *anodizing.* This is a combined electrical and chemical process which hardens and increases the thickness of the natural oxide coating on aluminum. It also permits dyeing of the metal in bright colors. Aluminum sheets may be covered with a baked enamel or lacquer finish. Such treated sheets are used for *shingles, siding, canopies, acoustic ceiling panels,* and *curtain-wall panels* (see Fig. 8-73).

A number of types of siding are made from aluminum sheet. Some consist of a single thickness of metal formed into the required shape, while others have a rigid insulation backing. In addition, a baked-on vinyl enamel is used to produce siding with a permanently colored surface in a wide range of colors. Vertical paneling is also made in similar style. Aluminum sheet for siding and paneling is from 0.02 to 0.025 in (0.5 to 0.6 mm) thick. Siding is made 9 and 12 in (225 and 300 mm) wide, in sections 12 ft (3.65 m) long, while vertical panels are made 12 and 16 in (300 and 400 mm) wide, in lengths of 8, 9, 10, 11, and 12 ft (2.4, 2.7, 3, 3.35, and 3.65 m). Many different profiles are available, ranging from those illustrated in Fig. 8-74 to the standard siding profile used in residential construction. (See Fig. 8-75.)

Aluminum shingles are made from sheet aluminum, approximately 0.020 in (0.5 mm) thick, in the form of a 9-in (225-mm) square. They are folded on all edges with reversed folds, so that adjacent shingles will interlock. Starters are made by cutting a shingle as shown in Fig. 8-76. Each shingle is fastened down with a single nail.

This type of shingle may be used on roofs with a slope of 14° or steeper.

Aluminum shingles are manufactured with a *plain surface,* with an *anodized finish,* or with a baked-on *vinyl-enamel finish* in a variety of colors. (See Fig. 8-77.)

Aluminum foil is used as a vapor barrier on walls and ceiling and as reflective insulation.

Table 8-14
ALUMINUM SHEET

Gauge No.	Nominal Thickness		Weight	
	Inches	Millimeters	lb/ft²	kg/m²
26	0.016	0.406	0.226	1.1
24	0.020	0.508	0.285	1.39
22	0.025	0.635	0.355	1.73
20	0.032	0.812	0.455	2.22
18	0.040	1.016	0.568	2.77
16	0.051	1.295	0.725	3.53
14	0.064	1.625	0.910	4.44
12	0.081	2.057	1.152	5.61

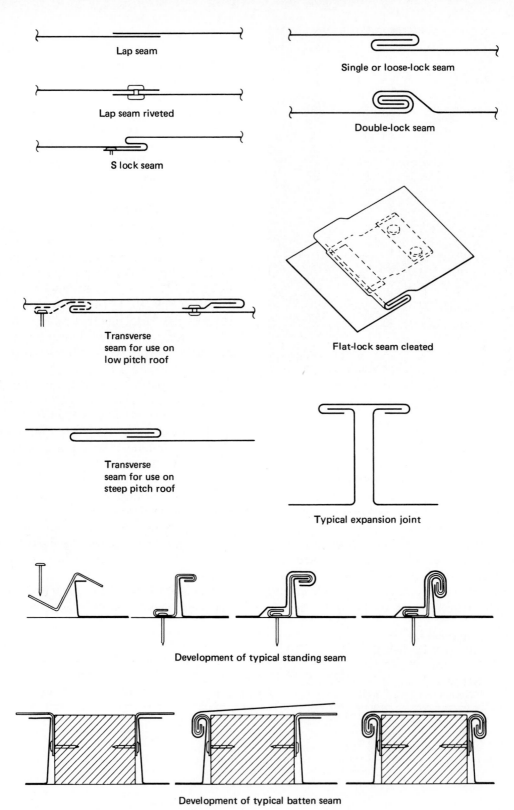

Lap seam

Single or loose-lock seam

Lap seam riveted

Double-lock seam

S lock seam

Transverse
seam for use on
low pitch roof

Flat-lock seam cleated

Transverse
seam for use on
steep pitch roof

Typical expansion joint

Development of typical standing seam

Development of typical batten seam

Fig. 8-71   Seams for aluminum sheets.

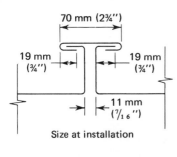

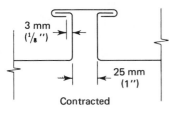

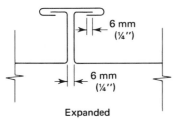

Fig. 8-72   Typical slip joint in aluminum.

70 mm (2¾'')

19 mm (¾'')   19 mm (¾'')

11 mm (⁷⁄₁₆'')

Size at installation

3 mm (⅛'')

25 mm (1'')

Contracted

6 mm (¼'')

6 mm (¼'')

Expanded

Fig. 8-73   Anodized aluminum curtain-wall framing.

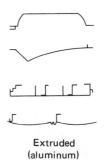

Extruded
(aluminum)

Fig. 8-74   Aluminum siding profiles.

Fig. 8-75   Aluminum siding and trim.

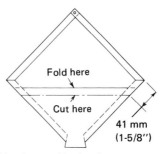

Fold here

Cut here

41 mm
(1-5/8'')

Fig. 8-76   Aluminum shingle shape.

Fig. 8-77 Aluminum shingled roof.

Copper

Most of the major copper-ore deposits in North America contain sulfides as the main mineral constituent. The commercially important copper sulfides are *chalcopyrite* ($CuFeS_2$), *bornite* (Cu_5FeS_4), and *chalcocite* (Cu_2S). In addition, some secondary minerals (formed by oxidation of copper ores) are also commercially important producers of copper. Two of the most common of these are *malachite* and *azurite*. The ores containing these minerals are usually low grade, often containing from 0.8 to 5 percent of the metal. Consequently, the first step in the production of copper is concentration of the mineral. The ore is first crushed and then ground in a ball mill (see Fig. 8-78), forming a pulp. To separate the valuable mineral from the waste rock, the flotation process is used. It depends on the principle that different minerals have different wetting characteristics. In the case of copper minerals, they are not easily wetted and can be carried in a froth to the surface of the pulp, while the waste materials fall to the bottom of the tank. (See Fig. 8-79.)

As the froth overflows, it is filtered, and the resulting product is concentrated copper ore. It may first require roasting to remove some of the sulfur, or it may be smelted directly in a reverberatory-type furnace. Here the charge of copper concen-trate, together with silica and lime or other suitable fluxes, is melted by burning oil, coal, or gas. The molten material separates into two layers, a *matte* of copper and iron sulfides with a layer of *slag* above. The slag is discarded, and the matte copper tapped off for further refining.

The next operation is carried out in a *converter*. The converting process is similar to the Bessemer process used in the steel industry. First, the iron in the matte is oxidized, forming a slag, which is removed. The sulfur is oxidized to form sulfur dioxide gas, which is discharged from the converter. The resulting *blister copper* is about 99 percent pure, but it still requires further refining before it can be used commercially. Blister copper is further refined to reduce its oxygen content, and when it has been reduced to about 0.04 percent, the resulting *tough-pitch copper* is poured into molds, which will form anodes for the final electrolytic process.

Electrolytic refining is done in acidproof tanks, through which is circulated a mixture of warm, diluted sulfuric acid and copper sulfate. The thick anodes are suspended in these tanks and separated by thin sheets of pure copper, called *starting sheets,* which act as cathodes. When an electric current is applied, the anodes slowly dissolve, and pure copper (about 99.9 percent pure) is deposited on the starting sheets. (See Fig. 8-80.)

These cathodes are then remelted and cast into

Fig. 8-78 Ball mills used for grinding copper ore. *(Canadian Copper & Brass Development Association)*

Fig. 8-79 Flotation process in reduction of copper ore. *(Canadian Copper & Brass Development Association)*

Fig. 8-80 Cooper cathodes raised from tank. *(Canadian Copper & Brass Development Association)*

wire bars, ingot bars, ingots, cakes, and billets, which can then be transformed into rod, wire, sheet, strip, tube, pipe, bar, and castings. (See Fig. 8-81.)

Some of them may also be used to produce a variety of copper alloys, the most important of

Fig. 8-81 Copper water and drainage lines. *(Canadian Copper & Brass Development Association)*

which are the brasses and bronzes, which contain primarily zinc and tin, respectively, and the alloys containing nickel.

Brasses are the most important of the alloys of copper. They are basically alloys of copper and zinc, although small amounts of other elements, particularly lead and tin, may be used to impart special properties. The zinc content may vary from 5 to about 40 percent, with a wide variety of colors and properties. Normal commercial brass contains 65 to 70 percent copper, although when tin, lead, or other elements are added, the copper content may be down to 60 percent. The most ductile sheet or strip alloy contains 70 percent copper and 30 percent zinc. Red brass, commercial bronze (a brass), and gilding metal, because of their rich colors, are used in architectural and hardware applications.

The addition of one or more elements to the brass results in the production of a wide range of useful alloys. The addition of about 3 percent lead to an alloy containing about 62 percent copper produces a free-cutting material which is widely used as rod in automatic screw machines. When about 2 percent lead and 38 percent zinc are added to 60 percent copper, an alloy is produced which is forgeable and easily machined. Naval brass, which contains about 0.75 percent tin in a 60 percent copper alloy, is strong and corrosion-resistant, while admiralty brass, containing 70 percent copper, 29 percent zinc, and 1 percent tin, is widely used for condenser tubes. Aluminum brass, which contains 77 percent copper, 21 percent zinc, and 2 percent aluminum, is particularly resistant to saltwater corrosion.

Special alloys, containing less than 60 percent copper and under 1 percent of one or more elements such as manganese, iron, and tin, are known as manganese bronzes. Because of their high strength they are used for such things as bolts, pump rods, and valve stems.

Bronzes are alloys of copper and tin, some of them, known as phosphor bronzes, containing up to 10 percent tin and a very small percentage of phosphorus. These are used in the production of springs.

Aluminum bronzes have no tin, but may contain up to about 10 percent aluminum and sometimes small amounts of other elements. They are particularly useful where high strength and corrosion resistance are required.

Silicon bronzes contain up to 3 percent silicon and small amounts of manganese, zinc, or iron. They have high tensile strength and are highly resistant to corrosion. They are used chiefly in the manufacture of high-strength bolts and screws, in making water tanks, as materials to be used in the chemical industry, and for sewage-treatment plants.

A number of copper alloys contain nickel as the main alloying ingredient. One of them is *nickel silver,* which contains 55 to 70 percent copper, 10 to 18 percent nickel, and small amounts of zinc. It is widely used as a base for silver plating. Another is *cupro nickel,* which contains nickel in the range of 10 to 30 percent. This material has high corrosion resistance and is especially useful in chemical plants and for condenser tubes. *Monel* contains about 68 percent nickel, 29 percent copper, and small amounts of iron and manganese. It is another highly corrosion-resistant material.

Table 8-15 lists a number of the more common copper alloys and their compositions, while Table 8-16 gives the physical properties of a number of these alloys.

Copper is an excellent outdoor metal from the standpoint of color as well as corrosion resistance. It first weathers to a brown coloring and then takes on a permanent light green patina. The green color can also be produced artificially, or the original copper color can be preserved by coating the metal with clear lacquer. (See Fig. 8-82.)

Copper has been used for centuries as roofing and is still considered to be one of the most satisfactory and enduring materials for metal roofing. Roofing copper may be soft-rolled or cold-rolled, the former being very easily worked, the latter stronger, harder, but less ductile. Copper roofing sheets are generally produced in four thicknesses or weights: 16, 20, 24, and 32 oz/ft^2 (4.9, 6.1, 7.3, and 9.8 kg/m^2). Roofing sheets are made 24, 30, and 36 in (600, 750, and 900 mm) wide in lengths of 8 and 10 ft (2.4 and 3 m).

Strip copper is also available for roofing in all four thicknesses, 10 to 20 in (250 to 500 mm) wide and 8 or 10 ft (2.4 or 3 m) long.

Rolled copper in 16-oz/ft^2 (4.9-kg/m^2) weight, from 6 to 20 in (150 to 500 mm) wide, in rolls of 80, 90, or 100 lb (36, 41, 45 kg), is also produced for roofing purposes.

Table 8-15
COMPOSITION OF SOME COPPER ALLOYS

Name	Nominal Composition, %
Copper	99.9+ copper
Everdur	95.8 copper, 3.1 silicon
Everdur casting alloy	94.9 copper, 4.0 silicon, 1.1 manganese
Normal commercial yellow brass	65–70 copper, 30–35 zinc
Commercial bronze	90 copper, 10 zinc
Gilding metal	95 copper, 5 zinc
Red brass	85 copper, 15 zinc
Muntz metal	60 copper, 40 zinc
Naval brass	60 copper, 39.5 zinc, 0.75 tin
Admiralty brass	70 copper, 29 zinc, 1 tin
Aluminum brass	77 copper, 21 zinc, 2 aluminum
Architectural bronze	56 copper, 41.5 zinc, 2.5 lead
Phosphor bronze	90 copper, 9.5 tin, 0.5 phosphorus
Nickel silver 10%	65 copper, 24.75 zinc, 10 nickel, 0.25 manganese
Nickel silver 13%	43.25 copper, 43.6 zinc, 13 nickel, 0.15 manganese
Nickel silver 15%	56.5 copper, 28.25 zinc, 15 nickel, 0.25 manganese
Cupro nickel	69–89 copper, 10–30 nickel, 0.75–1.25 iron, 0.25 manganese
Monel	29 copper, 68 nickel, 2.5 tin, 0.25 manganese

Table 8-16
PHYSICAL PROPERTIES OF COPPER AND COPPER ALLOYS

Copper Metal (And Nominal Composition)	Industry Alloy Number	Average Coefficient of Linear Thermal Expansion Per °F × 10⁻⁶ (68° to 572°)	Per °C × 10⁻⁶ (20° to 300°)	Density lb/in³ at 68°F	g/cm³ at 20°C	Specific Gravity	Modulus of Elasticity (Tension) psi × 10⁶	kg/mm² × 10³	Modulus of Rigidity psi × 10⁶	kg/mm² × 10³
Electrolytic copper Copper 99.90% min oxygen 0.04%	110	9.8	17.7	0.321–0.323	8.89–8.94	8.89–8.94	17	12	6.4	4.5
Phosphorized copper (high residual phosphorus) Copper 99.9% min phos. 0.015–0.040%	122	9.8	17.7	0.323	8.94	8.94	17	12	6.4	4.5
Gilding metal Copper 95% zinc 5%	210	10.0	18.1	0.320	8.86	8.86	17	12	6.4	4.5
Commercial bronze Copper 90% zinc 10%	220	10.2	18.4	0.318	8.80	8.80	17	12	6.4	4.5
Red brass Copper 85% zinc 15%	230	10.4	18.7	0.316	8.75	8.75	17	12	6.4	4.5
Low brass Copper 80% zinc 20%	240	10.6	19.1	0.313	8.67	8.67	16	11.2	6.0	4.2
Cartridge brass Copper 70% zinc 30%	260	11.1	19.9	0.308	8.53	8.53	16	11.2	6.0	4.2
Yellow brass Copper 65% zinc 35%	268	11.3	20.3	0.306	8.47	8.47	15	10.5	5.6	3.9
Muntz metal Copper 60% zinc 40%	280	11.6	20.8	0.303	8.39	8.39	15	10.5	5.6	3.9
Leaded commercial bronze Copper 89% zinc 9.25% lead 1.75%	314	10.2	18.4	0.319	8.83	8.83	17	12	6.4	4.5
Medium leaded brass Copper 65% zinc 34% lead 1%	340	11.3	20.3	0.306	8.47	8.47	15	10.5	5.6	3.9
High leaded brass Copper 65% zinc 33% lead 2%	342	11.3	20.3	0.306	8.47	8.47	15	10.5	5.6	3.9
Free-cutting brass Copper 61.5% zinc 35.5% lead 3%	360	11.4	20.5	0.307	8.50	8.50	14	9.8	5.3	3.7
Forging brass Copper 59% zinc 39% lead 2%	377	11.5	20.7	0.305	8.44	8.44	15	10.5	5.5	3.9
Architectural bronze Copper 57% zinc 40% lead 3%	385	11.6	20.9	0.306	8.47	8.47	14	9.8	5.3	3.7
Admiralty Copper 71% zinc 28% tin 1% arsenic or antimony 0.1% max	443–445	11.2	20.2	0.308	8.53	8.53	16	11.2	6.0	4.2
Naval brass Copper 60% zinc 39.25% tin 0.75%	464	11.8	21.2	0.304	8.41	8.41	15	10.5	5.6	3.9
Leaded naval brass Copper 60% zinc 37.5% tin 0.75% lead 1.75%	485	11.8	21.2	0.305	8.44	8.44	15	10.5	5.6	3.9
Phosphor bronzes 1.25% tin copper 98.7% tin 1.25% phos. 0.05%	502	9.9	17.8	0.321	8.89	8.89	17	12	6.4	4.5
5% tin copper 94.75% tin 5% phos. 0.25%	510	9.9	17.8	0.320	8.86	8.86	16	11.2	6.0	4.2

Table 8-16   (continued)

Copper Metal (And Nominal Composition)	In-dustry Alloy Num-ber	Average Coefficient of Linear Thermal Expansion		Density		Specific Gravity	Modulus of Elasticity (Tension)		Modulus of Rigidity	
		Per °F × 10⁻⁶ (68° to 572°)	Per °C × 10⁻⁶ (20° to 300°)	lb/in³ at 68°F	g/cm³ at 20°C		psi × 10⁶	kg/mm² × 10³	psi × 10⁶	kg/mm² × 10³
Phospor bronzes 8% tin copper 91.75% tin 8% phos. 0.25%	521	10.1	18.2	0.318	8.80	8.80	16	11.2	6.0	4.2
Aluminum bronze Copper 90.75% aluminum 7.25% silicon 2%	637	10.0	18.0	0.278	7.69	7.69	15	10.5	5.6	3.9
Silicon bronzes low silicon copper 98.5% silicon 1.5%	651	9.9	17.9	0.316	8.75	8.75	17	12	6.4	4.5
high silicon copper 97% silicon 3%	655	10.0	18.0	0.308	8.53	8.53	15	10.5	5.6	3.9
Manganese bronze Copper 58.5% zinc 39% iron 1.4% tin 1% manganese 0.1%	675	11.8	21.2	0.302	8.36	8.36	15	10.5	5.6	3.9
Aluminum brass Copper 77.5% zinc 20.5% aluminum 2% arsenic 0.1% max	687	10.3	18.5	0.301	8.33	8.33	16	11.2	6.0	4.2
Cupro-nickel alloys 90–10 copper 88.3% nickel 10% iron 1.3% manganese 0.4%	706	9.3	17.1	0.323	8.94	8.94	18	12.7	6,8	4.8
70–30 copper 68.9% nickel 30% iron 0.5% manganese 0.6%	715	9.0	16.2	0.323	8.94	8.94	22	15.5	8.3	5.8
Nickel-silver alloys 10% nickel copper 65% nickel 10% zinc 25%	745	9.1	16.4	0.314	8.69	8.69	17.5	12.3	6.6	4.6
18% nickel copper 65% nickel 18% zinc 17%	752	9.0	16.2	0.316	8.73	8.73	18	12.7	6.8	4.8
18% nickel copper 55% nickel 18% zinc 27%	770	9.3	16.7	0.314	8.70	8.70	18	12.7	6.8	4.8

SOURCE: Canadian Copper & Brass Development Association.

Standing and ribbed seams are preferred with copper roofing, since it has a relatively large expansion factor.

In most locations an attractive soft blue-green patina forms on copper so that its beauty is enhanced with age. This often results in its being chosen as the roofing material where dignity, warmth, and charm as well as long life are prime considerations.

Lead

A principal source of lead is ore containing galena, lead sulfide. It is first roasted to form lumps of lead oxide. The lead oxide is charged into a blast furnace with coke, iron oxide, and lime. The lead collects at the bottom of the furnace and is tapped off at intervals. Further refining, which is often necessary, is carried out by heating the lead in a reverberatory

Fig. 8-82 Copper siding and roofing.

furnace in the presence of air. Most of the impurities are oxidized and pass off as gases.

Lead is a soft, plastic, malleable metal used primarily in sheet form. It is used as flashing, in curtain-wall panels, and as roofing material. When exposed to the atmosphere it weathers to a soft, even gray tone. Lead is useful as a roofing material since it is very pliable and can be drawn and stretched over uneven surfaces. Sheet dimensions for roofing are usually limited to 24 × 48 in (600 × 1200 mm) because of weight. Ribbed seams are best suited for splicing roofing sheets.

Lead is used to cover sheets of steel and copper to take advantage of the stronger, lighter materials and yet retain the color of lead. It is highly resistant to acids, but if it must come in contact with fresh concrete, the contact side should be coated with a heavy coat of asphalt.

By mixing antimony with lead, hard lead is produced. It is not as pliable as normal lead and is used for gutters and castings.

Tin

The ore from which tin is commonly produced contains cassiterite, a tin oxide. A reverberatory furnace is used to reduce the ore, and the tin is further refined by electrolytic refining.

Because of its resistance to corrosion, tin is used largely to coat iron and steel roofing sheets. When coated with a mixture of 25 percent tin and 75 percent lead, the sheets are known as terneplate. Plates coated with pure tin are called bright tin-plate.

Zinc

Zinc is lighter and stiffer than lead but is affected by acids and has a high coefficient of expansion. Rolled sheet zinc is sometimes used for roofing and flashing, but zinc has a much wider application as a coating for steel roofing sheets.

GLOSSARY

alloy steel	A special steel, containing one or more added elements, which impart some special property to the steel.
anodize	Coat with a protective film by subjecting to electrolytic action.
bloom	The first stage in the formation of an ingot into a rolled steel shape.

bottom chord	Lower horizontal member of a steel joist or truss.
cementite	A hard brittle compound (Fe_3C) that when properly dispersed through a steel sample, increases the strength of the steel.
concentrated ore	Ore from which the major part of the impurities has been removed.
corrugated	Shaped into parallel, equally curved ridges and hollows.
cryolite	A mineral, sodium-aluminum fluoride.
dolomite	A limestone rich in magnesium carbonate.
eutectic	A three-phase reaction in which one liquid phase solidifies to produce two solid phases.
eutectoid	A three-phase reaction in which one solid phase transforms to two different solid phases.
extruded	Shaped by forcing through a die by pressure.
fluorspar	A mineral, calcium fluoride.
flux	A substance used to promote fusion.
ingot	A large mass of metal cast into some convenient shape.
matte	A crude mixture of sulfides formed in smelting.
patina	A film formed on copper by exposure or by treatment with acids.
pearlite	A two-phase layered material containing ferrite and cementite that occurs in steels cooled in the normal fashion or isothermally transformed at high temperatures.
petroleum coke	Residue left when petroleum is distilled to dryness.
pig iron	Basic iron from a blast furnace.
reverberatory furnace	A furnace in which the flame is reflected from the roof to the material being smelted.
slag	Waste material resulting from the refining of an ore.
trunnion	A projecting pivot.
tuyeres	The openings in the blast furnace wall through which preheated air is forced to preheat the charge.

REVIEW QUESTIONS

1. Explain briefly how a blast furnace reduces iron ore to metallic iron.

2. What purpose does the coke serve in the operation of a blast furnace?

3. What is the purpose of the limestone in the blast furnace?

4. Name the ingredients used to make steel in an open-hearth furnace, and indicate the part each plays in the process.

5. Give the average carbon content of low, medium, and high carbon steel, and outline the basic properties of each.

6. Draw neat sketches to illustrate the difference in cross-section between an S-shape and a W-shape beam.

7. Explain how a number of different weights per unit of length are produced, for a given nominal depth of W-shape beam.

8. What is the function of each of the following:
   a. A hot-strip mill
   b. A cold-reduction mill

9. What is meant by annealing, and what is the purpose of this process?

10. Why do wide-flange members, as nearly square as possible in cross-section, usually make the best columns?

11. Describe briefly how seamless pipe is made.

12. a. What is skelp?
    b. What is resistance welding?

13. a. What is deformed steel rod?
    b. What is the purpose of deforming rod?

14. Where and why is spiral reinforcing used?

15. Name two commonly used building products made from sheet steel.

16. a. Using diagrams, illustrate the three basic types of seams that are used in sheet metal roofing.
    b. Give reasons for using each of the three types of seam.

17. Why is lead useful as a roofing material?

18. List three common uses for aluminum structural shapes.

19. For what purposes are aluminum architectural shapes used?

20. Outline the difference between terneplate and bright tinplate.

SELECTED SOURCES OF INFORMATION

Alcan Ltd., Montreal, Que.
American Institute of Steel Construction, New York, N.Y.
American Iron & Steel Institute, New York, N.Y.
American Zinc Institute, Inc., New York, N.Y.
Anaconda American Brass Company, Waterbury, Conn.
Bethlehem Steel Co., Bethlehem, Pa.
Canadian Copper & Brass Development Association, Toronto, Ont.
Canadian Institute of Steel Construction, Toronto, Ont.
Dominion Foundries & Steel Ltd, Hamilton, Ont.
Lead Industries Association, New York, N.Y.
Rosco Metal Products Ltd., Toronto, Ont.
Sydney Steel Corporation, Sydney, N.S.
The Steel Company of Canada, Hamilton, Ont.
United States Steel Corporation, Pittsburgh, Pa.

REFERENCES

1. Allen, Dell K., *Metallurgy Theory and Practice,* American Technical Society, Chicago, Ill., 1969.
2. Keyser, Carl A., *Materials Science in Engineering,* 4th ed., Charles E. Merrill Publishing Co., Columbus, Ohio, 1986.
3. *The Making of Steel,* American Iron and Steel Institute, Washington, D.C., 1964.
4. Murphy, Glen, *Properties of Engineering Materials,* International Textbook Company, Scranton, Penna., 1957.

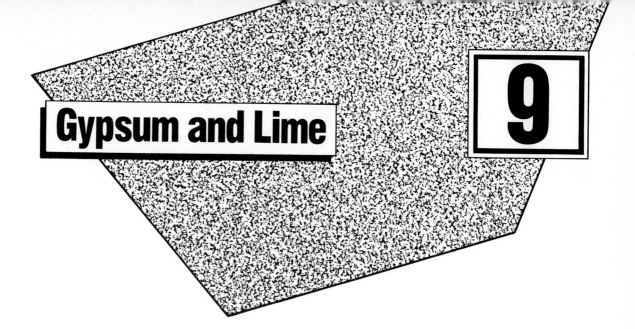

Gypsum and Lime

9

GYPSUM

Gypsum has been recognized as a valuable building material for several thousand years. The Greeks and the Egyptians both used it to advantage in structures which still stand.

As an interior finish, gypsum plaster is durable and versatile. Plaster surfaces can be troweled smooth, stippled, or sand finished and can be applied directly onto gypsum lath, metal lath, fiberboard plaster base, or directly over a masonry surface. Using lightweight aggregates, plaster can be given a textured surface to aid in sound insulation.

Gypsum board, the modern version of plaster interior finishing, provides a smooth, durable surface with a minimum amount of effort and expense. It is simple to install, provides good fire ratings, and can be painted, stippled, or papered. A substantial portion of all building finishes begin with gypsum wallboard. (See Fig. 9-1.)

Gypsum usually is found in rock formation in various parts of the world, notably in Canada, the United States, France, England, Italy, China, Russia, and areas of South America. The rock is crushed, ground, and calcined (heated), which drives off about 75 percent of the combined water, forming the hemihydrate known as plaster of paris. If this product is mixed with water, a chemical recombination takes place and the original rock structure is reformed.

Chemical Composition

Gypsum is a hydrous calcium sulfate with the chemical formula $CaSO_4(2H_2O)$, which means that it is a compound of lime, sulfur, and water:

$$CaSO_4(2H_2O) \rightarrow \begin{array}{l} \text{Calcium sulfate} \\ CaSO_4 \quad 79.1\% \\ + \\ 2H_2O \quad 20.9\% \\ \text{Water} \end{array} \left\{ \begin{array}{l} \text{Lime} \\ CaO \quad 32.5\% \\ + \\ SO_3 \quad 46.6\% \\ \text{Sulfur trioxide} \\ + \\ H_2O \quad 20.9\% \\ \text{Water} \end{array} \right.$$

Fig. 9-1   Interior gypsum board finish.

273

Gypsum is soluble in hydrochloric acid and also in about 500 parts of water; its specific gravity is 2.3. Anhydrite, calcium sulfate without combined water ($CaSO_4$), is often found closely associated with gypsum. It has little commercial value but will, in course of time, if exposed to air, absorb sufficient water (2 parts) to convert it into gypsum.

Production of Gypsum

Gypsum is very seldom found in the pure state but usually contains varying amounts of clay, limestone, silica, iron compounds, etc. In the pure state it is white, but combined with impurities, it may be gray, brown, or reddish brown. Some deposits of gypsum are found close to the surface of the earth; others are buried well below the surface.

Depending on the location of the deposit, gypsum is either mined or quarried. If the rock is near the surface, a stripping operation will allow the material to be removed by the open-pit quarrying method. If it is deeply buried, regular mining operations are necessary.

The raw material is shipped to a mill, where it is first passed through a heavy, jaw-type crusher, which reduces it to 2- to 3-in (50- to 75-mm) sizes. It is then further reduced in size in a hammer mill, to pieces of approximately $\frac{1}{2}$ in (13 mm) in diameter. In some mills, this material then goes to a rotary *calciner,* where it is heated to about 175°C, which drives off about 75 percent of the combined water in the gypsum, leaving the *hemihydrate* plaster of paris. This is the basic material from which many of the gypsum building materials are made.

In another process, the $\frac{1}{2}$-in (13-mm) material goes to a *Raymond mill,* where it is reduced to a fine powder, known as *land plaster.* The land plaster proceeds to a calcining kettle, where it is heated to about 165°C to drive off the combined water and produce plaster of paris.

Gypsum Plasters

PLASTER OF PARIS   Plaster of paris is made from carefully selected white rock. When mixed with water to form a paste, it sets in about 15 to 20 min. It is used for small patching jobs on plaster walls and for making molds; when it is mixed with lime putty according to directions, it makes a plaster finish coat which hardens fast and is free from shrinkage cracks.

KEENE'S CEMENT   If gypsum is subjected to a temperature of 400°C, which must be done in kilns, not kettles, it is completely dehydrated. When this material is ground and has had a positive catalyst such as alum added to it, it is known as Keene's cement. If this product is mixed with water to form a plaster, it sets slowly and becomes very hard. It is highly resistant to moisture penetration and is used where sanitary conditions or excessive moisture makes it necessary to specify a hard, impervious, smooth surface. About 1 ton (0.9 t) of Keene's cement, mixed with water and applied as a putty coat, will cover 400 to 500 yd² (335 to 420 m²) of wall surface.

CASTING PLASTER   This plaster is made from specially selected rock and ground much finer than regular plaster of paris. It is slower setting and cooler working, which makes it adaptable for ornamental molded plaster work. This technique requires considerable time to produce sharp, clear lines and extra-smooth surfaces associated with molded plaster. Fifty percent lime putty may be added for extra plasticity.

HARD WALL PLASTER   This is a neat gypsum plaster, containing hair or fiber, widely used to form the first (scratch) coat and the second (brown) coat on plastered walls and ceilings. It requires the addition of aggregate and water on the job. The aggregate may be natural sand or a lightweight aggregate such as vermiculite or perlite. A lightweight base-coat plaster is also produced which has the gypsum and aggregate already mixed together and requires only water.

When sand is to be used as the aggregate, 2 parts by weight of dry sand are mixed with 1 part of hard wall for the scratch coat on gypsum, wood, or metal lath. For the brown coat, 3 parts of sand are used to 1 part plaster.

Table 9-1 indicates the average covering capacity of base-coat plaster on various types of lath, using sand as the aggregate. (See Fig. 9-2.)

By increasing the amount of sand used per bag of hard wall, the plasterer can make the plaster cover a greater area but only at the expense of reducing its strength. Figure 9-3 shows the approximate strength of hard wall plaster containing varying amounts of sand.

Table 9-1
AVERAGE COVERING CAPACITY OF BASE-COAT PLASTER USING SAND AS AGGREGATE

Surface	Sand-to-Plaster	m²/t	yd²/ton
Brick and clay tile	3 to 1	150–185	165–200
Gypsum tile	3 to 1	215–235	235–255
Gypsum lath	2 to 1	205–220	225–240
Metal lath	2 to 1	95–125	105–135

CEMENT BOND PLASTER As the name implies, cement bond plaster is intended for application to concrete surfaces. Almost any finish plaster can then be applied over this base coat.

Cement bond plaster requires the addition only of water; the mixed material should be allowed to stand for at least 10 min before it is used. It is applied in two coats, totaling a $\frac{3}{8}$-in (9.5-mm) thickness on ceilings and a $\frac{5}{8}$-in (16-mm) thickness on walls. The surface should be roughened to receive the finish coat before the plaster begins to set. To cover from 99 to 132 yd² (83 to 110 m²) of surface, 1.1 tons (1 t) of plaster is needed.

Fig. 9-2 Plaster applied over gypsum lath by machine. *(Westroc Industries)*

FINISH PLASTER This material is made specially to produce the finish (putty) coat for plastered surfaces. It has to be mixed with hydrated lime putty and water. The lime putty is produced either by mixing hydrated lime and water or by slaking quicklime and using the resulting slaked lime putty. Finish plaster and putty are mixed in the proportion of 1 part plaster to 3 parts lime putty by volume or 1 part plaster to 2 parts dry hydrated lime by weight. Under average conditions 1 ton (0.9 t) of finish plaster with 2 tons (1.8 t) of dry hydrated lime will cover 1000 to 1400 yd² (836 to 1170 m²) of surface.

PREPARED FINISH PLASTER This type of plaster requires only water. It contains no lime, so the plaster surface can be decorated as soon as it is dry. It does not dry to the degree of whiteness of regular finish plaster and therefore is not recommended when the plaster surface is to be left unpainted. Usually 1.1 tons (1 t) of this plaster will cover from 385 to 440 yd² (322 to 368 m²).

TEXTURE PLASTER Similar in manufacture to prepared finish plaster, texture plaster is used when a rough (texture) surface is required. It is mixed in the proportion of 2 parts plaster to 1 part water by volume and applied in two coats over base-coat plaster or gypsum wallboard. The second or texture coat can be applied by trowel, brush, or sponge, depending on the texture desired. Generally, 11 lb (5 kg) of plaster will cover 10 to 20 ft² (0.93 to 1.86 m²), again depending on the kind of texture.

TEXTURE SPRAY Texture spray is a dry, gypsum-based material designed to cover minor imperfections and provide a uniform, durable, white surface over gypsum board, concrete, or plaster. It requires

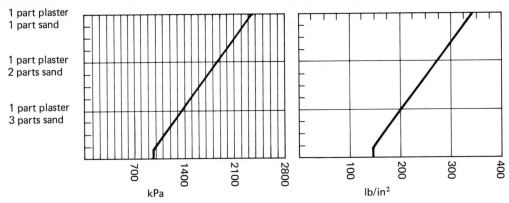

Fig. 9-3   Varying strengths in hard wall plaster.

only the addition of clean water at room temperature to prepare it for use. Application is by a spray machine designed for hard aggregate material, over surfaces that are smooth, clean, and primed with a good-quality white latex paint. Variations in texture may be obtained by varying the *water content, orifice size,* and *air pressure.* Less water, larger orifice size, and lower air pressure all produce heavier textures.

ACOUSTICAL PLASTER   Calcined gypsum is mixed with a lightweight mineral aggregate to make a type of finish plaster that has a high rate of sound absorption (see Table 9-2).

It requires only water for mixing and is applied over regular gypsum base-coat plasters in two coats, each about $\frac{1}{4}$ in (6 mm) thick. Generally, 1.1 tons (1 t) of acoustical plaster will cover about 110 yd^2 (92 m^2), $\frac{1}{2}$ in (12 mm) thick.

JOINT FILLER   Similar in manufacture and appearance to texture plaster, gypsum joint filler is used to make the paste for filling nail holes and covering joints in gypsum wallboard and also to make the adhesive used in laminating two sheets of board together.

When used as a filler, the material is mixed with lukewarm water in the proportion of approximately 17 pt (8 L) of water to 28 lb (12.75 kg) of filter. The mix should be allowed to stand for 30 min and can then be applied by hand with a broad spatula or by machine.

If it is to be used as an adhesive, 21 pt (10 L) of lukewarm water are mixed with $26\frac{1}{4}$ lb (11.9 kg) of dry filler. The mix should be allowed to stand for 30 min and can then be applied to the back of the board to be laminated in a thin layer. Usually 50 to 55 lb (22.5 to 25 kg) of dry filler is required to make enough adhesive to cover 1000 ft^2 (929 m^2) of wallboard.

Gypsum Boards

GYPSUM WALLBOARD   Gypsum wallboard is a highly fire-resistant board intended for both *sheathing* and *finishing* for interior walls and ceilings. It is made of a core of gypsum, covered on each side by a heavy, specially manufactured kraft paper. The

Table 9-2
ABSORPTION COEFFICIENTS OF ACOUSTICAL PLASTER FOR VARIOUS PITCHES OF SOUND

Thickness		2048 Cycles	1024 Cycles	512 Cycles	256 Cycles	128 Cycles	Reduction Coefficient
Inches	Milli- meters						
$\frac{1}{2}$	13	0.34	0.30	0.31	0.61	0.69	0.50
$\frac{3}{4}$	19	0.36	0.37	0.55	0.67	0.67	0.55

paper on the face side is ivory colored, while the back is gray.

The gypsum core is made up of the product of the calciner, into which is mixed a foaming agent to lighten the weight of the finished board, accelerators to speed up the set, paper pulp for reinforcement, and water. The resulting paste is poured in an even layer onto a moving belt of paper, topped off with another sheet of paper. By a continuous process, a sheet 4 ft (1200 mm) wide is produced, with reinforced, recessed edges. (See Fig. 9-4.) Common thicknesses are $\frac{3}{8}$, $\frac{1}{2}$, and $\frac{2}{3}$ in (10, 12, and 16 mm), and the continuous sheet is automatically cut into lengths of 4 to 16 ft (1200 to 4800 mm).

Gypsum wallboard has two classifications: Standard and Type X. When fire rating requirements exceed 30 min, Type X is normally required to obtain the higher ratings. When tested according to ASTM E119, Type X will provide a 60-min fire rating with a $\frac{5}{8}$-in (16-mm) thickness or a 45-min fire rating with a $\frac{1}{2}$-in (12.5-mm) thickness.

Gypsum wallboard is usually applied directly to the structural framing except when additional soundproofing is necessary. For that application, metal or wood furring may first be attached to the framing (to increase the wall cavity), to which the wallboard is then fastened. Depending on the fire rating, it can be applied in single or double layers. By taking advantage of the various combinations of thicknesses, a specified fire rating may be achieved without using excess material. When using the double-ply system it is recommended that the sheets on the outer layer be applied vertically for wall heights exceeding 8 ft 3 in (2500 mm) and horizontally for wall heights up to 8 ft 3 in. This will keep the number of joints to a minimum. Figure 9-5 illustrates the correct application of wallboard around openings.

Gypsum board may be fastened to the frame by single nailing, by double nailing, or with drywall

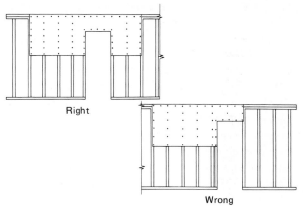

Fig. 9-5 Board application at openings.

screws. For the double-ply application, the two layers are laminated together with joint compound in addition to the nailing or screw fastening. Nails used should be annular ringed drywall nails, $1\frac{1}{4}$ to $1\frac{7}{8}$ in (32 to 48 mm) in length, depending on the thickness of the gypsum board and the fire rating required. For walls, spacing of the nails for single nailing is usually 8 in (200 mm) o.c. along the edges and 12 in (300 mm) in the field (intermediate studs between edges), but this can vary depending on the fire rating. For ceiling applications, nailing is usually 7 in (175 mm) o.c. but is reduced to 6 in (150 mm) for specific fire ratings. Double nailing, when appropriate [usually limited to single-thickness applications of $\frac{3}{8}$- and $\frac{1}{2}$-in (9.5- and 12.5-mm) wallboard], requires two nails 2 in (50 mm) apart every 12 in (300 mm).

Wallboard screws have greater holding power and may be spaced more widely than the nails. For walls, spacings normally used are 12 in (300 mm) along the edges and 16 in (400 mm) in the field. For ceilings, spacing is usually 12 in (300 mm) o.c. When wallboard is fastened to metal studs, screws must be used exclusively.

For laminated applications, the second layer is applied at right angles to the first and is bonded to the first using wallboard cement. It is kept in place with double-headed nails or cleats until the cement sets—usually 24 h. The nails or cleats are then removed and the holes patched with joint cement.

GYPSUM-BOARD PARTITIONS Partitions of gypsum board for non-load-bearing situations can be considered as semisolid or solid depending on the arrangement of the wallboard sections. Semi-

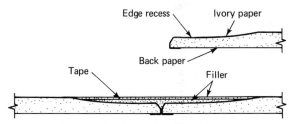

Fig. 9-4 Recessed edges of wallboard.

solid partitions are composed of two layers of wallboard separated by ribs spaced at regular intervals. Wood or metal runners, usually $1 \times 1\frac{1}{2}$ in (25 × 38 mm) are fastened to the wall and ceiling as required. (See Fig. 9-6.) Wallboard is nailed to one side of the runners, to which 1×6 in (25 × 150 mm) ribs made up of two $\frac{1}{2}$-in (12.5-mm) thick pieces of wallboard glued together are laminated with joint cement at 24 in (600 mm) o.c. To this, the last layer of wallboard is cemented and nailed to complete the partition. Using $\frac{5}{8}$-in (16-mm) thick Type X wallboard on this type of partition will provide a 60-min fire rating. For solid partitions, the space between the two outer sheets is filled with two thicknesses of $\frac{1}{2}$-in (12.5-mm) wallboard. This arrangement will provide a fire rating of 120 min.

Where improved sound insulation is required in a partition, double or triple solid partitions are used. A double solid partition consists of two layers of 1-in (25-mm) board supported by two $1 \times 1\frac{1}{2}$ in (25 × 38 mm) wood runners spaced 1 in (25 mm) apart. Each side is then covered with an additional layer of $\frac{1}{2}$-in (12.5-mm) wallboard. (See Fig. 9-7.) The triple solid partition is similar to the double solid except that the 1-in space in the center of the partition is filled with another layer of 1-in wallboard. In addition to better sound insulation, each of these partitions provides a 2-h fire rating.

Where pipes or other service installations must be placed in a partition, a greater depth is required. This may be provided by using two rows of $1\frac{5}{8}$-in (41-mm) metal studs, spaced the necessary distance apart and cross-braced with pieces of $\frac{1}{2}$-in (12-mm) gypsum board, 12 in (300 mm) wide, installed at the quarter points of the studs. (See Fig. 9-8.)

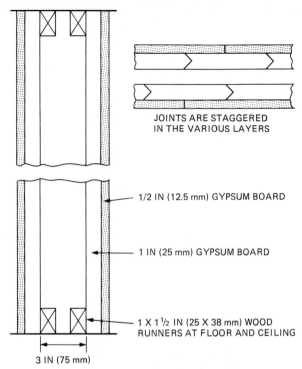

1/2 IN (12.5 mm) GYPSUM BOARD

1 IN (25 mm) GYPSUM BOARD

1 X 1½ IN (25 X 38 mm) WOOD RUNNERS AT FLOOR AND CEILING

JOINTS ARE STAGGERED IN THE VARIOUS LAYERS

3 IN (75 mm)

Fig. 9-7   Double solid gypsum board partition.

Finally, single or double layers of gypsum board are attached to the stud frame with screws or screws and cement. A sound-insulation blanket may be attached to the inner surface of one of the partition surfaces.

TAPING AND JOINT FILLING   Once the board is installed, it has to be prepared for final finishing. This is done by *taping* the joints and interior angles and applying *metal corner bead* to all external angles. (See Fig. 9-9.) Perforated tape is used, and it is applied by hand or machine (see Fig. 9-10) by bedding it in joint filler. After the filler is dry, a second, wider coat is applied, either by hand or by machine. (See Figs. 9-11 and 9-12.)

The internal angles are taped by folding a tape into the corner and bedding it in joint filler. A second, wider coat is applied after the first is dry. (See Fig. 9-12.) Finally, the joints are sanded lightly and the whole surface is sealed and painted.

DECORATED GYPSUM WALLBOARD   Gypsum wallboard is manufactured in $\frac{1}{2}$- and $\frac{5}{8}$-in (13- and 16-mm) thicknesses, which have one side surfaced with a fabric-backed vinyl sheet, printed in a variety

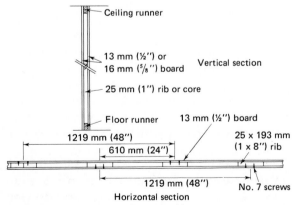

Ceiling runner

13 mm (½″) or 16 mm (⅝″) board

Vertical section

25 mm (1″) rib or core

Floor runner

13 mm (½″) board

1219 mm (48″)

610 mm (24″)

25 x 193 mm (1 x 8″) rib

1219 mm (48″)

No. 7 screws

Horizontal section

Fig. 9-6   Three-ply studless partition.

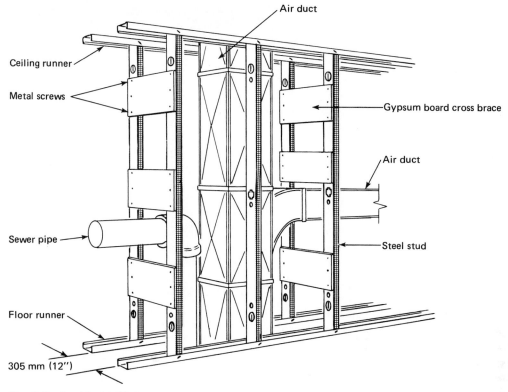

Fig. 9-8   Double partition.

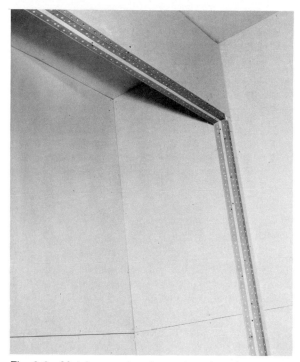

Fig. 9-9   Metal corner bead on external angles.   *(Westroc Industries)*

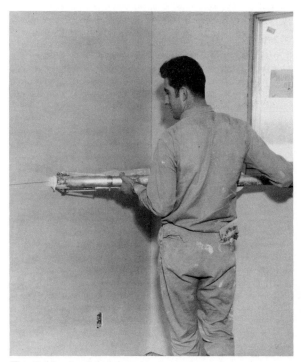

Fig. 9-10   Applying tape and cement with taping gun. *(Westroc Industries)*

Fig. 9-11   Gypsum board joints taped and filled.   *(Westroc Industries)*

Fig. 9-13   Gypsum board with wood grain vinyl surface.
(Gold Bond Building Products)

of simulated wood grain and fabric finishes. (See Figs. 9-13 and 9-14.) One type is made with a square, finished edge, one with a beveled, finished edge, and a third with loose flaps of vinyl left at each long edge.

The first two are applied vertically and nailed to a wood frame with colored nails (see Fig. 9-15) or secured with gypsum cement to a gypsum-board backing. The third type is applied vertically, using an adhesive at the intermediate supports and nails or screws at the edges. The joints are filled (see Fig. 9-16) and leveled, and the loose vinyl flaps cemented over the joint, one over the other. (See Fig.

9-17.) Finally, using a straightedge and sharp blade, the two flaps are trimmed to produce an invisible joint. (See Fig. 9-18.)

Fig. 9-12   Second coat of joint filler with mechanical applicator.   *(Westroc Industries)*

Fig. 9-14   Gypsum board with textured vinyl surface.
(Gold Bond Building Products)

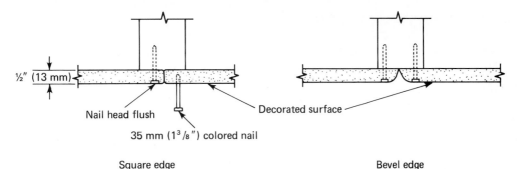

$\frac{1}{2}''$ (13 mm)

Nail head flush

35 mm ($1^3/_8''$) colored nail

Decorated surface

Square edge

Bevel edge

Fig. 9-15   Colored nails for decorated wallboard.

GYPSUM-BOARD RADIANT-HEATING PANELS

Available on the market are $\frac{5}{8}$-in (16-mm) gypsum-board panels which have radiant-heating cable embedded in them. An 18-ft (5.5-m) nonheating lead extends from the back of each panel so that the panels can be connected in parallel (see Fig. 9-19) to form a radiant-heating system for each room. Such panels should be used on ceilings only (see Fig. 9-20)—never on walls—and they cannot be cut or have fastenings applied to them except in areas indicated on the face of each panel.

In order to get efficient heating from such a system, adequate insulation in the space behind it is necessary. The specific depth of insulation required for best results in your area should be ascertained.

GYPSUM BACKER BOARDS   Gypsum backer boards, as the name implies, are boards which are intended for use as a base behind a facing material of some sort.

Regular backer board is an economical base layer for laminated construction. It is regular board width, up to 12 ft (3.65 m) long, with square edges, and available in two thicknesses: $\frac{3}{8}$ and $\frac{1}{2}$ in (9.5 and 12 mm).

Fire-resistant backer board is a type of gypsum board that meets Underwriters Laboratory requirements for 1-h fire-rated construction. It is made $\frac{5}{8}$ in (16 mm) thick, 24 in (600 mm) wide, and up to 12 ft (3.65 m) long, with tongue-and-grooved edges. A typical example of its use is shown in Fig. 9-21, where it is being used to fireproof a steel column. Four layers will provide a 4-h rating, three layers a 3-h rating, etc. By comparison, four layers of regular $\frac{1}{2}$-in (12-mm) board, used in a similar manner, will provide a 2-h fire rating.

Water-resistant backer board is a board made specifically to provide a suitable base for the adhesive application of plastic, ceramic, or metal wall tile in areas of high moisture, such as kitchens,

Fig. 9-16   Filling joint between vinyl-surfaced gypsum boards. *(Gold Bond Building Products)*

Fig. 9-17   Cementing vinyl flaps over joint. *(Gold Bond Building Products)*

Fig. 9-18   Making final joint in vinyl flaps. *(Gold Bond Building Products)*

Fig. 9-19 Wiring gypsum-board radiant-heating panels together. *(Gold Bond Building Products)*

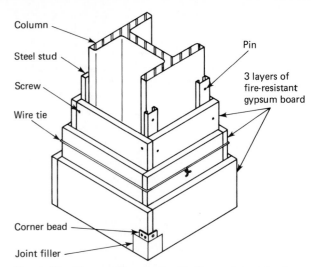

Fig. 9-21 Fireproofing steel with fire-resistant backer board.

shower stalls, tub enclosures, bathrooms, laundry rooms, etc. It consists of an asphalt-treated core covered with heavy, water-repellent paper on the back and an ivory paper on the face which does not require sealing before tile is applied. It is made standard width, $\frac{1}{2}$ or $\frac{5}{8}$ in (12 or 16 mm) thick, and up to 12 ft (3.65 m) long, with square or tapered edges.

Core board is a board made for gypsum solid-core partition systems, 1 in (25 mm) thick, 24 in (600 mm) wide, in lengths as required, with V-joint edges.

Fig. 9-20 Gypsum-board radiant-heating panels. *(Gold Bond Building Products)*

Gypsum sound-deadening board is a special gypsum backer board for sound-rated construction, $\frac{1}{4}$ in (6 mm) thick, 48 in (1200 mm) wide, and up to 12 ft (3.65 m) long, with square edges.

GYPSUM LATH   The same basic method of manufacture is used for gypsum lath as for wallboard. A gypsum core is covered on both sides with a heavy paper, but in the case of lath, the same paper is used for both back and front. Laths are 16 × 48 × $\frac{3}{8}$ in (400 × 1200 × 9.5 mm) and are usually packed six to a bundle.

They are applied in horizontal courses, with $1\frac{1}{4}$-in (32-mm) 13-gauge flatheaded blued nails, using four nails per stud. Joints in succeeding courses should be staggered, corners above openings and wide spaces between lath should be reinforced with metal lath, and internal angles should be reinforced with a corner bead.

This lath acts as a base for plaster, providing adhesion for gypsum plaster of about 6 psi (41 kPa) if properly applied.

Greater fire protection is provided by using perforated lath, which allows a heavier protective layer of plaster because of an added mechanical bond. Sound insulation can be increased and cracking can be reduced by clipping the lath to the frame.

In order to provide better insulation, gypsum lath and gypsum wallboard are sometimes made with a sheet of aluminum foil attached to the back. This sheet reduces radiant-heat losses in winter and keeps radiant heat from penetrating from the outside in summer. (See Fig. 9-22.)

VENEER PLASTER SYSTEMS   Veneer plaster systems consist of gypsum boards 48 in (1200 mm) wide, covered with a special, highly absorptive paper, which is the *plaster base,* covered with thinly troweled, *special-purpose plasters.* Two basic systems are available: a *one-coat* plaster system and a *two-coat* system. They may be used in all types of *ceiling* and *partition* construction, in both residential and commercial buildings.

The application of the plaster base is the same for both systems, using nails or screws as the fasteners. The joints may be covered with a mesh made for the purpose and fastened with staples (see Fig. 9-23), or dry-wall tape may be used, embedded in the special plaster.

The special-purpose plaster is mixed in a high-speed mechanical mixer according to instructions. Since the rate of set is fairly rapid, the size of mixed batches should be kept to not more than two bags of plaster.

The plaster is intended for application by trowel, and the use of conventional plastering machines is not recommended. (See Fig. 9-24.) In the one-coat system, the single coat of plaster applied is approximately $\frac{3}{32}$ in (2.5 mm) thick, while in the two-coat system, the combined thickness of the two coats is a minimum of $\frac{1}{8}$ in (3 mm). The same plaster can be used directly over masonry or over cast-in-place concrete, using a bonding agent. The temperature should be maintained at between 13 and 21°C in

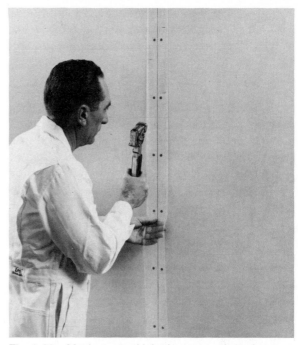

Fig. 9-23   Mesh-covered joint in veneer plastering system.   *(Gold Bond Building Products)*

Fig. 9-24   Thin plaster coat applied by trowel in veneer plastering system.   *(Gold Bond Building Products)*

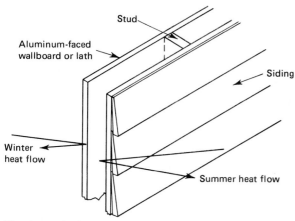

Fig. 9-22   Reflecting radiant heat.

Stud

Aluminum-faced wallboard or lath

Siding

Winter heat flow

Summer heat flow

the plastering area, and the plaster should not be allowed to dry quickly. The systems are not suitable where the plaster would be subject to weathering, direct water contact, or temperatures exceeding 52°C.

GYPSUM BOARD FOR EXTERIOR USE

Two types of gypsum board are manufactured for exterior use. One is a *regular-core* board, covered with water-repellent paper on both sides and intended for use as an exterior *sheathing* to be covered by some type of exterior finishing material. (See Fig. 9-25.)

Panels are produced $24 \times 96 \times \frac{1}{2}$ in ($600 \times 2400 \times 12$ mm), with the long edges tongue-and-grooved for a tighter fit. They are applied in horizontal courses, using $1\frac{3}{4}$-in (44-mm) galvanized roofing nails, spaced 8 in (200 mm) apart. Joints in succeeding courses should be staggered, and *let-in* wind bracing should be used for greater rigidity. Almost any type of exterior finish may be applied over gypsum sheathing, including siding, shingles, stucco, and brick veneer.

The other type of board is known as an exterior ceiling–soffit board, intended for use in exterior but protected locations. (See Fig. 9-26.) The *specially treated core* is covered on both sides with water-repellent paper. Panels are $\frac{1}{2}$ in (12 mm) thick, 48 in (1200 mm) wide, and from 8 to 12 ft (2.44 to 3.66 m) long.

DESIGN CONSIDERATIONS FOR GYPSUM-BOARD PRODUCTS

There are a number of design considerations which should be taken into account when such building elements as partitions, ceilings, column fireproofing, exterior curtain walls, and furring are to be made from gypsum board. They include the following:

1. Such elements will not significantly resist stresses imposed on them by structural movement, and they are subject to dimensional changes caused by changes in humidity and temperatures. Therefore gypsum-board surfaces should be isolated from all structural members, except the floor, by control joints of some type if the surfaces abut a structural member, wall, or ceiling of a different material, if the wall involved itself has a control joint in it, or if the construction changes within the plane of the building element involved.

2. In long partitions and wall furring surfaces, control joints should be provided at not more than 30 ft (9 m) o.c. Large ceiling areas should have control joints spaced not more than 50 ft (15 m) apart in either direction. The continuity of both the gypsum board and the supports should be broken at the control joints.

3. Where exterior curtain walls are made up of a metal stud frame covered by exterior gypsum-board sheathing and lath or gypsum board on the

Fig. 9-25 Gypsum board on metal studs as sheathing on an exterior wall.

Fig. 9-26 Gypsum soffit board used on exterior ceiling. *(Gold Bond Building Products)*

inside, the curtain wall should be divided into panels with control joints spaced not more than 10 ft (3 m) horizontally and vertically. Both interior and exterior sheathing material should be broken at the control joints. Where vertical and horizontal joints intersect, the vertical joints should be continuous, and the horizontal joint should abut it.

4. Dry-wall construction requires proper insulation of exterior walls, columns, and beams. This will minimize the possibility of partitions cracking due to the expansion or contraction of the structural members and will reduce shadowing and spotting problems in exterior walls. Such problems are caused by a temperature difference between the metal fasteners, metal studs, or furring members and the surrounding gypsum-board surface during periods of low temperature. This results in a greater accumulation of dirt over the fasteners and metal frame than on the surrounding surface. The intensity of the shadowing or spotting will vary directly with the temperature differential, as well as with the amount of airborne dirt or smoke.

5. Where any of the building elements mentioned are to be involved in sound control, the following factors should be considered:

a. The more massive the construction, the better its resistance to sound transmission.

b. Any openings in the construction, however small, will conduct airborne sound.

c. The introduction of a sound-absorbing material, such as mineral wool, between the wall surfaces will improve sound control.

d. The separation of the two opposing surfaces of a wall will help to reduce sound transmission.

6. During construction carried out in cold weather, controlled heat in the range of 13 to 21°C should be provided constantly while gypsum-board erection and joint-filling are being carried out. Ventilation should be provided to carry away excessive moisture, and during hot, dry weather, humidification of the air may be required to prevent the too rapid drying of joint filler.

Gypsum Roof Decking

A cast-in-place gypsum roof deck consists of what is known as a *reinforced-gypsum-concrete* slab, which may be cast on permanent form boards or used in a suspension system. The permanent forms may be supported directly by the structural frame—primary framing members—or by subpurlins, resting on the frame. (See Fig. 9-27.)

In the suspension system, continuous tension wires run from side to side across the subpurlins,

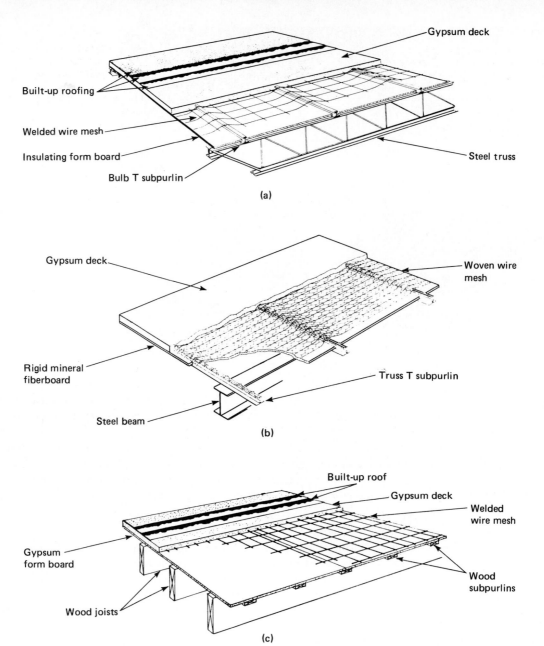

Built-up roofing

Welded wire mesh

Insulating form board

Bulb T subpurlin

Gypsum deck

Steel truss

(a)

Gypsum deck

Woven wire mesh

Rigid mineral fiberboard

Truss T subpurlin

Steel beam

(b)

Built-up roof

Gypsum deck

Welded wire mesh

Gypsum form board

Wood subpurlins

Wood joists

(c)

Fig. 9-27 Permanent form boards used in gypsum-concrete roof-deck construction. *(Owens-Corning Fiberglas)*

draping down at midspan to within not less than 12 mm ($\frac{1}{2}$ in) of the bottom of the slab. Temporary form boards hold the gypsum until the slab has set and is adequately strong. (See Fig. 9-28.)

Gypsum concrete is a factory-produced mixture of gypsum and shavings, wood chips, or mineral aggregate, which requires only the addition of water at the job site.

When permanent form boards are used, the gypsum is cast to a depth of not less than 2 in (50 mm) and reinforced with welded or woven wire mesh, as illustrated in Fig. 9-27. The form boards may be *gypsum board, insulating fiberboard, acoustical fiberboard, cement-asbestos board,* or *rigid mineral fiberboard.*

The maximum clear span of the slab between

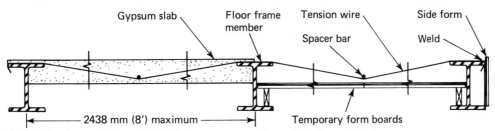

Fig. 9-28 Suspension system of gypsum-concrete roof-deck construction.

supports must not exceed 31 in (775 mm) when subpurlins and permanent form boards are used. If the form boards rest directly on the primary framing members, the center-to-center spacing of the members must not exceed 36 in (900 mm).

In the suspension system, the suspended decks should be hung from the primary framing members, the spacing of which must not exceed 96 in (2400 mm). The depth of the slab must be not less than 3 in (75 mm). In this system, the form boards will probably be of plywood, temporarily supported on T-head shores.

Such roof slabs are light in weight—normally the slab, form board, reinforcement, and subpurlins will not exceed 11.5 lb/ft² (56 kg/m²)—but relatively strong, supporting uniformly distributed loads of up to 700 lb/ft² (3400 kg/m²) when dry. They also offer good fire resistance: cast over gypsum, asbestos, or glass-fiber form boards, they are classed as noncombustible.

Gypsum Partition and Furring Tile

Gypsum tile for furring and partitions is made from specially calcined gypsum, to which is added about 5 percent wood fiber in the form of chips and sometimes some perlite, the wood chips for better strength and the perlite for reduced weight. Both solid and hollow tile is produced, in standard dimensions of 12 × 30 × 2, 3, 4, or 6 in (300 × 750 × 50, 75, 100, or 150 mm).

The thickness of tile used for partitions is determined largely by the ceiling height; 3- and 4-in (75- and 100-mm) tiles are generally used where the height does not exceed 15 ft (4.6 m). Two-inch (50-mm) solid tiles are used for partitions less than 10 ft (3 m) high and for ducts, shafts, etc. Either split or solid tiles may be used as furring against exterior walls.

Gypsum tiles are easily cut with a handsaw and are laid up with a mortar made from gypsum cement, sand, and water. Plaster grounds are nailed to the tile, while blocks can be spiked to tile ends to support wood trim, light fixtures, etc. Heavy fixtures can be supported by bolting through the wall.

LIME

Lime was commonly used in the past as a constituent of masonry mortar; today cement has largely replaced it for this purpose. It is still used, however, in the making of the finish or putty coat for interior plaster.

The lime used is hydrated or slaked lime, produced by slaking quicklime, which, in turn, is made by burning limestone. The limestone, calcium carbonate ($CaCO_3$), when subjected to heat in a shaft or kiln, breaks down into quicklime (CaO) and carbon dioxide (CO_2):

$$CaCO_3 + \text{heat} = CaO + CO_2$$

Calcium   Quicklime   Carbon
carbonate   dioxide

The quicklime is slaked by the addition of water to form hydrated lime, calcium hydroxide [$Ca(OH)_2$]:

$$CaO + H_2O = Ca(OH)_2$$

Quicklime   Water   Calcium
hydroxide

The hydrated lime is mixed with water to form a plastic, puttylike material to which is added gauging plaster, a gypsum product. This mixture is applied in a thin coat over the base plaster and troweled to a smooth finish. The setting of the gypsum gives the plaster its initial hardness and permits troweling to a smooth, hard finish. The lime in the putty begins to recarbonate, and this hardening process continues slowly for a long period of time.

287

The limestone used may be nearly pure calcium carbonate or it may consist of nearly equal parts of calcium carbonate and magnesium carbonate. If the stone contains at least 90 percent calcium carbonate, it is classified as a high-calcium limestone. If it contains more than 10 percent magnesium carbonate, it is classified as a magnesium limestone. If it has more than 25 percent magnesium carbonate, it is called dolomitic limestone.

Lime made from magnesium limestone slakes slower and with less heat than high-calcium limestones, and the resulting hydrated lime is more plastic and develops a better ultimate strength.

Slaked lime sets by gradually losing its water through evaporation and absorbing carbon dioxide, changing from $Ca(OH)_2$ to $CaCO_3$, calcium carbonate or limestone.

Although the use of finished lime may be limited as a construction material, its primary use is in its raw state as found in limestone. Large quantities of limestone are used in the manufacture of iron and cement.

GLOSSARY

cadmium	A noncorrosive metal used to coat nails.
catalyst	A substance which accelerates a chemical reaction without undergoing any significant change in itself.
corner bead	An expanded metal angle, used over gypsum board at external corners.
double-headed nails	Nails with two heads, spaced about $\frac{1}{2}$ in (13 mm) apart on the shank.
dry-wall tape	Wide, perforated paper tape used to cover joints in gypsum board construction.
gauging plaster	Gypsum plaster, added to lime putty to produce a finish plaster with the proper setting time.
hemihydrate	A hydrate containing half a molecule of water to one molecule of the other compound involved.
hydrated lime	An inert compound formed by the chemical combination of water and calcium oxide—quicklime.
let-in wind bracing	Diagonal bracing which is cut into the edges of framing members.
nail popping	The withdrawal of a nail from its seated position, resulting in a marring of the surface.
neat gypsum	Gypsum free from other compounds.
purlin	Roof-framing members which span the space between trusses.
slaked-lime putty	A paste made of hydrated lime and water.
spatula	Broad-bladed tool, used for applying cement or paste to a flat surface.
special-purpose plaster	A synthetic plaster, intended to be applied in a thin coat.
stippled plaster	Rippled plaster surface.
textured	Rough-surfaced.
vinyl	A synthetic material made from cellulose.

REVIEW QUESTIONS

1. What is the chemical difference between land plaster, plaster of paris, and Keene's cement?

2. For what particular purpose is Keene's cement commonly used?

3. Explain why casting plaster has to be a slow-setting plaster.

4. What are the results of increasing the amount of sand used per bag of hard wall when mixing plaster?

5. Give one advantage of prepared finish plaster over regular putty-coat plaster.

6. Describe briefly the process of filling and finishing a long-edge joint between two sheets of gypsum wallboard using gypsum joint filler.

7. **a.** What is meant by the laminated dry-wall system?
   b. What is the reason for horizontal application of wallboard?

8. What is the reason for the following:
   a. Perforations in gypsum lath
   b. Aluminum foil on the back of gypsum lath

9. Explain the difference between quicklime and slaked lime.

10. Describe three applications, using plaster as a finishing material, that will produce a textured surface.

SELECTED SOURCES OF INFORMATION

Canadian Gypsum Company, Limited, Toronto, Ont.
Celotex Corporation, Tampa, Fla.
Gypsum Association, Evanston, Ill.

National Gypsum Co., Buffalo, N.Y.
United States Gypsum Co., Chicago, Ill.
Westroc Industries, Ltd., Winnipeg, Man.

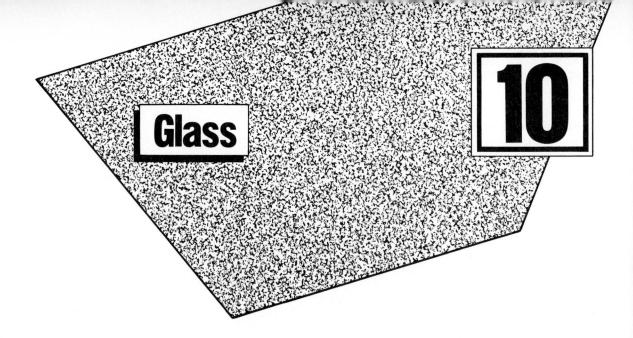

Glass

10

Of all the mass-produced materials that we use in everyday life, probably none has a more exciting background or adds more to modern living than glass. There is hardly a moment in our daily lives that glass in some form is not performing a service for us.

The art of glassmaking is very old, and today the industry uses basically the same raw materials as did the ancient glassmakers. However, the methods of manufacture have changed and improved, resulting in higher production rates, superior glass, and sheet sizes far greater than anything possible under older methods.

RAW MATERIALS

Glass is described as a soda-lime silicate; that is, it is made from silica (sand), soda, and lime. If sand and soda are melted together, they produce, on cooling, a hard, transparent, glassy substance known as sodium silicate (water glass) which is soluble in water. When lime is added to the mixture, the solubility of the sodium silicate is reduced, and when enough lime is added, a durable glass is obtained which will stand up to the weather and all strong acids except hydrofluoric.

Glass has two peculiar properties which influence the manufacturing process. First, glass does not have a definite melting point. When it is heated, it first softens so that it can be bent. Further heating brings it to the point when it becomes a thick, syrupy liquid, a state in which it can be worked. Finally, at still higher temperatures, it becomes a thin, watery liquid.

Second, above a certain temperature, known as the devitrification temperature, glass can be kept in a liquid condition without any change occurring. But if it is kept just below that temperature for any length of time, crystallization, or devitrification, occurs. It is therefore necessary, in any manufacturing process, to complete the operation before devitrification occurs.

MANUFACTURING

The commercial production of glass for use in construction evolved rather slowly compared to other materials because glass was produced by craftsmen in limited quantities primarily for use in glass blowing, cut glassware, and bottles. Production of plate glass in the United States did not begin until 1867, and that was not without some difficulty because of competition from Europe. Sheet glass production did not get established until the early 1900s when equipment was developed to produce glass in a continuous strip. Each method had its limitations, and not until the 1950s, when the production of float glass was developed, did the availability of large quantities of high-quality, inexpensive flat glass become a reality.

Sheet Glass

The raw materials, sand, soda, and limestone, are first ground to a fine state and mixed in the proper proportions. This mixture, which is called *frit,* is charged into the glass furnace (see Fig. 10-1) along with some broken glass (*cullet*).

During the initial melting stage a chemical reaction takes place among the three basic ingredients, resulting in a sticky mass full of bubbles. In the next stage, the temperature is raised so that the glass loses its viscous nature and becomes a watery liquid, allowing the gases forming the bubbles to rise to the surface. The third stage consists of cooling the glass down to a temperature at which the material is at the proper consistency to be drawn.

To form the glass into a sheet, it first passes from the furnace tank into a drawing kiln, of which there are usually four or five to a furnace. From here it is drawn up in the form of a sheet into a series of rollers. To start the drawing process a *bait* (an iron grille) is lowered into the glass in the kiln. When it has remained there for a short period, the molten glass sticks to the iron and the bait is slowly lifted,

drawing behind it a sheet of glass. When the leading edge of the sheet has passed between the first few pairs of rollers, the bait can be cracked off from the glass and the rollers will then draw up a continuous strip or sheet.

The success of this process lies in the provision of devices for maintaining the width of the ribbon of glass being drawn. Since it is in a plastic condition, the ribbon tends to taper off; if this were allowed to occur, the sheet would eventually stop drawing. Basically, these devices consist of knurled rollers which grip the edges of the glass and cool it sufficiently to prevent the tapering from taking place.

These sheets of flat drawn glass are cooled slowly in a cooling chamber known as an *annealing lehr.*

In some manufacturing processes the hot sheet of glass, after being drawn vertically from the surface of the tank, is bent over a roller and sent through the lehr horizontally. (See Fig. 10-2.) The process is illustrated diagrammatically from furnace to cutting table in Fig. 10-3. In another modern process, the sheet of glass is carried vertically up a tower which acts as an annealing lehr. At a height of about 30 ft (9 m), the sheet is cool enough to cut. This is done automatically, and the cut sheet is

Fig. 10-1 Charging raw materials into a glass furnace. *(Pilkington Bros., Ltd.)*

Fig. 10-2 A horizontal annealing lehr. *(Libbey-Owens-Ford Glass Co.)*

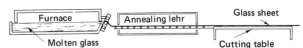

Fig. 10-3 Diagram of production of horizontally drawn sheet glass.

removed (see Fig. 10-4) and sent to be trimmed.

From the trimming table, the glass is sent to the warehouse, where it is examined, sorted, and finally cut into standard sizes.

Flat-drawn sheet glass can be drawn in thicknesses that range in weight from 18 to 32 oz/ft^2 (5.49 to 9.76 kg/m^2). This type of glass is used where perfect vision is not required but where cost is an important factor. The surface is good but never free from distortion, as the two surfaces are not perfectly parallel.

Sheet glass is produced in five nominal types: 18 oz, single-strength; 24 oz, double-strength; 32 oz; $\frac{3}{16}$-in-thick sheet; and $\frac{7}{32}$-in-thick sheet. Each type has a thickness tolerance: 18 oz, 0.079 to 0.087 in (2.00 to 2.21 mm); 24 oz, 0.108 to 0.165 in (2.74 to 3.10 mm); 32 oz, 0.150 to 0.165 in (3.81 to 4.19 mm); $\frac{3}{16}$ in, 0.177 to 0.201 in (4.50 to 5.11 mm); and $\frac{7}{32}$ in, 0.209 to 0.228 in (5.31 to 5.79 mm).

Each type is available in three quality ranges: AA, A, and B. AA sheet glass is specially selected flat glass that is used where superfine glass is required, usually for silvering. A sheet glass is selected glazing-quality flat glass used in applications where su-

perior quality glass is required such as picture framing. B sheet glass is suitable for all general glazing applications. Single-strength glass is not recommended for general glazing, and double-strength glass should not be used in areas exceeding 12 ft^2 (1.11 m^2) because of its flexibility.

Sizes for sheet glass are usually designated in *united units* (length plus width). Thus the maximum size for single-strength glass sheets of all qualities is 90 united in (2286 united mm) and for double-strength sheets 120 united in (3048 united mm).

Heavy sheet glass is used for glazing windows and doors where greater strength is required but where slight distortion is not objectionable. It is commonly used for display cases, shelving, window ventilators, furniture tops, and jalousies. It is made in two thicknesses, $\frac{3}{16}$ and $\frac{7}{32}$ in (4.75 and 5.5 mm), in AA, A, and B qualities. The $\frac{3}{16}$-in (4.75-mm) glass weighs about 40 oz/ft^2 (12.2 kg/m^2), and the $\frac{7}{32}$-in (5.5-mm) glass about 45 oz/ft^2 (13.7 kg/m^2). Both are cut to a maximum size of 76 × 120 in (1930 × 3048 mm).

Picture glass is used for covering pictures, photographs, maps, charts, projector slides, and instrument dials. It is made in three thicknesses, averaging 0.048, 0.063, and 0.075 in (1.2, 1.6, and 1.9 mm), in three qualities. In each case the maximum size cut is 60 united in (1524 united mm).

Plate Glass

In the manufacture of plate glass, molten glass flows from the furnace between rollers of the glassmaking machine. Because of this continuous-flow process, a greater range of thicknesses can be made than is possible with drawn glass. From the rollers, the sheet passes into a lehr for annealing.

As it emerges from the lehr, the blank has a rough surface, because it is drawn between metal rollers. It therefore passes to a twin grinder unit (see Fig. 10-5), which simultaneously grinds both surfaces of the continuous ribbon to make them smooth and parallel. (See Fig. 10-6.) At the end of the grinder line, the ribbon of glass is cut into large sections and passed under polishing heads (see Fig. 10-7) to give clear, undistorted vision and reflection.

Plate glass is produced in thicknesses of $\frac{1}{8}$ to $1\frac{1}{4}$ in (3 to 32 mm), although the special, thick glasses may be cast, rather than made by the continuous-

Fig. 10-4 Removing glass sheet cut at top of vertical annealing tower.

Fig. 10-5   Plate-glass blank passing from lehr to twin grinder.   *(Libbey-Owens-Ford Glass Co.)*

Fig. 10-6   Plate-glass twin grinder.   *(Libbey-Owens-Ford Glass Co.)*

Fig. 10-7   Plate glass passing under polishing heads. *(Libbey-Owens-Ford Glass Co.)*

flow process. However, in either case, the grinding and polishing are carried out by the same process.

Float Glass

From its beginning in the late 1950s, the production of flat glass using the float method has increased to the point where it has made sheet glass and plate glass production obsolete. The reason for this success is that it combines the fire finish of sheet glass with the perfect flatness of plate, while at the same time eliminating the time-consuming grinding and polishing operations required to produce plate glass. Figure 10-8 illustrates the basic layout of a float line.

In the manufacture of float glass, frit, the usual combination of raw materials, is fed into the charging end of the glass tank, where it is melted by an oil- or gas-fired furnace. The melted glass leaves the furnace and passes to a float bath, where it is supported on molten tin. Gravity keeps the molten tin perfectly level, and heat, applied from above, melts out any irregularities in the glass, resulting in a flat sheet of glass of uniform thickness.

As the ribbon of glass passes through the float bath, the heat is reduced until the glass is sufficiently hard to be fed onto the rollers of the lehr without marking the undersurface. In a modern glass plant, this whole operation is controlled by

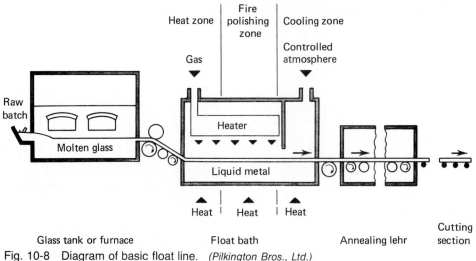

Fig. 10-8   Diagram of basic float line.   *(Pilkington Bros., Ltd.)*

closed-circuit television. (See Fig. 10-9.)

After leaving the lehr (see Fig. 10-10), the glass is cut into long lengths and transferred to a warehouse. There it is cut up automatically (see Fig. 10-11), inspected, and packed.

The float process does not lend itself to the effi-cient production of as broad a range of thicknesses as either the sheet-glass or plate-glass processes. But for those thicknesses for which the process is most suitable—$\frac{1}{8}$, $\frac{3}{16}$, and $\frac{1}{4}$ in (3, 4.5, and 6 mm)—it produces a fire-finished glass with flatter and more parallel surfaces than sheet glass.

Fig. 10-9   Closed-circuit control of float glass manu-facturing operation.   *(Libbey-Owens-Ford Glass Co.)*

Fig. 10-10 Ribbon float glass leaving annealing lehr. *(Libbey-Owens-Ford Glass Co.)*

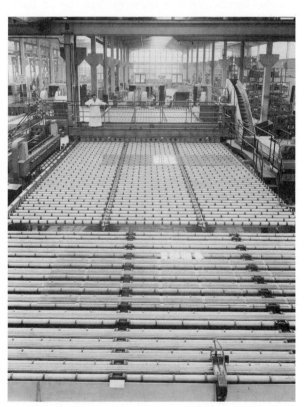

Fig. 10-11 Glass conveyor on automatic cutting line. *(Pilkington Bros., Ltd.)*

GLASS PROPERTIES

The primary purpose of glass in buildings is to allow the transmission of natural light into the interior without any undue discomfort to the occupants. Contemporary concepts such as energy efficiency, temperature control, security, and aesthetics must be dealt with effectively and efficiently when selecting and installing glass in today's buildings. Over the past three decades, the diversity of modern buildings has spurred the development of new methods and materials in the glass industry to deal with these varied and sometimes complex problems.

Strength Categories

ANNEALED GLASS   During the manufacturing process of flat glass (after the glass width and thickness have been established), the glass must be allowed to cool slowly to prevent residual stresses from building up in the glass cross-section. This slow cooling is known as *annealing* and occurs in the annealing lehr (see preceding sections dealing with the manufacture of flat glass). All flat glass that is produced in this manner is known as annealed glass. Annealed glass has a maximum surface compression strength of 2500 psi (24 MPa) maximum, and although it is relatively strong, it is limited in its use to locations where impact-type loads will not be encountered.

HEAT-STRENGTHENED GLASS   Glass fractures as a result of tension stresses that develop on the surface of the glass due to some loading. (Wind loads cause bending which produces tension stresses on the back face of a sheet of glass.) The concept of heat treatment is to produce compressive stresses at the surface of the glass while the center portion of the glass sheet is in tension (see Fig. 10-12). Any applied force must now overcome the induced compressive stresses before failure will occur. Heat-strengthened glass is annealed glass that has been heat treated to increase its strength by about two times. Its surface compression strength ranges between 2500 and 10,000 psi (24 to 69 MPa). Heat-treated glass has good resistance to solar-induced thermal stresses, hailstones, and cyclic wind loads.

TEMPERED GLASS   This is annealed glass that has undergone special heat treatment to increase its strength to four or five times. Tempered glass must have a minimum surface compressive strength of at least 10,000 psi (69 MPa). Glass of this type is used in areas such as entranceways, patio doors, and shower enclosures. If broken, the glass breaks into small cubical shapes, thus reducing the risk of injury.

Optical Properties

The amount of light transmitted varies with the thickness of the glass, surface finish, and type of coating. Clear glass, $\frac{1}{8}$ in (3 mm) thick, transmits 91 percent of average daylight, while glass 1 in (25 mm) thick transmits about 78 percent. Tables supplied by glass manufacturers give transmission ratings for all thicknesses of glass produced.

When solar radiation falls on glass and other partially transparent material, some of the incident energy is reflected, some is absorbed by the material, and the rest is transmitted to the inside of the building, resulting in a heat gain in the building. (See Fig. 10-13.) For ordinary windows, absorption is quite a small fraction and transmission much the largest part of the total energy involved. The reflection varies considerably with the angle of incidence—the angle between the light rays and a line perpendicular to the reflecting surface. The greater the angle of incidence, the greater the amount of energy reflected. Figure 10-14 shows the variation of the reflection, absorption, and transmission of solar radiation by a single sheet of ordinary glass in a south wall at 45° latitude.

Because clear glass allows a good portion of the sun's energy to pass, the energy gain in a building can be significant. Although this may be advantageous in the winter months, additional ventilating and air-conditioning capacity is necessary for the summer months to maintain a uniform and comfortable temperature inside the building. Conversely, the heat loss through clear glass is also

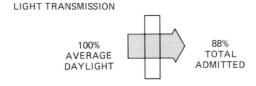

LIGHT TRANSMISSION

100% AVERAGE DAYLIGHT   88% TOTAL ADMITTED

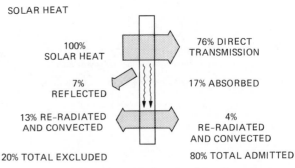

SOLAR HEAT

100% SOLAR HEAT

76% DIRECT TRANSMISSION

7% REFLECTED

17% ABSORBED

13% RE-RADIATED AND CONVECTED

4% RE-RADIATED AND CONVECTED

20% TOTAL EXCLUDED   80% TOTAL ADMITTED

Fig. 10-13   Solar transmission for $\frac{1}{4}$-in (6-mm) clear float glass—normal angle of incidence, no shade.

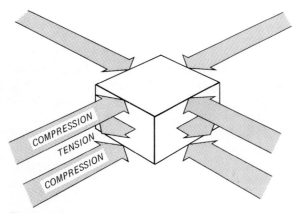

Fig. 10-12   Stresses in tempered glass.

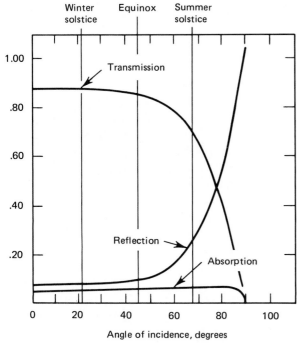

Fig. 10-14 Absorption, reflection, and transmission of a single sheet of ordinary glass in a south wall at 45° latitude.

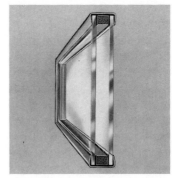

Fig. 10-15 Cutaway view of metal-edged insulating glass unit. *(Canadian Pittsburgh Industries, Ltd.)*

significant. The R value $[(°C \cdot m^2)/W]$ for a single sheet of clear glass based on a temperature difference between inside and outside of 39°C and an outdoor air velocity of 15 mi/h (24 km/h) at night is only 0.16 $[0.91 \ (ft^2 \cdot h \cdot °F)/Btu]$. This, of course, leads to greater heating costs. However, by using double-glazed hermetically sealed units the R value is increased to 0.30 (1.7) or nearly double that of a single pane. By using triple glazing with special coatings and tints on the individual panes, R values as high as 0.75 (4.3) can be obtained. This becomes a significant gain when a high-rise structure is being considered.

SPECIALTY GLASS

To increase the efficiency of glass components in a building, many innovative concepts have been developed in recent years.

Insulating Glass

Insulating glass consists of two or more lites of glass, separated by an air space, and joined at the edges to produce a hermetically sealed unit. Three methods of sealing are used. The most common method (see Fig. 10-15) consists of a metal spacer sealed between the lites and covered with a stainless steel frame. The air space, usually $\frac{1}{2}$ in (13 mm), is dehydrated with a drying agent to ensure no moisture build-up. Glass thicknesses used are normally $\frac{1}{8}$ or $\frac{1}{4}$ in (3 or 6 mm) and any combination of clear, tinted, heat-absorbing, or laminated glass can be used. There are many standard sizes available on the market as large as 102 × 142 in (2585 × 3600 mm).

Another method of sealing involves the use of a strip of lead sealed to the inner edges of the sheets (see Fig. 10-16). Both $\frac{1}{8}$- and $\frac{1}{4}$-in (3- and 6-mm) clear, tinted, and heat-absorbing glass can be used in a wide range of sizes.

The third method of sealing is an electrically fused, all-glass edge, such as shown in Fig. 10-17. Sheet glass of $\frac{3}{32}$- or $\frac{1}{8}$-in (2- or 3-mm) thickness is used, with an air space of $\frac{3}{16}$ in (4.75 mm).

The use of insulating units increases the thermal efficiency of the glass, reduces the amount of surface condensation, and provides sound insulation without greatly affecting the entry of natural light.

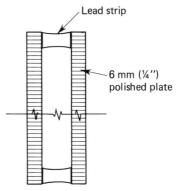

Fig. 10-16 Lead-sealed insulating glass unit.

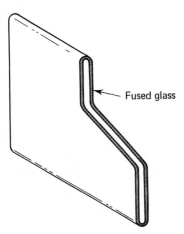

Fig. 10-17   All-glass seal.

Transparent Mirror Glass

This type of glass has been developed to act as either a mirror or a window, depending on the relative intensity of the light on either side. As one looks from a darkened room through the transparent mirror toward a light room, it is a window, but as one looks from the light side toward the dark side, it acts as a mirror. Such glass is used in doors of houses or apartments, in nurseries, in viewing windows of clinics and hospitals, and in security windows of banks, police stations, and department stores.

Reflective Glass

Reflective glass is an innovation in glassmaking, used to control glare and reduce solar heat. It is the product of a glass-coating process which is carried out in a large, rectangular vacuum chamber. The glass is coated with micro-thin layers of metallic films which provide the performance characteristics of the glass. It substantially reduces solar-heat gain by reflecting the sun's rays, resulting in savings in both the initial and operating costs of air-conditioning systems. The reduced light transmission also diminishes interior glare and brightness.

When reflective glass is viewed in daylight from outside, it reflects its surroundings with mirrorlike images. (See Fig. 10-18.) From the inside, as one looks out, the glass is transparent. At night the situation is reversed, with the glass becoming transparent from the outside and reflecting from the inside.

Reflective glass is used in four types of glass products: *single-pane unit, double-pane insulating*

Fig. 10-18   Reflective glass on high-rise building.

glass, laminated safety glass, and *tempered spandrel glass.* It is available in five basic colors: *gray, blue, silver, gold,* and *bronze* and can be specified in any one of three nominal light transmittances of 8, 14, or 20 percent. As a result, over fifty varieties of reflective glass are available for various requirements.

Tinted Glass

This type of glass is specially tinted to reduce solar heat and cut down glare, to provide a more restful atmosphere. It is available in two tints—*gray* and *bronze*—and is widely used for windows in homes, office buildings, libraries, etc. (See Fig. 10-19.)

Heat-Absorbing Glass

This glass is made by adding ingredients to the mix used in making regular glass so that the finished product is pale bluish green or gray. Because of its chemical composition, this glass absorbs a significant percentage of the sun's radiant energy, thus

Fig. 10-19 Tinted glass in enclosed pedestrian walkway.

reducing the build-up of heat within the building. Its color and the fact that it possesses lower light transmission than regular glass mean that glare and brightness in the room are reduced. This type of glass is quite widely used for glazing in office buildings, schools, and hospitals.

Patterned Glass

The manufacture of patterned glass is similar to that of regular glass except that patterned rolls are used to produce an irregular finish on the surface. Heat-treated, it is used in room dividers, office partitions, shower stalls, bathtub enclosures, and areas requiring privacy. Where higher fire ratings are required, patterned glass can be reinforced with wire mesh.

Spandrel Glass

Spandrel glass is $\frac{1}{4}$-in (6-mm) thick heat-treated glass coated on one side with a fired ceramic enamel or a ceramic frit producing an opaque panel. The ceramic enamel is fired to the exterior face producing a very durable and easily maintained surface. In the case of the ceramic frit, it is fired to the interior face for protection from the atmosphere and cleaning. (See Fig. 10-20.)

Glass covered with ceramic enamel can be used in standard glazing systems or as covering for insulated curtain-wall panels. Glass coated with the ceramic frit is not recommended for glazing applications without backup as the imperfections in the ceramic film may become visible. Both types can be used for most exterior applications quite successfully.

Fig. 10-20 Opaque panels of spandrel glass.

Laminated Glass

Laminated glass is made from two or more lites of glass bonded together with a film of polyvinyl butyral resin, a tough transparent plastic. Various glass combinations can be used to alter the final properties of the laminated section depending on the intended use, but the main reason for laminating glass in this manner is to increase its resistance to breakage. Laminated glass can be built up to a total thickness of $2\frac{1}{2}$ in (64 mm), capable of stopping a bullet from a high-powered rifle. Using tinted glass, solar radiation can be reduced significantly without increasing the total thickness of the glass.

By using tinted vinyl films, the solar heat gain can be reduced by almost 50 percent compared to that of heat-absorbing glass. Another important property of laminated glass using special vinyl film is that of fading control, that is, the filtering out of ultraviolet rays from the sun. Up to 99 percent of all ultraviolet light can be filtered out. This type of glass is used in store windows to protect displayed goods.

When used in insulating glass units, laminated glass is ideal for noise control applications, increased thermal performance, and added security. Typical applications are in airport control towers, radio and television control rooms, and intensive care units.

Because of its high resistance to breakage, laminated glass is used as safety glass in locations such as hockey rinks, gymnasiums, aquariums, and glazed domes, to mention just a few.

Low-Emission Glass

Low-emission glass, or Low-E glass as it is commonly known, is the latest development in heat transfer control through glass. Using special vacuum techniques, glass manufacturers coat ordinary glass with an ultrathin metallic coating. Although it is barely visible, the coating greatly improves the energy performance of the glass, especially if incorporated into double-glazing units.

Short wavelength energy from the sun passes easily through clear glazing and is absorbed by the building interior. It is then reradiated as heat but in a much longer wavelength known as far infrared radiation. This energy is absorbed by normal glazing and is re-radiated to the outside. The loss of heat through the glass in this manner is a waste of energy and must be supplemented by additional heat. The concept of Low-E glass is to absorb this energy, but instead of reradiating it to the outside, the coated glass reradiates the energy back inside, thus saving a good portion of the heat. A double-glazed unit incorporating Low-E glass has a comparable efficiency to that of a triple-glazed unit using conventional glass.

GLASS BLOCKS

Glass blocks, products of the glass industry, are comparable in many ways to unit masonry but have the added feature of transmitting light. They are made in two separate halves which are heat-sealed together to form a hollow unit with reasonably high thermal efficiency and sound insulation. The edge surfaces are coated with a gritty mortar bonding material.

Two general types of block are produced: functional and decorative. Functional blocks direct or diffuse the daylight which passes through them to improve the illumination of the building interior. Decorative blocks are chosen for their ability to contribute to an overall design plan and are not intended to be used as a major control of daylight.

Functional blocks are made in three styles or patterns, each with a specific purpose. A light-directing block (Fig. 10-21) directs incoming light upward toward the ceiling. It should always be used above eye level so that it cannot direct light into the eyes. Eye level is assumed to be approximately 6 ft (1.8 m) above the floor.

Fig. 10-21   Light-directing glass block.

Fig. 10-22   Light-diffusing glass block.   *(Pittsburgh-Corning Corp.)*

A light-diffusing block (see Fig. 10-22) diffuses incoming light evenly throughout the interior of the room. It may be used either above or below eye level. A third style is a general-purpose block.

Functional blocks are made in sizes of 8 × 8 in (200 × 200 mm) and 12 × 12 in (300 × 300 mm), both 4 in (100 mm) thick.

All these patterns and sizes are available with a white- or green-tinted fibrous glass insert in the block. The purpose of these inserts is to reduce brightness and instantaneous heat gain; such blocks should be used if direct sunlight strikes the panel during the day.

A complete line of architectural and decorative glass blocks is available in a wide range of styles and patterns, some of which are illustrated in Fig. 10-23. These glass masonry units provide almost unlimited design versatility when used in window openings and facades, as interior walls and divider panels and in many other architectural and decorative applications. Glass blocks may be used by themselves to build up curtain-wall panels, or they may be used in conjunction with other unit masonry.

SOLID GLASS BRICK

Another glass product, made by the manufacturers of glass block, is *glass brick*. Its primary purpose is the same as that of any other glass product, namely, to admit light into a building. Its ability to allow the undistorted passage of light is illustrated in Fig. 10-24. At the same time, because of its solid construction, it offers far greater protection against vandalism than conventional glass block or window glass. Physical characteristics of such units are outlined in Table 10-1.

Fig. 10-23   Some contemporary glass masonry units. *(Pittsburgh-Corning Corp.)*

Fig. 10-24   Light-transmitting ability of solid glass brick. *(Pittsburgh-Corning Corp.)*

Table 10-1
PHYSICAL PROPERTIES OF SOLID GLASS BRICK

Characteristic	Imperial	Metric
Sizes	8 × 8 × 3 in	200 × 200 × 75 mm
	5 × 5 × 3 in	125 × 125 × 75 mm
Weight	16.5 lb; 6.46 lb	7.47 kg; 2.9 kg
Density	149 lb/ft^3	2387 kg/m^3
Modulus of elasticity	10^7 psi	68947 MPa
Coefficient of expansion	0.0000047°F	0.0000026°C
Light transmission	80%	80%
Compressive strength	80,000 lb/in^2	552 MPa

GLOSSARY

blank	Unfinished sheet of plate glass.
ceramic frit	A durable material with a thermal coefficient of expansion compatible to glass. It is fire-fused to glass in different colors, producing an opaque surface.
devitrification	The change from a vitreous (glassy) condition to a crystalline condition.
dielectric	Nonconducting.
float bath	A large vat in which molten glass floats on molten metal.
hermetically sealed	Sealed by fusion.
***R* value**	A measure of resistance to thermal conductivity.
solar radiation	Energy radiating or traveling, as a wave motion, from the sun.

REVIEW QUESTIONS

1. Explain why glass must be cooled slowly.

2. Why is vision normally better through plate glass than through sheet glass?

3. How would you compare float glass and plate glass from the standpoint of thicknesses produced?

4. a. What is heat-absorbing plate glass?

b. Where is such glass used?

5. a. What is the reason for placing fibrous glass inserts in some glass blocks?

b. Where should such blocks be used?

SELECTED SOURCES OF INFORMATION

Ford Glass Limited, Toronto, Ont.
Globe-Amerada Glass Co., Chicago, Ill.
Guardian Industries Corp., Carleton, Mich.
Libbey-Owens-Ford Glass Co., Toledo, Ohio
Mississippi Glass Co., St. Louis, Mo.

Pilkington Bros. Ltd., St. Helens, England
Pittsburgh Corning Corp., Pittsburgh, Pa.
PPG Canada Inc., Toronto, Ont.
Solarpane Manufacturing Co., Regina, Sask.

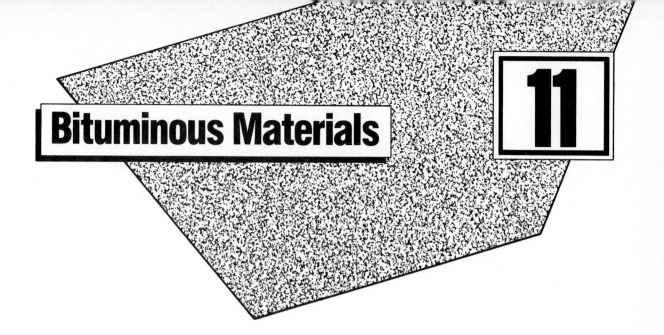

Bituminous Materials

11

The term "bitumen" is a generic name applied to various mixtures of hydrocarbons. They may be gaseous, liquid, semisolid, or solid in nature and are completely soluble in carbon disulfide. The most common materials within this family of bitumens are tars, pitches, and asphalts.

When destructive distillation is carried out on such materials as wood, coal, shale, peat, or bone, the resulting condensate is tar. Partial evaporation or fractional distillation of tar produces the solid or semisolid residue known as pitch. The most common material of this kind used in construction is coal-tar pitch.

Asphalts are dark brown or black solids or semisolids which are found in the natural state and are also produced by the refining of petroleum. Some of the best known deposits of natural asphalt are found in Trinidad, in an asphalt lake, and in Kentucky, Utah, Colorado, and California, where they include various forms. Some are semisolid, and some—rock asphalt and Gilsonite—are very hard. Today, however, more than 95 percent of the asphaltic materials used in North America are derived from the refining of petroleum. (See Fig. 11-1.)

Bitumens have a number of properties which make them useful in the construction industry. One is the tendency to adhere to a solid surface. This adhesiveness will depend on the nature of the surface and the state of the bitumen. For an adhesive to act, it must be able to wet a surface; bitumens have this ability in a fluid state, but the presence of water on the solid surface will prevent adhesion.

The water resistance of bitumens is important; in general it is very good. Under certain conditions water may be absorbed by minute quantities of inorganic salts in the bitumen or by fillers in it. There is very little difference in the absorption qualities of the pitches and the asphalts—both are very low.

TESTS OF FLOW PROPERTIES

The viscous or flow properties of bitumens are of importance, both at the high temperatures encountered in processing and application and at the low temperatures to which bitumens are subjected in service. Flow properties are very complex, and as a result, tests have been formulated to measure the consistency of the materials at temperatures comparable to those encountered during the service life of the bitumen.

Penetration Test

The penetration test measures the depth of penetration, in tenths of millimeters, of a weighted needle into a bitumen, during a given time period, at a known temperature. Commonly, a weight of

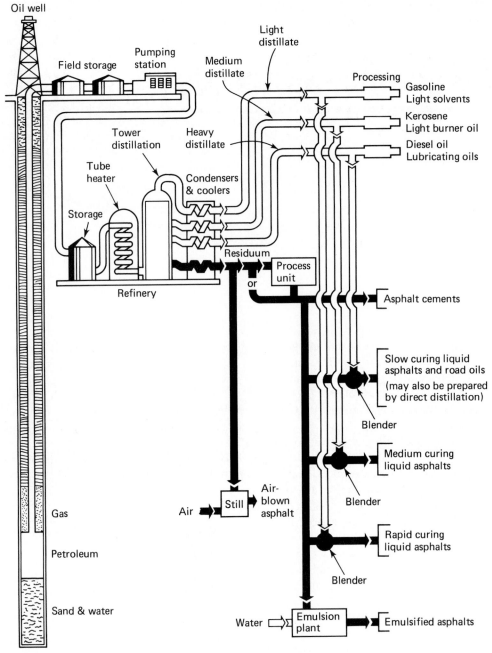

Fig. 11-1 Petroleum asphalt flowchart. (*Asphalt Institute*)

100 g is applied for 5 s at a temperature of 25°C. The penetration is a measure of hardness; typical results are approximately 10 for hard coating-grade asphalts, 15 to 40 for roofing asphalts, and up to 100 or more for waterproofing asphalts.

Softening-Point Test

The softening-point test measures the temperature, in degrees Celsius, at which a steel ball falls a known distance through the bitumen, when the test assembly is heated at a known rate. The test consists of allowing a steel ball of $\frac{3}{8}$-in (9.5-mm) diameter and weighing 3.5 g to sink 1 in (25.4 mm) through a disk of bitumen of $\frac{5}{8}$-in (16-mm) diameter and $\frac{1}{4}$ in (6 mm) thick, being held in a brass ring, while the whole assembly is heated at the rate of 5°C/min.

The softening-point value is used to grade bitumens into groups. Typical values would be as follows: up to 115°C for coating-grade asphalts, from 60 to 104°C for roofing asphalts, and down to 46°C for bituminous waterproofing materials.

Ductility Test

Ductility tests are conducted to determine the amount a bitumen will stretch at temperatures below its softening point. A briquet having a cross-sectional area of 1 in² (6.45 cm²) is placed in a tester and elongated at a rate of 5 cm/min at a temperature of 25°C. Ductility values range from 0 to over 150 cm, depending on the type of bitumen.

Viscosity Test

Viscosity tests are used to determine the flow characteristics of asphalts in the range of temperatures used during application. One measures the kinematic viscosity of asphalt cement at higher temperatures, such as 135°C, and is usually carried out with the aid of a gravity flow capillary viscometer. The result is the viscosity in *stokes* or *centistokes*.

Another test can be used to measure the viscosity of asphalt cements at lower temperatures, such as 60°C. A vacuum capillary viscometer is used in this case, and the result is recorded in *poises*. These and other tests are fully described in the *Asphalt Handbook*, published by the Asphalt Institute.

Flash-Point Test

The flash test indicates the temperature to which the asphalt cement can be safely heated without danger of instantaneous flash in the presence of an open flame. A brass cup is partially filled with the cement and heated at a prescribed rate. A small flame is played over the surface of the sample periodically, and the temperature at which an instantaneous flash is produced is designated as the *flash point*.

Thin-Film Oven Test

This test is used to obtain a general indication of the amount of hardening which may be expected to occur in an asphalt cement during the plant mixing operation. A 50-ml sample of cement is placed in a cylindrical pan 5.5 in (139.7 mm) in inside diameter and $\frac{3}{8}$ in (9.5 mm) deep. The sample and container are then placed on a rotating shelf in an oven and maintained at a temperature of 162.8°C for 5 h. The sample is then placed in a container used for the penetration test, and the results are taken. A full description of the test is given in ASTM Method of Test D1754.

Solubility Test

A solubility test is used to determine the bitumen content of asphalt cement. A measured amount of the cement to be tested is dissolved in carbon tetrachloride and the insoluble portion filtered out and measured. The result is given as a percentage of soluble content. This test is described in ASTM Method of Test D4.

TYPES OF BITUMENS
Tar and Pitch

Most of the tar and pitch used in construction is made by the distillation of coal. Tar is used to saturate felt paper and to coat kraft paper to render it waterproof. The coal-tar pitch is used in making pitch and gravel built-up roofs. Pitch will soften and flow at relatively low temperatures, so it should be applied only to roofs with a low slope. Coal-tar pitch oxidizes quite rapidly when exposed to ultraviolet rays of the sun and should always be protected by a coating of gravel or slag.

Asphalt

A large percentage of the asphalt used results from the refining of naphtha base crude oils, which produce aviation-grade gasoline, fuel oil, cold-test lubricating oils, and asphalt. The properties of this residual, known as straight-run asphalt, depend on the nature of the crude oil from which it was refined and the conditions of refining.

There are three main groups of asphalt products produced from straight-run asphalts: (1) hot asphalts, those softened by heat; (2) cutback asphalts, those dissolved in mineral solvents; and (3) emulsion asphalts, those dispersed or suspended in a water base.

HOT ASPHALTS Hot asphalt can be used directly or it can be processed further to produce a harder material. This can be done by a process in which air is blown through heated residual asphalt. Control of the process produces various degrees of hardness. Consistency can also be increased by using a pulverized mineral filler whose main purpose is to increase viscosity.

Hot asphalts have good resistance to the transmission of water and water vapor when they are applied to dry surfaces and the heating process is controlled.

Cold flow (the tendency for a piece of asphalt to flow, spread out, and lose its shape unless it is very cold) is inherent in all hot asphalts. Also, if stress is exerted on a piece of this type of asphalt, it will flow in a manner to relieve the stress.

Hot asphalts bond poorly to damp or wet surfaces, have relatively poor flexibility, oxidize under the sun's rays, and are brittle at low temperatures. As is the case with pitch, it is difficult to control the application thickness of hot asphalt.

CUTBACK ASPHALTS Cutback asphalts are of three types: No. 1, straight-run asphalt and solvent, with or without a small amount of fiber added; No. 2, heavily filled cutback, made by adding a large amount of filler and fiber to asphalt cut with solvent; and No. 3, primer-type cutback asphalt in solution with no filler or fiber.

These asphalts have poor bonding power on wet surfaces, but some of them have damp-bonding ability. No. 2 cutback generally has excellent vapor-barrier characteristics and increased weather resistance. Primer-type cutbacks are thin enough to penetrate the pores of masonry, wood, and paper to provide a firm bond for other bitumen applications. They are also used to wet surfaces such as metal for good adhesion. Primer-type cutbacks are made from soft, ductile asphalts, as well as harder-base asphalts, depending on requirements. The thin, penetrating types are used on dense surfaces, the harder, enamel types on metal, and the more viscous types on porous surfaces. None is intended to be used as a finish coating.

EMULSION ASPHALTS Emulsion asphalts are divided into three groups, depending on the type of emulsifier: (1) soap type, in which soap is used as the emulsifier; (2) clay-modified soap type, with a combination of soap and clay as emulsifier; and (3) clay-base type, with a mineral material, usually clay, as the emulsifier. The clay most commonly used for this purpose is bentonite.

The main advantage of emulsions over other bituminous products is that they are easy to handle; the addition of water is all that is necessary to decrease their viscosity. Drying involves, primarily, the loss of water by evaporation. No heating is required in their application and they have good bonding qualities, even to damp or wet surfaces. These asphalts, particularly the clay-base type, undergo less deterioration from weather exposure than other forms of bitumens.

USES OF BITUMENS

The use of bitumens in today's industrial world is very widespread. Table 11-1 lists some of those uses.

In general, the uses to which bitumens are put are controlled by their desirable qualities; their limitations control the methods of application and their performance. Their uses in construction are governed by the same general principles. The form in which the bitumen is used depends on the qualities and characteristics desired.

Waterproof Coatings and Membranes

Bitumens are widely used to provide a waterproof coating for walls and to make waterproof membranes in buildings and other structures. When hot-applied bitumens are used below grade, where they are not subject to high temperatures, types are used which have a low softening point—46 to 63°C—and a high penetration value—up to 85. When the bitumens are to be used above grade on vertical surfaces subjected to direct sunlight, a type with a higher softening point—93 to 104°C—and a lower penetration value—15 to 25—should be used. Cutbacks and emulsions, applied cold, are being used much more extensively for this purpose, with or without a felt membrane.

Asphalt Pavement

Asphaltic cutbacks and emulsions have their greatest use in road construction (see Fig. 11-2), road maintenance, and airport construction (see Fig. 11-3). This accounts for about 85 percent of the asphalt produced in North America.

Fig. 11-2 Pavements are large consumers of asphalt. *(Asphalt Institute)*

Asphalt in pavement acts as a binder for the aggregates (see Fig. 11-4); in this capacity as a cement, the asphalts are usually semisolid. Before it can be mixed with the gravel, crushed stone, or sand, the asphalt must be made liquid by heating, by cutting with solvent, or by emulsifying with water.

Lack of compatibility between different bitumens is a factor which requires attention. Though these reactions do not always occur, sometimes if asphalt is applied over pitch it will soften and flow off, leaving the pitch exposed. If pitch is applied over asphalt, the pitch may harden and crack. It is therefore advisable to avoid using these two bitumens together, if possible.

Fig. 11-3 Asphalt for airport pavement. *(Asphalt Institute)*

307

Table 11-1
SOME USES AND APPLICATION OF ASPHALT

AGRICULTURE

(Also see Buildings, Hydraulics, and Paving)
Cattle sprays
Dampproofing and waterproofing buildings, structures
Disinfectants
Fence post coating
Mulches
Mulching paper
Paved barn floors, barnyards, feed platforms, etc.
Protecting tanks, vats, etc.
Protection for concrete structures
Tree paints
Water and moisture barriers (above and below ground)
Wind and water erosion control
Weather modification areas

BUILDINGS

(Also see Industrial, Paving)

Floors
Dampproofing and waterproofing
Floor compositions, tiles, coverings
Insulating fabrics, papers
Step treads

Roofing
Asbestos felt
Building papers
Built-up roof adhesives, felts, primes
Caulking compounds
Cement waterproofing compounds
Cleats for roofing
Glass wool compositions
Insulating fabrics, felts, papers
Joint filler compounds
Laminated roofing, shingles
Liquid roof coatings
Plastic cements
Shingles

Walls, Siding, Ceilings
Acoustical blocks, compositions, felts
Architectural decoration
Asbestos cement panels, felt
Bricks
Brick siding
Building blocks, papers
Dampproofing coatings, compositions
Insulating board, fabrics, felts, paper
Joint filler compounds
Masonry coatings
Plaster boards
Putty, asphalt
Siding compositions
Soundproofing
Stucco base
Wallboard

Miscellaneous
Air-drying paints, varnishes
Artificial lumber
Ebonized lumber
Insulating paints
Plumbing, pipes
Treated awnings

HYDRAULICS AND EROSION CONTROL

Canal linings, sealants
Catchment areas, basins
Dam groutings
Dam linings, protection
Dike protection
Ditch linings
Drainage gutters, structures
Embankment protection
Groins
Jetties
Levee protection
Mattresses for levee and bank protection
Membrane linings, waterproofing
Reservoir linings
Revetments
Sand dune stabilization
Sewage lagoons, oxidation ponds
Swimming pools
Waste ponds
Water barriers

INDUSTRIAL

Aluminum Foil Compositions Using Asphalt
Backed felts
Conduit insulation, lamination
Insulating boards
Paint compositions
Papers
Pipe wrapping
Roofing, shingles

Automotive
Acoustical compositions, felts
Brake linings
Clutch facings
Floor sound deadeners
Friction elements
Insulating felts
Panel boards
Shim strips
Tacking strips
Underseal

Impregnated, Treated Materials
Armored bituminized fabrics
Asbestos compositions
Burlap impregnation
Canvas treating
Carpeting medium
Deck cloth impregnation
Fabrics, felts
Mildew prevention
Packing papers
Pipes and pipe wrapping
Planks
Rugs, asphalt base
Sawdust, cork, asphalt composition
Textiles, waterproofing
Tiles
Treated leather
Wrapping papers

Table 11-1 (continued)

Paints, Varnishes, etc.
Acidproof enamels, mastics and varnishes
Acid-resistant coatings
Air-drying paints, varnishes
Anticorrosive and antifouling paints
Antioxidants and solvents
Base for solvent compositions
Baking and heat-resistant enamels
Boat deck sealing compound
Lacquers, japans
Marine enamels

Electrical
Armature carbons, windings
Battery boxes, carbons
Electrical insulating compounds, papers, tapes, wire coatings
Junction box compound
Molded conduits

Compositions
Black grease
Buffing compounds
Cable splicing compound
Embalming
Etching compositions
Extenders, rubber, other
Explosives
Fire extinguisher compounds
Joint fillers
Lap cement
Lubricating grease
Pipe coatings, dips, joint seals
Plastic cements
Plasticizers
Preservatives
Printing inks
Well drilling fluid
Wooden cask liners

Miscellaneous
Belting
Blasting fuses
Briquette binders
Burial vaults
Casting molds
Clay articles
Clay pigeons
Depilatory
Expansion joints
Flower pots
Foundry cores
Friction tape
Fuel
Gaskets
Imitation leather
Mirror backing
Phonograph records
Rubber, molded compositions
Shoe fillers, soles
Table tops

PAVING
(Also see Hydraulics, Agriculture, Railroads, Recreation)

Airport runways, taxiways, aprons, etc.
Asphalt blocks
Brick fillers
Bridge deck surfacing
Crack fillers
Curbs, gutters, drainage ditches
Floors for buildings, warehouses, garages, etc.
Highways, roads, streets, shoulders
Parking lots, driveways
PCC Underseal
Roof-deck parking
Sidewalk, footpaths
Soil stabilization

RAILROADS
Ballast-treatment
Curve lubricant
Dust laying
Paved ballast, sub-ballast
Paved crossings, freight yards, station platforms
Rail fillers
Railroad ties
Tie impregnating, stabilization

RECREATION

Paved Surfaces for:
Dance pavilions
Drive-in movies
Gymnasiums, sports arenas
Playgrounds, school yards
Race tracks
Running tracks
Skating rinks
Swimming and wading pools
Tennis courts, handball courts

SOURCE: Asphalt Institute.

Fig. 11-4 Asphalt binder for aggregates in pavement. *(Asphalt Institute)*

LIQUID PAVING ASPHALTS Most of the liquid asphalts used for paving are cutbacks; three common types are used, depending on the type of solvent used. When gasoline is used as a solvent, a rapid-curing liquid asphalt is the result; kerosine produces a medium-curing asphalt; heavier fuel oils produce a slow-curing asphalt. These names refer to the rate at which solvent is lost, either during construction or after the pavement has been laid.

Each of these three types of asphalt is further subdivided into six grades (0 to 5) on the basis of differences in viscosity. Zero grade has the lowest viscosity in each case and runs freely at ordinary temperatures. Grade 5 material approaches semi-solid consistency. The differences in viscosity are obtained by varying the amount of solvent added in each case. Slow-curing liquid asphalts are also produced by refining a fluid asphalt-base stock to the required consistency for each S.C. grade.

The liquid asphalt to be selected for any given project depends on the construction conditions. In general, a rapid-curing grade can be used as a binder for open-graded aggregates that coat quickly during mixing or for surface treatments. Medium-curing grades are required for dense-graded aggregates, which require longer mixing time. Slow-curing grades are used with aggregates requiring a long mixing time and for projects where the pavement may have to be torn up and reworked from time to time.

ASPHALT PAVING CEMENTS The binders for the more expensive asphalt pavements are usually asphalt cements. These semisolid materials are also separated into grades having different ranges of hardness. To grade them, the penetration test is employed. The most common grades of asphalt cement in use are shown in Table 11-2. The 50 to 60 penetration grade is the hardest asphalt cement and the 150 to 200 grade is the softest.

Asphalt Canal Liner and Bank Erosion Control

The versatility of asphalt has led to its employment in many types of hydraulic structure, a typical one being a liner for canals. (See Fig. 11-5.) Mixes made with the harder asphalts have greater resistance to weed growth, transverse creep, and traffic damage; are less susceptible to temperature change; and are

Table 11-2
GRADES OF ASPHALT CEMENT

Grade	Penetration
1	50 to 60
2	60 to 70
3	70 to 85
4	85 to 100
5	100 to 120
6	120 to 150
7	150 to 200

Fig. 11-5 Asphalt concrete canal lining. *(Asphalt Institute)*

requires much the same type of asphalt concrete, often with wire reinforcement added, as for canal linings. The asphalt used should have penetration values of 60 to 100.

BUILDING PRODUCTS AND APPLICATIONS

Adhesiveness, durability, and waterproofing qualities, along with low cost, make bitumens useful in the manufacture of building materials that require water-resisting properties. Construction products manufactured using asphalt include flooring, prepared roofing, shingles, and insulating boards. Bitumen is also used as the bonding agent for the materials used in the various built-up roofing systems.

These applications require bitumens that have special properties. For saturated roofing felts, a bitumen with a low viscosity at the saturation temperature and with a flash point above that temperature is required. This type of asphalt has a softening temperature of about 60°C and yet must be able to withstand low temperatures reasonably well.

Prepared roofing products such as rolled roofing and shingles (see Fig. 11-7) are manufactured from asphalt-saturated felts coated with additional asphalt and a crushed mineral aggregate rolled into the asphalt coating. This type of asphalt is a No. 1 cutback with a softening point between 93 and 116°C. It is normally what is termed as an air-blown product having low penetration values—18 to 30

tough and lasting under extremes of weather. The paving grade asphalt should have a penetration rate of 60 to 70.

The use of asphalt in bank erosion control (see Fig. 11-6) presents the same type of problems and

Fig. 11-6 Bank erosion control using asphalt concrete. *(Asphalt Institute)*

Fig. 11-7 Triple-tab asphalt shingles with self-sealing adhesive strip.

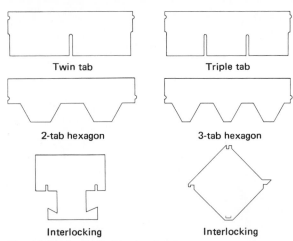

Twin tab   Triple tab

2-tab hexagon   3-tab hexagon

Interlocking   Interlocking

Fig. 11-8 Asphalt shingle shapes.

at 25°C—and low temperature susceptibility. Saturating and coating asphalts must be compatible.

Asphalt Shingles

Asphalt shingles are made from heavy rag felt, saturated with asphalt and coated with high-melting-point flexible asphalt. Ceramic-coated mineral granules are pressed into the asphalt coating on the exposed face to provide a fire-resistant surface. A number of weights and styles of shingles are made, each in a wide variety of colors. The weights refer to the weight of the quantity of shingles required to cover 100 ft^2 (9.29 m^2) of roof, traditionally known as a *square* of shingles.

This weight varies from 135 lb (61.15 kg) for light shingles to 325 lb (147.22 kg) for very heavy ones. Weights are varied by the following methods: altering the *thickness of the felt* used, altering the *amount of asphalt* absorbed by the felt, changing the *thickness of the asphalt coating,* and altering the *amount of mineral* used on the surface.

Shingle styles include a number of individual shapes, as well as a number of double- and triple-tab multiple shingles. (See Fig. 11-8.)

APPLICATION Most types of asphalt shingles can be used for reroofing over old shingles as well as for new applications. Roof slopes should be at least 18° for shingles of this type to give satisfactory service. Broad-headed roofing nails or staples are used to fasten them down, and manufacturers' instructions should be followed when shingles are being applied. To prevent damage by wind, the corners of exposed tabs should be cemented down with asphalt roofing gum.

Built-Up Roofing

Built-up roofing is a term applied to a type of roofing made by building up successive layers of felt paper and asphalt over a solid roof deck of some description. (See Fig. 11-9.)

It is generally recognized that there are five basic types of built-up roofing; modifications depend on the type of roof deck involved, the slope of the roof, and the length of time the roofing is expected to perform satisfactorily.

Fig. 11-9 Application of built-up roofing.

In many cases the first step is the application of a layer of rigid insulation of some kind. For example, in Fig. 11-10, foam-glass insulation is being laid in hot asphalt over the roof deck. In other cases the built-up roofing may be laid directly over the deck without insulation.

ROOFING TYPE NO. 1   Roofing type No. 1 consists of asphalted felt paper, asphalt and gravel, or slag and is intended for roof slopes from 2 to 14°.

With a wood deck, the first step is the application of a single layer of 5-lb (0.25-kg) dry sheathing paper, as illustrated in Fig. 11-11. The "5 lb" means 5 lb per 100 ft^2; the "0.25 kg" in this designation means 0.25 kg per square meter. Next, two layers of 15-lb (0.75-kg) asphalt-saturated felt paper is applied dry and nailed with broad-headed roofing nails. These are followed by three layers of 15-lb (0.75-kg) asphalt-saturated felt, each layer being sealed in place with hot asphalt at the rate of 20 lb/100 ft^2 (1 kg/m^2).

Next, a layer of hot asphalt is spread over the surface at the rate of about 65 lb/100 ft^2 (3.2 kg/m^2). If the slope is $\frac{1}{2}$ to 4°, use 60°C asphalt; if it is 4 to 8°, use 77°C asphalt; and if it is over 8°, use 99°C asphalt.

Finally, a layer of crushed slag or pea gravel is spread over the asphalt at the rate of 300 lb/100 ft^2

(15 kg/m^2) for slag or 400 lb/100 ft^2 (19.5 kg/m^2) for gravel. This type of roof should have a useful life of 20 years.

For nonwood decks or over an insulated surface, a similar grade of roofing is applied by sealing all layers of asphalt-impregnated felt paper in hot asphalt. (See Fig. 11-12.)

ROOFING TYPE NO. 2   Roofing type No. 2 consists of tarred felt paper, pitch, and gravel. It is intended for roofs with a slope of 0 to 6°.

Over a wood deck, the procedure is the same as with type No. 1 roofing, except that *tarred* rather than *asphalted* paper is used. The hot tar used between layers of paper should be applied at the rate of 25 lb/100 ft^2 (1.5 kg/m^2) and the hot tar topping at the rate of 80 lb/100 ft^2 (4 kg/m^2). Tar should be heated to not more than 204°C and applied at a temperature of not less than 177°C. Gravel or slag application is the same as for type No. 1 roofing.

ROOFING TYPE NO. 3   Roofing type No. 3 consists of asbestos felt, asphalt felt, and a smooth flood coat of asphalt. It is intended for roofs with a slope of from 3 to 34°. Over a wood deck, the dry sheathing paper consists of 9-lb (0.54-kg) waxed kraft. A single layer of 25-lb (1.2-kg) asphalt-saturated felt

Fig. 11-10   Foam glass insulation for roof deck. *(Pittsburgh-Corning Corp.)*

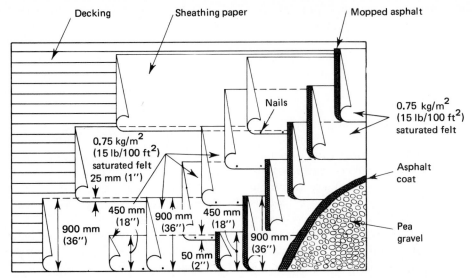

Fig. 11-11   Four-ply built-up asphalt roof over wood deck.

paper is laid over this, held in place with roofing nails. Next, two layers of 15-lb (0.75-kg) asphalt felt are applied, each layer being sealed in place with a 20-lb/100-ft² (1-kg/m²) mopping of hot asphalt. Next, two layers of 15-lb/100-ft² (0.75-kg/m²) asphalt-saturated asbestos paper are applied in the same way. Finally a flood coat, consisting of 25 lb per 100 ft² (1.2-kg/m²) of asphalt is applied, using the proper grade of asphalt for the roof slope, as specified under type No. 1.

ROOFING TYPE NO. 4   Roofing type No. 4 requires heavy, slate-surfaced roofing paper, as well as asphalt-saturated felts, and may be used on roofs with slopes from 10 to 34°. Over a wood deck, a single layer of 5-lb (0.25-kg) dry sheathing paper is first applied. Next comes a single layer of 15-lb (0.75-kg) asphalt-saturated felt, held in place with roofing nails. Over this are laid two layers of 15-lb (0.75-kg) asphalt felt and two layers of 120-lb (6.0-kg) slate-surfaced felt. Each of these is sealed in

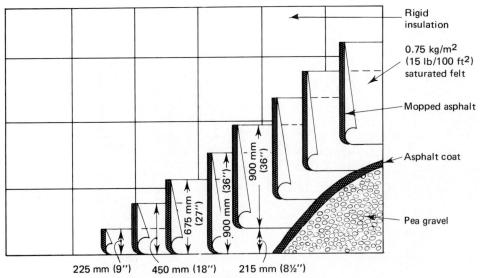

Fig. 11-12   Four-ply built-up roof over rigid insulation.

314

place with 20 lb/100 ft^2 (1 kg/m^2) of 99°C asphalt. This type of roofing is often recommended as a 10-year roof.

ROOFING TYPE NO. 5   Roofing type No. 5 involves what is known as the cold process. The felts are cold-process felts, saturated with cold asphalt emulsion, and the asphalt top coating is applied cold. Layers of felt are sealed together with asphalt adhesive. Roofing of this type is suitable for slopes from 1 to 34°. Over a wood deck, three layers of cold-process 53-lb (2.6-kg) felt paper are applied, fastened down with roofing nails and asphalt adhesive, at the rate of about 2.5 gal/100 ft^2 (1 L/m^2). This surface is covered with a layer of asphalt-fibrated emulsion, applied cold at the rate of 4 gal/100 ft^2 (1.6 L/m^2). This type of roofing is considered to have a useful life of 20 years.

Rolled Roofing

Rolled roofing consists of very heavy asphalt-saturated felt paper, with or without finely crushed slate embedded in one surface, put up in rolls. There are four basic types in this kind of roofing: (1) smooth roll, (2) mineral-surfaced roll, (3) pattern-edge roll, and (4) 19-in (475-mm) selvage.

SMOOTH ROLL   The smooth roll consists of asphalt-saturated felt ranging in weight from 45 to 65 lb/100 ft^2 (2 to 3 kg/m^2), covered with a smooth coating of asphalt.

MINERAL-SURFACED ROLL   The mineral-surfaced roll ranges from 90 to 120 lb/100 ft^2 (4 to 6 kg/m^2) and has a layer of crushed slate embedded in the asphalt surface coating. Both of these rolls are made 36 in (900 mm) wide.

PATTERN-EDGE ROLL   The pattern-edge roll is made in two widths—32 and 36 in (800 and 900 mm)—and consists of a 105-lb/100-ft^2 (5-kg/m^2) felt that is mineral-surfaced except for a 4-in (100-mm) band down the center. The roll is semi-cut on a pattern along this strip so that it produces 16 or 18 in (400 or 450 mm) wide patterned roofing strips. These are normally lapped 2 in (50 mm) when being applied to a roof.

SELVAGE ROLL   The 19-in (475-mm) selvage roll is made from felt weighing 140 to 150 lb/100 ft^2

(7 to 7.5 kg/m^2), in a strip 36 in (900 mm) wide. A 17-in-wide (425-mm-wide) band of this strip is mineralized, and the other 19 in (475 mm) is plain. When applied to a roof, each strip is lapped 19 in (475 mm) over the one below to present a completely mineralized surface and to provide double coverage.

SPRAYED-ON ASPHALT ROOFING

A new technique for the application of asphalt roofing involves the use of special equipment for applying the material. A special gun with three nozzles and a fiber-cutting chamber is used. Glass fibers are fed into the chamber, where they are cut to predetermined lengths and blown out through a center nozzle. Two side nozzles each deliver a spray of asphalt emulsion which coats the glass fibers and carries them to the deck to form a reinforced film of asphalt. (See Fig. 11-13.) The thickness of the film can be increased by repeated sprayings and will be determined by the weather conditions and the slope of the roof.

This type of roofing film is applied over regular base roofing felts and is particularly useful on roofs of irregular shapes. By this method a monolithic film be applied over the entire surface, regardless of the shape or contours.

Fig. 11-13   Sprayed-on asphalt roofing.   (Fintkote Co.)

ASPHALT FLOORING

Asphalt is the basic ingredient in two types of flooring: *asphalt mastic flooring* and *asphalt tile*.

Asphalt Mastic Flooring

Asphalt mastic flooring is made by mixing an emulsified asphalt with portland cement, sand, and gravel or crushed stone to form a plastic mixture. This is spread over the floor, screeded, compacted, and floated to a depth of $\frac{1}{2}$ in (12 mm).

The emulsified asphalt is a clay type—a dispersion of asphalt in water, held in suspension by a mineral colloid—a clay product. It has resiliency, adhesion, and masticity, but it does not flow under heat and is not toxic or flammable. The mix is usually made in the following proportions: 1 bag (40 kg) portland cement, $12\frac{1}{2}$ gal (47.3 L) emulsified asphalt, 2 ft^3 (56.6 L) clean, sharp sand, and 4 ft^3 (113.2 L) of hard, washed gravel chips.

This asphaltic mastic flooring can be applied over a wood, concrete, or steel base. In each case the base must be primed with the proper type of asphaltic primer. In addition, in the case of a wood base, a tack coat of asphalt emulsion should be applied over the primer.

The material may also be molded in form intersections of precast asphalt flooring, called *asphalt planks*. These are laid on a solid, level base and cemented down with an asphaltic bonding preparation.

Asphalt Tile

Asphaltic tiles are composed of asbestos fibers bound together by a blend of selected asphaltic binders. Pigments are added for color, and in some cases polystyrene plastic is added to produce a stronger tile. The ingredients are machine mixed and formed into sheets $\frac{1}{8}$ or $\frac{3}{16}$ in (3 or 5 mm) thick under pressure. The sheets are then precision cut into tiles of several sizes: 9×9 in (225×225 mm), 12×12 in (300×300 mm), and 18×24 in (450×600 mm). Feature strips 1 or 2 in (25 or 50 mm) wide and 18 in (450 mm) long are also produced.

A great range of colors and designs is produced, including a large number of insert designs. This makes possible an almost unlimited number of floor patterns possible with this type of tile. Asphalt tile can be laid over a wood, asphaltic mastic, or concrete base (including a concrete slab on grade) using an asphaltic adhesive. The surface must be smooth and even, since the asphalt tiles tend to be brittle and may crack on an uneven surface. These tiles are highly resistant to water but are not resistant to organic acids or petroleum solvents. Hence they are not satisfactory for many industrial uses.

FIBERBOARD

Insulation boards composed of asphalt-impregnated wood fibers are used in built-up roofing systems because of their ability to resist moisture and maintain their strength even when exposed to moisture. The boards are 24×48 in (600×1200 mm) in size and are available in thicknesses ranging from $\frac{1}{2}$ to 2 in (13 to 50 mm). Boards 1 in (25 mm) or thicker have shiplap edges to reduce ridging and heat loss.

GLOSSARY

asphalt mastic	A plastic flooring material containing asphalt.
destructive distillation	The process of decomposing a substance and collecting the resulting by-products.
emulsion asphalt	Asphalt suspended in a watery fluid.
fibrated emulsion	An asphalt emulsion containing mineral fiber.
flash point	The temperature at which a flammable material will break into a sudden flame.
flood coat	A heavy, poured-on coating of asphalt.
monolithic film	A film containing no joints.

pea gravel	Gravel with a maximum size of $\frac{1}{2}$ in (13 mm).
rag felt	Heavy paper made largely from rag fibers.
selvage	A specially formed edge.
viscosity	The physical property of a fluid or semifluid which allows it to offer continuous resistance to flow.

REVIEW QUESTIONS

1. Outline the difference between coal tar and coal-tar pitch.

2. Explain why it is important to know the flow properties of pitches and asphalts.

3. What are ductility tests designed to show?

4. Why should pitch be used only on roofs with very little slope?

5. What type of asphalt binds best to a damp or wet surface?

6. Explain what is meant by cutback asphalts.

7. Name two advantages of using emulsion asphalts.

8. What is meant by having a low viscosity at the saturation temperature?

9. What is the primary purpose of asphalt in a paving mix?

10. What are the basic differences between built-up and monoform roofing?

11. What is liquid-envelope roofing?

SELECTED SOURCES OF INFORMATION

Allied Materials Corporation, Oklahoma City, Okla.
American Bitumen & Asphalt Co., San Francisco, Calif.
The Asphalt Institute, College Park, Md.
British American Oil Company, Toronto, Ont.
Celotex Corporation, Tampa, Fla.
The Construction Materials Group of Domtar Inc., Montreal, Que.
The Flintkote Company of Canada Limited, Toronto, Ont.
Mastic Tile Corporation of America, Joliet, Ill.
The Tremco Mfg. Co., Cleveland, Ohio, and Toronto, Ont.

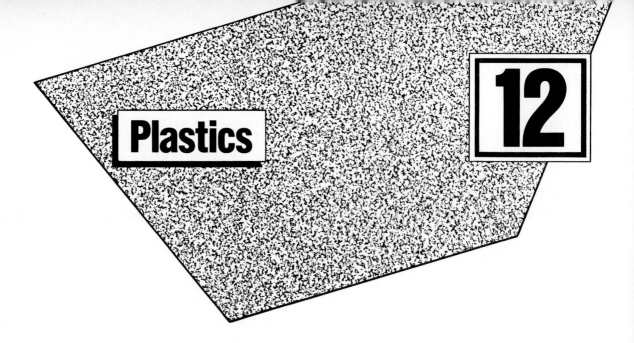

Plastics

12

The term *plastics,* as it is commonly used today, refers to a large group of synthetic materials which are made from a number of common substances such as coal, salt, oil, natural gas, cotton, wood, and water. For example, *furan resins* are made from *furfural,* a product obtained by acid hydrolysis of such waste by-products as oat hulls, corn cobs, and sugar cane bagasse. From these common substances, relatively simple chemicals, known as *monomers,* which are capable of reacting with one another, are produced. These are then built up into chainlike molecules (see Fig. 12-1) called polymers.

TYPES OF PLASTICS

The development of such products has increased to the point where there are now about 40 groups, or families, of plastics with commercial value, each with its own peculiar characteristics. For example, some may be light, others heavy; some heat-resistant, others softened by hot water; some hard, others soft; some clear, others opaque. Even within a family group there may be considerable differences between materials, brought about by changing the molecular weight and the chain formation. In addition, the properties of the basic polymer may be modified by the addition of plasticizers, fillers, color, and other chemicals.

Plastics have had a profound effect on nearly every facet of our society. The proliferation of plas-

tic end-products has meant that practically everyone is in almost daily contact with plastics in one form or another from birth to death. It would be difficult to imagine our life now without plastics. This growth is as pronounced in the construction field as elsewhere, and it is with plastics in this area that we are interested here.

All these materials fall into two general classifications: *thermoplastics* and *thermosetting plastics,* called *thermosets.* Thermoplastics become soft when heated and hard when cooled, regardless of the number of times the process is repeated. This is possible because thermoplastics have linear molecular chains (see Fig. 12-1*a*), which move in relation to one another when heated or cooled and

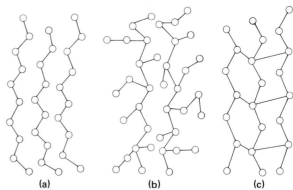

Fig. 12-1 Polymer molecules. *(a)* Linear, *(b)* branched, *(c)* cross-linked.

solidify into new shapes without any significant chain breakage occurring. Included in the thermoplastics are acrylics, cellulosics, polyethylene, polyvinyl chloride (PVC), polystyrene, polyallomers, polycarbonates, polyimide, polypropylene, polysulfone, phenylene oxide, nylons, methyl pentenes, ionomer, fluoroplastics, acetal and acrylonitrile butadiene styrene (ABS).

However, there are practical limits to the number of times that thermoplastics can be subjected to the heat-cool cycle. Too many cycles may result in the loss of color or plasticizer, which, in turn, affects the appearance or the properties of the product.

Thermosets are also chainlike in molecular structure and, before molding, very similar to thermoplastics. But the curing and hardening process involves the formation of cross-links between molecules in adjacent chains (see Fig. 12-1c) so that the result is a complex, interconnected network, in which the chains are no longer free to move. Thus the application of heat to these materials does not result in *plastic flow*—softening of the material. The thermoset group includes alkyds, aminos (urea and melamine formaldehyde), diallyl phthalate (DAP), epoxies, furan, phenolics, polyesters, polyurethane, and silicones.

PRODUCTION OF PLASTICS

The process of uniting monomers to form polymers is known as *polymerization* and is accomplished by either a *condensation* or an *addition* process. In the first process, monomers or groups of monomers unite chemically by the interaction of active units in each one. Often, in the process, water, alcohol, or hydrogen chloride may be eliminated as a by-product.

In the addition process, monomers attach themselves to one another in an end-to-end fashion. This repetition of units in a molecule may result in a chainlike, *linear* structure, a chain with *branches* or arms, or an interlaced structure with *cross-linked* units, forming network-type molecules (see Fig. 12-1). In the latter process—addition polymerization—the products formed have the same composition as the monomers from which they are produced.

The production of plastic products is divided into three steps that sometimes overlap. The manufacturer converts raw materials into basic plastic compounds in the form of granules, powder, beads, or liquid resins. The processor takes these basic compounds and forms them by one method or another into sheets, films, tubing, rods, and other solid or semisolid shapes. During this process the plastics are usually combined with one or more other materials in order to achieve certain desired physical properties in the product. Sometimes plasticizers are added for workability, fillers are added to produce bulk, fibers are added for strength and durability, or hardeners are used to induce setting. In addition, a plastic is sometimes combined with a conventional material to give it a special property. Finally, a fabricator makes finished plastic products.

Plastic products are formed by a number of methods which include *injection molding, blow molding, expandable bead molding, compression molding, transfer molding, rotational molding, form molding, extrusion thermoforming, laminating, casting,* and *calendaring.*

Injection Molding

In the injection-molding process, measured amounts of powder or granules are fed into the intake end of the heated barrel of a molding machine, as illustrated in Fig. 12-2, and forced forward by a ram. The material is spread out against the walls of the cylinder by a *spreader* or *torpedo* (see Fig. 12-2) and heated at temperatures of 300 to 650°F (149 to 343°C), so that by the time it reaches the nozzle it is liquefied and will flow. It is then forced through the nozzle under pressures of 5000 to 40,000 psi (34.5 to 275.75 MPa) into a closed, cold mold, where it cools and solidifies. Figure 12-3 illustrates a typical reciprocating-screw injection-molding machine, and Fig. 12-4 a rotary injection molder.

Almost all thermoplastics may be injection molded, and some thermosets are being similarly handled with modified machinery. Nylon, acrylics,

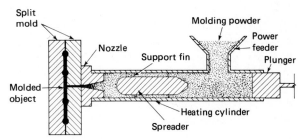

Fig. 12-2 Diagram of injection mold.

Fig. 12-3 Injection molding machine. *(Epco, Inc.)*

polyethylene, cellulosics, ABS, and polystyrene are the most widely used plastics for injection molding, and products made by this process include gears, knobs, wastebaskets, and kitchen and bathroom wall tile.

Blow Molding

Blow molding includes three processes: *extrusion-blow molding, injection-blow molding,* and *stretch-blow molding.* In the extrusion-blow molding process, an extruder produces a hollow tube, called a *parison* (see Fig. 12-5), which is captured between the two halves of a hollow mold. As the mold closes, the bottom end of the parison is sealed off and air is blown into the tube from the top, forcing it to expand to fit the inside surface of the mold. Figure 12-6 illustrates an extrusion-blow molding machine.

In the injection-blow molding process, the plastic

Fig. 12-4 Rotary injection molding machine for processing silicone rubber. *(Epco, Inc.)*

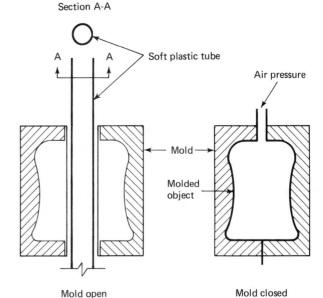

Fig. 12-5 Diagram of blow molding.

Fig. 12-6 Extrusion-blow molding machine. *(Ingersoll-Rand Co.)*

parison is injection molded on a steel rod instead of being extruded as a tube in open air. After the steel rod is withdrawn, the process is completed as with extrusion molding. Figure 12-7 is an example of an injection-blow molding machine.

Stretch-blow molding involves stretching the parison in the axial direction before blowing. In one process, the end of the parison is sealed off, a rod telescopes from the blowpin, presses against the closed end, and stretches it to size. Finally, the rod is withdrawn and the parison blown to shape. One style of stretch-blow molding machine is shown in Fig. 12-8.

Polyethylene is the most widely used plastic for blow molding, but polyvinyl chloride, polystyrene, and polypropylene are also being used. Bottles and water cans are typical blow-molded products.

Expandable Bead Molding

Expandable bead molding is a process used to produce lightweight products of polystyrene foam. Small granules of polystyrene, together with a small amount of an expanding agent, are placed in a rolling drum and steam heated. Heat softens the granules, and the expanding agent enlarges their size. When they have been pre-expanded to the desired density, which will usually be from 1 to 20 lb/ft^3 (16 to 320 kg/m^3), they are cooled and transferred

Fig. 12-7 Injection-blow molding machine. *(Ingersoll-Rand Co.)*

Fig. 12-8   Stretch-blow molding machine.   *(Ingersoll-Rand Co.)*

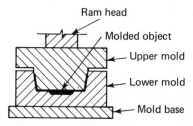

Fig. 12-10   Diagram of fully positive compression mold.

to a closed mold. (See Fig. 12-9.) Here they are again heated by steam, to about 135°C, and resoftened until they fuse together into a block. Flotation equipment, shipping containers, and rigid insulation are typical products.

Compression Molding

Compression molding is the simplest type of molding and the most common method by which thermosets are molded. A measured amount of powder is placed in a heated mold, which is then closed. Heat and pressure are applied to the plastic material, which melts and flows to all parts of the mold. There are three common mold designs: *flash, semipositive,* and *fully positive.* (See Fig. 12-10.) A flash mold is so called because a small amount of the melted plastic "flashes" out between the two halves of the mold as it is being closed. This flash seals the mold and allows the plunger to exert pressure on

the plastic within. In a fully positive mold, the ram moves down into a recess in the top of the mold, which prevents plastic from overflowing. Semipositive molds combine the flash and the fully positive techniques. Plastic dinnerware is commonly compression molded. Handles and knobs, radio and television cabinets, and furniture drawers are other common products of this type of molding.

Transfer Molding

Transfer molding differs from compression molding in that in the transfer molding process, the molding compound is liquefied outside the molding chamber in a *transfer* chamber. It is then transferred to the mold under pressure, through a tube called a *sprue* (see Fig. 12-11), and there the forming and setting takes place. Thermoset, rather than thermoplastic, materials normally are employed in transfer molding, phenolic being the most common, followed by melamine, urea, and epoxy thermosets. Typical articles made by this process are cups, bottle caps, and terminal block insulators.

Rotational Molding

Rotational molding is used to form hollow units with complex shapes and heavy walls. A premeasured amount of powder or liquid resin is placed

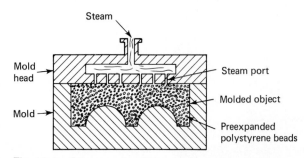

Fig. 12-9   Diagram of molding expandable polystyrene.

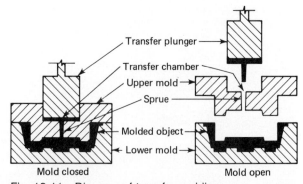

Fig. 12-11   Diagram of transfer molding.

322

in the bottom half of a cold mold, and the mold is closed. It is then rotated horizontally and vertically to distribute the material evenly over the inner mold surfaces, passed through an oven to heat and cure the plastic, cooled, and finally opened to eject the product. Most of the plastics used for blow molding are also used in rotational molding, and typical products so manufactured are tanks and heater ducts.

Form Molding

Foamed plastics are made by mixing an expanding agent with either granules or powder and then heating it. Heat melts the plastic and causes the formation of a gas which expands the molten material into a foamed structure. It is quickly cooled to set the material in its expanded state. Nearly all thermoplastics can be foamed, the most commonly used ones being polyethylene, polystyrene, and polyvinyl chloride. Both rigid and flexible foams may be made from thermoplastics. Examples of thermoplastic foam products are upholstery, insulation, and packaging fill.

A thermoset foam is made by mixing the appropriate resin with a curing agent and an expanding agent and then heating the mixture in a mold. The heat activates the expanding agent and subsequently the curing agent so that the expanded material is set in that state. By regulating the foaming and setting reactions, a variety of densities of foam may be produced. Thermoset foams are commonly made from epoxy, silicone, polyurethane, and phenolic plastics, and the usual products are thermal insulation, shock-absorbing pads, mattress pads, and furniture cushions.

Extrusion Thermoforming

Extrusion forming is used for mass-produced materials which have a constant cross-section, and it is done in two ways. The simplest way is the forcing of semiliquid plastic through a die of the proper size and shape, in a manner similar to that used for forming brick by extrusion. (See Fig. 12-12.) Sheets (thicknesses of over 10 mils), films (thicknesses up to 10 mils), tubes, rods, water hose, drainpipe, house siding, and molding trim are formed in this way. Polyethylene, PVC, ABS, cellulosics, and polystyrene are commonly used for this type of extrusion. The other extrusion method involves forcing wire, cable, or cord through a die along with the plastic, so that the material emerges with a plastic coating.

In the thermoforming process, sheet plastic is heated until soft and then forced against a cold mold surface, where it cools and hardens to shape. There are two principal methods of thermoforming. One involves the use of a vacuum to exhaust air from the inside of a closed mold (see Fig. 12-13) so that outside air pressure forces the plastic against the mold. In the other, air pressure is applied to the outside of a hot plastic sheet, stretched over the open side of a mold (see Fig. 12-14), forcing it into and against the mold. Thermoforming is limited to thermoplastics, and common materials so processed include cellulosics, acrylics, vinyls, styrenes, polyolefins, ABS, and PVC. Typical products include domed skylights, refrigerator and freezer door liners, washing-machine covers, automobile instrument and door panels, patterned light diffusers, toys, and aircraft parts.

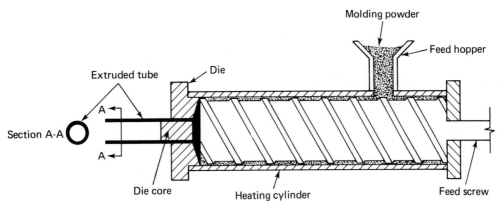

Fig. 12-12   Diagram of extrusion molding.

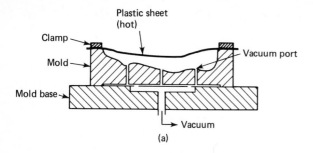

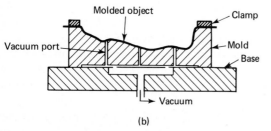

Fig. 12-13   Vacuum thermoforming. *(a)* Before vacuum applied, *(b)* after vacuum applied.

Laminating

Laminating, in general, consists of bonding together a number of layers of materials to form a single sheet. Two processes are involved. In one, the layers of material to be laminated—paper, cloth, glass fiber, or asbestos—are impregnated with a thermosetting resin and assembled to provide the proper thickness. They are then subjected to heat and pressure, which causes the resin to flow, and upon cooling, the laminate hardens into a solid sheet. Tubes are made by laminating a number of layers around a mandrel.

In the other process, a number of layers of one material are laminated together to form a sheet, and then a layer of a different material is laminated to one or both faces of that sheet. The most common product made by this process is *overlaid* plywood, which consists of a cellulose fiber sheet impregnated with a phenol-formaldehyde resin and laminated to a plywood sheet. (See Fig. 12-15.)

Epoxies, melamines, ureas, diallyl phthalate, and phenolics are all used in the first process to produce a wide variety of plain and patterned wall paneling, tabletop material, and industrial laminate board.

Casting

Casting is a simple process in which liquid plastics, with their appropriate curing agents, are poured into molds and set, with or without heat. In general, silicones, epoxies, polyesters, and polyurethanes are used in the casting process, with pipe, rods, and sheet being typical casting products.

Calendaring

Calendaring is really a form of extrusion, in which plastic material is fed to a pair of revolving rollers which extrude a thin film or sheet from between them. (See Fig. 12-16.) Normally, pressures in the roll gaps will be from 2000 to 3500 lb/linear in (357 to 625 kg/cm) of roll face for soft products and may be up to 6000 lb/linear in (1071 kg/cm) for thin, rigid material. Calendaring is usually a high-speed process, with speeds ranging from 30 to 300 ft/min (9 to 91 m/min), in which materials with a thickness of 0.002 in (0.05 mm), with a tolerance of about 0.001 in (0.025 mm), may be produced. With thicker materials, the surface of the sheet may be smooth or patterned, depending on the roller surface.

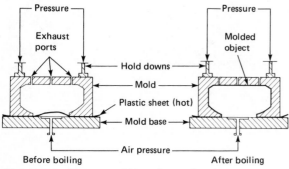

Fig. 12-14   Diagram of blow thermoforming.

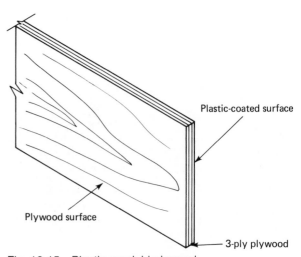

Fig. 12-15   Plastic overlaid plywood.

324

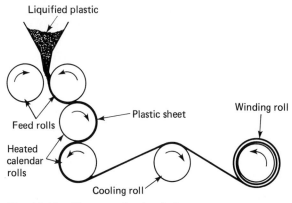

Fig. 12-16 Diagram of calendaring process.

Thermoplastics such as vinyls, polyolefins, cellulosics, and styrenes are used in calendaring, with polyvinyl chloride accounting for a large majority of the products. Such things as vapor barrier film, floor coverings, shower curtains, swimming-pool liners, construction hoardings, and automobile seat covers are common products.

PROPERTIES OF PLASTICS

The properties of many plastics make them desirable materials for use over a wide area of the construction field. Among those properties are *transparency* (acrylics, methyl pentenes, polycarbonates, ionomer, polysulfone), *resistance to discoloration* (acrylics), *good resistance to weathering* (acrylics, epoxy, silicone, polyvinyl chloride), *good dimensional stability* (fluoroplastics, polycarbonates, phenylene oxide, polyvinyl chloride, urea, melamine), *toughness* (cellulosics, ionomer, nylons, phenoxies, polycarbonates, polyethylene, phenylene oxide, polyvinyl chloride), *high impact resistance* (acrylics, ethyl cellulose, polypropylene, polyimide, polycarbonates), *abrasion resistance* (nylons, polyallomers, polyimide, polypropylene, urea, melamine, polyurethane), *low moisture absorption* (fluoroplastics, phenylene oxide, polypropylene, diallyl phthalate, silicone), *ductility* (phenoxies, acrylics, nylons), *good adhesive qualities* (epoxy, phenolics, amino resins), and *good resistance to chemicals* (nylons, polyethylene, phenylene oxide, polypropylene, polysulfone, diallyl phthalate). Most of them are lighter than conventional structural materials, and a number of them can be foamed to produce very lightweight products.

In addition, a number of these plastics have the property of being able to unite with another material in such a way as to combine the good qualities of all the partners. For example, when acrylonitrile and styrene monomers are copolymerized in the presence of butadiene rubber, the result is an ABS plastic possessing the chemical resistance of acrylonitrile, the ease of processing and the gloss of styrene, and the ability to absorb and disperse energy of impact of butadiene.

ADDITIVES FOR PLASTICS

Not all the properties of plastics are positive ones, and in many cases it is necessary to add a material to a plastic compound which will help it to overcome some tendency to failure or to reinforce another property. Among the materials which are added to plastics to improve their performance in some way are *antioxidants, antistatic agents, coloring agents, coupling agents, fillers, reinforcing agents, flame retardants, foaming agents, lubricants, plasticizers, preservatives, processing aids,* and *ultraviolet stabilizers.* For details concerning the need for these additives, their reactions with specific plastics, and the materials in common use which perform these various functions, consult the *Modern Plastics Encyclopedia,* a McGraw-Hill publication.

PLASTICS IN CONSTRUCTION

Plastics, with their wide range of properties—lightweight, strong, durable, corrosion-resistant, and weatherproof, to list a few—are ideal for construction applications. With the perfection of manufacturing processes, any size and shape can be produced quickly and accurately. Plastics are now being used as structural and nonstructural components, in composite applications, and as auxiliary materials.

Structural Applications

For structural purposes, a family of plastic materials produced by reinforcing the plastic with a fibrous mat are commonly used. About 90 percent of all reinforced plastics use *glass fiber,* but *jute, cotton, sisal, asbestos,* and *synthetic and metallic fibers* are also used. *Polyester resins* are used in about 85 percent of all reinforced plastics, the others being *epoxy, acrylic, melamine, phenolic, silicone, nylon, polystyrene,* and *polyvinyl chloride* resins.

CORRUGATED PANELS   One of the more common structural products is the glass-fiber-reinforced acrylic corrugated panel, which is not only transparent or translucent but also highly resistant to discoloration. Panels are available in various widths—18, 24, and 34 in (450, 600, and 850 mm), depending on the application and with $1\frac{1}{4}$- or $2\frac{1}{2}$-in (32- or 64-mm) corrugations. Lengths vary from 8 to 14 ft (2.4 to 4.3 m). Panels are available in a variety of colors.

Because these panels have good dimensional stability, as well as being strong and corrosion-resistant, their applications are many. They are used as roof panels, skylights, wall cladding, room dividers, and carport and patio covers.

FLAT SHEETS   Flat sheets of clear acrylic and polycarbonate plastic are used extensively as glazing materials. (See Fig. 12-17.) They are available in a variety of thicknesses, sizes, and finishes. Because of their light weight, high impact strength, and high light transmission values, these sheets are used in skylights, curtain walls, passive solar applications, pool enclosures, and greenhouses. In double glazing, they are about 12 percent more effective than glass when considering heat loss and 20 percent more effective when considering heat gain [based on two $\frac{1}{4}$-in (6-mm) lites with a $\frac{1}{2}$-in (12-mm) air space]. When sheets are laminated, they

Fig. 12-17   Clear acrylic sheets used as glazing for bus stop shelter.   *(Fibreglass R.P. Report)*

are very resistant to impact and are used where security must be considered. A $1\frac{1}{4}$-in (32-mm) thick laminate can withstand the impact from a .357 Magnum or a 12-gauge shotgun without any dangerous spalling.

THERMOFORMED SHAPES   Sheets may also be molded by the thermoform process into such roof shapes as those illustrated in Figs. 12-18 and 12-19. Figure 12-18 shows clear acrylic thermoformed into transparent roof domes for a showroom. The acrylic in the church domes shown in Fig. 12-19 has had a copper coloring added. Tinted acrylic sheets may be used as sunscreens to reduce solar heat, or the material may be used to make light control lenses for glare-free lighting. Transparent or translucent sheets may also be used for dome skylights. Acrylic sheets are textured or formed to produce spandrel panels, enclosure panels, and other exterior facings. (See Fig. 12-20.)

Plastic materials are widely used in the manufacture of sandwich panels used in curtain-wall construction. In some cases only the sandwich core is a plastic material, while in others both the core and one or both faces are of plastic. Some sandwich panels are made by bonding plastic sheets to an aluminum grid core (see Fig. 12-21). Plastics used for such panels include acrylics, polypropylene, polycarbonates, and polyesters because of their dimensional stability, high impact resistance, ability to withstand weathering, corrosion resistance, and, in the case of colored products, their ability to resist fading.

Reinforced acrylic is used to make the dome pans employed in forming a two-way rib or *waffle-type* concrete floor slab. In Fig. 12-22, glass-fiber-reinforced acrylic pans are shown in place, ready for the placing of a concrete slab.

GLASS-FIBER STRUCTURAL SHAPES   A relatively new use for fiber-reinforced plastic is in the manufacture of structural shapes. (See Fig. 12-23.) These shapes come in a wide variety of standard sizes, and nonstandard sizes and shapes are produced upon special request. Flat sheets are available in seven standard thicknesses ranging from $\frac{1}{8}$ to 1 in (3 to 25 mm) in thickness, in 4 × 8 ft (1.2 × 2.4 m) sheets. Nonstandard thicknesses and sizes can be made to order.

Fig. 12-18   Acrylic thermoformed roof domes.   *(Rohm & Haas)*

These shapes are produced by the *pultrusion process.* (See Fig. 12-24.) Glass-fiber rovings along with continuous strand mat are pulled through tanks of thermosetting resin and then through a curing and forming die to produce the structural shape. Glass placement, resin formulation, catalyst

Fig. 12-20   Plastic enclosure panels.

level, die temperature, and pull speed must be carefully regulated and monitored throughout the process.

The resin used can be tailor-made to suit particular requirements, but the three basic systems are *isophthalic polyester, vinyl ester,* and *epoxy.* The types of reinforcing fibers used are *glass-fiber rovings* and *continuous strand mat, graphite fibers,* and *aramid fibers.*

Fig.   12-19   Glass-fiber-reinforced   plastic   church domes.   *(Fibreglass R.P. Report)*

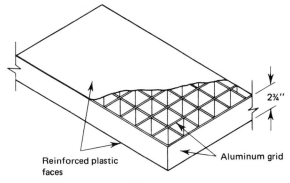

Fig. 12-21   Section of plastic-faced sandwich panel with aluminum grid core.

327

Fig. 12-22 Reinforced acrylic waffle pans. *(Fibreglass R.P. Report)*

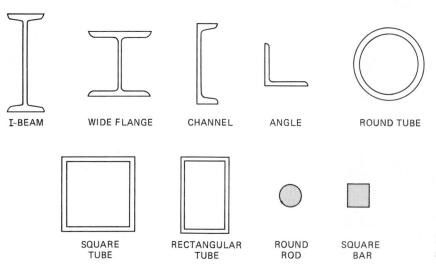

I-BEAM WIDE FLANGE CHANNEL ANGLE ROUND TUBE

SQUARE TUBE RECTANGULAR TUBE ROUND ROD SQUARE BAR

Fig. 12-23 Glass fiber structural shapes.

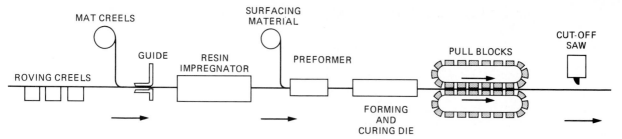

Fig. 12-24 Schematic of pultrusion process. *(Morrison Molded Fiber Glass Company)*

Sections produced by this method are most useful in areas where corrosion is a problem—water and sewage treatment plants, pulp and paper mills, and chemical plants. (See Fig. 12-25.) In addition to being corrosion-resistant, the material is nonconductive, nonmagnetic, and lightweight.

The material is extremely strong—stronger than steel when compared on a mass basis. Standard shapes have an ultimate tensile strength of 37,500 psi (258 MPa), while flat plate can develop 25,000 psi (172 MPa) when loaded in the longitudinal direction. It will not creep under long-term loads and has a coefficient of thermal expansion of 5×10^6 in/(in $\cdot$ °F) [9×10^6 mm/(mm $\cdot$ °C)], which is less than that of steel. The material can be sawn, drilled, routed, and turned on a lathe, but sections cannot be bent, rolled, or pressed as in steel. Connectors used to connect sections are screws, bolts, and adhesives. A combination of bolts and an adhesive produces the best results.

The material may be painted, but since it comes in standard colors, painting is usually not required. If painting is necessary, surfaces should be prepared by sanding or sandblasting. Most paints may be used with good results.

PLASTIC FOAM BOARDS   Rigid slabs of foamed plastic are finding increasing use for structural purposes. In Fig. 12-26, slabs of expanded polystyrene are used to form the roof deck for a hyperbolic

Fig. 12-25 Fiber-reinforced plastic structural sections used in corrosive environments. *(Morrison Molded Fiber Glass Company)*

329

Fig. 12-26 Rigid slabs of polystyrene used as roof decking. *(Dow Chemical Co.)*

paraboloid roof. Because of their flexibility, the slabs can be readily fitted to the contours of the roof. Later, the deck will be covered with a layer of concrete. In Fig. 12-27, similar rigid slabs are being used as decking but, in this case, over a steel cable frame.

Research is being carried out continually on the possibilities of further uses of plastics for structural components. Polystyrene is one material ideally suited for such purposes. It has rigidity, lightness, good impact resistance, and structural strength. Structural polystyrene items are stronger than com-

parable wood or metal ones. Like most plastics, it has the added advantage of being able to be molded into almost any desired shape. This could mean a reduction in the number of component parts required to form a given structure. Also, like many other plastics, polystyrene is resistant to shattering, is weather- and corrosion-resistant, and is dimensionally stable.

FABRICS Polyester and nylon fabrics, coated with PVC, provide an alternate method for enclosing large open areas. These fabrics, a result of space-age technology, are light, strong, durable, and remain pliable over large temperature changes. (See Fig. 12-28.)

A combination of glass-fiber fabric and a *Teflon* fluorocarbon resin has been used in fabric roof applications with much success. The glass-fiber fabric provides the strength for sustaining the necessary design loads, while the Teflon provides the flexibility, durability, and weather resistance. This type of coated fabric has been given a life expectancy of more than 20 years.

FOAMED INSULATION One of the most important uses of plastics in the construction industry is as insulation. *Polystyrene, polyurethane, phenolic resin,* and *vinyl resins* are the most common materials used in the manufacture of insulating materials.

Polystyrene and polyurethane are foamed by a patented process to about 40 times their original volume. Slabs are formed either by extrusion or by the molding process and a variety of sizes are man-

Fig. 12-27 Rigid foam plastic slabs for decking over a steel cable frame. *(Dow Chemical Co.)*

Fig. 12-28 Fabric structure.

ufactured, the most common being 24 × 96 in (600 × 2400 mm) in thicknesses of 1, 2, 3, and 4 in (25, 50, 75, and 100 mm). Polystyrene has a k (thermal conductivity) factor of about 0.25 and a density of 1.2 to 4.5 lb/ft^3 (19 to 72 kg/m^3), while polyurethane has a k factor of about 0.15 and a density of approximately 2 lb/ft^3 (32 kg/m^3). Both materials have extremely good insulation qualities and relatively high compressive strength and are flexible enough to be formed around curved surfaces.

Because of their high insulation values and resistance to moisture, these panels are used as perimeter insulation around foundation walls as well as for wall and roof insulation. (See Fig. 12-29.) These panels can also be used below grade for foundation protection against frost penetration without any detrimental effects to their insulation value. The panels are usually applied to walls with either cement mortar or a special plastic adhesive. Panels used as built-up roofing insulation are sometimes enclosed in a stiff paper covering so that asphalt adhesive can be used to cement them into place.

Another type of foamed insulation is one that is formulated on site using polyurethane or epoxy two-part resins. The process consists of injecting controlled amounts of resin liquid, a foaming catalyst, and a curing agent into the space to be insulated. The reaction forms a foam which expands and sets, filling the entire space. This type of insulation application is extremely useful when existing structures or installations are being retrofitted or upgraded.

Nonstructural Applications

Plastics have a large place in the manufacture of nonstructural materials used in construction. Materials falling into this category include wall and floor coverings, vapor and moisture barriers, flashing material, water stops, expansion-joint material, pipe and conduit, and a wide variety of hardware products.

RESILIENT FLOORING   A considerable number of floor coverings, both resilient and rigid, involve the use of plastics. Vinyl and vinyl-asbestos tile are resilient-type floor coverings in common use. Several very resilient floor coverings in sheet form are made partially or wholly of plastic. One such product consists of a sponge vinyl backing covered with a closely woven layer of synthetic fiber. A layer of colored vinyl covers the fibers and binds them to the backing, and a clear vinyl coating provides a tough wearing surface. A somewhat similar product is made by covering a backing of matted jute fibers with a thick, patterned coating of colored vinyl.

> **Vinyl tile**   Vinyl tile is made of a layer of vinyl plastic bonded to a flexible backing. Tiles are 6 × 9 in (150 × 225 mm) and 9 × 9 in (225 × 225 mm), in thicknesses of 0.08, 0.09, and 0.125 in (2, 2.4, and 3 mm). Feature strips 1 × 36 in (25 × 900 mm) and rolls 27, 45, and 54 in (675, 1125, and 1350 mm) wide are also available.
>
> Vinyl tiles may be applied to floors on or above grade and are laid in vinyl cement. For concrete floors on grade, a special waterproof cement is used. Vinyl is highly resistant to fats and oils, most acids, alkalis, and petroleum

Fig. 12-29   Foamed insulation board.

derivatives. A wide range of colors and designs is available.

Vinyl-cushioned flooring Vinyl-cushioned flooring is composed of a thick sponge vinyl backing covered with a layer of closely woven glass-fiber fabric to provide strength and stability. Over this is laid a layer of vinyl plastic imprinted with the color or colors desired, and finally a surface of clear vinyl is applied. These layers are bonded together by heat and result in a flexible flooring material approximately 0.15 in (3.8 mm) thick.

The flooring is produced in rolls 54 and 72 in (1350 and 1800 mm) wide and is laid in a special cement made for the purpose. Adjoining edges are joined with a special cement. Strong solvents should not be used for cleaning, and varnishes, shellacs, or lacquers should not be applied to the surface.

Linoleum Linseed oil is used as the binder in the manufacture of linoleum. It is oxidized by air treatment until it becomes a tough plastic substance somewhat like rubber. Powdered cork, resin gum, wood flour, and color pigments are then mixed with it, and the resulting mixture is spread over a burlap backing and rolled into sheets. Three thicknesses are made: $\frac{3}{32}$ in (2 mm) (A grade), $\frac{1}{8}$ in (3 mm) (AA grade), and $\frac{1}{4}$ in (6 mm) (AAA grade). It is produced in rolls 72 in (1800 mm) wide and as 9 × 9 in (225 × 225 mm) and 12 × 12 in (300 × 300 mm) linoleum tiles. Two types of roll linoleum are made: plain or battleship linoleum and inlaid linoleum. Plain linoleum is one single color, while inlaid linoleum is made up of several colors, which extend through to the burlap backing.

Linoleum can be laid on any wood floor above grade and can be laid over suspended concrete floors, providing they are dry. Two types of linoleum cement are used: plain for ordinary installations and waterproof cement for such locations as kitchens and bathrooms. Linoleum and linoleum tile should be laid over a thick felt paper base, which can be bonded to the subfloor with the same cement.

Cork tile Cork tile is made by mixing cork shavings with resin and compressing the plastic mixture into molds. Tiles are baked to set the resin. Two thicknesses of tile are produced: $\frac{3}{16}$ and $\frac{5}{16}$ in (4.5 and 8 mm). Sizes include 6-, 9-, and 12-in (150-, 225-, and 300-mm) squares and 6 × 12 in (150 × 300 mm) and 12 × 24 in (300 × 600 mm) rectangles.

The tiles are laid on floors above grade in a special adhesive and rolled down with a heavy roller. The surface is sanded and given a coat of filler and finally waxed.

Cork tiles are warm, quiet, and resilient but not as durable as many others. They resist water but not oils and grease.

Rubber flooring Rubber is used for flooring in the form of tiles. Synthetic rubber is used, since it has less tendency to oxidize than natural rubber. Pigments and plasticizers are mixed with the liquid rubber, and the mixture is rolled into sheets under pressure and cut into 6-, 9-, and 12-in (150-, 225-, and 300-mm) squares and 18 × 36 in (450 × 900 mm) rectangles, in thicknesses of $\frac{3}{32}$, $\frac{1}{8}$, and $\frac{3}{16}$ in (2, 3, and 4.5 mm).

Rubber tile is suitable for floors above grade and is laid in a rubber-base cement. It is very pliable and provides good resilience and relatively good sound absorption.

NONRESILIENT FLOORING Several hard-surface floor toppings involve the use of epoxy resins. A high-friction topping is made by applying a $\frac{1}{8}$- to $\frac{1}{4}$-in (3- to 6-mm) layer of the resin compound to a base floor and sprinkling sand or other abrasive material over the surface before curing takes place.

A smooth epoxy topping is produced by blending dry salt-free sand and white portland cement with the resin components. The mixture is troweled over a base floor primed with an epoxy-resin primer, to a depth of $\frac{1}{8}$ to $\frac{1}{4}$ in (3 to 6 mm).

A terrazzo topping can be produced by mixing small marble chips with the resin and spreading and leveling the mix with a trowel. After 24 h of curing, the surface can be ground, and the final grouting and polishing can be done in the next 48 h. (See Fig. 12-30.)

Plastic terrazzo In plastic terrazzo, an epoxy resin is used instead of portland cement paste as a binder for marble chips. A mixture of a liquid epoxy resin, inert filler, and color pig-

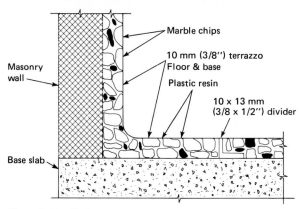

Fig. 12-30 Polyacrylate terrazzo.

ment is used as the resin component. A typical formulation consists of 100 lb (45.3 kg) of epoxy resin, 50 lb (22.65 kg) of fine calcium silicate, $2\frac{1}{4}$ lb (1 kg) of titanium dioxide, and $\frac{3}{4}$ lb (0.34 kg) of a mineral pigment. To this is added 10 lb (4.5 kg) of a hardening and curing agent, an aliphatic polymine. In this amount of binder, 450 lb (204 kg) of small marble chips may be used.

This plastic mixture is spread over the floor about $\frac{1}{4}$ in (6 mm) thick, after metal grid strips have been secured to the floor with an epoxy resin adhesive. After hardening (1 to 2 days after application), the topping can be ground smooth and polished.

This type of topping may be applied over a wood, concrete, or old terrazzo base. Mixes should be limited to about 100 lb (45 kg) total, because the mixture has a limited pot life—about 1 to $1\frac{1}{2}$ h at 24°C. This topping weighs about 3 lb/ft^2 (14.6 kg/m) and is $\frac{1}{4}$ in (6 mm) thick.

Plastic topping Epoxy resins, similar to those described above, are used to produce floor toppings in a variety of colors. The liquid resin, color pigment, and curing agent are mixed and spread over the surface in thicknesses of $\frac{1}{4}$ to $\frac{1}{2}$ in (6 to 12 mm). The material may be troweled smooth or left with a dimpled finish, as required. Application may be made over either a wood or a concrete base. Manufacturers' instructions must be followed as to the amount which may be mixed at one time and the thickness required for best service.

CARPETS The introduction of high-speed carpet-making machines and the development of a number of synthetic fabrics suitable for the manufacture of carpets have caused this product to become one of the most popular finish flooring materials in public and commercial, as well as residential, buildings.

The new machines—*tufting machines*—have made it possible to greatly accelerate the rate of production of carpet. Previously, the manufacturing processes included *weaving, looming, knitting,* and *needle punching.*

The introduction of the synthetic fabrics has provided an almost limitless supply of material, largely limited to *wool* until that time. The synthetic fibers introduced into the carpet industry include *rayon, nylon, acrylic, modacrylics, olefins (polypropylene),* and *polyesters.* Table 12-1 provides some basic information on modern carpet fabrics.

Tufted carpet A tufting machine is similar in principle to a sewing machine, but it sews any number of rows at a time, with hundreds of individual needles stitching simultaneously through a backing material as much as 15 ft (4.57 m) wide.

A secondary back is usually adhered to the carpet for added strength, dimensional stability, and tuft bind. In some cases, a high-density *foam-rubber, sponge, urethane,* or *vinyl* cushion may be used in place of the secondary back.

Carpet made on a tufting machine can be styled in several ways, such as *tweeds, solids,* and *stripes.* Pattern attachments on the machine produce high-low sculptured and embossed effects. Colorful designs may be printed over the pile, and multicolor effects may be achieved, either on the machine or by dyeing.

The pile may be cut to produce a *plush finish,* selectively sheared, for a *cut-and-loop* finish, or left completely uncut, for a *loop* finish.

Woven carpet Carpet weaving involves three basic carpet machines: *Velvet, Wilton,* and *Axminster* looms.

Velvet carpet uses the simplest of all carpet weaving techniques and is commonly available in solid colors. However, a wide range of color and texture variations is possible on a velvet loom. Included in the possible texture effects

Table 12-1
FIBERS USED IN CARPET MANUFACTURING

Characteristics	Generic Term					
	Acrylic	Modacrylic	Nylon	Olefin (Poly-propylene)	Polyester	Wool
Definition	Fiber-forming substance is any long-chain synthetic polymer composed of at least 85% by weight of acrylonitrile units.	Fiber in which fiber-forming substance is any long-chain synthetic polymer composed of less than 85% but at least 35% by weight of acrylonitrile units.	Fiber-forming substance is any long-chain synthetic polyamide having recurring amide groups as an integral part of the polymer chain.	Fiber in which fiber-forming substance is any long-chain synthetic polymer composed of at least 85% by weight of ethylene, propylene, or other olefin units.	Fiber in which fiber-forming substance is any long-chain synthetic polymer composed of at least 85% by weight of an ester of a dihydric alcohol and terephthalic acid.	Fiber in which amino acids units are combined into peptide chains possessing multi-dimensional stability resulting from hydrogen bonding and cross linking forces of cystine molecules through their sulfur bonds.
Standard moisture regain (%)	1.3 to 2.5	0.4 to 4	4 to 4.5	-8-	0.4 to 0.8	
Effects of heat	215–254°C sticking temperature	135–149°C sticking temperature	Sticks 160–190°C, melts 218°C	Melts 121–167°C	Sticks 230–235°C, melts 250–290°C	Scorches at 205°C, chars at 300°C
Specific gravity	1.16 to 1.18	1.31 to 1.37	1.14	0.90 to 0.96	1.38	
Effects of acids, alkalis, and solvents	Generally good resistance to mineral acids. Fair to good resistance to weak cold alkalis. Good resistance to common solvents.	Excellent resistance to highly concentrated acids. Unaffected by alkalis. Soluble in warm acetone.	Resistant to weak acids but decomposes in strong mineral acids. Alkalis have little or no effect. Soluble in phenol and formic acid.	Excellent resistance to most acids and alkalis. Generally soluble above 71°C in chlorinated hydrocarbons.	Good to excellent resistance to mineral acids. Some affected by concentrated sulfuric acid. Decomposes in alkalis at the boil. Generally insoluble in common solvents but soluble in some phenolic compounds.	Unaffected by mineral acids. Generally good resistance to weak cold alkalis. Resistance to organic solvents.
Dyestuffs used	Acid, basic cationic, chrome, direct, disperse, naphthol, neutral premetallized, and sulfur. Some fibers are solution dyed.	Basic, cationic, disperse, neutral premetallized, and vat.	Acid, direct disperse, and premetallized. Some fibers are now solution dyed.	Usually pigmented before extrusion. When modified can be dyed with selected dyestuffs.	Cationic, developed, and disperse.	Acid, premetallized, fiber reactant, chrome vats, and direct.
Resistance to mildew, aging, sunlight, and abrasion	Excellent resistance to mildew and aging and generally good resistance to sunlight and abrasion.	Not attacked by mildew. Good resistance to abrasion, sunlight, and aging but some loss in tensile strength may be noted in the case of Dynel upon prolonged exposure to sunlight.	Excellent resistance to mildew, aging, and abrasion. Some degradation may result from prolonged exposure to sunlight.	Not attacked by mildew. Good resistance to aging, abrasion, and indirect sunlight. Can be stabilized to give good resistance to direct sunlight.	Excellent resistance to mildew, aging, and abrasion. In some instances prolonged exposure to sunlight will result in some loss of strength.	Generally excellent resistance to aging and abrasion. Good fastness to sunlight and mildew.

SOURCE: Canadian Carpet Institute.

are *cut pile plushes, cut pile twist, pebbly uncut loop pile,* and *multilevel sculptured effects.*

A *Wilton* carpet loom is distinguished by its specialized jacquard system of perforated pattern cards, which regulate the feeding of different colored yarns onto the pile surface.

The number of colors possible on a Wilton loom is limited, but the jacquard system produces very accurate reproduction of intricate patterns. As weaving proceeds, one color at a time is drawn into the pile and the colors not required are buried beneath the surface. These buried yarns give additional body, resilience, and strength to Wilton carpet.

It is available in a wide range of multicolor patterns, as well as solids, and in numerous textures, including modern carved effects.

Axminster carpet is distinguished by an almost limitless choice of designs and colors. Patterns may be stylized, geometric, classic, modern, or floral.

Axminster looms are nearly as versatile as hand weaving. The pile is cut, with few exceptions, and almost all the yarn appears on the surface. Another distinguishing feature is the heavily ribbed back. The carpet can be rolled lengthwise but not the opposite way.

Loomed carpet Loomed carpet, produced on a modified upholstery machine, is also manufactured for commercial use. Because a permanently bonded sponge rubber back is an integral part of the carpet, it is known as a sponge-bonded high-density fabric. Pile yarns are normally limited to nylon, and width is limited to a 6-ft (1.8-m) maximum.

Loomed carpet has a tightly woven, extra-dense, level pile. Though it can be manufactured in solid colors, it is most commonly produced as multicolor tweeds.

Knitted carpet Knitted carpet, like woven carpet, is fabricated in one operation, face and back simultaneously. Backing yarns, stitching yarns, and pile yarns are looped together with three sets of needles. To give the carpet additional body, a coat of latex is applied to the back, and sometimes a secondary back, similar to those used in tufted carpet, is added in the finishing process.

Knitted carpet is usually in tweeds or solid colors, though some patterns are possible with machine modifications. Loop pile surface is most common, though cut pile plushes can be made, also with machine modifications.

Needle-punched carpet Needle-punched carpet is a flat, abrasion-resistant sandwich of unspun fibers normally covering a prewoven fabric core. The face and back are formed by hundreds of barbed needles punching through blankets of fiber to mesh them permanently together. The result is an extremely dense sheet, without pile, of considerable weight and thickness, which may be printed with colored designs. The material, which may have a high-density rubber cushion bonded to it, can be supplied in broad rolls, like other carpet, or in carpet tiles.

INTERIOR FINISHES Many interior finishing products are manufactured from various types of plastic. Plastic wall tiles in $4\frac{1}{4}$ and $8\frac{1}{2}$ in (108 and 216 mm) squares are made from polystyrene and urea formaldehyde resins in a wide range of colors. They are applied with special adhesives, and the joints are pointed with a special grout after the tiles are in place. (See Fig. 12-31.) They are not as durable as ceramic tiles but are less expensive.

Rigid panels or sheets in color and color patterns are made from styrene, acrylic, and vinyl plastic. Hardboard, plaster-board, and paperboard are plastic-coated or covered with a thin film of vinyl containing a printed pattern. Gypsum board and hardboard are also produced with one face clad in vinyl fabric.

Flexible vinyl sheets with textured patterns are available as wall covering. These are applied like wallpaper and are useful where high resistance to damage and low maintenance costs are important. Steel- and aluminum-backed vinyl sheets are produced which can be formed and shaped without damaging the vinyl covering.

Decorative plastic laminates are so called because they consist of a number of layers of material laminated together to form a sheet, one face of which contains a decorative pattern of some sort. The sheet which contains the pattern—the *decor* sheet—consists of a durable, pigmented, alpha-cellulose paper carrying a pattern which usually contains three colors in addition to that of the paper.

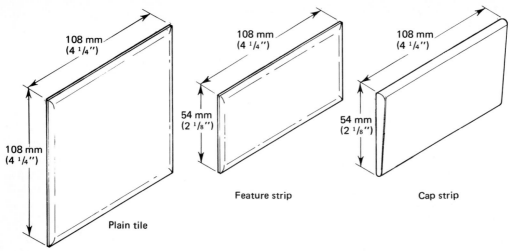

108 mm
(4 1/4″)

108 mm
(4 1/4″)

108 mm
(4 1/4″)

54 mm
(2 1/8″)

54 mm
(2 1/8″)

108 mm
(4 1/4″)

Plain tile

Feature strip

Cap strip

Fig. 12-31   Plastic wall tile.

The pattern may be applied by rotogravure printing, by silk screening, by letterpress, or even by hand drawing and painting. After the pattern has been applied, the sheet is impregnated with melamine resin solution and dried.

The back of the decor sheet is then bonded to at least seven sheets of a phenolic-impregnated kraft paper, while its face is overlaid with a sheet of alpha-cellulose tissue, impregnated with malamine resin. (See Fig. 12-32.) The whole assembly is bonded into a single, hard, durable, wear-, heat-, light-, and stain-resistant sheet under pressure of 1400 psi (9.65 MPa), at a temperature of about 140°C.

Common panel thicknesses of $\frac{1}{32}$, $\frac{1}{16}$, $\frac{1}{10}$, and $\frac{1}{8}$ in (0.75, 1.5, 2.5, and 3 mm) are used as cabinet and tabletop surfacers and as wall coverings, but industrial laminates can be made to order from $\frac{1}{8}$ to $1\frac{1}{2}$ in (3 to 38 mm) thick. Standard widths are 24, 30, 36, 48, and 60 in (600, 750, 900, 1200, and 1500 mm); lengths range from 5 to 12 ft (1.5 to 3.6 m). A great many colors and patterns are available, including a wide range of wood-grain patterns.

Plastic laminates are usually bonded to plywood or particle board using contact cement, providing a durable, easily maintained surface. Special moldings, either metal or plastic, are used as panel dividers, edgings, and corner trims (see Fig. 12-33). Plastic laminates are used on room dividers, countertops, wall panels (see Fig. 12-34), and desk tops, and in similar areas where surface durability is required.

Plastic wall fabrics and films of vinyl are used in much the same way as wallpaper. Molded sheets of plastic reinforced with glass fiber which simulate brick and stone may be used for either interior or exterior. Molded plastic acoustical tile, backed by wool or glass-fiber wool, has been introduced, along with opaque plastic ceiling tile for use with suspended ceiling systems.

A whole range of trim and molding materials, made from vinyl, conforms in general to their coun-

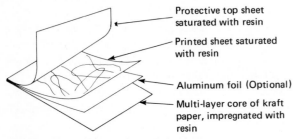

Protective top sheet saturated with resin

Printed sheet saturated with resin

Aluminum foil (Optional)

Multi-layer core of kraft paper, impregnated with resin

Fig. 12-32   Build-up of plastic laminate.

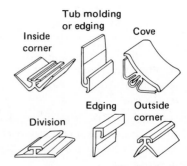

Inside corner

Tub molding or edging

Cove

Division

Edging

Outside corner

Fig. 12-33   Moldings used with plastic laminate wall panels.

Fig. 12-34   Wall panels covered with plastic laminate.

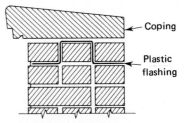

Fig. 12-35   Plastic parapet flashing.

terparts in wood. They are made in 8 ft (2400 mm) lengths, with a wood-grain finish in various colors, intended to harmonize with prefinished plywood or hardboard panels.

MOISTURE CONTROL   Films used as moisture and vapor barriers are commonly made from polyethylene and polyvinyl chloride in thicknesses of 2, 4, and 6 mils. Both transparent and black film are made, in widths of 3 to 20 ft (0.9 to 6 m). For use as flashing, polyvinyl chloride sheets are manufactured in three thicknesses: 0.02, 0.04, and 0.06 in (0.5, 1.02, and 1.5 mm), in standard rolls of 36 ft (11 m), 36 in (900 mm) wide; widths of 9, 18, 27, and 54 in (225, 450, 675, and 1375 mm) are also available. (See Fig. 12-35.)

Water stops (strips placed across construction joints in concrete walls to prevent water passage) and strips to be used to form control joints in concrete block walls are made from polyvinyl chloride. (See Fig. 12-36.)

Sheets of glass-fiber fabric are used in conjunction with a coating of thermosetting liquid resin to produce a waterproof membrane (see Fig. 12-37). A number of coats are used to provide the required thickness of film to ensure water tightness. This type of roof covering is tough, resilient, flexible, and resistant to both heat and abrasion.

Liquid plastic is also sprayed onto roof decks to form what is known as an envelope roofing. This liquid envelope consists of a pigmented, opaque vinyl plastic which is applied by means of a spray gun to form a continuous film 30 to 40 mils thick. It can be applied over almost any type of roof deck or existing roofing material with the exception of wood shingles. When it is to be used over an existing built-up roof, the surface should first be primed. This liquid-envelope type of roofing is particularly useful for roofs with irregular shapes or very steep slopes or both.

The plastic dries very quickly to form a film which, for a 40-mil thickness, has a tensile strength of about 500 psi (3.4 MPa) and an ultimate elongation of about 200 percent. The vinyl coat is highly resistant to commonly encountered industrial atmospheres containing dirt, grime, and mild acid fumes. It is also highly resistant to deterioration due to extended exposure to sunlight.

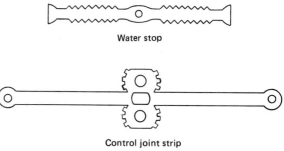

Water stop

Control joint strip

Fig. 12-36   Typical control strips.

Fig. 12-37   Glass fiber and liquid resin roofing.

Plastic Pipe

Several types of plastic are used to produce rigid and flexible pipe. Probably the largest single use for ABS plastics in the construction field is in the manufacture of rigid *drain, waste,* and *vent* (dwv) pipe and fittings. (See Fig. 12-38.) They are light in weight, easy to cut to length, and easy to assemble and install, using the proper ABS solvent cements. (See Fig. 12-39.) Rigid pipe is also made from PVC (see Fig. 12-40), fluoroplastics, and phenylene oxide. Flexible pipe and tubing are made from polyethylene and the vinyls. For example, polyvinylidene fluoride pipe is used in chemical processing equipment, because of its resistance to most chemicals and solvents. Extensive use is being made of both rigid and flexible pipe in water systems, with flexible pipe having some advantages because of the long lengths available and because its use may eliminate some fittings.

Some plastic fittings for flexible pipe are made to fit inside the pipe, with a clamp around the end to hold the fitting in place. (See Fig. 12-41.) A more recent development for small pipe fittings has been the *quick-connect* type of fitting (see Fig. 12-42), for which no clamps are necessary. Pipe and fitting are merely pushed together, and pulled to make the connection, as illustrated in Fig. 12-43.

Auxiliary Uses

Auxiliary uses of plastic in the manufacture and use of construction materials cover a wide field. These are uses in which the plastic plays a hidden or inconspicuous but important role.

FORMS FOR PRECAST CONCRETE   One important auxiliary use of plastics in construction is in the making of forms for precast concrete products. Such forms are particularly useful in situations in which a considerable number of identical shapes are required, as is often the case in architectural precast concrete design, where a number of identical wall panels will be used in a structure.

Such forms are light in weight, have greater strength per unit weight than most other materials, have almost unlimited design possibilities, are resilient, and have a high resistance to impact. The form model may be made of plaster of paris, clay, steel, or wood, with plaster of paris being a favorite medium because it lends itself to the development of complex forms.

On completion, the pattern is first sprayed with a nonbonding agent, such as polyvinyl alcohol, to prevent the resin from sticking to it. A plastic gel coat is then applied, which accurately reproduces the exact configuration of the mold. Next, the mold

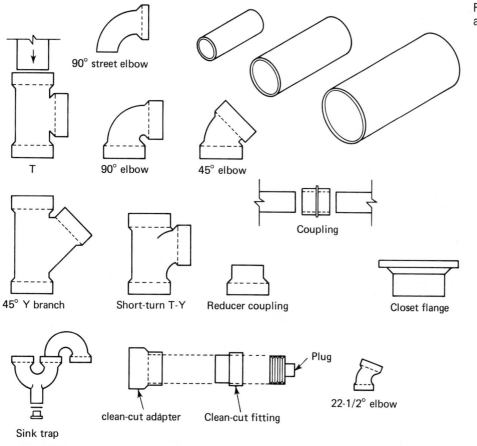

Fig. 12-38 Plastic pipe and fittings.

90° street elbow

T

90° elbow

45° elbow

45° Y branch

Short-turn T-Y

Reducer coupling

Coupling

Closet flange

Sink trap

clean-cut adapter

Clean-cut fitting

Plug

22-1/2° elbow

Fig. 12-39 ABS dwv pipe being assembled. *(Plastic Pipe Institute)*

Fig. 12-40 PVC dwv pipe being assembled. *(Allcraft Foundation; Photo by Bruce Tilden)*

body is built up to the desired thickness with glass fiber, a polyester resin, and a catalyst and allowed to cure, after which it is removed from the master pattern, ready for use.

ADHESIVES In the manufacture of plywood, chipboard, particle board and hardboard, *phenolic, urea formaldehyde, epoxy,* and *amino resins* are used for bonding *veneer layers, chips,* or *wood particles* into solid sheets. Similar adhesives are used extensively in the manufacture of glue-laminated beams and in the fabrication of wood trusses.

Epoxy, phenolic, and *amino resins* are used as adhesives where metal, glass, concrete, porcelain, or rigid plastics are involved. They are also used when adhesives, rather than nails or screws, are used to attach plywood or gypsum board to stud walls.

MATERIAL COATINGS Another important auxiliary use of plastics is as a coating for another material. Plywood, hardboard, and particle board are produced with a tough coating of *diallyl phthalate, amino resin, epoxy resin, phenolic resin, polyurethane,* or *polyvinyl chloride* to render them more waterproof and to produce a smooth, grainless paint surface. Similar resins are used to coat concrete forms to protect plywood, hardboard, and particle board from damage and to prevent the concrete from adhering to them. Plywood and laminated cedar siding are produced that are surfaced with a layer of melamine-impregnated kraft paper to produce a smooth waterproof paint surface.

Silicone, which has extremely good water-repellent properties and good chemical and physiological inertness, is used as a coating for exterior masonry to protect it from water penetration and to render it easier to clean.

Amino resins are used in the treatment of textiles—for example, draperies—to provide shrinkage control and render them water-repellent and heat-resistant.

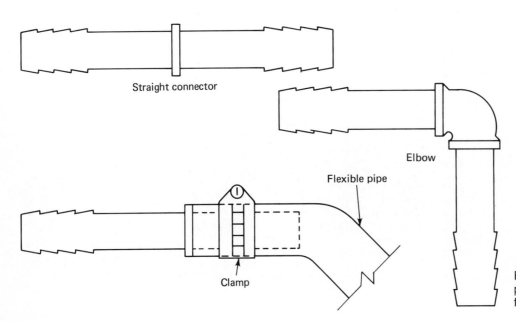

Straight connector

Elbow

Flexible pipe

Clamp

Fig. 12-41 Typical plastic connectors for flexible pipe.

Fig. 12-42 Quick-connection fittings. *(Bristol Products Co.)*

LIGHTS AND SUNSCREENS Acrylics, polycarbonate, polyvinyl chloride, ionomer resins, and polyesters are used in the manufacture of lighting fixtures, diffusers, lenses, and shields used in lighting systems. Sunscreens of colored acrylic or polycarbonate may reduce solar-heat gain, and thereby the air-conditioning load in a building, by as much as 50 percent.

PAINTS AND VARNISHES Plastics form the basis of various paints, enamels, lacquers, and varnishes. *Vinyl, polyurethane, acrylics, epoxy resins, cellulose acetate,* and *phenolic resins* are all used in the manufacture of coatings of this type.

Vinyl, epoxy resins, allyl resins, fluoroplastics, polypropylene, and *polyurethane* are used to coat the inside and/or outside surfaces of metal pipe to make it more resistant to rust and corrosion.

CAULKING AND SEALING COMPOUNDS Many of the caulking, sealing, and glazing compounds and expansion joint fillers are manufactured from synthetic resins. Premolded, foam-rubber-like expansion joint filler is made from expanded *polyvinyl chloride* and expanded *polyurethane* by the extrusion process. (See Fig. 12-44.)

Sealing, glazing, and caulking compounds are made from *acrylics, liquid polymer polysulfide* (see Fig. 12-44), and *butyl compounds (styrene butadiene),* normally applied by a caulking gun.

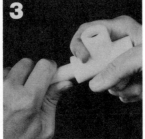

Fig. 12-43 To make a connection: (1) prepare, (2) push, (3) pull. *(Bristol Products Co.)*

Fig. 12-44 Using extruded caulking and polysulfide sealant. *(Thiokol Corp.)*

Polybutene-based glazing mastic is produced in ribbon form by extrusion. Other sealing compounds are made in two parts which are mixed on the job and poured as a liquid—which cures into a pliable sealer—into the space to be sealed.

MISCELLANEOUS AUXILIARY USES OF PLASTICS Other examples of auxiliary uses of plastics are (1) ABS resins for plumbing fixtures; (2) acetal homopolymers for plumbing fixtures, shower heads, valves, and fittings; (3) acetal copolymers for plumbing fixtures, diverter valves, and pumps; (4) epoxy resins for pipe and tank linings and heavy-duty floor and wall coatings over masonry, steel, and wooden surfaces; (5) fluoroplastics for pump linings, valve fittings, packing gaskets, and pipe-thread sealants; (6) ionomer resins for wire coating; (7) phenylene oxide for pumps and pump parts, water-sprinkler systems, shower heads, power-tool cases, and handles; (8) polyethylene for wire and pipe coating, filaments for carpeting, and backing for carpets; (9) silicones for lubricants and mold coatings (because of their release properties); and (10) nylons for tubing and extruded coatings.

GLOSSARY

acetal	Thermoplastic made by polymerization of trioxane with another material which provides carbon-to-carbon bonds.
acrylic	A glasslike thermoplastic resin made by polymerizing esters of acrylic acid.
aliphatic polymine	A polymerized compound containing a fatty substance.
alpha-cellulose	One of a group of cellulose compounds.
allyls	A family of esters based on allyl alcohol—monomers used as cross-linking agents in polymer resins.
amino	A compound containing the group NH_2.
asphalt mastic	A plastic flooring material containing asphalt.
blowpin	A fine nozzle through which air is blown.
calendaring	Pressing between rollers.
catalyst	A substance which speeds up a reaction without undergoing change itself.
cellulosic	A substance containing cellulose.
ceramic tile	Glazed clay tile.
epoxy resin	A class of thermosetting resins derived from certain special types of organic chemicals; specifically, epichlorhydrin and a double phenol.
ester	A compound formed by the substitution of a hydrocarbon radical for the acid hydrogen in an acid.
ethylene	A colorless gaseous hydrocarbon product.
extrusion	The forcing out of a material through an opening.
fluoroplastic	One of a family of polymers having some or all of the hydrogen replaced by fluorine.
hyperbolic paraboloid	Basically, a warped parallelogram.
impregnate	To soak or fill.
ionomer	A polymer in which the intermolecular structure is cross-linked by ionized carboxyl molecules.
melamine	A white crystalline compound made from calcium cyanamide.

melamine resin	A synthetic resin made by combining melamine and formaldehyde.
methyl pentene	A monomer used in the polymerization of polymethylpentene based on methyl alcohol.
mil	1/1000 in (0.0254 mm).
monolithic film	A film containing no joints.
nylon	A synthetic plastic made from coal, tar, and water.
phenol	A crystalline compound made by the distillation of organic substances such as wood or coal.
phenolic	A synthetic resin made by the reaction of a phenol with an aldehyde.
phenylene oxide	A polymer formulated by oxidation coupling of phenolic monomers.
plasticizer	An agent added to various plastics to make them softer and more flexible.
polycarbonate	A polyester made by linking certain phenols through carbonate groups.
polyester	A linear polymer made by linear linking of oxybenzoyl units.
polyethylene	A thermoplastic resin made by polymerizing ethylene.
polyimide	A polymer based on the combination of certain anhydrides with aromatic di-amines.
polymer	A compound consisting of the same elements, in the same proportions, as another, but with higher molecular weight.
polymerize	To change into another compound with higher molecular weight and different physical properties, by the union of two or more molecules of the same kind.
polyolefin	A polymer composed of open-chain hydrocarbons having double bonds.
polypropylene	A polymer produced by the linking of repeated propylene monomers.
polystyrene	A clear, colorless plastic resin, made by polymerizing styrene.
polysulfone	A polymer produced by the reaction of a sodium salt of propane with sulfone.
primer	A first coat used to prepare a surface for further treatment.
reciprocating screw	A screw which moves backward and forward like a piston.
resilient	Elastic, having the ability to regain its original shape after being deformed.
resin	A solid, semisolid, or liquid substance which may be a natural or a synthetic organic material.
rotogravure	A process of making prints by etched cylindrical plates fixed to the rollers of a rotary printing press.
sandwich panel	A panel made by enclosing a sheet or slab of material with facings of different material.
silicone	A synthetic resin made by polymerizing an organic silicon compound.
silk screen	A printing process in which semiliquid pigment is pressed through fine-meshed silk to form a given design on a surface below.
styrene	A liquid hydrocarbon made from cinnamic acid.
sulfone	A compound containing sulfur dioxide, united with carbon.
synthetic	A material formed by the artificial building up of simple compounds.
terrazzo	A type of flooring in which the surface consists of marble chips in irregular pattern.
thermal conductivity	Heat-transmitting ability.

transfer chamber	A container in which liquid is held to be transferred to a mold.
ultraviolet stabilizer	A material added to a plastic to make it more resistant to the degrading effects of ultraviolet light.
urea	A soluble crystalline compound made from carbon dioxide and ammonia and condensed with formaldehyde to produce urea-formaldehyde resin.
vinyl	A thermoplastic resin made by the polymerization of a vinyl compound such as vinyl acetate.

REVIEW QUESTIONS

1. **a.** Name the two general classes of synthetic plastics.

b. Describe the primary differences between these two classes.

2. **a.** List the three steps that are generally involved in the production of plastic products.

b. Explain why this system of production is usually employed.

3. Explain how transfer molding differs from compression molding.

4. **a.** What is meant by extrusion forming?

b. What types of products are formed in this way?

c. How do you differentiate between plastic sheets and plastic films?

5. Name five uses made of plastic laminates in building construction.

6. **a.** Outline the extent to which plastic products are used for structural purposes.

b. What do you consider to be the future of plastics in this field?

7. **a.** Give three reasons why plastic material has become important in thermal insulation.

b. List three methods of using plastic materials as insulation.

8. Give three reasons why plastic films are so widely uses as a moisture barrier.

9. Give three common uses of foamed-plastic building boards.

10. What is resilient flooring?

11. What are the differences between battleship linoleum and inlaid linoleum?

12. Outline the differences between tufted carpet and woven carpet.

13. **a.** What is meant by auxiliary uses of plastics?

b. Name four common auxiliary uses of plastics in construction.

SELECTED SOURCES OF INFORMATION

Armstrong Cork Co., Lancaster, Pa.
Canadian Carpet Institute, Montreal, Que.
CIBA-GEIGY Ltd., Toronto, Ont.
CIBA Products Company, Fairlawn, N.J.
Dominion Oilcloth & Linoleum Company, Ltd., Montreal, Que.
Domtar Construction Materials, Arborite Division, Montreal, Que.
Dow Chemical Co., Midland, Mich.
Dupont Canada, Inc., Toronto, Ont.
Fiberglas Canada Ltd., Toronto, Ont.
Genstar Building Materials Co., Irving, Tex.

Harris Manufacturing Co., Johnson City, Tenn.
Ingersoll-Rand, Nashua, N.H.
Modern Plastics Encyclopedia, McGraw-Hill Book Company, Inc., New York, N.Y.
Monsanto, St. Louis, Mo.
Morrison Molded Fiber Glass Company, Bristol, Va.
Thiokol, Chemical Division, Trenton, N.J.

REFERENCES

1. Beach, Norman E., *Plastic Laminate Materials: Their Properties and Usage,* Foster Publishing Company, Long Beach, Ca., 1967.
2. Lubin, George, *Handbook of Fiberglass and Advanced Plastics Composites,* Van Nostrand Reinhold Company, New York, 1969.
3. Morgan, Phillip, *Glass Reinforced Plastics,* 3d ed., Interscience Publishers, Inc., New York, 1961.
4. Shah, Vishu, *Handbook of Plastics Testing Technology,* John Wiley & Sons, New York, 1984.

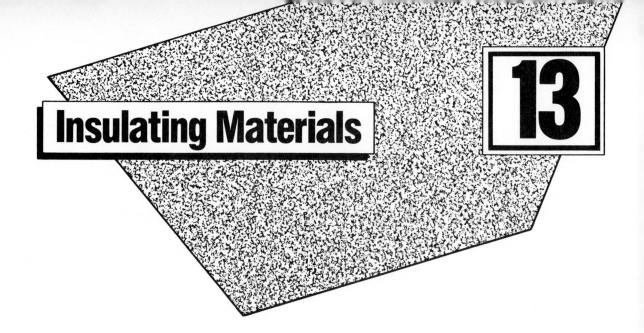

Insulating Materials

13

THERMAL INSULATION

The instability of supply of traditional energy supplies in the past few years and the high cost of alternative ones has had one positive effect on the industrial nations of the world—a realization of the importance of conservation. The construction industry has taken up the challenge through the development of new materials, building concepts, and improved workmanship in an effort to provide buildings that are as energy efficient as possible. The prime concern of building designers today is to ensure that the occupants and the equipment that they use will function at peak efficiency and comfort, and yet use the minimum amount of energy. In dealing with these concerns, it has become evident that proper installation of thermal insulation produces the most significant results for the money invested.

Heat Transfer

The transfer of heat always occurs from warm to cool. In buildings, where the ideal situation is to have a relatively stable temperature, two situations arise. In winter, energy must be used to maintain a comfortable temperature; without proper insulation, heat is lost to the colder outside air. In summer, when temperatures are usually higher outside than inside, the building interior must be cooled to keep it comfortable. The less insulation that is used, the greater are the costs for air-conditioning.

Heat is transferred in three ways: *conduction, convection,* and *radiation.* When a wall panel is subjected to a temperature differential, the wall feels cool to the touch on the warm side. The reason for this is that the inside heat is being conducted (led) from the warmer side to the cooler side. To prevent heat loss by conduction, materials that are poor conductors of heat must be used. Usually, the less dense the material, the better the resistance to heat loss by conduction.

Air that is heated expands and rises. During this movement, if it comes in contact with cooler surfaces, some of its energy is given up. This type of energy loss due to convection currents occurs inside of walls and ceilings that have overly large air spaces. To minimize this effect, air spaces should be kept relatively shallow—not over 1 in (25 mm)—and be divided into small, enclosed compartments. The convection currents set up in these confined spaces are insignificant and cause negligible heat loss.

Radiation is the third method of heat transfer. Heat that is absorbed by a wall panel will be radiated to the surrounding cooler air. One method of reducing the amount of radiated heat is to use reflective surfaces which prevent the absorption of heat.

Thermal Properties

In order to establish insulation values for the various materials, some means of designating their thermal properties is necessary. Some common terms that are used when dealing with insulation qualities of materials are as follows:

THERMAL CONDUCTIVITY k This is the term used to indicate the amount of heat that will pass through a unit of area of a material at a temperature difference of one degree. The lower the k value, the better the insulation qualities of the material. Units are the following:

$$(Btu \cdot in)/(h \cdot ft^2 \cdot °F) \qquad W/(m \cdot °C)$$

$\qquad$ U.S. Customary $\qquad\qquad\qquad$ Metric

CONDUCTANCE C Conductance indicates the amount of heat that passes through a given thickness of material:

$$Conductance = \frac{thermal\ conductivity}{thickness}$$

Units are:

$$Btu/(h \cdot ft^2 \cdot °F) \qquad W/(m^2 \cdot °C)$$

$\qquad$ U.S. Customary $\qquad\qquad$ Metric

For SI units, thickness is expressed in meters; in U.S. Customary units, thickness is expressed in inches.

THERMAL RESISTANCE (*RSI* FOR METRIC AND *R* FOR U.S. CUSTOMARY)   Thermal resistance is that property of a material that resists the flow of heat through the material. Resistance is the reciprocal of conductance:

$$R = \frac{1}{C}$$

Units are:

$$(hr \cdot ft^2 \cdot °F)/Btu \qquad (m^2 \cdot °C)/W$$

$\qquad$ U.S. Customary $\qquad\qquad$ Metric

The total thermal resistance of a building system is the sum of the individual thermal resistances of the materials used to make up that system. It is given the symbol R_t.

THERMAL TRANSMITTANCE U Thermal transmittance is the amount of heat that passes through all the materials in a system. It is the reciprocal of the total resistance:

$$U = \frac{1}{R_t}$$

Using proper measuring procedures, values can be established for these basic terms for the various materials that are used in the construction industry. Once these values are established, they can be used as guides to help designers choose the appropriate materials for a particular building application. Table 13-1 lists a few of the common materials and their thermal properties.

Kinds of Thermal Insulation

All the materials used to prevent heat losses are known as thermal insulation. There are nine basic kinds: *loose fill, blankets, batts, structural insulation board, slab* or *block insulation, reflective insulation, sprayed-on, foamed-in-place,* and *corrugated insulations.*

LOOSE FILL   Loose-fill insulation is generally bulky and can be divided into two main types; (1) fibrous and (2) granular. The fibrous type is made from mineral wool—*rock, glass,* or *slag wool*—or *vegetable fiber*—usually wood fiber. Granular insulations are made from expanded minerals such as *perlite* and *vermiculite* or from ground vegetable matter such as *granulated cork.*

BLANKET INSULATION   Blanket insulation is made from fibrous material, such as *mineral wool, wood fiber, cotton fiber,* or *animal hair,* manufactured in the form of a mat. Mats are made in various thicknesses and cut in a variety of widths, sometimes with a paper cover. (See Fig. 13-1.)

Fig. 13-1   Rolled blanket insulation.

Table 13-1
THERMAL PROPERTIES OF MATERIALS

	Thermal Resistance		Thermal Conductivity[a]	
	RSI	*R*	*k* (SI)	*k* (U.S. Customary)
Brick, clay, 4 in (100 mm)	0.07	0.42	1.43	9.52
Built-up roofing	0.08	0.44		
Concrete block, 8 in (200 mm):				
Cinder	0.30	1.72	0.67	4.65
Lightweight aggregate	0.35	2.00	0.57	4.00
Glass, clear, $\frac{1}{4}$ in (6 mm)	0.16	0.91	0.04	0.27
Gypsum sheathing, $\frac{1}{2}$ in (12.5 mm)	0.08	0.43	0.16	1.16
Insulation, per 1 in (25 mm):				
Fiberboard	0.49	2.80	0.051	0.36
Glass fiber	0.52	2.95	0.048	0.34
Expanded polystyrene	0.75	4.23	0.033	0.24
Rigid urethane	1.05	6.00	0.024	0.17
Vermiculite	0.36	2.08	0.069	0.48
Wood shavings	0.42	2.44	0.060	0.41
Moving air	0.03	0.17		
Particle board, $\frac{1}{2}$ in (12.5 mm)	0.11	0.62	0.114	0.81
Plywood, softwood, $\frac{3}{4}$ in (19 mm)	0.17	0.97	0.112	0.77
Stucco, $\frac{3}{4}$ in (19 mm)	0.02	0.11	0.95	6.82

[a] For SI values, thickness is in meters. For U.S. Customary values, thickness is in inches.

SOURCE: Values were obtained from various manufacturers' data. Complete lists are available from ASHRAE *Handbook of Fundamentals* and the National Research Council, Ottawa, Ont.

BATTS Batts are similar in basic manufacture to blankets, but they are restricted as to length, usually being 4 ft (1.2 m) or less. Some are paper covered, with paper tabs along the long edges for easier attachment to the frame, while others are made without a cover and fit between framing members by friction. (See Fig. 13-2.)

Fig. 13-2   Friction-fit insulation batts.

STRUCTURAL INSULATION BOARD Structural insulation board is made from a variety of substances, such as cane, wood, and mineral fibers. It is used for various purposes, such as exterior or interior sheathing, insulating roof decking, roof insulation board, interior finishing board, backer, and insulating from board.

SLAB INSULATION Slab or block insulation is made in rigid units, normally smaller in area than insulation board, though some of them may be made from two or more pieces of *insulation board* cemented together to make a thick slab. This type of insulation is also made from *cork, shredded wood and cement, mineral wool with binder, vermiculite and asphalt, cellular glass, foamed concrete, foamed plastic, cellular hard rubber,* or from *concrete made with perlite, vermiculite, or expanded clay* as aggregate.

REFLECTIVE INSULATION Reflective insulations are composed of metallic or other special surfaces with or without some type of backing. Unlike all others, reflective insulations rely on their surface characteristics, thickness of air space, temperature difference, etc., for their insulating value. It is important that reflective insulations be installed so that the reflective surface faces an air space of at least $\frac{3}{4}$ in (19 mm). Properly installed, they may also act as a vapor barrier.

SPRAYED-ON INSULATION Sprayed-on insulations are produced by mixing some fibrous or cellular material with an adhesive and blowing the mixture onto the surface to be insulated. Areas that are otherwise difficult to insulate because of their shape, location, etc., are treated in this manner.

FOAMED-IN-PLACE INSULATION Foamed-in-place, or *cellular mass*, insulation is made from synthetic liquid resins. Two ingredients are used which, when mixed, produce a foam which solidifies to fill the space into which the mixture was introduced.

CORRUGATED INSULATION Corrugated insulation is made from paper, corrugated and cemented into multiple layers. Some types are sprayed with an adhesive which hardens to give the product extra stiffness, while others are faced with foil to provide extra insulative values.

Description, Uses, and Application of Thermal Insulations

LOOSE-FILL INSULATIONS Fibrous loose-fill insulation is made by passing a stream of molten rock, glass, or slag through a jet of air. The jet blows the material into long, thin threads which solidify into a wool-like mass. This is packed into bags, ready for application. In some cases it is poured from bags into spaces between framing members, but more often it is blown into open and concealed spaces by compressed air. This will produce a more uniform and more compact job than can be obtained by hand methods. Mineral-wool-fill insulation does not support combustion, repeals vermin, and does not absorb moisture. Mineral-wool-filled partitions have been accorded a $1\frac{1}{2}$-h fire rating when faced with metal lath and plaster.

Vegetable fiber loose fill is usually made from wood shredded into a lightweight, fleecy insulating material. This is generally treated to make it moisture-resistant, fire-resistant, and vermin-repellent. Like mineral wool, this material can be placed by hand or blown into place.

Fibrous loose fill normally is applied over horizontal surfaces. In vertical spaces it may have a tendency to settle over a period of time, leaving an uninsulated space at the top. However, it is used to insulate walls of buildings that have been built without insulation. In such cases, holes are drilled in the wall between each pair of studs, a hose inserted, and the insulation blown in until the space is filled.

Mineral-type granular loose fill is made from either perlite or vermiculite. (See Chap. 2, section on lightweight aggregates, for description of perlite and vermiculite.)

The coarser sizes of perlite and sizes 1 and 2 of vermiculite are generally used as loose-fill insulation for sidewalls and ceilings, over suspended ceilings, between wood sleepers over a concrete floor slab, as a fill for the cores of concrete blocks, and for many other, similar uses.

BLANKET INSULATIONS Blanket insulations are made of felted fiber, usually of a mineral nature, manufactured to controlled thicknesses of 1, $1\frac{1}{2}$, 2, 3, and 4 in (25, 38, 50, 75, and 100 mm). A variety of blanket insulation widths are made; some to fit between framing members 16, 20 or 24 in (400, 500, or 800 mm) o.c.; others are wider. The wider material is often used to wrap pipe but may be used in other applications as well.

Some blankets are cut into 8-ft (2.4-m) lengths; others are put up in rolls of 40 to 100 ft (12.2 to 30.5 m) in length, depending on the thickness. Some are made with no covering at all; some have a paper backing on one side only; others are completely enclosed in an envelope. Those with no backing are made for a friction fit. Those with backing or envelopes are usually provided with a stapling flange on each side so that they may be stapled to the sides or edges of framing members. (See Fig. 13-3.)

Blankets are used to insulate large areas such as *sidewalls* in new construction, *overhead* in floored attics, *between joists* in unfloored attics, in *crawl spaces,* and over suspended ceilings.

BATT INSULATION Batts are similar to blankets in many respects except for length and the fact that

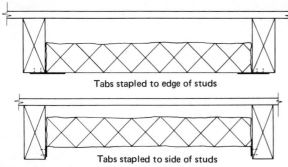

Tabs stapled to edge of studs

Tabs stapled to side of studs

Fig. 13-3 Blanket insulation installed.

they may be made in thicknesses up to $7\frac{1}{4}$ in (181 mm). They are used for the same purposes and in the same manner as blankets.

Batts are commonly rated according to their *R value* (thermal resistance) rather than their thickness, though the *R* value is related to the thickness of the material. Thus a batt may be rated from R5 (relatively low resistance to heat transmission) to R20 (very high resistance).

STRUCTURAL INSULATION BOARD Structural insulation boards are made from both *organic fiber*—wood, cane, or cork—and *synthetic fibers*—commonly glass-fiber-reinforced cellular isocyanurate.

In the case of wood and cane fiberboard, the raw material is first pulped, after which it is treated with waterproofing chemicals. The fibers are then formed into sheets of various thicknesses in a continuous process and cut into standard lengths. Some boards are impregnated with asphalt during the manufacturing process, some are given a coat of asphalt after they are made, and others are left plain.

Wood and cane fiberboard is used for several purposes, including the following: exterior wall sheathing, which is normally supplied in asphalt-impregnated square-edged panels $\frac{1}{2}$ in (12 mm) thick, 48 in (1200 mm) wide, and from 6 to 12 ft (1.8 to 3.6 m) long; shingle backer, consisting of asphalt-impregnated strips $\frac{5}{16}$ or $\frac{3}{8}$ in (8 or 9.5 mm) thick, $11\frac{3}{4}$, $13\frac{1}{2}$, 15, or $15\frac{1}{2}$ in (294, 338, 375, or 388 mm) wide, and 48 in (1200 mm) long; roof insulation, from $\frac{1}{2}$ to 3 in (12 to 75 mm) thick, in single or multiple layers and in several dimensions; interior wallboard, which is made $\frac{5}{16}$, $\frac{3}{8}$, and $\frac{1}{2}$ in (8, 9.5, and 12 mm) thick, in plain sheets 48 × 96 in (1200

× 2400 mm) and 48 × 120 in (1200 × 3000 mm).

Corkboard is made from granulated cork mixed with resin and pressed into sheets of several thicknesses, depending on their use. A common thickness is 3 in (75 mm), the board being used for roof insulation.

The synthetic fiberboard is made in thicknesses of $\frac{3}{8}$ to $1\frac{7}{8}$ in (9.5 to 47.5 mm), widths of 48 in (1200 mm), and lengths of 8, 10, and 12 ft (2.4, 3, and 3.6 m), although custom lengths are also available. The board is faced on both sides with aluminum foil facers, one of which has a white vinyl coating. This product is intended as ceiling material in commercial, agricultural, and industrial buildings using a suspended ceiling system (see Fig. 13-4) or as wall insulation in similar buildings. (See Fig. 13-5.)

A similar product, with a white-coated, embossed aluminum sheet either 0.019 or 0.032 in (0.48 or 0.81 mm) in thickness on one side is also available as a cladding material for industrial and commercial buildings.

Another product of the same family, without the white-coated face, is available for installation behind $\frac{1}{2}$-in (12-mm) gypsum board. The R value of this material ranges from 3 to 15, depending on the thickness.

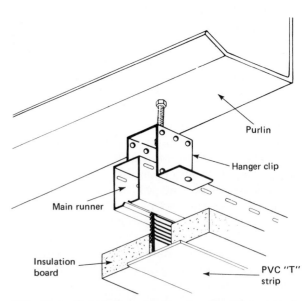

Fig. 13-4 Suspension system for insulation board. *(Celotex Corp.)*

Fig. 13-5 Synthetic-fiber structural insulation board. *(Celotex Corp.)*

RIGID-SLAB INSULATION This type of thermal insulation is so called because the units are relatively stiff and inelastic. In most cases inorganic materials are used in their manufacture. Insulations falling into this category include *mineral wool with binder, expanded plastic materials, cellular glass,* and *cellular hard rubber.*

The insulative value of these materials lies in the facts that the basic material is a nonconductor and that the finished product contains millions of isolated air cells. These characteristics make it an ideal insulation.

MINERAL WOOL WITH BINDER Mineral wool has been described previously under blanket and batt insulation. When this material has been mixed with a binder and processed or fixed to a rigid back, sheets are produced which are suitable for roof-deck insulation and similar applications.

EXPANDED PLASTIC Expanded-plastic insulation is made from expanded polystyrene and expanded polyurethane, extruded into slabs, normally 2×8 ft (600×2400 mm), 1, $1\frac{1}{4}$, $1\frac{1}{2}$, 2, $2\frac{1}{2}$, or 3 in (25, 32, 38, 50, 63.5, or 75 mm) thick. The material has an R value of 5 per 1 in (25 mm) of thickness and a k factor, at $24°C$, of 0.20.

Such insulation has many uses, including *exterior sheathing* (over a braced frame), *insulation over concrete* or *block walls* (applied with an asphalt adhesive), *insulation under built-up roof* (for which the material is available wrapped with asphalt-impregnated kraft paper), *cavity-wall insulation, roof decking* under concrete (if properly supported) (see Fig. 13-6), and *perimeter insulation.* (See Fig. 13-7.)

CELLULAR GLASS Cellular-glass insulation is made from expanded molten glass, which is cast

Fig. 13-6 Roof dome decked with expanded-poly-styrene insulation.

into block form and cut into slabs 12 × 18 in (300 × 450 mm) and 24 × 48 in (600 × 1200 mm), in thicknesses of $1\frac{1}{2}$ to 4 in (38 to 100 mm), and into hollow cylinders, intended for pipe insulation. (See Fig. 13-8.) It is a strong, rigid material, with a compressive strength of about 100 psi (689 kPa) and a density of 9 lb/ft³ (44 kg/m³). It has a *k* factor of 0.38 at 10°C and 0.40 at 24°C.

The usual method of application on flat surfaces is in hot asphalt or asphalt emulsion, as illustrated in Fig. 13-9. On vertical surfaces, it may be applied with mastic or held in place with pins cast into the backing. (See Fig. 13-10.)

CELLULAR HARD RUBBER   Cellular hard rubber is a synthetic material containing cells filled with nitrogen. It is formed into slabs of varying sizes and thicknesses which are used in a similar manner to other kinds of rigid-slab insulation.

INSULATING CONCRETE   Concrete, using as aggregate such lightweight materials as *vermiculite, perlite,* or *expanded clay,* is useful as an insulation because of the cellular structure of the aggregates. Cast in place, it becomes a rigid slab that possesses structural strength, as well as insulation value. This type of concrete is widely used as the base portion of a two-part concrete slab-on-grade floor and as an insulating roof deck.

It is particularly important to incorporate insulating concrete in the floor slab in cases which involve the casting of hot-water heating pipes into the floor. A typical system of this type is illustrated in Fig. 13-11.

REFLECTIVE INSULATION   Reflective insulation is made from such materials as aluminum or copper foil or sheet metal, with bright surfaces that reflect heat rather than absorb it.

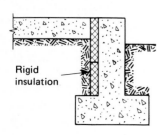

Rigid insulation

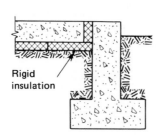

Rigid insulation

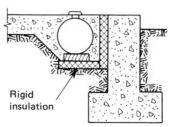

Rigid insulation

Fig. 13-7 Perimeter insulation.

Fig. 13-8 Cellular-glass-pipe insulation. *(Pittsburgh-Corning Corp.)*

Fig. 13-10   Cellular-glass insulation attached by pins.

Fig. 13-9 Cellular-glass insulation laid in asphalt.
(Pittsburgh-Corning Corp.)

Aluminum foil is produced in sheets or rolls and formed into battlike units, like that illustrated in Fig. 13-12. These are particularly useful for ceiling and floor application. Sheet foil is commonly made 36 in (900 mm) wide, and on stud walls it should be installed vertically for maximum benefit, draped back between each pair of studs to provide the needed air space in front of it.

Several materials, including gypsum lath and synthetic-fiber insulation board, are available with one side faced with aluminum foil to provide reflective insulation.

Special papers coated with a polished aluminum, pigmented heat-reflective coating are produced as reflective insulation. These are supplied either in single sheets or with two sheets laminated by an asphalt adhesive. This material can be used as one side of a mineral wool blanket.

Copper foil insulation is commonly made in the form of a thin paper core covered on one or both sides with copper.

Reflective insulation can be used in stud, rafter, and joist spaces; to insulate walls, roofs, ceilings, and floors; and for cold-storage work.

FOAMED-IN-PLACE INSULATION   This is a polyurethane product, made by combining a polyisocyanate and a polyester resin. Trichlorofluoromethane also can be used as a blowing agent in some cases, depending on the foam properties required.

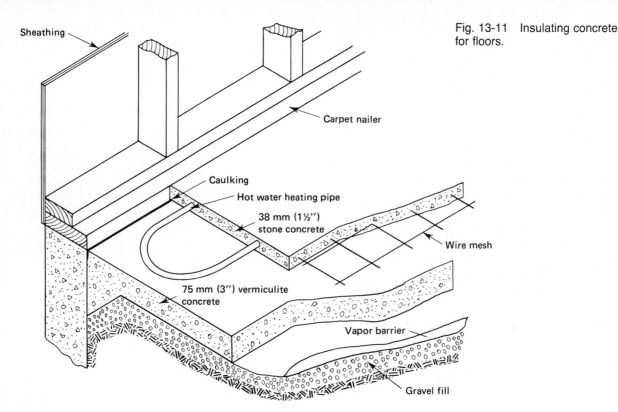

Fig. 13-11   Insulating concrete for floors.

Sheathing

Carpet nailer

Caulking

Hot water heating pipe

38 mm (1½'')
stone concrete

Wire mesh

75 mm (3'') vermiculite
concrete

Vapor barrier

Gravel fill

This type of insulation can be applied either by pouring or by spraying. In either case, the two basic ingredients are drawn from their containers, measured, and mixed by machine. When the pouring system is being used, a carefully measured amount of the mixture is deposited in an existing cavity. The mixture reacts and foams up to fill a predetermined portion of the space to be filled. This volume of foam is called a "lift" and normally is limited to

a height of about 14 in (350 mm). When the foam has set, a new lift is poured and the process repeated until the space is completely filled. The average density of this material when set is about 2 lb/ft^3 (32 kg/m^3).

The same materials are used for the spray application. A number of thin coats of foam are applied, one over the other, with sufficient time being left between each application for the foam to set up. By this system, any desired thickness of insulation can be applied, according to specifications.

SPRAYED-ON INSULATIONS   Several materials are used in this type of application, one of them being the *polyurethane foam* described above. Other common ones are *asbestos fiber* mixed with inorganic binders, *vermiculite aggregate* with a binder such as portland cement or gypsum, and *perlite aggregate* using gypsum as a binder. Machines are used for blowing these insulations into place; as a result, the shape or irregularity of the surface being insulated is of little consequence.

The use of polyurethane foam, vermiculite, and perlite are increasing, as the result of safety requirements which place severe restrictions on the use

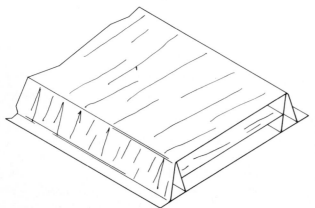

Fig. 13-12   Aluminum foil battlike unit.

of such materials as asbestos fiber containing toxic dusts.

Vermiculite or perlite with binders may be sprayed over a base of gypsum lath, base coat plaster, a masonry surface, or metal lath. (See Fig. 13-13.)

VAPOR INSULATION

The dampness that sometimes occurs inside buildings can be caused by penetration of moisture from the outside or by condensation of water vapor generated on the inside.

Protecting the interior of buildings against moisture penetration from outside involves well-known procedures. Protection against condensation of water vapor produced on the inside is a different matter and is perhaps not so well understood. Protection from the outside is provided by water-repellent materials which turn water aside and force it to return to the earth down the outside of the building. Moisture vapor, on the other hand, can permeate most ordinary building materials, such as wood, paper, lath, plaster, untreated brick, etc.

In addition, this moisture vapor will condense into water when its temperature is reduced by contact with a cool surface or cool air. Hence, high humidity in a building may result in condensation of water not only on the inside of walls and windows but also on the outside or within the exterior walls, ceiling, or roof.

Moisture vapor is inevitable in a building. Occupants, cooking, laundering, unvented fuel-burning devices, humidifiers, and evaporation from basement floors or earth in crawl spaces all produce moisture vapor. Some moisture can be eliminated at its source, and adequate ventilation will help carry it away. But this does not provide the answer to the problem of condensation on the inside of buildings or within the walls. If the inside surfaces of walls and windows are kept warm enough, condensation will not take place on them. Vapor can be kept from penetrating the exterior walls from the inside by an effective vapor barrier—vapor insulation—on the inside of exterior walls.

Vapor Barriers

Vapor barriers are materials which effectively retard or stop the flow of warm, moisture-laden air from

Fig. 13-13 Typical sprayed-on insulation.

inside a building outward through walls, ceilings, and floors to the colder, dryer outside atmosphere. (See Fig. 13-14.) Without a vapor barrier, warm, moist air, flowing outward through a wall, ceiling, or floor, could cool to the extent that some of the vapor would condense out as water and collect within the wall, etc., to the eventual detriment of the material in the structure.

Vapor barriers should be installed on the warm side of the insulation and present a continuous, impervious surface to the vapor pressure from within the building. Materials which effectively perform this function include polyethylene film, asphalt- or *wax-coated kraft paper, aluminum* or *other metal foil sheets,* and *paint coatings.*

POLYETHYLENE FILM   Polyethylene film is a chemically inert plastic, unaffected by acids, alkalis, and caustics, produced in rolls 3 to 20 ft (0.9 to 6 m) wide, in thicknesses of 2, 3, 4, and 6 mils. The film may be applied vertically in strips 36 in (900 mm) wide to stud walls, or sheets wide enough to cover the wall from top to bottom, with an overlap on both floor and ceiling, may be applied horizontally. Film should be applied lengthwise to ceiling joists, with a lap of at least the full thickness of the joists. On floors, the film is applied over the subfloor, with a lap up the walls.

ALUMINUM FOIL   Aluminum foil is used as a vapor barrier in several forms. One is the foil as a single sheet. Another is a thin layer of foil laminated

to a heavy backing of asphalt-impregnated kraft paper. Still another consists of two layers of foil laminated with asphalt cement.

COATED KRAFT PAPER   Kraft paper coated with asphalt or wax also acts as a vapor barrier. Sometimes two layers of paper are cemented with a continuous layer of asphalt. Whatever the material used, the same rule applies: the application should be continuous.

VAPOR BARRIER PAINT   In situations where it is desirable to insulate an existing building but it is not possible to install a conventional vapor barrier at the same time, it is possible to use a vapor barrier paint on the inner surfaces. Paint coatings which will act as a vapor barrier include *rubber emulsion, aluminum paint,* or two coats of *white lead and linseed oil.*

MOISTURE VAPOR CONTROL   In order to help control the moisture vapor problem, the indoor relative humidity should be kept within the limits shown in the Table 13-2. If no method of measuring humidity or automatically controlling humidities within given limits is available, the formation of moisture on windows may be taken as evidence of excessive humidity.

Moisture Barriers

Moisture barriers are materials which are used to prevent the entrance of moisture into a building from the outside or from the earth below.

Saturated felt paper may be used on outside walls as a moisture barrier. Such paper will shed water but will not prevent any moisture vapor which does reach the interior of a wall from escaping to the outside.

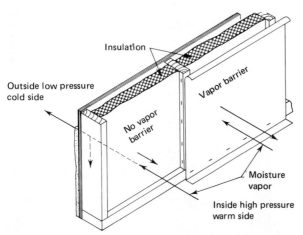

Fig. 13-14   Vapor barrier on warm side of wall prevents moisture vapor from penetrating wall.

Table 13-2
RELATIVE HUMIDITY LEVEL NEEDED TO CONTROL MOISTURE

Outside Temperature, °C	Maximum Inside Relative Humidity, %
Below −18	20
−18 to −7	30
−7 and over	40

Moisture from the earth can enter a building through a concrete slab on grade by traveling upward through the concrete slab; when it reaches the warm inner surface it evaporates and becomes water vapor. To prevent this, a moisture barrier should be laid between the earth and the concrete. *Polyethylene film* is an excellent material for this purpose, because it is impervious to the action of alkalis, decay, etc.

A 2-in (50-mm) layer of sand should be laid over the grade to provide a cushion for the film. Then the film is laid over the sand to form a continuous barrier to moisture. Material as wide as possible should be used; where joints have to be made, a wide overlap is necessary for complete protection. Four- or six-mil film should be used for this purpose because of its greater resistance to tearing and puncturing. If wire mesh reinforcement is being used, it is laid over the film before the slab is poured. In any case, great care must be taken to see that the barrier is not broken during the preparation for the concrete pour.

GLOSSARY

convection	Transfer of heat by moving masses of matter.
k factor	The unit rate of heat transmission.
perimeter insulation	Insulation installed around the outer walls or foundations of a building.
R value	The resistance of a material to heat flow.
structural insulation board	A building board with structural strength as well as insulation value.

REVIEW QUESTIONS

1. Give a concise definition of thermal insulation.

2. Give an example, other than the ones mentioned in the chapter, of each of the three methods of heat transfer.

3. Make a list of the nine basic kinds of thermal insulation, and beside each write the name of two products that fall into that category of insulation.

4. What is the difference between batt and blanket insulation?

5. Explain why it is important that a reflective-type insulation should face an air space of at least $\frac{3}{4}$ in (19 mm).

6. What is one disadvantage of using loose-fill insulation in a vertical space?

7. Give two advantages of sprayed-on thermal insulation.

8. Explain why it is necessary to prevent the penetration of moisture vapor into the walls of a building.

9. Why should vapor barriers be installed on the warm side of the insulation?

SELECTED SOURCES OF INFORMATION

Aluminum Company of Canada, Ltd., Montreal, Que.
Atlas Asbestos Company, Ltd., Toronto, Ont.
Dominion Rubber, Textile Division, Kitchener, Ont.
Dow Chemical Co., Midland, Mich.
Dow Chemical of Canada, Ltd., Sarnia, Ont.
Pal-O-Pak Insulation Company, Inc., Hartland, Wis.
Pittsburgh Corning Corporation, Pittsburgh, Pa.
The Celotex Corporation, Tampa, Fla.
United States Mineral Wool Company, Stanhope, N.J.
Vermiculite Institute, Chicago, Ill.
Zonolite Company, Chicago, Ill.

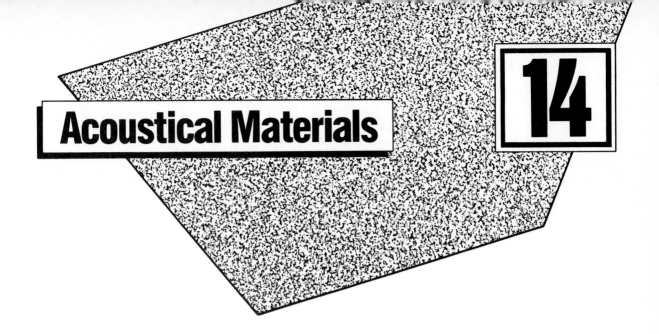

Acoustical Materials

14

This chapter focuses on the effects of sound in buildings and the method by which such sound can be controlled. Sound control is sought in order to (1) improve hearing conditions and reduce unwanted noise in any given room and (2) to control the transmission of sound from one room to another through walls, floors, and ceilings.

SOUND MECHANICS

Sound travels through the air as waves, in the form of small pressure changes occurring regularly above and below the normal atmospheric pressure. A sound wave is one *complete cycle of pressure variation,* as illustrated in Fig. 14-1.

The number of times that this cycle occurs in 1 s is the *frequency* of the wave, and the unit of measurement of frequency is called a *hertz* (Hz), which is equal to 1 cycle per second. The series of frequencies with which we are most concerned in acoustical work are 128, 256, 512, 1024, 2048, and 4096 Hz.

The average variation in pressure in a sound wave, above and below the normal, is called *sound pressure.* It is related to the loudness of a sound. That loudness, or strength, of a sound—its intensity—is measured in *decibels* (dB), and a reference sound intensity has been chosen for use with the

decibel scale. That intensity has been given a standard value of 10^{-16} W/cm^2. This amount of energy flow is very small, but a sensitive human ear can hear a sound of that intensity, which corresponds to 1 dB. Table 14-1 charts the decibel levels of a number of common sounds.

SOUND CONTROL

Sound control is largely accomplished by controlling reverberations, which in turn is accomplished by the use of products which have a much greater ability to *absorb* sound waves than most building materials.

The fraction of sound energy absorbed by a material, at a specific frequency, during each sound-wave reflection, is called the *sound-absorption*

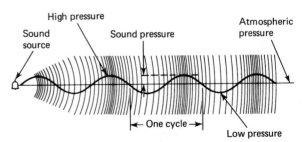

Fig. 14-1   Diagram of a sound wave.

Table 14-1
DECIBEL LEVELS OF COMMON SOUNDS

Decibels	Sound	Effect
120	Thunder, artillery	
110	Nearby riveter	Deafening
	Elevated train	
	Boiler factory	
100		
	Loud street noise	
90	Noisy factory	Very loud
	Truck (unmuffled)	
	Police siren	
80		
	Noisy office	
70	Average street noise	Loud
	Average radio	
	Average factory	
60		
	Noisy home	
50	Average office	Moderate
	Average conversation	
	Quiet radio	
40		
	Quiet home	
30	Private office	Faint
	Average auditorium	
	Quiet conversation	
20		
	Rustle of leaves	
10	Whisper	Very faint
	Soundproof room	
	Threshold of audibility	
0		

coefficient of that surface. Since most sounds contain a range of frequencies, it is necessary to use an *average* of the absorption coefficients when considering sound absorption. To obtain that average, it has been customary to average four coefficients from 250 to 2000 Hz inclusive and call the result the *noise-reduction coefficient* (NRC), which is expressed as a percentage. For example, some materials, such as glass, concrete, and masonry, would have an NRC rating of 0.05 or less. Some other materials might have a rating of 0.90 or better.

Materials which have a great ability to absorb sound are known as acoustical materials, and most of them can be classified into three groups: (1) acoustical tiles, (2) assembled acoustical units, and (3) sprayed-on acoustical materials.

ACOUSTICAL TILES

A majority of the tiles used for acoustical purposes are made from wood, cane, or asbestos fibers, mat-

ted and bonded into sheets of various thicknesses, ranging from $\frac{3}{16}$ to $1\frac{1}{4}$ in (5 to 32 mm). The sheets are cut into tiles of several sizes, including 12 × 12 in (300 × 300 mm), 12 × 24 in (300 × 600 mm), 16 × 16 in (400 × 400 mm), 16 × 32 in (400 × 800 mm), 24 × 24 in (600 × 600 mm), and 24 × 48 in (600 × 1200 mm). Edges may be square cut, beveled, or tongue-and-grooved.

These tiles are intended primarily for ceiling applications. They can be applied to solid surfaces with adhesives, nailed to furring strips attached to a ceiling frame or the underside of a solid deck (see Fig. 14-2), or installed in a suspended ceiling frame (see Fig. 14-3).

A great variety of designs, colors, and patterns are available. The acoustic openings in the surface of the tile in themselves provide many different designs. The openings may be holes drilled in uniform or random patterns or a combination of large drilled holes and tiny punched ones. (See Fig. 14-4.) The openings may be slots, striations, or fis-

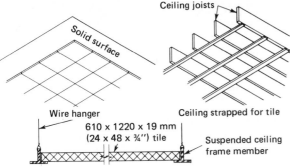

Fig. 14-2 Acoustical ceiling tile application.

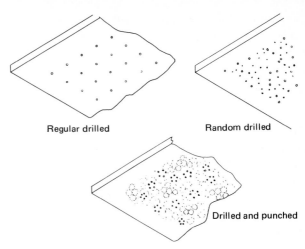

Fig. 14-4 Acoustical tile hole patterns.

sures, or the surface of the tile may be sculptured in various patterns. (See Fig. 14-5.) All ceiling tile comes with a factory-painted surface so that it does not require painting after installation. However, fiber tile can be repainted with a nonbridging paint without appreciable loss of acoustical properties.

The noise-reduction coefficient of tiles of this type is about 0.70, with some variations, depending on the particular material, the thickness of the tile, and the kind of pattern used.

Asbestos fiber tiles $12 \times 12 \times \frac{3}{4}$ in ($300 \times 300 \times 19$ mm) weigh approximately $1\frac{1}{4}$ lb (0.567 kg). Wood or cane fiber tiles are slightly lighter.

ASSEMBLED UNITS

Assembled units usually consist of some type of sound-absorbing material such as a rock-wool or

Fig. 14-3 Acoustical tile in suspended ceiling. *(Donn Products Ltd.)*

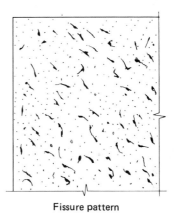

Fissure pattern

Striated pattern

Fig. 14-5 Acoustical tile surface patterns.

361

glass-fiber blanket fastened to an acoustically transparent facing. This facing is generally some type of rigid board, such as hardboard or asbestos board, or a metal sheet. The facings are perforated to allow the penetration of sound waves. (See Fig. 14-6.)

Such acoustical panels can be fastened to a wall over a framework of furring strips or suspended in front of the wall by some mechanical means. By varying the thickness of the sound-absorbing element and the spacing between the panels and the wall, some variation in the overall absorption and the absorption at different frequencies can be obtained. Sound-absorption coefficients vary with the thickness of the material, the type of facing, and the size and number of the perforations in the face.

SPRAYED-ON ACOUSTICAL MATERIALS

Two types of material are used for this kind of sound control application. One type consists of plaster made with vermiculite or perlite aggregate, and the other of a coating of mineral fiber mixed with an adhesive.

Vermiculite acoustical plaster is generally a premixed product, requiring only the addition of approximately 10 gal (45.5 L) of water per bag of mix. The plaster can be applied by hand or by machine spraying and will bond to any clean, firm, water-resistant surface such as base plaster, concrete, or steel. When it is applied by hand, usually two coats are used, a first coat at least $\frac{3}{8}$ in (9.5 mm) thick and a finish coat at least $\frac{1}{8}$ in (3 mm)

thick. When machine application is used, two, three, or four thin coats are applied so that the total thickness of plaster will be at least $\frac{1}{2}$ in (12 mm).

According to tests, the NRC for $\frac{1}{2}$ in (12 mm) thick acoustical plaster applied by trowel is 0.65, while for trowel-applied plaster 1 in (25 mm) thick, the NRC is 0.75. For machine-applied plaster $\frac{1}{2}$ in (12 mm) thick, the NRC is 0.55.

Perlite acoustical plaster is usually mixed on the job, using calcined gypsum as the binder. It also can be applied either by hand or by machine. Sound-reduction properties of perlite plaster are approximately the same as those of vermiculite.

The main advantage of using machine spraying as a means of application is that this method presents no difficulties in plastering over irregular surfaces, such as those presented in Fig. 14-7.

Acoustical treatment with mineral fiber involves the use of specially prepared mineral wool or asbestos fibers and an adhesive to hold them to the surface. It should be noted that, in most areas, there are stringent safety requirements which place restrictions on the use of such materials as asbestos fiber containing toxic dusts.

The fibers are prepared and mixed with an inorganic binding material, which helps to give them body, and packed in bags ready for application. The area to be covered is first primed with a thick coat of adhesive, and the fiber is then sprayed over the surface in one or more coats, depending on the

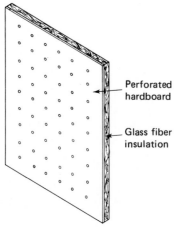

Fig. 14-6 Acoustical assembled unit.

Perforated hardboard

Glass fiber insulation

Fig. 14-7 Acoustical treatment on irregular surfaces. *(Columbia Acoustics & Fireproofing)*

thickness required. For thicknesses of over $\frac{1}{2}$ in (12 mm), at least two coats are used. Each coat is tamped to consolidate the fibers; the final surface can be sprayed with sealer or color. (See Fig. 14-8.)

Such material is very light; a 1-in (25-mm) coat weighs 9 to 12 oz/ft² (2.75 to 3.65 kg/m²). The NRC varies, depending on the thickness of the coat and the type of backing. Over solid backing, an unpainted $\frac{3}{4}$-in (18-mm) thickness has an NRC of from 0.60 to 0.70. Over metal lath backing, the same thickness, unpainted, has an NRC of from 0.80 to 0.90. A $1\frac{1}{2}$-in (36-mm) thickness, unpainted, over solid backing has an NRC of 0.90, while the coefficient of the same thickness, painted, is about 0.85.

SOUND-TRANSMISSION CONTROL

The transmission of sound from room to room through walls, floors, and ceilings takes place as a result of diaphragmatic vibration. The surface may be set in vibration through impact, such as a footstep, or by the action of sound waves striking it. The first is called impact transmission and the second airborne transmission. In either case sound waves of reduced intensity are generated in the room on the other side by the vibrating surface.

The sound-insulating efficiency of a wall or floor for airborne sound is called its transmission loss and is measured in decibels (Fig. 14-9). The transmission loss of any wall depends on the materials of which it is made and the method of construction.

Fig. 14-8   Mineral fiber acoustical treatment.

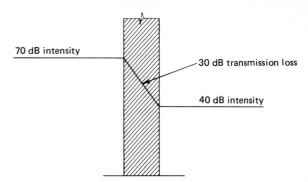

70 dB intensity

30 dB transmission loss

40 dB intensity

Fig. 14-9   Reduction in sound intensity level through a wall.

However, the transmission loss of any given wall varies considerably with the frequency of sound.

In order to be reasonably useful as an airborne-sound insulator, a wall should have a sound-transmission loss rating of at least 35 dB, and for dividing walls between apartments it is usually recommended that the transmission loss be 45 dB.

For solid masonry partitions, the transmission loss depends on the weight of the wall per unit area. For example, if a solid masonry partition which weighs 10 lb/ft² (49 kg/m²) and has a transmission loss of 26 dB has its weight doubled, the transmission loss will be increased by 9 dB. Each successive doubling of weight will add another 9 dB to the rating. Partitions made from porous concrete block have a superior transmission loss rating if they are plastered on at least one side and preferably on both.

In general, the effectiveness of single- or double-stud walls depends on the rigidity of the material in the wall and the method of construction. Figure 14-10 illustrates some types of partition and the approximate transmission-loss rating, in decibels, of each. Loose fill should not be used as sound insulation in a structurally separated double wall, since it acts as a bridge across the space and reduces the sound-insulation value.

Transmission of sound through floors may be either of the impact or airborne type. Solid floors of concrete or tile effectively reduce airborne transmission, losses being normally in the range of 40 to 60 dB for this type of floor. However, impact transmission is a problem with this as well as steel- or wood-frame floors, and special construction techniques are necessary to reduce this type of sound transmission.

Suspended ceilings provide high insulation, par-

Fig. 14-10 Approximate transmission losses through various partition constructions.

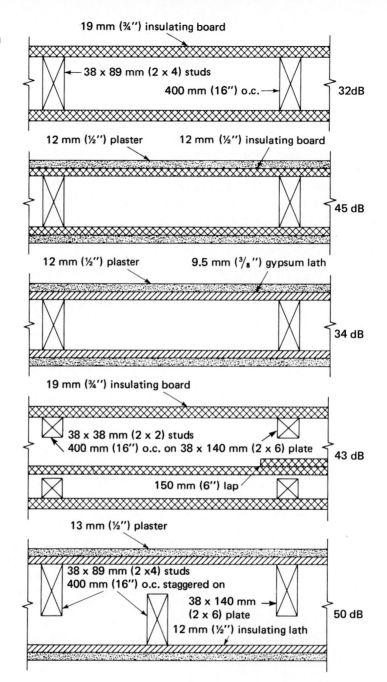

19 mm (¾″) insulating board

38 x 89 mm (2 x 4) studs

400 mm (16″) o.c.

32dB

12 mm (½″) plaster   12 mm (½″) insulating board

45 dB

12 mm (½″) plaster   9.5 mm (³/₈″) gypsum lath

34 dB

19 mm (¾″) insulating board

38 x 38 mm (2 x 2) studs
400 mm (16″) o.c. on 38 x 140 mm (2 x 6) plate

43 dB

150 mm (6″) lap

13 mm (½″) plaster

38 x 89 mm (2 x4) studs
400 mm (16″) o.c. staggered on

38 x 140 mm
(2 x 6) plate

50 dB

12 mm (½″) insulating lath

ticularly if resilient hangers are used. A floating floor over the structural floor also provides good impact insulation. (See Fig 14-11.) It may be a floor supported on springs, or it may be laid over a layer of resilient material such as wood or cane fiberboard or some type of rigid foamed insulation.

Wood-frame floors can be improved by providing an insulating cushion between the frame and the finished ceiling below or by separating the floor and ceiling frames. Figure 14-12 illustrates several possible ways of using insulating materials to improve the impact transmission losses through frame floors.

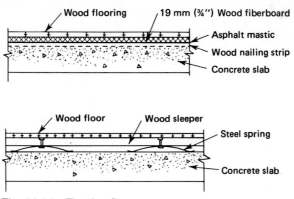

Fig. 14-11   Floating floors.

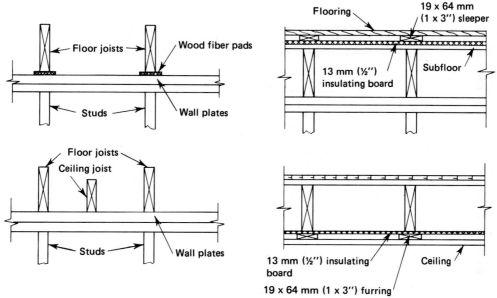

Fig. 14-12   Suggested methods for reducing impact transmission through wood frame floors.

GLOSSARY

diaphragmatic vibration	The vibration of a dividing membrane or surface.
striation	A narrow groove or channel.

REVIEW QUESTIONS

1. Explain briefly how a sound is generated.

2. Define the following terms:
   a. sound frequency
   b. sound intensity

3. a. List four major sound problems with which sound engineering is concerned.
   b. Explain what is meant by acoustical correction.

4. Explain how acoustical materials control excessive reverberation.

5. a. How do standard types of paint reduce the sound-absorbing qualities of acoustical tile?
   b. What is meant by a nonbridging paint?

6. Draw a careful sketch of a typical acoustical assembled unit.

7. What are the advantages of using machine-sprayed mineral fiber for sound control?

8. What is meant by the following terms:
   a. impact transmission?
   b. airborne transmission?

SELECTED SOURCES OF INFORMATION

Armstrong Cork Company, Lancaster, Pa.
Atlas Asbestos Company, Toronto, Ont.
Canadian Johns-Manville Co., Ltd., Montreal, Que.
The Celatex Corporation, Chicago, Ill.
Columbia Acoustics & Fireproofing Co., Stanhope, N.J.
Hermon, Hosmer Scott, Inc., Cambridge, Mass.
Insulation Board Institute, Chicago, Ill.
International Panel Boards, Ltd., Gatineau, Que.
Tectum Corporation, Columbus, Ohio
Vermiculite Institute, Chicago, Ill.

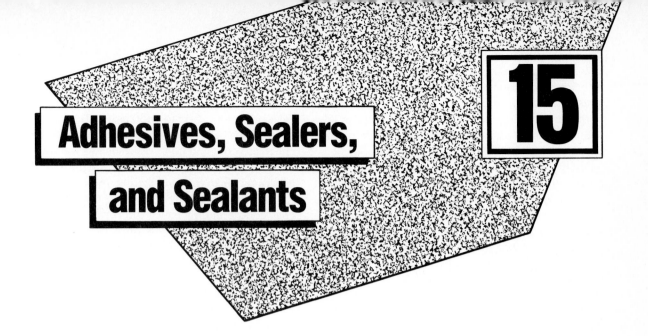

Adhesives, Sealers, and Sealants

15

All the materials described in this chapter, with one or two exceptions, have at least two common characteristics—cohesiveness and adhesiveness. Cohesiveness is the ability of particles of a material to cling tightly to one another. Adhesiveness is the ability of a material to fix itself and cling to an entirely different material.

ADHESIVES

The art of making and using glues of various kinds has been known for a very long time. Many of the materials used in ancient times were natural products, such as bitumen and tree resins, while others were made by hand by processes which were kept closely guarded secrets. It was not until the eighteenth century that the process of making glues began to develop industrially.

In the nineteenth century chemists and physicists began to take a serious interest in the chemical properties of glues, and it was this interest which sparked the development of the modern glue industry.

One of the early discoveries in the field of modern glues was the adhesive properties of nitrocellulose. This was the first adhesive known which was resistant to water. Today other synthetic adhesives have replaced nitrocellulose to a large extent. About the same time (in the mid-1800s) it was

found that rubber could be treated to make an adhesive. Such adhesives, which consist mainly of raw rubber dissolved in gasoline, are still used in the manufacture and repair of rubber products. New and improved methods of making and keeping animal glue, particularly fish glue, were also made during this period. This rediscovery of an old craft resulted in the production of a glue that continued to be of major importance until nearly halfway through the twentieth century.

The discovery of the first synthetic resin—phenolic resin—was announced in 1909. Some 20 years later a phenolic-resin glue had become well known as an adhesive for wood; the plywood industry still relies largely on phenolic adhesives as a bonding agent. In the 1930s another wood adhesive made from urea formaldehyde was developed. It has some advantages over phenolic adhesives (it is quick setting and produces a colorless glue line), but it is not as waterproof as the phenolics.

The growth of the plastics industry has resulted in the development of many new glues made from synthetic resins. They include resorcinol adhesives, polyvinyl acetate, neoprene phenolic cement, polyurethane adhesives, and epoxy-resin glues. Today many of the old glues, such as animal glue, casein glue, and asphalt adhesives, are still in use along with a wide variety of synthetic glues.

Whereas most of the older type adhesives were

367

intended for gluing wood, paper, leather, rubber, and cloth, some of the new synthetics will also bond to glass, steel, concrete, ceramics, and plastics. As a result, today there are glues for every conceivable purpose, and the glue chosen for a particular job will depend on its properties, the nature of the application, and the cost of the glue.

Animal glue is available in either solid or liquid form. Solid glue is melted and applied hot. It is slow setting and allows time for adjustment to the glue joint. Animal glue has excellent bonding properties with wood, leather, paper, or cloth, developing up to 12,000 psi (92.5 MPa) in shear. It has moderate resistance to heat and good resistance to cold but poor resistance to water. It cures by air drying at room temperatures.

Blood-albumin glue is a special animal glue made for use particularly with leather and paper. It has only very moderate bonding power with wood. It is usually sold as a dry powder which is mixed with water. It has fair resistance to both heat and cold but poor resistance to water. This type of glue will dry at room temperature or at a low heat of from 65 to 93°C. Its strength is considerably less than that of the animal glue described above.

Casein glue, made from protein materials, is a dry powder to be mixed with water. It has good bonding power for wood-to-wood or paper-to-wood applications and will develop the full strength of the wood in most situations. Casein glue has good dry heat resistance and moderate resistance to cold. It has moderate resistance to water but does not perform well when subjected to high humidity or wetting and drying cycles. It is subject to attack from molds, fungi, and other wood organisms. Casein glue will set at temperatures as low as 1.5°C but maximum strength is developed at about 21°C with moderate pressure.

Starch and dextrin glues are available in both dry and liquid state, the dry glue being mixed with water. They have good bond with paper or leather and fair bond with wood, but strength does not compare with those of animal or casein glues. They have fair resistance to heat and cold but poor resistance to water. They dry at room temperature.

Asphalt cements are thermoplastic materials made from asphalt emulsions or asphalt cutbacks. They have a good bond to paper and concrete and are used mainly for roofing applications and for laminating layers of wood fiberboard. They have

relatively poor resistance to heat but good resistance to cold and good water resistance.

Cellulose cements are thermoplastic in nature and have good bond to wood, paper, leather, or glass, developing up to 1400 psi (10.8 MPa) in shear with wood. They have moderate resistance to both heat and cold and good resistance to water. A common solvent is ethyl acetate. Cellulose cement cures by air drying and setting. (See Fig. 15-1.)

Chlorinated-rubber adhesive is usually a liquid; it has good bond for paper and fair bond with wood, metal, or glass. Strength does not compare with animal or casein glues. It has moderate resistance to heat, cold, and water but poor resistance to creep. It cures by drying at room temperature. The usual solvent is ketone.

Natural-rubber adhesives are usually latex emulsions or dissolved crepe rubber. They have a good bond with rubber or leather and fair bond with wood, ceramics, or glass, developing strengths of about 350 psi (2.7 MPa) in tension with wood. They have fair resistance to heat and cold, good resistance to water, but poor resistance to creep. Room temperature is sufficient for drying.

Nitrile or Buna N rubber adhesive is available in both thermoplastic and thermosetting types. It has good bond with wood, paper, porcelain enamel, and polyester film or sheet. The thermosetting type will develop up to 4000 psi (31 MPa) shear and the thermoplastic type up to 600 psi (4.6 MPa). It has good resistance to heat and cold and excellent water resistance, while its creep resistance is fairly

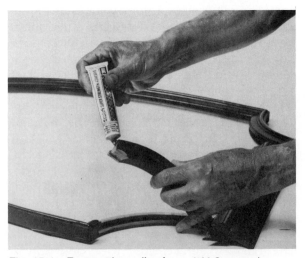

Fig. 15-1 Fast-setting adhesive. *(3M Company)*

good. This adhesive cures best under heat.

Urea formaldehyde resin glues are available in powder form, to be mixed with water, and in liquid form, which requires the addition of a hardener. They are thermosetting in nature, with excellent bond to wood, leather, or paper, having a shear strength up to 2,800 psi (21.5 MPa). They have good resistance to heat and cold and fair resistance to water. Creep resistance is good. These glues often behave unsatisfactorily on wood that is below 6 percent in moisture content. Heat is desirable for curing of some types of urea resin glue, while others cure satisfactorily at room temperature. Rapid curing can be achieved by the application of a high-frequency electric current directly to the joint. This technique is known as wood welding.

Phenolic resin glues are made in both dry and liquid form. They are thermosetting glues with excellent bond to wood and paper. Shear strengths up to 2800 psi (21.5 MPa) are developed. They have excellent resistance to heat, cold, creep, and water. Some set at room temperature, while others require a hot press. These hot-press glues are commonly used in the manufacture of plywoods. Other similar glues are combinations of phenol-formaldehyde, phenol-resorcinol, or resorcinol-formaldehyde. All are woodworking glues used in the manufacture of laminated wood structural members.

Melamine resins are thermosetting glues manufactured as a powder with a separate catalyst. They have excellent bond with wood or paper. Resistance to heat, cold, creep, and water are all excellent. Melamine resins are cured under hot press at 150°C. Melamine-formaldehyde resin glues are manufactured as a powder to be mixed with water and may be either hot-setting or intermediate-temperature-setting types.

Resorcinol resins are usually made as a liquid with a separate catalyst. They have good bond with wood or paper, developing shear strengths up to 1950 psi (15 MPa) with wood. They have very good resistance to heat, cold, and creep and are generally used where a waterproof joint is required. Some cure at room temperatures, while others require moderate heat, up to 75°C.

Epoxy-resin adhesives are among the most versatile of all the modern adhesives, since formulations of the material may be developed to suit a particular requirement. They are thermosetting in nature, manufactured in liquid form with a separate catalyst, the amount of catalyst added to the resin determining to a large extent the type of curing required.

They have excellent bond with wood, metal, glass, and masonry and excellent resistance to both heat and cold, while creep resistance and water resistance vary widely, depending on how the adhesive is compounded. With regular catalyst addition, curing is by hot press, up to 200°C, while increased catalyst addition results in an adhesive which will cure at room temperature.

Such adhesives have been widely used in the manufacture of laminated curtain-wall panels of all kinds for a number of years. More recently, the development of epoxy-based adhesives which can form very high-strength bonds between a variety of materials, including steel and concrete, has led to their increasing use in the construction industry.

Applications of such adhesives and mortars made from them include the bonding of prefabricated concrete elements in bridges, the bonding together of concrete sections of large-span roof-framing assemblies (see Fig. 15-2), and the joining of external steel reinforcement to concrete structures, both as repair measures and for new construction. Such

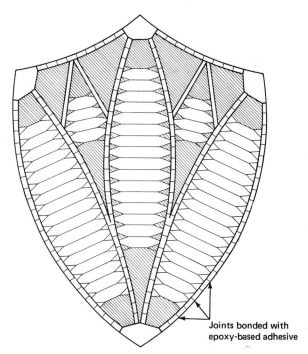

Joints bonded with epoxy-based adhesive

Fig. 15-2 Concrete skeleton of Velodrome viewed from above. *(CIBA-GEIGY)*

adhesives are used as the stress-transmitting medium for the bonding of new concrete to old and for the anchoring of prestressed cables in underground workings and tunnels. It would appear that a new group of alternatives is available to the conventional methods of joining many types of structural elements.

Polyvinyl-resin adhesives are usually in the form of an emulsion. They have good bond with wood or paper or vinyl plastics and reasonably good bond with metal. Shear strengths up to 1000 psi (7.5 MPa) are developed with wood. Resistance to cold is good, but heat, creep, and water resistance are only fair. These glues cure at room temperature.

Sodium silicate adhesives are liquids which have excellent bond with paper or glass and reasonably good bond with wood or metal. Resistance to heat, cold, and creep are good, but water resistance is poor. Some cure at room temperature, while others require moderate heat, in the 95°C range.

CONTACT CEMENTS

Contact cements are adhesives which provide an almost instant bond between surfaces to which a film of the adhesive has been applied and allowed to dry. A range of adhesives is made, each one designed to do a specific job, such as bonding *wood, leather, glass, plastic foams, plastic laminates, glass fiber, metals, vinyl,* or *rubber.* Most of them are *neoprene* products, though a *polychloroprene* base is used for those intended to bond plastic foams, and a few have a *synthetic rubber-resin* blended base.

Contact adhesives are produced in the form of an emulsion, the majority of them using water as the suspension medium, and may be applied by brush or roller. (See Fig. 15-3.) Generally the coverage will be at the rate of about 1 gal/360 ft^2 (1 L/8.8m^2).

Neoprene-rubber adhesives are essentially thermoplastic in nature, though they may have some thermosetting characteristics. They have excellent bond with wood, asbestos board, metals, glass, and some plastics, with strengths up to 1200 psi (9.25 MPa) in shear. They have good resistance to heat and cold and excellent resistance to water. Creep resistance is fairly good. Most of the contact cements used in the application of plastic laminates to walls or flat surfaces are neoprene-rubber prod-

Fig. 15-3   Contact cement.   *(3M Company)*

ucts. These adhesives are also used for cementing gypsum board to studs and ceiling joists and for laminating one layer of gypsum board to another.

SEALERS

Sealing compounds are products which are used to seal the surface of various materials against the penetration of water or other liquids or in some cases to prevent the escape of water through the surface. To do this they must have some adhesive qualities and the ability to fill the surface pores and form a continuous skin on the surface to which they are applied. In many applications the adhesion should be permanent, while in others it need be only temporary.

One common type of sealer is liquid asphalt, either in cutback form or as an asphalt emulsion. This type of sealer has several uses. One is to coat the outer surface of concrete below ground level to prevent the penetration of water to the interior through pores in the concrete. Another, similar use is to seal the inside surface of wooden or concrete water tanks. Another use is as a sealer or primer over a concrete slab before asphaltic tile adhesive is applied. Here the sealer prevents liquids from being withdrawn from the flooring or adhesive, allowing it to become dry and hard.

In order to be effective as a waterproofing membrane in many building-construction applications, sealers must be elastomeric in character. That is, they must be resilient enough to be able to expand over small cracks in the base surface without losing their effectiveness and be able to bridge joints between members without rupture, in case of movement at the joint.

Polysulfide polymers, which had previously been used as caulking materials, have more recently been developed as sealers. They have excellent adhesive qualities, are highly flexible and may be applied either by hand or by spray. They are being used on exterior walls of foundations, between two-course concrete slab floors, on roof decks, as swimming pool waterproofing, and under roof flashing.

These polysulfide-polymer sealers are two-component, chemically curing materials which are produced for either hand or machine mixing. The hand-mixed sealer has a work life of approximately 4 h at 24°C and 50 percent relative humidity, while the machine-mixed variety will have a work life of about 5 min under the same conditions. Curing time for the hand-mixed material is about 24 h at 24°C and 50 percent relative humidity, while curing time for the second variety is approximately 45 min.

A volume of 1 gal (4.75 L) of prepared sealer will cover approximately 25 ft² (2.32 m²) of surface, with a membrane of 60 mils thickness, which will expand and contract with the base without cracking, down to −40°C.

Another well-known sealer is a solution of sodium silicate. It is used to seal the inside surface of concrete liquid containers. The sodium silicate forms a gel-like film on the surface to prevent water penetration.

Various wax compounds are made in the form of emulsions to be sprayed over the surface of newly placed concrete. The wax oxidizes to form a continuous film which prevents the evaporation of water from the concrete. In this case the adhesion is only temporary. As the wax continues to oxidize it becomes hard and brittle and flakes or is worn off the concrete by traffic.

Other waxes are used to make sealers for concrete and terrazzo floors which prevent the penetration of oil and grease into the floor surface.

Liquid silicones are used as sealers over concrete, brick, and tile masonry to prevent the penetration of water into the surface. The absorption of water by masonry walls often leads to staining and efflorescence. The silicone sealers are particularly valuable for such applications because they are colorless and do not affect the appearance of the wall.

Sealers made from various oils and turpentine are used to seal wood surfaces before the application of paint or varnish. They penetrate into and are absorbed by the wood fibers so that the vehicle in paints and varnish will not be similarly absorbed. Similar sealers are used to seal wood which will not be painted against moisture penetration.

Other types of sealer made for wood are synthetic plastic products which form a film over the surface and allow better bonding of synthetic lacquers to wood.

Thin solutions of animal and casein glues are used to coat the surface of plaster and gypsum board under paint. These products are commonly known as wall sizing.

Epoxy-resin formulations are used as sealers over concrete, wood, or old terrazzo surfaces before epoxy-resin terrazzo is applied. The thin liquid adheres to and seals the old surface and provides a good bond for the new application. Similar sealers are used under concrete surface repairs.

SEALANTS

A *sealant* is a material used to fill the joint between two adjoining elements of a structure in order to render it moisture- and air-tight. Since earliest recorded history, men have used pitch or asphalt to seal—*caulk*—the joints between planks in wooden ships. Windows required a sealant—*glazing compound*—between their edges and the surrounding window frame.

The development of new building methods and, in particular, the widespread use of prefabricated panels and curtain-wall construction have brought about the development of dynamic materials which will provide permanent sealing of *moving* joints which occur in metal, glass, and masonry curtain-wall exterior cladding systems.

The areas in which these materials—*sealants*—will be used include *glazing, curtain walls* (see Fig. 15-4), *deck areas, concrete, masonry* (see Fig. 15-5), *stone, terrazzo flooring, quarry tile, skylights* (see Fig. 15-6), *window units* (see Fig. 15-7), and *metal roofs.* To be useful in such a

Fig. 15-4 Applying sealant to curtain wall. *(Thiokol Chemical Corp.)*

variety of functions, a sealant must have a number of specific properties:

1. It must be able to adhere to the surfaces with which it comes in contact.

2. It must remain workable over a considerable range of temperature.

3. It must be able to form a tough, elastic skin over the surface, while the interior of the mass remains flexible.

4. It must be able to stretch or elongate with changes that may occur in the width of the joint.

Fig. 15-5 Sealing coping block joint. *(Thiokol Chemical Corp.)*

Fig. 15-6 Sealing skylight with polysulfide elastomer. *(Thiokol Chemical Corp.)*

5. It must have good movement capability; that is, it must have movement in either extension or compression from the mean. (See Fig. 15-8.)

6. It must be able to recover well after having been extended or compressed.

7. It must have very low sensitivity to water.

8. It must have low volatility.

9. It must be able to provide good service performance.

The ability to recover differs quite widely in materials which may possess the other characteristics

Fig. 15-7 Sealing window-wall unit with polysulfide elastomer. *(Thiokol Chemical Corp.)*

mentioned above, and sealants may be classified into five groups, based on their recovery properties. These groups are as follows:

1. Mastics, having a recovery of 0 to 10 percent

2. Elastomastics, with a recovery of 10 to 49 percent

3. Elastomers, with a recovery rate of 50 to 100 percent

4. Elastoplastics, having a recovery rate of 0 to 100 percent

5. Plastics, also with a recovery rate of 0 to 100 percent

Generally speaking, mastics will have a maximum movement capability of plus or minus 5 percent; elastomastics, plus or minus 10 percent; elastomers, plus or minus 25 percent; elastoplastics, plus or minus 10 percent; and plastics, plus or minus 5 percent.

MASTICS

The mastic group of sealants includes *linseed oil putty, linseed oil–isobutylene caulks, mastic glazing and caulking compounds,* and *asphalt* and *polybutene sealants.*

Putty, made from finely ground calcium carbonate and raw linseed oil, tends to harden and become brittle with age and has no practical elongation value. It is used almost exclusively for glazing wood sash.

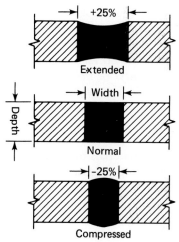

Fig. 15-8 Movement capability of good sealant.

Mastic glazing and caulking compounds and linseed oil–isobutylene caulks are composed of a number of materials blended to produce a sealer which has a longer elastic life than putty and may have an elongation rate up to 10 percent. They are oxidating-type sealants and can be used in exposed areas where painting over them may be desirable.

Asphalt and polybutene sealants are nonoxidizing types and set through evaporation of the solvent. They are useful where a skin is not required, as under flashings, between lapped joints, or in other hidden locations. Sealants made from medium molecular-weight polybutenes will remain soft indefinitely and produce elongations of about 50 percent.

ELASTOMASTICS

The elastomastic group includes the *butyl* sealants with a solvent base, *acrylic* sealants with solvent or emulsion base, *acrylic* sealants which are 100 percent solids, and *one-part polymercaptan.*

ELASTOMERS

Elastomers include *one- and two-part polysulfides* containing 100 percent solids, *one-part silicone* with 100 percent solids, *one- and two-part urethanes* with 100 percent solids, *vinyl chloride polymers,* and *butadiene-styrene copolymers.*

Polysulfide sealants have been used extensively over a longer period of time than most of the others in this group and are available in one-part and two-part systems. Two-part systems are made up of a base and an accelerator which must be combined and mixed before application. They are available in *nonsag* and *self-leveling* forms. The nonsag types are intended for joints in vertical surfaces, while the self-leveling ones are used for joints in horizontal surfaces. One-part systems are premixed and packaged in cartridges or bulk containers. The cartridges are for use in a caulking gun. (See Fig. 15-5.) Both the one- and two-part sealants are available in white, black, and a variety of colors.

Aluminum-colored polysulfide-based sealants have been in use for a number of years and are particularly popular for use with aluminum frame window units. Joints which are immersed in water or which will be wet for long periods of time should not be sealed with aluminum-colored sealants, which may be affected by a chemical reaction between lime in any of the materials and the aluminum, in the presence of water.

Silicone sealant is a one-part product which cures on exposure to air. It has excellent adhesion and can be used where high elongation properties are required. This sealant is available in a number of colors.

ELASTOPLASTICS

Butyl, neoprene, and *hypolon* (chlorosulfonated polyethylene) elastoplastic sealants are solvent types made with fillers and pigments and are thus available in a range of colors. They compare favorably with polysulfide sealants, though they do have higher rates of shrinkage. All have very high elongation ratings—in the range of 200 percent and better.

PLASTICS

The plastics include the high-molecular-weight sealant materials, which have been specially treated to be extruded as plastic or cellular sheets or strips. One disadvantage of most of them is that special adhesives are required to join strips and these may not be available in the field.

BACKUP MATERIALS

Good joint design requires the proper selection and use of *backup* materials for watertight performance of joints. A backup material is one which is placed behind or under the sealant, to perform a number of functions:

1. It controls the depth of sealant in the joint. (See Fig. 15-9.) There a polyurethane foam strip has been used as a backup in the joint.

2. It assists in the tooling of the sealant in the joint.

3. It may serve as a *bond-breaker,* to prevent the sealant from bonding to the back of the joint.

4. It may act as a temporary joint filler, in some cases.

5. It functions as a secondary protective barrier, after the sealant is applied.

6. It supports the sealant in horizontal deck joints which are subject to traffic.

Fig. 15-9   Polyurethane foam backup behind polysulfide sealant.   *(Thiokol Chemical Corp.)*

7. In glazing applications, backup material not only supports the sealant but also assists in positioning and cushioning the glass sections.

Backup materials may be divided into three classes according to the area in which they will be used:

Class 1.   These are for use on the main body of buildings and can be divided into two types: *A* and *B. Type A* materials are used primarily to control the depth of sealant in the joint. *Type B* materials are applied immediately after the joints are formed and serve as a temporary sealant until the primary sealant is applied, after which they serve as a secondary water stop. Type A materials include closed cell *polyethylene, urethane,* or *neoprene* rods, while Type B materials will normally be elastomeric tubing or rods of *butyl* or *neoprene.* Typical areas of application for both will be *joints between curtain wall panels* and *expansion joints* in buildings.

Class 2.   These are for use in glazing applications. Such materials must remain flexible to a temperature of at least $-26°C$, must not absorb water, and must have good recovery. Materials which may be included in Class 2 include *resilient and nonresilient tapes, curable sealants,* and *noncurable mastics,* where little movement is expected.

Class 3. These are for horizontal areas, such as sidewalks, patios, highways, floors, etc. They must not absorb water, must remain resilient to at least −26°C, and must have good recovery. They must also be able to support the sealant in traffic areas. Class 3 backups include extruded, *high-density flexible foams, corkboard, resin-impregnated fiberboard,* and *elastomeric tubing* or *rods.*

Figure 15-10 illustrates some typical uses of backup material with sealants in various types of joints.

In cases where the sealant has adhesive tendencies to the backup material, a *bond-breaker* must be used between them. There may be adhesion between the bond-breaker film and the backup, but none must be exhibited between the film and the sealant. A typical material used for this purpose is a strip of polyethylene film. (See Fig. 15-11.)

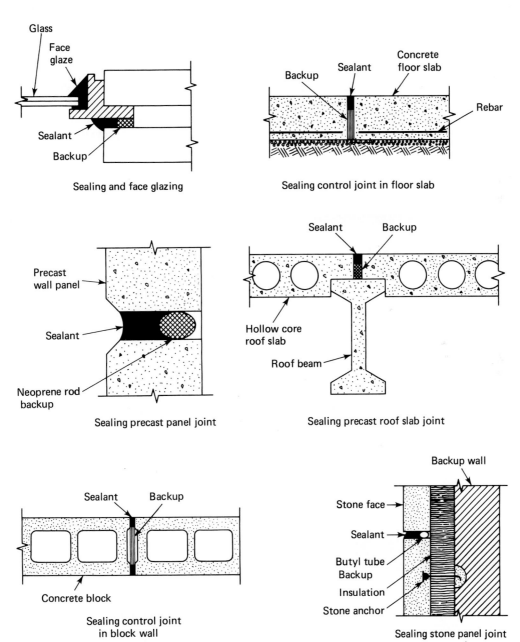

Fig. 15-10 Typical sealant and backup applications.

375

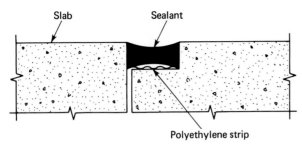

Fig. 15-11   Use of a bond-breaker strip.

JOINT DESIGN

Often the successful performance of other building components depends on the proper functioning of the joints between them. It is therefore important that careful attention be paid to the size of the joints and the selection, application, and maintenance of the sealants used in them.

The width of the joint to be used in any specific case depends on the calculated amount of movement at the joint and the type of sealant to be used.

The amount of movement at a joint is dependent on the coefficient of linear expansion of the panel materials involved and the temperature gradient which causes the movement. Then, by using the calculated amount of joint movement and such other factors as the anticipated temperature extremes, the elongation capability of the proposed sealant, and the temperature at the time of application, the recommended joint width may be determined.

The type of sealant to be used is important because wider joints are necessary with sealants of low movement capability than with those of higher capability, in order to prevent sealant failure.

GLOSSARY

albumin	One of a class of proteins derived from various animal and vegetable sources.
creep	Longitudinal movement due to external forces.
crepe rubber	Crude rubber in crinkled sheets.
dextrin	A soluble carbohydrate formed by the decomposition of starch.
efflorescence	A powdery surface crust formed as a result of the loss of water of crystallization.
elastomer	An elastic rubberlike substance.
emulsion	A dispersion of fine particles or globules of a liquid in a liquid.
nitrocellulose	Cellulose which has been treated with a nitrate.
phenolic resin	A synthetic resin made by treating phenol, a distillate of some organic substance, with an aldehyde, a liquid obtained from an alcohol by oxidation.
thermoplastic	Having the property of becoming plastic under heat and regaining rigidity under normal temperatures.
thermosetting	Having the property of becoming permanently rigid by the application of heat.

REVIEW QUESTIONS

1. Define the following terms:

   a. cohesiveness

   b. adhesiveness

2. What is the basic difference between thermosetting and thermoplastic adhesives?

3. List eight types of glue, and beside each give the name of one glue that belongs to that category.

4. a. What is meant by the creep resistance of a glue?

b. Name two glues which have high creep resistance and two which have poor or relatively poor creep resistance.

5. a. Explain what is meant by a contact adhesive.

b. Briefly outline the procedure for using such an adhesive.

6. What is wood welding? Give two examples of the use of this technique in industry.

7. Describe the basic function of sealing compounds, and give two examples of the use of these compounds in building construction.

8. Explain the difference between a glazing compound and a sealant.

9. a. List five basic qualities required of a sealant.

b. Explain why sealants have such an important place in building construction.

10. Explain what is meant by a backup material in a joint.

11. Outline six properties which a backup material must possess.

12. Explain how the recovery rate of a sealant affects the design width of a joint.

SELECTED SOURCES OF INFORMATION

Adhesive Products Corporation, New York, N.Y.
Canadian Industries, Ltd., Toronto, Ont.
The Flintkote Company of Canada, Ltd., Toronto, Ont.
Le Page's, Ltd., Toronto, Ont.
Minnesota Mining & Manufacturing of Canada, Limited, London, Ont.
Miracle Adhesive Corporation, Newark, N.J.
Monsanto Company, St. Louis, Mo.
Northern Adhesives, Inc., Brooklyn, N.Y.
Thiokol Chemical Corporation, Trenton, N.J.
Tremco Manufacturing Co., Toronto, Ont.

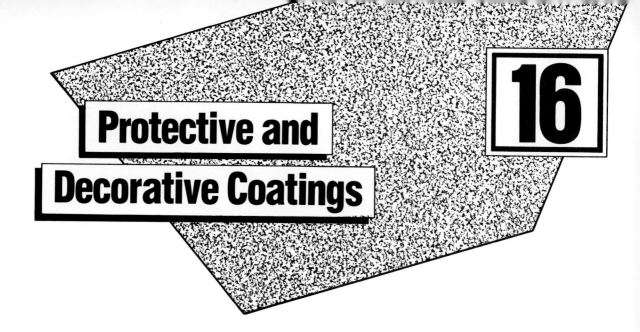

Protective and Decorative Coatings

16

For ages people have been painting their building materials to protect and decorate them. Today painting may be done for one or more of a number of reasons. They include decoration, sanitation, preservation, improved lighting effects, improved heating effects, improved working conditions, safety, and economy.

A group of materials has been developed for such purposes and included in it are paints, varnishes, enamels, shellac, lacquers, stains, fillers, and sealers. Each has special characteristics which have resulted in its being accepted for certain specific types of jobs.

PAINTS

While traditionally paint has been a material with an oil as one of the chief ingredients, many new advances have taken place in the paint industry in recent years. Oil-based paints are being supplemented by alkyd paint, resin-emulsion paint, metallic paint, and luminescent paint.

Surface Preparation

The application of protective and/or decorative coatings has certain limitations. The performance of any coating material is related directly to the thoroughness and quality of the preparation of the surface prior to application of the coating.

It is essential that the surface be thoroughly cleaned; *dirt, mildew, chemicals, oil, grease, scale, rust, marking compounds, efflorescence,* and *powdery residues* of all kinds must be removed. In the case of wood and masonry surfaces, not only should the surface be *dry,* but also the material itself must be dry; it should have a moisture meter reading of not more than 12. Tests should also be made on masonry surfaces to make sure that there is no alkalinity. The test can be made with a small strip of pink litmus paper. If the litmus paper turns blue or indigo, the surface is alkaline.

Cleaning Materials

Cleaning materials vary according to the type of surface to be cleaned and the material to be removed. *Soap, detergents,* and *solvent-type* cleaners as well as *wire brushes, scrapers, sandpaper, abrasives,* and *sand-blasting equipment* are all used in various situations. Some surfaces will require a special cleaner. For example, galvanized metal should be cleaned with an acetic acid wash before priming. The surface of structural steel should be treated with a phosphoric acid solution after it has been washed, to make it chemically clean and suitable for painting. Complete details on surface preparation may be obtained from any reputable paint manufacturer.

Primers

Primers are materials which are used as a first or base coat for many surfaces, to help cover discolorations on the surface and to provide a better bonding base for the subsequent coating. The material used as a primer will vary, depending on the type of base surface.

Aluminum surfaces should be primed with a *zinc chromate* primer. Do not use primers containing lead pigments for aluminum.

Copper surfaces do not require special primers to prevent corrosion, as the blue-green patina formed during early exposure acts as an inhibitor for further oxidation. However, if the copper surface is to be painted, *conventional metal primers* may be used, after the surface has been cleaned.

Galvanized metal may be primed with any good *metal primer* if it is first treated with the acetic acid wash. Otherwise, a special *galvanized-metal primer* should be used.

Structural-steel surfaces may require any one of a number of primers, depending on the type of exposure to which the surface will be subjected. *Oleoresinous primers* containing basic lead silicon, chromate, ferric oxide, titanium dioxide, dibasic lead phosphite or carbon black are used for either interior or exterior surfaces under normal exposure conditions. An *alkyd primer* containing red lead should be used for exterior steel surfaces subject to severe exposure conditions or for steel that is to be embedded in concrete. Steel which will be exposed to abnormal conditions, such as chemicals, condensation, or high humidity should be treated with a primer with hard-drying characteristics, such as an *epoxy metal primer* containing red lead.

Asbestos-cement surfaces should be primed with an *alkali-resistant primer,* a material containing synthetic rubber.

Asphalt and asphalt-coated surfaces require a primer which will prevent asphaltic materials from bleeding into top coats. *Shellacs* provide an adequate seal but produce a brittle film to which subsequent top coats may not adhere successfully. An alternative is to use a *ready-mixed aluminum primer* or a *latex emulsion sealer.*

Concrete surfaces below grade should be sealed against water penetration from below before they can be painted successfully. All concrete floors less than 2 years old or floors which have been troweled smooth with a steel trowel should be etched with *acid* before painting. A solution made up of 1 part concentrated muriatic acid and 3 parts water may be used. This type of treatment provides for better adhesion of paint and also neutralizes the alkalinity of the surface. Following this, the prime coat should be an *alkali-resistant chlorinated rubber paint.*

Concrete-block surfaces, dry and alkali-free, which are to be painted, require a *latex filler* type of primer. If the blocks show alkalinity, an *alkali-resistant primer* should be used.

Plaster and stucco surfaces that are dry and non-alkaline may be primed with a *latex emulsion sealer* or an *oleoresinous primer sealer.* If the surfaces are slightly damp and known to be alkaline, a *synthetic-rubber alkali-resistant primer* is used.

Wood surfaces require any one of the several different types of primer, depending on the type of wood and on the final finish to be applied:

1. For wood that is going to be finished with paint or enamel, the primer should be an *alkyd enamel undercoater.*

2. If hard, close-grained wood is to have a stained finish, the primer will be the *appropriate stain.*

3. For a natural or stained finish on soft, coarse-grained wood, the primer should be an *alkyd gloss varnish,* reduced 50 percent with mineral spirits.

4. For a natural or stained finish on hard, open-grained wood (for example, oak or ash), if the wood is to be filled, the primer will be a *natural paste wood filler.* If the wood is not to be filled, then the primer will be a *processed oil,* such as boiled linseed oil or tung oil.

5. For wood floors with a natural or stained finish, if close-grained wood, the primer will be a *processed oil;* if the wood is open grained, the primer will be a *natural paste wood filler.*

6. For a natural finish with extreme durability on open- or close-grained wood, the primer will simply be the first coat of a *polyester epoxy clear gloss finish.*

7. For an opaque enameled finish on close- or open-grained wood, the prime coat should be an *alkyd enamel,* reduced 25 percent with mineral spirits.

Brick and stone surfaces may require a clear surfacing material to prevent moisture penetration, to preserve the original color, or to facilitate future maintenance. In such a case, a clear silicone finish will normally be used.

Oil Paints

The fundamental components of an oil-base paint are: (1) body, (2) vehicle, (3) pigment, (4) thinner, and (5) drier.

The body of a paint is that solid, finely ground material which gives a paint the power to hide, as well as color, a surface. In white paints the body is also the pigment. The products most widely used for paint body are white lead, zinc oxide, lithopone, and titanium white.

White lead, basic carbonate of lead or basic sulfate of lead, is the most widely used paint body on the market. It reacts chemically and physically with linseed oil and for this reason will produce a durable paint when used alone with oil. It has good hiding power and, upon aging, leaves a good surface for repainting because of the gradual chalking that takes place. However, white lead is poisonous, and white-lead paint should be confined to outdoor applications, where the fumes are less dangerous to the painter. This paint also has a tendency to darken when exposed to hydrogen sulfide gas in the air.

Zinc oxide has desirable characteristics for paint and used in combination with white lead produces greater hardness and durability, better color retention, greater elasticity, and reduced chalking. It has less tendency to turn yellow than some other paint body materials. If the amount of zinc oxide used in outside paint is too great, there is a marked tendency for the paint to check and crack. Body for outside paint should not contain more than 20 percent zinc oxide. It is also important in the formulation of house paint for the control of mildew. Because of its resistance to yellowing, zinc oxide is finding greater use in the making of inside paints and enamels.

Lithopone is a paint body material made by mixing barium sulfide with zinc sulfate. It is most widely used in making interior paints.

Titanium white (titanium dioxide) is produced in three forms—anatase, rutile, and brookite—all of which have specific uses in paint formulation. Titanium dioxide retains color better than any paint body and is particularly useful in paint exposed to hydrogen sulfide fumes. Anatase titanium dioxide chalks quite freely, and, to a certain extent, this is a desirable characteristic, since it presents a better repainting surface. Rutile titanium dioxide is highly resistant to chalking and is used in exterior paints where the maximum chalking resistance and maximum resistance to discoloration are required.

Extenders are inert materials which are added to the paint body to increase the volume without duly increasing the cost. When mixed with oils, they have very little hiding power, but they are necessary in paints to prevent the active body material from settling to the bottom of the container in a solid mass. Good exterior paint should not contain more than 10 percent extender. Larger amounts will decrease durability and increase chalking. Calcium carbonate (known as whiting), ground silica, aluminum silicate, and barium sulfate are all used as extenders.

The paint vehicle is a nonvolatile fluid in which the solid body material is suspended. The vehicle should consist of from 85 to 90 percent drying oil and the remainder thinner and drier. The drying oils include linseed oil, soybean oil, fish oil, dehydrated castor oil, tung oil, perilla oil, and oiticica oil. Sometimes some synthetic resins are added to these to produce a harder film.

Linseed oil is expressed from flaxseed and is produced both as raw and boiled oil. Boiled linseed oil is raw oil which has been heat treated and had certain metallic driers added. Tung oil is obtained from the nuts of the Chinawood tree, perilla oil from the seeds of an oriental plant, perilla ocymoide, and oiticica oil from the seeds of a Brazilian tree. Castor oil is obtained from the seeds of the East Indian castor-oil plant. All of these are drying oils; that is, they oxidize when exposed to air, forming a hard, resinous mass which coats and protects the surface.

The different oils dry at different rates to varying degrees of hardness. Some are more resistant to moisture than others, and the dried films possess varying degrees of elasticity. Therefore the choice of vehicle to be used in a paint will depend on where it is to be used and the length of time to be allowed for drying. For example, raw linseed oil is slower drying but lighter colored than boiled oil. Tung oil produces a stronger film than linseed oil and, when properly processed, is more waterproof than linseed oil.

Pigments are the materials which give the paint its color. In the case of white paint, the body is the pigment. Color pigments are classified into two basic groups: natural pigments and synthetic or manufactured pigments.

Natural pigments are obtained from animal, vegetable, and mineral sources. Most of them are composed of natural mineral oxides such as iron oxide, chrome oxide, cobalt oxide, siennas, ochres, and umbers. Carbon black is also used as pigment. Many of the synthetic pigments are phthalocyanines (coal tar derivatives) similar to those used to make dyes.

The red pigments are red lead, vermilion, and red ochres. Brown pigments are burnt ochre, burnt sienna, and burnt umber. Yellow pigments include chromium oxide, zinc oxide, and cadmium oxide. Blue pigments are cobalt blue, Prussian blue, and ultramarine blue—all natural pigments—and a number of synthetic blue pigments. Green pigments include chrome green, viridian, and emerald green. Black pigments are carbon black and lampblack.

Thinners are volatile solvents, materials which have a natural affinity for the vehicle in the paint. They cause the paint to flow better; they evaporate when the paint is applied. One of the most common thinners for oil-based paints is turpentine, made by distilling gum from a number of pine trees. Some petroleum fractions, such as naphtha and benzene, are also used as thinners.

Driers are organic salts of various metals, such as iron, zinc, cobalt, lead, manganese, and calcium, which are added to the paint to accelerate the oxidation and hardening of the vehicle. Litharge, lead oxide, is a drier commonly used with lead-based paints; zinc sulfate and manganese oxide are used with zinc oxide–based paints.

Alkyd Paints

Alkyd paints are so called because of the synthetic resin—alkyd resin—used in the paint formulation. Alkyd resin is obtained by the combining of an alcohol and an acid. Alkyd paints are produced by combining a drying oil, such as linseed oil or dehydrated castor oil, with glycerine (the alcohol) and phthalic anhydride (the acid). The glycerine neutralizes the phthalic anhydride and the fatty acid in the oil. The ester molecules which form as a result of this neutralization then polymerize to form the paint body.

Styrenated oils are also used sometimes to produce paints that possess fast-drying and excellent adhesion characteristics. Such a formulation also has fairly good alkali resistance. In these cases the regular drying oil is either emulsified with the styrene or dissolved in it.

Alkyd paints in general have mild alkali resistance but excellent water resistance. They also have the ability to produce lighter colors and retain color better than paints with natural drying oils. Their speed of curing is at least equal to the curing of oil-based paints. Because of its excellent weathering ability, alkyd paint is particularly useful for porch and deck enamel and paints for other such exposed conditions. With modifications, it is used in making white baking enamel, such as is used on stoves, refrigerators, etc. Nonyellowing white finishes are obtained using soybean and castor oil in the alkyd, but linseed alkyds give faster drying times and tougher films.

Alkyd resins are also used as modifiers in other types of paints. They usually produce greater permanence and better adhesion properties. They may be mixed with latex paints, up to 20 to 50 percent alkyd. Altogether some 50 types of alkyds are used in paint manufacture.

Resin-Emulsion Paints

Resin-emulsion, or latex, paints are paints in which the vehicle is a synthetic-resin emulsion, usually made from one of four basic resin types: butadiene-styrene, polyvinyl acetate, epoxy resin, or acrylic resin.

The body of these paints is usually titanium dioxide or lithopone, and soybean proteins are added to the formulations, using butadiene-styrene and polyvinyl acetate to increase consistency and stability. Preservatives must then be added to prevent the proteins from allowing the formation of microorganisms. Extenders such as China clay may also be used. Pigments are more restricted than for oil paints because the emulsion is alkaline in nature. Pigments usually used include titanium white, lithopone, cadmium yellow, cadmium red, talc, mica, silica, lampblack, and some hydrocarbon colors. The thinner is water, and to it must be added a dispersing agent to keep the pigment and other materials suspended in the emulsion. These emulsion-based paints tend to foam, so a defoaming agent, usually tributyl phosphate, is added. Finally methyl cellulose is added to improve the flow qualities of the paint.

Polyvinyl acetate emulsions produce a much

tougher skin than the butadiene-styrene types and so can be used as exterior as well as interior paint. One of its most important applications is in exterior finishes for masonry and stucco. Neither of these types of paint can be applied to a glossy surface, and, in addition, both must be protected from freezing.

Acrylic- and epoxy-resin-emulsion paints require no oxidation to form a film and remain flexible after drying. They exhibit great resistance to weathering and no tendency to lose their adhesive qualities or color with age. They contain no protein and therefore are not subject to deterioration. However, they are more costly than other emulsion paints.

Metallic Paint

Metallic paint consists of a metallic pigment and a vehicle. The pigment is very fine flakes of aluminum, copper, bronze, zinc, or tin. They are suspended in a vehicle which may be a natural or synthetic varnish, a quick-drying lacquer, special bronzing lacquer, or bituminous-based vehicles, depending on where the paint is to be used.

Spraying is the best method of applying metallic paints as it permits the spreading of a uniform film and encourages even depositing of the metallic flakes. Metallic paints are used for many decorative purposes; aluminum paint in particular makes an excellent primer for exterior paints of other types.

Luminescent Paint

Luminescent paint is made by adding fluorescent and phosphorescent pigments to any one of a number of drier-free vehicles, including alkyd marine varnish, spirit varnish, or quick-drying lacquers. Color may also be incorporated into luminous paints.

Luminescent paints may be used in residential buildings to produce special effects. They are used in hospitals, schools, factories, hotels, etc., because their unique quality helps provide maximum safety.

Fire-Retardant Paint

Fire-retardant paint does not make a building fireproof, but what it does do is make it more difficult for a fire to spread. Some fire-retardant paints accomplish this by the fact that they have an inherent, slightly insulating effect; others by the fact that they are noncombustible. Another type releases a vapor, usually water or carbon dioxide, when heated and thus tend to smother the fire in the immediate area.

These are called *nonintumescent* fire-retardant coatings.

Others, *intumescent* coatings, may have some of the same values as the nonintumescents but also have an added insulating effect. When a surface coated with an intumescent paint is exposed to heat or fire, it puffs up and forms a thick, insulating crust which greatly retards the penetration of heat to the coated surface. This crust is composed of tiny air cells which build up to a thickness of about 0.3 in. It seals out the air, or oxygen, required for combustion so that only very intense exposure to heat will result in charring the undersurface.

A variety of these paints are available, with a vinyl, alkyd, polyurethane, epoxy, or solvent base. Both opaque and transparent products are manufactured in flat, semigloss, gloss, or satin finishes. They may be applied by brush, roller, or spray over a variety of surfaces such as wood, paper, acoustical tile, concrete, stucco, plaster, conventional paint, enamel, or varnish. Drying time to a dust-free condition will vary from 30 min to 2 h, depending on the particular product.

The degree of fire retardancy resulting from the use of these paints depends on the thickness of the paint film applied, and care should be taken to follow the manufacturer's directions when applying such a product. Coverage will vary from 50 to 500 ft^2/gal (3.5 to 12 m^2/L), depending on the particular type of paint used and the kind of surface to which it is applied.

Polyester-Epoxy Coatings

The need for heavier-bodied paint materials, particularly for use on masonry and concrete walls, for greater protection under a variety of extreme conditions, and for greater versatility has led to the development of polyester-epoxy coatings which contain a much higher percentage of solids than conventional paints. The coating system consists of a high-solids vinyl filler material, to be applied directly over a concrete block or other masonry surface, and a high-solids, pigmented polyester-epoxy topcoat (see Fig. 16-1).

The filler material may be applied by brush, roller, or spray at a thickness which will give approximately 16 mils of dry film. The top coating, available in either semigloss or gloss finish in approximately 90 different colors, will add another 6 mils of dry film to the coating.

Fig. 16-1 Polyester-epoxy coating system. *(Pittsburgh Paints)*

This coating system creates a tough, long-lasting finish which is highly resistant to water, grease, and many chemicals and which can be cleaned with harsh caustics. For this reason it is ideally suited to areas of heavy traffic such as schoolrooms, corridors, kitchens, cafeterias, and laboratories.

A similar top-coating material is available for a clear finish, in either gloss or semigloss. It is to be used over previously painted surfaces or to preserve the natural appearance of wood, brick, or stone. One or two coats may be required, depending on the porosity of the base and the degree of gloss required.

Both filler and top coating require overnight drying time before applying a second coat and approximately 2 weeks for complete cure.

Another system consists of a two-component coal-tar epoxy-resin product, which cures as a continuous film at room temperature. The film combines the characteristics of coal-tar pitch with the chemical resistance of epoxy resin, to provide good immersion and environmental resistance to both fresh and salt water. It is also highly resistant to many organic and inorganic acids, bases, and salts, to most petroleum products, as well as to hydrogen

sulfide liquors and sewage effluent. However, special equipment is required for application, and workers must be carefully protected against fumes, overspray, or spills.

Another epoxy-based protective material consists of a two-coat system in which the base or primer coat contains a high ratio of metallic zinc to the resin binder. Properly applied to a sand-blasted steel surface, the coating deposits a film containing up to 93 percent metallic zinc by weight. The application of the clear top coat may be delayed up to 3 months to help complete stabilization of the base. The resulting film provides protection for steel surfaces similar to that obtained by hot-dip galvanizing.

Still another specialty coating is made, containing chlorinated rubber. It is applied as a three-coat system to produce a film about 8 mils in thickness. Such a paint is useful in conditions of high humidity, in cold storage plants, or to control corrosion in many industrial situations, such as pulp plants, sewage treatment plants, etc. It is also useful as a vapor barrier on masonry surfaces. It should not be used in situations in which the coating will be in contact with animal or vegetable fats and oils. The recommended thinner for such a product is xylol, a derivative of benzine.

VARNISHES

Varnishes constitute a group of more-or-less transparent liquids which are used to provide a protective surface coating in much the same way as paints do. At the same time they allow the original surface to show but add a lustrous and glossy finish to it.

All varnishes have basically the same components as paints—body, vehicle, thinner, and drier. However, varnishes may be divided into three groups, depending on the type of material used to form the body: (1) natural-resin varnishes, (2) modified natural-resin varnishes, and (3) synthetic-resin varnishes.

Natural-Resin Varnishes

The body of this group of varnishes is made from natural resins obtained from certain trees. Some of the resins are exudations from living trees, while others are fossil resins—which usually are superior in quality. Among the resins used are Congo copals, Kauri gum from New Zealand, boea resins from the East Indies, Philippine manila resin, and Pontianak resin from Borneo. Some of these must be heat treated to produce an oil-soluble gum, while others are naturally soluble in oil. Rosin, a by-product from the distillation of turpentine, is also used to make varnish.

The vehicle used in varnish is one of a number of drying oils, the same oils which are used in the manufacture of oil-based paints. The resins are dissolved into the oil, and the mixture is heated to temperatures ranging from 260 to 315°C, depending on the amount of gloss required. Varnishes made from a combination of oil and natural resin are known as *oleoresinous* varnishes.

The best thinner for varnishes is *turpentine*, a distillate of gum from a group of pine trees. It evaporates slowly and gives varnish brushing and flowing qualities that no other solvent can give. It also aids oxidation of the drying oil by absorbing oxygen from the air and passing it on to the oil. *Mineral spirits, benzene,* and *naphtha* are also used as thinners.

Driers used in varnishes are essentially the same as those used in paints, namely organic salts of various metals. They speed the drying of varnishes by acting as a catalyst to the oxidation process.

Varnishes are often classified as *long-oil, medium-oil,* and *short-oil* varnishes, depending on the amount of oil used per unit of solid resin.

Long-oil varnish contains from 40 to 100 gal (180 to 455 L) of oil per 100 lb (45 kg) of resin. The result is a varnish which will produce a tougher, more durable and elastic film but which takes longer to dry and produces only moderate gloss. Marine and spar varnishes belong to this group. Tung oil is the oil most commonly used in making these varnishes, since it is particularly impervious to water.

Medium-oil varnishes contain from 12 to 40 gal (55 to 182 L) of oil per 100 lb (45 kg) of resin. They dry faster and have a harder film than long-oil varnishes but are not as impervious to water. Floor varnishes belong to this group.

Short-oil varnishes contain from 5 to 12 gal (23 to 55 L) of oil per 100 lb (45 kg) of resin. They dry quite rapidly and form a hard, brittle film which will not stand much rough usage. Rubbing and polishing varnishes belong to this group. They can be rubbed and polished to a high gloss or to a stain finish, depending on the finishing procedure.

Modified Natural-Resin Varnishes

This group of varnishes is made with a natural resin which has been altered by chemical action. Common resin is heat treated with glycerin to form an ester gum, and this gum is used as the body for the varnish. Generally speaking, this type of varnish is less expensive than oleoresinous varnishes.

Synthetic-Resin Varnishes

Synthetic resins are those produced by the plastics industry including nitrocellulose, phenolics, amino resins, alkyd resins, a number of vinyl resins, polyethylene, polystyrene, silicone, acrylic resins, and epoxy resins. Some of these are thermoplastic, and some are thermosetting. Many varnishes made with plastic resins reach their greatest potential only when baked.

The vehicle for synthetic-resin varnishes is often the same type of drying oil used with oleoresinous varnishes. However, synthetic drying oils have been developed, and in baking varnishes, liquid alkyd resin may be the vehicle.

Because of the great variety of resins used in synthetic varnishes, a wide range of solvents is required. Some are the same as those used in other varnishes. Coal-tar derivatives and high petroleum fractions are also used as solvents. Driers are the same as those used for other types of varnish.

ENAMELS

When pigment is added to a varnish, the result is an enamel. Any of the varnish types can be used, and the durability of the enamel depends to a large extent on the quality of the pigment. Since varnishes do not contain the opaque body material which paints do, enamels do not have high covering power; for best results they require an opaque undercoat. Baking enamels, made with synthetic resins, are used on most household appliances, curtain-wall panels of various kinds, aluminum shingles and siding, and various interior and exterior trim materials.

SHELLAC

Shellac is the only liquid protective coating containing a resin of animal origin. The resin is an exudation of the *lac* insect of India and Southeast Asia, deposited on the branches of trees.

The resin accumulations are collected, crushed, cleaned, and dissolved in alcohol to produce *orange shellac,* so called because of its color. By bleaching the resin, pure white shellac is produced.

Various grades of shellac are made by varying the amount of resin dissolved in a unit of solvent. These grades are known as *cuts;* a 4-lb (1.8-kg) cut means that the shellac contains 4 lb/gal (480 g/L) of lac resin.

The alcohol used is usually special denatured alcohol or proprietary denatured alcohol. The first type consists of a mixture of 100 gal (455 L) of ethyl alcohol and 5 gal (23 L) of methyl alcohol. Proprietary denatured alcohol consists of a mixture of 100 gal (455 L) of special denatured alcohol, 2 gal (9 L) denatured wood alcohol, 1 gal (4.5 L) ethyl acetate, and 1 gal (4.5 L) aviation gasoline.

Shellac dries quickly, is easy to apply, and produces a tough, elastic film on wood, metal, glass, cork, and leather. However, it should not be used on work exposed to outside conditions except as a sealer over knots and sap streaks under exterior paint.

Shellac finds considerable use as a seal coat over stains and fillers and is sometimes used as a complete finishing material by itself. This latter treatment, known as French polish, consists of many layers of shellac applied one over the other, using a linseed-oil-soaked applicating cloth.

The main disadvantages of shellac are that it will discolor under strong sunlight, and water containing alkali causes it to soften and whiten. The surface must be dry before shellac is applied and water should never be used to polish shellac.

LACQUERS

The material which we know today as lacquer is a comparatively new product made from synthetic materials to take the place of varnish for clear finishes. Most modern lacquer is based on nitrocellulose used in combination with natural or synthetic resins and plasticizers. These ingredients are dissolved in a mixture of volatile solvents which evaporate, leaving a film to form the protective coating.

While nitrocellulose alone will produce a clear film, it has poor adhesion, poor durability, and poor flexibility. As a result, natural or synthetic resins are added to nitrocellulose to improve adhesion and hardness and to give the lacquer gloss and film thickness. These resins include cellulose acetate, ethyl cellulose, alkyd resins, vinyl resins, epoxy resins, acrylic resins, polystyrenes, and many others.

Plasticizers counteract the tendency of resins to be brittle and allow lacquer to flow out on application. They also contribute to the body of the lacquer and its durability. Most common plasticizers are ester gums, but some nondrying and drying oils—camphor, dibutyl phthalate, and tricresyl phosphate—are also used.

The solvents used are quite complex since no single solvent will dissolve all the lacquer ingredients. In many cases from six to ten solvents are blended to produce a material capable of dissolving all the ingredients present. These solvents are usually grouped according to their boiling point into low, medium, and high boilers. The boiling points of each of these is about 100°C, 127°C, and 177°C, respectively. The proper blending of solvents affects setting time, flow, gloss, and freedom from bubbling in lacquers. The commonly used solvents include ethyl, butyl, isopropyl, and amyl acetate; acetone; and diethylene glycol.

In addition to these ingredients, thinners are mixed with lacquer just before application to reduce the consistency for spraying, to control the rate of drying, and to reduce the cost of lacquer. They include a group of alcohols—ethyl, butyl, amyl, and isopropyl—and a number of hydrocarbonic mixtures such as toluol, benzol, and xylol.

When another class of materials—pigments—are added to clear lacquer, the result is lacquer enamel, available in a wide range of colors.

Today a wide variety of clear and colored lacquers are manufactured to meet a great many special purposes:

1. Clear gloss lacquer. A clear lacquer that dries to a glossy finish in 1 to 4 h. It may be rubbed and polished with oil or water.

2. Clear flat lacquer. It is similar to gloss lacquer but dries without gloss. It is often used to produce satin effects.

3. **Tinting lacquer.** This is a concentrated colored lacquer mixed with clear lacquer to produce lacquer enamel.

4. **Brushing lacquer.** A slow-drying lacquer formulated specially for brush application.

5. **Bronzing lacquer.** This is a clear lacquer into which are mixed metallic pigments to produce metallic effects.

6. **Shading lacquer.** A slightly colored lacquer used to produce wood-color-tone effects on furniture.

7. **Water-white lacquer.** This is an exceptionally clear lacquer that produces a protective coating of greatest transparency over pale finishes.

8. **Dipping lacquer.** This is designed for application by the dip-tank method and is available both clear and in colors.

STAINS

Stains are materials used to apply color to wood surfaces. They are intended to impart color without concealing or obscuring the grain and not to provide a protective coating. They may be used to accentuate the color contrast of a wood grain, to even up color differences, or to imitate expensive wood colors on surfaces which lack desirable color or grain. There are a number of types of wood stain available, based on the kind of solvent used to dissolve the coloring matter—water-soluble stains, spirit-soluble stains, penetrating oil stains, non-grain-raising stains, and pigment wiping stains.

Water Stains

Water stains are synthetic dyes, many of which are coal-tar derivatives manufactured in powder form and in various strengths. They are dissolved in hot water at a specific rate in grams per liter (ounces per gallon), depending on the depth of color required.

Water stain is easy to apply by brush, sponge, dipping, or spray; it is nonfading and nonbleeding; and it gives deep, even penetration. However, it has a tendency to raise the grain of wood, thus roughening the surface and necessitating careful sanding. Water stain will air-dry in about 12 h or may be force-dried in from 2 to 4 h.

Spirit Stains

Spirit stains are made from dyes which are soluble in alcohol and are manufactured both in powder form and in ready-mixed liquid form.

This type of stain produces the brightest and strongest colors but is most susceptible to fading. It also tends to bleed and to raise the grain of wood. Because they dry rapidly, spirit stains are usually applied by spray; because of their high penetration quality, they are often used for refinishing, repair work, and for staining sap streaks. Drying time is usually from 15 min to 2 h.

Penetrating Oil Stains

This type of stain is made by dissolving oil-soluble dyes in coal-tar solvents such as toluol, benzol, or xylol and further thinning the vehicle with common petroleum solvents. Although they are available in powder form, oil stains are usually produced as a ready-mixed liquid.

Stain is easy to apply by the sponge, spray, or dip method, but the surface must be wiped after application to remove excess stain. Oil stains have a tendency to bleed into finish coats and are not as light-fast as water stains but have no tendency to raise the grain. Drying time varies from 1 to 24 h.

Non-Grain-Raising Stains

This type of stain is made using light-fast dyes which are soluble in such substances as glycols, alcohols, and ketones. It is designed to produce all the advantages of the stains previously mentioned with none of their disadvantages.

Non-grain-raising stains have moderate penetration, do not raise the grain of wood, and dry in from 15 min to 3 h. They do not run or bleed and, because of their fast-drying properties, are usually applied by spraying.

Pigment Wiping Stains

Stains of this type are made from translucent mineral pigments ground into a drying oil. They are applied by brushing or swabbing the surface with a cotton cloth and are allowed to set for various lengths of time after application.

They have good light resistance, no tendency to raise the grain, and good color uniformity. However, they lack the staining capacity of many other stains and, because they are not as transparent as some others, tend to obscure the fine grain of the wood.

FILLERS

Fillers are finishing materials which are used on wood surfaces, particularly those with open grain, to fill the pores and provide a perfectly smooth, uniform surface for varnish or lacquer. Filler is also used to impart color to the wood pores and so emphasize the grain.

There are two general types of fillers: paste fillers, which are used on open-grained woods, and liquid fillers, for close-grained woods. Paste wood fillers consist of a base or body, pigment, nonvolatile vehicle, and thinner. The body is generally a translucent, inert material (such as silica, some silicates, and carbonates of calcium and magnesium) which will fill the pores without staining the wood. Color pigment is usually umber, sienna, or similar colors which will give the filler the desired color. Sometimes a small quantity of dye solution may be used. The vehicle is a vegetable oil or special varnish with japan driers. Thinners are similar to those used in varnishes.

Filler is applied by brush, by spray, or by dipping and must be thinned to the proper consistency for the method of application used. It is then wiped off, across the grain, before it sets on the surface.

Liquid filler is generally a varnish with a small amount of body material added. It is used on medium, close-grained woods in essentially the same way as paste filler but has much less filling capacity.

SEALERS

The primary purpose of a sealer is to seal the surface of the wood and prevent the absorption of succeeding finish coats. It may be applied to bare wood that has been sanded smooth or applied over the stain or filler.

A sealer also tends to seal in the filler, blend the stain, stiffen any raised wood grain and thus make sanding easier, and form a bond between the wood and the finishing coats.

A number of materials are used as sealers, the proper one to use in a specific situation depending on the type of finish to be used.

Shellac is widely used as a sealer, thinned out to a 2- to 4-lb (0.9- to 1.8-kg) cut, depending on whether varnish or lacquer is to be used. Lacquer finish requires the thinner sealer. It dries rapidly, does not penetrate, and does not soften appreciably under newly applied lacquer or varnish. It does not, however, provide the best adhesion for finish coats and may show crazing tendencies under a thick finishing film.

Lacquer sealer is the type of sealer most commonly used under lacquer finishes. It consists primarily of the same type of resins from which lacquer is made, with plasticizers and solvent and, in addition, solid content in the form of zinc and calcium stearates. These are called sanding agents and increase the ease with which the sealer surface may be sanded when dry.

Varnish sealer is also available for use under varnish or lacquer. It is similar to varnish cutback until the material contains 30 to 35 percent solids. This type of sealer air-dries in about 8 h or may be force-dried in 1 to 2 h at 65°C. The surface must be sanded after the sealer is completely dry.

COLOR DYNAMICS

Color dynamics is a system of using colors which combines function and proper color use in decoration. It uses the knowledge of the effects of color on people, both physiologically and psychologically, and employs the principles of camouflage, contrast, and proportion to improve working conditions and increase working efficiency, reduce industrial hazards, reduce tension, improve study conditions, provide more congenial surroundings, induce a feeling of relaxation, and provide a nationally recognized system of color coding.

Color-dynamics concepts include the following:

1. Color can cause depression or happiness, tension or relaxation, depending on how it is used.

2. The proper use of color on machinery is a factor in worker safety.

3. The proper use of color in an industrial plant can improve production.

4. Color coding is a very useful industrial technique.

5. Color can be used to de-emphasize visual distractions.

6. Red may not always appear to be red.

7. The ability to recognize and interpret is greater when the right colors are used.

8. Color can improve the mood of individuals in various industrial, commercial, and social settings.

Detailed outlines of the use of color dynamics in general and specific color systems for a wide variety of living and working situations are available from several well-known paint manufacturing companies.

GLOSSARY

alkyd	Any of a group of thermoplastic synthetic resins.
anatase	With reference to the length of titanium white crystals.
brookite	Containing orthorhombic crystals.
chalking	Development of a chalklike surface.
crazing	The formation of minute cracks on the surface.
ochre	An earthy ore of iron.
oiticica	One of a family of South American trees.
perilla	A member of an Asiatic mint plant family.
rutile	Containing a little iron.
sienna	An earthy substance containing oxides of iron.
styrene	An unsaturated hydrocarbon.
titanium white	A white pigment containing the element titanium.
umber	A brown earth containing manganese and iron oxides.
viridian	A chromic oxide.
volatile solvent	A solvent which vaporizes easily.

REVIEW QUESTIONS

1. Explain what is meant by the following:
   a. the body of paint
   b. a paint vehicle
   c. pigment in a paint

2. Give one advantage and one disadvantage of using paint with white lead as the body.

3. What type of paint is best suited for an area in which the atmosphere contains hydrogen sulfide?

4. Give a concise definition of each of the following:
   a. a drying oil
   b. an extender
   c. a drier

5. Outline three advantages of using latex paints.

6. Suggest three specific uses for luminescent paint.

7. List three classes of varnish and give two specific uses for each kind.

8. Compare varnish and lacquer from the standpoint of each of the following:
   a. basic ingredients
   b. drying time
   c. method of application
   d. depth of film produced in one application

9. Outline the sequence of operations for finishing a piece of oak in a walnut color with a varnish surface.

SELECTED SOURCES OF INFORMATION

Borden Chemical Company, West Hill, Ont.
British American Paint Company, Victoria, B.C.
Canadian Industries, Ltd., Montreal, Que.
Canadian Pittsburgh Industries, Ltd., Montreal, Que.
CIBA Products Company, Fairlawn, N.J.
General Paint Corporation, Vancouver, B.C.
Le Page's, Ltd., Toronto, Ont.
Pittsburgh Paints, Pittsburgh, Pa.
Pratt & Lambert, Inc., Buffalo, N.Y.
Protection Products Manufacturing Co., Kalamazoo, Mich.
Samuel Cabot, Inc., Boston, Mass.
Shellac Information Bureau, New York, N.Y.
The Sherwin-Williams Company of Canada, Ltd., Montreal, Que.

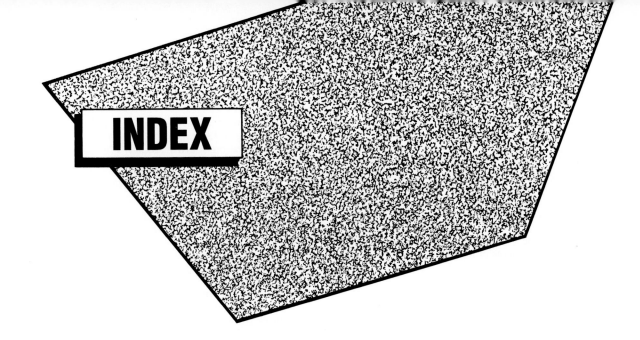

INDEX

394